Investigations in Algebra

Exploring with Logo

E. Paul Goldenberg, editor

Investigations in Algebra

Albert Cuoco

The MIT Press
Cambridge, Massachusetts
London, England

This book was set in Computer Modern by The MIT Press and printed and bound in the United States of America.

Library of Congress Cataloging-in-Publication Data

Cuoco, Albert.
    Investigations in algebra / Albert Cuoco.
       p.   cm.—Exploring with Logo.
    Includes bibliographical references.
    ISBN 0–262–03144–2. — ISBN 0–262–53071–6 (pbk.)
    1. Algebra—Computer-assisted instruction. 2. LOGO (Computer program language) I. Title. II. Series: Exploring with Logo.
QA159.C86 1990
512'.078—dc20
                                                89–49218
                                                  CIP

This book is for Micky and Alicia.

Contents

Series Foreword

The aim of this series is to enhance the study of topics in the arts, humanities, mathematics, and sciences with ideas and techniques drawn from the world of artificial intelligence—specifically, the notion that in building a computer model of a construct, one gains tremendous insight into that construct.

Each volume in the series presents a penetrating yet playful excursion through a single subject area—such as linguistics, visual modeling, music, number theory, or physics—written for a general audience.

E. Paul Goldenberg

Introduction

Thus I might say: the proof does not
serve as an experiment; but it does
serve as the picture of an experiment.

Ludwig Wittgenstein,
Remarks on the Foundations of Mathematics

I grew up in a family of tinkerers. Early on, I learned that playing with existing machines helps you learn how to design new machines and to predict their behavior. Everything we built, from flower boxes to go-carts to whole houses, was prefaced with long thought experiments in which we tried to turn our experiences into predictive metaphors. Some of these thought experiments were designed to help us understand why a new machine couldn't possibly work. I remember an involved conversation with my uncle (the quintessential *bricoleur*) in which he convinced me that it would be impossible to have a bicycle that was driven by an electric motor that was powered by a battery that was charged by a generator that was turned by a friction wheel that was attached to the wheel of the bicycle. I never could have followed his proof if I hadn't had some experience with bicycles and motors.

In school, this idea of using experiments to develop both conjectures and plausible arguments to support the conjectures was almost never discussed, and I arrived in high school thinking (like many people) that mathematics is a set of facts and procedures that have to be mastered. Luckily, my high school mathematics teacher saw things differently; he immersed his classes in carefully constructed problems that required pages of calculations. These calculations were really mathematical experiments, and wonderful patterns emerged from them. I began to understand something that wouldn't be clear to me for almost another decade: the heart of mathematical research is tinkering.

This book is about tinkering with mathematics. It offers you the chance to play with mathematical phenomena and to use your experiments to find patterns and explanations for the patterns. In order to tinker with the mathematics, it's necessary to build concrete models. These models are best constructed

Introduction

on a computer, and for many reasons I've chosen Logo as the programming language with which we'll conduct our mathematical investigations.

The book consists of alternating sections of exposition (where I try to explain something) and problems. The most important parts of the book are its problems, and they are divided into three types:

Exercises are problems that will help you become familiar with a certain topic. Like sit-ups, if you do them faithfully, it will be easier to do more interesting things.

Experiments are open-ended problems. They ask you to investigate a topic without giving you much direction. This is very much the way it is in "real life" mathematical research.

Projects are guided tours. They pose problems and then offer suggestions and hints. Some of the projects discuss topics that would have been more efficiently discussed in the expository sections, but doing so would have taken the fun away.

I've tried to resist the temptation to further classify the problems by difficulty, because things that seem difficult to me are often easy for other people. Still, I tagged a few problems with a sharp (#) when they seemed hard.

I said above that you'll be playing with mathematical phenomena, but I haven't yet said what the phenomena are. That's because the book really is about methods of mathematical investigation; the tinkering is much more important than the objects that are tinkered with. I chose the actual mathematical topics because they lend themselves to the kinds of investigations that come up in mathematical research, because they are special cases of topics that have been useful in contemporary mathematics, and because I find them fascinating (I could also say that the topics are extremely important, but that's just another way to say that I find them fascinating). The major topics in the book:

Functions. You probably have an idea of what the word function means in mathematics. We'll think of a function as a process that transforms "inputs" into "outputs" in a predictable way. A major goal of our discussion will be for you to learn to think of a function as an object that can be manipulated and transformed.

Mathematical induction. Mathematical induction is an extremely useful method of proof; it is a technique you can use to convince someone that patterns that are established by calculations will continue in cases where the calculations have not yet been carried out. Most of the time, we'll use it to show that two functions are "equal" (they produce the same output when given the same input).

Combinatorics. Combinatorics is a collection of techniques for establishing the number of ways that something can be done without actually making a list. For example, it allows you to find the number of three letter collections that you can make from our usual alphabet without actually listing the collections. Rather than make a systematic study of combinatorics, we'll consider several "counting problems," and we'll develop the machinery necessary to solve them.

Number theory. Number theory began as the study of the properties of whole numbers. We'll discuss prime numbers, common divisors, and several functions that can be used to study these notions. We'll finish with a version of the celebrated "Chinese remainder theorem" that can be modeled on your computer.

The book contains three parts, each divided into several sections. The focus of part I is on functions, the focus of part II is on combinatorics and mathematical induction, and part III concentrates on number theory. However, as you'll see, each part makes heavy use of the topics from the other two.

It might seem strange to you that the book is called *Investigations in Algebra*, but algebra means much more than the content of the high school courses with names like "Algebra II." A precise description of what mathematicians mean when they speak of algebra would take up almost as many pages as are in this book, but it's certainly true that you are doing algebra whenever you are reasoning about the properties of operations like addition and multiplication. To complicate matters, many of the topics from high school algebra (like trigonometry) are not part of algebra at all. Just remember that the important word in the title is "investigations".

It might also seem odd that Logo will be used to construct the models. That's because Logo is most often used in elementary school geometry. But Logo is an extremely powerful programming language, and what's more important, it is a close approximation to the language of mathematics. Our use of Logo will be confined to what might be called its *functional subset*; we won't use turtle graphics, assignment (MAKE and LOCAL), or any text formatting commands. By using Logo as an idiom for expressing mathematical ideas, you'll see many situations in which the actual construction of Logo procedures suggests mathematical results (and even methods of proof) that would be difficult to discover otherwise. Logo is not the only language that can be used this way, but the other candidates (like Logo's cousin Scheme) require more equipment than most people have.

There are a few prerequisites for reading this book. You'll have no trouble understanding things if

1. You have a mathematics background that includes "intermediate" algebra. This means that you should be able to expand things like

$$(X^2 - 2X + 1)(X - 3)(4X^3 - 3X)$$

You should be able to do a little factoring, and you should be able to find a common denominator and add algebraic fractions. You should also understand some very basic vocabulary about sets. For example, you should understand the following paragraph:

If $A = \{1\ 3\ -2\}$ and $B = \{2\ -2\ 3\ 6\}$, then the union of A and B (written $A \cup B$) is the set $\{1\ 3\ -2\ 2\ 6\}$, and the intersection of A and B (written $A \cap B$) is $\{3\ -2\}$. 1 is an element of A (shorthand: $1 \in A$) but it is not an element of B (shorthand: $1 \notin B$). $\{1\ 3\}$ is a subset of A (shorthand: $\{1\ 3\} \subset A$). $\{1\ 2\ 4\} = \{4\ 1\ 2\}$.

We'll use the symbol Z (for the German word *Zahlen*) to stand for the set of integers; that is, Z is the set of all whole numbers:

$$\{\ldots -2\ -1\ 0\ 1\ 2\ 3\ 4\ 5\ 6\ldots\}$$

The symbol R stands for the set of real numbers (that is, the set of all the coordinates of points on a number line). Z^+ stands for the set of positive integers (Z^+ is the set $\{1\ 2\ 3\ 4\ 5\ldots\}$).

2. You have an elementary knowledge of Logo programming. This means that you should understand the structure of the following procedure:

```
TO F :X
IF :X = 1 [OP 2]
OP (F :X - 1) + 3
END
```

This is not to say that you should be able to figure out the output of F 5 in your head (you can see this output by typing SHOW F 5), but you *should* understand how to use IF and OP. If you have used Logo only for turtle geometry, you might have to read the section on OP (or OUTPUT) in your Logo manual.

By working on the problems in the book, you'll soon develop your knack for Logo programming to the point where it takes no thought for you to throw together an experiment that can be run on your computer and that tests out one of your conjectures.

3. You have access to a computer and Logo. You won't need a color monitor or graphics, but you should have a fair amount of memory (say, 512K) and a reasonably fast machine (say, a Mac or an IBM compatible). This is because you'll want to keep a large number of procedures in your workspace, and many of our procedures will be very slow. If you can't get access to this kind of machine, you can get by with a II-E, a BBC, or a Commodore, but you'll have to worry more about conserving workspace and making things more efficient. The version of Logo that you use isn't very important. The procedures in the book are written in LCSI Logo for the IBM, and my students have worked through many of the problems using the British BBC Logo.

How to Use This Book

This book should be *worked through* rather than *read*. This means that you should study the expository sections and try to understand them. If you come across any Logo that you don't understand, refer to your Logo manual. If you are still confused, check the appendix of this book. If something isn't explained in the appendix, refer to Harvey (1985). (The references are cataloged by giving the last name of the author and the publication date; they are listed in the back of the book.) If the exposition contains a computer program, install it in your workspace and run it a few times. It's a good idea to keep all the programs from the section you are working on in your workspace; some procedures (like a version of the TAB procedure that is described in the appendix) should always be on hand. When I was writing part III, I needed close to 100 procedures in the workspace at once. If a procedure contains a line that is too long for the page, I use an arrow (→) to tell you that it continues on the next line. So

```
TO F :X
OP 3 * :X + →
:X * :X + 2
END
```

means

```
TO F :X
OP 3 * :X * :X + 2
END
```

Occasionally in the exposition I've put a stopsign symbol in the margin

and a warning (something like "close the book for a while and think about this") in the text. Ignoring these warnings can be hazardous to your intellectual health.

As far as the problems go, you should do all of the exercises. You should also read all the experiments and projects, think about how you would attack them, and *really* work on at least half of them. Often the exposition refers to the result of a previous problem. If you didn't happen to work on that one, you should take some time out to do so.

Some problems will take a great deal of time. Don't be concerned if you find yourself working on a problem for a few hours (or days); that's what is supposed to happen. Take some time to experiment with things that catch your eye (this is really where having a computer comes in handy). Real mathematics involves very long-term projects; in mathematical research some projects last longer than a lifetime, and they are only solved through the collaborative work of many people in the mathematical community. You'll learn much more if you spend lots of concentration on one problem than if you give superficial consideration to several. Don't worry about finishing the book; it's made of durable paper and it will last for a long time.

Acknowledgments

This book grew out of my work with students at Woburn High School in Woburn, Massachusetts. The students were taking a course called "Independent Study," which consists of a loosely structured environment in which the only objective is to work intensively on mathematical problems. They helped me develop many of the problems in the book, and they did something much more important: they taught me that the best thing a teacher can do for students is to help them discover things for themselves.

Stephanie Raggucci, Ken Bouley, Dan Girard, Paul Gonsalves, Mark Ingalls, Mike Kirk, Mark Saviano, Gloria Liu, Jon Britt, Mike Dango, Rob Reynolds, Fred Oey, and John Franson all contributed in different ways to the final form of the book. Ken Mungan worked through many of the problems and offered valuable hints about how to make them better. Lisa Haverty worked through the entire draft of the first two parts, and her suggestions for improving the exposition were invaluable. John Treacy returned to Woburn High ten years after graduation to show us how useful Logo could be in doing mathematics.

My colleagues at Woburn High were extremely supportive throughout the writing of the book. Jim Brennan, Elfreda Kallock, and Gail Bussone listened patiently to my ramblings about simplex locks and prime factorizations when they probably would have preferred to be correcting tests. Jim Foley, the principal of Woburn High, spends countless hours each year reconvincing the people downtown that the independent study program is worth funding.

Paul Goldenberg first convinced me to write a book around the independent study problems, and his encouragement and advice have been crucial to this project. His influence on the book extends far beyond the typical effects that a series editor brings about in the elements of the series. Paul and I had many mathematical conversations when I began writing part I, and these talks determined many of the directions that I took.

Terry Ehling and the staff at The MIT Press provided first-rate technical support and advice.

Part of the book was written while I was on sabbatical leave, and several people whom I met in my travels contributed unknowingly to the final product. Amasio Corsetti and his wonderful family opened up their home to us while we

15

were in Rome; Anna Maria's cuisine was inspirational. Elio and the technical experts at Metelliana in Cava de Tirreni revived my ailing computer, allowing me to continue work when the rest of Italy was on extended vacation.

Finally, this book is for Micky and Alicia. They shared the interior of a Volkswagen with cables and monitors and computers and books for four months in Europe. They helped me carry all this stuff in and out of dozens of pensiones, guest houses, and hotels. They gave me the time and the peace of mind to work, and they listened carefully when the work led nowhere. They took me on the most glorious picnics imaginable.

Part I

Functions

This part has two purposes. You will investigate the notion of a mathematical function. Mathematicians use functions to express relationships between mathematical objects (like numbers). You can't study methods for expressing relationships between objects without studying the objects themselves, so you'll also investigate some of the mathematical topics that we'll take up throughout this book. Think of this part as a preview of coming attractions.

Chapter 1

What Is a Function?

You have been using functions for years.

Sometimes you deal explicitly with functions. For example, many mathematics courses involve problems like these:

1. Sketch the graph of the function f for which $f(x) = x^2 + 6x - 7$.

2. If $f(x) = 3x - 2$, find $f(2)$, $f(2x)$, and all x so that $f(x) = 13$.

More often, you use functions implicitly. For example, you are probably using functional ideas when you

1. solve "word problems" in algebra courses,

2. convert one unit of measurement to another (like Fahrenheit to Celsius), and

3. make measurement calculations (like finding the area of a circle whose radius is 5).

Roughly, a function is a process that transforms input values to an output value in a predictable way. It can transform Fahrenheit values to Celsius values, it can transform the radius of a circle to its area, or it can transform your grades on a set of tests to a grade for the term. The input values can come from any set, but for now, we'll assume that the input values are real numbers (we'll change this requirement considerably later on). Similarly, the output values will be real numbers.

Because a function is a process that takes a number (or several numbers) as input and outputs another number in a predictable way, we'll think of a function as a certain type of *procedure*. Before making this more precise, let's look at a few examples of functions:

Example 1 Lots of functions are defined by mathematical formulas:

Chapter 1

```
TO F :X
OP 2 * :X
END
```

```
TO G :X
OP :X*:X + 6*:X - 7
END
```

or, say, the function that converts Fahrenheit to Celsius:

```
TO FAHRENHEIT.TO.CELSIUS :T
OP (:T - 32) * (5 / 9)
END
```

A good way to get familiar with a function is to "tabulate" it. A tabulation is just a chart that lists some inputs with the corresponding outputs. A tabulation for the above function F looks like this:

```
1 . . 2
2 . . 4
3 . . 6
4 . . 8
5 . . 10
```

We'll call this a "tabulation of F between 1 and 5." Logo can generate tabulations; in the appendix, there is a Logo procedure that will tabulate a function for you. It's called TAB, and you use it by typing

TAB "F 1 5

to see the tabulation of F between 1 and 5. After you install TAB in your workspace, try typing

TAB "G 2 23

or

TAB "FAHRENHEIT.TO.CELSIUS 32 212

The last tabulation will require some sort of scroll lock on your computer so that you can see a screenful at a time.

Tabulating functions is an important way to discover their properties, and TAB will be one of the major experimental tools in this book. Whenever you meet a new function, it is a good idea to TAB it over several intervals and to look for patterns.

Compare the way functions are defined in mathematics with the way they are defined in Logo. For example, suppose F is the function that takes a number and adds 3 to it. In mathematics we'd say something like this:

Let F be the function so that $F(X) = X + 3$

whereas in Logo, we'd write

```
TO F :X
 OP :X + 3
END
```

These two ways of defining the function are really not so different. Imagine someone who understands that a function is a process that takes a number as input and outputs another number in a predictable way, but doesn't understand you when you say,

Let F be the function so that $F(X) = X + 3$

You'd probably explain yourself by saying something like,

F is the function that takes whatever number you give it and outputs the number that is three more

or

To apply the function F to a number, simply add three to it

or

To apply F to X, output $X + 3$

That looks pretty much like the Logo definition.

If you ask someone to "calculate F(5)" (you say this: "calculate F of 5"), you'd expect an answer like "F(5) = 8" (the person would say this as: "F of 5 is 8," or "F of 5 equals 8").

You can ask a computer to calculate F(5) by typing

```
SHOW F 5
```

(you say this: "show me F of 5"), and you'll see

```
8
```

So, in Logo, we need to simply write

```
F 5
```

Chapter 1

for the mathematical notation F(5), but we'll still use the mathematical terminology for function application; this means that we will read

F 3

as "F of 3" or "F applied to 3."

Example 2 Functions can be defined in pieces. The absolute value function
returns the input if the input is positive, and it returns the opposite of the
input if the input is negative:

```
TO ABS :X
IF :X > 0 [OP :X]
OP -1*:X
END
```

TAB ABS between -5 and 10.

Example 3 Functions can have more than one input. This function outputs
the surface area of a rectangular box from the lengths of its sides:

```
TO AREA :LENGTH :WIDTH :HEIGHT
OP 2 * (:LENGTH * :WIDTH + :LENGTH * :HEIGHT
        + :WIDTH * :HEIGHT)
END
```

If you want to find the area of a box whose dimensions are 4, 3, and 7, you'd
type:

SHOW AREA 4 3 7

If I'm writing for you, I'll use the mathematical notation and say

$$\text{AREA}(4, 5, 7) = 166$$

or even

$\text{AREA}(4, 5, 7)$ outputs 166

The fact that we'll always think of a function as a concrete Logo procedure will be reflected in the way we *write* conventional mathematical
expressions. Whenever I write the name of a function, I'll use the "Logo

22

font" even if the function is used in a mathematical expression that is written for you and *not* meant to be typed at your computer. So, although most texts write something like this

Let F be the function so that $F(X) = 2X + 3$

we'll write

Let F be the function so that $F(X) = 2X + 3$

Example 4 Functions can be defined recursively. The following function gives a method for finding the units digit in a positive integer:

```
TO DIGIT :N
 IF :N < 10 [OP :N]
 OP DIGIT (:N - 10)
END
```

I said before that a function must compute its output in a "predictable way." For example, people don't consider the RANDOM procedure a function, because RANDOM 4 will return different values if it is called often enough.

In order to avoid things like the RANDOM procedure, we can define a function like this:

> *A function is a procedure* F *that takes one or more inputs,*
> *that outputs, and that has the property that any two calls to*
> F *with the same inputs returns the same output.*

Experiment 1.1 Write Logo versions of the following mathematical functions:

1. $F(X) = X^3 + 3X - 2$

2. $G(X) = 5X + 7$

3. $S(X) = F(X) + G(X)$

4. $V(X) = \begin{cases} F(X), & \text{if } X > 9 \\ S(X), & \text{otherwise} \end{cases}$

5. H(X) = F(X + .001)

6. W(X) = F(G(X))

7. D(X) = (F(X + .001) − F(X))/.001

8. J(X) = H(X − .001)

9. M(X) = 3X^2 + 3

Tabulate each function between 1 and 15. Remember how TAB works: for example, you type

TAB 1 H 1 15

Which ones have identical tabulations? Why? Do any functions have almost the same tabulations? Can you explain why?

Project 1.2 When you took Algebra 1, you probably solved dozens of silly problems like this:

Debbie bought some apples at 25 cents each, she ate two of them, and she sold the rest for 32 cents each. If her profit was $1.88, how many apples did she buy?

Of course, you could solve the problem the way you are supposed to solve such problems in algebra class, but let's look at it another way:

Suppose that Debbie bought 10 apples. Then her cost would be $2.50. She would sell 8 apples for a total of $2.56, so her profit would be 6 cents. Too small.

Suppose she bought 25 apples. Her cost would be $6.25, and she would sell 23 apples at 32 cents each for a total of $7.36. Her profit would be $1.11. Better, but still too small.

You could experiment with other guesses, and each time, you could calculate the corresponding profit by the same process:

To find the profit, take the number of apples, subtract 2, multiply *this* result by .32, and subtract from this the number you get by multiplying the number of apples by .25.

So, say, you write a function that calculates Debbie's profit in terms of the number of apples she buys. Then you tabulate this function between, say, 20 and 50. What is the solution to the original problem?

Exercise 1.3 Look at the `FAHRENHEIT.TO.CELSIUS` function given in this section. Write a `CELSIUS.TO.FAHRENHEIT` function.

Project 1.4 The Celsius scale is designed so that the Celsius temperature of freezing water is 0 degrees and the Celsius temperature of boiling water is 100 degrees. Therefore the `FAHRENHEIT.TO.CELSIUS` function can be thought of as a function that takes the set of numbers between 32 and 212 (freezing and boiling on the Fahrenheit scale), shifts the set down by 32 so that it becomes the set of numbers between 0 and 180, and then scales it down by a factor of $100/180 = 5/9$ so that it becomes the set of numbers between 0 and 100. The steps of the transformation can be visualized by these pictures:

Shift:

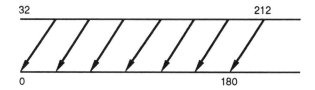

Figure 1.1

Scale down:

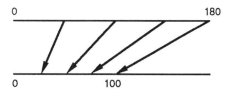

Figure 1.2

Suppose that you need a temperature scale (the `NEWGRADE` scale) where water freezes at 100 degrees and boils at 360 degrees. Write functions FAHREN-

...HEIT.TO.NEWGRADE and NEWGRADE.TO.FAHRENHEIT. How about CELSIUS.TO. NEWGRADE and NEWGRADE.TO.CELSIUS?

Exercise 1.5 Write a function HUNDREDS (in the style of the DIGIT function given in this section) that outputs the hundreds digit of a positive integer.

Experiment 1.6 Suppose that we think of N and K as nonnegative integers where K is less than or equal to N. Consider the following function of two variables:

$$\text{MYSTERY}(N,K) = \begin{cases} 1, & \text{if } N = K \text{ or if } K = 0 \\ \text{MYSTERY}(N-1,K) \\ \quad + \text{MYSTERY}(N-1,K-1), & \text{otherwise} \end{cases}$$

Implement the function in Logo. Calculate MYSTERY(5,2) by hand, and check your answer with the computer. Keep N constant (say, at 6) and write down MYSTERY(N,K) as K goes from 0 to N. Do you see why the outputs are symmetric around the middle output?

Two Important Functions

We'll build two closely related functions that will be very useful in our work. First, consider the following problem: We have a number system with N distinct digits. How many N digit numbers are there if no digit can be used more than once? For example, suppose $N = 3$, and our digits are 1, 2, and 3. Then we can form the following three digit numbers:

$$123, 132, 213, 231, 312, \text{ and } 321$$

So the answer to our problem, when $N = 3$, is 6. Note that the answer has nothing to do with the fact that we chose our digits to be 1, 2, and 3; there are 6 three digit "numbers" that can be formed from the digits $*$, $+$, and $\#$ (they are $*+\#$, $*\#+$, $+*\#$, $+\#*$, $\#*+$, and $\#+*$).

What about the case $N = 4$? We could list all the possibilities (try it), or we could reason like this: Suppose that the digits are 1, 2, 3, and 4. First, form all the possible three-digit numbers with 1, 2, and 3. There are 6 of these, and they are listed above. Each of these six numbers can be transformed into a four-digit number by inserting a 4 before the number, after the number or between two digits in the number. For example, 231 can be transformed into the four-digit numbers 4231, 2431, 2341, and 2314. In other words, each of the 6 three-digit numbers above yields 4 four-digit numbers, so the answer to our problem when $N = 4$ is $4 \cdot 6$, or 24.

How about $N = 5$? A brute force listing is becoming tedious, but the above idea allows us to imagine all the possibilities. There are 24 four-digit numbers from the digits 1, 2, 3, and 4. Each of them (like 2431) can be transformed into 5 five-digit numbers, so the answer to our problem for $N = 5$ is $5 \cdot 24$, or 120.

A general pattern emerges. The number of N digit numbers is N times the number of $(N - 1)$ digit numbers. Since the number of 1 digit numbers is 1, we have the following function:

```
TO COUNT.NUMBERS :N
 IF :N = 1 [OP 1]
 OP :N * (COUNT.NUMBERS :N - 1)
END
```

The above function is of fundamental importance in mathematics. It counts the number of rearrangements of N objects (we used digits). Take a good look at the calculation of COUNT.NUMBERS(4). We have

$$
\begin{aligned}
\texttt{COUNT.NUMBERS}(4) &= 4(\texttt{COUNT.NUMBERS}(3)) \\
&= 4(3(\texttt{COUNT.NUMBERS}(2))) \\
&= 4(3(2(\texttt{COUNT.NUMBERS}(1)))) \\
&= 4(3(2 \cdot 1))
\end{aligned}
$$

So COUNT.NUMBERS$(4) = 4 \cdot 3 \cdot 2 \cdot 1 = 24$, and similarly, COUNT.NUMBERS$(5) = 5 \cdot 4 \cdot 3 \cdot 2 \cdot 1$. In general, COUNT.NUMBERS(N) will output the product of all the whole numbers between N and 1.

Exercise 1.7 Implement COUNT.NUMBERS in terms of the PROD function of the appendix.

Of course, COUNT.NUMBERS will only work if we input a positive integer. We will also need to input 0 from time to time, and the function that acts like COUNT.NUMBERS but allows an input of 0 is called the "factorial" function. It is defined like this:

```
TO FACTORIAL :N
  IF :N = 0 [OP 1]
  OP :N * (FACTORIAL :N - 1)
END
```

The reason that we define the factorial of 0 to be 1 will become clear in part II. You should convince yourself that FACTORIAL(N) is still the product of all the numbers between N and 1 if N is a positive integer. Although we'll never need the fact, it's interesting that FACTORIAL can be further modified to accept real numbers (and even complex numbers). The resulting function is called the *gamma function*, and it turns up throughout mathematics.

The modifications that allow FACTORIAL to accept real number inputs are substantial (they require advanced techniques from calculus). The gamma function has the property that if N is a positive integer, the output at $N + 1$ is FACTORIAL(N). The output at 1/2 turns out to be $\sqrt{\pi}$, and the output at 3/2 is $\sqrt{\pi}/2$. The gamma function is discussed in Conway (1978), but the discussion assumes that the reader has taken a few semesters of calculus.

The mathematical notation for FACTORIAL(N) is $N!$, so that $5! = 120$.

Exercise 1.8 Predict the result of each expression, and then check it with your computer:

1. FACTORIAL(6) (you type: SHOW FACTORIAL 6)

2. 6 · FACTORIAL(5)

3. 8 · 7 · 6! (you type: SHOW 8 * 7 * FACTORIAL 6)

4. $\dfrac{9!}{5!\,4!}$

(you type: SHOW (FACTORIAL 9)/((FACTORIAL 5)*(FACTORIAL 4)))

5. $\dfrac{10!}{3!\,2!\,5!}$

Exercise 1.9 In your head, what is 1000001!/1000000!. What happens if you ask your computer to calculate this quotient. What's different between the way you do it and the way the computer does it?

Experiment 1.10 The `REMAINDER` function takes as inputs two integers A and B and outputs the remainder when A is divided by B. For example, `REMAINDER 16 10` outputs 6. Tabulate the following function:

```
TO F :N
 OP REMAINDER (FACTORIAL (:N - 1)) :N
END
```

What's going on?

Exercise 1.11 Suppose that you have N digits and that you want to form all K digit numbers (with no repeated digit) where K is some positive integer less than or equal to N. For example, suppose that we have the digits 1, 2, 3, 4, 5, 6, and 7. How many three-digit numbers are there? Once you figure this out, write a function (of two variables N and K) that solves the problem in general.

The next function we need is exponentiation. We need a function of two variables N and E that outputs the Eth power of N. We'll assume (for now) that E is a positive integer, so that the Eth power of N is simply

$$\underbrace{N \cdot N \cdot N \cdot N \cdots N}_{E \text{ times}}$$

Some versions of Logo have this function built in; others have it built in for a few special values of N (like the famous constant e which is approximately 2.7182818284590). You should check your version, but even if the function is there already, you should work through the following development (it uses important and enjoyable ideas).

Let's start with a special case: suppose that $N = 3$ and $E = 12$, so we want to compute 3^{12}. This would be easy if we knew the value of 3^{11}, because

$$3^{12} = 3 \cdot 3^{11}$$

Since $3^1 = 3$, we have the following method for computing 3^E:

```
TO POWER3 :E
 IF :E = 1 [OP 3]
 OP 3 * POWER3 (:E - 1)
END
```

If you are comfortable with this, you should have no trouble with the general case:

Chapter 1

```
TO POWER :N :E
  IF :E = 1 [OP :N]
  OP :N * POWER :N (:E - 1)
END
```

While we're at it, we might as well adjust POWER so that it accepts 0 as an exponent. Of course, an exponent of 0 can't be interpreted using the repeated multiplication model

$$N^E = \overbrace{N \cdot N \cdot N \cdot N \cdots N}^{E \text{ times}}$$

so we are free to define N^0 as we please. You probably learned in algebra that the convention is to take the 0th power of a nonzero number N to be 1. One of the reasons is that with the repeated multiplication model, it's clear that we have the following fact:

$$N^E N^F = N^{(E+F)} \tag{*}$$

and this fact is extremely useful in manipulating expressions that contain exponents. If we want this fact to remain true when $E = 0$, then we must insist that 0th powers are defined in such a way that the following identity holds:

$$N^0 N^F = N^{(0+F)}$$

Since $0 + F = F$, this becomes

$$N^0 N^F = N^F$$

Suppose that N and F are nonzero. Then we can divide both sides of this equation by N^F, and we find that $N^0 = 1$. In other words, if we want identity (*) to hold when $E = 0$, we must define the 0th power of a nonzero number to be 1. The power function now becomes

```
TO POWER :N :E
  IF :E = 0 [OP 1]
  OP :N * POWER :N (:E - 1)
END
```

The only trouble with this is that POWER 0 0 will output 1. The symbol 0^0 is ambiguous. On one hand, 0 to any power should be 0, and, on the other hand, any number to the 0 power should be 1. Most texts leave the symbol undefined. I once worked on a project in number theory where it was extremely convenient to define 0^0 as 1. Let's leave it that way; as long as you remember that POWER will always interpret the 0th power of 0 as 1, there won't be any trouble (if it bothers you, change the definition of POWER to handle POWER 0 0 as a special case). Do you see that if N is not 0, then POWER$(0, N)$ will output the correct answer (0)?

You probably know that POWER can be extended to negative and fractional exponents. The modification that allows negative exponents is straightforward (it will show up as an exercise later; you have enough machinery to do it now if you want to try it), but fractional exponents require ideas from calculus. It turns out that, even though we'll have no need for it, POWER can even be modified to accept all real (even complex) numbers as exponents.

I said on page 11 that the two functions that we now call FACTORIAL and POWER are closely related. A glance at their definitions

```
TO FACTORIAL :N
 IF :N = 0 [OP 1]
 OP :N * (FACTORIAL :N - 1)
END

TO POWER :N :E
 IF :E = 0 [OP 1]
 OP :N * (POWER :N :E - 1)
END
```

shows a striking similarity. More precisely, factorial involves repeated multiplication in which each factor is decreased by 1, and exponentiation involves repeated multiplication in which each factor remains the same.

Project 1.12 Write a function that expresses the idea of repeated multiplication with a generic decrement and length. In other words, write a function REP.MULT that takes three inputs N, D and L. The output of REP.MULT(N, D, L) should be

$$N(N - D)(N - 2D)(N - 3D) \cdots (N - (L - 1)D)$$

so that REP.MULT$(15, 2, 6)$ will output

$$15(15 - 2)(15 - 2 \cdot 2)(15 - 3 \cdot 2)(15 - 4 \cdot 2)(15 - 5 \cdot 2)$$
$$= 15 \cdot 13 \cdot 11 \cdot 9 \cdot 7 \cdot 5, \text{ or } 675675$$

In other words, if you type

SHOW REP.MULT 15 2 6

you'll see 675675.

If we ignore the troublesome special cases (FACTORIAL(0) and POWER(N, 0)), we can redefine our two functions in a way that makes their connection explicit:

TO FACTORIAL :N
OP REP.MULT :N 1 :N
END

and

TO POWER :N :E
OP REP.MULT :N 0 :E
END

Fix these modifications so that they handle the special cases.

Noticing that two functions (FACTORIAL and POWER) are instances of the same process (repeated multiplication) is an activity that is extremely close to the heart of most mathematicians. This activity is often described by the loosely defined word "abstraction." Roughly, abstraction is the act of finding similarities between seemingly different ideas. Another example of this phenomenon is to point out the similarity between SIGMA and the PROD function of the appendix (one is repeated addition and the other is repeated multiplication). Abstraction is important in mathematics for many reasons; three important ones are these:

1. *Efficiency.* If the mathematical objects A, B, and C are special cases of object D, then any fact that is true about object D is true about all the objects A, B, and C. For example, you learned in geometry that rectangles and rhombi are parallelograms. So any fact about parallelograms is true about rectangles and rhombi. This means that you don't have to prove that the diagonals of a rhombus bisect each other once you prove this fact for parallelograms. Whole branches of mathematics (like linear algebra) were created to investigate the properties of "abstract" objects that are defined by properties common to several concrete objects. The theorems in these disciplines are very powerful because they apply to a wide class of phenomena that occur in nature.

2. *Inspiration.* If you have discovered that objects A and B share some important properties, and if object B is well understood, you can look to object B to get ideas about facts that might be true about object A. For example, the arithmetic of the integers is very much like polynomial arithmetic. Granting this, we can ask questions like "What is the analogue for polynomials of the fact that every pair of integers has a greatest common divisor?" Of course, there is no guarantee that facts about B will lead to insights about A, but this technique is used every day to discover new mathematics.

3. *Beauty.* There is something compelling about the fact that FACTORIAL and POWER are instances of a more general process; finding new connections between ideas gives you a sense of aesthetic satisfaction. Poets, musicians, computer programmers, and mathematicians (among others) are constantly trying to capture the essence of the processes that are central to their work. This search is driven in part by the fact that these underlying principles are often elegant and intellectually pleasing.

Project 1.13 Formulate your solution to exercise 1.11 in terms of REP.MULT.

Project 1.14 Suppose that you have N digits and that you want to form all K digit numbers, but this time, you allow a digit to be repeated any number of times. For example, suppose you have the digits 1 and 2, and you want to form all three-digit numbers. They are

$$111, 112, 121, 122, 211, 212, 221, \text{ and } 222$$

In general, how many such K digit numbers can you form with N digits?

 # Project 1.15 Look carefully at the definition of REP.MULT, and explain why the following statement is true:

Suppose that N, D, D' and L are positive integers so that $N > (L-1)D'$ and $D < D'$. Then

$$\text{REPMULT}(N, D', L) > \text{REP.MULT}(N, D, L)$$

Use this fact to show that for $N > 1, N^N > N!$.

 # Exercise 1.16 Suppose that N, M, D, and L are positive integers. Show that

$$\text{REP.MULT}(N, D, L) \cdot \text{REP.MULT}(M, 0, L) = \text{REP.MULT}(MN, MD, L)$$

Deduce that $N_N N! = \text{REP.MULT}(N^2, N, N)$

Operations on Functions

It is often useful to combine functions in various ways. For example, take another look at exercises 1.3 and 1.4. First, you wrote a function CEL-SIUS.TO.FAHRENHEIT. Then you wrote a function FAHRENHEIT.TO.NEWGRADE. The last part of the problem was to write a function CELSIUS.TO.NEWGRADE. Now, one solution to the problem is to work out the scale and shift changes from scratch; if you did this, you probably came up with something like

```
TO CELSIUS.TO.NEWGRADE :C
OP (13/5) * :C + 100
END
```

Here's a version that takes no work

```
TO CELSIUS.TO.NEWGRADE :C
OP FAHRENHEIT.TO.NEWGRADE (CELSIUS.TO.FAHRENHEIT :C)
END
```

Let's look at another example. Suppose that F is the function

```
TO F :X
OP :X * :X + 3 * :X - 2
END
```

and we want to write the function H so that $H(X) = F(2X + 1)$. One way to do this is to do the algebraic calculations that simplify $F(2X + 1)$.

$$F(2X + 1) = (2X + 1)^2 + 3(2X + 1) - 2 = 4X^2 + 10X + 2$$

So H is defined like this:

```
TO H :X
OP 4 * :X * :X + 10 * :X + 2
END
```

Of course, there is no need to do all this work; you could simply write

```
TO H :X
 OP F (2 * :X + 1)
END
```

There is even a better idea here. We could define a function G:

```
TO G :X
 OP 2 * :X + 1
END
```

so that we have

```
TO H :X
 OP F (G :X)
END
```

The function H is called the *composite* of F and G, and we can think of composition as an operation that takes two functions and outputs their composite. Such an operation is called a "higher-order function," and we will meet several of them in this book. We can approximate this higher-order function in Logo with the following useful tool:

```
TO COMPOSITE :F :G :X
 OP (APPLY :F (APPLY :G :X)
END
```

Then, using the above notation, we have

```
TO CELSIUS.TO.NEWGRADE :C
 OP COMPOSITE "FAHRENHEIT.TO.NEWGRADE →
            "CELSIUS.TO.FAHRENHEIT :C
END
```

and

```
TO H :X
 OP COMPOSITE "F "G :X
END
```

Chapter 1

Exercise 1.17 Sometimes it is helpful to view a function as a composite of other functions. For example, if we define the following functions

```
TO SCALE :X
OP (5/9) * :X
END
```

```
TO SHIFT :X
OP :X - 32
END
```

then we have

```
TO FAHRENHEIT.TO.CELSIUS :T
OP COMPOSITE "SCALE "SHIFT :T
END
```

Write CELSIUS.TO.FAHRENHEIT in this style.

Exercise 1.18 Find a simple way to write the following function:

```
TO SIMPLE :X
OP COMPOSITE "FAHRENHEIT.TO.CELSIUS ←
"CELSIUS.TO.FAHRENHEIT :X
END
```

Project 1.19 If F and G are functions, we define the sum of F and G to be the function that takes an input X and outputs $F(X)+G(X)$. Use COMPOSITE as a model to write a procedure ADD that approximates this higher-order operation of function addition.

Notice that I say that COMPOSITE "approximates" function composition. The reason is that in real life, the composite of two functions is another function. So, if $F(X)=2X$ and $G(X)=X+3$, I'd like

COMPOSITE "F "G

to output "the function that takes an input X and outputs $2X+6$." Without a great deal of fuss, it's not possible in most versions of Logo to write functions that output other functions.

 # Exercise 1.20 Look at the procedure H above. If I change the definition of F, does H change? Is H a function?

 # Exercise 1.21 Most versions of Logo have "prefix" versions of addition and multiplication. They are equivalent to

```
TO F SUM :A :B          TO PRODUCT :A :B
  OP :A + :A              OP :A * :B
END                     END
```

Use SUM an PRODUCT to write a higher-order function COLLECT that captures the similarities between the SIGMA and PROD functions of the appendix. Implement SIGMA and PROD using this abstract procedure. COLLECT should take a "binary operation" as one of its inputs; play with binary operations besides SUM and PRODUCT, like

```
TO BIN :X :Y
  OP 1 + (:X/:Y)
END
```

Exercise 1.22 Modify POWER so that it accepts negative exponents. Recall the definition:

If E is a positive integer,

$$N^{-E} = \frac{1}{N^E}$$

Why is negative exponentiation defined in this way?

Chapter 2

Equal Functions

Think of a function as a processor; it takes an input (for now, let's just worry about functions with one input), and it processes that input in a certain way to arrive at an output. A function can thus be visualized as a machine:

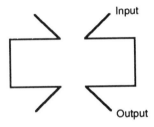

Figure 2.1

For example, consider the function

```
TO F :X
  IF :X > 2 [OP :X - 2]
  OP 2 - :X
END
```

If you drop the number 6 into the input hopper of the machine, the machine churns out 4 (try typing SHOW F 4); if you drop in 1, the machine produces a 1, and if you feed it a −3.5, you get back 5.5 (see figure 2.2).

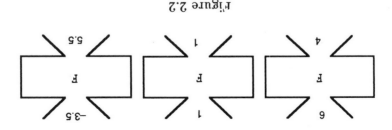

Figure 2.2

Using this processor model, you can think of equal functions as functions that define the same machine (we'll formulate a more precise definition shortly). For example, if you experiment with these two functions (by, say, tabulating them)

```
TO G :X                     TO H :X
OP ABS (:X - 2)             OP SQRT (:X-2) * (:X-2)
END                         END
```

you'll see that even though they each look very different from F, all three functions seem to define the same processor. (Can you prove this?)

Thinking of equal functions as functions that define the same processor leads us to a first stab at a definition of function equality

Definition of Equal Functions (First Try)   If F and G are functions, we say that F = G if F(X) =G(X) for all inputs X.

Before pointing out a subtle flaw in this definition, let me point out something that is perfectly valid but often causes confusion. Many people look at a definition like this and say that it is nonsense because it·defines equality in terms of itself. In other words, the definition is supposed to give meaning to the word "equality" (F = G), and it does this by using the notion of equality (F(X) = G(X)). You probably learned in geometry class that you should never define a word in terms of itself; definitions shouldn't be "circular." However, the above definition isn't circular because the symbol "=" means two different things in the two places that it is used in the definition. In the phrase "F = G," we are talking about equality of functions; this is the notion that we are try-ing to define. In the phrase "F(X) = G(X)," we are talking about equality of real numbers, and everyone knows what that means. So the definition gives meaning to function equality by explaining it in terms of number equality, and there's nothing circular about that. The only thing that might be confusing is that the same symbol ("=") is used in two different ways inside the same sentence. We could use a symbol different from "=" when talking about about function equality. This would be silly for the following reasons:

1. Besides equal functions and equal numbers, people talk about other kinds of equality in mathematics (equal sets, equal points, equal triangles, equal polynomials, etc.). Giving a new symbol in each instance of equality would make the mathematics unreadable. People have no trouble (most of the time) figuring out the meaning of a word from its context; why should mathematical symbols be any different?

2. Using the same symbol for different ideas suggests that the ideas share a common property; it is a means for expressing abstraction. So, rather than looking at the two uses of "=" above as sources of confusion, you should look at them as an attempt to clarify the meaning of equal functions.

What is the subtle flaw in our definition "if F and G are functions, we say that F = G if $F(X) = G(X)$ for all inputs X"? Consider the following two functions:

```
TO Q :X                    TO R :X
 IF :X = 1 [OP 3]           OP 4 * :X - 1
 OP (Q :X - 1) + 4         END
END
```

Tabulate each function between, say, 1 and 20. Do you get the same thing? How about between 100 and 200? Is $Q(320) = R(320)$? It seems that both functions give the same output for a given input, although Q takes much longer to calculate its output than R does for big numbers. Is $Q(1.5) = R(1.5)$? A problem arises. $R(1.5) = 5$, but Q doesn't output at all when we input 1.5 (eventually, the computer will produce an "out of space" message; why?). Clearly Q and R do not define the same processor, so we wouldn't want to call Q and R equal.

The flaw in our definition, then, is that even though F and G may never "disagree" by outputting different values for the same input, F and G may still fail to be equal because they are defined on different "domains." By the domain of a function, we mean the set of all inputs that cause the function to output. So the domain of Q above is the set of positive integers, whereas the domain of R is the set of real numbers. Using this domain concept, we have a better definition of function equality.

Definition of Equal Functions (Second Try) If F and G are functions, we say that F = G if

1. F and G have the same domain,

2. $F(X)=G(X)$ for all X in this common domain.

What happens if you have a function defined in Logo and you input a number that is not in its domain? Logo will complain, and the kind of error message often tells you why the number is not in the domain. For example, if F is defined like this:

TO F :X
 OP 1/(SQRT (:X - 1))
END

try typing

SHOW F 2

SHOW F 1

SHOW F 0

SHOW F 3.5

SHOW F -3.5

What is the domain of F?

Another example: Suppose that F is defined like this:

TO F :X
 IF :X = 2 [OP 1]
 OP (F :X - 1) + 4
END

Try typing

```
SHOW F 4

SHOW F 3

SHOW F 2

SHOW F 1

SHOW F 0

SHOW F 3.5

SHOW F -2
```

What is the domain of F?

Experiment 2.1 Use Logo to help you find the domain for each function:

1. ```
   TO F :X
     OP :X * :X
   END
   ```

2. ```
   TO G :X
     OP 3/:X
   END
   ```

3. ```
   TO H :X
     IF :X = 0 [OP 4]
     OP (H :X - 1) + 3
   END
   ```

4. ```
   TO K :X
     IF :X = -1 [OP -2]
     OP (K :X - 1) +3
   END
   ```

5. ```
   TO L :X
     IF :X < -1 [OP -2]
     OP (L :X - 1) + 3
   END
   ```

6. ```
   TO M :X
     OP 3/(:X - 4)
   END
   ```

7. ```
   TO N :X
     IF :X = 4 [OP 0]
     OP 3/(:X - 4)
   END
   ```

8. ```
   TO P :X
     IF :X > 2 [OP :X + 2]
   END
   ```

9. ```
   TO Q :X
     IF :X < 0 [OP :X]
     OP 3 + (Q :X - 1)
   END
   ```

10. ```
    TO R :X
      OP 3 + (R :X)
    END
    ```

11. SQRT (this is a primitive)

Exercise 2.2 If F and G are functions, describe the domain of the composite of F and G in terms of the domains of F and G. You might want to use the following functions as examples:

```
TO F: X
  OP (F :X - 1) + 2
  END

TO G: X
  IF :X = 1 [OP 3]
  OP :X * X - 3
  END
```

Functions Equal on a Set

Recall the functions Q and R:

```
TO Q: X
  IF :X = 1 [OP 3]
  OP (Q :X - 1) + 4
  END

TO R: X
  OP 4 * :X - 1
  END
```

We know that Q and R are not equal because the domain of Q is the set of positive integers whereas the domain of R is the set of real numbers. Still, it seems that if X is a positive integer, $Q(X) = R(X)$. If this is true, we say that "Q = R on the set of positive integers." More generally, we can say the following:

Definition of Functions Equal on a Set If F and G are functions and S is a subset of both the domain of F and the domain of G, we say that "F = G on S" if $F(X) = G(X)$ for every X in S.

By the way, the above functions Q and R *are* equal on the set of positive integers. Here's why (these ideas will be refined in part II): Take a positive integer, like 6. From the definition of Q, we have

$$Q(6) = Q(5) + 4$$
$$= (Q(4) + 4) + 4 = Q(4) + 2 \cdot 4$$
$$= (Q(3) + 4) + 2 \cdot 4 = Q(3) + 3 \cdot 4$$
$$= (Q(2) + 4) + 3 \cdot 4 = Q(2) + 4 \cdot 4$$
$$= (Q(1) + 4) + 4 \cdot 4 = 3 + 5 \cdot 4 = 23 = R(6)$$

Try this for Q(8).

Let's move up one level of abstraction. Instead of Q(8) or Q(6), let's use our technique to calculate Q(N) where N is some positive integer:

$$\begin{aligned}
Q(N) &= Q(N-1) + 4 \\
&= Q(N-2) + 4 + 4 = Q(N-2) + 2 \cdot 4 \\
&= Q(N-3) + 4 + 2 \cdot 4 = Q(N-3) + 3 \cdot 4 \\
&= Q(N-4) + 4 + 3 \cdot 4 = Q(N-4) + 4 \cdot 4 \\
&= Q(N-5) + 5 \cdot 4 \\
&= Q(N-6) + 6 \cdot 4 \\
&\vdots \\
&= Q(N-K) + K \cdot 4 \\
&\vdots \\
&= Q(1) + (N-1) \cdot 4
\end{aligned}$$

I got the last line by continuing the pattern (in every line, the thing you take Q of and the thing you multiply by 4 add up to N). If you want to be more formal, replace K in "$=Q(N-K)+K\cdot 4$" by $N-1$. So, eliminating all the middle steps, we have

$$\begin{aligned}
Q(N) &= Q(1) + (N-1) \cdot 4 \\
&= 3 + 4N - 4 = 4N - 1 = R(N)
\end{aligned}$$

Project 2.3 Use this technique to show that the following two functions are equal on the set of positive integers:

```
TO V :X                    TO G :X
 IF :X = 1 [OP 2]           OP 5 * :X - 3
 OP (V :X - 1) + 5         END
END
```

For what positive integer(s) X does the above technique fail to work? Are the functions still equal at this (these) integer(s)?

Exercise 2.4 Find a simple function (like the G in the previous exercise) that is equal to the following function on the set of positive integers:

Chapter 2

```
TO W :X
  IF :X = 1 [OP 5]
  OP (W :X - 1) + 7
END
```

Project 2.5 We have been defining quite a few functions via the following skeleton:

```
TO GEN.FCN :X
  IF :X = 1 [OP ?]
  OP (GEN.FCN :X - 1) + ??
END
```

Make this skeleton into a generic function generator by introducing two more inputs: B (the "base case" that replaces the "?" in F) and I (the "increment" that replaces the "??" in F). So the F of exercise 2.2 is

```
TO F :X
  OP GEN.FCN 3 2 :X
END
```

the V of project 2.3 is

```
TO V :X
  OP GEN.FCN 2 5 :X
END
```

and the W of exercise 2.4 is

```
TO W :X
  OP GEN.FCN 5 7 :X
END
```

If you keep B and I constant, and you let $G(X) = \text{GEN.FCN}(B, I, X)$, find a simple function (defined without recursion) that is equal to G on the set of positive integers.

Suppose that we have a function in mind. For example, we're thinking of the function that outputs the absolute value of its input. We can implement this function in Logo in many ways. For example,

```
TO F :X
 IF :X > O [OP :X]
 OP -1 * :X
END

TO G :X
 OP SQRT :X * :X
END
```

The functions F and G are equal. We'll sometimes express this fact by saying that F and G are both "Logo models" for the absolute value function. Rather than writing down a fussy definition for a Logo model (actually trying to do that could get us into a philosophical tangle), let's leave the notion vague. When I say,

> Build a Logo model for the function that squares its input

you'll know to type something like

```
TO F :X
 OP :X * :X
END
```

at your computer.

Project 2.6 Suppose S is a function defined on the positive integers by the rule: $S(N)$ is the sum of all the integers between 1 and N. Model S in Logo (you might want to use the SIGMA function of the appendix). Can you find a simple function T that is equal to S on the set of positive integers? (Hint: Tabulate your Logo model and look at the outputs.)

Exercise 2.7 Why are the following functions not equal?

```
TO F1 :X              TO F2 :X
 OP :X + 3             OP (:X * :X + 4 * :X + 3)/(:X + 1)
END                   END
```

Make them equal by inserting an IF statement in F2.

Exercise 2.8 Write a function K that is equal to

```
TO H :X
 OP :X + 4
END
```

at all real numbers except 6; make k(6) = 20.

Experiment 2.9 Let S be the function defined like this:

```
TO S :X
  IF :X > 0 [OP 1]
  IF :X < 0 [OP -1]
  OP 0
END
```

S is called the "signature function"; it tells you the sign (or signature) of a number. Let F be defined like this:

```
TO F :X
  OP S (:X * :X)
END
```

and let ONE be this function:

```
TO ONE :X
  OP 1
END
```

Is F equal to ONE?

Exercise 2.10 Write a function L with the following properties:

1. The domain of L is the set of all real numbers except 6.

2. On its domain, L is equal to H where H is defined like this:

```
TO H :X
  OP :X + 4
END
```

Proving Functions Equal

Proving two functions equal can be a tricky task. Sometimes you can prove that two functions are equal by showing that they are defined by algebraically equivalent expressions. For example, consider the following two functions:

```
TO F1 :X                      TO F2 :X
 OP :X * :X + 3 * :X + 2       OP (:X + 2) * (:X + 1)
END                           END
```

Now, the domain of each function is the set of all real numbers. Since $X^2 + 3X + 2 = (X + 2)(X + 1)$ for all real numbers X (do you remember how to prove this fact?), the functions are equal.

Sometimes, you can do a "case analysis." For example, suppose that we have

```
TO A :X                       TO B :X
 IF :X > 0 [OP :X]             OP SQRT :X * :X
 OP -1 * :X                   END
END
```

Now, both functions have the real numbers as a domain. To show that they have the same output, notice that the function A is defined in pieces. One piece is the set of real numbers X so that $X > 0$ (the positive real numbers). On this set, A simply outputs the value of its input. What about B? Well, if you take a positive number, square it, and then take the square root, you end up right where you started. In other words, if $X > 0$, $\text{SQRT}(X^2) = X$ (is this true for negative numbers?). So A = B on the set of positive real numbers. On the set of nonpositive numbers, A outputs the opposite of its input. How about B? Well, if you take a negative number (or 0), square it, and take its square root, you also end up with its opposite. To see this, note that if $X < 0$, $-X > 0$. So

$$B(X) = \text{SQRT}(X^2) = \text{SQRT}(-X)^2 = -X$$

(remember that $-X$ is positive, so its square root is itself). Since A = B on both the set of positive real numbers and the set of nonpositive real numbers, A = B.

We will often deal with functions defined on $\mathbf{Z}^+$ by recursive definitions. Reasoning about such functions requires some interesting counting techniques; we'll take up some of these techniques in depth in part II. Here's a preview of the kinds of things you'll find there.

When mathematician Carl Gauss (1777–1855) was in elementary school, his class was told to add up the numbers between 1 and 100 (teachers have always loved to use mathematical calculations as a method for crowd control). Rather than doing the arithmetic, Gauss found a pattern. Looking at the sum

$$1 + 2 + 3 + 4 + 5 + \cdots + 96 + 97 + 98 + 99 + 100$$

he added the first number to the last $(1 + 100 = 101)$, the second number to the next to last $(2 + 99 = 101)$, and realized that adding pairs equidistant from the ends always yields 101. Since there are 50 pairs, the sum is $50 \cdot 101 = 5050$. Let's use Gauss' idea (*first plus last times half the number of terms*) to look again at project 2.6. We have this function S that adds the numbers between 1 and its input. One way to define S (without SIGMA) is

```
TO S :N
  IF :N = 1 [OP 1]
  OP :N + (S :N - 1)
END
```

Another way to view Gauss' technique is to write the output of S in two ways:

$$s(N) = 1 + 2 + 3 + \cdots + (N - 1) + N$$
$$s(N) = N + (N - 1) + (N - 2) + \cdots + 2 + 1$$

Now add these two equations by adding every term in the top equation to the term directly below it; you should get

$$2s(N) = \overbrace{(N + 1) + (N + 1) + (N + 1) + \cdots + (N + 1) + (N + 1)}^{N \text{ times}}$$

So

$$2s(N) = N(N + 1) \quad \text{and} \quad s(N) = \frac{N(N + 1)}{2}$$

This gives us a function equal to S on the set of positive integers:

```
TO S? :N
  OP :N * (:N + 1) / 2
END
```

Many theorems in mathematics amount to statements about the equality of two functions, and variations on the above techniques for proving functions equal (algebraic manipulation, case analysis and counting) will show up throughout this book.

More Examples

Sometimes the fact that two functions are equal on a set can come as a surprise. Here are some examples of unobvious function equalities that you'll establish (either now or in the remaining sections):

Example 1 This example uses the REMAINDER primitive. If A and B are positive integers, REMAINDER(A, B) is the remainder that is left when A is divided by B. So

```
SHOW REMAINDER 15 6
```

produces 3. We'll study this function in depth in part III; one of the most beautiful and systematic treatments of its properties is in Gauss' classic work in number theory, *Disquistiones Arithmeticae*, published in 1801. Consider the following functions:

```
TO DIVIS :N
 IF REMAINDER :N 7 = 0 [OP 0]
 OP 1
END

TO FE :N
 OP REMAINDER (POWER :N 6) 7
END
```

The first function simply tests its input for divisibility by 7; numbers that are divisible by 7 cause an output of 0, and all others cause an output of 1. The second function outputs the remainder of the sixth power of its input on division by 7. Surprisingly,

```
DIVIS = FE on Z+
```

Check it out by tabulation. It's fairly easy (isn't it?) to see why the functions agree on multiples of 7. The fact that they agree on numbers not divisible by 7 is a special case of a theorem due to Pierre Fermat (1601-1665), known as "Fermat's little theorem." We'll prove it in part III.

Experiment 2.11 Suppose you generalize DIVIS and FE as follows:

```
TO DIVIS :N :M
  IF REMAINDER :N :M = 0 [OP 0]
  OP 1
END
```

```
TO FE :N :M
  OP REMAINDER (POWER :N :M-1) :M
END
```

Is DIVIS = FE on Z^+ if you keep $M = 5$? How about $M = 6$? $M = 9$? Experiment with different values of M; for what values of M does it seem that DIVIS = FE on Z^+?

Example 2 Let CTS be the function that counts the number of two-element subsets of an N element set. For example, CTS(5) = 10 because a five-element set, say, {1,2,3,4,5}, has 10 two-element subsets; they are

$$\{1,2\},\{1,3\},\{1,4\},\{1,5\},\{2,3\},\{2,4\},\{2,5\},\{3,4\},\{3,5\}, \text{ and } \{4,5\}$$

It turns out that on Z^+, CTS is equal to the following function:

```
TO PAIRS :N
  OP :N * (:N - 1)/2
END
```

Exercise 2.12 Prove this using the following idea. We can count the two-element subsets of $\{1,2,3,4\ldots N\}$ using the scheme

Group 1. Sets that "start" with 1:

$$\{1,2\},\{1,3\},\{1,4\},\ldots,\{1,N\} \text{ (there are } N - 1 \text{ of these)}$$

Group 2. Sets that "start" with 2 but aren't counted in group 1:

$$\{2,3\},\{2,4\},\{2,5\},\ldots,\{2,N\} \text{ (there are } N - 2 \text{ of these)}$$

Group 3. Sets that "start" with 3 but aren't in groups 1 and 2:

$$\{3,4\},\{3,5\},\{3,6\},\ldots,\{3,N\} \text{ (there are } N - 3 \text{ of these)}$$

Group $N - 1$. Sets that "start" with $N - 1$ but aren't contained in groups 1 through $N - 2$:

$\{N - 1, N\}$ (there is one of these)

Now use project 2.6.

Finally, there are functions that are conjectured equal but whose equality has yet to be established. For example, consider the following baroque function FT:

FT(N) is the number of ordered triples of positive integers (X, Y, Z) so that

$$X^N + Y^N = Z^N$$

FT is a very mysterious function. It isn't at all clear, for example, which numbers are in the domain of FT. Of course, FT$(0) = 0$ because there are no triples (X, Y, Z) for which

$$X^0 + Y^0 = Z^0$$

On the other hand, 1 isn't in the domain of FT; FT(1) doesn't output because there are infinitely many triples (X, Y, Z) of positive integers so that

$$X + Y = Z$$

Surprisingly, 2 is also missing from the domain of FT. This is because there are infinitely many triples (the "Pythagorean triples") so that

$$X^2 + Y^2 = Z^2$$

This is a consequence of the algebraic identity

$$(a^2 - b^2)^2 + (2ab)^2 = (a^2 + b^2)^2$$

Simply choose positive integers a and b with $a > b$, and you have a Pythagorean triple by putting

$$X = a^2 - b^2, \quad Y = 2ab, \quad \text{and} \quad Z = a^2 + b^2$$

In 1983 the German mathematician Gerd Faltings produced a brilliant piece of work that has as one of its consequences that the domain of FT includes all integers greater than 2. In other words, FT will output for inputs of 3, 4, 5 .... Using Faltings' result, we can state one of the most famous unproved conjectures in mathematics:

> *On the set of integers greater than 2,* FT *is equal to the following function:*

```
TO C :X
 OP O
END
```

This conjecture says that if N is an integer > 2, then there are no triples of positive integers (X, Y, Z) for which

$$X^N + Y^N = Z^N$$

The statement is known as the Fermat conjecture. Fermat claimed that he had a proof for it, but he never wrote it down. Over the past 350 years many mathematicians have devoted their careers to the conjecture, and whole branches of mathematics have been developed to attack it. Despite all this work the Fermat conjecture remains an open problem in mathematics.

I should mention that there is a school of mathematics that would deny the existence of my function FT. People who adhere to this "constructivist" point of view maintain that because no one can give a procedure (in any language) for computing $FT(N)$ in a finite number of steps, FT doesn't exist. Of course, if someone were to establish the Fermat conjecture this week, the existence of FT would go unquestioned (FT would equal C). On the other hand, suppose that someone proved this week that for any N, $FT(N) < 5$. The constructivists would still deny the existence of FT until a procedure is developed to calculate the value of $FT(N)$ (0, 1, 2, 3, 4, or 5) explicitly. You can find a description of the constructivist philosophy of mathematics in Stewart (1986).

Exercise 2.13 Prove that the following two functions are equal:

```
TO  V :X
 IF :X > 2 [OP :X - 2]
 OP 2 - :X
END

TO U :X
 OP SQRT ((:X - 2) * (:X - 2))
END
```

Project 2.14 Define a function E so that

$$E(N) = 1 + 3 + 5 + \cdots + (2N - 1)$$

for all positive integers N. Find a simple function that is equal to E on $\mathbf{Z}^+$. Prove that your functions are equal. (Hint: First model E in Logo using project 2.6 as a guide. To find a simple function equal to E on $\mathbf{Z}^+$, tabulate E. For the proof, mimic Gauss' technique.)

Exercise 2.15 By an *array*, I mean a square of numbers. So here are some 2×2 arrays:

$$\begin{pmatrix} 1 & 2 \\ 3 & 4 \end{pmatrix} \begin{pmatrix} 3 & -1 \\ 4 & 8 \end{pmatrix} \begin{pmatrix} 9 & 0 \\ 2 & 2 \end{pmatrix}$$

How many numbers show up in an $N \times N$ array? The "diagonal" of a 3×3 array is shown in the picture:

How many numbers belong to the diagonal of an $N \times N$ array? How many numbers do not belong to the diagonal of an $N \times N$ array? How many numbers are "above" the diagonal of an $N \times N$ array? Use this result to give a proof that your solution to project 2.6 is correct.

Experiment 2.16 Consider the following functions:

```
TO M :X :N
 IF :N = 0 [OP 1]
 OP 1 + (:X * (M :X :N-1))
END

TO Q :X :N
 IF :N = 0 [OP 1]
 OP (POWER :X :N) + (Q :X :N-1)
END

TO P :N
 OP ((POWER :X :N+1) - 1)/(:X - 1)
END

TO M' :X            TO Q' :X            TO P' :X
 OP M :X 5           OP Q :X 5           OP P :X 5
END                 END                 END
```

Tabulate M', Q', and P'. What seems to be going on? What if 5 is replaced by another positive integer? (# Any proofs?)

Chapter 3

Functions That Extend Tables

The problem is to find a simple function that agrees with a table on the first few positive integers. For example, suppose we have the following "input-output" table:

I	O
1	3
2	7
3	11
4	15
5	19

Of course, there are many functions that behave like this table. Here's one that interprets the table exactly:

```
TO MIMIC.THE.TABLE :X
  IF :X = 1 [OP 3]
  IF :X = 2 [OP 7]
  IF :X = 3 [OP 11]
  IF :X = 4 [OP 15]
  IF :X = 5 [OP 19]
END
```

This really isn't what I have in mind. MIMIC.THE.TABLE is certainly a simple function, but I'd like the domain of our "solution function" to be at least $\mathbf{Z}^+$. Well, how about this?

```
TO MIMIC.THE.TABLE :X
 IF :X = 1 [OP 3]
 IF :X = 2 [OP 7]
 IF :X = 3 [OP 11]
 IF :X = 4 [OP 15]
 IF :X = 5 [OP 19]
 OP :X
END
```

It works, but all the IF's give the function a contrived flavor. Besides, the table sets up a definite pattern, and it's this pattern that we want to capture. Of course, one person's pattern is another person's chaos (something the writers of standardized tests have conveniently ignored over the years), and the above functions are perfectly legitimate, although uninteresting, solutions to our problem. Here's another solution that isn't uninteresting:

```
TO MONSTER :X
 OP (-75 + 712 * :X + 450 * (POWER :X 2) - 170 →
 * (POWER :X 3) + 30 * (POWER :X 4) - 2 * (POWER :X 5)) →
 / 315
END
```

If you tabulate it, you'll see that MONSTER does indeed agree with our table (except for any round-off error that might creep into your machine's arithmetic). Type

```
TAB "MONSTER 1 10
```

to see what I mean. So, does MONSTER solve our problem? Do you think that MONSTER is the simplest function that agrees with our table? By now, you've probably come up with at least one simpler solution (especially if you have worked on project 2.5). In addition to its complexity, there is another problem with MONSTER. Like MIMIC.THE.TABLE, MONSTER doesn't capture any of the obvious patterns in the table (once again, keep in mind that the phrase "obvious patterns" is difficult to pin down). For example, the output column of the table increases by 4 for each increase of 1 in the input. So, if this is what we're after, the output for 6 should be 23, and MONSTER(6) is slightly more than 22. Things get worse for larger inputs; check it out.

Most of the people that I show this table to see one of two patterns. About half of them see the pattern mentioned above: any output is 4 more than the previous one. So, to get the output for 3, you go back to 2, look at the output for 2, and add 4. The only special case is the output for 1 (there is nothing to "go back" to), and here you just declare the output to be 3. This leads to the following function:

```
TO F :X
 IF :X = 1 [OP 3]
 OP (F :X - 1) + 4
END
```

Almost everyone who doesn't think of the table this way comes up with the idea that the output can be obtained from the input by multiplying by 4 and subtracting 1. Looking at the table in this way yields

```
TO G :X
 OP 4 * :X - 1
END
```

A little experimentation (tabulate both functions between, say, 1 and 20) shows that F and G seem to agree on positive integers outside the table, and the technique that we developed in the last chapter can be used to prove that, in fact, F = G on Z^+. We'll say that F and G "extend" our table; F extends the table to Z^+, and G extends the table to **R**. Of course, MONSTER extends the table to **R** too, but it gives a different (and less natural) extension than the one given by G. There are infinitely many extensions of our table to **R** (or to Z^+).

Arithmetic Sequences

We have been working with a particularly simple table: consecutive outputs differ by 4. The extension to Z^+ given by F is an example of what is called an arithmetic (pronounced *ar-ith-met-ic* with the accent on the "met") sequence; F is called an arithmetic sequence because each output of F is obtained from the previous one by the arithmetic operation of "adding 4." The general definition is

> An "arithmetic sequence with first term 'a' and common dif-
> ference 'd'" is the function F defined on Z^+ so that

$$F(N) = \begin{cases} a, & \text{if } N = 1 \\ F(N-1) + d, & \text{if } N > 1 \end{cases}$$

The function is described as a "sequence" because its domain is $\mathbf{Z}^+$. This means that its outputs can be arranged in a list (or sequence) like this:

$$[F(1) \ F(2) \ F(3) \ F(4) \ F(5)\ldots]$$

The numbers in the list (the outputs of the function) are sometimes called the "terms" of the sequence. The d in the definition is called the "common difference" because it is the difference between successive outputs of the function.

Every arithmetic sequence is defined by a recursive function of the form:

```
TO F :N
 IF :N = 1 [OP a]
 OP (F :N-1) + d
END
```

So, for example, the sequence

$$[2 \ 5 \ 8 \ 11 \ 14\ldots]$$

is defined by

```
TO H :X
 IF :X = 1 [OP 2]
 OP (H :X - 1) + 3
END
```

Of course, arithmetic sequences can have all kinds of numbers as outputs; write out the first few terms of this sequence:

```
TO S :N
 IF :N = 1 [OP 6]
 OP (S :N-1) + (-5)
END
```

or this sequence:

```
TO T :X
 IF :X = 1 [OP SQRT 2]
 OP (T :X-1) + .1
END
```

When we looked at the table corresponding to the arithmetic sequence

```
TO F :X
 IF :X = 1 [OP 3]
 OP (F :X - 1) + 4
END
```

we came up with a nonrecursive method for defining the same sequence:

```
TO G :X
 OP 4 * :X - 1
END
```

This function is called a "closed form" representation for F. It agrees with F on $\mathbf{Z}^+$, so it can be thought of as an extension of F to $\mathbf{R}$. Our first project is to find a method for generating a closed form version for any arithmetic sequence. Before I go into the details, you might want to try this for yourself (it is essentially the same as project 2.5).

Suppose that F is an arithmetic sequence with first term a and common difference d. Then successive terms are obtained by "adding d":

$$F(1) = a$$
$$F(2) = F(1) + d = a + d$$
$$F(3) = F(2) + d = (a + d) + d = a + 2d$$
$$F(4) = F(3) + d = (a + 2d) + d = a + 3d$$
$$F(5) = a + 4d$$
$$F(6) = a + 5d$$
$$\vdots$$
$$F(20) = a + 19d$$
$$\vdots$$

This gives us the idea for a closed form version for F:

Theorem 3.1 The arithmetic sequence with first term a and common difference d has the closed form

$$\mathbf{F}(N) = a + (N - 1)d$$

Of course, the a and d in this function are supposed to stand for actual real numbers. So, for example, the sequence

```
TO H :N
 IF :N = 1 [OP 4]
 OP (H :N - 1) + 8
END
```

has $a = 4$ and $d = 8$. It has the following closed form:

```
TO J :X
 OP 4 + (:X - 1) * 8
END
```

Both functions generate the same table:

I	O
1	4
2	12
3	20
4	28
5	36

Looking at the table, you may see that the output is 4 less than 8 times the input. This is equivalent to the formula that defines J because $4 + (X - 1) \cdot 8 = 8X - 4$.

The proof of theorem 3.1 amounts to showing that two functions (the recursive version and the closed form version) are equal on $\mathbf{Z}^+$. You can use the techniques of chapter 2 to convince yourself of this fact; a more formal way to see this equality will be developed in the next part.

Exercise 3.1 Find recursive and closed form representations for the arithmetic sequence $\mathbf{F}$ defined by each set of conditions:

1. $a = 3, d = 7$

2. $a = 1, d = 1$

3. $a = 23, d = -4$

4. $a = .23, d = -.04$

5. the outputs of F are $[12 \quad 15 \quad 18 \quad 21 \ldots]$

6. $F(N) - F(N-1) = 4$, $F(1) = 5$

7. $F(N) - F(N-1) = 5$, $F(3) = 5$

8. $F(N-1) - F(N) = 4$, $F(1) = 5$

9. $F(1) = 3$, $F(2) = 7$

10. $F(1) = 4$, $F(5) = 24$

11. $F(5) = 29 \; F(9) = 53$

Project 3.2 We have seen that the arithmetic sequence with first term a and difference d has a closed form representation as a function T where $T(N) = a + (N-1)d$. T can be simplified; it can be written as $T(N) = dN + (a-d)$, a function defined by a "degree one polynomial in N." So, the sequence $[4 \; 16 \; 28 \; 40 \; 52 \ldots]$ ($a = 4$ and $d = 12$) has a closed form representation: $T(N) = 12N - 8$. Is the converse true? That is, does every function of the form $F(N) = mN + p$ define an arithmetic sequence? Try it with a few values for m and p. For example, if m is 4 and p is 5, tabulate the function F:

```
TO F :N
  OP 4 * :N + 5
END
```

Can you write a recursive model for F? Can you recover a and d from m and p? (# Can you write a procedure that recovers a and d from F?)

Project 3.3 Consider our favorite table:

I	O
1	3
2	7
3	11
4	15
5	19

We now know that the table can be extended to $\mathbf{Z}^+$ by the arithmetic sequence

```
TO F :X
 IF :X = 1 [OP 3]
 OP (F :X - 1) + 4
END
```

and it can be extended to $\mathbf{R}$ by the closed form version

```
TO G :X
 OP 4 * :X - 1
END
```

In an attempt to find a new closed form extension for the table, I came up with this:

```
TO BEAST :X
 OP (3/24) * (:X - 2) * (:X - 3) * (:X - 4) * (:X - 5) + →
    (-7/6) * (:X - 1) * (:X - 3) * (:X - 4) * (:X - 5) + →
    (11/4) * (:X - 1) * (:X - 2) * (:X - 4) * (:X - 5) + →
    (-15/6) * (:X - 1) * (:X - 2) * (:X - 3) * (:X - 5) + →
    (19/24) * (:X - 1) * (:X - 2) * (:X - 3) * (:X - 4)
END
```

First, let me tell you how the BEAST was born. I formed the expression

$$? \cdot (X - 2)(X - 3)(X - 4)(X - 5) +$$
$$?? \cdot (X - 1)(X - 3)(X - 4)(X - 5) +$$
$$??? \cdot (X - 1)(X - 2)(X - 4)(X - 5) +$$
$$???? \cdot (X - 1)(X - 2)(X - 3)(X - 5) +$$
$$????? \cdot (X - 1)(X - 2)(X - 3)(X - 4)$$

where the question marks will be filled in in a minute. Consider this whole expression as the sum of five "terms"; the terms are the expressions on each line. Now, suppose that the value of X is 1. Then all but the first term are 0, and the first term has value

$$? \cdot (1-2) \cdot (1-3) \cdot (1-4) \cdot (1-5) =$$

$$? \cdot (-1) \cdot (-2) \cdot (-3) \cdot (-4) = ? \cdot 24$$

Now, when the value of X is 1, I want the entire expression to have value 3 (from the table), so I make ? equal to 3/24. Next I want the expression to have value 7 when the value of X is 2. Well, when $X = 2$, every term but the second vanishes, and the second term has value

$$?? \cdot (2-1) \cdot (2-3) \cdot (2-4) \cdot (2-5) =$$

$$?? \cdot (1) \cdot (-1) \cdot (-2) \cdot (-3) = ?? \cdot -6$$

so I make ?? −7/6.

The other missing coefficients are determined in the same way. Try forming the **BEAST** for this table:

I	O
1	5
2	11
3	17
4	23

Because the table has only four entries, each term will have only three factors.

The remarkable thing about **BEAST** is that it seems to extend the table in exactly the same way as the closed form for the arithmetic sequence that the table defines (tabulate **BEAST** between 1 and 20 to see what I mean). Is this true? Can you prove it? Does **BEAST** give a new formula for the closed form representation of an arithmetic sequence? If you take the messy expression that defines **BEAST**, multiply it out and simplify, what happens? (Try this for the table above; if you love to calculate, try it for the five entry table at the start of this project.) If you have a table that defines an arithmetic sequence, how many terms of the table do you have to use in the formation of **BEAST** in order to produce a function that extends the table to all of $\mathbf{Z}^+$ (you want the extension to still be an arithmetic sequence)? What about nonarithmetic sequences? If you look at the table

I	O
1	1
2	4
3	9
4	16

does the BEAST function for this table extend the "obvious" pattern to Z^+?

Project 3.4 Is 1296 a term in the arithmetic sequence whose first term is 4 and whose common difference is 17? Write a predicate IN.SEQ? that takes three inputs: A (the first term of a sequence), D (the common difference in the sequence) and M (the number to be tested). Typing

SHOW IN.SEQ? 4 17 1296

produces TRUE if 1296 is a term in the sequence

$$[4\ 21\ 38\ 55\ldots]$$

and FALSE otherwise. (Note: IN.SEQ? should work even if A and D are not integers. If you restrict yourself to the case where A and D are integers, this problem is easier (why?) Maybe you should try this case first).

Write a function TERM.NUM that takes the three inputs A, D, and M (just like IN.SEQ?). TERM.NUM outputs -1 if M isn't in the sequence whose first term is A and whose common difference is D. If M is in this sequence, TERM.NUM outputs the "number of the term" that is equal to M (that is, the number that you have to input to the arithmetic sequence in order to get M).

Project 3.5

1. How many even numbers are there between 1 and 100?

2. How many multiples of 3 are there between 5 and 1900?

3. How many multiples of 17 are there between 23 and 5000?

4. Write a function that counts the number of multiples of N that are between the integers A and B.

Experiment 3.6 Consider the arithmetic sequence

```
TO F :X
 IF :X = 1 [OP 9]
 OP (F :X - 1) + 4
END
```

Are there any multiples of 5 among the terms of F? Are there any multiples of 6 among the terms of F? Are there any multiples of 9 among the terms of F? How can you tell if there are any multiples of N among the terms of F. If F has first term a and common difference d (a and d are integers), how can you tell if there are any multiples of N among the terms of F?

Experiment 3.7 Using the ADD function of project 1.15, investigate the following statement:

> *The sum of two arithmetic sequences is another arithmetic sequence*

For example, if F and G are the sequences

```
TO F :N                      TO G :N
 IF :N = 1 [OP 6]             OP 4 * :N + 7
 OP (F :N-1) + 5             END
END
```

Then is the sequence

```
TO SEQ :N
 OP ADD "F "G :N
END
```

an arithmetic sequence? Investigate the following statement:

> *The composite of two arithmetic sequences is another arithmetic sequence*

Experiment 3.8 If multiplication of functions is defined in the obvious way, is the product of two arithmetic sequences another arithmetic sequence?

Experiment 3.9 Consider the two arithmetic sequences

```
TO F :N                    TO G :N
  IF :N = 1 [OP 3]           IF :N = 1 [OP 7]
  OP (F :N-1) + 5            OP (G :N-1) + 8
END                        END
```

If you tabulate both sequences, you'll find some common outputs. Write a function whose Nth output is the Nth common output for F and G. This function is called the "intersection" of F and G. Does the intersection of F and G define an arithmetic sequence? Can you find two arithmetic sequences whose intersection is empty? If two arithmetic sequences intersect, is their intersection another arithmetic sequence?

Project 3.10 A friend showed me an interesting problem* whose solution depends on the following function:

$$P(N) = \begin{cases} 1, & \text{if } N = 10 \\ 0, & \text{if } N = 1 \\ .5(P(N+1) + P(N-1)), & \text{if } 1 < N < 10 \end{cases}$$

The domain of P is the set $\{1, 2, 3, 4, 5, 6, 7, 8, 9, 10\}$. If you model this definition in Logo, it doesn't work (why?). It turns out, however, that this definition produces a simple function. Here's how I found an alternate method for defining P in a way that does tabulate

$$P(2) = \frac{1}{2}(P(3) + P(1)) = \frac{1}{2}P(3) \qquad (\text{because } P(1) = 0)$$

$$P(3) = \frac{1}{2}(P(4) + P(2))$$

$$= \frac{1}{2}(P(4) + \frac{1}{2}P(3))$$

$$= \frac{1}{2}P(4) + \frac{1}{4}P(3)$$

So

---

* The problem is this: You are on the seventh story of a ten-story building. There is one elevator, and it is equally likely to go up one floor as it is to go down one floor. If you plan to get off only at the first floor or the tenth floor, what is the probability that you'll get off on the tenth floor? In our notation, the answer is P(7). See Alison Birch (Birch 1988) for more details.

$$\frac{3}{4}P(3) = \frac{1}{2}P(4)$$

Multiply both sides by $\frac{4}{3}$, and we have

$$P(3) = \frac{2}{3}P(4)$$

Let's try it again:

$$P(4) = \frac{1}{2}(P(5) + P(3))$$

$$= \frac{1}{2}(P(5) + \frac{2}{3}P(4))$$

$$= \frac{1}{2}P(5) + \frac{1}{3}P(4)$$

So

$$\frac{2}{3}P(4) = \frac{1}{2}P(5)$$

and

$$P(4) = \frac{3}{4}P(5)$$

A pattern emerges. Carry out this process for a few more N's; it seems to work. This leads to the function

```
TO Q :N
 IF :N = 10 [OP 1]
 OP ((:N - 1) / :N) * Q (:N + 1)
END
```

Suppose for a minute that P really is equal Q on the integers between 1 and 10. If you tabulate Q between 1 and 10, a pleasant surprise pops up: Q (and hence P) can be extended to $\mathbf{Z}^+$ by an arithmetic sequence. Try it.

Notice two things:

Chapter 3

1. Unless you go through the calculation that I outlined for every N between 2 and 9, you can't be sure that $P = Q$ on the set of integers between 1 and 10. One way to eliminate all this tedious calculation is to reason like this: You are trying to establish that the pattern

$$P(N) = \frac{(N-1)}{N} P(N+1)$$

holds for all N between 2 and 9. Suppose that you have shown that

$$P(K) = \frac{(K-1)}{K} P(K+1)$$

for some number K between 2 and 9. Then the next calculation will go like this:

$$P(K+1) = \frac{1}{2}(P(K+2) + P(K))$$

$$= \frac{1}{2}(P(K+2)) + \frac{1}{2}P(K)$$

$$= \frac{1}{2}(P(K+2)) + \frac{1}{2}\frac{K-1}{K}P(K+1)$$

$$= \frac{1}{2}(P(K+2)) + \frac{K-1}{2K}P(K+1)$$

So, collecting all the $P(K+1)$'s on the right-hand side,

$$\frac{K+1}{2K}P(K+1) = \frac{1}{2}P(K+2)$$

and

$$P(K+1) = \frac{K+1}{K}P(K+2)$$

and the pattern will continue to the next step. This kind of argument, where a generic calculation is used to show that a pattern continues, is very useful; you should spend some time going over it.

2. Q doesn't extend the table to $\mathbf{Z}^+$. It uses recursion to define $Q(N)$ in terms of $Q(N+1)$, so the "base case" of the function is the upper limit of its domain. Of course, you can get a bigger upper limit (now that you know the closed form for P); for example, we can define Q up to 19 by

```
TO Q :N
 IF :N = 19 [OP 2]
 OP ((:N-1)/:N) * Q(:N+1)
END
```

There are other ways to extend P. For example, one of my students came up with this:

```
TO L :N
 OP (1 + (10 - :N) * L(:N - 1))/(11 - :N)
END
```

Try to figure out how she got this. It looks like this function should be defined on all of $\mathbf{Z}^+$ (it doesn't use "upward recursion"); tabulate it to see what happens.

Here's another idea: Originally, we were looking for a function P so that

$$P(N) = .5(P(N+1) + P(N-1))$$

Solve this for $P(N+1)$; you'll find that

$$P(N+1) = 2P(N) - P(N-1)$$

Moving down one level, this says that

$$P(N) = 2P(N-1) - P(N-2)$$

Try to implement this in Logo; you'll need to worry about the first few outputs. Try this same technique with the formula that is in Q's definition. That is, solve

$$Q(N) = \left(\frac{N-1}{N}\right) Q(N+1)$$

for $Q(N + 1)$, and rewrite Q accordingly.

Try to come up with another method for extending the table for P (different from the ones we have talked about) to larger values of N.

Playing with a concrete sequence like this teaches you a great deal about sequences in general, and more important, it helps you develop strategies for investigating properties of general sequences. Besides, it's fun.

Exercise 3.11 Show that if F is any arithmetic sequence and N is an integer greater than 1, then

$$F(N) = .5(F(N + 1) + F(N - 1))$$

Exercise 3.12 Suppose that G is a function defined by

$$G(N) = \begin{cases} 2, & \text{if } N = 1 \\ 35, & \text{if } N = 11 \\ .5(G(N + 1) + G(N - 1)), & \text{if } 2 < N < 11 \end{cases}$$

Find a Logo model for G and extend G to $\mathbf{Z}^+$.

Series

Consider the arithmetic sequence T with first term 3 and common difference 8. It tabulates in this way:

N	$T(N)$
1	3
2	11
3	19
4	27
5	35
6	43
$\vdots$	

Using T, we can form a new sequence S, which is called the "series associated with T."

N	$S(N)$	
1	3	$(= T(1))$
2	14	$(= T(1) + T(2))$
3	33	$(= T(1) + T(2) + T(3))$
4	60	$(= T(1) + T(2) + T(3) + T(4))$
5	95	$(= T(1) + T(2) + T(3) + T(4) + T(5))$
6	138	$(= T(1) + T(2) + T(3) + T(4) + T(5) + T(6))$

$\vdots$

So, the Nth output in the table is the sum of the first N terms from T. Of course, this table doesn't define an arithmetic sequence, but we can easily define a function that agrees with the table on $\mathbf{Z}^+$. In fact, the series can be defined in this way:

```
TO SERIES  :N
 OP SIGMA "T 1 :N
END
```

And, in general, we can define the series associated with any sequence SEQ (even if SEQ isn't an arithmetic sequence) by

```
TO SERIES :SEQ :N
 OP SIGMA :SEQ 1 :N
END
```

Experiment 3.13 Suppose F is the arithmetic sequence whose first term is 3 and whose common difference is 5. Define G as the series associated with F:

```
TO G :N
 OP SERIES "F :N
END
```

Tabulate G, and try to find a closed form for G. Change F to another arithmetic sequence (say, with first term 5 and common difference 8), and repeat the experiment. Can you do this for a generic arithmetic sequence?

The actual calculation in SERIES is mapped out in SIGMA; if you don't care about the details of the calculation, you can leave these details hidden inside SIGMA (in fact computer scientists would consider this a healthy use of abstraction). I'm sure you have noticed that SERIES is very slow to output for numbers of moderate size. Let's see if we can find a simpler model (say, a closed form) for SERIES. To do this, let's first uncover what SIGMA is hiding; recall its definition:

```
TO SIGMA :F :A :B
 IF :A > :B [OP 0]
 OP (APPLY :F :A) + (SIGMA :F (:A+1) :B)
END
```

To develop another recursive method for defining SERIES, start with our table for T:

N	T(N)
1	3
2	11
3	19
4	27
5	35
6	43

If S is the associated series, the table for S is

N	S(N)
1	3
2	14
3	33
4	60
5	95
6	138

Suppose that we combine the tables:

N	S(N)	T(N)
1	3	3
2	14	11
3	33	19
4	60	27
5	95	35
6	138	43

Now, if you compare outputs, you see that

$$S(1) = T(1),$$
$$S(2) - S(1) = T(2)$$
$$S(3) - S(2) = T(3)$$
$$S(4) - S(3) = T(4)$$
$$\vdots$$

In other words, the "successive differences" between the terms of S are precisely the terms of T (see experiment 3.20 and projects 3.21 and 3.22 for an introduction to the fascinating topic of successive differences). If you think about it, the reason that this pattern continues becomes clear:

$$S(N) = \underbrace{T(1) + T(2) + T(3) + \cdots + T(N-1)}_{} + T(N)$$
$$= S(N-1) + T(N)$$

This leads to the following method for calculating series:

```
TO NEW.SERIES :F :N
 IF :N = 1 [OP APPLY :F 1]
 OP (APPLY :F :N) + (NEW.SERIES :F :N-1)
END
```

It might not seem important right now, but SERIES and NEW.SERIES really *do* outline different processes for calculating the sum of N terms in a sequence. Suppose, for example, that you want to calculate S(4) above. Then the calls to SERIES "T 3 (which is just SIGMA "T 1 3) can be visualized like this:

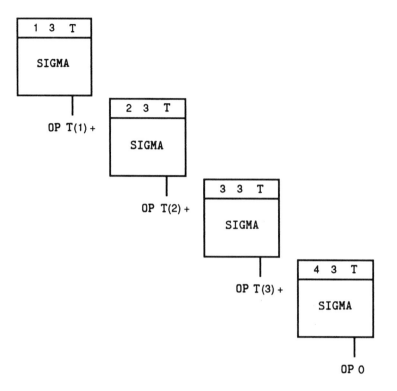

Figure 3.1

So SERIES describes the calculation of S(3) as

$$S(3) = T(3) + T(2) + T(1)$$

(Actually, SERIES describes the calculation as $0 + T(3) + T(2) + T(1)$.)

Now, if you write out the call sequence for NEW.SERIES, you'll find that it describes the calculation of S(3) as

$$S(3) = T(1) + T(2) + T(3)$$

Of course, both functions lead to the same result, but the recipes for arriving at this result are different.

How about a closed form for the series attached to F? For general sequences, this is a very interesting problem. We'll only consider the case when F is an arithmetic sequence. Before we start looking for general principles, you should do a little more brute force calculating.

Exercise 3.14 In these exercises, tabulate the series associated to each arithmetic sequence (it might help to tabulate the sequence as well). To tabulate the series associated with F, for example, write a function F':

```
TO F' :N
 OP SERIES :F :1 :N
END
```

And then type

```
TAB "F' 1 20
```

Look for general strategies:

1.
```
TO F :N
  IF :N = 1 [OP 1]
  OP (F :N-1) + 2
END
```

2.
```
TO T :N
  OP 2 * :N
END
```

3.
```
TO G :N    (Hint: Look at Gauss' method in the last section.)
  OP :N
END
```

4.
```
TO H :N
  IF :N = 1 [OP 6]
  OP (H :N - 1) + 5
END
```

5.
```
TO K :N
  OP 3 * :N - 2
END
```

6.
```
TO M :X
  IF :X = 1 [OP 0]
  OP (M :X - 1) + (1/9)
END
```

7.
```
TO N :X
  OP 8 * :X + 7
END
```

If you have finished the above exercise, you probably have a good idea about how to find a closed form for the series associated with an arithmetic sequence. If you do, close the book and try to write a closed form version of SERIES; I'm about to fill in the details.

Suppose that T is an arithmetic sequence with common difference d. We want to write a function S that is defined by the formula

$$S(N) = T(1) + T(2) + T(3) + \cdots + T(N-1) + T(N)$$

Keep N fixed for a minute. We know that for any integer $K > 1$,

$$T(K) = T(1) + (K-1)d$$

(*the Kth term is the first term plus $K-1$ differences*), but suppose that we want to use "upward recursion." That is, if $K < N$, how is $T(K)$ related to $T(N)$? Well,

$$T(N-1) = T(N) - d$$
$$T(N-2) = T(N-1) - d = T(N) - 2d$$
$$T(N-3) = T(N-2) - d = T(N) - 3d$$
$$\vdots$$
$$T(1) = T(N - (N-1)) = T(N) - (N-1)d$$

Now, the trick is to calculate $S(N)$ two ways using SERIES and NEW.SERIES. More precisely,

$$S(N) = \text{NEW.SERIES}(T, N) = T(1) + T(2) + \cdots + T(N-1) + T(N)$$
$$S(N) = \text{SERIES}(T, N) = T(N) + T(N-1) + \cdots + T(2) + T(1)$$

Now, use the above "upward recursion" calculation to rewrite the second expression, and use theorem 3.1 to rewrite the first expression:

$$S(N) = T(1) + (T(1) + d) + \cdots$$
$$+ (T(1) + (N-2)d) + (T(1) + (N-1)d)$$

and

$$S(N) = T(N) + (T(N) - d) + \cdots$$
$$+ (T(N) - (N-2)d) + (T(N) - (N-1)d)$$

Look at these two equations. If you add them, the left-hand sides add to $2S(N)$. What about the right-hand sides? Add each term to the one below it; you get

$$T(1) + T(N) = T(1) + T(N)$$
$$(T(1) + d) + (T(N) - d) = T(1) + T(N)$$
$$(T(1) + 2d) + (T(N) - 2d) = T(1) + T(N)$$
$$\vdots$$
$$(T(1) + (N - 2)d) + (T(N) - (N - 2)d) = T(1) + T(N)$$
$$(T(1) + (N - 1)d) + (T(N) - (N - 1)d) = T(1) + T(N)$$

So the terms on the right-hand side add in pairs to $T(1)+T(N)$. This is exactly the insight that Gauss used to add the numbers from 1 to 100; he noticed that the sum of pairs equally spaced from the ends of the sequence is constant. How many pairs are there? Convince yourself that there are N of them. This means that the right-hand sides add to $(T(1) + T(N))N$. But this is $2S(N)$, so

$$2S(N) = (T(1) + T(N))N$$

and

$$S(N) = \frac{(T(1) + T(N))N}{2}$$

In other words, the value of the series for an arithmetic sequence is "the first term plus the last term times half the number of terms." The translation into Logo is natural:

```
TO ARITH.SERIES :T :N
 OP ((APPLY :T 1) + (APPLY :T :N)) * N / 2
END
```

Suppose that F is the arithmetic sequence with first term 2 and common difference 7. One way to model F is

```
TO F :N
 IF :N = 1 [OP 2]
 OP (F :N - 1) + 7
END
```

For this model of F, calculate the first 30 terms of the series for F using SERIES, NEW.SERIES, and ARITH.SERIES. Which is faster to output? What if you use the closed form for F instead of the above model?

From here it is easy to get a closed form representation for the series associated with any arithmetic sequence. Suppose that T has first term a and common difference d, and suppose that we let S stand for the series for T. Then we have

$$
\begin{aligned}
\text{S}(N) &= \frac{((\text{T}(1) + \text{T}(N))N}{2} \\
&= \frac{(a + (a + (N-1)d)N}{2} \quad (\text{T}(N) = a + (N-1)d \text{ by theorem 3.1}) \\
&= \frac{(2a - d + N)N}{2} \\
&= \frac{1}{2}(N^2 + (2a - d)N)
\end{aligned}
$$

So we have the following result:

Theorem 3.2 The series for the arithmetic sequence with first term a and common difference d has the following closed form:

$$
\text{S}(N) = \frac{1}{2}(N^2 + (2a - d)N)
$$

As in theorem 3.1, this theorem gives a recipe for determining the closed form for a particular series; a and d stand for actual real numbers.

Project 3.15 Write a function GEN.CF.ARITH.SERIES that takes two inputs T (an arithmetic sequence) and N. GEN.CF.ARITH.SERIES(T, N) outputs the Nth term in the series associated with T using the method of theorem 3.2. (Hint: You'll need to calculate the first term and the common difference. The first term is just T(1), and the common difference is just T(2) − T(1).)

Experiment 3.16 Let F be an arithmetic sequence with associated series S. Investigate the following statement:

$$
\text{S}(19) = 19\text{F}(10)
$$

by trying it out with some actual functions F.

Exercise 3.17

1. Find the sum of 20 terms of the arithmetic sequence whose first term is 3 and whose common difference is 5.

2. Find the sum of all even integers between 6 and 267.

3. Find the sum of all multiples of 3 between 1 and 400.

4. What is the sum of all the integers between 1 and 400 that are not divisible by 3?

5. Find the sum of all the integers between 1 and 1000 whose last digit is either 3, 5, or 0.

Experiment 3.18 We have seen that the arithmetic sequence with first term a and difference d has a series with a closed form representation as a function S where

$$S(N) = \frac{1}{2}(N^2) + \frac{(2a - d)}{2}N$$

which is a "degree two polynomial in N." Is the converse true? That is, is every function of the form

$$Q(N) = aN^2 + bN + c$$

a closed form representation for an arithmetic series? It looks like we might have to take $c = 0$ (why?). Let's try an example. Suppose

$$Q(N) = 3N^2 + 2N$$

We'll form the "successive difference" table:

N	$Q(N)$	$Q(N+1) - Q(N)$
1	5	11
2	16	17
3	33	23
4	56	29
5	85	
$\vdots$		

It looks like the successive differences for Q form an arithmetic sequence. Investigate this phenomenon. Is there an arithmetic sequence T so that

$$Q(N) = \text{SERIES}(\text{T}, N)$$

How about other degree two functions Q? Do the successive differences always produce an arithmetic sequence? Does Q represent the closed form version of the associated series? If so, why? If not, how is Q related to this closed form function? Is it necessary to assume that $c = 0$?

Project 3.19 Use the above experiment to find an extension of this table to $\mathbf{Z}^+$:

I	O
1	6
2	27
3	64
4	117
5	186

Can you extend it to $\mathbf{Z}^+$ (if you haven't already)?

Project 3.20 Use repeated successive differences to find an extension of this table to $\mathbf{Z}^+$:

I	O
1	17
2	34
3	101
4	248
5	505
6	902

Chapter 4

A Function Whose Existence Depends on the State of the Art

What determines a function? Since two functions are equal if they have the same domain and if they produce the same output when fed something from this common domain, a function is determined by two things: its domain and its behavior on this domain. To understand a function, then, you must know its domain; a function whose domain cannot be determined is "an object about which nothing can be said."*

Look at the following object:

```
TO HAILSTONE :N
 IF :N = 1 [OP 1]
 IF EVEN? :N [OP HAILSTONE :N/2]
 OP HAILSTONE 3 * :N + 1
END
```

---

* The phrase is due to Nicholas Bourbaki (Bourbaki 1968). The notion of an object about which nothing can be said is full of paradox (if you say "nothing can be said about X," aren't you saying something about X?).

By the way, Nicholas Bourbaki is a good example of an object with questionable existence; Bourbaki never existed as a mathematician (the name was borrowed from an obscure figure in the Polish military). Bourbaki is the fabrication of a group of French mathematicians who tried to give a systematic development of all of mathematics from a single point of view. The title of their (his?) work is *Elements of Mathematics*, the same title that Euclid (possibly another fabrication) used to carry out the same mission around 300 B.C. Thirty years ago people took the Bourbaki myth very seriously. No one hinted at Bourbaki's nonexistence in print, and people dedicated books to this "master of a generation of mathematicians."

EVEN? is the predicate that outputs TRUE if N is an integer divisible by 2 and outputs FALSE otherwise:

```
TO EVEN? :N
 OP REMAINDER :N 2 = 0
END
```

The input to HAILSTONE is supposed to be a positive integer. What is the output of HAILSTONE(7)? Well,

$$
\begin{aligned}
\text{HAILSTONE}(7) &= \text{HAILSTONE}(22) \quad (7 \text{ is odd, so we call HAILSTONE}(3 \cdot 7 + 1)) \\
&= \text{HAILSTONE}(11) \quad (22 \text{ is even, so we call HAILSTONE}(22/2)) \\
&= \text{HAILSTONE}(34) \\
&= \text{HAILSTONE}(17) \\
&= \text{HAILSTONE}(52) \\
&= \text{HAILSTONE}(26) \\
&= \text{HAILSTONE}(13) \\
&= \text{HAILSTONE}(40) \\
&= \text{HAILSTONE}(20) \\
&= \text{HAILSTONE}(10) \\
&= \text{HAILSTONE}(5) \\
&= \text{HAILSTONE}(16) \\
&= \text{HAILSTONE}(8) \\
&= \text{HAILSTONE}(4) \\
&= \text{HAILSTONE}(2) \\
&= \text{HAILSTONE}(1) \\
&= 1
\end{aligned}
$$

The name HAILSTONE is due to Brian Hayes (his article in *Scientific American* gives a nice account of the history of this topic; see Hayes 1984). So HAILSTONE(7) = 1. In fact, if N is any number in the domain of HAILSTONE, HAILSTONE(N) = 1. So, on its domain, HAILSTONE is equal to the function that is identically 1:

```
TO ONE :N
 OP 1
END
```

The problem is that no one knows exactly what the domain of HAIL-STONE is. Are there numbers that cause HAILSTONE to fail to output? This would happen, for example, if in the calculation of HAILSTONE(N), we visited the same number (larger than 1) twice (why?). Playing with HAILSTONE (as we have written it) isn't much fun; you simply type SHOW HAILSTONE 9, for example, and you sit back and wait for a 1 to show up. Try it.

But will a 1 always show up? The "$3N + 1$ conjecture" says that it will; it says that the domain of HAILSTONE is $\mathbf{Z}^+$. As of now (March 1990), no one has established the conjecture. So, if we don't know HAILSTONE's domain, can we say anything about HAILSTONE? Is HAILSTONE a function?

There are some things that we can say about HAILSTONE. For example, any power of 2 causes HAILSTONE to output. For example, HAILSTONE(64) = HAILSTONE(32) = HAILSTONE(16) = HAILSTONE(8) = HAILSTONE(4) = HAIL-STONE(2) = HAILSTONE(1) = 1. So there are infinitely many numbers in the domain of HAILSTONE (the powers of 2), and the $3N + 1$ conjecture would be settled if someone could show that calling HAILSTONE with any input eventually causes a call to HAILSTONE with an input that is a power of 2. For example, HAILSTONE(5) = HAILSTONE(16), and this will cause HAILSTONE to output.

Experiment 4.1 By modifying HAILSTONE, we can keep track of some interesting phenomena. For example, suppose we want to know the length of a number's "path" (the number of calls to HAILSTONE necessary to cause HAILSTONE to output). For example, 7 produces a path of length 17. We can write PATHLENGTH so that it outputs a number's path length when the input to HAILSTONE becomes 1:

```
TO PATHLENGTH :N
 OP PL :N 1
END

TO PL :N :LENGTH
 IF :N = 1 [OP  :LENGTH]
 IF EVEN? :N [OP PL :N/2 :LENGTH + 1]
 OP PL 3 * :N + 1 :LENGTH + 1
END
```

If you type SHOW PATHLENGTH 64, you'll see

7

which means that HAILSTONE(64) has a path length of 7.

Tabulate PATHLENGTH between 1 and 200. Which numbers have the longest path? How long is the longest path?

Experiment 4.2 Another interesting modification of HAILSTONE is to calculate a number's "height," the largest number in a number's path. Write a HEIGHT function that outputs a number's height. Tabulate the heights of all numbers between 1 and 200. Which numbers reach the largest height? What is the largest height? What can you say about a number if the height of the number is itself?

Experiment 4.3 Suppose G is the sequence

```
TO G :N
 OP ((POWER 2 2 * :N) - 1)/3
END
```

Investigate the following statement:

> The outputs of G are in the domain of HAILSTONE

Find some other sequences that take values in HAILSTONE's domain.

Experiment 4.4 The function PATH outputs a number's entire path as a list:

```
TO PATH :N
 IF :N = 1 [OP [1]]
 IF EVEN? :N [OP SE :N (PATH :N/2)]
 OP SE :N (PATH 3*:N + 1)
END
```

(If you are not familiar with SE, see the appendix.) The path for 7 can be seen by typing SHOW PATH 7. Experiment with some numbers (try some big numbers). Does the PATH(N) change in any regular way if you, say, double N? Is there a pattern in the PATH's of numbers that are outputs of an arithmetic sequence? Does the maximum number in a path (the path's "height") lie near the middle of the path? If every path contains a power of 2, the "$3N + 1$" conjecture is true. Does every path contain an output of a certain fixed arithmetic sequence? Is there more than one arithmetic sequence with this property?

Experiment 4.5 Why is HAILSTONE so interesting? Why not use other functions, such as

```
TO GRINDSTONE :N
 IF :N = 1 [OP 1]
 IF EVEN? :N [OP GRINDSTONE :N/2]
 OP GRINDSTONE 2 * :N + 1
END
```

or

```
TO STONEWALL :N
 IF :N = 1 [OP 1]
 IF EVEN? :N [OP STONEWALL :N/2]
 OP STONEWALL 3 * :N - 1
END
```

Show that GRINDSTONE grinds out paths of infinite length, whereas STONE-WALL confines some numbers to circular paths. Try some other HAILSTONE-like functions. Can you find any that behave like HAILSTONE?

The problem of determining HAILSTONE's domain has been attacked from many angles. One recent result, due to Korec and Znam (1987), implies that every number's HAILSTONE path contains an an element from the path of some output from the following arithmetic sequence:

```
TO F :N
 IF :N = 1 [OP 2]
 OP (F :N - 1) + 9
END
```

In fact, they give infinitely arithmetic sequences with this property (for example, the sequence whose first term is 4 and whose common difference is some power of 3). The $3N + 1$ conjecture would be settled, then, if one could show that the outputs of F, for example, were in the domain of HAILSTONE.

For a summary of the technical results about the $3N + 1$ conjecture, see the paper by Lagarias (1985).

There is a myth that mathematics deals with a fixed and ancient body of facts. The truth is that mathematical research is often concerned with half understood, mysterious objects like HAILSTONE that produce conjectures and give birth to other half understood objects. Many times the conjectures claim the the object under study is, in fact, quite trivial (if the $3N + 1$ conjecture is true, HAILSTONE is nothing other than ONE), but even if the objects do turn out to be very simple, the methods that need to be developed to establish this simplicity are often powerful.

What do you think about HAILSTONE? If the $3N + 1$ conjecture hasn't been established by the time you read this, is HAILSTONE a function? If you say no, suppose that the conjecture is established next week. Will HAILSTONE suddenly become a function, or was it a function all along, waiting to be discovered? Suppose that someone proves that the $3N + 1$ conjecture cannot ever be proved or disproved using mathematical methods. Then what can you say about HAILSTONE?

Part II

Counting and
Mathematical Induction

How can you be sure that two different-looking functions are equal on $\mathbf{Z}^+$?

In how many ways can you write 47 as a sum of distinct positive integers, each of which is less than 10?

In how many ways can you assign the numbers [1 2 3 4 ... 10] to the numbers [1 2 3 4]?

If you expand the expression $(3X + 2Y)^{12}$, what is the sum of the coefficients?

What is the sum of the first 20 powers of 2?

How many 3-element subsets of a 14-element set are there?

How are all of the above questions related?

In this part, we'll develop some general methods to answer these questions.

Chapter 5

Mathematical Induction

What Is Mathematical Induction?

Consider a set S of positive integers that satisfies the following two conditions:

1. 5 is in S.

2. If a number N is in S, then $N + 3$ is also in S.

The conditions that define S allow us to generate elements in S: By condition 2, since 5 is in S, $5 + 3 = 8$ is in S. Since 8 is in S, $8 + 3 = 11$ is in S. Since 11 is in S, $11 + 3 = 14$ is in S. We can keep calculating elements in S, adding 3 each time; S contains the number 5 and all numbers that you can get from 5 by adding to it any number of 3's. So S contains the set of outputs of the arithmetic sequence whose first term is 5 and whose common difference is 3:

$$[5 \ 8 \ 11 \ 14 \ 17 \ 20 \ 23 \ldots]$$

Exercise 5.1 Could the above set S contain anything else?

Exercise 5.2 Suppose that T is a set of positive integers with the following properties:

1. 3 is in T.

2. If a number K is in T, then $2K$ is also in T.

Write a function whose outputs are all in T, and generate ten elements of T. Describe the outputs of your function in words.

Exercise 5.3 Suppose that S is a set of positive integers with the following properties:

1. 3 is in S.

2. If the numbers N and M are in S, $N + M$ is also in S.

Describe S in words.

Exercise 5.4 Suppose that R is a set of positive integers with the following properties:

1. 3 is in R, and 4 is in R.

2. If the numbers N and M are in R, $N + M$ is also in R.

Which positive integers are not necessarily in R?

Exercise 5.5 Suppose that U is a set of positive integers with the following properties:

1. 27 is in U.

2. If N is an even number in U, then $N/2$ is also in U.

3. If N is an odd number in U, then $3N + 1$ is in U.

Which positive integers are in U?

The above exercises show that a subset of $\mathbf{Z}^+$ can be generated by two conditions:

1. Specify one or more elements of the set.

2. Show how to obtain new elements of the set from old ones.

Of course, there are other ways to generate subsets of $\mathbf{Z}^+$, but when you define a set by giving some elements of the set and a rule for generating new elements from old, you are giving an "inductive definition" of the set. So, for example, here are two ways to define the same subset of $\mathbf{Z}^+$:

Inductive definition. E is the set of positive integers that can be generated from these two properties:

1. 2 is in E.

2. If N is in E, then $N + 2$ is in E.

Noninductive definition. E is the set of positive integers divisible by 2.

Exercise 5.6 Give an inductive definition for the following sets:

1. The set of positive integers divisible by 3.

2. The set of positive integers that are one more than a multiple of 5.

#3. The set of perfect squares.

Exercise 5.7 Give a noninductive definition of the following sets:

1. The set of positive integers S that has the properties

   (a) 3 is in S, and

   (b) if N is in S, then $N + 2$ is in S.

2. The set of positive integers S so that

   (a) 5 is in S, and

   (b) if K is in S, then $2K$ is in S.

3. The set of positive integers T so that

   (a) 3 is in T, and

(b) if M is in T, M^2 is also in T.

Subsets of $\mathbf{Z}^+$ are closely related to sequences. Remember that a sequence is a function whose domain is $\mathbf{Z}^+$ (in the last section we studied arithmetic sequences and their associated series). The connection between subsets of $\mathbf{Z}^+$ and sequences is that given a sequence, we get a subset of $\mathbf{Z}^+$ by looking at its outputs. It is also true that every subset of $\mathbf{Z}^+$ is the output set of some sequence (see project 5.10 for some special cases). For example, the sequence

```
TO F :X
 IF :X = 1 [OP 1]
 OP (F :X - 1) + 2 * :X
END
```

generates the subset S of $\mathbf{Z}^+$:

$$S = \{1\ 5\ 11\ 19\ 29\ 41\ldots\}$$

Now, our method for defining a set inductively translates naturally into the method we used in part I to give a recursive definition for a sequence. To define a sequence F, we

1. specified $F(1)$, and

2. showed how to obtain $F(N)$ from $F(N-1)$.

For example, suppose we have a sequence H with the properties that $H(1)$ is 4, and for all other positive integers N, $H(N)$ is $3 + H(N-1)$. Then the outputs of H form the set of positive integers S defined by the conditions

1. 4 is in S, and

2. if N is in S, $N+3$ is also in S.

Exercise 5.8 Give inductive definitions for the set of outputs for each sequence. If possible, give a noninductive definition as well.

1. ```
TO F :X
   IF :X = 1 [OP 6]
   OP (F :X - 1) + 5
   END
```
```

2. ```
TO H :X
   IF :X = 1 [OP 3]
   OP (H :X - 1) * 2
   END
```

3. ```
TO G :X
   IF :X = 1 [OP 1]
   OP :X * (G :X - 1)
   END
```

Experiment 5.9 Consider the following sequence:

```
TO F :N
 IF :N = 1 [OP 1]
 IF :N = 2 [OP 1]
 OP (F :N - 1) + (F :N - 2)
END
```

F is called the *Fibonacci sequence*. It's great fun to play with this sequence. For example, tabulate the consecutive differences for F. How about the consecutive quotients for F: that is,

$$\frac{F(N+1)}{F(N)}$$

#Can you find a noninductive way to describe this sequence?

Project 5.10 Find a sequence whose set of outputs is precisely the given set:

1. The set of all positive multiples of 5

2. The set of all positive integers whose units digit is 3

#3. The set of positive integers that are not divisible by 5

#4. The set $\{1, 3, 4, 10\}$

Here's an inductive definition that is the cornerstone of this part:

> Suppose that S is a set of positive integers that has these two properties:

   1. 1 is in S.

   2. If N is in S, then $N + 1$ is also in S.

Think about this for a minute. If 1 is in S, then by the second condition, 2 is in S. So, again by the second condition, 3 is in S. Write a sequence I whose outputs form the set S by mimicking S's inductive definition, and tabulate I for a while. Are you convinced that $S = \mathbf{Z}^+$? This is exactly what the principle of mathematical induction says:

Principle of Mathematical Induction Suppose that S is a set of positive integers that has these two properties:

1. 1 is in S.

2. If N is in S, then $N + 1$ is also in S.

Then S is all of $\mathbf{Z}^+$.

We'll make no attempt to prove this statement. Instead, we'll take the principle of mathematical induction as an obvious property of $\mathbf{Z}^+$; as you'll see below, the principle of mathematical induction is just an abstraction of some properties that are common to many calculations.

> The principle of mathematical induction can be proved by assuming some other equally obvious properties of $\mathbf{Z}^+$. For example, you can prove the principle of mathematical induction by assuming that every non-empty subset of $\mathbf{Z}^+$ has a smallest element, and, in fact, the principle of mathematical induction is equivalent to this "smallest element" property. The branch of mathematics known as set theory studies the logical connections of the principle of mathematical induction to other statements about $\mathbf{Z}^+$. In many treatments of set theory, a version of the principle of mathematical induction is actually used to define $\mathbf{Z}^+$.

The principle of mathematical induction says that a subset of $\mathbf{Z}^+$ that contains 1 and has the property that it contains the "successor" of each of its elements contains all positive integers. What can the principle of mathematical induction be used for? It is used to show that a subset of $\mathbf{Z}^+$ is in fact all of $\mathbf{Z}^+$, and many problems that we have already met can be solved by showing that a set of positive integers is all of $\mathbf{Z}^+$.

For example, suppose that we want to show that the closed form for

```
TO F :X
 IF :X = 1 [OP 3]
 OP (F :X - 1) + 5
END
```

is

```
TO G :X
 OP 5 * :X - 2
END
```

In part I, we carried out some calculations that were designed to give a convincing argument that $F = G$ on $\mathbf{Z}^+$, but the argument made the subtle assumption that certain patterns in the calculations would continue indefinitely. The principle of mathematical induction gives us a way to make this type of argument precise.

To show that these two functions are equal on $\mathbf{Z}^+$, we reason as follows. Let Q be the set of positive integers on which F and G are equal. We'll show that $Q = \mathbf{Z}^+$. To do this, we need only show that 1 is in Q, and that whenever N is in Q, then $N + 1$ is also in Q. Let's spell out the previous three sentences in detail

Q is the set of integers on which F and G are equal. What does this *mean*? It means that K is in Q if and only if $F(K) = G(K)$. So, to see if a number is in Q, we need only check that F and G both output the same thing when fed this number. For example, 5 is in Q because $F(5)$ and $G(5)$ are both 23, as you can easily check.

We will prove that $Q = \mathbf{Z}^+$ by showing two things:

1. 1 is in Q.

2. If N is in Q, then $N + 1$ is also in Q.

Well, is 1 in Q? That is, is $F(1) = G(1)$? Yes. It is clear from F's definition that $F(1) = 3$, and $G(1) = 5 \cdot 1 - 2 = 3$ also.

Next, we want to show that every time Q contains a number N, it also contains the number $N + 1$. So suppose that N is in Q, and let's try to use this assumption to show that $N + 1$ is also in Q. Since N is in Q, we know that $F(N) = G(N)$. We want to use this fact to prove that $F(N+1) = G(N+1)$ (because $F(N + 1) = G(N + 1)$ is what you need to be able to say that $N + 1$ is in Q).

Looking at G's definition, we see that $G(N+1) = 5(N+1)-2$, so $G(N+1) = 5N + 3$. How about $F(N + 1)$? Well, look at F's definition:

```
TO F :X
 IF :X = 1 [OP 3]
 OP (F :X - 1) + 5
END
```

If X has value $N + 1$, we see that

$$F(N + 1) = F(N) + 5$$

but since N is in Q, $F(N) = G(N)$, so

$$
\begin{aligned}
F(N + 1) &= G(N) + 5 \\
&= (5N - 2) + 5 \qquad \text{(because } G(N) = 5N - 2\text{)} \\
&= 5N + 3 \\
&= G(N + 1)
\end{aligned}
$$

So $N + 1$ is in Q. We have satisfied both hypotheses of the principle of mathematical induction; we have shown that

1. 1 is in Q, and

2. if N is in Q, then $N + 1$ is also in Q.

This means that $Q = \mathbf{Z}^+$. Since Q is the set of positive integers N for which $F(N) = G(N)$, we have shown that $F = G$ on $\mathbf{Z}^+$.

A Less Formal Approach

I apologize for the long-winded exposition in the above proof; if the proof seems contrived, it's because I spelled out every step in detail. No one writes inductive proofs this way (a proof that uses the principle of mathematical induction is called an "inductive proof"), but it's important to go through a detailed example like this one at least once in your life.

As I read the proof, it seems stuffy and artificial. It almost seems that informal arguments like the ones we made in part I are more natural and more convincing. Let's see if we can find a method of arguing that is as precise as the above one and as convincing as the informal ones.

Suppose we have a function F defined like this:

```
TO F :X
 IF :X = 1 [OP 3]
 OP (F :X - 1) + 7
END
```

If we type

```
TAB "F 1 10
```

we see

```
1  . . . 3
2  . . . 10
3  . . . 17
4  . . . 24
5  . . . 31
6  . . . 38
7  . . . 45
8  . . . 52
9  . . . 59
10 . . . 66
```

Even if we didn't recognize this as an arithmetic sequence, we would probably conjecture that $F = G$ on Z^+ where G is defined like this:

```
TO G :X
 OP 7 * :X - 4
END
```

If we type

```
TAB "G 1 10
```

we see

```
1  . . . 3
2  . . . 10
3  . . . 17
4  . . . 24
5  . . . 31
```

```
6  . . . 38
7  . . . 45
8  . . . 52
9  . . . 59
10 . . . 66
```

We could tabulate F and G up to 100, and we'd get the same tabulations. Mathematical induction can be thought of as a method to convince someone that if F and G tabulate the same up to some number (like 100), then they will also tabulate the same up to the next number (101), and the convincing takes place without actually carrying out the tabulation. To convince someone of this fact, we could argue like this:

Suppose F and G tabulate the same up to 100; then, in particular, $F(100) = G(100)$. Look at the definitions of F and G:

```
TO F :X                     TO G :X
 IF :X = 1 [OP 3]            OP 7*:X - 4
 OP (F :X - 1) + 7          END
END
```

Now, $F(101) = F(100) + 7$ (because of the way F is defined)

$\qquad\qquad = G(100) + 7$ (because $F(100) = G(100)$)

$\qquad\qquad = (7 \cdot 100 - 4) + 7$ (because of the way G is defined)

$\qquad\qquad = 7 \cdot 100 + 7 - 4$

$\qquad\qquad = 7(100 + 1) - 4$

$\qquad\qquad = 7 \cdot 101 - 4$

$\qquad\qquad = G(101)$ (because of the way G is defined)

So, if $F(100)$ were the same as $G(100)$, then $F(101)$ would be the same as $G(101)$.

There is actually nothing special about 100 in this calculation. We could use the same calculation to convince someone that if F and G tabulate the same up to some number N, then they would also tabulate the same up to $N + 1$, and we would not have to carry out the tabulation to convince them. Here's what we could say:

Suppose F and G tabulate the same up to N; then we'd know that $F(N) = G(N)$. Look at the definition of F and G:

```
TO F :X                      TO G :X
 IF :X = 1 [OP 3]             TO G :X
 OP (F :X - 1) + 7            OP 7*:X - 4
END                          END
```

Now, $F(N+1) = F(N) + 7$ (because of the way F is defined)

$\qquad\qquad = G(N) + 7$ (because $F(N) = G(N)$)

$\qquad\qquad = (7 \cdot N - 4) + 7$ (because of the way G is defined)

$\qquad\qquad = 7 \cdot N + 7 - 4$

$\qquad\qquad = 7(N+1) - 4$

$\qquad\qquad = 7(N+1) - 4$

$\qquad\qquad = G(N+1)$ (because of the way G is defined)

So, if $F(N) = G(N)$, then $F(N+1) = G(N+1)$.

The principle of mathematical induction simply says that because of this argument, F and G are equal on $\mathbf{Z}^+$.

> Here are the details of the connection between the above argument and a full blown proof by mathematical induction: Let Q be the set of positive integers on which F and G are equal. Because of our tabulation, 1 is in Q; in fact, the integers between 1 and 10 are all in Q because our tabulation shows that F and G output the same for integer inputs between 1 and 10. Assume that they tabulate the same up to N; that is, assume that N is in Q. Then we proved that they would tabulate the same up to $N+1$; that is, we proved that $N+1$ would be in Q. This means that Q is all of $\mathbf{Z}^+$, so $F = G$ on $\mathbf{Z}^+$.

So you can think of the principle of mathematical induction (at least when it is used to show that two functions are equal on $\mathbf{Z}^+$) as something that says:

> If two functions tabulate the same for the first few positive integers, and if you can prove that any equal tabulation can be extended by one more input, then the functions are equal on $\mathbf{Z}^+$.

An inductive proof that two functions F and G are equal on $\mathbf{Z}^+$ therefore consists of two parts:

1. An initial tabulation to show that F and G are equal up to a certain point.

2. An argument (involving the way F and G are defined) that convinces your audience that any tabulation can be extended by one more input.

Before we state this in a formal way, let's work out a few more examples.

Let's give an inductive proof to show that the sum of the integers between 1 and N is $\frac{N(N+1)}{2}$. This amounts to showing that the following two functions are equal on $\mathbf{Z}^+$:

```
TO F :N                     TO G :N
 IF :N = 1 [OP 1]            OP :N * (:N + 1) / 2
 OP :N + (F :N - 1)         END
END
```

Look at the tabulations:

```
TAB "F 1 5


1 . . . 1
2 . . . 3
3 . . . 6
4 . . . 10
5 . . . 15
```

and

```
TAB "G 1 5


1 . . . 1
2 . . . 3
3 . . . 6
4 . . . 10
5 . . . 15
```

Suppose that we tabulated further than 5; suppose that we tabulated up to some number, like 46, and F(46) was the same as G(46) (try it if you like). Then, without tabulating, F(47) would have to equal G(47). Here's why:

$$G(47) = \frac{47 \cdot 48}{2}$$

(why?), and from F's definition,

$$F(47) = 47 + F(46) \qquad \text{(by the way } F \text{ is defined)}$$

$$= 47 + G(46) \qquad \text{(we are assuming that } F(46) = G(46))$$

$$= 47 + \frac{46 \cdot 47}{2}$$

$$= \frac{2 \cdot 47}{2} + \frac{46 \cdot 47}{2}$$

$$= \frac{2 \cdot 47 + 46 \cdot 47}{2}$$

$$= \frac{47 \cdot (2 + 46)}{2}$$

$$= \frac{47 \cdot 48}{2}$$

$$= G(47)$$

There's nothing special about 46 in this calculation. Suppose that we tabulated up to N and that $F(N)$ was the same as $G(N)$. Then the tabulations would also have to be the same up to $N + 1$, because

$$G(N + 1) = \frac{(N + 1)(N + 2)}{2}$$

(why?), and from F's definition,

$$F(N + 1) = (N + 1) + F(N) \qquad \text{(by the way } F \text{ is defined)}$$

$$= (N + 1) + G(N) \qquad \text{(we are assuming that } F(N) = G(N))$$

$$= (N + 1) + \frac{N \cdot (N + 1)}{2}$$

$$= \frac{2 \cdot (N + 1)}{2} + \frac{N \cdot (N + 1)}{2}$$

$$= \frac{(2 \cdot (N + 1) + N \cdot (N + 1))}{2}$$

$$= \frac{N^2 + N + 2N + 1}{2}$$

$$= \frac{N^2 + 3N + 1}{2}$$

$$= \frac{(N+1)(N+2)}{2}$$
$$= G(N+1)$$

So any tabulation on which F and G are equal can be extended by one more input. Since F and G tabulate the same up to 5, we know that they will tabulate the same up to 6. Since they tabulate the same up to 6, they'll tabulate the same up to 7. "Inductively," F and G will tabulate the same up to any number; F = G on $\mathbf{Z}^+$.

In the above proof, we use the assumption that $F(N) = G(N)$ to prove that $F(N+1)$ is the same as $G(N+1)$. The assumption that $F(N) = G(N)$ is called the "inductive hypothesis."

Another example: Suppose we want a closed form for

```
TO F :X
 IF :X = 1 [OP 2]
 OP (F :X - 1) + (POWER 2 :X)
END
```

If I type

```
TAB "F 1 6
```

I see

```
1 . . . 2
2 . . . 6
3 . . . 14
4 . . . 30
5 . . . 62
6 . . . 126
```

This almost looks like powers of 2. If I define a temporary function TEMP

```
TO TEMP :X
 OP POWER 2 :X
END
```

and type

```
TAB "TEMP 1 6
```

I see

```
1 . . . 2
2 . . . 4
3 . . . 8
4 . . . 16
5 . . . 32
6 . . . 64
```

Notice that the outputs of F seem to be 2 less than a power of 2, but to get the right power of 2, you have to increase the input by 1. So, for example, to get F(3), take the fourth power of 2 (16) and subtract 2. This leads to a conjecture; if we define G as

```
TO G :X
 OP (POWER 2 (:X + 1)) - 2
END
```

then $F = G$ on $\mathbf{Z}^+$. Well, an initial tabulation of G gets us hoping:

```
TAB "G 1 6
```

produces

```
1 . . . 2
2 . . . 6
3 . . . 14
4 . . . 30
5 . . . 62
6 . . . 126
```

Suppose that F and G tabulated the same up to N; that is, suppose that $F(N)$ and $G(N)$ were the same. Then F and G would have to tabulate the same up to $N + 1$. Here's why:

$$
\begin{aligned}
\mathrm{F}(N + 1) &= \mathrm{F}(N) + 2^{(N+1)} & \text{(by the way F is defined)} \\
&= \mathrm{G}(N) + 2^{(N+1)} & \text{(by the inductive hypothesis)} \\
&= (2^{(N+1)} - 2) + 2^{(N+1)} \\
&= 2^{(N+1)} + 2^{(N+1)} - 2 \\
&= 2 \cdot 2^{(N+1)} - 2 \\
&= 2^{(N+2)} - 2 \\
&= \mathrm{G}(N + 1)
\end{aligned}
$$

So any tabulation on which F and G are equal can be extended by one more input, and since they tabulate the same up to 6, they'll tabulate the same up to every positive integer N; F = G on $\mathbf{Z}^+$.

One more example: Suppose that F is defined like this:

```
TO F :X
 IF :X = 1 [OP 3]
 OP (F :X - 1) + (POWER 3 :X)
END
```

If I type

```
TAB "F 1 6
```

I see

```
1 . . . 3
2 . . . 12
3 . . . 39
4 . . . 120
5 . . . 363
6 . . . 1092
```

Looking at the previous example for inspiration, let's try

```
TO TEMP :X
 OP (POWER 3 (:X + 1)) - 3
END
```

Then

```
TAB "TEMP 1 6
```

produces

```
1 . . . 6
2 . . . 24
3 . . . 78
4 . . . 240
5 . . . 726
6 . . . 2184
```

The outputs of TEMP are too big. But it looks like they are too big in a predictable way; it looks like TEMP is exactly twice F. If that were true, we could find a formula for F like this:

$$\text{If } \texttt{TEMP}(X) = 2\texttt{F}(X), \text{ then}$$

$$3^{(X+1)} - 3 = 2\texttt{F}(X), \text{ so}$$

$$\frac{3^{(X+1)} - 3}{2} = \texttt{F}(X)$$

So we conjecture that F = G on $\mathbf{Z}^+$ where G is defined like this:

```
TO G :X
 OP ((POWER 3 (:X + 1)) - 3)/2
END
```

To prove it, you can check that F and G tabulate the same up to, say, 7. Suppose inductively that they tabulate the same up to N. Then

$$\begin{aligned}
F(N+1) &= F(N) + 3^{(N+1)} \\
&= G(N) + 3^{(N+1)} \\
&= \frac{3^{(N+1)} - 3}{2} + 3^{(N+1)} \\
&= \frac{3^{(N+1)} - 3 + 2 \cdot 3^{(N+1)}}{2} \\
&= \frac{3 \cdot 3^{(N+1)} - 3}{2} \\
&= \frac{3^{(N+2)} - 3}{2} \\
&= G(N+1)
\end{aligned}$$

and F and G would tabulate the same up to $N + 1$. Since F and G tabulate the same up to 7, they'll tabulate the same forever. That is, F = G on $\mathbf{Z}^+$.

In the above examples, we used the principle of mathematical induction to prove that functions are equal on $\mathbf{Z}^+$. We will often use the principle of mathematical induction this way, so we might as well state a streamlined version of it that is specifically designed to prove that two functions are equal on $\mathbf{Z}^+$. Notice that the length of our initial tabulation is quite arbitrary; sometimes we tabulated up to 10, sometimes up to 5, or 6 or 7. If you think about it, the initial tabulation is just to get things rolling; it can be as short or as long as we like, but it has to include (at least) a tabulation "up to" 1. Since this is the minimum requirement, we can state an efficient version of the principle of mathematical induction that lets you prove that two functions are equal on $\mathbf{Z}^+$.

The Principle of Mathematical Induction for Functions Suppose that F and G are two functions whose domains contain $\mathbf{Z}^+$, and suppose that F and G satisfy the following two conditions:

1. $F(1) = G(1)$.

2. Whenever $F(N) = G(N)$, $F(N + 1) = G(N + 1)$.

Then $F = G$ on $\mathbf{Z}^+$.

Using the principle of mathematical induction in this form eliminates the need to deal with "the set Q" (the set of positive integers on which $F = G$), so it often makes for cleaner arguments. Remember, though, that the principle of mathematical induction is really a way to show that a subset of $\mathbf{Z}^+$ is all of $\mathbf{Z}^+$; in complicated or delicate situations, we'll always use the original formulation.

Before we look at some other types of inductive proofs, you should try proving some functions equal using the principle of mathematical induction. The following problems give you some samples.

Exercise 5.11 Give a closed form for each function (you can arrive at the closed form by a tabulation, by the results in part I, or by other methods). Then prove that your closed form is equal to the given function on $\mathbf{Z}^+$ by the principle of mathematical induction:

```
1. TO F :N
     IF :N = 1 [OP 3]
     OP (F :N-1) + 5
   END
```

```
2. TO H :X
     IF :X = 1 [OP 1]
     OP (H :X-1) + 2 * :X-1
   END
```

```
3. TO J :X
     IF :X = 1 [OP 2]
     OP (J :X-1) * 2
   END
```

```
4. TO K :X
     IF :X = 1 [OP 4]
     OP (K :X-1) + (POWER 4 :X)
   END
```

```
5. TO L :X                         6. TO G :X
     IF :X = 1 [OP 1]                   IF :X = 1 [OP 4]
     OP (L :X-1) + (POWER 5 :X)         OP (G :X-1) + 3 * :X
   END                               END
```

Exercise 5.12 Give a recursive form for each function (you can arrive at the recursive form by a tabulation, by the results in Part I, or by other methods). Then prove that your recursive form is equal to the given function on $\mathbf{Z}^+$ by the principle of mathematical induction:

1. $F(X) = 3X + 1$
2. $G(X) = 4X - 1$
3. $H(X) = X^2$
4. $J(X) = X(X + 1)$
5. $K(X) = 2X - 1$
6. $L(X) = 2^X + X$

There's another way to think of the principle of mathematical induction. It can be looked at as a method for capturing what is common to a whole stream of calculations. Here's an example:

Consider the following function:

```
TO F :X
 IF :X = 1 [OP 3]
 OP (F :X - 1) + 2 * :X
END
```

Is there a closed form? There's nothing like a tabulation to give you inspiration

X	$F(X)$
1	3
2	7
3	13
4	21
5	31
6	43
7	57
8	73
9	91
10	111

So how about this?

```
TO G :X
 OP :X * (:X + 1) + 1
END
```

Let's prove that **F** = **G** on $\mathbf{Z}^+$ by using the principle of mathematical induction for functions. We need to prove two things:

1. $F(1) = G(1)$. Well, $F(1) = 3$ and $G(1) = 1 \cdot (1 + 1) + 1 = 3$, too. In fact, just for emotional security, a tabulation shows that **F** and **G** are equal for inputs up to 15.

2. Whenever $F(N) = G(N)$, we also have $F(N+1) = G(N+1)$ (any tabulation can be extended by one more input). So suppose that we have tabulated **F** and **G** up to N, and we have found that $F(N) = G(N)$. Does this imply that $F(N + 1) = G(N + 1)$? Well,

$$G(N + 1) = (N + 1) \cdot (N + 2) + 1$$

and

$$
\begin{aligned}
F(N + 1) &= F(N) + 2(N + 1) \\
&= G(N) + 2(N + 1) &&\text{(the inductive hypothesis)} \\
&= (N(N + 1) + 1) + 2(N + 1) &&\text{(because } G(N) = N(N + 1) + 1) \\
&= (N(N + 1) + 2(N + 1)) + 1 \\
&= (N + 1)(N + 2) + 1 \\
&= G(N + 1)
\end{aligned}
$$

So there we have it. Since $F(1) = G(1)$, and since we can prove that $F(N + 1) = G(N + 1)$ whenever $F(N) = G(N)$, the principle of mathematical induction for functions assures us that **F** = **G** on $\mathbf{Z}^+$.

Now, this argument is really just a technique for generically carrying out calculations like those we used in part I. For example, let's write out several outputs of **F**, simplifying as we go:

$F(1) = 3 = 2 + 1$

$F(2) = F(1) + 2 \cdot 2 = (2 + 1) + 2 \cdot 2 = (2 + 2 \cdot 2) + 1 = 2 \cdot (2 + 1) + 1$

$\qquad = 2 \cdot 3 + 1$

$F(3) = F(2) + 2 \cdot 3 = (2 \cdot 3 + 1) + 2 \cdot 3 = (2 \cdot 3 + 2 \cdot 3) + 1 = 3 \cdot (2 + 2) + 1$

$\qquad = 3 \cdot 4 + 1$

$F(4) = F(3) + 2 \cdot 4 = (3 \cdot 4 + 1) + 2 \cdot 4 = (3 \cdot 4 + 2 \cdot 4) + 1 = 4 \cdot (3 + 2) + 1$

$\qquad = 4 \cdot 5 + 1$

$F(5) = F(4) + 2 \cdot 5 = (4 \cdot 5 + 1) + 2 \cdot 5 = (4 \cdot 5 + 2 \cdot 5) + 1 = 5 \cdot (4 + 2) + 1$

$\qquad = 5 \cdot 6 + 1$

$F(6) = F(5) + 2 \cdot 6 = (5 \cdot 6 + 1) + 2 \cdot 6 = (5 \cdot 6 + 2 \cdot 6) + 1 = 6 \cdot (5 + 2) + 1$

$\qquad = 6 \cdot 7 + 1$

$\qquad \vdots$

You get the idea. Once the calculation gets going, it becomes mechanical and predictable. Without carrying out the details, can't you picture the calculation of $F(7)$ in your head? Aren't you certain that if you did the calculation, you'd find that $F(7) = 7 \cdot 8 + 1$? And, if this is the output for $F(7)$, can't you picture using this fact in the calculation of $F(8)$? Here it is:

$$\begin{aligned} F(8) &= F(7) + 2 \cdot 8 = (7 \cdot 8 + 1) + 2 \cdot 8 \\ &= (7 \cdot 8 + 2 \cdot 8) + 1 = 8 \cdot (7 + 2) + 1 \\ &= 8 \cdot 9 + 1 \end{aligned}$$

Imagine that you could keep going forever: you could calculate $F(9)$ from $F(8)$ (and it would come out to be $9 \cdot 10 + 1$), you could calculate $F(10)$ from $F(9)$ (and it would come out to be $10 \cdot 11 + 1$); eventually you would find that $F(104) = 104 \cdot 105 + 1$, and from this you could calculate that $F(105) = 105 \cdot 106 + 1$, and so on. The generic calculation in the principle of mathematical induction that takes you from the inductive hypothesis to the "next step" is just a snapshot of the infinite stream of calculations outlined above. It captures the similarity between the process that lets you use the fact that $F(23) = 23 \cdot 24 + 1$ to prove $F(24) = 24 \cdot 25 + 1$ and the process that lets you use the fact that $F(104) = 104 \cdot 105 + 1$ to prove that $F(105) = 105 \cdot 106 + 1$. It is an abstraction of what is similar among all the calculations in our infinite stream of calculations. It says:

Okay. Suppose I've done this N times and I've found that

$$F(N) = N(N+1) + 1$$

Then I can calculate $F(N+1)$ using the definition of F,

$$\begin{aligned}
F(N+1) = F(N) + 2(N+1) &= (N(N+1) + 1) + 2(N+1) \\
&= (N(N+1) + 2(N+1)) + 1 \\
&= (N+1)(N+2) + 1 \\
&= (N+2) + 1
\end{aligned}$$

and this is the next calculation in my infinite list of calculations.

When I use the principle of mathematical induction to prove that $F = G$, I'm thinking of the calculation of $F(N)$ in a certain way. I'm thinking of the above string of calculations. I calculate $F(4)$ by using

1. the recursive call in F that relates $F(4)$ to $F(3)$,

2. the value of $F(3)$ that has already been computed, and

3. algebraic simplification.

At the Nth step I manipulate the output of F until it is identical with the corresponding output of G, and then I move on to the next calculation, substituting $G(N)$ wherever I see $F(N)$. This "simplify as you go" method is by no means the only way to think of the calculation of $F(N)$.

Another way is to develop a model of what the computer is doing when you ask it for $F(N)$ (it doesn't make any difference what your particular computer is actually doing; this discussion is to help you understand mathematical induction, not how a computer works).

Here's our function

```
TO F :X
 IF :X = 1 [OP 3]
 OP (F :X - 1) + 2 * :X
END
```

Suppose that you ask the machine for $F(4)$. This sets up the sequence of function calls shown in figure 5.1.

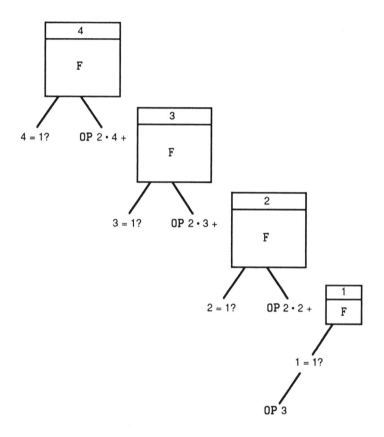

Figure 5.1

At this point the computer "unstacks"; $F(1)$ evaluates to 3. $F(2)$ evaluates to $3+2\cdot2 = 7$, $F(3)$ evaluates to $7+2\cdot3 = 13$, and $F(4)$ evaluates to $13+2\cdot4 = 21$. If we write out these calculations but delay the evaluation until the end, we see that

$$F(4) = 3 + 2 \cdot 2 + 2 \cdot 3 + 2 \cdot 4$$

Similarly,

$$F(5) = 3 + 2 \cdot 2 + 2 \cdot 3 + 2 \cdot 4 + 2 \cdot 5$$
$$F(6) = 3 + 2 \cdot 2 + 2 \cdot 3 + 2 \cdot 4 + 2 \cdot 5 + 2 \cdot 6$$
$$F(7) = 3 + 2 \cdot 2 + 2 \cdot 3 + 2 \cdot 4 + 2 \cdot 5 + 2 \cdot 6 + 2 \cdot 7$$
$$\vdots$$
$$F(N) = 3 + 2 \cdot 2 + 2 \cdot 3 + 2 \cdot 4 + 2 \cdot 5 + \cdots + 2 \cdot N$$

Now, we can do some symbolic manipulation on this expression

$$
\begin{aligned}
F(N) &= 3 + \quad\ 2 \cdot 2 + 2 \cdot 3 + 2 \cdot 4 + 2 \cdot 5 + \cdots + 2 \cdot N \\
&= 1 + 2 \cdot 1 + 2 \cdot 2 + 2 \cdot 3 + 2 \cdot 4 + 2 \cdot 5 + \cdots + 2 \cdot N \\
&= 1 + 2(1 + 2 + 3 + 4 + 5 + \cdots + N) \\
&= 1 + 2\left(\frac{N(N+1)}{2}\right) \\
&= 1 + N(N+1) \\
&= G(N)
\end{aligned}
$$

Have we eliminated mathematical induction from our argument? No. It shows up in two places. Before I tell you where it shows up, try to find the uses of mathematical induction in the above calculation for yourself.

STOP

The first use is simple to spot: Why does

$$1 + 2 + 3 + 4 + 5 + \cdots + N = \frac{N(N+1)}{2}$$

Because we proved it by mathematical induction. Of course, you could argue with me about this; you could say that Gauss' method ("first plus last times half the number of terms") gives a noninductive way to sum the numbers between 1 and N. Think about that. Does Gauss' method bypass the principle of mathematical induction?

The second use of the principle of mathematical induction is more subtle. In our argument, we showed that

$$F(4) = 3 + 2 \cdot 2 + 2 \cdot 3 + 2 \cdot 4$$

and then we said that similarly,

$$F(5) = 3 + 2 \cdot 2 + 2 \cdot 3 + 2 \cdot 4 + 2 \cdot 5$$
$$F(6) = 3 + 2 \cdot 2 + 2 \cdot 3 + 2 \cdot 4 + 2 \cdot 5 + 2 \cdot 6$$
$$F(7) = 3 + 2 \cdot 2 + 2 \cdot 3 + 2 \cdot 4 + 2 \cdot 5 + 2 \cdot 6 + 2 \cdot 7$$
$$\vdots$$
$$F(N) = 3 + 2 \cdot 2 + 2 \cdot 3 + 2 \cdot 4 + 2 \cdot 5 + \cdots + 2 \cdot N$$

Now, you could easily check (using the method we used to get the expression for $F(4)$) that

$$F(5) = 3 + 2 \cdot 2 + 2 \cdot 3 + 2 \cdot 4 + 2 \cdot 5$$

and that

$$F(6) = 3 + 2 \cdot 2 + 2 \cdot 3 + 2 \cdot 4 + 2 \cdot 5 + 2 \cdot 6$$

But how do you conclude that

$$F(N) = 3 + 2 \cdot 2 + 2 \cdot 3 + 2 \cdot 4 + 2 \cdot 5 + \cdots + 2 \cdot N$$

If you were forced to write out the details, you'd find yourself using mathematical induction! Here's a sketch:

We want to prove that for all N in $\mathbf{Z}^+$,

$$F(N) = 3 + 2 \cdot 2 + 2 \cdot 3 + 2 \cdot 4 + 2 \cdot 5 + \cdots + 2N$$

or, rewriting the above expression, we want to prove that

$$F(N) = 1 + 2 \cdot 1 + 2 \cdot 2 + 2 \cdot 3 + 2 \cdot 4 + 2 \cdot 5 + \cdots + 2 \cdot N$$
$$= 1 + 2(1 + 2 + 3 + 4 + 5 + \cdots + N)$$

So we claim that F is equal to H on $\mathbf{Z}^+$, where H is defined like this:

```
TO H :X
 OP 1 + 2 * (S :N)
END

TO S :N
 IF :N = 1 [OP 1]
 OP :N + (S :N - 1)
END
```

The proof that $F = H$ on $\mathbf{Z}^+$ is an exercise in using the principle of mathematical induction for functions.

Project 5.13 Consider the following functions:

```
TO F :X
 IF :X = 1 [OP 3]
 OP (F :X - 1) + 2 * :X
END

TO H :X
 OP 1 + 2 * (S :X)
END

TO S :N
 IF :N = 1 [OP 1]
 OP :N + (S :N - 1)
END
```

Show that $F = H$ on $\mathbf{Z}^+$.

Project 5.14 Suppose that F is the function

```
TO F :X
 IF :X = 1 [OP 3]
 OP (F :X - 1) + 3 * :X
END
```

Show that on $\mathbf{Z}^+$,

$$F(N) = 3(1 + 2 + 3 + \cdots + N)$$

Hint: Define G like this:

```
TO G :N
 OP 3 * H :N
END

TO H :N
 IF :N = 1 [OP 1]
 OP :N + (H :N - 1)
END
```

Show that $\mathbf{F} = \mathbf{G}$ on $\mathbf{Z}^+$.

Summations

Many functions that we have been playing with are just summations of very simple functions. If $\mathbf{F}$ is a function, we can get another function $\mathbf{G}$ by defining

$$\mathbf{G}(N) = \mathbf{F}(1) + \mathbf{F}(2) + \mathbf{F}(3) + \mathbf{F}(4) + \cdots + \mathbf{F}(N)$$

or by using Logo representations

```
TO G :X
 OP SIGMA "F 1 :X
END
```

There is a convenient mathematical notation for this process of summing the outputs of a function $\mathbf{F}$; it looks like this:

$$\sum_{K=1}^{N} \mathbf{F}(K)$$

This is read "the sum as K goes from 1 to N of $\mathbf{F}(K)$." The symbol $\sum$ is the Greek letter sigma (the analogue of the Roman S), suggesting a summation. So, for example,

$$\sum_{K=1}^{5} F(K) \text{ means } \mathbf{F}(1) + \mathbf{F}(2) + \mathbf{F}(3) + \mathbf{F}(4) + \mathbf{F}(5)$$

and

$$\sum_{K=1}^{4} 2K + 1 \text{ means } (2 \cdot 1 + 1) + (2 \cdot 2 + 1) + (2 \cdot 3 + 1) + (2 \cdot 4 + 1)$$

Project 5.15 For each function F, let

$$G(X) = \sum_{K=1}^{X} F(K)$$

Find a closed form for G (and prove that your closed form is equal to G on $\mathbf{Z}^+$). Hint: You can define G using SIGMA:

```
TO G :X
 OP SIGMA "F 1 :X
END
```

Tabulate G and look for patterns. The following fact about summations is often useful in problems like these:

$$\sum_{K=1}^{N+1} F(K) = \left(\sum_{K=1}^{N} F(K) \right) + F(N + 1)$$

1. ```
TO F :X
   OP 5
END
```

2. ```
TO F :X
   IF :X = 1 [OP 3]
   OP 5
END
```

3. ```
TO F :X
   IF :X = 1 [OP -1]
   OP (F :X - 1) + 10
END
```

4. ```
TO F :X
   OP 3 * :X
END
```

5. ```
TO F :X
   OP 5 * :X
END
```

6. ```
TO F:X
   OP 2 * :X - 1
END
```

7. ```
TO F :X
   OP 12 * :X + 12
END
```

8. ```
TO F :X
   OP POWER 2 :X
END
```

#9. ```
TO F :X
   OP 6 * :X * :X
END
```
```

Project 5.16 Suppose that F is defined like this:

```
TO F :X
 IF :X = 1 [OP 2]
 OP (F :X - 1) + 2 * :X
END
```

Then suppose that G accumulates the outputs of F:

```
TO G :X
 OP SIGMA "F 1 :X
END
```

Find a closed form for G and prove that your closed form is equal to G on $\mathbf{Z}^+$ by the principle of mathematical induction.

Notice that if $H(X) = 2X$, then F can also be defined in this way:

```
TO F :X
 OP SIGMA "H 1 :X
END
```

So F accumulates the outputs of H, and G accumulates the outputs of F. Find a closed form for the function J that accumulates the outputs of G:

```
TO J :X
 OP SIGMA "G 1 :X
END
```

(and prove that your closed form agrees with J on $\mathbf{Z}^+$). Can you go one level higher?

The principle of mathematical induction is one of the most useful tools in mathematics. Many of the new results that are obtained in mathematics each year use inductive proofs in a fundamental way. Many published proofs are written in a style where the proof is sketched and the details are left to the reader. More often than not, these details are most easily completed by an inductive argument.

> On the other hand, you don't want to go around proving everything by the principle of mathematical induction. For example, you could prove that
> $$X^2 - 3X + 2 = (X - 2)(X - 1)$$

on $\mathbf{Z}^+$ by mathematical induction, but it is much simpler to use high school algebra. And even when inductive proofs are called for, they are often easiest to understand when they are written in an informal style. Later in part II, we'll use mathematical induction to establish some counting techniques; after a while, you won't even notice the use of induction in these "combinatorial arguments."

Knowing about mathematical induction is not only an important prerequisite for understanding someone else's mathematics, it's an important means of discovering your own mathematics. The examples and problems in this section are good models for how mathematical discovery comes about:

You investigate the properties of a mathematical object by making some concrete calculations; let's say the object is a function. So you tabulate this function, and in the process of tabulating it, you notice a pattern in the function's outputs that wasn't obvious from the function's definition. This leads you to a conjecture about an alternative way of calculating the function's outputs. The proof that this alternative definition agrees with your function on $\mathbf{Z}^+$ is embedded in your calculations, and when you try to explain why the pattern continues from one output to the next, you find yourself outlining an inductive proof. Perhaps you can generalize your result to a general class of functions (say, arithmetic sequences); if this happens, the proof of your general result will most likely be an inductive one.

This process is really at the heart of mathematical research. It involves a combination of calculation, pattern recognition, abstraction of the basic ideas in the calculation, proof (generic calculation) and generalization; very often, inductive ideas show up in natural ways. By the way, facility in each of these aspects of research can be developed with practice; people who say that mathematical talent is inborn are wrong.

Other Forms of Mathematical Induction

Because of its central importance, you should work at inductive proofs until they seem very natural to you. The next set of problems shows you some variations on the principle of mathematical induction.

Project 5.17 (*Induction for function inequality*) Suppose you tabulate these two functions:

```
TO F :N                          TO G :N
 IF :N = 1 [OP 1]                 OP POWER :N 3
 OP (F :N - 1) + :N * :N         END
END
```

F adds up the squares of the integers between 1 and its input, and G cubes its input. Of course, F isn't equal to G on Z^+, but it seems that G's output is always greater than F's (except at 1, where both F and G output 1). In other words, it seems that $F \leq G$ on Z^+ (function inequality on a set is defined exactly the same way as function equality on a set). There are several ways to prove that $F \leq G$ on Z^+; one way is to use mathematical induction. In other words, we can show that

1. $F(1) \leq G(1)$, and

2. whenever $F(N) \leq G(N)$, we also have $F(N+1) \leq G(N+1)$.

Do you see that these two conditions imply that $F \leq G$ on Z^+? If this isn't clear, go back to the original principle of mathematical induction; let Q be the set of positive integers N so that $F(N) \leq G(N)$. Proving that $F \leq G$ on Z^+ amounts to showing that $Q = Z^+$, and for this, we could show that

1. 1 is in Q (that is, $F(1) \leq G(1)$), and

2. whenever N is in Q (whenever $F(N) \leq G(N)$), we also have that $N+1$ is in Q (we also have $F(N+1) \leq G(N+1)$).

Now, for the proof:

1. $F(1) = 1$, and $G(1) = 1$ too, so $F(1) \leq G(1)$.

2. Suppose $F(N) \leq G(N)$. Then we use the definition of F to reason this way:

$$F(N+1) = F(N) + (N+1)^2 \leq G(N) + (N+1)^2$$
$$\text{(because } F(N) \leq G(N))$$

Because $G(N) = N^3$,

$$F(N+1) \leq N^3 + (N+1)^2 = N^3 + N^2 + 2N + 1$$

But N is a positive integer, so

$$N^3 + N^2 + 2N + 1 \leq N^3 + 3N^2 + 3N + 1$$
$$\text{(because } N^2 \leq 3N^2 \text{ and } 2N \leq 3N)$$

Finally, $N^3 + 3N^2 + 3N + 1 = (N+1)^3$. Combining the above calculations, we find that

$$\mathrm{F}(N+1) \leq (N+1)^3 = \mathrm{G}(N+1)$$

and this shows that $\mathrm{F} \leq \mathrm{G}$ on $\mathbf{Z}^+$.

There is another (perhaps more elegant) way to see that $\mathrm{F} \leq \mathrm{G}$ on $\mathbf{Z}^+$. For any positive integer N, we know that

$$1^2 \leq N^2$$
$$2^2 \leq N^2$$
$$3^2 \leq N^2$$
$$4^2 \leq N^2$$
$$\vdots$$
$$(N-1)^2 \leq N^2$$
$$N^2 \leq N^2$$

If you add up these inequalities, you'll find that

$$1^2 + 2^2 + 3^2 + 4^2 + \cdots + (N-1)^2 + N^2$$
$$\leq N^2 + N^2 + N^2 + N^2 + \cdots + N^2$$

Now, the left-hand side is just $\mathrm{F}(N)$, and the right-hand side is the sum of N N^2's, which is just $N \cdot N^2$ or N^3. So $\mathrm{F}(N) \leq N^3 = \mathrm{G}(N)$, and $\mathrm{F} \leq \mathrm{G}$ on $\mathbf{Z}^+$.

Which argument do you like? Does the second proof avoid the use of mathematical induction? Does either proof give you an insight into the fact that $\mathrm{F}(N) = \mathrm{G}(N)$ only when $N = 1$?

Prove that $2^N \leq (N+1)!$ for all positive integers N.

Project 5.18 (*Induction from a certain point*) Sometimes we have a set of positive integers that isn't all of $\mathbf{Z}^+$ but only excludes a few numbers. For example, consider the F of the above discussion, and the function G:

```
TO F :N
 IF :N = 1 [OP 1]
 OP (F :N - 1) + :N * :N
END

TO G :N
 OP (POWER :N 3) - 2 * (POWER :N 2) + :N
END
```

A tabulation shows that F isn't equal to G. It also shows that G's output is larger than F's once the input is 4 or larger. In other words, it seems that $F \leq G$ on the set of integers greater than or equal to 4:

$$F \leq G \text{ on } \{4\ 5\ 6\ 7\ 8 \cdots\}$$

The proof is fairly straightforward if we use this variation on the principle of mathematical induction:

Principle of Mathematical Induction (More General Form)

Suppose that K is an integer, and Q is a set of integers with the following two properties:

1. K is in Q.

2. Whenever an integer N is in Q, we also have that $N + 1$ is also in Q.

Then Q contains all integers greater than or equal to K.

(Note that this general form of the principle of mathematical induction even allows us to assume that K is less than 0.) So, we can prove that $F(X) < G(X)$ if X is 4 or greater by showing that

1. $F(4) < G(4)$, and

2. whenever $F(N) < G(N)$ for some integer N (where N is bigger than 4), we also have that $F(N + 1) < G(N + 1)$.

I'll leave the details to you.

Experiment 5.19 Investigate the following functions:

```
TO F :X                      TO G :X
 OP POWER 2 :X                 OP (FACT :X)/2
END                          END
```

FACT is the factorial function of part I:

```
TO FACT :N
  IF :N = 0 [OP 1]
  OP :N * (FACT :N - 1)
END
```

Find a subset of $\mathbf{Z}^+$ on which $F \leq G$, and prove your assertion.

Project 5.20 (*Strong induction*)   In chapter 3 we worked with the following function P:

```
TO P :N
  IF :N = 1 [OP 0]
  IF :N = 2 [OP 1/9]
  OP 2 * (P :N - 1) - (P :N - 2)
END
```

A tabulation led us to conjecture that P was equal on $\mathbf{Z}^+$ to R where R is defined like this:

```
TO R :N
  OP (:N - 1)/9
END
```

Let's try to prove the functions equal on $\mathbf{Z}^+$ by the principle of mathematical induction. First of all, $P(1) = 0$ and $R(1) = 0$. So far, so good. Suppose that $P(N) = R(N)$. Then

$$P(N + 1) = 2P(N) - P(N - 1)$$

This is unlike the situations we have seen before because $P(N+1)$ is defined in terms of the two previous outputs from P, and that causes some problems. First of all, the above equation makes no sense if N is 1; it says that

$$P(2) = 2P(1) - P(0)$$

and 0 isn't in the domain of P. In addition to checking that $P(1) = R(1)$, we need a separate calculation to show that $P(2) = R(2)$. Both P and R output 1/9 at 2, so we are all set. The failure to notice when an inductive argument requires the verification of several "base cases" is the source of many examples of "false inductions" (see project 6.24).

Returning to the proof, we suppose that $N > 1$ and that $P(N) = R(N)$. Then

$$P(N + 1) = 2P(N) - P(N - 1)$$
$$= 2R(N) - P(N - 1)$$

Now what? We can replace $R(N)$ by $(N - 1)/9$, but that's as far as we'll get. Of course, if you think of the principle of mathematical induction as a shorthand for an infinite stream of calculations, you know that you would have never arrived at the fact that $P(N) = R(N)$ without first having arrived at the fact that $P(N - 1) = R(N - 1)$. Would this help? Well, look at the point where we got stuck:

$$P(N + 1) = 2P(N) - P(N - 1)$$
$$= 2R(N) - P(N - 1)$$
$$= \frac{2(N - 1)}{9} - P(N - 1)$$

If we could say that $P(N - 1) = R(N - 1)$, we could continue like this:

$$P(N + 1) = 2P(N) - P(N - 1)$$
$$= 2R(N) - P(N - 1)$$
$$= \frac{2(N - 1)}{9} - P(N - 1)$$
$$= \frac{2(N - 1)}{9} - R(N - 1)$$
$$= \frac{2(N - 1)}{9} - \frac{(N - 2)}{9}$$
$$= \frac{N}{9}$$

The last step came from algebraic simplification. Since $R(N + 1) = N/9$, this would show that $P(N + 1) = R(N + 1)$.

There is a variation of the principle of mathematical induction that allows you to assume the inductive hypothesis "all the way down"; it looks like this:

Principle of Mathematical Induction Suppose that Q is a set of positive integers with the following two properties:

1. 1 is in Q.

2. Whenever the positive integers between 1 and N are in Q, we also have that $N + 1$ is in Q.

Then $Q = \mathbf{Z}^+$.

It should be clear that this version of the principle of mathematical induction is true. Indeed, condition 2 of its definition is stronger than condition 2 of the principle of mathematical induction that we have been using until now (it allows you to use the fact that all the integers between 1 and N are in Q to prove that $N + 1$ is in Q). So the "traditional" principle of mathematical induction can be used to establish this strong principle of mathematical induction. It turns out that the two versions are actually equivalent. If you think about it, this "strong induction" is closer in spirit to the "extending the tabulation by one more input" point of view that we used to prove that two functions are equal. (If F and G tabulate the same up to N, isn't F equal to G for all integers between 1 and N?)

This variation of the principle of mathematical induction is typically used when you are dealing with a function whose output at N depends on the outputs at several integers less than N, as in the above example. Here's another example. Consider the following two functions defined on positive integers:

```
TO F :N                     TO G :N
 IF EVEN? :N [OP  :N/2]       IF :N = 1 [OP 2]
 OP 2 * :N                    IF :N = 2 [OP 1]
END                          IF EVEN? :N [OP (G :N - 2) + 1]
                             OP (G :N - 2) + 4
                            END
```

Tabulate them, and you'll see that they seem to be equal on $\mathbf{Z}^+$. (Notice that some numbers show up twice as outputs. Is there a pattern to the "distribution" of these double outputs?) Prove that F $=$ G on $\mathbf{Z}^+$. (Hint: You'll need to consider two cases in going from the inductive hypothesis to the fact that $F(N + 1) = G(N + 1)$.)

Project 5.21 Suppose you had a set of integers Q with the following properties:

1. The integer K is in Q.

2. Whenever an integer N is in Q, the integer $N-1$ is also in Q.

What can you say about Q?

This version if the principle of mathematical induction is useful when dealing with a function whose definition uses "upward recursion." For example, consider the following function:

```
TO F :X
 IF :X = 10 [OP 1]
 OP (F :X + 1) + 10
END
```

Find the domain of F, and find a closed form representation that agrees with F on this domain. Prove that your closed form works.

The next project is used in later sections.

#**Project 5.22** (*Double induction*)   This project uses the same ideas as project 5.16. Suppose F is the very simple function that always outputs 1:

```
TO F :M
 OP 1
END
```

Let F_1 be the function that accumulates the values of F so that

$$F_1(M) = \sum_{K=1}^{M} F(K)$$

```
TO F1 :M
 OP SIGMA "F 1 :M
END
```

$$
\begin{aligned}
\text{Now } F_1(M) &= F(1) + F(2) + F(3) + \cdots + F(M) \\
&= \underbrace{1 + 1 + 1 + \cdots + 1}_{M \text{ times}} \\
&= M
\end{aligned}
$$

So $F_1(M) = M$ for all M. Suppose that F_2 accumulates F_1's outputs so that

$$F_2(M) = \sum_{K=1}^{M} F_1(K)$$

```
TO F2 :M
 OP SIGMA "F1 1 :M
END
```

A tabulation of F_2 suggests a closed form. In fact a calculation shows that

$$F_2(M) = F_1(1) + F_1(2) + F_1(3) + \cdots + F_1(M)$$
$$= 1 + 2 + 3 + \cdots + M$$
$$= \frac{M(M+1)}{2}$$

Suppose that F_3 accumulates the outputs of F_2 so that

$$F_3(M) = \sum_{K=1}^{M} F_2(K)$$

```
TO F3 :M
 OP SIGMA "F2 1 :M
END
```

Then

$$F_3(M) = F_2(1) + F_2(2) + F_2(3) + \cdots + F_2(M)$$
$$= \frac{1 \cdot (1+1)}{2} + \frac{2 \cdot (2+1)}{2} + \frac{3 \cdot (3+1)}{2} + \cdots \frac{M(M+1)}{2}$$
$$= \frac{1}{2}(1 \cdot 2 + 2 \cdot 3 + 3 \cdot 4 + \cdots + M(M+1))$$

How about a closed form for F_3? A tabulation shows

M	$F_3(M)$
1	1
2	4
3	10
4	28
5	35
6	56
7	84
8	120
9	165
10	220

Take some time to play with this. I'm about to tell you how I came up with a closed form, so you shouldn't read on until you've worked at this on your own for a while.

One way to guess at a closed form is to look at the closed forms for F, F_1 and F_2:

$$F(M) = 1$$

$$F_1(M) = M$$

$$F_2(M) = \frac{M(M+1)}{2}$$

This isn't much information, but when I looked at it, I noticed that F_1 is a degree 1 polynomial in M, and F_2 is a degree 2 polynomial in M (if you multiply out the numerator of the expression for F_2, it becomes $M^2 + M$). Perhaps the closed form for F_3 would be something like

$$\frac{\text{a degree 3 polynomial in } M}{\text{something}}$$

Well, if the numerator for F_1 is M, and the numerator for F_2 is $M(M+1)$, perhaps the numerator for F_3 should be $M(M+1)(M+2)$. I checked this out by tabulating a temporary function G_3:

```
TO G3 :M
 OP :M * (:M + 1) * (:M + 2)
END
```

Try it. You don't get the same outputs as F_3 produces, but you get exactly six times these values! So we modify G_3:

```
TO G3 :M
 OP :M * (:M + 1) * (:M + 2)/6
END
```

and we conjecture that $F_3 = G_3$ on $\mathbf{Z}^+$. The proof, of course, is a proof by the principle of mathematical induction. Try it.

We can keep up the good work and consider F_4:

```
TO F4 :M
 OP SIGMA "F3 1 :M
END
```

If we have really discovered a pattern, then F_4 should equal G_4 on $\mathbf{Z}^+$ where

$$G_4(M) = \frac{M(M + 1)(M + 2)(M + 3)}{\text{something}}$$

Define G_4 temporarily as

```
TO G4 :M
 OP :M * (:M + 1) * (:M + 2) * (:M + 3)
END
```

Tabulate this, and compare with F_4. You'll see that we have to divide G_4's outputs by 24, so we modify G_4,

```
TO G4 :M
 OP :M * (:M + 1) * (:M + 2) * (:M + 3)/24
END
```

and we conjecture that $G_4 = F_4$ on $\mathbf{Z}^+$. Can you prove it?

Let's list the results that we have obtained so far:

$$\mathbf{F}(M) = 1$$

$$\mathbf{F}_1(M) = \mathbf{F}(1) + \mathbf{F}(2) + \cdots + \mathbf{F}(M) = M$$

$$\mathbf{F}_2(M) = \mathbf{F}_1(1) + \mathbf{F}_1(2) + \cdots + \mathbf{F}_1(M) = \frac{M(M+1)}{2}$$

$$\mathbf{F}_3(M) = \mathbf{F}_2(1) + \mathbf{F}_2(2) + \cdots + \mathbf{F}_2(M) = \frac{M(M+1)(M+2)}{6}$$

$$\mathbf{F}_4(M) = \mathbf{F}_3(1) + \mathbf{F}_3(2) + \cdots + \mathbf{F}_3(M) = \frac{M(M+1)(M+2)(M+3)}{24}$$

Is there a pattern in the denominators? Letting $D(N)$ stand for the denominator of the closed form for $\mathbf{F}_N$, we see that

N	$D(N)$
1	1
2	2
3	6
4	24

Could it be that the denominator for the Nth level accumulator is just the factorial of N? If this is so, we have arrived at a delightful theorem:

Let $\mathbf{F}_1(M) = M$. Define a sequence of functions

$$\{\mathbf{F}_1, \mathbf{F}_2, \mathbf{F}_3, \ldots, \mathbf{F}_N \ldots\}$$

by the rule

$$\mathbf{F}_N(M) = \sum_{K=1}^{M} \mathbf{F}_{(N-1)}(M)$$

Then for all positive integers N and M,

$$\mathbf{F}_N(M) = \frac{M(M+1)(M+2)(M+3)\cdots(M+N-1)}{N!}$$

Notice that we are dealing with two variables (N and M) here. Let's define a sequence of functions $\mathbf{G}_N$ by

$$G_N(M) = \frac{M(M+1)(M+2)(M+3)\cdots(M+N-1)}{N!}$$

The numerator of $G_N(M)$ is the product of all the integers between M and $M + N - 1$.

We want to prove that for every positive integer N, $F_N = G_N$ on $\mathbf{Z}^+$. We will prove this (of course) by the principle of mathematical induction; we will "induct on N."

If $N = 1$, we have that

$$F_1(M) = M$$

and

$$G_1(M) = \frac{M}{1!}$$

(Why is the numerator just "M"?)

So F_1 and G_1 are equal on $\mathbf{Z}^+$. Suppose that, for some N, $F_N = G_N$ on $\mathbf{Z}^+$. We want to conclude that $F_{(N+1)} = G_{(N+1)}$ on $\mathbf{Z}^+$. In other words, we want to use the fact that $F_N = G_N$ on $\mathbf{Z}^+$ to show that for all positive integers M,

$$F_{(N+1)}(M) = G_{(N+1)}(M)$$

So we are now thinking of N as being fixed. We have two functions ($F_{(N+1)}$ and $G_{(N+1)}$), and we want to prove that they are equal on $\mathbf{Z}^+$. As usual, we'll use the principle of mathematical induction; this time we'll induct on M (this is exactly how you proved that $F_4 = G_4$).

Before we go on, think about what we are doing. We want to show that $F_N = G_N$ on $\mathbf{Z}^+$ for all N. We have shown that $F_1 = G_1$ on $\mathbf{Z}^+$. We then assume that we have worked our way up to level N; that is, we assume that for some particular N, $F_N = G_N$ on $\mathbf{Z}^+$. We now want to use this fact to show that $F_{(N+1)} = G_{(N+1)}$ on $\mathbf{Z}^+$. (Imagine that we have just shown that $F_3 = G_3$ on $\mathbf{Z}^+$, and we are about to use this fact to show that $F_4 = G_4$ on $\mathbf{Z}^+$.) But what is the typical way to show that two functions are equal on $\mathbf{Z}^+$? By using the principle of mathematical induction. So we want to use the assumption that $F_N = G_N$ on $\mathbf{Z}^+$ to show that

1. $F_{(N+1)}(1) = G_{(N+1)}(1)$, and

2. if, for some M, $F_{(N+1)}(M) = G_{(N+1)}(M)$, then we also have $F_{(N+1)}(M+1) = G_{(N+1)}(M+1)$.

Now,

$$F_{(N+1)}(M) = \sum_{K=1}^{M} F_N(K)$$

and

$$G_{(N+1)}(M) = \frac{M(M+1)(M+2)\cdots(M+N)}{(N+1)!}$$

(Make sure that you understand why the last factor in the numerator for $G_{(N+1)}(M)$ is $(M+N)$.)

So

$F_{(N+1)}(1) = F_N(1)$ (sum goes from 1 to 1)

        $= G_N(1)$ (by inductive hypotheses in "outer" induction on N)

        $= 1$

The last equality is due to the fact that

$$G_N(M) = \frac{M(M+1)(M+2)(M+3)\cdots(M+N-1)}{N!}$$

so

$$G_N(1) = \frac{1\cdot 2\cdot 3\cdots(1+N-1)}{N!} = \frac{N!}{N!} = 1$$

Since

$$G_{(N+1)}(1) = \frac{1\cdot 2\cdot 3\cdots(1+N)}{(N+1)!} = \frac{(N+1)!}{(N+1)!} = 1$$

we have that $F_{(N+1)}(1) = G_{(N+1)}(1)$.

This takes care of the first part of our objective.

> Don't read this parenthetical note if you are following the argument so far. It's easy to forget where you are in an argument like this. Remember, we are trying to use the fact that $F_N = G_N$ on $\mathbf{Z}^+$ to show that

1. $F_{(N+1)}(1) = G_{(N+1)}(1)$, and
2. if, for some M, $F_{(N+1)}(M) = G_{(N+1)}(M)$, then we also have that
   $F_{(N+1)}(M + 1) = G_{(N+1)}(M + 1)$.

We have just used the fact that $F_N = G_N$ on $\mathbf{Z}^+$ to show that

$$F_{(N+1)}(1) = G_{(N+1)}(1)$$

and we are about to use the fact that $F_N = G_N$ to show that if, for some M, $F_{(N+1)}(M) = G_{(N+1)}(M)$, then we also have that

$$F_{(N+1)}(M + 1) = G_{(N+1)}(M + 1)$$

Next, suppose that $F_{(N+1)}(M) = G_{(N+1)}(M)$ for some M. We'll show that this implies that $F_{(N+1)}(M + 1) = G_{(N+1)}(M + 1)$.

Now, remember how $F_{(N+1)}(M + 1)$ is defined:

$$F_{(N+1)}(M + 1) = \sum_{K=1}^{M+1} F_N(K)$$

$$= \left(\sum_{K=1}^{M} F_N(K) \right) + F_N(M + 1)$$

$$= F_{(N+1)}(M) + G_N(M + 1)$$

Here we are using the inductive hypothesis on N to replace $F_N(M + 1)$ by $G_N(M + 1)$, and we are using the definition of $F_{(N+1)}$ to replace the summation by $F_{(N+1)}(M)$. Now, the inductive hypothesis on M is that $F_{(N+1)}(M) = G_{(N+1)}(M)$. So, using both inductive hypotheses, we find that

$$F_{(N+1)}(M + 1) = G_{(N+1)}(M) + G_N(M + 1).$$

The rest is algebra. Notice that

$$G_{(N+1)}(M) = \frac{M(M + 1) \cdots (M + N)}{(N + 1)!}$$

and

$$G_N(M + 1) = \frac{(M + 1)(M + 2) \cdots (M + N)}{N!}$$

Add the above identities to conclude that

$$F_{(N+1)}(M+1) = \frac{M(M+1)\cdots(M+N)}{(N+1)!} + \frac{(M+1)(M+2)\cdots(M+N)}{N!}$$

$$= \frac{(M+1)(M+2)\cdots(M+N)}{N!}\left(\frac{M}{N+1}+1\right)$$

$$= \frac{(M+1)(M+2)\cdots(M+N)(M+N+1)}{(N+1)!}$$

and this last expression is exactly the formula for $G_{(N+1)}(M+1)$.

The above argument is very involved, and it is probably a good idea to work through it a few times. The reason that we needed the double induction here is that we were trying to prove two sequences of functions (the F_N's and the G_N's) equal. In general, when you are trying to prove that two sequences of any kinds of objects are equal, you use the principle of mathematical induction; you assume that the Nth term in one sequence is equal to the Nth term in the other sequence (in our case, you assume that $F_N = G_N$), and you use this to prove that the $(N+1)$st terms are equal. But in this case, the $(N+1)$st terms are functions on $\mathbf{Z}^+$, and the typical way to prove two such functions equal is to use the principle of mathematical induction.

Another way to think about our theorem is to think about how the F_N's and the G_N's could be represented in Logo. How do you represent a sequence of functions in Logo? Consider the sequence of F_N's:

$$[F_1\ F_2\ F_3\ \ldots]$$

Try to imagine a higher order function S that has this sequence as its output set. In other words, S is a function that takes a number (say, 3) as input, and outputs a function (F_3, in our case). So $S(4) = F_4$, $S(6) = F_6$, and so on. Notice that $S(2)$ is a function, so the expression $(S(2))(4)$ makes sense; it stands for $F_2(4)$ or 10. Now, it is rather difficult to build a faithful model of S in Logo (How do you write a function that outputs another function?), but we can approximate S by thinking of S as a function of two inputs: Think of $S(2, 4)$ as $F_2(4)$; $S(5, 1)$ is $F_5(1)$, and so on. So we want S to take two inputs N and M, and we want $S(N, M)$ to be $F_N(M)$. Think about what this means. $F_N(M)$ is the sum of the outputs of $F_{(N-1)}$ between 1 and M, so

$$S(N, M) = \sum_{K=1}^{M} F_{(N-1)}(K)$$

But $F_{(N-1)}(M)$ is precisely $S(N-1, M)$, so

$$S(N, M) = \sum_{K=1}^{M} S(N-1, K)$$

The only exception to this formula is when $N = 1$; when $N = 1$, $S(1, M)$ is $F_1(M)$, which is M. If $N > 1$, it seems that we should be able to implement S using SIGMA, but notice that we are summing a function of two variables, holding the first variable constant (at $N - 1$) and letting the second variable increase from 1 to M. This can be done in Logo; one way is to modify SIGMA to accept a function of two variables. But I'd like you to look at the function S without hiding the details of the recursion in a SIGMA procedure. How would you express

$$S(N, M) = S(N-1, 1) + S(N-1, 2) + \cdots + S(N-1, M-1) + S(N-1, M)$$

in Logo? Notice that the sum of all the terms except the last one

$$S(N-1, 1) + S(N-1, 2) + S(N-1, 3) + \cdots + S(N-1, M-1)$$

is just $S(N, M-1)$. So $S(N, M) = S(N, M-1) + S(N-1, M)$. The only special case here is when $M = 1$, and then, $S(N, 1) = F_N(1)$. In the midst of the long inductive proof above, we did prove that $F_N(1) = 1$ for all N, but we can give another simple proof of this fact right here: Since $F_N(M) = M$, $F_1(1) = 1$. Suppose that $F_N(1) = 1$ for some N. Then

$$F_{(N+1)}(1) = \sum_{K=1}^{1} F_N(K) = F_N(1) = 1$$

so $F_N(1) = 1$ for all N by mathematical induction.

We now know the following things about S:

1. $S(1, M) = M$ for all M.

2. $S(N, 1) = 1$ for all N.

3. $S(N, M) = S(N, M - 1) + S(N - 1, M)$ if $N > 1$ and $M > 1$.

Think about what this says for the corresponding F_N's. The Logo representation for S is a direct translation of the above three facts:

```
TO S :N :M
 IF :N = 1 [OP :M]
 IF :M = 1 [OP 1]
 OP (S :N :M - 1) + (S :N - 1 :M)
END
```

We now have a function that captures some important features of the F_N's. We can recover the F_N's from S one at a time:

```
TO F3 :M
 OP S 3 :M
END
```

What's more important is that S makes the nature of the abstract notion of a sequence of functions where each function accumulates the outputs of its predecessor very concrete.

Recall the definition of the G_N's:

$$G_N(M) = \frac{M(M + 1)(M + 2)\ldots(M + N - 1)}{N!}$$

Suppose we want to write a function P of two variables N and M so that $P(N, M)$ is $G_N(M)$. You should try doing this in the style that led us to S.

There is another way to look at the G_N's. Notice that

$$\begin{aligned}
G_N(M) &= \frac{M(M + 1)(M + 2)\cdots(M + N - 1)}{N!} \\
&= \frac{(M + N - 1)\cdots(M + 2)(M + 1)M}{N!} \\
&= \frac{(M + N - 1)!}{N!(M - 1)!}
\end{aligned}$$

So we could express P as

```
TO P :N :M
 OP (FACT :M + :N - 1) / ((FACT :N) * (FACT :M - 1))
END
```

Now, the theorem that $F_N = G_N$ on $\mathbf{Z}^+$ for all N can be rephrased this way:

$$\text{For all } N \text{ and } M, \text{ } S(N, M) = P(N, M)$$

Look at the particularly simple characterization that led us to the Logo representation for S:

1. $S(1, M) = M$ for all M.

2. $S(N, 1) = 1$ for all N.

3. $S(N, M) = S(N, M - 1) + S(N - 1, M)$ if $N > 1$ and $M > 1$.

I claim that the same properties hold for P:

1. $P(1, M) = M$ for all M.

2. $P(N, 1) = 1$ for all N.

3. $P(N, M) = P(N, M - 1) + P(N - 1, M)$ if $N > 1$ and $M > 1$.

You should prove this using the representation of P in terms of factorials:

$$P(N, M) = \frac{(M + N - 1)!}{N!(M - 1)!}$$

Some Thought Questions

1. Does the fact that both S and P satisfy properties 1, 2, and 3 above imply that $P(N, M) = S(N, M)$ for all N and M?

2. If your answer to question 1 is yes, how would you prove it?

3. If your answer to question 1 is yes, have we eliminated the use of mathematical induction? Have we eliminated the double induction?

4. Now, fix N. We have two definitions for G_N:

$$G_N(M) = \frac{(M + N - 1)!}{N!(M - 1)!}$$

and

$$G_N(M) = \frac{M(M+1)(M+2)\cdots(M+N-1)}{N!}$$

Do these formulas define exactly the same function G_N?

5. For what values of M and N does S output? Justify your answer.

#Project 5.23 This project is for people who have done project 5.22. Using the notation of that project, use the closed forms for F_2 and F_3 to find a closed form for SUM.SQUARES:

```
TO SUM.SQUARES :N          TO SQUARE :M
 OP SIGMA "SQUARE 1 :N       OP :M * :M
END                        END
```

Project 5.24 Consider the following two functions:

```
TO F :X                    TO G :X
 IF :X = 1 [OP 0]            OP (:X - 1) * (:X + 2) / 2
 IF :X = 2 [OP 1]          END
 OP :X + (F :X - 1)
END
```

Now, $F(1) = G(1)$. Suppose that $F(N) = G(N)$ for some N. Then

$$\begin{aligned}
F(N+1) &= (N+1) + F(N) \\
&= (N+1) + G(N) \\
&= (N+1) + (N-1)(N+2)/2 \\
&= N(N+3)/2 \\
&= G(N+1)
\end{aligned}$$

So $F = G$ on $\mathbf{Z}^+$. Tabulate each function. What's wrong here?

Chapter 6

Application 1: The Tower of Hanoi and Related Curiosities

Our first application of mathematical induction arises from the study of an intriguing puzzle called the Tower of Hanoi. The puzzle consists of three pegs driven into a piece of wood; on one of the pegs, we stack some disks, all of different sizes, with the largest disk on the bottom.

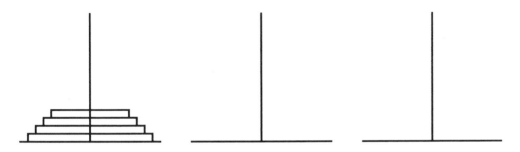

Figure 6.1

The object is to move all the disks from the first peg to the second peg by moving only one disk at a time but never placing a larger disk on top of a smaller one. Try it. You can build a Tower of Hanoi without much trouble, or you can write a set of procedures that allows you to manipulate disks on the computer screen.

The object of our investigation is to answer the following question:

> *How many disk transfers does it take to solve the puzzle if the stack contains N disks?*

Of course, it can take as many moves as you want, but that's not what I mean by the question. We want the minimum number of transfers necessary to solve the puzzle. Before reading on, you should try stacks of 3, 4, and 5 disks; try to solve each case as efficiently as possible.

We'll develop an inductive method for solving our problem (and, it turns out, for solving the actual Tower of Hanoi puzzle).

Let's make C be the "complexity function" for our puzzle: $C(N)$ is the number of disk transfers required to move a stack of N disks from one peg to another.

Label the pegs A, B and C. We'll call A the "source," B the "target," and C the "spare." Label the disks using any scheme. Say, the top disk is labeled "1," and the disks are numbered consecutively from 1 to N. Suppose that $N = 1$; that is, suppose we have a stack of 1 disk. Then to move this stack, we simply pick it up and put it on the target: one move, so $C(1) = 1$.

Inductively, suppose we know $C(N)$. That is, we know how many disk transfers are required to move a stack of N disks from one peg to another. Imagine a stack of $N + 1$ disks on peg A. Eventually, we'll have to transfer the bottom disk to the target peg (B), and (because the bottom disk is the largest) when we move it, none of the top N disks can be on peg B. Of course, none of them can be on peg A either (otherwise, the biggest disk would be covered). So, when we move the bottom disk from the source to the target, the top N disks must have already been moved to the spare peg (C). So, to move a stack of $N + 1$ disks from the source to the target with the minimum number of disk transfers, we should

1. move the top N disks from the source to the spare (this requires $C(N)$ moves), as in figure 6.2,

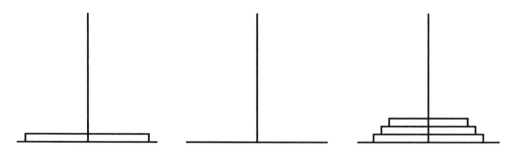

Figure 6.2

2. move the bottom disk from the source to the target (1 move), as in figure 6.3, and

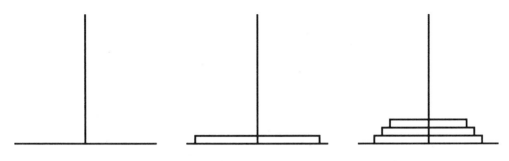

Figure 6.3

3. move the top N disks from the spare to the target (this requires $C(N)$ moves), as in figure 6.4.

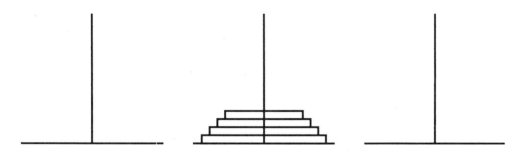

Figure 6.4

This does it. The number of transfers for $N + 1$ disks is

$$C(N) + 1 + C(N)$$

or

$$C(N + 1) = 2C(N) + 1$$

Our complexity function is

```
TO C :N
 IF :N = 1 [OP 1]
 OP 2 * C (:N - 1)  +  1
END
```

Tabulate it, find a closed form for it, and prove that your closed form is correct by mathematical induction.

Exercise 6.1 Suppose that you had a stack of 64 disks. How many transfers would it take to solve the puzzle? If you started on January 1 at 12:01 A.M., and if you could make one transfer each second, when would you finish the puzzle?

Before continuing, let's exploit the method we used to construct C to drive a procedure that actually prints out the moves needed to solve the puzzle. We'll use some built-in Logo list-processing functions. More precisely, you should be familiar with the Logo functions

LAST, BUTLAST, BL, LIST, and COUNT

An acquaintance with SE will also be helpful. If you are not familiar with these, take some time now to read the appendix.

We'll build a procedure MOVE that takes a list of disks and the names of the source peg, the target peg, and the spare peg as inputs. The procedure gives you instructions for moving the disks from the source to the target. Assume that the first object in the list stands for the top disk so that

MOVE [1 2 3] "A "B "C

prints the following instructions:

```
MOVE 1 FROM A TO B
MOVE 2 FROM A TO C
MOVE 1 FROM B TO C
MOVE 3 FROM A TO B
MOVE 1 FROM C TO A
MOVE 2 FROM C TO B
MOVE 1 FROM A TO B
```

Notice that this sequence of transfers follows the inductive model that we used to define C:

1. Move all but the bottom disk from the source to the spare:

```
MOVE 1 FROM A TO B
MOVE 2 FROM A TO C
MOVE 1 FROM B TO C
```

2. Move the bottom disk from the source to the target:

```
MOVE 3 FROM A TO B
```

3. Move all but the bottom disk from the spare to the target:

```
MOVE 1 FROM C TO A
MOVE 2 FROM C TO B
MOVE 1 FROM A TO B
```

The Logo procedure is a natural model of this method:

```
TO MOVE :DISK.STACK :SOURCE :TARGET :OTHER
 IF ONE.DISK? :DISK.STACK
    [(PR "MOVE :DISK.STACK "FROM :SOURCE "TO :TARGET) STOP]
 MOVE TOP :DISK.STACK :SOURCE :OTHER :TARGET
 MOVE BOTTOM :DISK.STACK :SOURCE :TARGET :OTHER
 MOVE TOP :DISK.STACK :OTHER :TARGET :SOURCE
END
```

If there is one disk in the *DISK.STACK*, a message to simply move the disk is printed. Otherwise, the TOP of *DISK.STACK* is moved from the source to the spare. Then the BOTTOM of *DISK.STACK* is moved from the source to the target. Finally, the TOP of the stack is moved from the spare to the target. The predicate ONE.DISK? is simply

```
TO ONE.DISK? :STACK
 OP (COUNT :STACK) = 1
END
```

Because we think of MOVE as a procedure whose first input is a list, we have

```
TO BOTTOM :STACK
 OP ( LIST LAST :STACK )
END
```

TOP is just BL:

```
TO TOP :STACK
 OP BL :STACK
END
```

The procedure MOVE looks like a simple translation of the idea behind our construction of C, but there is a lot to think about in order to figure out how MOVE works. It would be worth your while to trace

```
MOVE [1 2 3] "A "B "C
```

carefully by hand.

It's also great fun to modify MOVE so that, rather than printing out instructions, it actually draws the disk transfers on the screen.

Experiment 6.2 If the tower has N disks, how many times does the Kth disk get transferred?

An interesting article about the Tower of Hanoi (and its variations) is in *Scientific American* (Dewdney 1984).

Geometric Sequences and Series

Back to mathematics (MOVE is one of the few procedures in this book that isn't a function).

Recall the function C:

```
TO C :N
 IF :N = 1 [OP 1]
 OP 2 * C (:N - 1)  +  1
END
```

A closed form for C is

```
TO CLOSED.C :N
 OP (POWER 2 :N) - 1
END
```

Can we generalize this fact? Look at D:

```
TO D :N
 IF :N = 1 [OP 1]
 OP 3 * D (:N - 1) + 1
END
```

Is this another version for D?

```
TO CLOSED.D :N
 OP (POWER 3 :N) - 1
END
```

If you tabulate D and CLOSED.D, you'll see that CLOSED.D has to be modified:

```
TO CLOSED.D :N
 OP ((POWER 3 :N) - 1) / 2
END
```

If you try more examples, you'll see a pattern emerge; try it before reading on.

The pattern is captured in the following theorem:

Theorem 6.1 The following two functions:

```
TO C :N :B
 IF :N = 1 [OP 1]
 OP :B * (C :N - 1 :B) + 1
END
```

and

```
TO CLOSED.C :N :B
 OP ((POWER :B :N) - 1) / (:B - 1)
END
```

are equal for all pairs (N, B) where N is a positive integer and B is any real number except 1.

The proof is by induction on N. That is, we keep B constant (and not equal to 1), and we prove that for all integers $N > 0$,

$$C(N, B) = \text{CLOSED.C}(N, B)$$

If $N = 1$, both functions output 1 (CLOSED.C outputs $\dfrac{B^1 - 1}{B - 1}$). Suppose that for some N,

$$C(N, B) = \text{CLOSED.C}(N, B)$$

Let's use this equality to show that

$$C(N + 1, B) = \text{CLOSED.C}(N + 1, B)$$

Well,

$$
\begin{aligned}
C(N + 1, B) &= B \cdot C(N, B) + 1 && \text{(by the way C is defined)} \\
&= B \cdot \text{CLOSED.C}(N, B) + 1 && \text{(by the inductive hypothesis)} \\
&= B\frac{(B^N - 1)}{B - 1} + 1 && \text{(by the way CLOSED.C is defined)} \\
&= \frac{B^{(N+1)} - B + B - 1}{B - 1} && \text{(by algebra)} \\
&= \frac{B^{(N+1)} - 1}{B - 1} = \text{CLOSED.C} \quad (N + 1, B)
\end{aligned}
$$

Is it clear to you that CLOSED.C will not accept 1 as a second input? What is a closed form for $C(N, 1)$?

There is another way to look at C. To keep the notation down, let's suppose that $B = 3$, so that C can be defined this way:

```
TO C :N
  IF :N = 1 [OP 1]
  OP 3 * (C :N - 1) + 1
END
```

Then

$$C(1) = 1$$

$$C(2) = 3C(1) + 1 = 3 + 1$$

$$C(3) = 3C(2) + 1 = 3(3 + 1) + 1 = 3^2 + 3 + 1$$

$$C(4) = 3C(3) + 1 = 3(3^2 + 3 + 1) + 1 = 3^3 + 3^2 + 3 + 1$$

$$C(5) = 3C(4) + 1 = 3(3^3 + 3^2 + 3 + 1) = 3^4 + 3^3 + 3^2 + 3 + 1$$

and, inductively,

$$C(N) = 3^{(N-1)} + 3^{(N-2)} + \cdots + 3^2 + 3 + 1$$

It seems that our original function C can also be defined in this way:

```
TO NEW.C :N :B
 IF :N = 1 [OP 1]
 OP (POWER :B :N - 1) + NEW.C :N - 1 :B
END
```

In other words, it seems that we have a theorem:

Theorem 6.2 $C(N, B) = $ NEW.C(N, B) for all positive integers N and all real numbers B.

Exercise 6.3 Prove theorem 6.2 by induction on N.

Exercise 6.4 Modify SIGMA so that it handles functions of more than one input (refer to the appendix if you get stuck), and define NEW.C using SIGMA.

By theorems 6.2 and 6.1, then, we have the following interesting facts:

$$1 + 2 + 2^2 + 2^3 + \cdots + 2^{(N-2)} + 2^{(N-1)} = \frac{(2^N - 1)}{(2-1)} = 2^N - 1$$

$$1 + 3 + 3^2 + 3^3 + \cdots + 3^{(N-2)} + 3^{(N-1)} = \frac{(3^N - 1)}{(3-1)} = \frac{(3^N - 1)}{2}$$

$$1 + 4 + 4^2 + 4^3 + \cdots + 4^{(N-2)} + 4^{(N-1)} = \frac{(4^N - 1)}{(4-1)} = \frac{(4^N - 1)}{3}$$

$$1 + 5 + 5^2 + 5^3 + \cdots + 5^{(N-2)} + 5^{(N-1)} = \frac{(5^N - 1)}{(5-1)} = \frac{(5^N - 1)}{4}$$

and so on.

There is another way to see this using algebra: To multiply out the two polynomials

$$(X - 1)(1 + X + X^2 + X^3 + \cdots + X^{(N-1)})$$

you multiply everything in the second polynomial by X:

$$X + X^2 + X^3 + \cdots + X^{(N-1)} + X^N$$

Then you multiply everything in the second polynomial by -1,

$$-1 - X - X^2 - X^3 - \cdots - X^{(N-1)}$$

and then you add

$$\begin{array}{l} X + X^2 + X^3 + \cdots + X^{(N-1)} + X^N \\ \underline{-1 - X - X^2 - X^3 - \cdots - X^{(N-1)}} \\ -1 \qquad\qquad\qquad\qquad\qquad\quad + X^N \end{array}$$

So

$$(X - 1)(1 + X + X^2 + X^3 + \cdots + X^{(N-1)}) = X^N - 1$$

The above identity is called the "cyclotomic identity." It is true for polynomials, so it becomes a true statement when X is replaced by any number B. In other words, we have the following result:

Theorem 6.3 If B is any real number and N is a positive integer, then

$$(B - 1)(1 + B + B^2 + B^3 + \cdots + B^{(N-1)}) = B^N - 1$$

Notice that B can be 1 in this theorem.

> The word "cyclotomic" means "circle dividing"; the connection between geometry and the polynomial $X^N - 1$ goes back at least to Gauss. When Gauss was seventeen years old, he realized that the problem of constructing a regular 17-sided polygon using only a straightedge and compass (or, as Gauss thought of it, of dividing a circle into 17 equal arcs using only these tools) was equivalent to the problem of expressing the roots of $X^{17} - 1 = 0$ in terms of square roots. He managed to do this, and he went on to give a precise description of the numbers N for which it is possible to divide a circle into N equal arcs using only straightedge and compass. The description involves certain kinds of prime numbers called *Fermat primes*; we'll meet them in part III. The revolutionary connections between algebra, geometry, and number theory that Gauss made are described in *Disquisitiones Arithmeticae*, first published in 1801 (see Gauss 1965 for an English translation).

Recall one of our C functions (with base 3):

```
TO C :N
 IF :N = 1 [OP 1]
 OP 3 * (C :N - 1) + 1
END
```

Suppose we drop off the "+1" when C calls itself. Then we get a function that is very familiar:

```
TO G :N
 IF :N = 1 [OP 1]
 OP 3 * (G :N - 1)
END
```

If you tabulate G, you'll see this:

I	O
1	1
2	3
3	9
4	27
5	81

So (as an easy induction shows) $G(N) = 3^{(N-1)}$.

What if we modify G by changing the base case?

```
TO G :N
  IF :N = 1 [OP 4]
  OP 3 * (G :N - 1)
END
```

Then a tabulation suggests that $G(N) = 4 \cdot 3^{(N-1)}$ (and an induction establishes it). In general, if a and r are numbers, the function

```
TO G :N
  IF :N = 1 [OP a]
  OP r * (G :N - 1)
END
```

is called the *geometric sequence* with first term a and common ratio r (of course, the above definition of G is just a template for a geometric sequence; a and r have to be replaced with actual numbers). If we write the terms of the sequence in a list, we have

$$a, ar, ar^2, ar^3, ar^4, \ldots, ar^N, ar^{(N+1)}, \ldots$$

a is called the "first term," and r is the "common ratio" (it is the ratio of any two consecutive terms). For example,

$$3, 6, 12, 24, 48, \ldots$$

is the geometric sequence with first term 3 and common ratio 2. The Logo model for this sequence is

```
TO SEQ :N
  IF :N = 1 [OP 3]
  OP 2 * (SEQ :N - 1)
END
```

These things are called "geometric" sequences because each term is obtained from the previous one by multiplying by a constant factor. Our Western mathematical traditions are heavily influenced by the mathematics of Greece that developed around 300 B.C.; the Greek mathematicians performed multiplication on real numbers by interpreting real numbers as lengths. They multiplied these lengths by a geometric process that uses a theorem from geometry (if a line is parallel to one side of a triangle, then it divides the other two sides proportionally). Multiplication was thus considered a geometric operation, while addition (of integers, at least) was an arithmetic operation.

Exercise 6.5 If G is a geometric sequence with first term A and common ratio R, show that

$$G(N) = AR^{(N-1)}$$

Experiment 6.6 Of course, the first term and the common ratio of a geometric sequence don't need to be integers.

1. Find the tenth term of the geometric sequence whose first term is 4 and whose common ratio is 3.

2. Find the first ten terms of the geometric sequence whose first term is 4 and whose common ratio is -3.

3. Find the first ten terms of the geometric sequence whose first term is -4 and whose common ratio is 3.

4. Find the first ten terms of the geometric sequence whose first term is -4 and whose common ratio is -3.

5. A geometric sequence is called "alternating" if consecutive terms have opposite signs. What determines if a geometric sequence is alternating?

6. Find the first ten terms of the geometric sequence whose first term is -4 and whose common ratio is .5.

7. Find the first ten terms of the geometric sequence whose first term is -4 and whose common ratio is .5.

8. Find the 100th term of the geometric sequence whose first term is 1 and whose common ratio is -1. What is the sum of the first 100 terms of this sequence?

Experiment 6.7 A geometric sequence G is called "convergent" if $G(N)$ gets closer to 0 as N gets bigger. Give examples of several convergent sequences. How can you tell if a geometric sequence is convergent? Are there are any alternating convergent geometric sequences?

#Project 6.8 Is 1296 a term in the geometric sequence whose first term is 4 and whose common ratio is 2? Write a predicate `IN.SEQ?` that takes three inputs: A (the first term in the sequence), R (the common ratio), and M (the number to be tested). You can assume for this project that A and R are integers (and R is positive). Write a function `TERM.NUM` that takes the same three inputs and outputs -1 if M is not in the sequence and K if M is the Kth term in the sequence.

What about geometric series? If `G` is a geometric sequence with first term A and common ratio R, the associated series is `S` where

```
TO S :N
 OP SIGMA "G 1 :N
END
```

If R isn't 1, we can apply the cyclotomic identity to find

$$S(N) = G(1) + G(2) + G(3) + \cdots + G(N)$$
$$= A + AR + AR^2 + \cdots + AR^{(N-1)}$$
$$= A(1 + R + R^2 + R^3 + \cdots + R^{(N-1)})$$
$$= A\frac{R^N - 1}{R - 1}$$

What happens if $R = 1$?

Just for future reference, let's record these facts as a theorem:

Theorem 6.4 If `G` is a geometric sequence with first term A and common ratio R, and if `S` is the associated series, then

$$S(N) = A\frac{R^N - 1}{R - 1} \qquad \text{if } R \text{ isn't 1}$$
$$S(N) = NA \qquad \text{if } R = 1$$

Exercise 6.9

1. Find the sum of the first twenty powers of 2, of -2, of 5, and of -5.

2. Find the sum of the first twenty-five powers of 3, of -3, of $1/3$, and of $-1/3$.

3. Find the sum of all the powers of 5 less than 1000.

#Project 6.10 Sometimes (here, perhaps, and in real life) you need to sum a "weighted series"; that is, you might want to add up something like this:

$$1 + 2 \cdot 2 + 3 \cdot 2^2 + 4 \cdot 2^3 + 5 \cdot 2^4 + \cdots + N \cdot 2^{(N-1)}$$

Call the value of this series V. Before reading the hint, build a Logo model for V, tabulate it, and try to find a closed form for V.

Hint: To obtain a closed form for V, write V like this:

$$\begin{aligned}
V = 1 + 2 + 2^2 + 2^3 + 2^4 + \cdots + 2^{(N-1)} + \\
2 + 2^2 + 2^3 + 2^4 + \cdots + 2^{(N-1)} + \\
2^2 + 2^3 + 2^4 + \cdots + 2^{(N-1)} + \\
2^3 + 2^4 + \cdots + 2^{(N-1)} + \\
2^4 + \cdots + 2^{(N-1)} + \\
\cdot \\
\cdot \\
\cdot \\
+ 2^{(N-1)}
\end{aligned}$$

Now add up the series on each line. The respective sums are

$$2^N - 1, \ 2^N - 2, \ 2^N - 4, \ 2^N - 8, \ 2^N - 16, \ldots \text{ and } 2^N - 2^{(N-1)}$$

When you add these up, you'll get

$$N2^N - (1 + 2 + 2^2 + 2^3 + 2^4 + \cdots + 2^{(N-1)}) = (N-1)2^N + 1$$

If you know any calculus, you can also get this formula by looking at the derivative of the function

$$G(X) = 1 + X + X^2 + \cdots + X^N = \frac{X^{(N+1)} - 1}{X - 1}$$

in two ways and then by replacing X by 2.

Can you find a simple formula for the weighted series

$$1 + 2R + 3R^2 + 4R^3 + \cdots + NR^{(N-1)}$$

Is the case $R = 1$ special? Do you get an interesting result if $R = -1$?

Experiment 6.11 Establish a closed form for WS:

$$\text{WS}(N) = 2 + 3 \cdot 2 \cdot 2 + 4 \cdot 3 \cdot 2^2 + 5 \cdot 4 \cdot 2^3 + 6 \cdot 5 \cdot 2^4 + \cdots + N(N-1)2^{(N-2)}$$

Experiment 6.12 Is there a relationship between the series associated with the geometric sequence whose first term is A and whose common ratio is R and the series associated with the geometric sequence whose first term is A and whose common ratio is $-R$? Look at the quotient and the difference of these two series. What happens if you do other things to R? How about changing R to $2R$?

Experiment 6.13 Find three numbers that are both the first three terms of an arithmetic sequence and the first three terms of a geometric sequence. Can you characterize all such triples?

Convergence

Suppose that G is the geometric sequence with first term 1 and common ratio 1/2:

```
TO G :N
 OP (POWER 0.5 :N - 1)
END
```

Then suppose we build the associated series

```
TO GEO.SERIES :N
 OP SIGMA "G 1 :N
END
```

When I tabulate GEO.SERIES, I see this:

```
1  . . . 1
2  . . . 1.5
3  . . . 1.75
4  . . . 1.875
5  . . . 1.9375
6  . . . 1.96875
7  . . . 1.984375
8  . . . 1.9921875
9  . . . 1.99609375
10 . . . 1.998046875
11 . . . 1.999023438
12 . . . 1.999511719
13 . . . 1.999755859
14 . . . 1.99987793
15 . . . 1.999938965
16 . . . 1.999969482
17 . . . 1.999984741
18 . . . 1.999992371
19 . . . 1.999996185
20 . . . 1.999998093
```

It looks like, as the inputs to GEO.SERIES get bigger, the outputs from GEO.SERIES get closer to 2.

Project 6.14 Investigate this phenomenon. Why is the output for GEO.SERIES never bigger than 2? Can you make the output from GEO.SERIES as close as you want to 2 by making the input big enough? How big must the input to GEO.SERIES be in order for the output to be within .001 of 2? Within .0001? Within .000001? Write a predicate CLOSE.ENOUGH? that takes two numbers and a "tolerance" as input; CLOSE.ENOUGH? outputs TRUE if the two numbers are within the tolerance of each other and FALSE otherwise. For example,

CLOSE.ENOUGH? (GEO.SERIES 4) 2 .2

outputs TRUE (because GEO.SERIES(4) and 2 are within .2 of each other), whereas

CLOSE.ENOUGH? (GEO.SERIES 3) 2 .2

outputs FALSE. (Hint: The distance between two numbers is the absolute value of their difference.) Use CLOSE.ENOUGH? to write a function that takes a tolerance as input and outputs the first integer N so that GEO.SERIES(N) is within this tolerance of 2.

Because the outputs of GEO.SERIES in the above project can be made as close to 2 as we please, we say that "GEO.SERIES converges to 2," or "the limit of GEO.SERIES is 2." This idea applies to any sequence (that is, to any function defined on $\mathbf{Z}^{+}$), and the technical definition is

Definition 6.5 If F is a sequence, we say that "F converges to the number L" (or "the limit of F is L") if we can make F(N) as close as we want to L by making N big enough.

Here's an even more technical version:

Definition 6.5′ If F is a sequence, we say that "F converges to the number L" (or "the limit of F is L") if, given any positive tolerance T, you can make F(N) and L within T of each other by making N big enough.

So the "convergent geometric" sequences of experiment 6.7 converge to 0.

Experiment 6.15 Can a geometric sequence converge to anything except 0?

Project 6.16 Which geometric series are convergent? Here's a bare-bones GEO.SERIES that allows you to vary the first term and the common ratio:

```
TO GEO.SERIES :A :R :N
 IF :N = 1 [OP :A]
 OP :A * (POWER :R :N - 1) + GEO.SERIES :A :R :N - 1
END
```

If you think of A and R as constants, GEO.SERIES is a function of N. We'd like to tabulate GEO.SERIES for various choices of A and R, and to do this, you need to modify TAB so that it accepts functions (like GEO.SERIES) that require three inputs. This is done in the appendix, and if you look there, you'll see the Logo code for the extended version of TAB that allows the function to take "extra" inputs. You use it like this:

TAB "GEO.SERIES [2 3] 1 10 will tabulate the geometric series whose first term is 2 and whose common ratio is 3 between 1 and 10. (You can use this generalized TAB with functions that take only one input; if F is such a function, you simply type TAB "F [] 1 10.)

Using this generalized TAB experiment with several geometric series, and come up with a conjecture about which geometric series are convergent.

If a geometric series converges, what does it converge to? Hint: If you want to come up with a formula for the limit of a geometric series by using tabulations, it might help to tabulate the series associated with the sequence whose first term is 1 and whose ratio is 1/2. Then keep the first term at 1 and change the ratio to 1/3, then 1/4, then 1/5, and then 1/8. Then try a ratio of 2/3 or 3/4, or 5/6. After you have figured out a formula for the series for a sequence that starts with 1, you can tackle the case of any first term using the fact that

$$A + AR + AR^2 + AR^3 + AR^4 + AR^5 = A(1 + R + R^2 + R^3 + R^4 + R^5)$$

#When you arrive at a conjecture, prove that your answer is correct.

Can a geometric series converge to L though some of its terms are bigger than L and some of its terms are smaller than L?

Project 6.17 In general, a tabulation tells you when a sequence seems to be converging. Once you have your alleged limit L, it would be good to have a tool that tells you how many terms in a given interval are within a given tolerance of L. For example, what follows is a set of functions that supports the function NUMBER.OF.TERMS.CLOSE.TO.

NUMBER.OF.TERMS.CLOSE.TO(L, F, A, B, T)

outputs the number of outputs of F between A and B that lie within T of the alleged limit L. For example, if we define the function EXAMPLE

```
TO EXAMPLE :N
 OP GEO.SERIES 1 .5 :N
END
```

then typing

```
SHOW NUMBER.OF.TERMS.CLOSE.TO 2 "EXAMPLE 1 20 .01
```

produces 16 because there are sixteen terms of EXAMPLE between 1 and 20 that are within .01 of 2 (check it by tabulating EXAMPLE between 1 and 20). If you type

```
SHOW NUMBER.OF.TERMS.CLOSE.TO 2 "EXAMPLE 1 30 .01
```

the output is 26, which implies that all the terms between 20 and 30 are within .01 of 2. Here's the complete routine:

```
TO NUMBER.OF.TERMS.CLOSE.TO :LIMIT :F :A :B :TOLERANCE
 OP HELPER :LIMIT :F :A :B :TOLERANCE 0
END

TO HELPER :L :F :A :B :T :TALLY
 IF :A > :B [OP :TALLY]
 IF CLOSE.ENOUGH? (APPLY :F :B) :L :T →
    [OP HELPER :L :F :A :B - 1 :T :TALLY + 1]
 OP HELPER :L :F :A :B - 1 :T :TALLY
END
```

So, *TALLY* starts out at 0. If $F(B)$ is within the tolerance T of L, we increase *TALLY* by 1; otherwise, we leave *TALLY* alone, and try $F(B-1)$. The support is

```
TO CLOSE.ENOUGH? :A :B :T
 OP (ABS (:A - :B)) < :T
END

TO ABS :X
 OP SQRT (:X * :X)
END
```

Of the first 100 terms of EXAMPLE, how many are within .001 of 2? How many terms (among the first 100) of the geometric series with first term 3 and common ratio .1 are within .001 of the limit of the series?

What is the limit of the following sequence?

```
TO F :N
 IF :N = 1 [OP 4]
 OP SQRT (F :N - 1)
END
```

#How about this one?

```
TO F :N
 IF :N = 1 [OP 1]
 OP 1 + SQRT (F :N - 1)
END
```

Of course, sequences can converge very slowly, and tabulations (and the function NUMBER.OF.TERMS.CLOSE.TO) only give experimental evidence about the existence of limits. For example, Euler (1707–1783) loved the following function:

```
TO EULER :N
 OP SIGMA "EU  1 :N
END

TO EU :M
 OP 1 / (POWER :M 2)
END
```

Does EULER have a limit? What is it? How many terms out of the first 100 are within .001 of your guess? (The actual evaluation of EULER's limit involves some advanced calculus; see Ireland and Rosen 1982 for details).

Here's another example to think about. How many of the first 100 terms of the series associated with F:

```
TO F :N
 IF :N = 1 [OP 1]
 OP -1 * (F :N - 1)
END
```

are within .1 of 1? Within .1 of 0?

#Project 6.18 All this talk about convergent sequences requires that we have an idea of when two numbers are close. We've been brought up with an idea of closeness (for real numbers) that is embodied in our predicate CLOSE.ENOUGH?:

```
TO CLOSE.ENOUGH? :A :B :T
 OP (ABS (:A - :B)) < :T
END
```

During the second half of the nineteenth century, it became apparent that other kinds of CLOSE.ENOUGH?'s can be very useful. For example, if we restrict ourselves to the integers, we can say that two integers are "5-close" if their difference is divisible by a high power of 5. To be precise, write a function ORD that outputs the highest power of 5 that divides evenly into its input. So ORD 250 will output 3 (because 5^3 is a factor of 250 and 5^4 isn't). (Hint: You might try using REMAINDER.)

One way to redefine CLOSE.ENOUGH? is

```
TO CLOSE.ENOUGH? :N :M :T
 OP (POWER 5 -1*(ORD (:N - :M))) < :T
END
```

Explain this in words. It says that 125 and 25 are "within" .05 of each other (or as Hensel, 1861–1941, would say: 125 and 25 are within .05 of each other "in the realm of 5"), although 125 and 124 aren't even within .5 of each other. Using this version of CLOSE.ENOUGH? leads to some results that seem very strange at first. For example, in the "real world," the series associated with the geometric sequence whose first term is 4 and whose common ratio is 5 doesn't converge (successive outputs grow without bound). But, in the realm of 5, the sequence converges to 0, and the series converges. What is the "limit" of the series? Hint: Use the formula for the limit of a geometric series developed in project 6.16. Note: after you modify CLOSE.ENOUGH?, NUMBER.OF.TERMS.CLOSE.TO should work fine (of course, it will give you the number of terms that are 5-close to L).

Investigate the 5-convergence of the series associated with the sequence

```
TO F :N
 IF :N = 1 [OP -12]
 OP (-5) * (F :N - 1)
END
```

For a more detailed account of 2-closeness, see my article "Making a Divergent Series Converge" (Cuoco 1984).

Chapter 7

Counting Subsets

In Massachusetts there is a weekly lottery. To play the lottery, you pick six numbers between 1 and 36. How many ways are there to do this? Another way to ask this question is this:

How many 6-element subsets of a 36-element set are there?

It turns out there are very many (close to 2,000,000), so it wouldn't be feasible to find the number of possibilities by listing them all. We need to develop some techniques for "counting without counting," that is, for finding the number of objects of a given type without listing them. The branch of mathematics that is concerned with efficient counting techniques is called *combinatorics*, and in this chapter we'll look at some combinatorial methods for finding the number of subsets of a given size from a given set. In the remaining chapters of this part II, we'll apply our results to some intriguing problems.

Before we worry about subsets of a given size, let's look at a less technical question. Given a set with a finite number of elements, how many subsets does it have? For example, suppose our set is $\{A\ B\ C\}$. Before we start counting, we'll agree that every set is a subset of itself and that the empty set, denoted by $\emptyset$, is a subset of every set. There are many ways to count the subsets of $\{A\ B\ C\}$. For example, you could list the subsets according to their size:

0 element subsets: $\emptyset$		1
1 element subsets: $\{A\}\{B\}\{C\}$		3
2 element subsets: $\{A\ B\}\{A\ C\}\{B\ C\}$		3
3 element subsets: $\{A\ B\ C\}$		1
total	....	8

So there are 8 subsets. This method is too cumbersome for large sets. Another way to count the subsets is to pick out one element, say C, and to classify a subset according to whether or not it contains C:

Subsets that don't contain C

∅
{A}
{B}
{A B}

Subsets that contain C

{C}
{A C}
{B C}
{A B C}

Here are two things to notice:

1. The subsets of {A B C} that don't contain C are just the subsets of {A B}.

2. Every subset that contains C can be obtained from a subset that doesn't contain C by "adjoining C":

$$∅ \quad \overrightarrow{\text{adjoin } C} \quad \{C\}$$

$$\{A\} \quad \overrightarrow{\text{adjoin } C} \quad \{A\ C\}$$

$$\{B\} \quad \overrightarrow{\text{adjoin } C} \quad \{B\ C\}$$

$$\{A\ B\} \quad \overrightarrow{\text{adjoin } C} \quad \{A\ B\ C\}$$

This method (let's call it the "distinguished element" method) suggests an inductive way to count the subsets of an N element set. You simply pick an element, and you classify each subset by whether or not it contains this distinguished element. The number of subsets that don't contain the distinguished element is the same as the total number of subsets of an $N - 1$ element set, and each subset that does contain the distinguished element can be obtained by adjoining the distinguished element to a subset that doesn't contain it. So an N element set has exactly twice as many subsets as an $N - 1$ element set. The only special case is the empty set, which has 0 elements and one subset (itself). This translates naturally into a function that counts the subsets of an N element set:

```
TO COUNT.SUBSETS :N
  IF :N = 0 [OP 1]
  OP 2 * (COUNT.SUBSETS :N - 1)
END
```

A tabulation of `COUNT.SUBSETS` suggests the following theorem:

Theorem 7.1 A set with N elements has 2^N subsets.

You should prove this. The proof amounts to showing that `COUNT.SUB-SETS` is equal to `C.S` on the set $\{0\ 1\ 2\ 3\ldots\}$, where `C.S` is defined like this:

```
TO C.S :N
  OP POWER 2 :N
END
```

which is an easy induction.

> 1. Isn't it fortunate that we defined 2^0 to be 1?
>
> 2. Does the proof that `COUNT.SUBSETS` is equal to `C.S` on the set of non-negative integers really require mathematical induction? Look carefully at the definition of `POWER`.

Theorem 7.1 tells us how many subsets a set has. Now let's look at the finer question of determining the number of subsets of a given size in a given set S. Imagine a function that would do this counting. It would need two inputs: the size of the set S, and the size of the subsets we want to count. Let's call our function B and suppose that

> $B(N, K)$ is the number of K-element subsets of an N-element set.

The implicit assumptions here are that N is any nonnegative integer (we'll allow N to be 0), and K is any nonnegative integer less than or equal to N. These assumptions will be in force for the rest of this chapter. Several of B's outputs are easy to determine. For example,

1. $B(N, 0) = 1$ for all N. This is because any set S has only one 0 element subset, namely, $\emptyset$.

2. $B(N, N) = 1$ for all N. This is because an N element set S has only one N element subset, namely, S itself.

Before we develop some general methods for determining B, you should play with some examples.

Exercise 7.1 Determine the following outputs for B by actually counting subsets:

1. $B(3, 2)$ 2. $B(4, 1)$
3. $B(4, 2)$ 4. $B(7, 1)$
5. $B(5, 2)$ 6. $B(5, 3)$
7. $B(6, 3)$ 8. $B(23, 1)$
9. $B(6, 5)$ 10. $B(8, 7)$

Exercise 7.2 Give an argument to justify each statement:

1. $B(N, 1) = N$ for all $N > 0$.
2. $B(N, N - 1) = N$ for all $N > 0$.

Experiment 7.3 Calculate each pair of outputs for B:

1. $B(4, 3)$ and $B(4, 1)$
2. $B(5, 3)$ and $B(5, 2)$
3. $B(3, 2)$ and $B(3, 1)$
4. $B(6, 4)$ and $B(6, 2)$

Do you have a conjecture?

There are some things we can say about B before we have an algorithm to calculate its outputs. For example,

Theorem 7.2 $B(N, K) = B(N, N - K)$.

Here's "combinatorial" proof of this fact (a combinatorial proof is an argument based on counting):

$B(N, K)$ is the number of K element subsets of an N element set. Every K element subset determines a unique $N - K$ element subset (the elements that are "left out" of the the K element subset), and every $N - K$ element subset determines a unique K element subset (the elements that are left out of the $N - K$ element subset). So the number of K element subsets is the same as the number of $N - K$ element subsets; that is, $\text{B}(N, K) = \text{B}(N, N - K)$.

This kind of argument can be difficult to follow until you've had a little practice, so let's look at a specific example. Suppose that $N = 6$ and $K = 2$. We want to prove that $\text{B}(6, 2) = \text{B}(6, 4)$. So we are interested in a 6-element set, say, $S = \{A\ B\ C\ D\ E\ F\}$, and we want to show that there are just as many 2-element subsets as there are 4-element subsets. The proof outlines a method for pairing off the 2-element subsets and the 4-element subsets in a one-to-one manner. It tells us to pair every 2-element subset Q with its "complement" (the subset of S containing the elements that are not in Q). So we match $\{A\ C\}$ with $\{B\ D\ E\ F\}$. To make things explicit, figure 7.1 shows the whole story.

So every 2-element subset determines a 4-element subset. It's also easy to see that if my list of 2-element subsets is complete (is it?) then the list of 4-element subsets is also complete, because if there were a 4-element subset that didn't show up on the above list, its complement would be a 2-element subset that would be missing from my (supposedly complete) list.

The combinatorial proof is just a sketch for how you would go about making the above lists. Until you are comfortable with such arguments, you should probably carry out the actual counting that these proofs outline (with an explicit example). After a while, you'll be able to simply imagine the explicit calculations without having to write them down, and pretty soon, you'll be writing your own combinatorial arguments. Of course, you can often eliminate combinatorial proofs by using more formal strategies (mathematical induction, for example), but being able to give an explanation for a phenomenon in two styles (say, combinatorial and inductive) will give you a better insight into the phenomenon than if you look at it from a single point of view.

How can we represent our function B in Logo? Because $\text{B}(N, 0) = 1$ and $\text{B}(N, N) = 1$, we could begin like this:

```
TO B :N :K
 IF :K = 0 [OP 1]
 IF :K = :N [OP 1]
 ...
END
```

$\{A\ B\}$ $\overrightarrow{\text{is paired with}}$ $\{C\ D\ E\ F\}$

$\{A\ C\}$ $\overrightarrow{\text{is paired with}}$ $\{B\ D\ E\ F\}$

$\{A\ D\}$ $\overrightarrow{\text{is paired with}}$ $\{B\ C\ E\ F\}$

$\{A\ E\}$ $\overrightarrow{\text{is paired with}}$ $\{B\ C\ D\ F\}$

$\{A\ F\}$ $\overrightarrow{\text{is paired with}}$ $\{B\ C\ D\ E\}$

$\{B\ C\}$ $\overrightarrow{\text{is paired with}}$ $\{A\ D\ E\ F\}$

$\{B\ D\}$ $\overrightarrow{\text{is paired with}}$ $\{A\ C\ E\ F\}$

$\{B\ E\}$ $\overrightarrow{\text{is paired with}}$ $\{A\ C\ D\ F\}$

$\{B\ F\}$ $\overrightarrow{\text{is paired with}}$ $\{A\ C\ D\ E\}$

$\{C\ D\}$ $\overrightarrow{\text{is paired with}}$ $\{A\ B\ E\ F\}$

$\{C\ E\}$ $\overrightarrow{\text{is paired with}}$ $\{A\ B\ D\ F\}$

$\{C\ F\}$ $\overrightarrow{\text{is paired with}}$ $\{A\ B\ D\ E\}$

$\{D\ E\}$ $\overrightarrow{\text{is paired with}}$ $\{A\ B\ C\ F\}$

$\{D\ F\}$ $\overrightarrow{\text{is paired with}}$ $\{A\ B\ C\ E\}$

$\{E\ F\}$ $\overrightarrow{\text{is paired with}}$ $\{A\ B\ C\ D\}$

Figure 7.1

Now, we need a method for reducing the calculation of any $B(N, K)$ to the two cases that we know (second input 0 or equal inputs). Think about this for a while before you read on.

One way to think about calculating outputs for B is to use the distinguished element method. Look at a specific example: Suppose we want to find $B(6, 4)$.

We want the number of 4-element subsets of a 6-element set. Suppose our set is $S = \{A\ B\ C\ D\ E\ F\}$. Let's classify our 4-element subsets by whether or not they contain F. So, we'll look at two kinds of 4-element subsets of S: those subsets that contain F, and those that don't. This time, we won't try to set up a pairing between our two types; we'll just try to calculate the number of each type separately.

How many subsets of S have 4 elements and don't contain F? This is just the number of 4-element subsets of $\{A\ B\ C\ D\ E\}$, and this is just B$(5,4)$.

How many subsets of S have 4 elements and do contain F? How would you build such a subset? You'd start like this:

$$\{\,\_\,\_\,\_\,F\}$$

and then you'd fill in the blanks with 3 elements from $\{A\ B\ C\ D\ E\}$. In other words, the number of 4-element subsets of S that contain F is the same as the number of 3-element subsets of $\{A\ B\ C\ D\ E\}$, and this is just B$(5,3)$.

We have shown that

$$\text{B}(6,4) = \text{B}(5,4) + \text{B}(5,3)$$

The method we used to arrive at this fact is perfectly general:

Theorem 7.3 (*Pascal's (1623–1662) identity*) If $N > K \geq 1$, we have

$$\text{B}(N,K) = \text{B}(N-1, K-1) + \text{B}(N-1, K)$$

Proof: B(N, K) counts the number of K-element subsets of an N-element set. Suppose that S is a set with N elements, and pick a distinguished element, say, D from S. Then the K-element subsets of S break up into two types:

Type 1. K-element subsets that don't contain D

Type 2. K-element subsets that contain D

So

$$\text{B}(N,K) = (\text{the number of subsets of type 1})$$
$$+ (\text{the number of subsets of type 2})$$

Now, to form a subset of type 1, we must pick K elements from $N - 1$ elements (because we can't use D), so there are B$(N-1, K)$ subsets of type 1. To form a subset of type 2, we start with D, and we throw in $K - 1$ other elements of S. These $K - 1$ elements are chosen from $N - 1$ elements (everything but D), so there are $B(N - 1, K - 1)$ subsets of type 2. In other words,

$$B(N, K) = B(N - 1, K - 1) + B(N - 1, K)$$

and this is what we wanted to prove.

Exercise 7.4 Use this line of reasoning to prove the following statement: If N, K and J are nonnegative integers so that $K + J \leq N$, then

$$B(N, K + J) = B(N, K) + B(N - K, J)$$

Theorem 7.3 allows us to finish our Logo model for B.

Model 1 Version for B

```
TO B :N :K
 IF :K = 0 [OP 1]
 IF :K = :N [OP 1]
 OP (B :N - 1 :K - 1) + (B :N - 1 :K)
END
```

The first thing to notice about this representation of B is that it is extremely slow to output. Also notice that some rather small inputs to B will cause your computer to run out of space (the calculation of the Massachusetts lottery number $B(36, 6)$ is out of the question in most versions of Logo; my version gives erratic error messages). The following project takes a closer look at the complexity involved in computing the model 1 B's output.

Project 7.5 If I trace the computation of $B(5, 3)$ by hand, I can arrange my calculations like this:

$B(5, 3) =$

| $B(4, 2)$ | | | $+$ | | | $B(4, 3) =$ | | |
| $B(3, 1)$ | | $+$ | | $B(3, 2)$ | | $+$ | | $B(3, 2)$ | | $+$ | | $B(3, 3)$ |

$B(5, 3) =$

$B(4, 2)$ $+$ $B(4, 3) =$

$B(3, 1)$ $+$ $B(3, 2)$ $+$ $B(3, 2)$ $+$ $B(3, 3)$

$B(2, 0) + B(2, 1) +$ $B(2, 1) +$ $B(2, 2) + B(2, 1) +$ $B(2, 2) + 1$

1 $+ B(1, 0) + B(1, 1) + B(1, 0) + B(1, 1) + 1$ $+ B(1, 0) + B(1, 1) + 1$ $+ 1$

1 $+ 1$ $+ 1$ $+ 1$ $+ 1$ $+ 1$ $+ 1$ $+ 1$ $+ 1$ $+ 1$

Here, I go from one line to the next by placing beneath each call to B the result of applying Pascal's identity (or a 1, if the second input to B is 0 or if the inputs to B are equal). Notice, for example, that $B(2,1)$ is calculated three times. It turns out that there are 19 calls to B involved in my calculation of $B(5,3)$. How many calls to B are made in the calculation of $B(6,3)$? In the calculation of $B(5,4)$? In the calculation of $B(7,3)$? Look at your calculations and explain why the following statement is true:

The number of calls to B that are made in the computation of $B(N, K)$ is at least as big as $B(N, K)$.

#Suppose we define the complexity function $C(N, K)$ like this:

$C(N, K)$ = the number of calls to B in the calculation of $B(N, K)$

So $C(N, N) = 1$, and $C(N, 0) = 1$. Also $C(5, 3) = 19$, and $C(6, 3) = 39$. Write a Logo representation for C. (Hint: Use Pascal's identity.)

We'll soon find some other Logo representations for B that are more efficient (run faster and take up less memory), but the model 1 definition, based on Pascal's identity, is the basic tool used to investigate properties of B. For example,

Project 7.6 Give an inductive proof of theorem 7.2 (if $N \geq K \geq 0$, $B(N, K) = B(N, N - K)$).

Hint: If $N = 0$, then $K = 0$, and the identity is immediate. Suppose that, for some M, we have

$$B(M, K) = B(M, M - K)$$

for all K between 0 and M. To prove the assertion for $N = M + 1$, consider two cases:

1. $K = M + 1$. Is $B(M + 1, M + 1)$ the same as the following?

$$B(M + 1, (M + 1) - (M + 1))$$

2. $K < M + 1$. Then $K \leq M$, and, by Pascal's identity,

$$B(M + 1, K) = B(M, K) + B(M, K - 1)$$

By the inductive hypothesis,

$$B(M, K) = B(M, M - K)$$

$$B(M, K - 1) = B(M, M - (K - 1)) = B(M, M + 1 - K)$$

So

$$\begin{aligned}
B(M + 1, K) &= B(M, M - K) + B(M, M + 1 - K) \\
&= B(M, M + 1 - K - 1) + B(M, M + 1 - K)
\end{aligned}$$

Now, use Pascal's identity on this last sum to find that it is equal to $B(M + 1, M + 1 - K)$.

The mathematical notation for $B(N, K)$ is $\binom{N}{K}$. Using this notation, Pascal's identity becomes

$$\binom{N}{K} = \binom{N - 1}{K - 1} + \binom{N - 1}{K}$$

If we arrange the outputs of B in the following triangular array,

$$\binom{0}{0}$$

$$\binom{1}{0} \binom{1}{1}$$

$$\binom{2}{0} \binom{2}{1} \binom{2}{2}$$

$$\binom{3}{0} \binom{3}{1} \binom{3}{2} \binom{3}{3}$$

$$\binom{4}{0} \binom{4}{1} \binom{4}{2} \binom{4}{3} \binom{4}{4}$$

$$\binom{5}{0} \binom{5}{1} \binom{5}{2} \binom{5}{3} \binom{5}{4} \binom{5}{4} \binom{5}{5}$$

$$\binom{6}{0} \binom{6}{1} \binom{6}{2} \binom{6}{3} \binom{6}{4} \binom{6}{4} \binom{6}{5} \binom{6}{6}$$

we get the celebrated "Pascal's triangle." Because $B(N, 0) = 1$ and $B(N, N) = 1$, each row of the triangle starts and ends with 1. Pascal's identity says that any other number in the triangle is the sum of the two numbers above it. So the first few rows of Pascal's triangle can be easily written down:

$$
\begin{array}{ccccccccccccc}
 & & & & & & 1 & & & & & & \\
 & & & & & 1 & & 1 & & & & & \\
 & & & & 1 & & 2 & & 1 & & & & \\
 & & & 1 & & 3 & & 3 & & 1 & & & \\
 & & 1 & & 4 & & 6 & & 4 & & 1 & & \\
 & 1 & & 5 & & 10 & & 10 & & 5 & & 1 & \\
1 & & 6 & & 15 & & 20 & & 15 & & 6 & & 1
\end{array}
$$

By convention, we call the row of Pascal's triangle that contains a single 1 the "zeroth" row, and we number the rows accordingly; the first row is [1 1], the second row is [1 2 1], and so on. Also we number the entries of each row starting with 0, so that if we know the Nth row of Pascal's triangle, we can read off the various values of $B(N, K)$ as K goes from 0 to N. For example, looking at the sixth row above, we see that

$$\binom{6}{2} = 15, \binom{6}{3} = 20, \text{ and } \binom{6}{0} = 1$$

A More Efficient Method for Calculating B

It seems that constructing Pascal's triangle up to the Nth row and then reading across the row is a more efficient way of computing $B(N, K)$ than the calculation involved in the model 1 definition. One reason for this is that, in Pascal's triangle, we compute a row of the triangle by using the previous row (and not by winding our way back to the base cases of second input 0 or equal inputs). This eliminates a great deal of duplication in our calculations; in the model 1 calculation of $B(5, 3)$, $B(2, 1)$ is calculated three times, whereas in computing $B(5, 3)$ from Pascal's triangle, we calculate $B(2, 1)$ only once. Let's build a Logo representation of the method that we use to generate Pascal's triangle so that we can find a more efficient model for B.

We have not been very concerned with computational efficiency up to now, and we won't often worry about it. Our goal is to build Logo models for mathematical phenomena so that we can do mathematical experiments. In some cases, however, the lack of efficiency of our models will actually get in the way of our experiments, and in these cases, we'll have to worry about issues of efficiency. The function B is important enough that we should have a workable model for it (at least so that it can handle inputs of modest size). Besides, it's sometimes fun to find ways to eliminate significant amounts of computation.

In our method for generating Pascal's triangle, we'll treat each row as a list of numbers. So the third row of Pascal's triangle will be represented as the list [1 3 3 1]. We'll begin by writing a function that takes any row of Pascal's triangle as input and outputs the next row. Then we'll write a PASCAL function that takes an input N and outputs the Nth row of Pascal's triangle. Finally, we'll build a new model of B that computes $B(N, K)$ by finding the appropriate element in the Nth row of Pascal's triangle. We'll write our functions using the Logo functions

FIRST, BUTFIRST (BF), SENTENCE (SE), and ITEM.

As usual, if you see something that you are not familiar with, start by looking at the appendix.

Our first function GEN.PAS models an algorithm designed by one of my students to generate rows of Pascal's triangle. It takes two inputs I (the input row) and O (the eventual output). The value of I is a particular row of Pascal's triangle, say the fifth row: [1 5 10 10 51]; O starts out as the empty list []. The procedure outlines a scheme for transforming I into [1] while transforming O into the "interior" of the next row of Pascal's triangle; in our case this would be [6 15 20 15 6]. GEN.PAS then outputs the list you get by taking this transformed O and adjoining 1's to the front and back of it (using SE). The transformation is carried out by repeated applications of the following substitution scheme:

Calculate the sum of the first two elements of I.

Replace O with the list obtained by adjoining this sum to the back of O.

Replace I by the BUTFIRST of I.

This gives a recipe (or algorithm) for reducing I to [1] while inflating O to the interior of the next row of Pascal's triangle. Here is how it converts the fifth row of Pascal's triangle to the sixth:

	O	*I*
Step 1.	[]	[1 5 10 10 5 1]
Step 2.	[6] (1 + 5)	[5 10 10 5 1]
Step 3.	[6 15] (10 + 5)	[10 10 5 1]
Step 4.	[6 15 20]	[10 5 1]
Step 5.	[6 15 20 15]	[5 1]
Step 6.	[6 15 20 15 6]	[1]

Now, if we adjoin 1's to the front and back of *O*, we have the sixth row of Pascal's triangle. Here is the function GEN.PAS:

```
TO GEN.PAS :I :O
 IF EMPTYP BF :I [OP (SE 1 :O 1)]
 OP GEN.PAS (BF :I) (SE :O (FIRST :I) + (SECOND :I))
END

TO SECOND :L
 OP FIRST BF :L
END
```

If you type

```
SHOW GEN.PAS [1 3 3 1] []
```

you'll see

```
[1 4 6 4 1]
```

Since we'll always start off with [] as the value for *O*, we can tidy GEN.PAS like this:

```
TO GEN.PAS1 :ROW
 OP GEN.PAS :ROW []
END
```

Type

```
SHOW GEN.PAS1 [1 4 6 4 1]
```

The PASCAL function takes an input N and outputs the Nth row of Pascal's triangle. If N is 0, PASCAL simply outputs [1]; otherwise, it generates the Nth row from row $(N-1)$ using GEN.PAS1:

```
TO PASCAL :N
 IF :N = 0 [OP [1]]
 OP GEN.PAS1 (PASCAL :N - 1)
END
```

If you're confused by this, think of it this way:

```
PASCAL(3) = GEN.PAS1 (PASCAL(2))
          = GEN.PAS1 (GEN.PAS1 (PASCAL(1)))
          = GEN.PAS1 (GEN.PAS1 (GEN.PAS1 (PASCAL(0))))
          = GEN.PAS1 (GEN.PAS1 (GEN.PAS1([1])))
          = GEN.PAS1 (GEN.PAS1([1 1]))
          = GEN.PAS1([1 2 1])
          = [1 3 3 1]
```

In this calculation I replaced PASCAL(3) by GEN.PAS1(PASCAL(2)); in this expression, I replaced PASCAL(2) by GEN.PAS1(PASCAL(1)) and I replaced PASCAL(1) by GEN.PAS1(PASCAL(0)); finally I replaced PASCAL(0) by [1]. The unstacking is done using the definition of GEN.PAS1.

You should try PASCAL out. Try typing

```
SHOW PASCAL 36
```

We can now write a new version of B that finds $B(N, K)$ by reading across the Nth row of Pascal's triangle. Since the first entry of the Nth row is $B(N, 0)$, we have that

$$B(N, 0) = \text{ITEM } 1 \ (\text{PASCAL}(N))$$
$$B(N, 1) = \text{ITEM } 2 \ (\text{PASCAL}(N))$$

and inductively,

$$B(N, K) = \text{ITEM } (K + 1) \ (\text{PASCAL}(N))$$

So we obtain a new version of B.

Model 2 Version for B

```
TO B :N :K              TO PICK :M :L
 OP PICK :K  (PASCAL :N)  OP ITEM (:M + 1) :L
END                     END
```

Exercise 7.7 How many different numbers can be bet in the Massachusetts lottery? Suppose you wrote each of these numbers of a separate sheet of paper. If a 500-sheet stack of paper is about 1.5 inches high, how high would your stack containing all the possible lottery numbers be? If you could place one bet every 10 seconds for 8 hours each day, how many days would it take you to cover all the possibilities?

Experiment 7.8 Find a simple formula for $B(N, 2)$. Prove that your formula is correct.

Exercise 7.9 There are 12 distinct points on a circle. How many chords do the points determine? How many chords are determined by N points on a circle?

Exercise 7.10 How many diagonals are there in a 12-sided polygon? (A diagonal is any segment that connects two vertices that aren't already connected by a side.) How many diagonals are there in an N-sided polygon?

Project 7.11 What is the sum of the numbers in the Nth row of Pascal's triangle? Give a combinatorial proof for your assertion. (Hint: use theorem 7.1 and the definition of $\binom{N}{K}$.) Give an inductive proof of your assertion. (Hint: Use Pascal's identity.)

Project 7.12 (For those of you who have completed the last part of project 7.5), here's a sequel. The complexity function for the model 1 version of B could be defined in this way:

```
TO C :N :K
 IF :K = 0 [OP 1]
 IF :K = :N [OP 1]
 OP (C :N - 1 :K - 1) + (C :N - 1 :K) + 1
END
```

Of course, C is just as hard to compute as B is. But, if we arrange the outputs of C in a triangle, we get

$$
\begin{array}{ccccccccccccc}
& & & & & & 1 & & & & & & \\
& & & & & 1 & & 1 & & & & & \\
& & & & 1 & & 3 & & 1 & & & & \\
& & & 1 & & 5 & & 5 & & 1 & & & \\
& & 1 & & 7 & & 11 & & 7 & & 1 & & \\
& 1 & & 9 & & 19 & & 19 & & 9 & & 1 & \\
1 & & 11 & & 29 & & 39 & & 29 & & 11 & & 1
\end{array}
$$

Write a model 2 version of C. What is $C(36, 6)$?

From now on, we'll be dealing with quite a few functions that take more than one input. We'd like to be able to sum such functions "against the last input"; in other words, we want to compute something like

$$C(5,0) + C(5,1) + C(5,2) + C(5,3) + C(5,4) + C(5,5)$$

Here we keep the first input to C fixed at 5, and we accumulate the outputs as the second input goes from 0 to 5. The Logo code for this extended SIGMA is given in the appendix, and it allows you to sum a function of several variables against the last variable. Here's an example of how to use it.

Type

SHOW SIGMA "B 5 0 5

to see

$$\sum_{K=0}^{5} B(5, K)$$

If you have a function that only takes one input, you can still use the new SIGMA; just call SIGMA "F [] 1 10. If you have a function of, say, three inputs, you can pass the first two in as a list. For example, if H is a function of three inputs, then typing

SHOW SIGMA "H [2 4] 1 3

will produce the value of $H(2,4,1) + H(2,4,2) + H(2,4,3)$.

#Project 7.13 This project is designed to help you find a function that gives the sum of the numbers in the Nth row of the complexity triangle of project 7.12. In other words, we want to compute

$$S(N) = \sum_{K=0}^{N} C(N, K)$$

We can write a Logo model of S by using our more flexible version of SIGMA:

```
TO S :N
 OP SIGMA "C :N O :N
END
```

Find a simple formula for S; prove that your version of S is correct.

Hints: Here are several lines of attack. There is no need to follow them in order, and it might be better to ignore them.

1. In project 7.5 we saw that

$$C(N, K) \geq B(N, K)$$

so the sum across the Nth row of the complexity triangle is at least as big as the sum across the Nth row of Pascal's triangle, and in project 7.11, we saw that the sum across the Nth row of Pascal's triangle is 2^N. So let $T(N) = S(N) - 2^N$, and tabulate T.

2. Try to find a recursive form for S before you look for a closed form.

3. Use project 6.10.

Project 7.14 This project also makes use of the generalized SIGMA. Consider the following function H:

```
TO H :N :BASE :K
 OP (B :N :K) * (POWER :BASE :K)
END
```

So

$$H(5,3,2) = \binom{5}{2} 3^2$$

For a given N and $BASE$, we can accumulate H's outputs:

$$\sum_{K=0}^{N} H(N, BASE, K)$$

This is really a function of N and $BASE$; call it ACC.H. So

$$\text{ACC.H}(5,3) = \binom{5}{0} 3^0 + \binom{5}{1} 3^1 + \binom{5}{2} 3^2 + \binom{5}{3} 3^3 + \binom{5}{4} 3^4 + \binom{5}{5} 3^5$$

We can model ACC.H in Logo using our generalized summer:

```
TO ACC.H :N :BASE
 OP SIGMA "H (SE :N :BASE) 0 :N
END
```

Find a simple formula for ACC.H (as a function of N and $BASE$), and prove that your formula is correct. Does your formula work if $BASE = 1$ (see project 7.11)? Does it work if $BASE = -1$?

Project 7.15 Suppose that M and N are positive integers, and suppose that K is a nonnegative integer less than or equal to M and less than or equal to N. Verify the following fact for several values of M, N, and K:

$$\binom{M}{0}\binom{M}{K} + \binom{M}{1}\binom{M}{K-1} + \binom{M}{2}\binom{M}{K-2} +$$

$$\binom{M}{3}\binom{M}{K-3} + \cdots + \binom{M}{K}\binom{N}{0} = \binom{M+N}{K}$$

Give two proofs that the fact is true in general.

Hints:

1. *Verification.* Define a function of four variables:

```
TO F :N :M :K :J
 OP (B :N :J) * (B :M :K - :J)
END
```

Then use **SIGMA** to get the sum in question:

```
TO S :M :N :K
 OP SIGMA "F (SE :M :N :K) O :K
END
```

Now, check that, for example,

SHOW S 7 5 4

produces the same result as

SHOW B 12 4

For more evidence, you can **TAB**ulate S (keeping M and N constant and varying K) by using the generalized **TAB** from the appendix.

2. *Combinatorial Proof.* Suppose we have two sets S and T; S has M elements, and T has N elements. Suppose further that S and T have no elements in common so that, if Q is the union of S and T, Q has $M + N$ elements. Then to pick a K-element subset of Q, you could

pick no elements from S and $\quad K \quad$ elements from T, or you could
pick 1 element from S and $K - 1$ elements from T, or you could
pick 2 elements from S and $K - 2$ elements from T, or you could

$\vdots$

pick K elements from S and $\quad$ no $\quad$ elements from T

3. *Inductive Proof.* Induct on M. If $M = 1$, K is either 0 or 1, and each case is easy to handle. If the fact is true for some value of M, use Pascal's identity to write

$$\binom{M+1}{0}\binom{N}{K} + \binom{M+1}{1}\binom{N}{K-1} + \binom{M+1}{2}\binom{N}{K-2}$$
$$+ \cdots + \binom{M+1}{K}\binom{N}{0}$$

as two sums that can be handled by the induction hypothesis.

Experiment 7.16 Let W be the square of B:

```
TO W :N :K
 OP POWER (B :N :K) 2
END
```

Then using our generalized SIGMA, define R:

```
TO R :N
 OP SIGMA "W :N O :N
END
```

Show that R(N) is the same as B(X, Y) for some X and Y depending only on N. Hint: Use project 7.15 and theorem 7.2.

A Third Method for Calculating B

There is another model for B that is often useful, especially for hand calculations. This third model for B expresses B in terms of the factorial function:

```
TO FACT :N
 IF :N = 0 [OP 1]
 OP :N * (FACT :N-1)
END
```

> If your computer has a hard time computing the output of FACT for inputs bigger than 30, try this version:
>
> ```
> TO FACT :N
>  OP FACT.HELPER :N 1
> END
>
> TO FACT.HELPER :N :P
>  IF :N = 0 [OP :P]
>  OP FACT.HELPER (:N - 1) :N * :P
> END
> ```
>
> For an explanation of why this doesn't cause Logo to run out of space, see Harvey (1985, ch. 10).

In chapter 1 (exercise 1.11) you looked at the problem of determining the number of K-digit numbers that can be formed from N digits. The answer was

$$N(N-1)(N-2)\cdots(N-K+1)$$

Let's call this function $\text{D}(N, K)$. Notice that $\text{D}(N, K)$ can be written as $N!/(N-K)!$. For example,

$$D(9,4) = 9\cdot 8\cdot 7\cdot 6 = \frac{9\cdot 8\cdot 7\cdot 6\cdot 5\cdot 4\cdot 3\cdot 2\cdot 1}{5\cdot 4\cdot 3\cdot 2\cdot 1}$$
$$= \frac{9!}{(9-4)!}$$

What is the difference between the number of K-digit numbers that can be formed from N digits and the number of K-element subsets of an N element set? Clearly, the number of K-digit numbers is larger than the number of K-element subsets, because each K-element subset gives rise to several K-digit numbers. For example, suppose our "digits" are $\{A\ B\ C\ D\ E\}$. Now, there are $\binom{5}{3} = 10$ three-element subsets; each three-element subset gives rise to 6 three-digit numbers. For example, $\{A\ B\ E\}$ gives rise to

$$ABE, AEB, BAE, BEA, EAB, EBA$$

So there are $10\cdot 6 = 60$ three-digit numbers that can be obtained from five digits (this agrees with our function D: $\text{D}(5,3) = 5!/2! = 120/2$). Why does each three-element subset give rise to six digits? In part I we looked at exactly this question: We have three symbols A, B, and E, and we want to count all the three-digit numbers from these symbols (with no repeated digit); the answer is 3! (or 6). Similarly, how many digits does a four-element subset generate? 4! (or 24). In general, each K-element subset generates $K!$ digits, so we have the following relation between B and D:

$$K!\,\text{B}(N,K) = \text{D}(N,K) = \frac{N!}{(N-K)!}$$

Solving for $\text{B}(N, K)$,

$$\text{B}(N,K) = \frac{N!}{K!(N-K)!}$$

This gives rise to a third model for B.

Model 3 Version for B

```
TO B :N :K
 OP (FACT :N) / ((FACT :K) * (FACT (:N - :K)))
END
```

This version of B is even faster on my computer than the model 2 version. It's also easy to use for hand calculations of outputs of B if you are a little careful about canceling. For example, suppose you want the number of possible bets in the Massachusetts lottery, B(36, 6). The model 3 version of B asks us to calculate

$$B(36,6) = \frac{36!}{6!\,30!}$$

This looks like a significant amount of calculation (36! is bigger than 2^{35}, which is beyond the precision of most hand calculators). However, if we think of B(36, 6) like this:

$$B(36,6) = \frac{36 \cdot 35 \cdot 34 \cdot 33 \cdot 32 \cdot 31 \cdot 30!}{6 \cdot 5 \cdot 4 \cdot 3 \cdot 2 \cdot 1 \cdot 30!}$$

then the 30!'s cancel, and we are left with a manageable calculation.

Exercise 7.17 Use the model 3 version of B and some manipulations with factorials to give algebraic proofs of the following facts:

1. $B(N, K) = B(N, N - K)$.
2. $B(N, 0) = B(N, N) = 1$.
3. $B(N, 2) = N(N - 1)/2$.
4. $B(N, K) = B(N - 1, K - 1) + B(N - 1, K)$.

When I was in school, the model 3 version of B was the first version we saw. Then we derived all the pertinent facts about B (like the above ones) by manipulating factorials. Which method for deriving these facts (combinatorial or algebraic) do you like?

Exercise 7.18 Modify the model 3 version of B so that it cancels the larger factorial in the denominator of $B(N, K)$ with part of the numerator. (Hint: Recall REP.MULT of part 1.) Does this improve the operation of B?

A Final Method

There are many interesting ways to make the calculation of B efficient (see, for example, the article "Computing Binomial Coefficients" by Goetgheluck 1987).

Here's a method that is simple, beautiful, and fast.

Model 4 Version for B

```
TO B :N :K
 OP B.HELPER :N :K 0 1
END

TO B.HELPER :N :K :COUNTER :HOLDER
 IF :COUNTER > :K - 1 [OP :HOLDER]
 OP B.HELPER :N :K :COUNTER + 1 :HOLDER →
               * (:N - :COUNTER) / (:COUNTER + 1)
END
```

Why does this work? Why is it so fast (compared to, say, the model 3 version of B)?

For a reason that we'll discuss in the next section, the outputs of B are called "binomial coefficients." There is really no convention about the name of the function B, and this causes some awkwardness in spoken mathematics. Some people refer to $\binom{N}{K}$ as "the binomial coefficient N over K" (a real mouthful), some people say "N over K" (easy to confuse with N/K), and still others say "N K" (very hard to understand); finally, some people call it "N choose K" (because you are picking K things from N). There are several important functions without names in mathematics; such creatures can't exist in Logo.

These final projects investigate some interesting variations and applications of binomial coefficients.

Project 7.19 In project 7.12 we modeled the complexity function C by

```
TO C :N :K
 IF :K = 0 [OP 1]
 IF :K = :N [OP 1]
 OP (C :N - 1 :K - 1) + (C :N - 1 :K) + 1
END
```

The following function GEN.BIN includes both B and C as special cases:

```
TO GEN.BIN :N :K :INC
 IF :K = 0 [OP 1]
 IF :K = :N [OP 1]
 OP (GEN.BIN :N - 1 :K - 1 :INC) →
       + (GEN.BIN :N - 1 :K :INC) + :INC :INC
END
```

GEN.BIN$(N, K, 0)$ = B(N, K), and GEN.BIN$(N, K, 1)$ = C(N, K). Investigate GEN.BIN. For example, can you write model 2 versions of GEN.BIN? What is the sum of the entries across the Nth row of the GEN.BIN triangle? Is there a version of GEN.BIN in terms of FACT?

Project 7.20 Let's take another look at project 5.22. We defined a sequence of functions F_N by the rules

1. $F_0(M) = 1$ for all M

2. $\displaystyle F_N(M) = \sum_{K=1}^{M} F_{(N-1)}(K)$ for $N > 0$

We proved (in two different ways) that for $N > 0$ and for $M \geq 1$, $F_N(M)$ had a simple model:

$$F_N(M) = \frac{(M + N - 1)!}{N!(M - 1)!}$$

We now know that this can be written as a binomial coefficient:

$$F_N(M) = \binom{M + N - 1}{M - 1}$$

So

$$F_1(M) = \binom{M}{M - 1} = M$$

$$F_2(M) = \binom{M + 1}{M - 1} = \frac{(M + 1)!}{(M - 1)!\, 2!} = \frac{(M + 1)M}{2}$$

and so on. The second part of the definition of F_N,

$$F_N(M) = \sum_{K=1}^{M} F_{(N-1)}(K)$$

becomes

$$\binom{N+M-1}{M-1} = \sum_{K=1}^{M} \binom{N+K-2}{K-1} \qquad (*)$$

Identity $(*)$, when written out, looks very interesting:

$$\binom{N+M-1}{M-1} = \binom{N-1}{0} + \binom{N}{1} + \binom{N+1}{2} + \binom{N+2}{3}$$

$$+ \cdots + \binom{N+M-2}{M-1}$$

For example, suppose that $N = 6$ and $M = 4$. Then we have

$$\binom{9}{3} = \binom{5}{0} + \binom{6}{1} + \binom{7}{2} + \binom{8}{3}$$

Look at what this says in Pascal's triangle:

```
                        1
                    1       1
                1       2       1
            1       3       3       1
        1       4       6       4       1
    1       5      10      10       5       1
  1     6      15      20      15       6      1
1     7     21      35      35      21      7      1
1   8    28      56      70      56      28     8     1
1   9   36     84     126     126     84    36    9    1
```

If you start at any 1 along the left-hand side of the triangle, and you add the numbers along the diagonal starting with your 1, the sum up to any number is the entry in the triangle below that number to the left. Check it out with several examples. Notice that if you start with $\binom{1}{0}$, we have

$$\binom{1}{0} + \binom{2}{1} + \binom{3}{2} + \cdots + \binom{N}{N-1} = \binom{N+1}{N-1}$$

or

$$1 + 2 + 3 + \cdots + N = \frac{N(N+1)}{2}$$

which is Gauss' formula for the sum of the first N integers.

If you write out what identity (∗) says for entries in Pascal's triangle, you see that it can be expressed as

$$\sum_{J=0}^{M} \binom{H+J}{J} = \binom{H+1+M}{M} \qquad (\ast\ast)$$

Here H is the number of the row you start at, and M is the number of entries that you move down the diagonal.

Let's call identity (∗∗) the "hockey stick theorem." Prove the hockey stick theorem using the ideas from this section. Hint: By Pascal's identity,

$$\binom{9}{3} = \binom{8}{3} + \binom{8}{2}$$

Now apply Pascal's identity again to $\binom{8}{2}$.

Is the hockey stick theorem still true if you start at the right-hand border of the triangle? For example, are

$$\binom{2}{2} + \binom{3}{2} + \binom{4}{2} + \binom{5}{2} + \binom{6}{2} + \binom{7}{2} + \binom{8}{2} = \binom{9}{3}?$$

Can you write out an identity like (∗∗) that expresses this fact in general?

Project 7.21 There are many interesting facts hidden in Pascal's triangle. Find a diagonal with the property that the sum of any two consecutive numbers on the diagonal is a perfect square. Find a diagonal with the property that the differences between numbers that are "almost consecutive" (elements on the diagonal that are separated by one entry of the diagonal) are perfect squares. Prove these facts. Come up with a few facts of your own.

You can find a discussion of some other interesting patterns in Pascal's triangle in the article "Looking into Pascal's Triangle: Combinatorics, Arithmetic, and Geometry" (Hilton 1987).

Experiment 7.22 Find a closed form for the function SQUARE.SUM:

```
TO SQUARE.SUM :N
 OP SIGMA "SQUARE [] 1 :N
END

TO SQUARE :N
 OP :N * :N
END
```

(I've written SQUARE.SUM in terms of our modified SIGMA; that's why the second input to SIGMA is [].)

Hint: You can do this by playing around with tabulations of SQUARE.SUM and related functions. Another way is to look at the F_2 and F_3 functions of project 5.22:

$$F_2(M) = \sum_{K=1}^{M} K = \frac{M(M+1)}{2}$$

and

$$F_3(M) = \sum_{K=1}^{M} \frac{K(K+1)}{2} = \frac{M(M+1)(M+2)}{6}$$

Now, express SUM.SQUARES in terms of F_2 and F_3.

Find a closed form for ALT.SUM.SQUARES:

```
TO ALT.SUM.SQUARES :N
 OP SIGMA SIGNED.SQUARE [] 1 :N
END

TO SIGNED.SQUARE :N
 OP (POWER -1 :N + 1) * (SQUARE :N)
END
```

Why is the function called ALT.SUM.SQUARES?

The numbers

$$F_2(M) = \frac{M(M+1)}{2}$$

are called "triangular numbers" because they represent the sum of the first M integers. Such a sum can be represented as the number of dots on a triangle:

```
. . . . .   5 +
. . . .     4 +
. . .       3 +
. .         2 +
.           1      = F_2(5) = 5(5+1)/2 = 15.
```

$$. \quad 1 \qquad = F_2(5) = \frac{5(5+1)}{2} = 15.$$

Using this idea, you can find a delightful derivation of the closed form for `ALT.SUM.SQUARES` (it uses only pictures—no words or symbols) in Logothetti (1987).

Project 7.23 A "partition" of a positive integer N is a set of positive integers whose sum is N. For example, $\{1\ 3\ 4\}$ is a partition of 8. For this project, partitions will have no repetitions, so we won't allow $\{1\ 1\ 3\}$ as a partition of 5. Let P be the function of two variables that is defined like this:

$P(N, M) =$ the number of partitions of M whose elements are between 1 and N.

For example, $P(4, 6) = 2$ because 6 can be written as a sum of numbers less than or equal to 4 in two ways:

$$6 = 4 + 2$$

$$6 = 3 + 2 + 1$$

Find the output for

1. $P(4, 7)$
2. $P(4, 8)$
3. $P(5, 8)$
4. $P(10, 6)$
5. $P(7, 7)$
6. $P(6, 7)$
7. $P(6, 6)$

Why are the following statements true?

1. $P(N, M) = 0$ if $M > N(N + 1)/2$
2. $P(N, M) = P(N - 1, M)$ if $M < N$

We want to allow M and N to be 0. Why do these conventions make sense:

$$P(N, 0) = 1 \text{ for all nonnegative } N$$
$$P(0, M) = 0 \text{ for all positive } M$$

If we allowed M to be negative, what would the rules be?

Give a combinatorial argument for the following statement:

$$P(N, M) = P(N - 1, M - N) + P(N - 1, M)$$

Find a Logo model for P. Make your model as efficient as possible. In particular, can you come up with an algorithm for generating one row of the "partition array" from the previous one, where the partition array is defined like this?

$P(0,0)\ P(0,1)\ P(0,2)\ P(0,3)\ P(0,4)\ P(0,5)\ P(0,6)\ P(0,7)\ldots$

$P(1,0)\ P(1,1)\ P(1,2)\ P(1,3)\ P(1,4)\ P(1,5)\ P(1,6)\ P(1,7)\ldots$

$P(2,0)\ P(2,1)\ P(2,2)\ P(2,3)\ P(2,4)\ P(2,5)\ P(2,6)\ P(2,7)\ldots$

$P(3,0)\ P(3,1)\ P(3,2)\ P(3,3)\ P(3,4)\ P(3,5)\ P(3,6)\ P(3,7)\ldots$

$\vdots$

Is there any symmetry in this array?

Project 7.24 Suppose that you have two finite sets

$$S = \{A\ B\ C\ D\} \quad \text{and} \quad T = \{1\ 2\ 3\}$$

How many functions can you build that have domain S and produce outputs from T?

For example, here are two such functions:

```
TO F :X                      TO G :X
 IF :X = "A [OP 1]            IF :X = "A [OP 1]
 IF :X = "B [OP 1]            IF :X = "B [OP 2]
 IF :X = "C [OP 2]            IF :X = "C [OP 1]
 IF :X = "D [OP 3]            IF :X = "D [OP 1]
END                          END
```

Note that we don't have to use all the possible elements in T as outputs. To build a function from S to T, we choose an output for A (there are 3 of these), an output for B (there are 3 of these), and output for C (there are 3 of these), and an output for D (there are 3 of these). So altogether there are $3 \cdot 3 \cdot 3 \cdot 3$ possible functions.

If this isn't clear to you, think of it this way: To build a function you have three choices for the output at A: 1, 2, or 3. So, a function could start out like this:

```
TO F :X
 IF :X = "A [OP 1]
 ⋮
END
```

or

```
TO F :X
 IF :X = "A [OP 2]
 ⋮
END
```

or

```
TO F :X
 IF :X = "A [OP 3]
 ⋮
END
```

So far we have started three functions. But each of these three functions gives rise to three other functions because we can complete the next part of the definition for each of our F's in three ways (by sending B to 1, 2, or 3). This gives us nine starts. But then we can add a third step to each of our nine functions in three ways, ...

Give a combinatorial argument to support the following statement:

> If S has N elements and T has M elements, there are M^N functions whose domain is S and whose outputs come from T.

#A function from S to T that uses all the elements of T as outputs is called "surjective" or "onto." For example, the function F above is onto (the word *onto* is a shortcut for saying "F is a function from S onto T"), while G isn't onto. How many functions from a 4-element set to a 3-element set are onto? How many functions from an N-element set to an M-element set are onto?

Hint: Suppose S has 7 elements and T has 5 elements:

$$S = \{A\ B\ C\ D\ E\ F\ G\} \quad \text{and} \quad T = \{1\ 2\ 3\ 4\ 5\}$$

There are 57 functions whose domain is S and whose outputs come from T. So the number of onto functions is 5^7 minus the number of functions from S to T that "miss something" in T. When I first thought about this, I reasoned that there are $B(5,1) = 5$ ways to pick an element to miss in T; for each of these misses, there are 4^7 functions that have domain S and take outputs from the 4 elements that are left in T. So, I thought, there should be

$$5^7 - B(5,1) \cdot 4^7$$

onto functions from S to T. But this is a negative number, so it couldn't be right. Then I realized that $B(5,1) \cdot 4^7$ counts some non-onto functions more than once. For example, the function

$$
\begin{array}{l}
A \longrightarrow 1 \\
B \longrightarrow 2 \\
C \longrightarrow 1 \\
D \longrightarrow 2 \\
E \longrightarrow 3 \\
F \longrightarrow 3 \\
G \longrightarrow 3
\end{array}
$$

is counted as one of the 4^7 functions that miss 4 and also as one of the 4^7 functions that miss 5. In other words, by subtracting off $B(5,1)4^7$ from 5^7,

I've subtracted off the functions that miss two or more elements of T twice. So I should add the number of these functions back on. Well, there are $B(5, 2)$ ways to pick two elements of T to miss, and for each of these two element choices, there are 3^7 functions from S to the remaining three elements of T. So, can my answer be

$$5^7 - B(5, 1)4^7 + B(5, 2)3^7$$

No, because this has added back twice the number of functions that miss three elements. I should subtract off the number of functions that miss three elements; now, is the answer this:

$$5^7 - B(5, 1)4^7 + B(5, 2)3^7 - B(5, 3)2^7$$

If you've followed me so far, you see that I need one more adjustment:

$$5^7 - B(5, 1)4^7 + B(5, 2)3^7 - B(5, 3)2^7 + B(5, 4)1^7$$

This is the number of onto functions from a 7-element set to a 5-element set; it can be written as

$$B(5, 0)5^7 - B(5, 1)4^7 + B(5, 2)3^7 - B(5, 3)2^7 + B(5, 4)1^7 + B(5, 5)0^7$$

Using the symmetry of Pascal's triangle, this can be written as

$$B(5, 5)5^7 - B(5, 4)4^7 + B(5, 3)3^7 - B(5, 2)2^7 + B(5, 1)1^7 + B(5, 0)0^7$$

Generalize this argument as follows:

Define the function TERM by

```
TO TERM :N :M :K
 OP (POWER -1  (:M - :K)) * (B :M :K) * (POWER :K :N)
END
```

and let O be defined like this:

```
TO O :N :M
 OP SIGMA "TERM (SE :N :M) O :M
END
```

Give a combinatorial argument to prove that $O(N, M)$ is the number of onto functions whose domain is an N-element set taking outputs in an M-element set. What is the output of $O(N, M)$ if $M > N$? If $M = N$?

For an application of this project to a problem in probability, see Birch (1988).

Chapter 8

Application 2: The Binomial Theorem

In this chapter, we look at an interesting problem from algebra that can be solved using the methods of chapters 5 through 7.

Here is the algebra problem:

If N is a nonnegative integer, expand $(X + Y)^N$

For example,

$$(X + Y)^0 = 1$$
$$(X + Y)^1 = (X + Y)$$
$$(X + Y)^2 = (X + Y)(X + Y) = X^2 + 2XY + Y^2$$

To find $(X + Y)^3$, we calculate as follows:

$$(X + Y)^3 = (X + Y)(X + Y)(X + Y)$$
$$= (X + Y)(X + Y)^2$$
$$= (X + Y)(X^2 + 2XY + Y^2)$$

Now, to do this last calculation, we multiply everything in $X^2 + 2XY + Y^2$ by X, and we multiply everything in $X^2 + 2XY + Y^2$ by Y, and then we collect like terms:

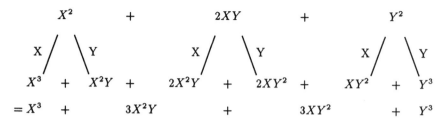

An inductive pattern emerges. To calculate $(X+Y)^4$, we multiply every term in $(X+Y)^3$ by X and by Y, and we collect terms:

$$X^3 \quad + \quad 3X^2Y \quad + \quad 3XY^2 \quad + \quad Y^3$$

$$X^4 \quad + X^3Y + 3X^3Y \quad + \quad 3X^2Y^2 + 3X^2Y^2 \quad + \quad 3XY^3 + XY^3 + Y^4$$

$$= X^4 \quad + \quad 4X^3Y \quad + \quad 6X^2Y^2 \quad + \quad 4XY3 \quad + Y^4$$

Imagine the calculation of $(X+Y)^5$. The terms would be

$$X^5, X^4Y, X^3Y^2, X^2Y^3, XY^4, Y^5$$

and the coefficient for each term would come from the contributions that you'd get by multiplying each term in $X^4 + 4X^3Y + 6X^2Y^2 + 4XY^3 + Y^4$ by X and by Y. So you'd get

1 X^5

5 X^4Y's   (one from $X^4 \cdot Y$ and four from $4X^3Y \cdot X$)

10 X^3Y^2's $(4X^3Y \cdot Y + 6X^2Y^2 \cdot X)$

10 X^2Y^3's $(6+4)$

5 XY^4's $(4+1)$

1 Y^5

    Notice that the coefficients in $(X+Y)^N$ are obtained from the coefficients of $(X+Y)^{(N-1)}$ in exactly the same way that the Nth row of Pascal's triangle is obtained from the $(N-1)$st row. Since the coefficients of $(X+Y)$ are [1 1], mathematical induction guarantees that the coefficients of $(X+Y)^N$ will be precisely the same as the entries in the Nth row of Pascal's triangle.

This is essentially the content of the binomial theorem (it's called the binomial theorem because it gives a method for raising a binomial $(X + Y)$ to a power). It says that the expansion of $(X + Y)^N$ is a sum of $N + 1$ terms:

$$X^N, X^{(N-1)}Y, X^{(N-2)}Y^2, \ldots, XY^{(N-1)}, Y^N$$

and the coefficients of these terms come from the Nth row of Pascal's triangle.
So

$$(X + Y)^8 = X^8 + 8X^7Y + 28X^6Y^2$$
$$+ 56X^5Y^3 + 70X^4Y^4 + 56X^3Y^5 + 28X^2Y^6 + 8XY^7 + Y^8$$

There are many ways to prove the binomial theorem; here's an informal proof that is fairly convincing.

It's pretty clear that the terms in $(X + Y)^N$ are

$$X^N, X^{(N-1)}Y, X^{(N-2)}Y^2, \ldots, XY^{(N-1)}, Y^N$$

Suppose that the coefficient of $X^{(N-K)}Y^K$ is $\mathrm{L}(N, K)$, so that

$$(X + Y)^N = \mathrm{L}(N, 0)X^N + \mathrm{L}(N, 1)X^{(N-1)}Y + \mathrm{L}(N, 2)X^{(N-2)}Y^2$$
$$+ \cdots + \mathrm{L}(N, N - 1)XY^{(N-1)} + \mathrm{L}(N, N)Y^N$$

Then by the method we used to obtain $(X + Y)^5$ from $(X + Y)^4$, we see that

$$\mathrm{L}(N, K) = \begin{cases} 1 & \text{if } K = 0 \text{ or } K = N \\ & \text{(these are the coefficients} \\ & \text{of } X^N \text{ and } Y^N) \\ \mathrm{L}(N - 1, K - 1) + \mathrm{L}(N - 1, K) & \text{otherwise} \end{cases}$$

But these are precisely the equations that define the binomial coefficients $\mathrm{B}(N, K)$, so

$$\mathrm{L}(N, K) = B(N, K)$$
$$= \text{the } K\text{th entry in the } N\text{th row of Pascal's triangle.}$$

We can make things a little tighter by eliminating language like "it's pretty clear that ..." and "by the method we used to obtain $(X+Y)^5$ from $(X+Y)^4$." Doing this leads us to an argument that uses mathematical induction. First, let's state the theorem in precise notation:

Theorem 8.1 (*The binomial theorem*)   If N is a nonnegative integer, then

$$(X + Y)^N = \sum_{K=0}^{N} \binom{N}{K} X^{(N-K)} Y^K$$

Proof: We'll induct on N. If $N = 0$, the theorem says that

$$(X + Y)^0 = \binom{0}{0} X^0 Y^0$$

which is certainly true. If you think that the case $N = 0$ is too trivial, look at the case $N = 1$; it says that

$$(X + Y)^1 = \binom{1}{0} X^1 Y^0 + \binom{1}{1} X^0 Y^1$$

Once again, this is clearly true.

Suppose the theorem is true for some integer M; that is, suppose that

$$(X + Y)^M = \binom{M}{0} X^M + \binom{M}{1} X^{(M-1)} Y + \binom{M}{2} X^{(M-2)} Y^2$$

$$+ \cdots + \binom{M}{M-1} X Y^{(M-1)} + \binom{M}{M} Y^M$$

To form $(X + Y)^{(M+1)}$ from $(X + Y)^M$, take the expression on the right-hand side, multiply everything by X and by Y, and collect terms using Pascal's identity:

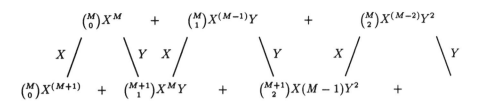

$$+ \quad \cdots \quad + \quad \binom{M}{M-1}XY^{(M-1)} \quad + \quad Y^M$$

$$\cdots \qquad + \qquad \binom{M+1}{M}XY^M \quad + \quad \binom{M}{M}Y^M$$

Since $\binom{M}{0} = \binom{M+1}{0}$ and $\binom{M}{M} = \binom{M+1}{M+1}$, we get the desired formula when $N = M + 1$.

This proof is just an abstract description of our method for computing $(X + Y)^6$ from $(X + Y)^5$. But there is another way to think about $(X + Y)^6$; it goes like this:

Say you have to do a polynomial multiplication by hand; suppose you want to compute

$$(4X^3 + 6X^2 - 5X + 2)(2X^4 + 3X^2 + 2X - 3)$$

Of course, you could multiply everything out by brute force and collect up like terms. Or, you could reason that the product is a polynomial of degree 7, and you could construct the product term by term:

Where will the X^7 term come from? It will come from $(4X^3)(2X^4)$ (and nowhere else), so the X^7 term is $8X^7$.

Where will the X^6 term come from? Well, you can get an X^6 from $(6X^2)(2X^4)$ (and nowhere else), so the X^6 term is $12X^6$.

Where will the X^5 term come from? Here we have more choices:

$$(4X^3)(3X^2) = 12X^5, \quad \text{and}$$

$$(-5X)(2X^4) = -10X^5$$

So the X^5 term is $2X^5$.

Similarly, we can look for the term of any degree by taking all possible combinations of terms (one from the first polynomial and one from the second) whose product has that degree.

We can use this same method with $(X + Y)^6$:

$$(X + Y)^6 = (X + Y)(X + Y)(X + Y)(X + Y)(X + Y)(X + Y)$$

Now, when we multiply this out, we'll get a sum of terms. Each term will come from taking either an X or a Y from each parenthesis. For example, if we pick an X from the first four parentheses and a Y from the last two, we get an X^4Y^2 term. Of course, there are other ways to get an X^4Y^2 term; you could pick an X from the first, second, fourth, and sixth parentheses, and a Y from the third and fifth parentheses. All these X^4Y^2 terms will be collected, and the coefficient of X^4Y^2 in the final expansion will just be the number of X^4Y^2 terms that show up. How many are there? To get an X^4Y^2, we pick two terms from the six $(X + Y)$ terms and designate these as "Y parentheses"; the other four terms are "X parentheses". So, there are $\binom{6}{2}X^4Y^2$ terms, because there are $\binom{6}{2}$ ways to pick two $(X + Y)$ terms as Y parentheses. (What would have happened if, instead of counting the number of X^4Y^2 terms by counting the number of Y parentheses, you counted the number of X^4Y^2 terms by counting the number of X parentheses?) Similarly, there are $\binom{6}{5}XY^5$ terms, and in general,

$$(X + Y)^6 = \binom{6}{0}X^6 + \binom{6}{1}X^5Y + \binom{6}{2}X^4Y^2 +$$
$$\binom{6}{3}X^3Y^3 + \binom{6}{4}X^2Y^4 + \binom{6}{5}XY^5 + \binom{6}{6}Y^6$$

Exercise 8.1 Give a similar combinatorial proof of the general binomial theorem.

The fact that the $\binom{N}{K}$ show up as coefficients in the expansion of $(X + Y)^N$ is the reason that they are called binomial coefficients.

Exercise 8.2 In the binomial theorem, X and Y can be replaced by any expressions. So, for example,

$$(3X + 2Y)^6 = \sum_{K=0}^{6} \binom{6}{K}(3X)^{(6-K)}(2Y)^K$$

Write this out and simplify the coefficients. What is the sum of the coefficients? How could you have predicted this by simply looking at the expression $(3X + 2Y)^6$?

Of course, the binomial theorem also applies to differences as well as to sums, so

$$(2X - Y)^6 = (2X + (-Y))^6 = \sum_{K=0}^{6} \binom{6}{K}(2X)^{(6-K)}(-Y)^K$$

$$= \sum_{K=0}^{6} (-1)^K (2X)^{(6-K)} Y^K$$

What is the sum of the following coefficients? Why?

$$\binom{6}{0}(2X)^6 - \binom{6}{1}(2X)^5 Y + \binom{6}{2}(2X)^4 Y^2 - \binom{6}{3}(2X)^3 Y^3 +$$

$$\binom{6}{4}(2X)^2 Y^4 - \binom{6}{5}(2X) Y^5 + \binom{6}{6} Y^6$$

Project 8.3 This project applies the binomial theorem to the problem of project 7.14. The problem is to find a simple formula for

$$\text{ACC.H}(N, BASE) = \sum_{K=0}^{N} \binom{N}{K}(BASE)^K$$

For example, theorem 7.11 says that

$$\sum_{K=0}^{N} \binom{N}{K} = 2^N$$

Another way to see this is to use the binomial theorem:

$$2^N = (1+1)^N = \sum_{K=0}^{N} \binom{N}{K} 1^{(N-K)} 1^K$$

$$= \sum_{K=0}^{N} \binom{N}{K}$$

Here is yet another example:

$$0 = (1-1)^N = \sum_{K=0}^{N} \binom{N}{K} 1^{(N-K)} (-1)^K$$

$$= \sum_{K=0}^{N} (-1)^K \binom{N}{K}$$

$$= \binom{N}{0} - \binom{N}{1} + \binom{N}{2} - \binom{N}{3} + \binom{N}{4} - \cdots + (-1)N \binom{N}{N}$$

So the alternating sum of any row of Pascal's triangle is 0.

Generalize the above two arguments so that you can use the binomial theorem to justify your formula for ACC.H.

Project 8.4 Let's return again to project 5.22. We had a sequence of functions F_N defined by

$$F_0(M) = 1 \text{ for all } M, \text{ and for } N > 0$$

$$F_N(M) = \sum_{K=0}^{M} F_{(N-1)}(K)$$

Suppose we "weight" the sum using the binomial coefficients as weights; that is, we define

$$F_0(M) = 1 \text{ for all } M, \text{ and for } N > 0$$

$$F_N(M) = \sum_{K=0}^{M} \binom{M}{K} F_{(N-1)}(K)$$

Just as in project 5.22, to model the situation in Logo, we consider a function S of two inputs so that $S(N, M) = F_N(M)$:

```
TO S :N :M
 IF :N = 0 [OP 1]
 OP SIGMA "Q (SE :N - 1 :M) 0 :M
END

TO Q :N :M :X
 OP (B :M :X) * (S :N :X)
END
```

1. How can this work? S is defined in terms of Q, and Q is defined in terms of S.

2. Why does $S(N, M) = F_N(M)$ for all N and M?

3. Can you eliminate the need for Q? That is, can you define S so that it only calls B and (perhaps) SIGMA?

4. Find a simple formula for $S(N, M)$ by tabulating S (you'll have to use the generalized TAB that tabulates functions of two inputs against one of the inputs), and use project 8.3, the binomial theorem, or anything else to prove that your formula is correct.

Project 8.5 Suppose we modify the functions in the previous project by defining

$$F_0(M) = M \text{ for all } M, \text{ and for } N > 0$$

$$F_N(M) = \sum_{K=0}^{M} \binom{M}{K} F_{(N-1)}(K)$$

Write out the expression for the first few F's. For example,

$$F_1(M) = \sum_{K=0}^{M} \binom{M}{K} K$$

$$= 0\binom{M}{0} + 1\binom{M}{1} + 2\binom{M}{2} + \cdots + M\binom{M}{M}$$

Build a Logo model of the function S so that $S(N, M) = F_N(M)$, and find a closed form for S. Prove that your simple formula is correct. Modify your

Logo model by changing the base function F_0 (or $S(0, M)$) while keeping the inductive relation

$$F_N(M) = \sum_{K=0}^{M} \binom{M}{K} F_{(N-1)}(K)$$

the same. Can you get some interesting results?

Experiment 8.6 Experiment with the following function:

```
TO G :N
 OP (N + 1) * (SIGMA "W :N 0 :N)
END

TO W :M :L
 OP (B :M :L) / (:L + 1)
END
```

Write out an expression for G without using SIGMA (in both Logo and mathematics). Find a closed form for G. Prove that your formula is correct. Hint: if you use the binomial theorem, you might want to use facts like

$$\binom{N+1}{K} = \frac{N+1}{N+1-K} \binom{N}{K}$$

which follow easily from the model 3 version of B (the one that uses factorials).

Project 8.7 The only real number whose fifth power is 1 is 1. However, imagine a number system in which there are other numbers that satisfy the equation

$$X^5 - 1 = 0$$

besides 1. Suppose that P is such a number. That is, P is not 1 but $P^5 = 1$. What would the value of

$$\sum_{K=0}^{4} \binom{5}{K} (P-1)^K$$

be? Why is it difficult to interpret this expression if $P = 1$?

#**Experiment 8.8** In the spirit of project 5.22, suppose we define

$$F_0(M) = 2^M$$

and

$$F_N(M) \sum_{K=0}^{M} F_{(N-1)}(K)$$

A Logo model for this function sequence is

```
TO S :N :M
 IF :N = 0 [OP POWER 2 :M]
 OP SIGMA "S :N-1 1 :M
END
```

Find a simple formula for S.

Project 8.9 Consider the following functions:

```
TO F :N
 OP SIGMA "D [] 1 :N
END

TO G :N
 OP SIGMA "D1 :N 1 :N
END

TO D :K
 OP POWER 3 :K
END

TO D1 :N :K
 OP (B :N :K) * (POWER 3 :K)
END
```

What is the difference between F and G? Establish an inequality between F and G, and prove that your inequality is correct. (Hint: Use the binomial theorem, the cyclotomic identity, and mathematical induction.)

Chapter 9

Application 3: Locks and Partitions

In this chapter, we'll consider two problems with closely related solutions.

We will also expand our use of Logo in a somewhat different direction. Until now we have been using Logo procedures to model mathematical functions whose inputs and outputs are numbers. In this chapter we'll want to look at other kinds of mathematical objects (like sets), and we'll study functions whose inputs and outputs are these more general creatures. This means that we'll make more extensive use of Logo's list-processing functions; if you see something unfamiliar, refer to the appendix.

Mathematics has grown enormously over the past two centuries. One reason for this growth is the widespread use of higher-order functions (like SIGMA) that capture the similarities among many special functions. Another reason is the use of general data objects as domains for functions. It takes a little effort to get used to the idea of a function that takes, for example, a collection of sets as input and produces another collection of sets as output, but the payoff (in intellectual satisfaction alone) is worth the trouble. The end result of this march toward higher degrees of procedural and data abstraction is the actual removal of the distinction between functions and the objects they work on.

Back to our two problems. Brian Harvey told me about the first problem, and my first incorrect solution to it led to a solution of the second problem. Brian's "Simplex lock" problem is this (see Harvey 1987 for a somewhat different treatment of the problem):

The Simplex company makes a door lock with five buttons numbered 1, 2, 3, 4, and 5. The lock is opened by the correct sequence of pushes, and a "push" is a set of buttons that are depressed together. Here are six possible combinations:

1. [[1] [2 3] [5]]
2. [[2 3] [1] [5]]
3. [[1] [2 3] [4] [5]]
4. [[1] [2 3 4] [5]]
5. [[1] [2] [3] [4] [5]]
6. [[1 2 3 4 5]]

I've represented each combination as a list of pushes; each push is represented as a sublist of the combination. Note that the combination in example 2 is different from the combination in example 1, but it's not different from [[3 2] [1] [5]], because both of these lists stand for the combination:

Push 2 and 3 together, then push 1, and then push 5

Notice also that a button can only be used once in a combination, and you don't have to use all five buttons in a combination.

Brian's problem is to find the number of possible combinations in a Simplex lock.

We'll work through several ways to look at the problem. Of course, the problem is interesting not because we want to gain entrance to locked rooms, but because the solution involves some very beautiful mathematics. Like many problems in mathematics, the answer isn't anywhere near as interesting as the ideas that lead up to the answer. So, if it seems like we are developing a great deal of machinery to use on such an unimportant problem, just remember that it's the machinery that we're really after; the problem is just an excuse to play.

After several false starts (one of them actually led somewhere, as we'll see at the end of this chapter), and after a couple letters to Brian, the following ideas emerged:

The number of possible combinations is a function of the number of buttons; you can easily imagine a lock with four buttons or with six buttons. Say, we let

LOCK(N) = the number of possible combinations in an N-button Simplex lock

Maybe we can relate LOCK(N) to LOCK($N - 1$). Just to be sure, we better look at some small values for N:

LOCK(0) = 1 (a lock with no buttons has only one combination: the door is always open)

LOCK(1) = 2 (a lock with one button has two possible combinations: the door is open, or push the single button)

If you try to calculate LOCK(2) and LOCK(3), you see that things get out of hand very quickly. Before you read on, try to find a strategy for calculating the outputs of LOCK. (If you put some time into this, the rest of the discussion will go much more smoothly, and you will probably find a way to calculate LOCK that is different from mine.)

(STOP)

Part of the complication lies in the fact that you don't have to use all the numbers from 1 to N in a combination for an N-button lock. Perhaps we should look a function that might be more tractable; let's set

> $S(N) =$ the number of possible combinations on an N-button Simplex lock that use all N buttons

So $S(0) = 1$ (why?), $S(1) = 1$ (why?). $S(2) = 3$ because there are three combinations on a two-button lock that use all 2 buttons; they are

$$[\ [1] \ [2] \ ], \ [\ [2] \ [1] \ ], \text{ and } [\ [2 \ 1] \ ]$$

Exercise 9.1 Figure out the value of $S(3)$ by counting combinations.

Here's an important insight: $S(N)$ doesn't depend on how you label the buttons. So in a five-button lock there are $S(2)$ ($= 3$) combinations that you can get from using exactly the buttons 1 and 4, and there are 3 more combinations that use the buttons 3 and 4. In fact there are $B(5, 2) \cdot S(2)$ (or 30) combinations that use exactly two buttons. Feel a theorem coming on?

Theorem 9.1

$$\text{LOCK}(N) = \sum_{K=0}^{N} \binom{N}{K} S(K)$$

Proof: Look at what this says for $N = 5$:

$$\text{LOCK}(5) = \binom{5}{0}S(0) + \binom{5}{1}S(1) + \binom{5}{2}S(2) + \binom{5}{3}S(3) + \binom{5}{4}S(4) + \binom{5}{5}S(5)$$

This counts the number of combinations on a 5-button lock by adding the number of combinations that use exactly 0 buttons, exactly 1 button, exactly 2 buttons, exactly 3 buttons, exactly 4 buttons, and exactly 5 buttons. The number of combinations that uses exactly 4 buttons, for example, is $B(5, 4) \cdot S(4)$

211

because, to build a 4-button combination, you must first pick 4 buttons to use (this can be done in B(5,4) ways) and then forming all combinations on these 4 buttons (this can be done in S(4) ways).

In general, in an N button lock you can calculate LOCK(N) by

1. picking a number K between 0 and N,

2. picking K buttons from the N buttons on the lock,

3. forming all possible combinations that use these buttons, and

4. adding all these answers as K goes from 0 to N.

Now, 2 can be done in B(N, K) ways and 3 can be done in S(K) ways, so we want to add the numbers B(N, K)·S(K) as K goes from 0 to N, and that's exactly what the statement of the theorem does.

The theorem looks pleasing, but all it does is express one function (LOCK) that we don't know in terms of another function (S) that we don't know. Still, the theorem will solve our problem if we find a way to calculate S, and S looks like it might be a little easier to deal with than LOCK (again, this is because in S the number of buttons is fixed, whereas in LOCK, you can use any number of buttons up to the number of buttons on the lock).

Generating the Combinations

One way to calculate S(N) is to actually generate the combinations that use all N buttons. Of course, as N grows, this becomes difficult, but maybe we can find an algorithm for generating the combinations that can be modeled in Logo. I'm about to describe one such algorithm, so close the book if you want to find a method for yourself.

Here's how I generated the combinations using Logo. Actually, I worked most of this out by hand because I wasn't near a computer at the time that I was working on the problem. Still, I thought about the problem in Logo, and when I finally got around to using a computer, my notes translated easily into actual Logo functions. Logo is not only a valuable tool for doing mathematical experiments; it's also a wonderful medium for expressing mathematical ideas.

First, I needed to represent the combinations in Logo. I've already told you how I did this. A push is a list:

[2 3 4] or [1] or [1 2]

Don't forget that [2 3 4] is the same push as [4 2 3]. A combination is just an ordered list of pushes:

[[1 2] [3 4]] or [[2 3] [5 6 7]] or [[ ]]

Of course, you can't tell by looking at a combination exactly how many buttons are in the lock, but this wasn't a problem because I wanted to calculate S (which counts the combinations that use all the buttons).

Finally, for a given N, I imagined the list of all combinations that use all N buttons; I called this COMB.LIST(N). For example, there are three combinations on a 2-button lock that use all the buttons:

[[1] [2]]

[[2] [1]]

[[1 2]]

So COMB.LIST(2) outputs

[[[1] [2]] [[2] [1]] [[1 2]]]

Similarly, COMB.LIST(1) is

[[[1]]]

and COMB.LIST(0) is

[[]]

S can easily be calculated once we know COMB.LIST:

```
TO S :N
 OP COUNT COMB.LIST :N
END
```

It seemed reasonable to try to compute `COMB.LIST` inductively, so I imagined a function `EXT` (for EXTend) that would take a combination in `COMB.LIST`(N) and produce a part of `COMB.LIST`$(N + 1)$. Of course, such a function `EXT` couldn't produce a single combination in `COMB.LIST`$(N + 1)$ because there are many more combinations in `COMB.LIST`$(N + 1)$ than in `COMB.LIST`(N). So I wanted `EXT` to take a combination in `COMB.LIST`(N) and to output a list of combinations in `COMB.LIST`$(N + 1)$.

Say, I take an element of `COMB.LIST`(2)

```
[ [1] [2] ]
```

How can I extend this to an element of `COMB.LIST`(3)? I have to throw in a 3, and there are five places to put it.

1. Before the first push: `[ [3] [1] [2] ]`
2. Before the second push: `[ [1] [3] [2] ]`
3. At the end of the whole combination: `[ [1] [2] [3] ]`
4. With the first push: `[ [3 1] [2] ]`
5. With the second push: `[ [1] [3 2] ]`

So `[ [1] [2] ]` EXTends to 5 elements of `COMB.LIST`(3), and

```
EXT ( [ [1] [2] ] ) =
```

```
[ [[3] [1] [2]] [[3 1] [2]] [[1] [3] [2]] [[1] [3 2]] [[1] [2] [3]] ]
```

Lists like this are difficult to read, so I often use `DISPLAY`

```
TO DISPLAY :L
 IF EMPTYP :L [STOP]
 SHOW FIRST :L
 DISPLAY BF :L
END
```

Then

```
DISPLAY [[[3] [1] [2]] [[3 1] [2]] [[1] [3] [2]] →
        [[1] [3 2]] [[1] [2] [3]]]
```

prints out the following display:

```
[[3] [1] [2]]
[[3 1] [2]]
[[1] [3] [2]]
[[1] [3 2]]
[[1] [2] [3]]
```

My idea is simple. To EXT a combination, say, C', on $N - 1$ buttons, insert N as a separate push in all the "spaces" between the pushes (and at the front and back) in C', and then adjoin N to each push in C'. If C' contains K pushes, then it has $K + 1$ spaces, so EXT(C') will contain $2K + 1$ different combinations.

Notice that to calculate the EXT of a combination in COMB.LIST($N - 1$), I "inflate" each push in the combination in two ways:

1. I insert the single push [N] before the push.

2. I adjoin N to the buttons in the push.

Now, to build a Logo model for EXT, I wrote a function INFLATE that works on a single push:

```
TO INFLATE :TYPE :N :PUSH
 IF :TYPE = 1 [OP LIST (LIST :N) :PUSH]
 OP (LIST SE :N :PUSH)
END
```

INFLATE's first input is the type of inflation desired (1 or 2, as above); N is the number we want to inflate the push with, and *PUSH* is the push to be inflated:

```
SHOW INFLATE 1 4 [1 2]
```

produces

```
[ [4] [1 2] ]
```

and

```
SHOW INFLATE 2 4 [1 2]
```

produces

```
[ [4 1 2] ]
```

Next, I worked on the extension of a whole combination. The idea is to take a combination, say, [[1] [2 3] [4]], and to perform the following four steps:

1. Form the list of combinations that are obtained by inflating each push in the original combination using a type 1 inflation:

   [[[5][1] [2 3] [4]] [[1] [5][2 3] [4]] →
   [[1] [2 3] [5][4]]]

2. Form list of the single combination that is formed by adjoining the push [5] to the end of the combination:

   [[[1] [2 3] [4] [5]]]

3. Form the list of combinations that are obtained by inflating each push in the original combination using a type 2 inflation:

   [[[5 1] [2 3] [4]] [[1] [5 2 3] [4]] [[1] [2 3] [5 4]]]

4. Combine the results in the above three steps into a list:

   [[[5] [1] [2 3] [4]] [[1] [5] [2 3] [4]] →
   [[1] [2 3] [4] [5]] →
   [[5 1] [2 3] [4]] [[1] [5 2 3] [4]] [[1] [2 3] [5 4]]]

Let's call these four steps the EXT algorithm.

When speaking about combinations, I prefer the more suggestive name LENGTH to COUNT, so

```
TO LENGTH :COMB
 OP COUNT :COMB
END
```

For example,

```
SHOW LENGTH [ [1 2] [3] [4 5] ]
```

produces 3.

This next function EXTENDS a combination in COMB.LIST(N) to a list of combinations in COMB.LIST($N+1$). It INFLATEs each push using either a type 1 or a type 2 inflation (so it accomplishes both strategies 1 and 3):

```
TO EXTEND :TYPE :N :COMB
 OP EXPAND :TYPE :N :COMB  1
END

TO EXPAND :TYPE :N :COMB :PLACE
 IF :PLACE > LENGTH :COMB [OP []]
 OP FPUT (SETITEM :PLACE :COMB (INFLATE :TYPE :N →
      (ITEM :PLACE :COMB))) EXPAND :TYPE :N :COMB :PLACE + 1
END
```

The inputs to EXPAND are the type of inflation to be performed to each push, the number that will be used in the inflation (the new button), the combination to be inflated, and a counter, *PLACE*, that starts with 1 and increases by 1 with each call to EXTEND; *PLACE* marks the push that is currently being inflated. The *PLACE* element of COMB is replaced with its inflation, and the resulting combination is adjoined to the front of the output list. (SETITEM(M, OB, L) outputs the list obtained by replacing the Mth item of L with OB; if your Logo doesn't have a SETITEM, write one (or see the appendix). This is an interesting exercise in list processing.) The finished product behaves like this:

```
DISPLAY EXTEND 1 5 [ [1] [2 3] [4]]

[[5] [1] [2 3] [4]]
[[1] [5] [2 3] [4]]
[[1] [2 3] [5] [4]]
```

```
DISPLAY EXTEND 2 5 [ [1] [2 3] [4]]

[[5 1] [2 3] [4]]
[[1] [5 2 3] [4]]
[[1] [2 3] [5 4]]
```

Finally, EXT forms a list from three lists of combinations:

1. From the type 1 extension of COMB

2. From the list of the single combination obtained by adjoining [N] to the end of COMB

3. From the type 2 extension of COMB

So EXT models step 4 of the EXT algorithm

```
TO EXT :N :COMB
 OP (SE (EXTEND 1 :N :COMB) (LIST (LPUT (LIST :N) :COMB)) →
         (EXTEND 2 :N :COMB))
END
```

EXT acts like this:

```
DISPLAY EXT 5 [[1] [2 3] [4]]

[[5] [1] [2 3] [4]]
[[1] [5] [2 3] [4]]
[[1] [2 3] [5] [4]]
[[1] [2 3] [4] [5]]
[[5 1] [2 3] [4]]
[[1] [5 2 3] [4]]
[[1] [2 3] [5 4]]
```

The rest is much easier. When speaking about lists of combinations, let's use the names FIRST.COMB and REST.COMBS to talk about the first combination in the list and the list of all but the first combination:

```
TO FIRST.COMB :L
 OP FIRST :L
END

TO REST.COMBS :L
 OP BF :L
END
```

These conventions allow us to think about lists of combinations rather than about lists of lists.

INDUCE takes a new button and a list of combinations and outputs the new list of combinations obtained by applying EXT to each combination in the list:

```
TO INDUCE :N :COMBLIST
 IF EMPTYP :COMBLIST [OP []]
 OP SE (EXT :N FIRST.COMB :COMBLIST) →
       INDUCE :N REST.COMBS :COMBLIST
END
```

Finally, we can INDUCE COMB.LIST($N - 1$) to COMB.LIST(N):

```
TO COMB.LIST :N
 IF :N = 0 [OP [[]] ]
 IF :N = 1 [OP [[[1]]] ]
 OP INDUCE :N COMB.LIST :N - 1
END
```

Watch how it generates one COMB.LIST from the previous one:

DISPLAY COMB.LIST 3

```
[[3] [2] [1]]
[[2] [3] [1]]
[[2] [1] [3]]
[[3 2] [1]]
[[2] [3 1]]
[[3] [1] [2]]
[[1] [3] [2]]
[[1] [2] [3]]
[[3 1] [2]]
[[1] [3 2]]
[[3] [2 1]]
[[2 1] [3]]
[[3 2 1]]
```

DISPLAY COMB.LIST 4

```
[[4] [3] [2] [1]]
[[3] [4] [2] [1]]
[[3] [2] [4] [1]]
[[3] [2] [1] [4]]
[[4 3] [2] [1]]
[[3] [4 2] [1]]
[[3] [2] [4 1]]
[[4] [2] [3] [1]]
[[2] [4] [3] [1]]
[[2] [3] [4] [1]]
[[2] [3] [1] [4]]
[[4 2] [3] [1]]
[[2] [4 3] [1]]
[[2] [3] [4 1]]
[[4] [2] [1] [3]]
```

```
[[2] [4] [1] [3]]
[[2] [1] [4] [3]]
[[2] [1] [3] [4]]
[[4 2] [1] [3]]
[[2] [4 1] [3]]
[[2] [1] [4 3]]
[[4] [3 2] [1]]
[[3 2] [4] [1]]
[[3 2] [1] [4]]
[[4 3 2] [1]]
[[3 2] [4 1]]
[[4] [2] [3 1]]
[[2] [4] [3 1]]
[[2] [3 1] [4]]
[[4 2] [3 1]]
[[2] [4 3 1]]
[[4] [3] [1] [2]]
[[3] [4] [1] [2]]
[[3] [1] [4] [2]]
[[3] [1] [2] [4]]
[[4 3] [1] [2]]
[[3] [4 1] [2]]
[[3] [1] [4 2]]
[[4] [1] [3] [2]]
[[1] [4] [3] [2]]
[[1] [3] [4] [2]]
[[1] [3] [2] [4]]
[[4 1] [3] [2]]
[[1] [4 3] [2]]
[[1] [3] [4 2]]
[[4] [1] [2] [3]]
[[1] [4] [2] [3]]
[[1] [2] [4] [3]]
[[1] [2] [3] [4]]
[[4 1] [2] [3]]
[[1] [4 2] [3]]
[[1] [2] [4 3]]
[[4] [3 1] [2]]
[[3 1] [4] [2]]
[[3 1] [2] [4]]
```

```
[[4 3 1] [2]]
[[3 1] [4 2]]
[[4] [1] [3 2]]
[[1] [4] [3 2]]
[[1] [3 2] [4]]
[[4 1] [3 2]]
[[1] [4 3 2]]
[[4] [3] [2 1]]
[[3] [4] [2 1]]
[[3] [2 1] [4]]
[[4 3] [2 1]]
[[3] [4 2 1]]
[[4] [2 1] [3]]
[[2 1] [4] [3]]
[[2 1] [3] [4]]
[[4 2 1] [3]]
[[2 1] [4 3]]
[[4] [3 2 1]]
[[3 2 1] [4]]
[[4 3 2 1]]
```

You can see how each combination is EXTended, and you can even trace how each push is INFLATEd.

Well, we have a Logo model for S; S(N) simply counts the number of combinations in COMB.LIST(N). Calculating S(N) takes a great deal of time, and using this version of S to calculate the outputs of LOCK (by theorem 9.1) would take even longer. LOCK(N) is the weighted sum of the S(K) as K goes from 0 to N, and the weights are the binomial coefficients (whose calculation involves even more computation). Still, this version of S works, and you can use it (if you are patient) to investigate the Simplex lock problem.

Even though our version of S calculates S's outputs by brute force, there is a glimmer of elegance in our blueprint for extending COMB.LIST($N - 1$) to COMB.LIST(N). It turns out that the EXT algorithm (and mathematical induction) can be used to construct a beautiful version of S that counts the combinations without actually listing them.

Counting the Combinations

We've seen that if C' is a combination on $N - 1$ buttons, then the number of extensions of C' to a combination on N buttons is one more than twice the number of pushes in C'. The way we have represented combinations in Logo lends itself to an easy method for counting pushes. If C' is

```
[ [1 2] [3 4 5] [6] [7 8] ]
```

then the number of pushes in C' is just the LENGTH of C' (in our case, it is 4).

Suppose, for the sake of example, that N is 4 and we want to calculate S(4); instead of counting up each of the 75 combinations in COMB.LIST(4), we could run through COMB.LIST(3) (only 13 combinations), calculate

$$2 \cdot \text{LENGTH}(C') + 1$$

for each combination C' in the list (this is the number of extensions that C' has in COMB.LIST(4)), and add the results. We have been using $N = 4$ as the number of buttons, but our idea is perfectly general. In other words, to calculate S(N), we could use this model:

```
TO NEW.S :N
 OP S.HELPER :N COMB.LIST :N - 1
END

TO S.HELPER :N :L
 IF EMPTYP :L [OP 0]
 OP 2 * (LENGTH FIRST.COMB :L) + 1 + S.HELPER :N REST.COMBS :L
END
```

Try it. Is it faster than the old model for S?

Let's generalize this idea a bit. First of all, there is a similarity between S and NEW.S if you look at things in the right light; NEW.S adds up $2 \cdot \text{LENGTH}(C) + 1$ for each C in COMB.LIST($N - 1$), and S can be viewed as a function that adds up a "1" for each C in COMB.LIST(N). More precisely, if you evaluate the function

```
TO G :X
 OP 2 * :X + 1
END
```

at the length of each combination in `COMB.LIST(3)` and add the outputs, you get the same thing as if you evaluate the function

```
TO ONE :X
  OP 1
END
```

at the length of each combination in `COMB.LIST(4)`. Both calculations give you S(4) or 75.

The similarity between these two calculations is that in both cases, you sum the outputs of a function not as the inputs grow from A to B but as the inputs run over a set that is indexed by the elements of a list (in this case, the inputs are the lengths of the combinations in a list of combinations). These kind of general summations ("summations over a set" rather than "summations over an interval") come up very often in mathematics. A general purpose list summer is given in the appendix, but here we want something even *more* specialized. Let's write a Logo model that captures the similarity between the summations used above. While we're at it, we might as well allow the function that we sum to take more than one input

```
TO SIGMA.L :F :EXTRA :LIST.OF.COMBS
  IF EMPTYP :LIST.OF.COMBS [OP 0]
  OP (APPLY :F SE :EXTRA (LENGTH FIRST.COMB :LIST.OF.COMBS)) →
      + ( SIGMA.L :F :EXTRA REST.COMBS :LIST.OF.COMBS )
END
```

The mathematical notation for this kind of summation is

$$\text{SIGMA.L}(F, E, L) = \sum_{C \in L} \text{F}(E, \text{LENGTH}(C))$$

You read this "the sum of $\text{F}(E, \text{LENGTH}(C))$ as C ranges over L."

Using this abstraction, we can express `S` and `NEW.S` from a single point of view:

Theorem 9.2 The following two functions are equal on $\mathbf{Z}^+$:

```
TO S :N
 OP SIGMA.L "ONE [] COMB.LIST :N
END

TO NEW.S :N
 OP SIGMA.L "G [] COMB.LIST :N - 1
END
```

The advantage of **NEW.S**, of course, is that it is a summation over a much smaller list than the list involved in the calculation of S. Can we reduce the work even more? Let's try to calculate $S(N)$ as a sum over the lengths of the combinations in COMB.LIST$(N-2)$.

We can calculate $S(N)$ by summing **ONE** over the lengths of the combinations COMB.LIST(N) or by summing G over the lengths of the combinations in COMB.LIST$(N-1)$. Now, each combination in COMB.LIST$(N-1)$ is an extension of some combination in COMB.LIST$(N-2)$. Suppose that C is a combination in COMB.LIST$(N-1)$, and suppose that C is an extension of some C' in COMB.LIST$(N-2)$. Since we want to add up the outputs of

```
G(LENGTH(C))
```

over COMB.LIST$(N-1)$ by looking at the various C's in COMB.LIST$(N-2)$, we should compare the lengths of C and C'. The relation is simple:

If C is obtained from C' by inserting the new push $[N-1]$ (as in steps 1 and 2 of the **EXT** algorithm), then

$$\text{LENGTH}(C) = \text{LENGTH}(C') + 1$$

whereas if C is obtained from C' by throwing $N-1$ into an already existing push of C' (as in part 3 of the **EXT** algorithm), then

$$\text{LENGTH}(C) = \text{LENGTH}(C')$$

Let's break **EXT**(C') into two sublists:

> **EXT!**(C') is the list of extensions of C' in which the length goes up by 1.

> **EXT!!**(C') is the list of extensions of C' in which the length stays the same.

If you look at our Logo model for EXT:

```
TO EXT :N :COMB
 OP (SE (EXTEND 1 :N :COMB) (LIST (LPUT (LIST :N) :COMB)) →
        (EXTEND 2 :N :COMB))
END
```

EXT!(C') comes from

"EXTEND 1 :N :COMB"   and   "LIST (LPUT (LIST :N) :COMB"

but EXT!!(C') comes from

"EXTEND 2 :N :COMB"

As a specific example, if C' is

[[1 2] [3]]

then EXT!(C') is

[[[4] [1 2] [3]] [[1 2] [4] [3]] [[1 2] [3] [4]]]

and EXT!!(C') is

[[[4 1 2] [3]] [[1 2] [3 4]]]

Because C' has one more "space" than its length, we see that

$$\text{COUNT}(\text{EXT!}(C')) = \text{LENGTH}(C') + 1$$

There are also as many type 2 extensions of C' as there are pushes in C', so

$$\text{COUNT}(\text{EXT!!}(C')) = \text{LENGTH}(C')$$

Notice that I use COUNT when I talk about the number of combinations in EXT!(C') or EXT!!(C') because these things are lists of combinations (LENGTH is reserved for the combinations themselves.)

Now, we want to add up the outputs of G over the lengths of the combinations in COMB.LIST$(N - 1)$. That is, we want to calculate

$$\sum_{C \in \text{COMB.LIST}(N-1)} G(\text{LENGTH}(C))$$

Since every combination in COMB.LIST$(N-1)$ is either in an EXT!(C') or in an EXT!!(C') for some C' in COMB.LIST$(N-2)$, we can calculate the above sum by the following method:

1. For each C' in COMB.LIST$(N-2)$, calculate EXT!(C') and EXT!!(C') (this gives two lists for each C').

2. Calculate the sum of the G$((\text{LENGTH}(C))$ over each of these lists (this gives two numbers for each C').

3. Add these numbers over all C's in COMB.LIST$(N-2)$.

In other words, we'll calculate

$$\sum_{C \in \text{COMB.LIST}(N-1)} G(\text{LENGTH}(C))$$

using this identity:

$$\sum_{C \in \text{COMB.LIST}(N-1)} G(\text{LENGTH}(C))$$

$$= \sum_{C' \in \text{COMB.LIST}(N-2)} \left(\sum_{C \in \text{EXT!}(C')} G(\text{LENGTH}(C)) + \sum_{C \in \text{EXT!!}(C')} G(\text{LENGTH}(C)) \right)$$

which is the sum of two "double sums,"

$$\sum_{C' \in \text{COMB.LIST}(N-2)} \sum_{C \in \text{EXT!}(C')} G(\text{LENGTH}(C))$$

and

$$\sum_{C' \in \text{COMB.LIST}(N-2)} \sum_{C \in \text{EXT!!}(C')} G(\text{LENGTH}(C))$$

Let's call these two sums the "contributions" from EXT! and EXT!!.

Just in case this isn't perfectly clear, let's work it out in some detail. Suppose that $N = 5$ so that $N - 1 = 4$ and $N - 2 = 3$.

First, let's look at the contribution of EXT!

If C' is [[3] [2] [1]], then EXT!(C') is

[[[4] [3] [2] [1]] [[3] [4] [2] [1]] [[3] [2] [4] [1]] [[3] [2] [1] [4]]]

Each of these combinations has length 4 (1 more than the length of C'), so G outputs $2 \cdot 4 + 1 = 9$ on the length of each of them; this list contributes $4 \cdot 9$ or 36 to the calculation.

Similarly, we'll get 36 when we sum over the lengths of the combinations in the EXT! of [[2] [3] [1]], of [[3] [1] [2]], of [[1] [3] [2]], of [[1] [2] [3]], and of [[2] [1] [3]]. This is because these combinations have length 3, so the elements of their EXT!'s each have length 4 (causing G to output 9). Also the length 3 causes each EXT! to contain 4 combinations, and this forces the sum over each EXT! to be $4 \cdot 9$ or 36.

Suppose that C' is [[3 2] [1]]. Then EXT!(C') is

[[[4] [3 2] [1]] [[3 2] [4] [1]] [[3 2] [1] [4]]]

Each of these combinations has length 3 (1 more than the length of C'), so G outputs $2 \cdot 3 + 1 = 7$ on the length of each of them; this list contributes $3 \cdot 7$ or 21 to the calculation.

Similarly, we'll get 21 when we sum over the lengths of the combinations in the EXT! of [[2] [3 1]], of [[3 1] [2]], of [[1] [3 2]], of [[3] [2 1]], and of [[2 1] [3]]. This is because these combinations have length 2, so the elements of their EXT!'s each have length 3 (causing G to output 7). Also the length 2 causes each EXT! to contain 3 combinations, and this forces the sum over each EXT! to be $3 \cdot 7$ or 21.

The only C' we haven't considered is [[3 2 1]], and because it has length 1, the combinations in its EXT! have length 2, causing G to output 5. There are also 2 combinations in its EXT!, contributing $2 \cdot 5$ or 10 to the calculation.

In this example, then, EXT! contributes 352 to the calculation of S(5) (I get this from adding up all the 36's, 21's, and the 10). What's more important is that a pattern emerges that allows us to calculate the contribution of any EXT!. Notice that for any C' in COMB.LIST(3), any combination in EXT!(C') has length 1 more than LENGTH(C'). So the contribution from EXT!

$$\sum_{C' \in \text{COMB.LIST}(3)} \sum_{C \in \text{EXT!}(C')} \text{G}(\text{LENGTH}(C))$$

can be written like this:

$$\sum_{C' \in \text{COMB.LIST}(3)} \sum_{C \in \text{EXT!}(C')} \text{G}(\text{LENGTH}(C') + 1)$$

Now, this inner sum just adds up the same number (namely, $\text{G}(\text{LENGTH}(C') + 1)$) once for each C in $\text{EXT!}(C')$; in other words, the inner sum is just

$$(\text{COUNT}(\text{EXT!}(C')))(\text{G}(\text{LENGTH}(C') + 1))$$

But we have seen that the COUNT of $\text{EXT!}(C')$ is also equal to

$$\text{LENGTH}(C') + 1$$

because there are this many "spaces" in C' that can hold the extra push. This means that the contribution of EXT! to our calculation is

$$\sum_{C' \in \text{COMB.LIST}(3)} (\text{LENGTH}(C') + 1)(\text{G}(\text{LENGTH}(C') + 1))$$

You should work this out by hand. Write down the 13 combinations in COMB.LIST(3), and for each combination C', calculate

$$(\text{LENGTH}(C') + 1)(\text{G}(\text{LENGTH}(C') + 1))$$

Then add up all these numbers. You 'll get 352.

How about EXT!!? The same kind of analysis can be used; here's a sketch of the details:

Suppose that C' is [[3] [2] [1]]. Then $\text{EXT!!}(C')$ is

[[[4 3] [2] [1]] [[3] [4 2] [1]] [[3] [2] [4 1]]]

each of these combinations has length 3 (the same as the length of C'), so G outputs $2 \cdot 3 + 1 = 7$ on the length of each of them; this list contributes $3 \cdot 7$ or 21 to the calculation.

Similarly, we'll get 21 when we sum over the lengths of the combinations in the EXT!! of [[2] [3] [1]], of [[3] [1] [2]], of [[1] [3] [2]], of [[1] [2] [3]], and of [[2] [1] [3]]. This is because these combinations have length 3, so the elements of their EXT!!'s each have length 3 (causing G to output 7). Also the length 3 causes each **EXT!!** to contain 3 combinations, and this forces the sum over each **EXT!!** to be $3 \cdot 7$ or 21.

The other cases are the same. If a C' has length K, the combinations in **EXT!!**(C') also have length K, and there are precisely K combinations in **EXT!!**(C'). So the contribution of **EXT!!**

$$\sum_{C' \in \text{COMB.LIST}(3)} \sum_{C \in \text{EXT!!}(C')} \text{G(LENGTH}(C))$$

can be simplified to

$$\sum_{C' \in \text{COMB.LIST}(3)} \sum_{C \in \text{EXT!!}(C')} \text{G(LENGTH}(C'))$$

which is the same as

$$\sum_{C' \in \text{COMB.LIST}(3)} \text{COUNT(EXT!!}(C')) \text{ G(LENGTH}(C))$$

and since $\text{COUNT(EXT!!}(C')) = \text{LENGTH}(C')$, this becomes

$$\sum_{C' \in \text{COMB.LIST}(3)} \text{LENGTH}(C') \cdot \text{G(LENGTH}(C'))$$

If you work this out by hand, you'll get 189. (This means that S(5) is $189 + 352$ or 541, but you probably knew that already.)

Putting the contributions of **EXT!** and **EXT!!** together, we see that S(5) is

$$\sum_{C' \in \text{COMB.LIST}(3)} (\text{LENGTH}(C') + 1)(\text{G(LENGTH}(C') + 1)) +$$

$$\sum_{C' \in \text{COMB.LIST}(3)} (\text{LENGTH}(C'))(\text{G(LENGTH}(C'))) =$$

$$\sum_{C' \in \text{COMB.LIST}(3)} (\text{LENGTH}(C'))(\text{G(LENGTH}(C'))) + (\text{LENGTH}(C')+1)(\text{G(LENGTH}(C')+1))$$

There is nothing special about the number 5 here; I used it simply as an example to keep the notation down. You should convince yourself that the contributions of **EXT!** and **EXT!!** are calculated in exactly the same way for 6 buttons, or for any number of buttons. In other words,

Theorem 9.3 S(N) is given by

$$\sum_{C' \in \text{COMB.LIST}(N-2)} (\text{LENGTH}(C'))(\text{G}(\text{LENGTH}(C')))+(\text{LENGTH}(C')+1)(\text{G}(\text{LENGTH}(C')+1))$$

Project 9.2 Carefully prove this theorem. Hint: Mimic the above derivation for $N = 5$. Use the fact that

$$S(N) = \sum_{C \in \text{COMB.LIST}(N-1)} \text{G}(\text{LENGTH}(C))$$

and break this up into a contribution from EXT! and EXT!!.

Notice that if I define G_2 like this:

```
TO G2 :X
 OP :X * (G :X) + (:X + 1) * G(:X + 1)
END
```

then theorem 9.3 says that S can be modeled as

```
TO S :N
 OP SIGMA.L "G2 [] COMB.LIST :N - 2
END
```

So we have three methods for modeling S:

```
TO S :N
 OP SIGMA.L "ONE [] COMB.LIST :N
END
```

and

```
TO S :N
 OP SIGMA.L "G [] COMB.LIST :N - 1
END
```

and

```
TO S :N
 OP SIGMA.L "G2 [] COMB.LIST :N - 2
END
```

Can we find a function G_3 so that S can be defined as

```
TO S :N
 OP SIGMA.L "G3 [] COMB.LIST :N - 3
END
```

Yes. Look carefully at the above discussion that outlined a method for reducing the

```
SIGMA.L "G [] COMB.LIST :N - 1
```

model to the

```
SIGMA.L "G2 [] COMB.LIST :N - 2
```

model.

The most important things to notice are that we never once used any special property of G (except that it was a function), and we never assumed anything special about N (except that it was a positive integer). The argument works fine if N is 5, 6, or 234. And the argument works fine if G is any function at all; G could be defined like this:

```
TO G :X
 OP 3 * :X - 2
END
```

or like this:

```
TO G :X
 OP 5 * (POWER :X 3) + 4 * (POWER :X 2) + 12
END
```

or (as we used it above) like this:

```
TO G :X
 OP 2 * :X + 1
END
```

As long as we define G_2 as

```
TO G2 :X
 OP :X * (G :X) + (:X + 1) * G(:X + 1)
END
```

then the discussion shows that typing

SHOW SIGMA.L "G [] COMB.LIST 8

will produce the same thing as typing

SHOW SIGMA.L "G2 [] COMB.LIST 7

In general, we have

Theorem 9.4 If G is any function, and G′ is defined as

```
TO G' :X
 OP :X * (G :X) + (:X + 1) * G (:X + 1)
END
```

Then the following two functions are equal on $\mathbf{Z}^+$:

```
TO T :N
 OP SIGMA.L "G [] COMB.LIST :N
END
```

and

```
TO NEW.T :N
 OP SIGMA.L "G' [] COMB.LIST :N - 1
END
```

The proof really is contained in the special case that we worked out; it amounts to looking at the sum over $\text{COMB.LIST}(N)$ as a sum over the EXTensions of combinations in $\text{COMB.LIST}(N-1)$.

Before moving up one level of abstraction, let's clean up one detail. We know that the following calls produce the same output:

1. SIGMA.L "ONE [] COMB.LIST 6

2. SIGMA.L "G [] COMB.LIST 5

By theorem 9.4, a call to SIGMA.L "ONE [] COMB.LIST 6 is the same as a call to SIGMA.L "Q [] COMB.LIST 5 where Q is defined as

```
TO Q :X
 OP :X * (ONE :X) + (:X + 1) * (ONE :X + 1)
END
```

Exercise 9.3 Prove that Q = G. Hint: What is ONE(*anything*)?

Theorem 9.4 gives us a general method for calculating $S(N)$; it says that we can model S like this:

```
TO S :N
 OP ...
END
```

where the "..." can be replaced by any of the following lines:

```
SIGMA.L "ONE [] COMB.LIST :N
```

or

```
SIGMA.L "G [] COMB.LIST :N - 1
```

or

```
SIGMA.L "G2 [] COMB.LIST :N - 2
```

or

```
SIGMA.L "G3 [] COMB.LIST :N - 3
```

where G_3 is defined as

```
TO G3 :X
 OP :X * (G2 :X) + (:X + 1) * (G2 :X + 1)
END
```

In fact we can keep reducing the input to COMB.LIST by 1 while we transform the function in a certain way.

The notion of "transforming the function in a certain way" can be made precise with a higher-order function. I call this higher-order function PSI (this is how you say the Greek letter that I've used to name it), and PSI looks like this:

```
TO PSI :F :E :X
 OP (:X * APPLY :F SE :E :X) + (:X + 1) →
              * (APPLY :F SE :E :X + 1)
END
```

Notice that I allow PSI to work on functions that take some extra inputs. If you ignore the extra inputs, you can think of PSI(G) as the function that takes X to

$$X(\mathsf{G}(X)) + (X+1)\mathsf{G}(X+1)$$

So we can define all our functions like this:

```
TO G :X
 OP PSI "ONE [] :X
END

TO G1 :X
 OP PSI "G [] :X
END

TO G2 :X
 OP PSI "G1 [] :X
END

TO G3 :X
 OP PSI "G2 [] :X
END

TO G4 :X
 OP PSI "G3 [] :X
END
```

and so on. We have a sequence of functions on our hands; as usual, we'll represent the sequence as a function of two inputs:

```
TO G :N :X
 IF :N = 0 [OP ONE :X]
 OP PSI "G :N - 1 :X
END
```

We can summarize our results in a particularly elegant form:

Theorem 9.5 S can be modeled as

```
TO S :N
 OP ...
END
```

where the "..." can be replaced with any of the following:

```
SIGMA.L "G 0 COMB.LIST :N
SIGMA.L "G 1 COMB.LIST :N - 1
SIGMA.L "G 2 COMB.LIST :N - 2
SIGMA.L "G 3 COMB.LIST :N - 3
SIGMA.L "G 4 COMB.LIST :N - 4
SIGMA.L "G 5 COMB.LIST :N - 5
                    ⋮
SIGMA.L "G :N COMB.LIST :N - :N
```

This tells us that we can calculate $S(N)$ by summing more complicated functions over smaller and smaller lists. You should try it out to see how real the savings in time is when you reduce the input to COMB.LIST by 1. For example, try these calls:

```
SHOW SIGMA.L "G 0 COMB.LIST 5
SHOW SIGMA.L "G 1 COMB.LIST 4
SHOW SIGMA.L "G 2 COMB.LIST 3
SHOW SIGMA.L "G 3 COMB.LIST 2
SHOW SIGMA.L "G 4 COMB.LIST 1
SHOW SIGMA.L "G 5 COMB.LIST 0
```

Notice that the last one is very fast.

In general, we can model S as

```
TO S :N
 OP SIGMA.L "G :N COMB.LIST 0
END
```

But COMB.LIST(0) is just [[]]; it has one combination and the length of that combination is 0. This means that

```
SIGMA.L "G :N COMB.LIST 0
```

can be replaced by "G :N 0," and this is one of my all time favorite results.

Theorem 9.6 The function S can be defined like this:

```
TO S :N
 OP G :N 0
END

TO G :N :X
 IF :N = 0 [OP 1]
 OP PSI "G :N - 1 :X
END

TO PSI :F :E :X
 OP (:X * APPLY :F SE :E :X) + (:X + 1) →
            * (APPLY :F SE :E :X + 1)
END
```

Try out this version of S. Tabulate S between 0 and, say, 10, and keep your table for future reference. The fact that such a simple function can quickly count the combinations in COMB.LIST(N) is just delightful, and it demonstrates the power of abstract methods in mathematics.

The function G is a wonderful topic for investigation; before we return to the Simplex lock problem, take some time to play with it. The next projects might give you some ideas.

Project 9.4 We used the function G above simply to calculate outputs for S. If N is any integer, $S(N) = G(N, 0)$. What about other inputs for G? There are at least 2 ways to look at this question: we can keep the second input to G constant and vary the first input, or we can keep the first input to G constant and vary the second input. Let's see what happens if we keep the second input constant and vary the first. Say, we tabulate $G(N, 1)$ for a few values of N. Does a new (and perhaps faster) definition for S emerge? Can you prove it? Hint: Look at the definition of PSI. It gives you the identity:

$$G(N, X) = X G(N - 1, X) + (X + 1) G(N - 1, X + 1)$$

#Can you find anything interesting in the tabulation of $G(N, 2)$? Of $G(N, 3)$?

Next, we can keep the first input to G constant and vary the second. Can you find a closed form for $G(1, X)$? For $G(2, X)$? For $G(3, X)$? Is there a pattern in these closed forms?

How about some identities involving G and S? For example, prove that for $N > 2$,

$$S(N + 1) = S(N) + 2(G(N - 1, 2))$$

Can you find other interesting facts?

Project 9.5 How do the $S(N)$'s grow? Can you estimate the size of $S(N)$ (say, between two consecutive powers of 10) without calculating $S(N)$? The $S(N)$'s are just the $G(N, 0)$'s. How fast do other outputs of G grow? For example, how fast do the $G(N, 2)$'s grow?

The Solution to the Lock Problem

Recall that LOCK(N) is the number of combinations on an N-button lock ($S(N)$ is the number of combinations that use all N buttons). We saw in theorem 9.1 that

$$\text{LOCK}(N) = \sum_{K=0}^{N} \binom{N}{K} S(K)$$

Exercise 9.6 Model LOCK in Logo.

If we compare the tabulations of LOCK and S, an interesting phenomenon arises:

N	$S(N)$	LOCK(N)
0	. . . 1	. . . 1
1	. . . 1	. . . 2
2	. . . 3	. . . 6
3	. . . 13	. . . 26
4	. . . 75	. . . 150
5	. . . 541	. . . 1082

By the way, we've solved the original Simplex lock problem; there are 1082 combinations.

It looks as if, for $N > 0$, LOCK(N) = 2S(N). Can you think of a reason why this might be so? Tabulate a bit more; it seems that something might be going on.

Let's work backward; that is, let's suppose that LOCK(N) is equal to 2S(N). Compare this to the result of theorem 9.1:

$$\text{LOCK}(N) = \sum_{K=0}^{N} \binom{N}{K} \text{S}(K)$$

When written out, this says:

$$\text{LOCK}(N) = \binom{N}{0}\text{S}(0) + \binom{N}{1}\text{S}(1) + \binom{N}{2}\text{S}(2) + \cdots$$
$$+ \binom{N}{N-1}\text{S}(N-1) + \binom{N}{N}\text{S}(N)$$

The last term in the sum is just S(N). So, if LOCK(N) were equal to 2S(N), we'd have

$$2\text{S}(N) = \binom{N}{0}\text{S}(0) + \binom{N}{1}\text{S}(1) + \binom{N}{2}\text{S}(2) + \cdots + \binom{N}{N-1}\text{S}(N-1) + \text{S}(N)$$

Subtract S(N) from both sides, and we would have

$$\text{S}(N) = \binom{N}{0}\text{S}(0) + \binom{N}{1}\text{S}(1) + \binom{N}{2}\text{S}(2) + \cdots + \binom{N}{N-1}\text{S}(N-1) \quad (**)$$

The right-hand side of this equation is the number of combinations on N buttons that use fewer than N buttons (think of the proof of theorem 9.1 to see why). The left-hand side is the number of combinations on N buttons that use all N buttons. In other words, to prove that LOCK(N) is twice S(N), it's enough to prove the following statement:

Theorem 9.7 On a lock with N buttons, there are exactly as many combinations that use all N buttons as there are combinations that use fewer than N buttons.

Experiment 9.6 Write a Logo model for the right-hand side of (**). Use tabulations to experimentally verify (**) for values of N between 1 and 10.

We'll prove theorem 9.7 by setting up a function PROJ (for PROJection) between COMB.LIST(N) (the combinations on an N-button lock that use all N buttons) and the set of combinations on an N-button lock that use fewer than N buttons. This function will be "one-to-one" in the sense that different inputs to PROJ will produce different outputs, and it will be "onto" in the sense of project 9.24 (that is, every combination on an N-button lock that uses fewer than N buttons will be an output from PROJ for some input in COMB.LIST(N)). In other words, PROJ will be a one-to-one correspondence between COMB.LIST(N) and the set of combinations on an N button lock that uses fewer than N buttons. If you have two finite sets and a one-to-one correspondence between them, then the two sets have the same number of elements, so we will be done once we define PROJ and show that it is one-to-one and onto.

Defining PROJ is easy:

```
TO PROJ :COMB
 OP BL :COMB
END
```

In other words, PROJ takes a combination and "forgets" its last push. So, if $N = 3$,

```
PROJ([[3] [2] [1]]) = [[3] [2]]
PROJ([[2] [3] [1]]) = [[2] [3]]
PROJ([[2] [1] [3]]) = [[2] [1]]
PROJ([[3 2]][1]])   = [[3 2]]
PROJ([[2] [3 1]])   = [[2]]
PROJ([[3] [1] [2]]) = [[3] [1]]
PROJ([[1] [3] [2]]) = [[1] [3]]
PROJ([[1] [2] [3]]) = [[1] [2]]
PROJ([[3 1] [2]])   = [[3 1]]
PROJ([[1] [3 2]])   = [[1]]
PROJ([[3] [2 1]])   = [[3]]
PROJ([[2 1] [3]])   = [[2 1]]
PROJ([[3 2 1]])     = [[]]
```

Does the above example set up a one-to-one correspondence between COMB.LIST(3) and the set of combinations on a 3-button lock that use fewer than 3 buttons?

Now that we have PROJ, let's verify that it is one-to-one and onto:

1. PROJ is one-to-one. If two elements in COMB.LIST(N) produce the same output from PROJ, then they must be identical except (possibly) in their last pushes. Imagine two combinations C and D on N buttons that use

all N buttons and are identical except possibly in their last pushes. Then their last pushes must be the same also because, if you know all but the last push in C, then the last push in C must include every button that doesn't show up in the known pushes.

(For example, suppose that C and D are in COMB.LIST(5) and that they both produce the same output from PROJ; suppose that

```
PROJ(C) = [[1 2] [3]]
PROJ(D) = [[1 2] [3]]
```

Then C and D must both be [[1 2] [3] [4 5]] because you can only "complete" C and D by adding a single push, and C and D must use all 5 buttons.)

2. PROJ is onto. Imagine a combination C' on an N button lock that doesn't use all the buttons. Take all the buttons that don't show up in any push of C' and put them into a new push. Adjoin this push to C', and call the resulting combination C. Then C is in COMB.LIST(N), and PROJ(C) = C'.

Project 9.7 Write a Logo model of the function that takes a combination C' on an N button lock that uses fewer than N buttons as input and outputs the combination C in COMB.LIST(N) that is defined by the formula

$$\text{PROJ}(C) = C'$$

The function will also need N as an input. If you call your solution INV.PROJ (for "INVerse PROJection"), it should satisfy the following two properties:

1. PROJ(INV.PROJ(C', N)) = C' for all combinations C' on N buttons that use fewer than N buttons.

2. INV.PROJ((PROJ(C)), N) = C for all C in COMB.LIST(N).

Note: This project probably requires some involved list processing.

Let's summarize our major results:

Theorem 9.8 The number of combinations on a Simplex lock with N buttons is LOCK(N), where LOCK(N) = 2S(N), and S is defined in either of these two equivalent ways:

1.
```
TO S :N
  IF :N = O [OP 1]
  OP SIGMA "TERM :N O :N-1
END
```

```
TO TERM :N :K
 OP (B :N :K) * (S :K)
END
```

Or in mathematical notation

$$S(0) = 1$$

and for $N > 1$,

$$S(N) = \sum_{K=0}^{N-1} \binom{N}{K} S(K)$$

2.
```
TO S :N
  OP G :N O
END
```

```
TO G :N :X
 IF :N = 1 [OP 1]
 OP PSI "G :N - 1 :X
END
```

```
TO PSI :F :E :X
 OP :X * (APPLY :F SE :E :X) + (:X + 1) →
                * (APPLY :F SE :E :X + 1)
END
```

Furthermore, $S(N)$ is the number of combinations on an N-button lock that use all N buttons.

This is quite a theorem. Every one of its assertions is unobvious, and it expresses some beautiful relationships between seemingly unrelated ideas. In addition it suggests some interesting new questions.

Project 9.8 The fact that S can be defined inductively by

$$S(0) = 1$$

and for $N > 1$,

$$S(N) = \sum_{K=0}^{N-1} \binom{N}{K} S(K)$$

gives you the impression that there must be some interesting identities involving S. Find some. For example, show that for $N > 2$,

$$S(N) = (N+1)\binom{N}{0}S(0) + N\binom{N}{1}S(1) + (N-1)\binom{N}{2}S(2)$$

$$+ \cdots + 3\binom{N}{N-2}S(N-2)$$

Hint: Take the expression

$$S(N) = \sum_{K=0}^{N-1} \binom{N}{K} S(K)$$

and replace $S(N-1)$ on the right by its expansion in terms of the $S(K)$ for K between 0 and $N-2$.

 # Project 9.9 We know that $S(N) = G(N, 0)$. Is the relation:

$$S(N) = \sum_{K=0}^{N-1} \binom{N}{K} S(K)$$

true for other inputs to G? Is it true that

$$G(N, X) = \sum_{K=0}^{N-1} \binom{N}{K} G(K, X)$$

for all values of X? If so, prove it. If not, is it true for any values of X except 0? If so, find them. If not, is anything like this true if $X = 1$? If $X = 2$?

Project 9.10 The sequence $S(N)$ has a striking similarity to a sequence that shows up throughout mathematics. Consider this version of S

$$S(0) = 1$$

and for $N > 1$,

$$S(N) = \sum_{K=0}^{N-1} \binom{N}{K} S(K)$$

You can write this as

$$S(0) = 1$$

and for $N \geq 0$,

$$S(N + 1) = \sum_{K=0}^{N} \binom{N+1}{K} S(K)$$

Now, let's change this definition slightly; define the function BERN:

$$\text{BERN}(0) = 1$$

and for $N \geq 0$,

$$\sum_{K=0}^{N} \binom{N+1}{K} \text{BERN}(K) = 0$$

The numbers BERN(N) are called *Bernoulli numbers*. It shouldn't be at all clear that this definition allows you to compute these numbers, but a few hand calculations clear things up.

$N = 0$:

BERN$(0) = 1$

$N = 1$:

$$\binom{2}{0} \text{BERN}(0) + \binom{2}{1} \text{BERN}(1) = 0$$

$1 \cdot \text{BERN}(0) + 2 \cdot \text{BERN}(1) = 1$, so

$1 + 2 \cdot \text{BERN}(1) = 0$, and

$$\text{BERN}(1) = -\frac{1}{2}$$

$N = 2$:

$$\binom{3}{0} \text{BERN}(0) + \binom{3}{1} \text{BERN}(1) + \binom{3}{2} \text{BERN}(2) = 0, \text{ so}$$

$$1 \cdot \text{BERN}(0) + 3 \cdot \text{BERN}(1) + 3 \cdot \text{BERN}(2) = 0, \text{ so}$$

$$1 \cdot 1 + 3 \cdot \left(\frac{-1}{2}\right) + 3 \cdot \text{BERN}(2) = 0, \text{ and}$$

$$\text{BERN}(2) = \frac{1}{6}$$

$N = 4$:

$$1 \cdot 1 + 4 \cdot \left(\frac{-1}{2}\right) + 6 \cdot \left(\frac{1}{6}\right) + 4 \cdot \text{BERN}(3) = 0, \text{ and}$$

$$\text{BERN}(3) = 0$$

Model BERN in Logo; tabulate it and see what you can see. Which Bernoulli numbers are zero? Positive? Negative? Any proofs?

The nonzero Bernoulli numbers aren't integers (except at $N = 0$), but they are rational numbers (that is, they are quotients of integers). Your Logo model of BERN will represent the Bernoulli numbers as decimals (rounded off, for large N). Most (but not all) of the mathematical properties of Bernoulli numbers result from properties of their numerators and denominators; in order to experiment with Bernoulli numbers effectively, we'd have to build a Logo model that gave us the exact value of the output of BERN (say, as a list consisting of the numerator and the denominator of the fraction).

Pseudocombinations

When I first thought about the Simplex lock problem, I didn't take into account the fact that the order of the pushes in a combination counts. That is, I looked at

```
[ [1 2] [3] [4] ]
```

as the same combination as

[[3] [1 2] [4]]

I proceeded as above, inductively building up the number of "combinations" on N buttons from the number on $N-1$ buttons. The resulting solution gives the wrong answer the to the Simplex lock problem (it is too small), and that's a shame, because the analogue of the function S in my wrong solution is much easier to understand than the real S.

Luckily, it turns out that my wrong S is mathematically important, so I have an excuse to show it to you. Let's work through the construction first, and then I'll show you how to transport this lock talk into something that actually shows up in textbooks on "discrete mathematics."

Imagine, then, a Simplex lock in which the order of the pushes doesn't count. We let P.LOCK(N) (for Pseudo-LOCK) be the number of combinations on N buttons and let P(N) be the number of combinations on N buttons that use all N buttons. Just as in theorem 9.1, we see that

$$ \text{P.LOCK}(N) = \sum_{K=0}^{N} \binom{N}{K} \text{P}(K) $$

because $\binom{N}{K}$P(K) counts the number of ways you can pick K buttons from N and then form all the combinations that use these K buttons. So, just as before, we'll concentrate on the calculation of P(N). Before I go on, try to find an analogue of PSI that reduces the calculation of P(N) to a sum of some simple function over P.COMB.LIST($N-1$) (P.COMB.LIST is, of course, the list of pseudocombinations).

The situation is much simpler for pseudocombinations. Suppose, for example, that we have the pseudocombination

[[1] [2 3] [4]]

in P.COMB.LIST(4). Remember, the order in which I have listed the pushes is insignificant. To extend it to an element of P.COMB.LIST(5), we look at the EXT! and the EXT!!. Now, the EXT! of [[1] [2 3] [4]] is formed by throwing in the new push [5]. But now it doesn't matter where we put it. In other words, the EXT! of [[1] [2 3] [4]] is the single combination

[[5] [1] [2 3] [4]]

In general, each pseudocombination C' in P.COMB.LIST($N - 1$) will have exactly one combination in its EXT!, and this new combination will have length LENGTH(C') + 1.

Next, what about the EXT!! of a pseudocombination in P.COMB.LIST($N - 1$)? To form the EXT!! of [[1] [2 3] [4]] we put a 5 into each of the existing pushes, and there are three ways to do this. So, the situation for EXT!! is the same for pseudocombinations as it is for combinations: every combination C' in P.COMB.LIST($N - 1$) has as many pseudocombinations in its EXT!! as its length, and these new pseudocombinations have the same length as C'.

If this isn't clear to you, you should work out some concrete example. How would you have to modify our INFLATE and EXT functions so that our Logo model would generate pseudocombinations instead of combinations?

We can now mimic our previous derivation (using a little hindsight). Suppose that F is any function, and suppose we want to calculate

$$\sum_{C \in \text{P.COMB.LIST}(N)} \text{F}(\text{LENGTH}(C))$$

then we can split our sum:

$$\sum_{C \in \text{P.COMB.LIST}(N)} \text{F}(\text{LENGTH}(C))$$

$$= \sum_{C' \in \text{P.COMB.LIST}(N-1)} \left(\sum_{C \in \text{EXT!}(C')} \text{F}(\text{LENGTH}(C)) + \sum_{C \in \text{EXT!!}(C')} \text{F}(\text{LENGTH}(C)) \right)$$

which is the sum of two "double sums":

$$\sum_{C' \in \text{P.COMB.LIST}(N-1)} \sum_{C \in \text{EXT!}(C')} \text{F}(\text{LENGTH}(C))$$

and

$$\sum_{C' \in \text{P.COMB.LIST}(N-1)} \sum_{C \in \text{EXT!!}(C')} \text{F}(\text{LENGTH}(C))$$

But this time, for each C' in P.COMB.LIST($N - 1$), EXT!(C') is a single combination, of length LENGTH(C') + 1. Also, EXT!!(C') contains LENGTH(C')

pseudocombinations, all of length $\text{LENGTH}(C')$. So the first double sum becomes

$$\sum_{C' \in \text{P.COMB.LIST}(N-1)} \sum_{C \in \text{EXT!}(C')} \text{F}(\text{LENGTH}(C') + 1)$$

$$= \sum_{C' \in \text{P.COMB.LIST}(N-1)} \text{F}(\text{LENGTH}(C') + 1)$$

(Again, this is because the inner sum (over $\text{EXT!}(C')$) contains only one element.)

The second double sum simplifies to

$$\sum_{C' \in \text{P.COMB.LIST}(N-1)} \sum_{C \in \text{EXT!!}(C')} \text{F}(\text{LENGTH}(C'))$$

$$= \sum_{C' \in \text{P.COMB.LIST}(N-1)} (\text{LENGTH}(C'))(\text{F}(\text{LENGTH}(C')))$$

Combining these two simplifications yields

$$\sum_{C \in \text{P.COMB.LIST}(N)} \text{F}(\text{LENGTH}(C))$$

$$= \sum_{C' \in \text{P.COMB.LIST}(N-1)} (\text{LENGTH}(C'))(\text{F}(\text{LENGTH}(C'))) + (\text{F}(\text{LENGTH}(C') + 1))$$

This leads to the following result (compare with theorem 9.4):

Theorem 9.9 If F is any function, and F_1 is defined as

```
TO F1 :X
 OP :X * (F :X) + F(:X + 1)
END
```

then the following two functions are equal on $\mathbf{Z}^+$:

```
TO T :N
 OP SIGMA.L "F [] P.COMB.LIST :N
END
```

and

247

```
TO NEW.T :N
 OP SIGMA.L "F1 [] P.COMB.LIST :N - 1
END
```

This theorem leads to the higher-order function CHI (compare it with PSI):

```
TO CHI :F :E :X
 OP :X * (APPLY :F SE :E :X) + (APPLY :F SE :E :X + 1)
END
```

Essentially, if F is any function, CHI(F) is the function that takes X to

$$X \cdot F(X) + F(X + 1)$$

whereas PSI(F) is the function that takes X to

$$X \cdot F(X) + (X + 1) \cdot F(X + 1)$$

If F is any function, F_1 can be defined as

```
TO F1 :X
 OP CHI "F [] :X
END
```

Now, P.LOCK(N) is just the sum of ONE over the lengths of the elements of P.COMB.LIST(N), so (just as with combinations) we are led to a sequence of functions that is modeled by the Logo function

```
TO F :N :X
 IF :N = 0 [OP 1]
 OP CHI "F :N - 1 :X
END
```

and to the following result (compare it with theorem 9.5):

Theorem 9.10 P can be modeled as

```
TO P :N
 OP ...
END
```

where the "..." can be replaced with any of the following:

```
SIGMA.L "F 0  P.COMB.LIST :N
SIGMA.L "F 1  P.COMB.LIST :N - 1
SIGMA.L "F 2  P.COMB.LIST :N - 2
SIGMA.L "F 3  P.COMB.LIST :N - 3
SIGMA.L "F 4  P.COMB.LIST :N - 4
SIGMA.L "F 5  P.COMB.LIST :N - 5
    ⋮
SIGMA.L "F :N P.COMB.LIST :N - :N
```

Finally, noting that P.COMB.LIST(0) is [[]], we have the analogue of theorem 9.6.

Theorem 9.11 The function P can be defined like this:

```
TO P :N
 OP F :N 0
END

TO F :N :X
 IF :N = 0 [OP 1]
 OP CHI "F :N - 1 :X
END

TO CHI :F :E :X
 OP (:X * APPLY :F SE :E :X) + (APPLY :F SE :E :X + 1)
END
```

We can now investigate P.LOCK; recall that

$$P.LOCK(N) = \sum_{K=0}^{N} \binom{N}{K} P(K)$$

We can model this in Logo in the usual way:

```
TO P.LOCK  :N
 OP SIGMA "TERM :N 0 :N
END

TO TERM :N :K
 OP (B :N :K) * (P :K )
END
```

```
TO P :N
 OP F :N 0
END

TO F :N :X
 IF :N = 0 [OP 1]
 OP CHI "F :N - 1 :X
END
```

Just for the fun of it, I tabulated P.LOCK and P together; look what happened:

N	P.LOCK(N)	P(N)
1	. . . 2	. . . 1
2	. . . 5	. . . 2
3	. . . 15	. . . 5
4	. . . 52	. . . 15
5	. . . 203	. . . 52
6	. . . 877	. . . 203
7	. . . 4140	. . . 877
8	. . . 21147	. . . 4140

At this point, Logo ran out of space, but the evidence is intriguing. Anyone looking at the table would guess at the following conjecture:

Conjecture P(N) = P.LOCK($N - 1$) for $N > 1$.

Well, it's true, and the next project will help you prove it.

Project 9.11 Prove that P(N) = P.LOCK($N - 1$) for $N > 1$. Hint: Set up a one-to-one correspondence P.PROJ between P.COMB.LIST(N) and the set of pseudocombinations on $N - 1$ buttons. One way to do this is to let P.PROJ(C) be the pseudocombination obtained from C by forgetting the push that contains N.

Notice that since

$$\text{P.LOCK}(N) = \sum_{K=0}^{N} \binom{N}{K} \text{P}(K)$$

we have that

$$\text{P.LOCK}(N-1) = \sum_{K=0}^{N-1} \binom{N-1}{K} \text{P}(K)$$

Using the result of the above project, we have the following result:

Theorem 9.12 The function P can be defined as

$$\text{P}(0) = 1$$

and for $N > 0$,

$$\text{P}(N) = \sum_{K=0}^{N-1} \binom{N-1}{K} \text{P}(K)$$

Take some time to play with the function P. It doesn't grow nearly as fast as S, so maybe you can find some patterns.

I used the function `P.LOCK` to count the number of combinations in my defective model of a Simplex lock; it's really of little interest. Notice, however, that `P.LOCK` doesn't enter into the statement of theorem 9.12; the theorem simply sets up an inductive definition for the function P. And the function P does count something interesting; it counts the number of "partitions" of a set with N elements.

Partitions

We used the word partition in project 7.23; a partition of a positive integer N is a set of positive integers that add up to N. A partition of a set S is defined similarly.

Definition 9.13 If S is a finite set, a "partition of S" is a collection of nonoverlapping subsets of S whose union is S.

For example, if S is the set $\{A\ B\ C\}$, then S has 5 partitions:

$\{\{A\}\{B\}\{C\}\}$

$\{\{A\ B\}\{C\}\}$

$\{\{A\ C\}\{B\}\}$

$\{\{B\ C\}\{A\}\}$

$\{\{A\ B\ C\}\}$

Of course, the labels that we use to name the elements of S are of no importance; neither is the order in which we list the subsets in a partition. So the partition $\{\{B\}\{A\}\{C\}\}$ is the same partition of $\{A\ B\ C\}$ as $\{\{A\}\{B\}\{C\}\}$. Sound familiar?

Here's the punch line: A partition of the set $\{1\ 2\ 3 \ldots N\}$ is nothing other than what we have called a "pseudocombination on a lock with N buttons that uses all N buttons". Think about this for a minute.

The number of partitions on a set with N elements is therefore $P(N)$. Let's state this as a theorem:

Theorem 9.14 The number of partitions of an N element set is $P(N)$ where

$$P(0) = 1$$

and for $N > 0$,

$$P(N) = \sum_{K=0}^{N-1} \binom{N-1}{K} P(K)$$

The proof of this result isn't at all obvious without the aid of the "useless" intermediate function P.LOCK, and I would never have thought of P.LOCK if I was thinking simply about partitions. (How would you describe the set of pseudocombinations on N buttons (that use all of them or fewer than all of them) in terms of partitions?) Sometimes you get more mileage from an "incorrect" approach to a problem than from a "correct" one.

Project 9.12 Recall that the function P can also be defined like this:

```
TO P :N
 OP F :N 0
END

TO F :N :X
 IF :N = 0 [OP 1]
 OP CHI "F :N - 1 :X
END

TO CHI :F :E :X
 OP (:X * APPLY :F SE :E :X) + (APPLY :F SE :E :X + 1)
END
```

Show that P is equal to Q on $\mathbf{Z}^+$ where Q is defined as

```
TO Q :N
 IF :N = 0 [OP 1]
 OP F :N - 1 1
END
```

In other words, show that for $N > 1$, $F(N,0) = F(N-1,1)$. Why is Q faster than P?

Experiment 9.13 Let R be the function defined like this:

$$R(N,X) = \sum_{K=0}^{N} \binom{N}{K} P(K) X^K$$

Build a Logo model for R. Compare R with F for several values of N and X, and develop a conjecture. #Prove your conjecture. Does your conjecture give an explanation for the fact that the following definitions of P yield the same function?

1. $$P(0) = 1$$

   and for $N > 0$, $$P(N) = \sum_{K=0}^{N-1} \binom{N-1}{K} P(K)$$

2.  ```
    TO P :N
      OP F :N 0
    END


    TO F :N :X
     IF :N = 0 [OP 1]
     OP CHI "F :N - 1 :X
    END


    TO CHI :F :E :X
     OP (:X * APPLY :F SE :E :X) + (APPLY :F SE :E :X + 1)
    END
    ```

3.  ```
    TO P :N
     IF :N = 0 [OP 1]
     OP F :N - 1 1
    END


    TO F :N :X
     IF :N = 0 [OP 1]
     OP CHI "F :N - 1 :X
    END


    TO CHI :F :E :X
     OP (:X * APPLY :F SE :E :X) + (APPLY :F SE :E :X + 1)
    END
    ```

Part III

Number Theory

In part II we developed mathematical induction and combinatorics as tools for investigation. Both of these techniques involve counting: They depend on and express some very basic (but hard to formalize) properties of the positive integers.

Number theory consists of a higher-level investigation of the integers and related systems. Until now, we have been using the integers as an "auxiliary set," as a kind of abacus that allowed us to keep track of where we were in our calculations. Number theory takes up **Z** itself as an object of study.

The difference is difficult to pin down precisely, but questions in number theory have a certain flavor. In discussing Pascal's triangle, we asked combinatorial questions such as

What is the sum of the entries in the Nth row?

A number-theoretic question would be something like

Which entries in Pascal's triangle are divisible by 8?

When we investigated the Simplex lock, we asked many questions about the outputs of the function S. A number theorist might wonder if any outputs from S are prime numbers.

The above examples illustrate an important theme in number theory: primes and divisibility. Not every question in number theory centers around this idea, but a great many (including most of the ones we'll discuss in this part) do.

The techniques that are developed in number theory can be widely applied. For example, number-theoretic methods can be used to investigate the following problems from geometry:

1. Find an integer-sided triangle, one of whose angles is 60 degrees.

2. Which values of A and I will cause the picture produced by

```
TO INSPI :A :I
 FD 10 RT :A
 INSPI :A + :I :I
END
```

    to have exactly six "nodes?"

3. Can you construct a regular seven-sided polygon using only a straightedge and compass?

In part III we'll barely scratch the surface of number theory. We'll concentrate on questions of divisibility, developing some of the classical results from the theory of arithmetic. The techniques we develop can be used to investigate many different ideas, and they can be transported to "number systems" that are different from **Z**.

Number theory is one of the oldest branches of mathematics. Euclid, in about 300 B.C., recorded many of the major number-theoretic results of the time; it's clear that the subject was already highly developed. Many people get the impression from their high school geometry course that Euclid's *Elements* was solely concerned with geometry; on the contrary, three of the thirteen books (*VII, VIII,* and *XII*) were concerned with number theory and algebra. Most of our results from parts I and II concerning arithmetic and geometric sequences and series show up in the these three books of Euclid.

From the beginning, number theory has been concerned with intricate and beautiful calculations, so it is no surprise that computers are playing increasingly important roles in modern number theory. If you look at the titles of the talks given at a modern-day meeting of number theorists, you'll see that a great deal of research uses computers to implement algorithms that are deeply rooted in number theory. This wasn't so even a decade ago. In this part III, we'll look at some of these important algorithms, and we'll model most of them in Logo. As usual, we'll use our models to experiment with the objects we are studying (in this case the objects are integers), but you should be aware of some facts. First, some important new results arise from applying classical number-theoretic results to very large integers (see the discussion in the next paragraph); in these cases, we will be able to understand the applications in principle, but we certainly won't have the computing power to deal with numbers of the size that are used in real life. Second, the algorithms themselves will be slow (even on integers of moderate size). Although we'll try to make them as efficient as possible, an in-depth study of how to make them substantially more efficient would require a long excursion into computer science. Finally, **Z** is a very sly domain. The integers are notorious for giving experimenters a false sense of certainty, and it is not uncommon to verify experimentally a result in a huge number of cases only to find that it is false (one famous conjecture was verified for the first few billion integers before it was found to be false).

Until recently, number theory was considered one of the most esoteric branches of mathematics. Most of the great mathematicians in history have done research in number theory, but the discipline was always considered far removed from real-world applications. Recently, this has changed; it was discovered that some classical results in number theory could be used to construct codes (the kind used for keeping secrets) that are essentially unbreakable in a reasonable length of time with current computers and with what we currently know about techniques for factoring an integer. The basic idea is that by using number theoretic results, it is fairly easy to construct large integers that are very difficult to factor, and the codes can only be broken by factoring these numbers. Although we won't explicitly construct such codes, one of the things that we'll do in this part is to develop the number theory that you'll need to understand the essential ideas behind how these codes are built (a good treatment of the application of number theory to cryptography can be found in Koblitz 1987).

Chapter 10

Primes and Divisors

In any discussion of number theory, you have to start somewhere. That is, you have to assume certain facts about the integers. Different treatments start at different places. Some books start by assuming a great deal (say, all of the results from a first course in calculus); others derive the basic laws of arithmetic from more elementary principles. We'll start somewhere in between.

Let's start by assuming that **Z** sits inside the rational number system. You can think of the rational number system as the system of numbers that your computer uses; rational numbers can be represented as decimals, and **Z** consists of all the "whole" rational numbers (the rational numbers with no digits to the right of the decimal point). **Z** is closed under addition, subtraction and multiplication. This means that the sum of two integers is another integer, that the difference between two integers is another integer, and that the product of two integers is another integer. **Z** is *not* closed under division, however. To see this take, for example, 13 and 4. Both are integers, but their quotient is 3.25, which is not an integer. These "closure" properties will most often be used when we have equations such as

$$B = AN + AD$$

In this equation, if we know that B, A, and N are integers, then we can conclude that AD is also an integer. This is because $AD = B - AN$; since A and N are integers, so is AN; since AD is the difference between two integers, AD is also an integer. Can we also conclude that D is an integer?

We'll also assume that we have a version of Logo that can add, subtract, multiply, and divide, and that we have the functions FLOOR, QUOT and MOD. In many versions of Logo (including the one I'm using) you have to build your own FLOOR, QUOT, and MOD. First, let me explain how FLOOR is supposed to work.

FLOOR returns the integer part of its input. One way to think about this is to think of a number line:

$$-7 \quad -6 \quad -5 \quad -4 \quad -3 \quad -2 \quad -1 \quad 0 \quad 1 \quad 2 \quad 3 \quad 4 \quad 5 \quad 6 \quad 7 \quad 8 \quad 9$$

Every rational number X is caught between two consecutive integers N and $N + 1$ on the number line. FLOOR(X) returns N (the greatest integer that is less than or equal to X). In particular, note that

```
SHOW FLOOR 4.23
```

produces 4, and that

```
SHOW FLOOR -4.23
```

produces -5.

Most versions of Logo have an INT function; in some instances, INT is exactly the same as FLOOR (it is in the BBC version of Logo, for example). In other Logos, INT acts like FLOOR on positive integers, but INT(-4.23) returns -4 (this is the case in the version of LCSI Logo that I'm using). So I have to put in the following fix:

```
TO FLOOR :N
 IF :N > 0 [OP INT :N]
 IF :N = INT :N [OP :N]
 OP (INT :N) - 1
END
```

Exercise 10.1 FLOOR gets its name because it locates a rational number between two consecutive integers and returns the smaller integer in this pair (the "floor" of the pair). Write a function CEILING that returns the larger integer in this pair. For example,

$$\text{CEILING}(3.21) = 4$$

$$\text{CEILING}(5) = 5$$

$$\text{CEILING}(-4.1) = -4$$

then write a function CLOSEST that returns the nearest integer to its input (in some versions of Logo, these things might be built in; write them anyway).

Experiment 10.2 Investigate the following statements (X and Y are rational numbers):

1. $\text{FLOOR}(X + Y) = \text{FLOOR}(X) + \text{FLOOR}(Y)$.

2. If N is an integer, $\text{FLOOR}(X + N) = \text{FLOOR}(X) + N$.

3. $\text{FLOOR}(XY) = (\text{FLOOR}(X))(\text{FLOOR}(Y))$.

4. If N is an integer, $\text{FLOOR}(XN) = (\text{FLOOR}(X))N$.

Give proofs for the true statements, and try to modify the false statements so that they become true.

The QUOT function is meant to take two integers B and A as inputs. We'll assume that A is nonzero. $\text{QUOT}(B, A)$ outputs the "whole number quotient" that is obtained when B is divided by A:

```
?SHOW QUOT 13 4
3
?SHOW QUOT 16 8
2
?SHOW QUOT 121 5
24
?SHOW QUOT 12 15
0
```

In other words, $\text{QUOT}(B, A)$ locates B/A between two consecutive integers, and it returns the smaller integer in the pair. So QUOT's definition is easy.

```
TO QUOT :B :A
 OP FLOOR (:B/:A)
END
```

Some Logos have something close to QUOT built in. If yours does, make sure that it is equal to the above QUOT for all kinds of integer inputs. In particular, note that

$$\text{QUOT}(13, 4) \quad = \quad 3$$

$$\text{QUOT}(13, -4) \quad = -4$$

$$\text{QUOT}(-13, -4) = \quad 3$$

$$\text{QUOT}(-13, 4) \quad = -4$$

Suppose for a minute that A is a positive integer. Then, if B is any integer, $\mathtt{QUOT}(B, A)$ is the integer N that can be obtained by writing B/A as

$$\frac{B}{A} = N + D$$

where D is some decimal that is nonnegative but strictly less than 1 (think of B/A on a number line). Multiply both sides of the above equation by A; you'll find that

$$B = NA + DA$$

Note that DA is an integer (because B and AN are integers). Also because

$$0 \leq D < 1 \quad \text{and} \quad 0 < A$$

we know that

$$0 \leq DA < A$$

Exercise 10.3 Use you $\mathtt{QUOT}$ function to find the integer DA in the above discussion if $B = 13$ and $A = 4$. If $B = 12$ and $A = 4$. If $B = 4$ and $A = 15$. If $B = -43$ and $A = 15$.

The integer DA is what we want to call the $\mathtt{MOD}$ of B and A; it is simply $B - NA$:

```
TO MOD :B :A
 OP :B - (QUOT :B :A) * :A
END
```

Notice that $\mathtt{QUOT}$ and $\mathtt{MOD}$ are related by the equation

$$B = (\mathtt{QUOT}(B, A))A + \mathtt{MOD}(B, A)$$

for all pairs of integers B and A. If B and A are positive, then $\mathtt{QUOT}$ and $\mathtt{MOD}$ are just the usual whole number quotient and remainder when B is divided by A; for example,

$$
\begin{array}{r}
3 \\
5 \overline{)\; 17} \\
15 \\
\hline
2
\end{array}
$$

so $\mathtt{QUOT}(17,5)$ is 3 and $\mathtt{MOD}(17,5)$ is 2.

You have used $\mathtt{REMAINDER}$ several times in parts I and II. It might be that your $\mathtt{REMAINDER}$ function is the same as $\mathtt{MOD}$, but you should check it with all kinds of integer inputs (in particular, when B is negative and A is positive).

Let's summarize some important results.

Theorem 10.1 If B is any integer and A is a positive integer, then

1. $\mathtt{QUOT}(B, A)$ is an integer,

2. $\mathtt{MOD}(B, A)$ is an integer,

3. $0 \le \mathtt{MOD}(B, A) < A$, and

4. $B = ((\mathtt{QUOT}(B, A))A + \mathtt{MOD}(B, A)$.

Experiment 10.4 For each choice of A and B, find $\mathtt{QUOT}(B, A)$ and $\mathtt{MOD}(B, A)$, and verify parts 3 and 4 of theorem 10.1:

1. $A = 4,\ B = 7$

2. $A = 4,\ B = 8$

3. $A = 3,\ B = 11$

4. $A = 11,\ B = 3$

5. $A = 11,\ B = 11$

6. $A = 8,\ B = 2$

7. $A = 6,\ B = -9$

8. $A = 6,\ B = -5$

9. $A = 6,\ B = -12$

10. $A = 6,\ B = 0$

For what numbers A and B is $\text{MOD}(B, A) = 0$? For what numbers A and B is $\text{QUOT}(B, A) = 0$?

The word MOD is short for "modulo," a word that was used by Gauss in *Disquisitiones*. The word is from the Latin verb that means "to measure." Roughly speaking, if we use 5 as a measure on the number line

then 17 is two more than a marked number (15), so Gauss would say that

$$17 \text{ is } 2 \text{ modulo } 5$$

Another way to say this is "17 is 2 more than a multiple of 5," or "17 is 2, except for a multiple of 5." This custom of thinking of "modulo" as "except for" has added a rich flexibility to the word. Mathematicians often say things like

I can prove this theorem modulo one conjecture

or even

Modulo a rainstorm, we'll have a picnic this afternoon

One important consequence of theorem 10.1 is that if A is a positive integer, then any integer B can be written as an integer, $\text{QUOT}(B, A)$, times A plus a remainder, $\text{MOD}(B, A)$, that is between 0 and $A - 1$. It turns out that $\text{QUOT}(B, A)$ and $\text{MOD}(B, A)$ are the only two integers with this property.

#Project 10.5 Suppose that B is any integer and that A is a positive integer. If Q is $\text{QUOT}(B, A)$ and R is $\text{MOD}(B, A)$, then we know two things:

1. $B = QA + R$.

2. $0 \leq R < A$.

Show that Q and R are the only pair of integers with these properties. That is, show that if Q' and R' are integers so that

1. $B = Q'A + R'$ and

2. $0 \leq R' < A$,

then $Q = Q'$ and $R = R'$.

Hints:

1. Suppose that R and R' were not equal; say, $R > R'$. Take the equations

   $B = QA + R$ and

   $B = Q'A + R'$,

   and subtract them. You'll find that

   $0 = (Q - Q')A + R - R'$

   This can be written as

   $(Q' - Q)A = R - R'$

   This means that $R - R'$ would be a multiple of A. But $R - R'$ would be positive (why?) and strictly less than A (why?). This can't happen (why?), so R must equal R'.

2. If $R = R'$, our equations

   $$B = QA + R \quad \text{and} \quad B = Q'A + R'$$

   become

   $$B = QA + R \quad \text{and} \quad B = Q'A + R$$

   Subtract and conclude that $Q = Q'$.

#Experiment 10.6 Investigate the following statements. (All numbers are integers, and A is a positive integer.)

1. $\text{MOD}(X + KA, A) = \text{MOD}(X, A).$

2. $\text{MOD}(X + Y, A) = \text{MOD}(X, A) + \text{MOD}(Y, A).$

3. $\text{MOD}(X + Y, A) = \text{MOD}((\text{MOD}(X, A) + \text{MOD}(Y, A)), A).$

4. $\text{MOD}(XY, A) = (\text{MOD}(X, A))(\text{MOD}(Y, A)).$

5. $\text{MOD}(XY, A) = \text{MOD}((\text{MOD}(X, A))(\text{MOD}(Y, A)), A).$

To check 5, for example, type

```
SHOW MOD 7*6 5
```

and

```
SHOW MOD (MOD 7 5) * (MOD 6 5) 5
```

Can you supply proofs for any that seem true?

A purist might say that we are assuming too much when we assume that **Z** lies inside the rational numbers; arithmetic should be developed using only the arithmetic operations that output integers (such as +, *, and −, but not /). So our definition of QUOT

```
TO QUOT :B :A
 OP FLOOR (:B / :A)
END
```

would be tarnished (in the purist's view) because it uses division. We can fix that. Let's assume for now that B and A are positive. Then we can define $\text{QUOT}(B, A)$ by locating B between two successive multiples of A:

```
TO PURIST'S.QUOT :B :A
 IF :B < :A [OP 0]
 OP QUOT.HELPER :B :A 1
END

TO QUOT.HELPER :B :A :C
 IF AND (NOT :B < :C * :A) (:B < :C * (:A + 1) [OP :C]
 OP QUOT.HELPER :B :A :C + 1
END
```

Exercise 10.7 Fix PURIST'S.QUOT so that it handles positive and negative inputs.

Do you think that PURIST'S.QUOT is better (in any sense) than our original QUOT? It does remove the use of division, but it introduces another worry: Why does it stop? The fact that any positive B can be located between two consecutive multiples of a positive A is not easy to prove (its proof would certainly require the existence of something at least as fancy as division), and in one form or another, this idea is often taken as an axiom ("Archimedes' axiom").

Project 10.8 Write a version of FLOOR that doesn't use INT. Hint: Treat the case of a positive input first; for this case, use something like Archimedes' axiom as a guarantee that a function that locates its input between two consecutive integers will actually stop.

Well, this is all the equipment that we'll need for a while, so let's get started.

Divisibility and Primes

Young children are taught in school to build factor trees for positive integers. For example, to factor 72, you could write

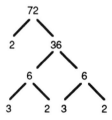

Figure 10.1

The idea in building these trees is that the numbers at the ends of the two branches emanating from any node should each be bigger than 1 and should multiply together to give you that node. So, $72 = 2 \cdot 36$, $36 = 6 \cdot 6$, and so on. The final result is that

$$72 = 2 \cdot 3 \cdot 2 \cdot 3 \cdot 2 = 2^3 \cdot 3^2$$

This activity exhibits one of the central themes in number theory: the factorization of integers. It also makes implicit use of two important facts from number theory:

1. The process will stop. That is, every node in the tree leads to a node in which no further factorization can be found (in the above example, this happens when you get to a 3 or to a 2). The set of these "stop nodes" is the set of "prime factors" of the original integer; in our example, this set is

$$\{2\ 3\ 2\ 3\ 2\}$$

2. If two people discover two different trees for the same integer, the set of prime factors will be the same. For example, another tree for 72 is

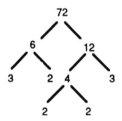

Figure 10.2

The set of prime factors is again {3 2 2 2 3}.

Let's prove these two facts. The first fact leads us to consider the notion of prime number, and this idea will occupy us for the rest of this section. The second fact is known as the "fundamental theorem of arithmetic"; we'll take it up in the next section.

Imagine any factor tree. Let's say, for the sake of example, that we start with 72. Because we allow only integers bigger than 1 as nodes, and because the product of the nodes at the ends of the branches emanating from 72 must be 72, the two branches emanating from 72 must end with nodes that are strictly smaller than 72. In other words, 72 must be connected to two numbers that are at most 71 (in reality, they have to be considerably less). Now, these two numbers must be connected to numbers that are at most 70, and inductively, we see that the whole tree can have no more than 72 "levels" (how many nodes can it have?). So the process stops.

At what kind of integers does it stop? It stops at integers bigger than 1 that are "irreducible," that is, at integers that can't be factored. Such integers, like 3, 5, 13, or 101 are called primes. The notion of prime number is central to number theory, and it depends on the idea of *divisibility*.

If A and B are integers, we say that "B is divisible by A" or "A is a factor of B" if there is an integer C so that $B = CA$. So 50 is divisible by 10, but 51 is not divisible by 11. Note that 50 is also divisible by -5 (because $50 = (-10)(-5)$). Think about how you would model this divisibility predicate in Logo. One way would be to model the definition; to see if DIVIS?(B, A) is true (at least for positive B and A), you could compute all the multiples of A up to B,

$$A, 2A, 3A, \ldots, (\text{FLOOR}(B/A))A$$

and see if any of them yield B. Or, you could use this:

```
TO DIVIS? :B :A
  OP (MOD :B :A) = 0
END
```

Experiment 10.9 Notice that every integer is a factor of 0. (If A is any integer, can you find an integer C so that $0 = CA$?). So 0 has infinitely many factors. Is 0 a factor of any integers? Which ones? Notice that 1 is a factor of any integer (why?). Are there any other integers that are factors of every integer? Which ones? How many positive factors does 15 have? 12? 36? 101? 100?

If DIVIS?(B, A) is true, we say that "A divides B." In this context, the word "divides" doesn't stand for a function (it doesn't mean "divide B by A"); it stands for a fact ("it is true that A is a factor of B"). So 14 divides 52, but 56 doesn't divide 102. The mathematical notation for "divides" is a vertical bar, so

$$14 \mid 52 \quad \text{but} \quad 56 \nmid 102.$$

You can read the sentence "14 | 52" as "14 divides 52" or "14 is a factor of 52." Notice that if A and B are positive integers and $A \mid B$, then A is less than or equal to B. So, if A is a proper factor of B (that is, $A \mid B$ but A is not equal to B), then A is strictly less than B. We'll often use this fact without comment (we used it above when we argued that factor trees must stop).

Experiment 10.10 Investigate each statement by writing it in words, by trying it out with a few examples and then by justifying the true statements by using the definition of "divides." All numbers are integers.

1. $A \mid A$

2. If $A \mid B$, then $B \mid A$

3. If $A \mid B$ and $B \mid C$, then $A \mid C$

4. If $A \mid B$ and $B \mid A$, then $A = B$

5. If $A \mid B$, then $A^2 \mid B^2$

6. If $A \mid 2B$, then $A \mid B$

7. If $A^2 \mid B^2$, then $A \mid B$

Using these ideas, we can give a first attempt at a definition of prime number

Definition 10.2 Let P be an integer not equal to 1 or -1. We say P is a prime number if the only factors of P are P, 1, $-P$, and -1.

So 7 is a prime number because the only factors of 7 are 7, 1, -7, and -1. To prove this, you would have to simply pass all the nonzero integers N between -7 and 7 through the DIVIS?$(7, N)$ test to see that 7 has no other factors. Why would it not be necessary to try integers outside the range of -7 to 7?

In most of our work, we'll be concerned with positive primes and with positive factors. In testing 101 for primality, I'd like to be able to test it for divisibility by integers between 1 and 101 (rather than between -101 and 101). Here's why we can do just that.

The numbers 1 and -1 are special in our story; they are the "units" in **Z**. A unit in a number system is a number whose reciprocal is also in that system. For example, though 3 is an integer, its reciprocal (1/3) is not an integer, so 3 is not a unit in **Z**. However, the reciprocal of 1 is 1 (an integer) and the reciprocal of -1 is -1 (an integer), so 1 and -1 are units in **Z**. Convince yourself that **Z** doesn't have any other units.

One proof of the fact that the only units in **Z** are 1 and -1 uses basic facts about inequalities. Suppose that K is a unit different from 1 and -1. K can't be 0 (why?), so K must be greater than 1 or less than -1. Suppose that K is greater than 1 (the other case is handled similarly). If K' is the reciprocal of K, then $KK' = 1$. But K' must be positive (since K is and their product is), and it must also be greater than 1 (if $K' = 1$ and $KK' = 1$, then K would equal 1). Take the inequality

$$K > 1$$

and multiply both sides by the positive integer K':

$$KK' > K'$$

But $KK' = 1$ and $K' > 1$, so this is a contradiction.

The importance of units in number theory is that they are factors of every number. This means that you can insert the product of a unit and its reciprocal at will in any factorization:

$$18 = 6 \cdot 3 = 6 \cdot 1 \cdot 1 \cdot 3 = 6 \cdot -1 \cdot 3 \cdot -1 = 6 \cdot 3 \cdot -1 \cdot -1 \cdot -1 \cdot -1$$

and so on. This is one reason that we don't allow units to be primes in definition 10.2. If we called 1 and -1 primes, then there would be no chance that the set of prime factors of 72 would be unique; one person could call it $\{2\ 3\ 2\ 3\ 2\}$, while another could call it

$$\{2\ 3\ 2\ 3\ 2\ 1\ 1\ -1\ -1\ -1\ -1\}$$

The fact that a pair of -1's can be inserted in any factorization implies that if A is a factor of B, then $-A$ is also a factor of B. For example, 14 divides 52 because

$$52 = 14 \cdot 3$$

It follows that

$$52 = -1 \cdot 14 \cdot -1 \cdot 3 = -14 \cdot -3$$

so -14 is also a factor of 52.

This allows us to use a less awkward definition of prime number:

Definition 10.3 Let P be an integer not equal to 1 or -1. We say P is a prime number if the only positive factors of P are P and 1. Numbers that are not prime are called "composites."

Let's simplify things even more: unless we explicitly say otherwise, whenever we use the word "prime," we'll mean "positive prime." So the first few primes are 2, 3, 5, 7, 11, 13, 17, 19, and 23. Why is 2 the only even prime?

Project 10.11 Show that every integer N has a prime factor. Hint: We can assume that N is positive (why?). If N is prime, then it has a prime factor (itself). If N is not prime, it can be written as $N = MM'$ where M and M' are integers bigger than 1 and less than N. Use induction and part 3 of experiment 10.8.

Primality Tests

How can you tell if a number is prime? This question has always fascinated mathematicians, and it remains the object of a great deal of current research. For small numbers, like 37, you can simply try all the possible divisors. For larger numbers, like 877, you can use a computer to do all the checking. For very large numbers like

$$618970019642690137449562111$$

(which happens to be prime), checking all possible factors is out of the question, and more sophisticated methods (and very powerful computers) are needed. We'll develop some primality tests that work for all integers, but we'll only apply our tests to numbers of reasonable size.

Let's write a PRIME? predicate that simply checks for divisibility.

Our first attempt simply tries all possible factors of N between 2 and $N - 1$:

```
TO PRIME? :N
 OP PRIME.HELPER :N 2
END
```

```
TO PRIME.HELPER :N :K
 IF :K > :N - 1 [OP "TRUE]
 IF DIVIS? :N :K [OP "FALSE]
 OP PRIME.HELPER :N :K + 1
END
```

Try it out. It works fine for small numbers or if the input has a small prime as a factor, but it really begins to slow down for primes bigger than 100 (try SHOW PRIME? 877). It's clear that PRIME? outlines a process that requires too much work. For example, the only even prime is 2, and PRIME? tests its input for divisibility by 2, 4, 6, ... Why not toss out even numbers right away?

```
TO PRIME? :N
 IF EVEN? :N [OP "FALSE]
 OP PRIME.HELPER :N 3
END

TO PRIME.HELPER :N :K
 IF :K > :N - 1 [OP "TRUE]
 IF DIVIS? :N :K [OP "FALSE]
 OP PRIME.HELPER :N :K + 2
END

TO EVEN? :N
 OP DIVIS? :N 2
END
```

What have we done? We first test a number for divisibility by 2; if it is divisible by 2, we pronounce it composite (so PRIME?(2) outputs FALSE, a slight bug in our predicate). If it isn't divisible by 2, we test it for divisibility by 3, 5, 7, 9, 11, and all odd numbers less than the number. This should cut the execution time for large odd prime inputs in about half; try it for 877. Notice that there is still a great deal of inefficiency in our method; if a number isn't divisible by 3, there is no need to test it for divisibility by 9, 15, ... Hold onto this thought; we'll come back to it in project 10.17. For now, let's leave this defect in our algorithm, and let's improve our method in a different direction.

You have probably realized by now that, in testing N for primality, you don't have to try all the odd possible factors less than $N - 1$; most people speed things up like this

```
TO PRIME? :N
 IF EVEN? :N [OP "FALSE]
 OP PRIME.HELPER :N 3
END

TO PRIME.HELPER :N :K
 IF :K > :N/2 [OP "TRUE]
 IF DIVIS? :N :K [OP "FALSE]
 OP PRIME.HELPER :N :K + 2
END
```

The idea is that you only need to test N for divisibility up to $N/2$. Why is this? (Although most people see that it works, many people have a hard time explaining why you only need to go up "half way.") If you think about the reason that this improvement works, you realize that a much better improvement can be made.

Suppose we are testing 101 for primality. Our previous predicate PRIME? tests 101 for divisibility by

> 2, 3, 5, 7, 9, 11, 13, 15, 17, 19, 21, 23, 25, 27, 29, 31, 33, 35,
> 37, 39, 41, 43, 45, 47, 49, 51, 53, 55, 57, 59, 61, 63, 65, 67, 69,
> 71, 73, 75, 77, 79, 81, 83, 85, 87, 89, 91, 93, 95, 97 and 99.

Our improved PRIME? tests 101 for divisibility by about only half as many numbers; it tries for divisibility by

> 2, 3, 5, 7, 9, 11, 13, 15, 17, 19, 21, 23, 25, 27, 29, 31, 33, 35,
> 37, 39, 41, 43, 45, 47, and 49.

The reason why this works is that if 101 has a factor M bigger than 49, then it must also have a factor smaller than 49 because the product of two numbers bigger than 49 is (much) bigger than 101. In other words, if $101 = MM'$ and M is bigger than 49, then M' must be smaller than 49, and M' will show up on our list of factors less than 101/2. Think about this for a minute; do you see that the same argument can cut back the list of possible factors even more?

The truth is that if 101 has a factor bigger than 11, then it must also have a factor smaller than 11 because the product of two numbers each bigger than 11 is bigger than 11^2 or 121. In other words, if $101 = MM'$ and M is bigger than 11, then M' must be smaller than 11, so we only have to test 101 for divisibility by 2, 3 , 5, 7, and 9. This is quite a savings. Let's try this argument with another number.

In testing 877 for primality, our PRIME? predicate will test it for divisibility by 2, 3, 5, 7, 9, 11, ..., 437. In reality we need to test it for divisibility by

2, 3, 5, 7, 9, 11, 13, 15, 17, 19, 21, 23, 25, 27, and 29

because if 877 has an odd factor M greater than or equal to 31, then $877 = MM'$ and M' must be smaller than 31 (the product of two numbers each bigger than 31 is bigger than 31^2 or 961). Once again, quite a savings.

Well, how high must we go in testing N for primality? We should try all possible divisors until we reach a number M so that $MM > N$; in other words, we should try all numbers up to the greatest integer M that is less than or equal to SQRT(N). This yields a significant improvement for large odd primes:

```
TO PRIME? :N
 IF EVEN? :N [OP "FALSE]
 OP PRIME.HELPER :N 3
END

TO PRIME.HELPER :N :K
 IF :K > SQRT :N [OP "TRUE]
 IF DIVIS? :N :K [OP "FALSE]
 OP PRIME.HELPER :N :K + 1
END
```

Going up only to the square root of the number being tested means that we can test a number as big as 10,000 for primality in around 50 steps (the square root of 10,000 is 100, and we only try odd divisors).

Exercise 10.12 Take some time to play with our versions of PRIME?. Time each of them on a large prime (say, 997). Which is fastest when the input is 998? How about 131? 3043? Describe the inputs for which our final version is significantly faster. For what kinds of inputs does it not make much difference? In testing 137 for primality, our fastest version of PRIME? uses the integers 2, 3, 5, 7, 9, and 11 as trial divisors. What is the largest number that PRIME? will test with these same trial divisors?

It is often useful to have a list of primes (for example, as data for an experiment). Suppose that PRIMES.UPTO(N) is the list of primes between 2 and N. One way to generate PRIMES.UPTO(N) is to simply take each element in the list

$$[1\ 2\ 3\ldots N]$$

and test it for primality. The list of elements that "test positive" for primality is `PRIMES.UPTO`(N). The function `PRIME.LIST` tests each element in any list for primality:

```
TO PRIME.LIST :L
 IF EMPTYP :L [OP []]
 IF PRIME? (FIRST :L) [OP FPUT (FIRST :L) PRIME.LIST BF :L]
 OP PRIME.LIST BF :L
END
```

The output of

```
PRIME.LIST [16 17 101 34 877]
```

is [17 101 877]. To generate the list of primes less than 20, you would call

```
PRIME.LIST [2 3 4 5 6 7 8 9 10 11 12 13 14 15 16 17 18 19 20]
```

and the output would be [2 3 5 7 11 13 17 19]. Rather than constructing the input list to `PRIME.LIST` by hand, we could use the following function:

```
TO LIST.UPTO :N
 IF :N = 1 [OP []]
 OP SE (LIST.UPTO :N - 1) :N
END
```

We then have

```
TO PRIMES.UPTO  :N
 OP PRIME.LIST LIST.UPTO :N
END
```

So what are the primes less than 100? Less than 500? 1000?

Exercise 10.13 Rewrite `PRIMES.UPTO` so that it doesn't have to use a list generator like `LIST.UPTO`.

Exercise 10.14 Write a function `ODDLIST.UPTO` that generates a list consisting all odd numbers between 3 and N.

PRIME.LIST is an example of a general process that can be described as a sieve (or, in the language of the appendix, a filter); to sieve a list with a given predicate, you simply apply the predicate to each element in the list, and you output the list of elements at which the predicate outputs TRUE. For example, we could ask for the list of all numbers less than, say, 1000 that are divisible by 3. Then we could sieve the list

$$[1\ 2\ 3\ \dots\ 1000]$$

with the predicate DIVIS.BY.THREE? where

```
TO DIVIS.BY.THREE? :N
 OP DIVIS? :N 3
END
```

This general method can be modeled in Logo:

```
TO SIEVE :PRED :E :L
 IF EMPTYP :L [OP []]
 IF APPLY :PRED (SE :E FIRST :L) →
    [OP FPUT FIRST :L (SIEVE :PRED :E BF :L)]
 OP SIEVE :PRED :E BF :L
END
```

I built in some flexibility by allowing the predicate to take more than one input (E is the list of extra inputs). So we can define PRIMES.UPTO like this:

```
TO PRIMES.UPTO :N
 OP SIEVE "PRIME? [] LIST.UPTO :N
END
```

Project 10.15 A composite of SIEVEs can be used to filter a list with several predicates. If you wanted to find all the numbers less than 100 that were divisible by 3 and by 7, you could type

```
SHOW SIEVE DIVIS? 3 (SIEVE DIVIS? 7 LIST.UPTO 100)
```

Can you generate this list by SIEVEing LIST.UPTO(100) with a single predicate? Use SIEVE (and appropriate combinations of predicates) to generate the following lists of numbers up to 100:

1. Divisible by 5 and by 7

2. Divisible by 7 and by 9

3. Divisible by 6 and by 8

4. Divisible by 7 or by 3

5. Divisible by 6 or by 10

6. Prime and of the form $4K + 1$

Which of the above lists can be generated by SIEVEing the list with a single predicate? Which list has more elements: the list of primes (less than 100) of the form $3K + 1$ or the list of primes (less than 100) of the form $3K + 2$? Does this same inequality hold if you look at primes up to 500?

Experiment 10.16 Some numbers, like 100, can be written as the sum of two perfect squares (64 + 36). By using a composite of two SIEVEs, generate the list of primes less than 500 that can be written as the sum of two squares. What makes these primes different from the primes that are not the sum of two squares?

In calculating PRIMES.UPTO(N), every number from 1 to N is tested for primality. This means that we must find the smallest factor (greater than 1) of each number between 1 and N. There is another beautiful method for generating the list of primes less than a given integer; it's called the Sieve of Eratosthenes (around 230 B.C.), and it does for PRIMES.UPTO what our best improvement did for PRIME?. It works like this: Suppose we want all the primes less than 40. We form the list of all the integers between 2 and 40:

[2 3 4 5 6 7 8 9 10 11 12 13 14 15 16 17 18 19 20 21 22 23 24
25 26 27 28 29 30 31 32 33 34 35 36 37 38 39 40]

From this list we cross out all the numbers divisible by 2 (except for 2 itself):

[2 3 5 7 9 11 13 15 17 19 21 23 25 27 29 31 33 35 37 39]

The next number on the list (3) isn't divisible by anything smaller than itself (or it would have been crossed out), so it is prime. Leave 3 and delete everything on the list divisible by 3:

[2 3 5 7 11 13 17 19 23 25 29 31 35 37]

The next number on the list (5) isn't divisible by anything smaller than itself (or it would have been crossed out), so it is prime. Leave 5 and delete everything on the list divisible by 5:

[2 3 5 7 11 13 17 19 23 29 31 37]

The next number on the list (7) isn't divisible by anything smaller than itself (or it would have been crossed out), so it is prime. Leave 7 and delete everything on the list divisible by 7; when you try to do this, you notice that there aren't any multiples of 7 on the list. This is because

$$7 \cdot 2, \; 7 \cdot 3, \; 7 \cdot 4, \; 7 \cdot 5, \; \text{and} \; 7 \cdot 6$$

have already been crossed out (these numbers are divisible by 2, 3 or 5), and the next multiple of 7 (49) is bigger than 40. Similarly, 11, not being divisible by any smaller number, is prime, and its multiples have already been deleted from the list. Inductively, we see that the remaining numbers in the list (the ones that are "caught by the sieve") are all prime. So, to generate PRIME.LIST(N) by Eratosthenes' method, we only have to find the smallest factors of the integers up to SQRT(N), and for large N, this translates into a significant savings of time.

To model Eratosthenes' sieve in Logo, imagine a function ERATOSTHENES that takes two lists I and O as input. I starts out as the list of integers between 2 and N, and O starts out as []. ERATOSTHENES sieves I and transforms O into the list of primes between 2 and N. More precisely, suppose that I starts out as

$I =$ [2 3 4 5 6 7 8 9 10 11 12 13 14 15 16 17 18 19 20 21 22 23 24 25 26 27 28 29 30 31 32 33 34 35 36 37 38 39 40]

and O starts out as

$O =$ []

After ERATOSTHENES SIEVEs I for divisibility by 2, we have

$I =$ [3 5 7 9 11 13 15 17 19 21 23 25 27 29 31 33 35 37 39]

and

$O =$ [2]

Next, **ERATOSTHENES** SIEVEs I for divisibility by 3 (and LPUTs 3 onto O):

$I = [5\ 7\ 11\ 13\ 17\ 19\ 23\ 25\ 29\ 31\ 35\ 37]$

and

$O = [2\ 3]$

Finally, **ERATOSTHENES** SIEVEs I for divisibility by 5 (and LPUTs 5 onto O):

$I = [7\ 11\ 13\ 17\ 19\ 23\ 29\ 31\ 37]$

and

$O = [2\ 3\ 5]$

At this point, everything left in I is prime (each number is bigger than SQRT(40) and is not divisible by anything smaller than itself), so **ERATOSTHENES** can just output the SEntence of O and I:

[2 3 5 7 11 13 17 19 23 29 31 37]

These are the primes less than 40. The idea in **ERATOSTHENES** is to move the **FIRST** element of I over to O while replacing I with the **SIEVE** of the **BF** of I using the predicate that tests for nondivisibility by the **FIRST** element of I. Here are the details:

```
TO NOT.A.FACTOR? :F :N
 OP NOT DIVIS? :N :F
END

TO ERATOSTHENES :I :O
 IF FIRST :I > SQRT (LAST :I) [OP SE :O :I]
 OP ERATOSTHENES →
     (SIEVE "NOT.A.FACTOR? (FIRST :I) BF :I) (LPUT FIRST :I :O)
END
```

ERATOSTHENES gives us a fairly quick way to generate lists of primes, so we'll change PRIMES.UPTO to

```
TO PRIMES.UPTO :N
 OP ERATOSTHENES LIST.UPTO :N []
END
```

Compare this version of PRIMES.UPTO with our original one (generate, say, the list of primes between 1 and 100). Do you notice a difference in speed? Do we need to put in a fix for the special prime 2?

Project 10.17 Most books on programming take a more computerish approach to ERATOSTHENES. A typical idea is this: To SIEVE the list

[2 3 4 5 6 7 8 9 10 11 12 13 14 15 16 17 18 19 20 21 22 →
  23 24 25 26 27 28]

for primes, keep the 2 and replace every second number after it by 0:

[2 3 0 5 0 7 0 9 0 11 0 13 0 15 0 17 0 19 0 21 0 23 0 25 →
  0 27 0]

Then, keep 3 and change every third number after that to 0 (some have already been changed):

[2 3 0 5 0 7 0 0 0 11 0 13 0 0 0 17 0 19 0 0 0 23 0 25 0 0 0]

Next, keep 5 and change every fifth number after that to 0 (some have already been changed):

[2 3 0 5 0 7 0 0 0 11 0 13 0 0 0 17 0 19 0 0 0 23 0 0 0 0 0]

Finally, since 7 > SQRT(30), we can eliminate the 0's from our list; what remains is the list of primes less than 30. The idea here is that counting by K's (crossing out every Kth entry) is supposed to be faster than testing for divisibility. Discuss the validity of this statement. Model this method in Logo, and compare it to our original ERATOSTHENES.

Project 10.18 Our first improvement on PRIME? came with the realization that if a number isn't divisible by 2, then there is no sense testing it for divisibility by 4, 6, 8, or any other even number. Similarly, if a number isn't divisible by 3, there is no sense testing it for divisibility by 6, 9, 12, or any other multiple of 3. In general, if N isn't divisible by J, then it isn't divisible by any multiple of J. This fact is a corollary of the following result from experiment 10.9:

> If A, B, and C are integers so that $A \mid B$ and $B \mid C$, then $A \mid C$

The proof of the above fact follows from the definition of divisibility.

If $A \mid B$, then $B = AK$ for some integer K. If $B \mid C$ then $C = BK'$ for some integer K'. But then

$$C = BK' = AKK' = A \text{ (something)}$$

so $A \mid C$.

Use this result to prove that if N isn't divisible by K, then it isn't divisible by any multiple of K.

So, in testing 101 for primality, our best version of PRIME? tests it for divisibility by

2, 3, 5, 7, and 9

We don't need to test 101 for divisibility by 9 (9 is already ruled out as a factor when we rule out 3), so we can pronounce 101 prime if it isn't divisible by 2, 3, 5, and 7. And these are the only divisors that we'd need to try in testing any number between 49 and 120 for primality.

In testing 877 for primality, our best version of PRIME? tests it for divisibility by

2, 3, 5, 7, 9, 11, 13, 15, 17, 19, 21, 23, 25, 27, and 29

What can we eliminate? We don't need to test for divisibility by 9, 15, 21 or 27 (any number divisible by one of these is already divisible by 3), and we can also get rid of 25. So 877 is composite or prime depending on whether or not it has a factor from the list

2, 3, 5, 7, 11, 13, 17, 19, 23, and 29

Furthermore these are the only trial divisors that we'd need to try in testing any number between 529 and 960 for primality.

In general, our best version of PRIME? tests a number N for primality by seeing if it isn't divisible by 2 or by any odd integers between 3 and SQRT(N). We have just seen that we can eliminate any of these trial divisors that are multiples of smaller ones. What remains? Precisely the set of primes between 2 and SQRT(N). So we have the following algorithm:

The positive integer N is prime if it isn't divisible by any prime that is less than or equal to SQRT(N)

Model the algorithm in Logo. Hint: Change our `PRIME.HELPER` predicate so that it runs through a list of trial divisors; that is, change

```
TO PRIME.HELPER :N :K
 IF :K > SQRT :N [OP "TRUE]
 IF DIVIS? :N :K [OP "FALSE]
 OP PRIME.HELPER :N :K + 1
END
```

to

```
TO PRIME.HELPER :N :FACTORLIST
  ⋮
END
```

Then, to test 877 (or any number between 529 and 961) for primality, we could type

```
SHOW PRIME.HELPER 877 [2 3 5 7 11 13 17 19 23 29]
```

Then we modify `PRIME?` like this:

```
TO PRIME? :N
 OP PRIME.HELPER :N PRIMES.UPTO SQRT :N
END
```

Is this modification worth it? Compare it for speed against our old version of `PRIME?` Can you describe the numbers at which one version is faster than the other? Can you explain why?

Infinitely Many Primes

Notice that `PRIMES.UPTO` outputs the same list for inputs between 337 and 346. It's conceivable that the output from `PRIMES.UPTO` eventually stabilizes; in other words, it might happen that the list of primes is finite. Euclid showed that this doesn't happen:

Theorem 10.4 There are infinitely many primes.

Euclid's proof shows how to take any list of primes and produce a prime not on the list. Suppose you have a list of K primes:

$$[P_1 \ P_2 \ \ldots \ P_K]$$

Let N be 1 more than the product of these primes:

$$N = (P_1 P_2 P_3 \ldots P_K) + 1$$

Then N is bigger than any of the P's, so if N is prime, we have produced a prime not on our list. But if N isn't prime, it has a prime factor P (from project 10.10). Now, P can't be one of the primes on our list, because each of these leave a remainder of 1 when you divide them into N (this is because $N = (P_1 P_2 \ldots P_K) + 1$, so $\text{MOD}(N, P_I) = 1$ for any of the P_I). In other words, either N is itself a prime that isn't on our list or it is divisible by a prime that isn't on our list.

Experiment 10.19 Euclid's proof suggests the following question: If you take the elements in PRIMES.UPTO(N), multiply them together and add 1, is the answer always a new prime? Try it for $N = 2, 3, 4, 5$ and 6. Is it always true?

There are other proofs of Euclid's result, but Euclid's original proof is one of the simplest and most appealing arguments in all of mathematics. The fact that there are infinitely many primes is responsible for many of the interesting questions in number theory; it means that the set of primes is a rich place for investigation. For example, there are many good questions about the "distribution" of primes; here's a sample:

1. It seems that the primes "thin out" after a while. For example, there are 168 primes less than 1000, so .168 of the numbers between 1 and 1000 are prime. There are only 78498 primes less than 1,000,000, so the ratio here is only .078498. Does this phenomenon persist? Is there a good estimate (say, a function of N) for the number of primes less than N?

2. Even though there are infinitely many primes, can you find long sequences of integers in which there are no primes? For example, none of the integers between 338 and 346 is prime. Is there a sequence of 100 consecutive composites?

3. Are there simple functions that output only primes?

4. How many primes are outputs of familiar functions? For example, if **F** is an arithmetic sequence with first term 1 and common ratio 4, are there infinitely many primes among the terms of **F**?

5. How many primes have a special form? For example, how many primes are the sum of two perfect squares? How many primes are the difference of two perfect squares?

6. If you look at `PRIMES.UPTO(100)`, you notice that primes often come in "pairs": 2 and 3, 5 and 7, 11 and 13, 17 and 19, 29 and 31, 41 and 43, and 71 and 73. How many pairs of these "twin primes" are there?

There are many other similar questions; you can certainly come up with a few of your own. The frustrating (and intriguing) thing about these questions is that though they all sound straightforward, some of them are easy to answer while others are incredibly difficult to deal with. For example, question 2 is not difficult, and question 3 depends on your definition of "simple." Question 5 is moderately difficult (see experiment 10.15). Question 1 has been settled; Gauss had experimental evidence for the answer, but it wasn't until the end of the last century that J. Hadamard and C. de la Valle Poussin established theoretically that the size of `PRIMES.UPTO(`N`)` can be estimated with fairly good precision for large N. The proof uses advanced techniques (some of which had to be invented for this problem). Question 4 has only partly been settled. For example, Peter Dirichlet (a student of Gauss) showed that every arithmetic sequence whose first term has no factor in common with its common difference contains infinitely many primes as outputs. His proof requires very advanced methods (in the next section, we'll look at another proof of theorem 10.4 that contains some of the spirit of Dirichlet's proof). For functions other than arithmetic sequences, much less is known. Question 6 is still open in spite of the work of many people; current mathematical methods have so far led to dead ends when applied to this twin prime question.

Project 10.20 Given any positive integer N, find a method for generating N consecutive composite integers. Hint: Start your search at $N!$. The location of the smallest starting point for a string of N composites is investigated in Polites (1988).

Experiment 10.21 Consider the quadratic function

```
TO F :X
 OP (POWER :X 2) + :X + 41
END
```

Tabulate F between 1 and, say, 20. What do you notice about the outputs? Does this phenomenon always occur?

Exercise 10.22 Show that the function

```
TO F :X
 OP 2 * :X + 1
END
```

produces infinitely many primes.

Experiment 10.23 Someone once told me that the function F that is defined like this

```
TO F :N
 OP :N * (TERM :N) + 2 * (1 - TERM :N)
END

TO TERM :N
 OP MOD (POWER (FACT.MOD :N - 1 :N) 2) :N
END

TO FACT.MOD :N :M
 IF :N = 0 [OP 1]
 OP MOD :N * (FACT.MOD :N - 1 :M) :M
END
```

generates only primes for positive values of N, *and*, if P is a prime, $P = \mathrm{F}(N)$ for some positive integer N. Tabulate F and explain why this claim is a cruel joke. Later in this section, we'll see why this works.

Project 10.24 Consider the function MERSENNE:

```
TO MERSENNE :N
 OP (POWER 2 :N) - 1
END
```

P. Mersenne (1588–1648) was concerned with those outputs of MERSENNE that are prime (the "Mersenne primes"). Investigate this question. Show that if MERSENNE(N) is prime, then N must be prime. Hint: use the cyclotomic identity from chapter 6 to show that

$$2^{MN} - 1 = (2^M - 1)(2^{M(N-1)} + 2^{M(N-2)} + \cdots + 2^M + 1)$$

Mersenne believed that if MERSENNE(N) is prime, then

MERSENNE(MERSENNE(N))

is also prime. Verify this for several Mersenne primes. In 1953 it was shown that even though MERSENNE(13) is prime, MERSENNE(MERSENNE(13)) is composite.

Experiment 10.4 Consider the function FERMAT:

```
TO FERMAT :N
 OP (POWER 2 :N) + 1
END
```

A Fermat prime is an output of FERMAT that is prime. Develop a conjecture about the kinds of inputs to FERMAT that produce Fermat primes. Can you prove anything?

Project 10.25 Show that an arithmetic sequence cannot output only prime numbers.

Project 10.26 Use Euclid's argument to show that the Nth prime number is at most $2^{2^N} - 1$. Hint: Use induction on N.

Chapter 11

Greatest Common Divisor and the Fundamental Theorem of Arithmetic

In this chapter, we'll prove that every integer can be written as a product of primes in essentially one way. This theorem is known as the "fundamental theorem of arithmetic," and it will be crucial to our work. It's not too hard to show that every integer can be written as a product of primes; it's the "essentially one way" part of the theorem that will take some work. This "unique factorization" property of **Z** hinges on an important result (theorem 11.8) of Euclid, and this result in turn depends on some facts about greatest common divisors for pairs of integers.

Greatest Common Divisor

Given two positive integers A and B, we can ask for their common divisors. For example, the common divisors of 24 and 36 are 1, 2, 3, 4 and 6. 6 is the greatest common divisor of 24 and 36 in two senses of the word "greatest". First of all, 6 is the largest integer that divides both 24 and 36. Furthermore, 6 is a "greatest" divisor of 24 and 36 in the sense that any integer that divides both 24 and 36 must also divide 6 (6 is greatest with respect to *divisibility*). This second meaning of the word "greatest" is perhaps not as familiar to you as the first meaning, but it turns out to be the best way to think about greatest common divisors (it is more portable to other number systems). Here it is:

Definition 11.1 If A and B are integers, we say that D is a greatest common divisor of A and B if D satisfies these two properties:

1. $D \mid A$ and $D \mid B$.

2. IF $C \mid A$ and $C \mid B$, then we also have that $C \mid D$.

In other words, a greatest common divisor of A and B is a common factor of A and B that is a multiple of every other common factor of A and B. Notice that 24 and 36 have another greatest common divisor besides 6: -6. In general, greatest common divisors are determined only up to multiplication by units. This means that if, in $\mathbf{Z}$, D is a greatest common divisor of A and B, the $-D$ is another greatest common divisor of A and B. Since $\mathbf{Z}$ has only two units (1 and -1), two integers A and B can only have two greatest common divisors. To avoid confusion, when we speak of the greatest common divisor of integers A and B, we'll always mean the positive greatest common divisor of A and B, and we'll denote this number by $\mathrm{GCD}(A, B)$. For example,

$$\mathrm{GCD}(12, 16) = 4$$

$$\mathrm{GCD}(12, 24) = 12$$

$$\mathrm{GCD}(-180, 120) = 60$$

$$\mathrm{GCD}(34, 67) = 1$$

To show how this definition is applied in theoretical situations, let's prove that if A and B are integers, then $\mathrm{GCD}(A, B) = \mathrm{GCD}(A, A + B)$. For example, we are claiming that $\mathrm{GCD}(12, 16) = \mathrm{GCD}(12, 28)$ (both GCDs are 4). Suppose that D is the greatest common divisor of A and B. Then we know two things:

1. $D \mid A$ and $D \mid B$.

2. If $C \mid A$ and $C \mid B$, then $C \mid D$.

We want to prove that D is also the greatest common divisor of A and $A + B$. To do this, we must show two things; we must show that

1'. $D \mid A$ and $D \mid (A + B)$, and

2'. if $C \mid A$ AND $C \mid (A + B)$, then $C \mid D$.

Well, clearly $D \mid A$ (this is part of what it means for D to be the GCD of A and B). So, to establish 1', we need only show that $D \mid (A + B)$. But since $D \mid A$ and $D \mid B$, there are integers K and K' so that $A = DK$ and $B = DK'$. This means that

$$A + B = DK + DK' = D(K + K') = D \cdot (\textit{something})$$

so $D \mid (A + B)$. This establishes 1'.

For 2', suppose that C is some integer that divides both A and $A + B$. Then there exist integers J and J' so that $A = CJ$ and $A + B = CJ'$. This last equation can be solved for B and manipulated like this:

$$B = CJ' - A = CJ' - CJ = C(J' - J) = C \cdot (\textit{something})$$

so $C \mid B$. Since $C \mid B$ and $C \mid A$, and since D is the greatest common divisor of A and B, $C \mid D$, this establishes 2'.

In proofs like this, the main strategy is to substitute the definition of greatest common divisor (definition 11.1) whenever you see the phrase "greatest common divisor" and to substitute the definition of "divides" ($X \mid Y$ if there is an integer Z so that $Y = XZ$) whenever you see the word "divides."

Here's another example. Let's show that that if A and B are positive and $A \mid B$, then $\text{GCD}(A, B) = A$.

First of all, note that $A \mid A$ and $A \mid B$, so A is a common divisor of A and B. Next suppose that C is any common divisor of A and B. Then $C \mid A$ and $C \mid B$. In particular, $C \mid A$. So any common divisor of A and B must divide A, and hence A is the greatest common divisor of A and B.

Exercise 11.1 Prove that if B is any positive integer, $\text{GCD}(0, B) = B$.

Exercise 11.2 Prove that if A and B are integers, then $\text{GCD}(A, B) = \text{GCD}(A, B - A)$.

Experiment 11.3 True or false: If A and B are integers and K is any other integer, then $\text{GCD}(A, B) = \text{GCD}(A, B + KA)$.

There is one case where our definition of GCD doesn't hold up. Because any integer divides 0, $\text{GCD}(0, 0)$ doesn't make sense. We can either leave $\text{GCD}(0, 0)$ undefined (we'll never need it) or, if you don't like loose ends, we can define $\text{GCD}(0, 0)$ to be 0 (think of this as an analogy with the fact that if A is positive, $\text{GCD}(A, A) = A$).

Exercise 11.4 Prove that if $A > 0$, $\text{GCD}(A, A) = A$.

How can we model GCD in Logo? One way, of course, to find $\text{GCD}(A, B)$ would be to form the list of all the factors of A and the list of all the factors of B, and then to find the largest factor common to both lists. This is not a good idea for two reasons:

1. Finding factors is very time-consuming.

2. This method uses the first interpretation of the word "greatest," not the one that is used in definition 11.1; it would be difficult to model this algorithm in number systems where there is no simple notion of size.

Euclid's Algorithm

In the seventh book of Euclid's *Elements*, there is a beautiful recursive algorithm for finding $GCD(A, B)$ that doesn't require the knowledge of any factors of A or B. This gem was invented over twenty centuries before computers; mathematicians have been thinking inductively for a long time. Here's how Euclid's algorithm works.

First, convince yourself that

$$GCD(A, B) = GCD(-A, B) = GCD(A, -B) = GCD(-A, -B)$$

so we can assume that A and B are nonnegative.

If $A = 0$, then $GCD(A, B) = B$ (because $B \mid 0$ if B is positive and, if B is 0, because we defined $GCD(0, 0)$ to be 0). Suppose that $A > 0$.

Let Q be $QUOT(B, A)$, and let $R = MOD(B, A)$. Then, by theorem 10.1,

1. $B = QA + R$, and

2. $0 \leq R < A$.

Euclid first shows that $GCD(A, B) = GCD(R, A)$. Try this for a few examples before reading on. That is, check experimentally that

$$GCD(A, B) = GCD(MOD(BA), A)$$

for several values of A and B. For example, check that

$$GCD(12, 22) = GCD(10, 12)$$
$$GCD(10, 12) = GCD(2, 10)$$
$$GCD(26, 28) = GCD(2, 26)$$
$$GCD(432, 21) = GCD(12, 21)$$

Note that if B is smaller than A, $\texttt{MOD}(B, A) = B$, so, in this case, the claim that $\texttt{GCD}(A, B) = \texttt{GCD}(\texttt{MOD}(BA), A)$ simply says that $\texttt{GCD}(A, B) = \texttt{GCD}(B, A)$.

In general, suppose that $D = \texttt{GCD}(A, B)$ and $D' = \texttt{GCD}(R, A)$. Then D and D' are positive integers, and we want to show that $D = D'$. We'll show that $D = D'$ by showing that $D \mid D'$ and $D' \mid D$. (See part 4 of experiment 10.10, and remember that D and D' are assumed to be positive.)

Suppose that $C \mid A$ and that $C \mid B$. Then there are integers K and J so that $A = CK$ and $B = CJ$. But because

$$R = B - QA = CJ - QCK = C(J - QK)$$

C also divides R. This means that any common divisor of A and B is also a divisor of R. So any common divisor of A and B is also a common divisor of R and A. It follows from definition 11.1 that any common divisor of A and B is a divisor of D'. But D is a common divisor of A and B, so $D \mid D'$.

Suppose next that $C \mid R$ and that $C \mid A$. Then there are integers K and J so that $R = CK$ and $A = CJ$. But because

$$B = QA + R = QCJ + CK = C(QJ + K)$$

C also divides B. This means that any common divisor of R and A is also a divisor of B. So any common divisor of R and A is also a common divisor of A and B. It follows from definition 11.1 that any common divisor of R and A is a divisor of D. But D' is a common divisor of R and A, so $D' \mid D$.

Again, since we have shown that $D \mid D'$ and $D' \mid D$ and since D and D' are positive, we can conclude that $D = D'$.

The above argument is typical of the kinds of proofs that you find in most mathematics texts; it consists of a sequence of statements, each backed up by some previously established fact. In trying to understand such a proof, it always helps to keep a concrete example on hand. Let's work through the above argument in the case where $A = 124$ and $B = 1028$. Then $Q = 8$ and $R = 36$, because

$$1028 = 8 \cdot 124 + 36$$

We claim with Euclid that $\texttt{GCD}(124, 1028) = \texttt{GCD}(36, 124)$. Suppose that

$$\texttt{GCD}(124, 1028) = D \text{ and } \texttt{GCD}(36, 124) = D'$$

Then any common factor of 124 and 1028 divides D, and any common factor of 36 and 124 divides D'. From the equation

$$1028 = 8 \cdot 124 + 36$$

you can see that any factor of 36 and 124 is also a factor of 1028 (why?). Well, D' is a factor of 36 and 124, so D' is a factor of 1028. But D' is also a factor of 124, so it is a common factor of 124 and 1028. By the statement we agreed to in the first line of this paragraph, $D' \mid D$. Similarly, from the equation

$$36 = 1028 - 8 \cdot 124$$

you can see that any factor of 124 and 1028 is also a factor of 36 (why?). Well, D is a factor of 124 and 1028, so D is a factor of 36. But D is also a factor of 124, so it is a common factor of 36 and 124. By the statement we agreed to in the first line of this paragraph, $D \mid D'$.

We've gone to enough trouble to prove this fact that we might as well declare our result as a theorem:

Theorem 11.2 If A and B are positive integers with $0 < A$, then

$$\mathrm{GCD}(A, B) = \mathrm{GCD}(\mathrm{MOD}(B, A), A)$$

Now, Euclid's algorithm uses the above theorem and the fact that $\mathrm{MOD}(B, A)$ is nonnegative and strictly less than A to calculate like this:

$$
\begin{aligned}
\mathrm{GCD}(124, 1028) &= \mathrm{GCD}(\mathrm{MOD}(1028, 124), 124) \\
&= \mathrm{GCD}(36, 124) = \mathrm{GCD}(\mathrm{MOD}(124, 36), 36) \\
&= \mathrm{GCD}(16, 36) = \mathrm{GCD}(\mathrm{MOD}(36, 16), 16) \\
&= \mathrm{GCD}(4, 16) = 4
\end{aligned}
$$

The process stopped because $4 \mid 16$, so that $\mathrm{GCD}(4, 16) = 4$. Suppose for a minute that you didn't realize that $4 \mid 16$, and you carried out the calculation one step further:

$$
\begin{aligned}
\mathrm{GCD}(124, 1028) &= \mathrm{GCD}(36, 124) \\
&= \mathrm{GCD}(16, 36) \\
&= \mathrm{GCD}(4, 16) \\
&= \mathrm{GCD}(0, 4) \\
&= 4
\end{aligned}
$$

If you wanted to do this calculation by hand, you could arrange your steps like this:

```
              8
       ┌──────────
  124  )  1028
          992      3
          ────  ┌──────
           36   )  124
                   108     2
                   ────  ┌──────
                    16   )   36
                            32     4
                            ───  ┌──────
                              4  )   16
                                    16
                                    ──
                                     0
```

At each step, the remainder becomes the new divisor and the previous divisor becomes the new dividend (the number inside the division box). It's clear that the process stops in this example, but how do we know that it will always stop? Before you read on, try to answer this question. It might help you to work out the next exercise by hand.

Exercise 11.5 Find the GCD of each pair by using Euclid's algorithm:

1. GCD(188, 1024)

2. GCD(189, 1024)

3. GCD(1717, 505)

4. GCD(940, 5120)

So why does the process stop? Look at a Logo model for GCD:

```
TO GCD :A :B
 IF :A = 0 [OP :B]
 OP GCD (MOD :B :A) :A
END
```

(Euclid would have loved this.) If we trace the calls to GCD in the calculation of GCD(188, 1024), we obtain

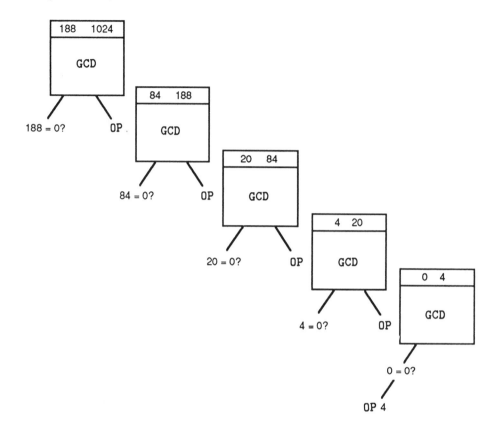

Figure 11.1

Do you see that the first input to GCD gets smaller with each call? The reason for this is that at each step, the first input to GCD is the remainder that you get when the second input to GCD at the previous step is divided by the first input to GCD in the previous step. If this is confusing, look at figure 11.2 (which shows a piece of the calculation in figure 11.1).

At the step where you call GCD(20, 84), the first input to GCD is 20, and 20 is MOD(188, 84); it is the "remainder when the second input to GCD at the previous step" (188) is "divided by the first input to GCD at the previous step" (84). Now, by theorem 10.1, the remainder in a division (of positive integers) is smaller than the divisor, so each first input to GCD is strictly smaller than the previous one. So the first inputs to GCD form a sequence of positive integers with the property that each term is strictly smaller than the previous one. If

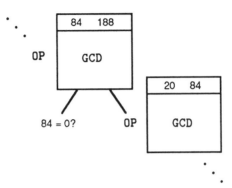

Figure 11.2

the sequence starts out with A, then in at most A steps, a term in the sequence will be 0, and this will cause GCD to output. We have proved the following theorem:

Theorem 11.3 The function

```
TO GCD :A :B
 IF :A = 0 [OP :B]
 OP GCD (MOD :B :A) :A
END
```

outputs the greatest common divisor of A and B for all nonnegative integers A and B.

Check out the theorem with several examples; try typing

```
SHOW GCD 12 16
```

or

```
SHOW GCD 1028 3124
```

Experiment 11.6 Is the theorem still true if A or B is allowed to be negative?

Experiment 11.7 Find the result of each calculation using your Logo model for GCD. Look for theorems.

1. GCD$(70, 110)$
2. GCD$(35, 55)$
3. GCD$(210, 330)$
4. GCD$(70, 110 - 70)$
5. GCD$(70, 110 + 70)$
6. GCD$(70 \cdot 70, 110 \cdot 110)$
7. GCD$(27, 36)$
8. GCD$(63, 36)$
9. GCD$(135, 36)$
10. GCD$(207, 36)$
11. GCD$(17, 19)$
12. GCD$(11, 17)$

Experiment 11.8 Use several values of A and B (include some large integers) as data to discuss each statement. If a statement isn't true for all values of A and B, for what values is it true?

1. $3 \cdot \text{GCD}(A, B) = \text{GCD}(3A, 3B)$
2. $\text{GCD}(A, B) = \text{GCD}(A, B - A)$
3. $(\text{GCD}(A, B))^2 = \text{GCD}(A^2, B^2)$
4. $\text{GCD}(A, 2B) = \text{GCD}(A, B)$
5. $\text{GCD}(A, A + 1) = 1$
6. $\dfrac{AB}{\text{GCD}(A, B)}$ is divisible by A and by B
7. If A and B are different prime numbers, $\text{GCD}(A, B) = 1$
8. If K is any integer, $\text{GCD}(A, B) = \text{GCD}(A, B + AK)$
9. If K is any integer, $\text{GCD}(A, B) = \text{GCD}(A, A + BK)$

Can you prove any of your conjectures?

Experiment 11.9 Play with the following function:

```
TO F :A :B
 OP (:A * :B) / (GCD :A :B)
END
```

Can you give a simple description of F's outputs?

Experiment 11.10 The greatest common divisor for three integers is defined just like the greatest common divisor for two integers. Find the greatest common divisor for

1. 12, 16 and 20

2. 120, 90 and 330

Does this function output the greatest common divisor of its inputs?

```
TO PERHAPS :A :B :C
 OP GCD (GCD :A :B) :C
END
```

Explain.

#Project 11.11 Prove that if C, A and B are positive integers, then

$$\text{GCD}(CA, CB) = C(\text{GCD}(A, B))$$

Hint: Suppose that $0 < A \leq B$. Euclid's algorithm says that

$$\text{GCD}(CA, CB) = \text{GCD}(\text{MOD}(CB, CA), CA)$$

Now if you knew that $\text{MOD}(CB, CA) = C(\text{MOD}(B, A))$, you could say that

$$\text{GCD}(CA, CB) = \text{GCD}(C(\text{MOD}(B, A)), CA)$$

This last expression is of the form $\text{GCD}(C \cdot (something), C \cdot (something\ else))$, where "*something*" is smaller than A and "*something else*" is smaller than B. Inductively, (this is really the "strong induction" technique of part II), you can write this as

$$C(\text{GCD}(\text{MOD}(B, A), A))$$

which, by theorem 11.3, is $C(\text{GCD}(A, B))$. So, to make the proof complete, you must

1. tighten up the strong induction (show that the result holds for small values of A and B, for example), and

2. show that $\text{MOD}(CB, CA) = C(\text{MOD}(B, A))$. For this, use theorem 10.1 and project 10.5.

In chapter 12 we'll be able to give a much easier proof that $\text{GCD}(CA, CB) = C(\text{GCD}(A, B))$.

Use this result to show that if A and B are even, then

$$\text{GCD}(A, B) = 2\text{GCD}(\frac{A}{2}, \frac{B}{2})$$

Experiment 11.12 Is the following function equal to GCD?

```
TO GCF :A :B
 IF :A = 0 [OP :B]
 IF :B < :A [OP GCF :B :A]
 OP GCF :B - :A :A
END
```

Why or why not?

Working the Algorithm Backward

If you think of GCD as a function of two inputs, Euclid's algorithm gives an extremely clever way to transform A and B into their GCD. It is natural to wonder if there is a more traditional model for GCD. That is, perhaps $\text{GCD}(A, B)$ is given by some simple expression in A and B, like

$$3A + 2B$$

or

$$A^2 - 3B$$

or

$$\frac{AB^3}{(2A + B)}$$

or something like that.

Let's look for some simple way to write $\mathrm{GCD}(A, B)$ in terms of A and B, and let's start by looking at the calculation of $\mathrm{GCD}(124, 1028)$:

$$
\begin{array}{r}
8 \\
\hline
124 \overline{)\ 1028} \\
992 \\
\hline
36
\end{array}
\quad
\begin{array}{r}
3 \\
\hline
124 \\
108 \\
\hline
16
\end{array}
\quad
\begin{array}{r}
2 \\
\hline
36 \\
32 \\
\hline
4
\end{array}
\quad
\begin{array}{r}
4 \\
\hline
16 \\
16 \\
\hline
0
\end{array}
$$

The best thing to do is to play with the numbers. If we write out the result of each division (in the format of theorem 10.1), we see that

$$1028 = 8 \cdot 124 + 36$$

$$124 = 3 \cdot 36 + 16$$

$$36 = 2 \cdot 16 + 4$$

The numbers of interest here are 1028, 124, and their GCD, 4. It looks like we should be able to express the output of GCD (that is, 4) in terms of the inputs (124 and 1028). Solve each of the above identities for the remainders:

1. $36 = 1028 - 8 \cdot 124$

2. $16 = 124 - 3 \cdot 36$

3. $4 = 36 - 2 \cdot 16$

Next, work backward (a sure sign that mathematical induction is in the wings), substituting the last number in each equation with the expression for it given in the previous equation:

$$4 = 36 - 2(124 - 3 \cdot 36)$$

(Before we carry on, note that this implicitly expresses 4 in terms of 36 and 124; since 36 can be expressed in terms of 1028 and 124, we should be able to express 4 in terms of 1028 and 124.)

So

$$4 = 36 - 2 \cdot 124 + 6 \cdot 36$$
$$= 7 \cdot 36 - 2 \cdot 124.$$

Now, use equation 1:

$$4 = 7 \cdot 36 - 2 \cdot 124$$
$$= 7(1028 - 8 \cdot 124) - 2 \cdot 124$$
$$= 7 \cdot 1028 - 56 \cdot 124 - 2 \cdot 124$$
$$= 7 \cdot 1028 - 58 \cdot 124$$

So $\text{GCD}(124, 1028) = -58 \cdot 124 + 7 \cdot 1028$. Of course, the coefficients -58 and 7 won't work for every A and B, but it looks like there is a general method here that will allow us to write $\text{GCD}(A, B)$ as

$$(something) \cdot A + (something\ else) \cdot B.$$

Before we get too confident, we'd better try another example. Let's write $\text{GCD}(216, 3162)$ as a combination of 216 and 3162. By Euclid's algorithm, $\text{GCD}(216, 3162) = 6$.

$$
\begin{array}{r}
14 \\
216 \overline{\smash{\big)}\, 3162} \\
\underline{3024}
\end{array}
$$

$$
\begin{array}{r}
1 \\
138 \overline{\smash{\big)}\, 216} \\
\underline{138}
\end{array}
$$

$$
\begin{array}{r}
1 \\
78 \overline{\smash{\big)}\, 138} \\
\underline{78}
\end{array}
$$

$$
\begin{array}{r}
1 \\
60 \overline{\smash{\big)}\, 78} \\
\underline{60}
\end{array}
$$

$$
\begin{array}{r}
3 \\
18 \overline{\smash{\big)}\, 60} \\
\underline{54}
\end{array}
$$

$$
\begin{array}{r}
3 \\
6 \overline{\smash{\big)}\, 18} \\
\underline{18} \\
0
\end{array}
$$

If we write out the identities (solving for each remainder) we find that

$$138 = 3162 - 14 \cdot 216$$
$$78 = 216 - 1 \cdot 138$$
$$60 = 138 - 1 \cdot 78$$
$$18 = 78 - 1 \cdot 60$$
$$6 = 60 - 3 \cdot 18$$

Now, work backward:

$$6 = 60 - 3 \cdot 18$$
$$= 60 - 3(78 - 1 \cdot 60) = 4 \cdot 60 - 3 \cdot 78$$
$$= 4(138 - 1 \cdot 78) - 3 \cdot 78 = 4 \cdot 138 - 7 \cdot 78$$
$$= 4 \cdot 138 - 7(216 - 1 \cdot 138) = 11 \cdot 138 - 7 \cdot 216$$
$$= 11(3162 - 14 \cdot 216) - 7 \cdot 216 = 11 \cdot 3162 - 161 \cdot 216$$

So $\text{GCD}(216, 3162) = -161 \cdot 216 + 11 \cdot 3162$.

It looks like we can always make it work. So, although it won't happen that there are fixed numbers F and S so that, for any A and B,

$$\text{GCD}(A, B) = FA + SB$$

(can you prove this?), we can probably show that $\text{GCD}(A, B)$ can be written as

$$(something) \cdot A + (something\ else) \cdot B$$

where the "*something*" and the "*something else*" depend on A and B. In other words, the above calculations exhibit a general method for finding the output of two functions that we could call FIRST.COEFF ("the first coefficient") and SECOND.COEFF (each of which take two integers as input) so that GCD is equal to the following function:

```
TO EXPLICIT.GCD :A :B
 OP ((FIRST.COEFF :A :B) * :A) + ((SECOND.COEFF :A :B) * :B)
END
```

For example,

FIRST.COEFF$(216, 3162) = -161$ and SECOND.COEFF$(216, 3162) = 11$
(because $\text{GCD}(216, 3162) = -161 \cdot 216 + 11 \cdot 3162$) and

FIRST.COEFF$(124, 1028) = -58$ and SECOND.COEFF$(124, 1028) = 7$
(because $\text{GCD}(124, 1028) = -58 \cdot 124 + 7 \cdot 1028$)

Notice that there are other choices for the outputs of FIRST.COEFF and SECOND.COEFF(for example, $4 = 970 \cdot 124 - 117 \cdot 1028$), but we are looking for the functions that capture the essence of the above calculations.

You may ask, "Isn't every number a combination of any two given numbers for some choice of coefficients?" No, because, for example, you can't find two integers D and E so that

$$5 = D \cdot 2 + E \cdot 6$$

The reason is that the right-hand side of this expression is always divisible by 2, and the left-hand side is odd. So the existence of FIRST.COEFF and SECOND.COEFF isn't immediate.

We'll show that these functions exist by building Logo models for them. Before you read on, think about how you would model FIRST.COEFF and SECOND.COEFF in Logo. When I first thought about this question, it seemed that the Logo models would be very complicated; after studying a few hand calculations, a simple strategy (based on theorem 11.2) emerged that works like a charm. Close the book for a while and see what you can find.

STOP

Look again at the equations that we used to write $\text{GCD}(216, 3162) \,(= 6)$ as a combination of 216 and 3162:

$$6 = 60 - 3 \cdot 18$$
$$= 60 - 3(78 - 1 \cdot 60) = 4 \cdot 60 - 3 \cdot 78$$
$$= 4(138 - 1 \cdot 78) - 3 \cdot 78 = 4 \cdot 138 - 7 \cdot 78$$
$$= 4 \cdot 138 - 7(216 - 1 \cdot 138) = 11 \cdot 138 - 7 \cdot 216$$
$$= 11(3162 - 14 \cdot 216) - 7 \cdot 216 = 11 \cdot 3162 - 161 \cdot 216$$

Eliminate all the distracting arithmetic:

$$6 = 60 - 3 \cdot 18$$
$$= 4 \cdot 60 - 3 \cdot 78$$
$$= 4 \cdot 138 - 7 \cdot 78$$
$$= 11 \cdot 138 - 7 \cdot 216$$
$$= 11 \cdot 3162 - 161 \cdot 216$$

Notice that not only is 6 a combination of 216 and 3126, it is also a combination of 18 and 60, of 60 and 78, of 78 and 138, and of 138 and 216. Do the pairs of numbers

$$(18, 60) \ (60, 78) \ (78, 138) \ (138, 216) \ (216, 3162)$$

have any significance? Look at our original calculation

```
              14
        ┌─────────
   216 ) 3162
         3024        1
        ─────    ┌─────────
         138  )  216
               138        1
              ─────    ┌─────────
               78   )  138
                      78        1
                     ─────   ┌─────────
                      60   )  78
                             60        3
                            ─────   ┌─────────
                             18   )  60
                                    54        3
                                   ─────   ┌─────────
                                    6    )  18
                                           18
                                          ────
                                            0
```

The sequence

$$(216, 3162) \to (138, 216) \to (78, 138) \to (60, 78)$$
$$\to (18, 60) \to (6, 18) \to (0, 6)$$

is just the sequence of remainders and divisors in Euclid's algorithm (and each divisor is the previous remainder). Now, the equations

$$6 = 60 - 3 \cdot 18$$
$$= 4 \cdot 60 - 3 \cdot 78$$
$$= 4 \cdot 138 - 7 \cdot 78$$
$$= 11 \cdot 138 - 7 \cdot 216$$
$$= 11 \cdot 3162 - 161 \cdot 216$$

show that 6 is a combination of the numbers in every pair except the last two in the above sequence, and 6 is also a combination of the numbers in these pairs:

$$6 = 0 \cdot 0 + 1 \cdot 6$$
$$6 = 1 \cdot 6 + 0 \cdot 18$$

We could think of the complete calculation as

$$6 = 0 \cdot 0 + 1 \cdot 6$$
$$= 1 \cdot 6 + 0 \cdot 18$$
$$= 1 \cdot 60 - 3 \cdot 18$$
$$= 4 \cdot 60 - 3 \cdot 78$$
$$= 4 \cdot 138 - 7 \cdot 78$$
$$= 11 \cdot 138 - 7 \cdot 216$$
$$= 11 \cdot 3162 - 161 \cdot 216$$

Theorem 11.2 guarantees that every pair in our sequence has the same GCD. Perhaps we can figure out the outputs of FIRST.COEFF and SECOND.COEFF for any pair in the sequence

$$(216, 3162) \to (138, 216) \to (78, 138) \to (60, 78)$$
$$\to (18, 60) \to (6, 18) \to (0, 6)$$

from the outputs of FIRST.COEFF and SECOND.COEFF for the next pair in the sequence. Then we could work down to the last pair (0,6), where we know that the coefficients are 0 and 1. Well, how do you go from one term in the sequence to the next? Euclid's algorithm tells us that successive pairs are related like this:

$$\cdots \longrightarrow (S, T) \longrightarrow (\texttt{MOD}(T, S), S) \longrightarrow \cdots$$

Suppose that we start with nonzero integers A and B, and let $R = \texttt{MOD}(B, A)$ and $Q = \texttt{QUOT}(B, A)$ so that

$$B = QA + R \quad \text{and} \quad 0 \le R < A$$

Then the above sequence for finding $\texttt{GCD}(A, B)$ starts out like this:

$$(A, B) \longrightarrow (R, A) \longrightarrow \cdots$$

Now, if $D = \texttt{GCD}(A, B)$, then $D = \texttt{GCD}(R, A)$ (this is the reason that Euclid's algorithm works, and it is the content of theorem 11.2). Suppose we know how to write D as a combination of R and A; that is, suppose we have numbers X and Y so that

$$\texttt{FIRST.COEFF}(R, A) = X \text{ and } \texttt{SECOND.COEFF}(R, A) = Y$$

This means that

$$D = XR + YA$$

Can we use this information to write D as a combination of A and B? Certainly. We have

$$
\begin{aligned}
D &= XR + YA \\
&= X(B - QA) + YA \\
&= XB - XQA + YA \\
&= (Y - XQ)A + XB
\end{aligned}
$$

If you think about it, this is exactly what we did when we unwound Euclid's algorithm for $A = 216$ and $B = 3162$; in that example, $Q = 14$, $R = 138$, and $D = 6$. Suppose someone told you that

$$6 = 11 \cdot 138 - 7 \cdot 216$$

Then, because $3162 = 14 \cdot 216 + 138$, you would know that

$$6 = 11(3162 - 14 \cdot 216) - 7 \cdot 216 = 11 \cdot 3162 - 161 \cdot 216$$

Returning to the general case, we have

$$D = (Y - XQ)A + XB$$

In other words, FIRST.COEFF$(A, B) = Y - XQ$, and SECOND.COEFF$(A, B) = X$. If you look up what X, Y, Q and R are, you see that we have found an inductive relation:

$$\text{FIRST.COEFF}(A, B) = \text{SECOND.COEFF}(\text{MOD}(B, A), A)$$
$$- (\text{FIRST.COEFF}(\text{MOD}(B, A), A))(\text{QUOT}(B, A))$$

and

$$\text{SECOND.COEFF}(A, B) = \text{FIRST.COEFF}(\text{MOD}(B, A), A)$$

The base case is when $A = 0$ (so that GCD$(A, B) = B$), and then

$$\text{FIRST.COEFF}(A, B) = 0, \text{ and SECOND.COEFF}(A, B) = 1$$

Here are the details:

```
TO FIRST.COEFF :A :B
 IF :A = 0 [OP 0]
 OP (SECOND.COEFF (MOD :B :A) :A) →
     - (FIRST.COEFF (MOD :B :A) :A) * (QUOT :B :A)
END

TO SECOND.COEFF :A :B
 IF :A = 0 [OP 1]
 OP FIRST.COEFF (MOD :B :A) :A
END
```

This pair of functions can cause you to scratch you head; FIRST.COEFF calls SECOND.COEFF which calls FIRST.COEFF, which calls .... How can this work? Since $0 \leq \text{MOD}(B, A) < A$, the sequence of first inputs to these functions is strictly decreasing. If we start with A, then after at most A steps, the first input becomes 0, and the functions output. We have established the following result:

Theorem 11.4 If A and B are positive integers, then $GCD(A, B)$ can be written as $XA + YB$ for some integers X and Y. In fact, the outputs of the following functions give one choice of values for X and Y:

```
TO FIRST.COEFF :A :B
 IF :A = 0 [OP 0]
 OP (SECOND.COEFF (MOD :B :A) :A) →
     - (FIRST.COEFF (MOD :B :A) :A) * (QUOT :B :A)
END
```

```
TO SECOND.COEFF :A :B
 IF :A = 0 [OP 1]
 OP FIRST.COEFF (MOD :B :A) :A
END
```

This theorem implies that the function EXPLICIT.GCD

```
TO EXPLICIT.GCD :A :B
 OP ((FIRST.COEFF :A :B) * :A) + ((SECOND.COEFF :A :B) * :B)
END
```

is equal to GCD for all positive values of A and B.

The fact that the GCD of two integers can be written as a combination of the two integers is one of the cornerstones of arithmetic in **Z**. As we'll soon see, it its crucial to the proof of the uniqueness part of the fundamental theorem of arithmetic.

Experiment 11.13 How much of the theorem remains true if we allow A or B to be negative?

Exercise 11.14 For each choice of A and B, write $GCD(A, B)$ as a combination of A and B:

1. $A = 12$ and $B = 16$
2. $A = 4$ and $B = 10$
3. $A = 9$ and $B = 24$
4. $A = 14$ and $B = 65$
5. $A = 28$ and $B = 130$
6. $A = 108$ and $B = 188$
7. $A = 3214$ and $B = 303$

Experiment 11.15 What happens to the outputs of FIRST.COEFF and SECOND.COEFF if you double the inputs? Triple the inputs? Multiply the inputs by K? Can you explain why?

#Project 11.16 One day, by mistake, instead of typing

```
TO FIRST.COEFF :A :B
 IF :A = 0 [OP 0]
 OP (SECOND.COEFF (MOD :B :A) :A) →
        - (FIRST.COEFF (MOD :B :A) :A) * (QUOT :B :A)
END
```

and

```
TO SECOND.COEFF :A :B
 IF :A = 0 [OP 1]
 OP FIRST.COEFF (MOD :B :A) :A
END
```

I typed

```
TO F.COEFF :A :B
 IF :A = 0 [OP 3]
 OP (S.COEFF (MOD :B :A) :A) →
        - (F.COEFF (MOD :B :A) :A) * (QUOT :B :A)
END
```

and

```
TO S.COEFF :A :B
 IF :A = 0 [OP 1]
 OP F.COEFF (MOD :B :A) :A
END
```

Of course, this changed the outputs of my two functions, but to my surprise, the following function

```
TO WRONG.EXPLICIT.GCD :A :B
 OP ((F.COEFF :A :B) * :A) + ((S.COEFF :A :B) * :B)
END
```

still did the right thing. Why?

Inflated by my discovery, I decided to be even more radical; I tried

```
TO F.COEFF :A :B
 IF :A = 0 [OP 1]
 OP (S.COEFF (MOD :B :A) :A) →
         - (F.COEFF (MOD :B :A) :A) * (QUOT :B :A)
END
```

and

```
TO S.COEFF :A :B
 IF :A = 0 [OP 0]
 OP F.COEFF (MOD :B :A) :A
END
```

Imagine my surprise when I tried

```
TO WRONG.EXPLICIT.GCD :A :B
 OP ((F.COEFF :A :B) * :A) + ((S.COEFF :A :B) * :B)
END
```

What happens here? Are there simple descriptions of these new $F.COEFF(A, B)$ and $S.COEFF(A, B)$? Can you prove it? Using the new F.COEFF and S.COEFF, I define F and S like this:

```
TO F :A :B :K
 OP (FIRST.COEFF :A :B) + :K * (F.COEFF :A :B)
END
```

```
TO S :A :B :K
 OP (SECOND.COEFF :A :B) + :K * (S.COEFF :A :B)
END
```

Show that the following function:

```
TO H :A :B :K
 OP ((F :A :B :K) * :A) + ((S :A :B :K) * :B)
END
```

outputs the GCD of its first two inputs (no matter what value you give to the third input).

One of the major applications of theorem 11.4 is when A and B have no common factor other than 1. Such integers are called "relatively prime."

Relatively Prime Integers

Definition 11.5 Two integers A and B are "relatively prime" if their only positive common factor is 1.

The term relatively prime is perhaps unfortunate because many people think that relatively prime numbers have to be prime numbers. But, for example, 14 and 39 are relatively prime, and 8 and 15 are relatively prime. The term "relatively prime" applies to pairs of integers; think of RELATIVELY.PRIME? as a predicate that requires two inputs. It outputs TRUE if its inputs have "nothing to do with each other" in the sense that they have no common factors, and it outputs FALSE if its inputs have a common factor other than 1. A Logo model for RELATIVELY.PRIME? might check factors of one number against factors of another number, or it could simply apply Euclid's algorithm:

```
TO RELATIVELY.PRIME? :A :B
 OP (GCD :A :B) = 1
END
```

Exercise 11.17 Which pairs are relatively prime?

1. 12 and 18   2. 12 and 15
3. 12 and 707   4. 13 and 65
5. 21 and 119   6. 7 and 17
7. 1994 and 2631   8. 25 and 32
9. 216 and 3162

As an example of how to use the definition, let's prove the following theorem that we'll use later.

Theorem 11.6 If P is a prime and P is not a factor of A, then P and A are relatively prime.

Proof: Suppose that P and A have a common factor C other than 1. Because $C \mid P$, C must equal P (P is a prime, so its only factors are 1 and P). Because C is a factor of A, P is a factor of A (because $C = P$), and this contradicts the fact that P is not a factor of A. So the only common factor of P and A is 1, and P and A are relatively prime.

Experiment 11.18 Discuss each statement. Try to justify the true ones:

1. If P and Q are distinct positive primes, then P and Q are relatively prime.

2. If N is even and M is odd, then N and M are relatively prime.

3. If P is a prime and N is an integer greater than 1 so that P and N are not relatively prime, then $P \mid N$.

4. If A and B are relatively prime and $A \mid BC$, then $A \mid C$.

5. If A and B are relatively prime and B and C are relatively prime, then A and C are relatively prime.

Suppose that A and B are relatively prime. Then (look at how we defined `RELATIVELY.PRIME?`), $\mathrm{GCD}(A, B) = 1$. By theorem 11.4, we can find integers X and Y so that $XA + YB = 1$. That's important:

Theorem 11.7 If A and B are relatively prime integers, then there exist integers X and Y so that

$$XA + YB = 1$$

In fact, we can take X to be

`FIRST.COEFF`(A, B)

and Y to be

`SECOND.COEFF`(A, B)

Earlier we gave an example to show that not every integer can be written as a combination of two given integers. The example we used was that 5 can't be written as a combination of 2 and 6. The reason was that that every combination of 2 and 6 has to be divisible by any common factor of 2 and 6 (like 2). It turns out that this is the only obstacle. In other words, suppose that A and B are relatively prime and that C is any integer. Then C can be written as a combination of A and B. To see this, write 1 as a combination of A and B:

$$1 = XA + YB$$

Then multiply both sides by C:

$$C = CXA + CYB = (CX)A + (CY)B$$

So C is a combination of A and B. For example, suppose that $A = 4$ and $B = 15$, and suppose we want to write 125 as a combination of A and B. First write 1 as a combination of 4 and 15 (using, for example, FIRST.COEFF$(4, 15) = 4$ and SECOND.COEFF$(4, 15) = -1$):

$$1 = 4 \cdot 4 + -1 \cdot 15$$

Multiply both sides by 125:

$$125 = 500 \cdot 4 - 125 \cdot 15$$

Project 11.19 Model this algorithm in Logo. That is, write two functions GENERAL.FIRST.COEFF and GENERAL.SECOND.COEFF that each take three inputs A and B (assumed to be relatively prime), and an integer C. The outputs should be such that

$$C = (\text{GENERAL.FIRST.COEFF}(A, B, C))A$$
$$+ (\text{GENERAL.SECOND.COEFF}(A, B, C))B$$

What happens if you accidentally choose A and B so that they are not relatively prime?

So, if A and B have no common factor other than 1, then A and B "generate" **Z** in the sense that every integer is a combination of A and B.

Experiment 11.20 What do A and B generate if they are not relatively prime? For example, suppose $A = 15$ and $B = 21$. Write a function that takes two inputs X and Y and outputs $X \cdot 15 + Y \cdot 21$. Try all kinds of inputs to your function (positive and negative); what kind of outputs do you get? What if you change 15 and 21 to 12 and 20? Any conjectures? Any proofs?

Euclid's Lemma and the Fundamental Theorem

There is an extremely important property that distinguishes prime numbers from composites. In fact, this property is sometimes taken as the definition of a prime number, and it will be the essential ingredient in our proof that the prime factorization of an integer is unique. If N is a composite number, then it is quite possible for N to be a factor of a product without N being a factor of either of the numbers in the product. For example, 6 is a factor of $8 \cdot 21$ ($8 \cdot 21 = 168 = 6 \cdot 28$), but 6 is neither a factor of 8 nor a factor of 21. This is because the "3" in the 6 is a factor of 21 and the "2" in the 6 is a factor of 8. Primes, on the other hand, can't be broken down into pieces, so you can't have part of a prime dividing 8 while another part divides 21. The proof of this fact isn't hard using the machinery that we have developed so far, but it isn't immediate (it doesn't follow, for example, from the definition of prime). It requires something like theorem 11.7. Before reading the proof, read the statement and try to find a proof on your own.

STOP

Theorem 11.8 If P is a prime and $P \mid AB$, then either $P \mid A$ or $P \mid B$ (or both).

Here is a beautiful proof that can be found in Euclid: Suppose P is a factor of AB. Then $AB = PK$ for some integer K. If P is a factor of A, there is nothing to prove (we want to show that P is either a factor of A or of B). So, suppose that P is not a factor of A; then we'll show that P is a factor of B. Since P is not a factor of A, theorem 11.6 tells us that P and A are relatively prime. But then theorem 11.7 tells us that you can find integers X and Y so that

$$1 = XA + YP$$

Multiply both sides by B:

$$B = BXA + BYP$$
$$= ABX + PYB$$
$$= PKX + PYB \qquad (\text{remember: } AB = PK)$$
$$= P(KX + YB)$$

So $B = P \cdot (something)$ (the "*something*" is $KX + YB$), and P is a factor of B.

It's hard to underestimate the importance of this theorem in number theory. It is usually known as Euclid's lemma (a good rule of thumb is that any theorem that has a name has proved very useful in mathematics).

> A "lemma" is a technical theorem that is used to prove other theorems. The German word for lemma is *hilfsatz* which translates as "helping theorem." Can you think of another English word that contains "lemma"? Is there a connection between your word and the mathematical use of "lemma"?

Euclid's lemma helps make precise the intuitive notion that primes are the building blocks of arithmetic. In addition the proof that we borrowed from Euclid is extremely attractive. The following project gives you a chance to use Euclid's idea again:

Project 11.21 Prove the following generalization of theorem 11.8:

> If N is an integer that is relatively prime to A and $N \mid AB$, then $N \mid B$

(Hint: Model the proof of theorem 11.8.) Why do I say that this is a generalization of Theorem 11.8?

Project 11.22 Show that if P and Q are distinct primes and if E is a positive integer, then P and Q^E are relatively prime. (Hint: Use induction on E. If $E = 1$, you want to show that P and Q are relatively prime, and that follows by using the definition of "prime" and the definition of "relatively prime". Suppose that P and Q^E are relatively prime; then write $Q^{(E+1)}$ as $Q^E Q$, and use theorem 11.8.)

Project 11.23 Prove the following extension of Euclid's lemma:

> If P is a prime and $P \mid ABC$, then P has to divide at least
> one of the integers A, B or C

(Hint: $ABC = A(BC)$, and if $P \mid A(BC)$, either $P \mid A$ or $P \mid BC$. If $P \mid A$, we're done. If $P \mid BC$, ...)

Show inductively that if P divides a product of K integers, then P must divide at least one of the factors.

Exercise 11.24 Suppose that P, Q, and Q' are primes and that $P \mid QQ'$. What can you conclude?

As I said above, theorem 11.8 is the key ingredient in proving the fundamental theorem of arithmetic; in fact, it is equivalent to this theorem (in the sense that either theorem can be used to prove the other), and you probably already see the connection between the two theorems. The development of the fundamental theorem that you'll find in most modern number theory books goes something like this:

Theorem 11.9 (*The fundamental theorem of arithmetic—usual version*) If N is any nonzero integer, then N can be written as a product of primes. The prime factorization of N is unique up to the order of the factors (and the insertion of units).

Before I outline a proof, make sure you understand what the theorem says. It tells us the following:

1. If N is a nonzero integer, N can be written as a product of primes. This is something that schoolchildren take for granted when they build their factor trees, and the proof of this fact is precisely the proof that factor trees stop. It is written out in chapter 10.

2. If someone in Canada factors 300 into primes, and if someone in Hungary factors 300 into primes, then the two people will get the same answer. By the "same answer," I mean that each person will say that 300 is divisible by 2 (twice), by 3, and by 5 (twice). Of course, the person from Canada might say that

   $$300 = 2^2 \cdot 3 \cdot 5^2$$

   and the person from Hungary might say that

   $$300 = -1 \cdot 2 \cdot 3 \cdot 5 \cdot 2 \cdot 5 \cdot -1$$

   but these two factorizations are essentially the same. Most schoolchildren (and others) take this for granted too, but, as we'll see, the proof is not so simple as the proof of 1. You should realize here that it is essential to use only primes (and units) in our factorizations of integers if we want any chance of uniqueness. It is certainly not true that every number can be factored into composites in only one way; for example, $168 = 8 \cdot 21$ and $168 = 6 \cdot 28$.

So the theorem tells us that every integer can be factored into primes in only one way. Given a real live integer N (like 88577), the theorem says nothing about how you can actually find this unique way to write N as a product of primes. There is a great deal of current research devoted to finding efficient factoring algorithms.

Here's a sketch of a proof of the fundamental theorem.

We want to show that every nonzero integer N can be factored into primes in essentially one way. Well, we already know that every nonzero integer can be factored into primes, so we have to show that this can only be done in one way. Suppose that N is a positive integer (if N is negative, we'll simply have to insert a factor of -1); imagine writing N as a product of primes (without any factors of "1"). Some of the primes might be the same, but that's all right. Think of 150; you'd write it as $5 \cdot 2 \cdot 3 \cdot 5$. In general, you could write N as

$$N = P_1 P_2 P_3 \ldots P_K$$

Imagine that someone in the next room also factors N into primes, and she comes up with

$$N = Q_1 Q_2 Q_3 \ldots Q_J$$

This implies that

$$P_1 P_2 P_3 \ldots P_K = Q_1 Q_2 Q_3 \ldots Q_J$$

This can be written as

$$P_1 \cdot (something) = Q_1 Q_2 Q_3 \ldots Q_J$$

So P_1 is a factor of the product $Q_1 Q_2 Q_3 \ldots Q_J$. Since P_1 is a prime, it must, by the extended version of Euclid's lemma (project 11.23), be a factor of one of the Q's. But each of the Q's are primes, so the only way that this can happen is for P_1 to actually equal one of the Q's. In other words, you could scan your colleague's factorization of N and find a P_1. Then P_1 and this special Q (which is just an alias for P_1) could be canceled from both sides of

$$P_1 P_2 P_3 \ldots P_K = Q_1 Q_2 Q_3 \ldots Q_J$$

and you could proceed inductively, arguing that P_2 must be among the Q's, canceling P_2 from both sides, and so on. Eventually, all the P's or all the Q's will be gone. In fact, they must both disappear at the same step, because, if they didn't, one side would become 1 while the other side was still a product of primes greater than 1. So the two factorizations of N would really be the same.

When I think of this proof, I imagine two people factoring N into primes in two different rooms. Later, they play a game (much like a card game) where each person tries to guess the other person's factors ("Do you have a 17?" etc.). Every time you guess a factor correctly, both of you cancel that factor, and you get to guess again. Euclid's lemma guarantees that the game is loaded; the first person to play always wins, and in fact the first person to play is the only person who ever guesses.

Another Proof of the Fundamental Theorem

I'd like to show you another proof of the fundamental theorem that is closer in spirit to Euclid's original statement of the theorem and that at the same time makes use of the Logo models we have developed so far. The theorem is important enough to justify two proofs, and this new proof requires a new and very useful function. So make believe that you didn't know that the fundamental theorem was true.

In Book 9 of Euclid's *Elements*, we find the following proposition:

> *If a number be the least that is measured by prime numbers, it will not be measured by any other prime except those originally measuring it.*

In this context, "A is measured by B" means "$B \mid A$." This is another instance of Greek mathematics using geometry to do arithmetic. The model is that numbers are represented as lengths, so 3 measures 21 because, if you have a stick of length 3 and a stick of length 21, you will be able to use the shorter stick to measure the larger stick with nothing "left over." (Was this idea that led Gauss to say that 21 is 0 "in the measure 3"?) So we could state Euclid's theorem this way:

> *If a number is the least that is divisible by prime numbers, then it will not be divisible by any other primes except those originally dividing it.*

The hypothesis of the statement (*"if a number is the least that is divisible by prime numbers"*) means

> Suppose you have the smallest number N that is divisible by some collection of primes.

Although Euclid's statement (and his proof) didn't concern itself with multiple factors, we won't demand that the primes in our collection be distinct. Suppose you have the smallest number that is divisible by 5, 2, 3, 3, and 5. We'll take this to mean that we have the smallest number that is divisible by 5^2, 3^2, and 2. The conclusion is that such a number is not divisible by any prime except 5, 2, and 3. By the way, what is the smallest number that is divisible by 5, 2, 3, 3, and 5?

Euclid's statement gives a poetic description of one aspect of the uniqueness part of the theorem; what's more important is that it contains the germ of a very high-level description of the prime factorization of an integer. Euclid's statement focuses on the primes in the factorization rather than on the number being factored. Combined with the fact that every number can be factored into primes, it sets up a one-to-one correspondence between the "collections of primes" and the positive integers, and it foreshadows some powerful techniques in number theory (the so-called "local" methods) that weren't fully developed until the early part of this century. Roughly speaking, number theorists often investigate a certain conjecture about integers by focusing in on one prime at a time. Euclid's statement can be transformed into a particularly elegant example this principle. In fact, if we turn Euclid's statement on its head (and return our focus to the number being factored), we find a method for factoring that can be modeled in Logo, that can be applied to any integer (although it will not be practical for large numbers), and that will lead us naturally to a proof of the fundamental theorem.

In the prime factorization of 300, we see that 300 is divisible by 2, 3 and 5. In fact it is divisible by 5 "twice," so 300 is "more divisible" by 5 than it is by 3. Let's refine our DIVIS? predicate into a function that, rather than telling us whether or not N is divisible by a prime P, tells us exactly "how divisible" by P N is.

Suppose that N is a positive integer and P is a prime. If I form the powers of P

$$1, P, P^2, P^3, P^4, P^5, \ldots$$

then one of these powers, say, P^M, is the highest power of P that divides N because eventually the powers of P are larger than N (what is the only number divisible by every power of P?). We call this integer M the P-order of N, written $\text{ORD}_P(N)$. So, $\text{ORD}_P(N) = E$ means that

$$P^E \mid N \quad \text{but} \quad P^{(E+1)} \nmid N$$

For example,

$$\text{ORD}_5(300) = 2$$
$$\text{ORD}_3(300) = 1$$
$$\text{ORD}_7(300) = 0$$
$$\text{ORD}_{17}(867) = 2$$
$$\text{ORD}_2(1024) = 10$$

Calculating P-orders of integers is a mechanical process. For example, suppose I want $\text{ORD}_3(1134)$. One way to calculate this is to write down the powers of 3 until they get larger than 1134 (that is, up to 3^6), and to test 1134 for divisibility by each of these powers of 3. Finding this highest power of 3 that divides 1134 can also be carried out using an inductive scheme that counts the number of times 3 divides 1134. You could reason like this:

Well, 1134 is divisible by 3,

$$1134 = 3 \cdot 378$$

so 1134 is divisible by one more power of 3 than 378 is; that is,

$$\text{ORD}_3(1134) = 1 + \text{ORD}_3(378)$$

Similarly, $378 = 3 \cdot 126$, so 378 is divisible by one more power of 3 than 126 is; that is,

$$\text{ORD}_3(378) = 1 + \text{ORD}_3(126)$$

Similarly,

$$\text{ORD}_3(126) = 1 + \text{ORD}_3(42) \text{ (because } 126 = 3 \cdot 42)$$
$$\text{ORD}_3(42) = 1 + \text{ORD}_3(14)$$
$$\text{ORD}_3(14) = 0$$

So

$$\begin{aligned}
\text{ORD}_3(1134) &= 1 + \text{ORD}_3(378) \\
&= 1 + (1 + \text{ORD}_3(126)) \\
&= 1 + (1 + (1 + \text{ORD}_3(42))) \\
&= 1 + (1 + (1 + (1 + \text{ORD}_3(14)))) \\
&= 1 + (1 + (1 + (1 + 0))) = 4
\end{aligned}$$

In project 11.18 you built a model for the ORD_5 function. We can write the general ORD function to model the above algorithm:

```
TO ORD :P :N
 IF NOT DIVIS? :N :P [OP 0]
 OP 1 + ORD :P (:N / :P)
END
```

So, for example,

```
SHOW ORD 5 150
```

produces 2, while

```
SHOW ORD 5 151
```

produces 0.

Exercise 11.25 Why is 0 not in the domain of the second input to ORD? In many number theory books, $\text{ORD}_P(0)$ is defined as "$+\infty$." Why is that consistent with our Logo model? Why is it consistent with the fact that every integer is a factor of 0?

Experiment 11.26 Find the result of each expression using your Logo model for ORD to help with the calculations. Look for theorems.

1. $\text{ORD}_7(49)$
2. $\text{ORD}_7(42)$
3. $\text{ORD}_7(49 \cdot 42)$
4. $\text{ORD}_7(49 + 42)$
5. $\text{ORD}_5(250)$
6. $\text{ORD}_5(75)$
7. $\text{ORD}_5(250 \cdot 75)$
8. $\text{ORD}_5(250 + 75)$

(continued on next page)

9. $\text{ORD}_5(50)$ 10. $\text{ORD}_5(75 \cdot 50)$

11. $\text{ORD}_5(75 + 50)$ 12. $\text{ORD}_{11}(121)$

13. $\text{ORD}_{11}(1331)$ 14. $\text{ORD}_7(7^{12})$

15. $\text{ORD}_7(11 \cdot 13 \cdot 17 \cdot 23)$ 16. $\text{ORD}_5(7^{12})$

So, if P is a prime and A is a nonzero integer, $\text{ORD}_P(A)$ is the number E so that $P^E \mid A$ but $P^{(E+1)}$ is not a factor of A; put another way, $\text{ORD}_P(A)$ is the highest power to which P can be raised to give a factor of A. If you think about how our Logo model for ORD works, you'll see that if

$$E = \text{ORD}_P(N)$$

then

$$N = P^E U \qquad \text{where } P \nmid U.$$

In other words, if N is any integer, N can be written as

$$N = P^{\text{ORD}_P(N)} U \qquad \text{where } P \nmid U.$$

The converse of this fact is also true: If

$$N = P^E U \qquad \text{where } P \mid U$$

then $\text{ORD}_P(N) = E$.

To see this, suppose that $N = P^E U$ where $P \mid U$. Then $P^E \mid N$ (because N is $P^E \cdot (something)$). If $P^{(E+1)}$ does not divide N, then $E = \text{ORD}_P(N)$, as we claim. For the sake of argument, suppose that $P^{(E+1)}$ is a factor of N. Then

$$N = P^{(E+1)} S$$

for some integer S. Since N is also $P^E U$, we would have

$$P^E U = P^{(E+1)} S$$

We could then divide both sides of this by P^E to conclude that

$$U = PS$$

so P would divide U, and that can't happen. We have proved the following theorem:

Theorem 11.10 If $N = P^E U$ where $P \nmid U$, then $E = \text{ORD}_P(N)$.

Notice that if N and P are relatively prime, then $\text{ORD}_P(N) = 0$. Now, recall Euclid's theorem:

> *If a number is the least that is divisible by prime numbers, then it will not be divisible by any other prime except those originally dividing it.*

Suppose that N is the smallest number that is divisible by all the primes in some list L of primes. What can we say about N? Some of the primes in L might be the same; suppose that the *distinct* primes in L are

$$P_1, P_2, P_3, \ldots, P_K$$

and suppose that there are E_1 P_1s in L, E_2 P_2s in L, ..., and E_K P_Ks in L. We can say that N is divisible by $P_1^{E_1}$, $P_2^{E_2}$, ..., and $P_K^{E_K}$. Because N is "the least" number with these properties, we can say that N isn't divisible by anything else. In particular, N isn't divisible by any prime that isn't in L, and the highest power of each of the P_Is that divides N is precisely E_I. In other words,

$$\text{ORD}_{P_1}(N) = E_1, \text{ORD}_{P_2}(N) = E_2, \ldots, \text{ORD}_{P_K}(N) = E_K$$

and for all other primes P, $\text{ORD}_P(N) = 0$.

So we know the P-order of N for all primes P (most of these ORDs are 0). Do we know N?

For example, suppose we want a positive integer N so that $\text{ORD}_5(N) = 2$, $\text{ORD}_3(N) = 2$, $\text{ORD}_2(N) = 1$ and $\text{ORD}_P(N) = 0$ for all other primes. We have what's called a local knowledge of N; we know what N looks like if we focus in on one prime at a time. We know that

$$N = 25 \cdot (\textit{something that isn't divisible by 5})$$

$$N = 9 \cdot (\textit{something that isn't divisible by 3})$$

$$N = 2 \cdot (\textit{something that isn't divisible by 2})$$

$$N \quad \text{isn't divisible by any prime except 2, 3, and 5.}$$

Can we piece this information together to get a "global" picture of N? In particular,

1. Does $25 \cdot 9 \cdot 2$ fit the bill? Make sure that you understand why it isn't obvious that N can be written this way (my students tell me that one of the things they've learned about doing mathematics is never to assume that something is obvious); for example, 60 is divisible by 6 and by 20, but you can't conclude that $60 = 6 \cdot 20$. So there is something special about the fact that, in our discussion, the factors are powers of primes.

2. How many values of N work? If we insist that N is positive, is N completely determined by its P-order at each prime P?

Both of the above questions are worthy of investigation. If the general answer to the first one is yes, we have a very appealing description of how to piece together local information about a positive integer to recreate the integer. We also have a method for factoring a number into primes: To factor N into primes, raise each prime P to the $\text{ORD}_P(N)$ power and multiply all the answers together. That sounds silly. There are infinitely many primes, so how can you multiply infinitely many prime powers together? The point is that for most, indeed for all but a finite number, of primes P, N will have 0 as a P-order. In fact, if P is bigger than N, $\text{ORD}_P(N)$ is 0 (and $P^{\text{ORD}_P(N)}$ is 1). So, the only primes that could possibly make a "contribution" to N are the primes in `PRIMES.UPTO`(N). To say that a number is the product of all the primes, each raised to the highest power for which the prime divides the number, isn't so silly after all; it becomes a conjecture that can be tested in Logo. Let's do it; let's see if a number N is the product of its "local components."

Envision a function that takes a number N and a list of primes L as inputs. It outputs the product of all the primes P in L, each raised to the $\text{ORD}_P(N)$ power. For example, if N is 180 and L is [3 5 7 13], the function outputs

$$3^{\text{ORD}_3(180)} \cdot 5^{\text{ORD}_5(180)} \cdot 7^{\text{ORD}_7(180)} \cdot 13^{\text{ORD}_{13}(180)} = 3^2 \cdot 5^1 \cdot 7^0 \cdot 13^0$$
$$= 3^2 \cdot 5 = 45$$

Let's call 45 the "trace" of 180 on L. This `TRACE` function is easy to model in Logo:

```
TO TRACE :N :L
 IF EMPTYP :L [OP 1]
 OP (POWER (FIRST :L) (ORD FIRST :L :N)) * (TRACE :N BF :L)
END
```

Now, we can multiply together all possible contributions to N by simply taking the TRACE of N on PRIMES.UPTO(N):

```
TO PRODUCT.OF.LOCAL.COMPONENTS :N
 OP TRACE :N PRIMES.UPTO :N
END
```

Tabulate this function. It seems that PRODUCT.OF.LOCAL.COMPONENTS has a very uninteresting tabulation, and that is one of the most interesting facts in number theory.

Theorem 11.11 (*The fundamental theorem of arithmetic—a version that Euclid would have liked*) If N is an integer greater than 1, then

$$\text{PRODUCT.OF.LOCAL.COMPONENTS}(N) = N$$

That is, if N is a positive integer, then

$$N = \prod_{P \in \text{PRIMES.UPTO}(N)} P^{\text{ORD}_P(N)}$$

and this is essentially the only way to write N as a product of powers of primes. (This "product notation" is discussed briefly in the appendix.)

I like this statement of the theorem much better than the usual version. It tells you that every number can be factored into primes by giving you an explicit way to think about the factorization, it really gets at the idea that primes are the "building blocks" of $\mathbf{Z}$, and it shows the central importance of the ORD function.

As usual, the word "essentially" in the theorem means that any other factorization of N will be the same as the one given in the theorem except for the order of the factors and the number of unit factors. Notice that the formula given in the theorem

$$N = \prod_{P \in \text{PRIMES.UPTO}(N)} P^{\text{ORD}_P(N)}$$

when applied to a particular N (like 12), contains a few unit factors; it factors 12 as

$$12 = 2^{\text{ORD}_2(12)} \cdot 3^{\text{ORD}_3(12)} \cdot 5^{\text{ORD}_5(12)} \cdot 7^{\text{ORD}_7(12)} \cdot 11^{\text{ORD}_1 1(12)}$$
$$= 2^2 \cdot 3 \cdot 1 \cdot 1 \cdot 1$$

We could remove these unit factors if, instead of taking the product over PRIMES.UPTO(N), we took the product over the sublist L of PRIMES.UPTO(N) that contains the actual prime factors of N (what we'll call the "support" of N in a later section).

We'll prove the theorem (using some properties of ORD) shortly, but right now, assume that the theorem is true and take some time to play with this beautiful result. The next project will be used repeatedly in the rest of the book.

Project 11.27 The function PRODUCT.OF.LOCAL.COMPONENTS outlines a process in which an integer N is torn apart into prime powers, and these pieces are then multiplied back together to output N. It would be nice to climb into the workings of PRODUCT.OF.LOCAL.COMPONENTS so that we could watch the factoring in action. The following function lets you actually see the factors of N that come from a list of primes L:

```
TO FACTOR.LIST :N :L
 IF EMPTYP :L [OP []]
 OP FPUT (SE FIRST :L ORD FIRST :L :N) FACTOR.LIST :N BF :L
END
```

For example, FACTOR.LIST 180 [3 5 7 11 23] outputs

[[3 2] [5 1] [7 0] [11 0] [23 0]]

Modify FACTOR.LIST so that it doesn't include pairs at which the P-order is 0.

Hint: Before you do

   FPUT (SE FIRST :L ORD FIRST :L :N) FACTOR.LIST :N BF :L

test N for divisibility by the first element of L; if it isn't divisible, simply output FACTORLIST with inputs N and BF(L).

Take this modified FACTOR.LIST and write a FACTOR function that outputs the list of all pairs [P E] where P is a prime that divides N and E is ORD$_P(N)$. It should work like this:

```
?SHOW FACTOR 1960
[[2 3] [5 1] [7 2]]
```

because $1960 = 2^3 \cdot 5 \cdot 7^2$.

Use your function to factor each number into primes:

1. 72   2. 81   3. 864 4. 202 5. 239 6. 514

7. 120 8. 720 9. 576

Experiment 11.28 Use the FACTOR function that you wrote in the above project to answer the following question: What restrictions must you impose on A and B to ensure that FACTOR(AB) contains the same pairs as SE(FACTOR(A), FACTOR(B)) (but not necessarily in the same order)? In other words, suppose I define

```
TO F :A :B
 OP FACTOR (:A * :B)
END
```

and

```
TO G :A :B
 OP SE (FACTOR :A) (FACTOR :B)
END
```

Try typing

```
SHOW F 3 4
```

and

```
SHOW G 3 4
```

or

```
SHOW F 12 35
```

and

```
SHOW G 12 35
```

or

```
SHOW F 12 15
```

and

```
SHOW G 12 15
```

When do the outputs of F and G contain the same pairs? How about in general?

Exercise 11.29 Modify FACTOR so that it does the right thing for negative inputs.

The proof that I have in mind of this version of the fundamental theorem involves an important property of the ORD function. Here are the details:

If you look at the following table, a conjecture stands out:

A	$ORD_5(A)$	B	$ORD_5(B)$	AB	$ORD_5(AB)$
10	1	50	2	500	3
15	1	10	1	150	2
8	0	250	3	2000	3
125	3	10	1	1250	4

Theorem 11.12 If P is a prime and A and B are integers, then

$$ORD_P(AB) = ORD_P(A) + ORD_P(B).$$

Before you read on, try to find your own proof.

One way to think about this is to imagine calculating the right-hand side of the above equation.

Suppose that $ORD_P(A) = E$ and $ORD_P(B) = E'$.

Then $A = P^E U$ and $B = P^{E'} U'$ where P is not a factor of U and P is not a factor of U'.

So

$$AB = P^E U P^{E'} U' = P^{(E+E')} U U'.$$

Now, $P \nmid UU'$ because if P were a factor of UU', then by Euclid's lemma, P would have to divide U or U', and it doesn't divide either of them. This means that

$$AB = P^{(E+E')}(\text{something that isn't divisible by } P)$$

But this means that $E + E'$ is the highest power of P that divides AB, so

$$\text{ORD}_P(AB) = E + E' = \text{ORD}_P(A) + \text{ORDP}(B)$$

Project 11.30 If P is a prime and N and M are positive integers, prove that

$$\text{ORD}_P(M^N) = N\,\text{ORD}_P(M).$$

Hint: Induct on N.

What does this say about $\text{ORD}_P(Q^N)$ where Q is a prime and

1. Q is different from P, or

2. $Q = \text{P}$?

Project 11.31 If $P, P_1, P_2, \ldots$ and P_K are primes and $E_1, E_2, \ldots$ and E_K are positive integers, show that

$$\text{ORD}_P(P_1^{E_1} P_2^{E_2} \ldots P_K^{E_K})$$
$$= E_1\text{ORD}_P(P_1) + E_2\text{ORD}_P(P_2) + \cdots + E_K\text{ORD}_P(P_K)$$

Hint: Use induction on K.

If the P_Is are all different, what is $\text{ORD}_P(P_1^{E_1} P_2^{E_2} \ldots P_K^{E_K})$ if

1. P is not among the P_I's

2. P is one of the P_I's (say, $P = P_J$)

Now we can prove our alternate version of the fundamental theorem. Suppose that N is a positive integer. From `PRIMES.UPTO(N)`, sift out the list L of primes that actually divide N.

Let's suppose that L is the list $[P_1\ P_2\ P_3\ \ldots\ P_K]$, and let's suppose further that $\text{ORDP}_1(N) = E_1, \ldots, \text{ORD}_{PK}(N) = E_K$. We want first to show that

$$N = P_1^{E_1}\ P_2^{E_2}\ P_3^{E_3}\ \ldots\ P_K^{E_K}$$

(That is, we want to show that N is the product of its local components.)

Since $\text{ORD}_{P_1}(N) = E_1$, we know that $P_1^{E_1}$ divides N. That is,

$$N = P_1^{E_1} U_1$$

for some integer U_1. Apply ORD_{P_2} to both sides of this identity:

$$\text{ORD}_{P_2}(N) = \text{ORD}_{P_2}(P_1^{E_1}U_1)$$

or

$$\text{ORD}_{P_2}(N) = \text{ORD}_{P_2}(P_1^{E_1}) + \text{ORD}_{P_2}(U_1)$$

Now $\text{ORD}_{P_2}(N)$ is E_2, and $\text{ORD}_{P_2}(P_1^{E_1}) = E_1\text{ORD}_{P_2}(P_1) = E_10 = 0$, so our identity becomes: $E_2 = \text{ORD}_{P_2}(U_1)$, and this means that $U_1 = P_2^{E_2}U_2$ for some integer U_2.

Take the identity $N = P_1^{E_1}U_1$, and substitute $P_2^{E_2}U_2$ for U_1. We now have

$$N = P_1^{E_1}P_2^{E_2}U_2$$

You get the idea. Next apply ORD_{P_3} to both sides of this identity, argue as above, and conclude that

$$N = P_1^{E_1}P_2^{E_2}P_3^{E_3}U_3$$

After K steps, we'll end up with

$$N = P_1^{E_1}P_2^{E_2}P_3^{E_3}\ldots P_K^{E_K}U_K$$

Now, U_K is a positive integer that can't have any prime factors because, if U_K is divisible by some prime not among the $P_1, P_2, \ldots, P_K$, then N would be divisible by a prime that is not in L (and that's silly: L was defined to be the list of primes that actually divide N), and if U_K is divisible by one of the primes in L, say P_J, then that would increase the P_J-order of N beyond E_J. It follows that U_K must be 1 and that

$$N = P_1^{E_1}P_2^{E_2}P_3^{E_3}\ldots P_K^{E_K}$$

or

$$N = \prod_{P \in L} P^{\text{ORD}_P(N)}$$

This establishes the correctness of our special factorization of N. How about uniqueness? Imagine that N could be factored into primes in "another way," and let Q be any prime in this alternate factorization (so that Q is a factor of N). Then

$$\text{ORD}_Q(N) = \text{ORD}_Q(P_1^{E_1} P_2^{E_2} P_3^{E_3} \ldots P_K^{E_K})$$
$$= E_1 \text{ORD}_Q(P_1) + E_2 \text{ORD}_Q(P_2) + \cdots + E_K \text{ORD}_Q(P_K)$$

Now, each term in this sum looks like $E_J \text{ORD}_Q(P_J)$. If Q is not equal to P_J, this term is 0, and if $Q = P_J$, this term is E_J. If Q is a factor of N, $\text{ORD}_Q(N)$ must be positive. The only way for this to happen is for Q to be equal to some P_J, and then Q is a factor of N exactly E_J times (so, N is not measured by any prime except those originally measuring it). Simply put, our factorization is unique.

Using the Fundamental Theorem

In chapter 12 we'll use the fundamental theorem to obtain new facts about arithmetic in **Z**. The idea behind most applications of the theorem is to think of integers as they look when they are factored into primes. For example, the fundamental theorem allows us to give an alternate version of the definition of relatively prime integers:

Definition 11.5′ Two integers A and B are "relatively prime" if the prime factorizations of A and B contain no primes in common.

Here's another example. In project 11.21 you proved that if N and A are relatively prime and if $N \mid AB$, then $N \mid B$. Here's a proof of the same thing using the fundamental theorem:

Think of N, A, and B as they look when they are factored into primes. Since N and A are relatively prime, the primes that divide N do not show up in the factorization of A. But they do show up in the prime factorization of AB because $N \mid AB$. But, to get the prime factorization of AB, you simply take the prime factorizations of A and B and multiply them together. So, the only way that the primes dividing N can show up among the primes dividing AB is for them to show up among the primes dividing B. In other words, $N \mid B$.

We'll make this argument tighter in chapter 12. For now, just try to understand it in broad strokes and don't worry about the details. This special case might help:

Suppose that N is 20 and A is 21, and suppose that B is some integer so that $N \mid AB$. Think of how things look when they are factored into primes:

$$N = 2^2 \cdot 5$$

$$A = 3 \cdot 7$$

$$B = ????$$

Then $AB = 3 \cdot 7 \cdot ????$. Now for N to be a factor of AB, the prime factorization of AB must contain two 2's and a 5. Well, you won't get any help from A; it only contains a 3 and a 7. So the two 2's and the 5 must be among the ????. In other words, B is divisible by $2^2 \cdot 5$, so B is divisible by N.

Here are some more examples to think about:

Experiment 11.32 Use your FACTOR factorer to develop a conjecture about the kinds of exponents that can turn up in the factorization of perfect squares, perfect cubes, and perfect Nth powers. Use these ideas to show that if A and B are positive integers so that

$$A^2 = 2B^2$$

then A and B are each even.

Experiment 11.33 Suppose that A and B are integers and D is their greatest common divisor. Use FACTOR to compare the factorizations for A, B, and D. Develop a conjecture about the relationship among $\text{ORD}_P(A)$, $\text{ORD}_P(B)$, and $\text{ORD}_P(D)$ for any prime P.

Project 11.34 Show that if A and B are relatively prime and if C is an integer that is divisible by A and by B, then C is divisible by AB. Hint: Factor everything into primes. If A and B are not relatively prime and C is divisible by A and by B, is C still divisible by AB?

Project 11.35 Suppose that R, M, and M' are three integers so that R and M are relatively prime and R and M' are relatively prime. Show that R and MM' are relatively prime. Hint: No prime factor of R shows up in the prime factorization of M and the same is true for M'. Could a prime dividing R show up in the prime factorization of MM'?

Finally, here's a project that develops another property of the ORD function:

Project 11.36 We know that the ORD of a product is the sum of the ORDs. How about the ORD of a sum? If we reason formally, we could proceed like this:

Suppose that A and B are integers and P is a prime. Suppose further that $\text{ORD}_P(A) = E$ and $\text{ORD}_P(B) = E'$. Then $A = P^E U$ and $B = P^{E'} U'$, and P is not a factor of U or of U'. We have

$$A + B = P^E U + P^{E'} U'$$

Now on the right-hand side, if $E \leq E'$, we can factor out a P^E, whereas if $E' \leq E$, we could factor out a $P^{E'}$. So we could write $A + B$ as $A + B = P^{(\textit{smaller of } E \textit{ and } E')} \cdot (\textit{something})$, and that might lead us to conjecture that $\text{ORD}_P(A + B)$ is the smaller of E and E'; that is, the following might be a theorem.

Conjecture: $\text{ORD}_P(A + B)$ is the smaller of $\text{ORD}_P(A)$ and $\text{ORD}_P(B)$.

To experiment with this conjecture, we need to model the "smaller than" function in Logo.

```
TO MIN :X :Y
 IF :X < :Y [OP :X]
 OP :Y
END
```

Now, fill in the tabulation of figure 11.3 (we'll use $P = 5$ as an example).

The last experiment in the tabulation produces a disappointment:

$$\text{ORD}_5(50 + 75) = 3, \text{ whereas } \text{MIN}(\text{ORD}_5(50), \text{ORD}_5(75)) = 2$$

What went wrong? Well,

$$50 + 75 = 5^2 2 + 5^2 3 = 5^2(2 + 3)$$

and another 5 (the $2 + 3$) shows up. Prove that this can only happen when A and B have the same P-ord.

A	$\mathrm{ORD}_5(A)$	B	$\mathrm{ORD}_5(B)$	$\mathrm{MIN}(\mathrm{ORD}_5(A), \mathrm{ORD}_5(B))$	$A + B$	$\mathrm{ORD}_5(A+B)$
10		20				
6		20				
15		15				
25		5				
125		50				
50		75				

Figure 11.3

Hint: If the P-ords are different, suppose that $A = P^E U$ and $B = P^{E'} U'$ and $E < E'$. Then

$$A + B = P^E(U + P^{(E-E')}U')$$

where $E - E' > 0$. Prove that $\mathrm{ORD}_P(U + P^{(E-E')}U') = 0$ (by showing that if P were a factor of $U + P(E - E')U'$, then P would have to be a factor of U).

We can salvage part of our conjecture:

Theorem 11.13 If P is a prime and A and B are integers, then

$$\mathrm{ORD}_P(A + B) \geq \mathrm{MIN}(\mathrm{ORD}_P(A), \mathrm{ORD}_P(B))$$

and if $\mathrm{ORD}_P(A)$ is different from $\mathrm{ORD}_P(B)$, then the above inequality is in fact an equality.

Since Euclid, the fundamental theorem has been the central model for what mathematicians call "structure theorems." The structure of **Z** (at least that part of **Z**'s structure that comes from multiplication) is completely known in principle: There are these special "building blocks" called prime numbers, and every integer can be uniquely decomposed (up to a unit factor) into a product of these building blocks. There are hundreds of other such theorems in mathematics; all of them take a certain class of objects and describe how each object in the class can be represented (and in how many ways) as a combination of certain special objects. One reason that people search out such theorems is that the ancestor of all of them, the fundamental theorem of arithmetic, has proved to be so useful in number theory.

Most people take the fundamental theorem for granted. By the time students get to junior high school, they just naturally assume that every integer can be factored into primes, and it hardly ever occurs to them to wonder whether or not there is more than one way to do this for a given integer. That's because the fundamental theorem has become so ingrained in our culture; it is difficult to imagine a course in arithmetic that goes beyond paper and pencil techniques for doing calculations and that doesn't use the fundamental theorem.

Taking the fundamental theorem for granted can get you into trouble. In the middle of the last century, Gabriel Lamé presented a proof of the Fermat conjecture to the Acadèmie des Sciences de Paris. Recall that the conjecture says that if N is an integer > 2, then there are no positive integers X, Y, and Z so that

$$X^N + Y^N = Z^N$$

A hole in the proof was soon found, and it turned out that the error was much more than a simple bug; it was an essential difficulty that couldn't be overcome. Lamé's proof has been discovered in one form or another many times over the past two centuries. It is based on an application of the fundamental theorem of arithmetic (see project 11.32) that implies that if an integer is the Eth power of another integer, then every prime power in the prime factorization of the integer is also an Eth power. For example, 1728 is the cube of 12, so when you factor 1728 into primes, every prime will show up to a power that is divisible by 3. To be precise,

$$1728 = 2^6 \cdot 3^3$$

Now, in Lamé's proof of the Fermat conjecture, you assume that you have a solution to the Fermat equation for some $N > 2$:

$$A^N + B^N = C^N$$

It is possible to factor the right-hand side of this equation, but the factors are not integers; they come from another number system which we can call $\mathbf{Z}'$. The factors can even be shown to be prime in $\mathbf{Z}'$. Lamé argued that since the right-hand side of this equation is an Nth power, then each prime in the factorization of the left side must show up to a power that is divisible by N. He could then show that this wasn't the case; some prime factors of the left-hand side were not showing up as Nth powers. He concluded that a solution to the Fermat equation could not exist. The hole in the proof is that it assumes that the factorization of numbers in $\mathbf{Z}'$ can only be done in one way (or that $\mathbf{Z}'$ has a fundamental theorem of arithmetic), and many people showed that this was not the case.

Quite a few historians are convinced that Fermat's celebrated "proof" also contained Lamé's error, so it is possible that assimilation into Western culture of one of the oldest theorems in number theory was partly responsible for the three-century search for the proof of one of number theory's most intriguing results. But the search has been worth it. Over the past three hundred years a whole branch of number theory, the theory of algebraic numbers, was developed to attack the Fermat conjecture. Algebraic number theory is one of the most beautiful branches of mathematics, and its powerful techniques will continue to find applications (and attract researchers) long after its central problem has been solved.

It is probably hard to imagine a number system in which a number can be factored into primes in more than one way, but they exist and are very important in algebraic number theory. Here's an example that is not very useful in applications but contains all the essential features of a system without unique factorization.

Suppose we are allowed to work only with even numbers; our number system is now $\mathbf{Z}'$:

$$\mathbf{Z}'' = \{\ldots -6, -4, -2, 0, 2, 4, 6, 8, \ldots\}$$

Then the usual laws of arithmetic apply (we can add, subtract, and multiply), and all the definitions of this chapter make sense. Divisibility is defined in the usual way, so that $4 \mid 8$ because $4 \cdot 2 = 8$. Note, however, that 2 does not divide 6 because there is no even integer C so that $2C = 6$. Also there are no units in $\mathbf{Z}'$. The definition of prime stays the same, but the set of primes is different. In $\mathbf{Z}'$, 2 is prime, but so are 6, 10, 14, and 18 (why?). In $\mathbf{Z}'$, I can factor some numbers into primes in more than one way; for example,

$$420 = 30 \cdot 14$$
$$420 = 70 \cdot 6$$

Of course, the reason for this quirky arithmetic in $\mathbf{Z}'$ is easy to understand. If we allow for all integers (not just even ones) in our factorizations, then our two factorizations of 420 look like this:

$$420 = (15 \cdot 2) \cdot (7 \cdot 2) = (5 \cdot 3 \cdot 2) \cdot (7 \cdot 2)$$

$$420 = (35 \cdot 2) \cdot (3 \cdot 2) = (5 \cdot 7 \cdot 2) \cdot (3 \cdot 2)$$

So, when we supply the "missing factors," the two factorizations become the same.

It was E. Kummer, as early as 1844, who realized that this "missing factors" idea had potential to resolve the problem of nonunique factorization in more general number systems, and with this abstraction came the birth of modern algebraic number theory. Kummer's idea was that if you have a number system $\mathbf{Z}'$ in which you can factor a number N into primes in two different ways:

$$N = PP'$$

$$N = QQ'$$

then perhaps there are these "ideal numbers" or "ghost factors" that exist (not in $\mathbf{Z}'$ but in some "extension" of $\mathbf{Z}'$) so that, for example,

$$P = GG'$$
$$P' = G''G'''$$

and

$$Q = GG''$$
$$Q' = G'G'''$$

This idea proved to be a very productive one, and Kummer's theory evolved into a theory of ideals that has become one of the cornerstones of twentieth century mathematics.

So the lack of a fundamental theorem about unique decomposition into primes in certain number systems has had quite an effect on the development of mathematics. So has the existence of such a theorem in number systems like $\mathbf{Z}$. It has led to many deep facts about arithmetic, and many of these facts have become models for what arithmetic should look like in other systems.

Chapter 12

Applications of the Fundamental Theorem

It's one thing to know why something works, but it's often quite another thing to know how to use it. In this chapter, you'll become good friends with the fundamental theorem. The idea is to learn to think about integers in terms of their prime factorizations. By the end of the chapter, you probably won't be thinking of the fundamental theorem as simply a theorem; instead, it will stand for a whole approach to thinking about integers. Of course, along the way you'll meet some new friends.

We'll need many of the functions from previous sections, and we'll also make extensive use of the following higher-order functions from the appendix:

```
TO L.SIGMA :F :E :L
 IF EMPTYP :L [OP 0]
 OP (APPLY :F SE :E FIRST :L) + (L.SIGMA :F :E BF :L)
END
```

`L.SIGMA` simply sums a function F (with possible extra inputs E) over a list L. For example, if H is defined like this

```
TO H :X :Y :Z
 OP :X + 3 * :Y - 4 * :Z
END
```

and if you wanted the value of

$$H(3, 4, 5) + H(3, 4, 1) + H(3, 4, 17) + H(3, 4, -1)$$

you could type

```
SHOW L.SIGMA "H [3 4] [5 1 17 -1]
```

The sum of the first five integers can be seen by typing

```
SHOW L.SIGMA "ID [] [1 2 3 4 5]
```

where $\text{ID}(X) = X$.

If the function that you are summing takes only two inputs, you can sum it against the second one and pass the first one in as a number (rather than a list); for example, if $F(X, Y) = X + 2Y$, typing either of the following should produce the same number

```
SHOW L.SIGMA "F 3 [1 4 2 7]
```

```
SHOW L.SIGMA "F [3] [1 4 2 7]
```

The multiplicative version of L.SIGMA is L.PROD; it calculates a function's outputs at each element of a list and multiplies the answers together

```
TO L.PROD :F :E :L
 IF EMPTYP :L [OP 1]
 OP (APPLY :F SE :E FIRST :L) * (L.PROD :F :E BF :L)
END
```

In chapter 10, we SIEVEd a list with a predicate. Let's return to the more standard terminology; FILTER filters a predicate over a list (it outputs the sublist of the input list that consists of all the elements in the input list for which the predicate is TRUE:

```
TO FILTER :PRED :E :L
 IF EMPTYP :L [OP []]
 IF APPLY :PRED (SE :E FIRST :L) →
    [OP FPUT FIRST :L (FILTER :PRED :E BF :L)]
 OP FILTER :PRED :E BF :L
END
```

The Local-to-Global Theorem

In this chapter, when we think of a number, we'll think of the way that number looks when it is factored into primes. We'll say that a prime P "occurs" in A if, when you factor A into primes, P is one of the factors (in other words, if $P \mid A$). To see the prime factorization of an integer, we can use the FACTOR function that was the object of project 11.27; one way to define it is

```
TO FACTOR.LIST :N :L
 IF EMPTYP :L [OP []]
 IF DIVIS? :N (FIRST :L) [OP FPUT →
    ( SE FIRST :L ORD FIRST :L :N ) FACTOR.LIST :N BF :L]
 OP FACTOR.LIST :N BF :L
END

TO FACTOR :N
 OP FACTOR.LIST :N PRIMES.UPTO :N
END
```

For example, typing

```
SHOW FACTOR 45
```

produces

```
[[3 2] [5 1]]
```

because $45 = 3^2 \cdot 5$

By thinking about integers as products of prime powers, we'll be able to look at many of the ideas in the previous chapter in a new light. For example, if $A \mid B$, what can you say about the primes that occur in A in relation to the primes that occur in B? Well, if $A \mid B$, there is an integer C so that $B = AC$. Suppose that P is any prime. Then

$$\mathrm{ORD}_P(B) = \mathrm{ORD}_P(AC) = \mathrm{ORD}_P(A) + \mathrm{ORD}_P(C)$$

Now, since P-orders are not negative, $\mathrm{ORD}_P(C)$ is nonnegative. This means that

$$\mathrm{ORD}_P(A) \leq \mathrm{ORD}_P(B)$$

This is true for every prime P. In other words, the only primes that can show up in the factorization of A are the primes that show up in the factorization of B, and they can occur up in A with an exponent that is never larger than the exponent with which they occur in B. Let's state this as a theorem.

Theorem 12.1 If $A \mid B$, then the primes that divide A are among the primes that divide B. Furthermore, for any prime P,

$$\text{ORD}_P(A) \le \text{ORD}_P(B)$$

Of course, for most primes P, both $\text{ORD}_P(A)$ and $\text{ORD}_P(B)$ will be 0. The thrust of the theorem is that the only factors of $5^2 \cdot 7^3 \cdot 11^1$ are the numbers you can form by taking a product $5^A \cdot 7^B \cdot 11^C$ where A is 0, 1 or 2, B is 0, 1, 2 or 3, and C is 0 or 1.

Project 12.1 Is the converse true? That is, suppose that A and B are integers and $\text{ORD}_P(A) \le \text{ORD}_P(B)$ for all primes P. Does A divide B? Hints: Try a few examples (is $5^2 \cdot 7 \cdot 17^2$ a factor of $5^3 \cdot 7 \cdot 11^2 \cdot 17^3$?); in each case, write out the prime factorization of A and the prime factorization of B. How can you describe the "inflating factor" that will multiply with A to give B.

The fundamental theorem is often used to show that two integers are equal (I'm thinking of the alternate formulation of the fundamental theorem (theorem 11.11) here). If A is an integer, A is the product of its local components with the possible insertion of unit factors. This means that if A and B have the same local components (that is, if $\text{ORD}_P(A) = \text{ORD}_P(B)$ for all primes P), then A and B can differ at most by a sign (from the unit factors). Put another way, if A and B have the same local components and the same sign, then they must be equal.

Theorem 12.2 (*The local-to-global theorem*) If A and B are integers with the same sign, and if $\text{ORD}_P(A) = \text{ORD}_P(B)$ for all primes P, then $A = B$.

Project 12.2 Suppose that X and Y are positive integers so that for every prime P, $\text{ORD}_P(X) = 2\text{ORD}_P(Y)$. Show that $X = Y^2$. Hint: By the above theorem, it's enough to show that $\text{ORD}_P(X) = \text{ORD}_P(Y^2)$ for every prime P. But $2\text{ORD}_P(Y) = \text{ORD}_P(Y^2)$.

Let's take another look at the greatest common divisor function. The most practical method for calculating the GCD of two integers A and B is to use Euclid's algorithm; it is simple, fast, and delightful to think about. In the last chapter, we saw a (slower) variation on this idea; we can calculate the GCD of A and B by calculating numbers X and Y so that the desired GCD is $XA+YB$. In experiment 11.33 you looked at yet another method, based on the fundamental theorem, that is slowest of all but theoretically very important. The idea is to determine the P-orders (for all primes P) of $\text{GCD}(A, B)$ from the P-orders of A and B. From the fundamental theorem, if we know the P-orders of $\text{GCD}(A, B)$, we know $\text{GCD}(A, B)$. Let's look at an example:

Suppose that A and B are two integers that we have factored into primes; let's say that A is $2^2 \cdot 5^2 \cdot 7 \cdot 11^2$ and B is $2 \cdot 3 \cdot 5^3 \cdot 7^2$. Don't multiply these numbers out; the idea is to reason with the prime factorizations. Suppose that D is the GCD of A and B. Then $D \mid A$ and $D \mid B$, and any other divisor of both A and B divides D. What primes can show up in D? Since $D \mid A$, if P is a prime dividing D, P must be 2, 5, 7, or 11. Since $D \mid B$, if P is a prime dividing D, P must be 2, 3, 5, or 7. So, if P is a prime dividing D, P must be 2, 5, or 7. Since we want D to "absorb" every other common divisor of A and B, D had better be divisible by as many factors of 2, 5 and 7 as possible. Well, by theorem 12.1, all the P-orders of D are bounded by the P-orders of A and also by the P-orders of B. This means that, for example,

$$\text{ORD}_5(D) \leq 2 \quad \text{(the 5-order of } A)$$

and

$$\text{ORD}_5(D) \leq 3 \quad \text{(the 5-order of } B)$$

So

$$\text{ORD}_5(D) \leq 2 \quad \text{(the minimum of 2 and 3)}$$

Since $\text{ORD}_5(D)$ must be as big as possible, D must be divisible by 5^2. Similarly, $\text{ORD}_2(D)$ must be as big as possible; it can't be bigger than 1 (this is $\text{ORD}_2(B)$), so it must be 1. Comparing the 7-orders of A and B, we see that $\text{ORD}_7(D)$ is cannot be greater than 1 (this is $\text{ORD}_7(A)$), so $\text{ORD}_7(D) = 1$. Since we know the P-order of D for each prime P, we know D:

$$D = 5^2 \cdot 2 \cdot 7$$

This strategy works in general. If we are given the prime factorizations of two numbers, we can read off the prime factorization of their GCD. If, for example,

$$A = 2^3 \cdot 5^2 \cdot 13^2 \cdot 17^3 \cdot 23 \cdot 101$$

and

$$B = 2^2 \cdot 3^2 \cdot 5^4 \cdot 11 \cdot 17^6 \cdot 23 \cdot 37^2 \cdot 101$$

then

$$\text{GCD}(A, B) = 2^2 \cdot 5^2 \cdot 17^3 \cdot 23 \cdot 101$$

We can give a precise description of this method using ORD.

Theorem 12.3 If A and B are integers, and $D = \text{GCD}(A, B)$, then for all primes P,

$$\text{ORD}_P(D) = \text{MIN}(\text{ORD}_P(A), \text{ORD}_P(B))$$

where **MIN** is defined like this:

```
TO MIN :X :Y
 IF :X < :Y [OP :X]
 OP :Y
END
```

In other words, the P-order of the GCD of A and B is the minimum of the P-orders of A and B.

Many people are confused at first by functions like MIN. MIN simply outputs the smaller of its two inputs; if the inputs are equal, it outputs their common value. So

$$\text{MIN}(3, 5) = 3$$

$$\text{MIN}(3, 2) = 2$$

$$\text{MIN}(100, 100) = 100$$

$$\text{MIN}(3, (\text{MIN}42)) = 2$$

and

$$\text{MIN}(\text{ORD}_3(18), \text{ORD}_3(162)) = 2$$

(because $\text{ORD}_3(18)$ is 2 while $\text{ORD}_3(162)$ is 4).

A similar function is MAX:

```
TO MAX :X :Y
 IF :X > :Y [OP :X]
 OP :Y
END
```

Experiment 12.3 Give a simple description of the following function.

```
TO I :X :Y
 OP (MIN :X :Y) + (MAX :X :Y)
END
```

Prove that your description is correct.

Theorem 12.3 outlines a new method for calculating $\text{GCD}(A, B)$ (it tells you how to find all the local components of $\text{GCD}(A, B)$); how can we model this method in Logo? There are several ways. You can search the lists $\text{FACTOR}(A)$ and $\text{FACTOR}(B)$ for common primes (and then take the smallest exponent). This closely models the theorem but takes a long time to output. Another method is to assume that A and B are positive (again, we can do this because $\text{GCD}(A, B) = \text{GCD}(-A, B) = \ldots$). You can then look at each prime in $\text{PRIMES.UPTO}(A)$; for each P in this list, you can calculate the smaller of $\text{ORD}_P(A)$ and $\text{ORD}_P(B)$ (this minimum power might be 0) and raise P to this power. Then you can output the product of all such prime powers. Of course, you can use $\text{PRIMES.UPTO}(B)$ instead of $\text{PRIMES.UPTO}(A)$; the best thing to do is to use $\text{PRIMES.UPTO}(\text{MIN}(A, B))$.

Think of this GCD function in two parts: first you compute the appropriate power of a prime P

```
TO MINTERM :A :B :P
 OP (POWER :P (MIN (ORD :P :A) (ORD :P :B)))
END
```

and then you multiply all these local components together (considering only those primes between 1 and the smaller of A and B).

```
TO GCF :A :B
 OP L.PROD "MINTERM (SE :A :B) PRIMES.UPTO (MIN :A :B)
END
```

I've used the name GCF ("greatest common factor") so that we don't confuse this process with the one described by Euclid's algorithm. Of course, GCF is equal to GCD on positive integers, but GCD outlines a process for computing its output that is much more efficient than the one described in GCF.

On the other hand, thinking about greatest common divisors using the GCF function is often fruitful. For example, in project 11.11 you were asked to show that if A, B and C are positive integers, then

$$\text{GCD}(CA, CB) = C \cdot \text{GCD}(A, B)$$

using only Euclid's algorithm. This can be a nasty piece of business. But if we use the algorithm in GCF, the local-to-global theorem, and the fact that the ORD of the product is the sum of the ORDs, then the argument is much cleaner. Here are the details.

Since $\text{GCD}(CA, CB)$ and $C \cdot \text{GCD}(A, B)$ are both positive, it's enough to show (by the local-to-global theorem) that they are equal "locally"; that is, it's enough to show that if P is any prime, then $\text{ORD}_P(\text{GCD}(CA, CB))$ and $\text{ORD}_P(C \cdot \text{GCD}(A, B))$ are the same.

Well,

$$\text{ORD}_P(\text{GCD}(CA, CB)) = \text{MIN}(\text{ORD}_P(CA), \text{ORD}_P(CB))$$
$$= \text{MIN}(\text{ORD}_P(C) + \text{ORD}_P(A), \text{ORD}_P(C) + \text{ORD}_P(B))$$

and

$$\text{ORD}_P(C \cdot \text{GCD}(A, B)) = \text{ORD}_P(C) + \text{ORD}_P(\text{GCD}(A, B))$$
$$= \text{ORD}_P(C) + \text{MIN}(\text{ORD}_P(A), \text{ORD}_P(B))$$

We'll be all set once you do the next project.

Project 12.4 Show that if X, Y, and Z are positive integers, then

$$\text{MIN}(X + Y, X + Z) = X + \text{MIN}(Y, Z)$$

Hint: Use the definition of MIN, and break up your argument into three cases:

1. $Y < Z$

2. $Y > Z$

3. $Y = Z$

Use basic facts about inequality; for example, if $Y < Z$, then $X + Y < X + Z$.

As another example, let's show that if A and B are positive integers, then

$$(\text{GCD}(A, B))^2 = \text{GCD}(A^2, B^2)$$

Well, let P be any prime. Then

$$\text{ORD}_P((\text{GCD}(A, B))^2) = 2\text{ORD}_P(\text{GCD}(A, B))$$
$$= 2\text{MIN}(\text{ORD}_P(A), \text{ORD}_P(B))$$

and

$$\text{ORD}_P(\text{GCD}(A^2, B^2)) = \text{MIN}(\text{ORD}_P(A^2), \text{ORD}_P(B^2))$$
$$= \text{MIN}(2\text{ORD}_P(A), 2\text{ORD}_P(B))$$

so we'll be all set once you do the next exercise.

Exercise 12.5 Show that if X and Y are positive integers, then

$$2\text{MIN}(X, Y) = \text{MIN}(2X, 2Y)$$

Project 12.6 Verify each statement for some specific numbers using tabulations and other tools; then justify each statement.

1. If A and B are relatively prime, $\text{GCD}(KA, KB) = K$
2. $(\text{GCD}(A, B))^3 = \text{GCD}(A^3, B^3)$
3. $\text{GCD}(A + B, B) = \text{GCD}(A, B)$
4. $B \mid \text{GCD}(AB, B)$
5. $\text{GCD}(A, A + B) \mid B$

Hint: Use any Logo model to do the experiment, but when you think about these statements, think of GCD as the process outlined in GCF, think of the fundamental theorem, and think of the local-to-global theorem. Are any of these statements easier to think about if you use the actual definition of greatest common divisor (definition 11.1)?

#Project 12.7 How would you define the greatest common divisor for more than two integers? Write a Logo model for your definition. Your function should take a list of integers as input. (Hint: You can either give an inductive description that reduces the problem of calculating the GCD of a list of numbers to the problem of calculating the GCD of of two numbers, or you can model the construction of GCF above.) If your function uses GCD, try substituting GCF wherever you see GCD in your definition. Does it make a difference? Should it?

Can the greatest common divisor of three integers be written as a combination of the three integers? If so, can you calculate the coefficients? What does it mean for a list of integers to be relatively prime? Write a predicate that models your definition.

Least Common Multiple

A notion that is analogous to greatest common divisor is "least common multiple." A common multiple of A and B is an integer M that is divisible by both A and B. For example, 48 is a common multiple of 4 and 6. So is 36. So is -60. A least common multiple of 4 and 6 is 12 because every other common multiple of 4 and 6 is also a multiple of 12 (4 and 6 have another least common multiple; what is it?).

Definition 12.4 If A and B are integers, an integer M is a least common multiple of A and B if

1. $A \mid M$ and $B \mid M$, and

2. if N is any integer so that $A \mid N$ and $B \mid N$, then $M \mid N$.

By convention, we'll always take our least common multiples to be positive.

Suppose that A is $2^2 \cdot 5^2 \cdot 7^3 \cdot 11^2$ and B is $2 \cdot 3 \cdot 5^3 \cdot 7^2$. What is the least common multiple of A and B? If M is divisible by A, the whole prime factorization of A must occur in M:

$$M = 2^2 \cdot 5^2 \cdot 7^3 \cdot 11^2 \cdot (something)$$

Now, look at this expression with an eye to "inflating" it as little as possible to make it divisible by B. Well, M contains more than enough 2s, and it contains just enough 7s. It needs a 3 and an extra 5. So M now looks like this:

$$M = 2^2 \cdot 5^2 \cdot 7^3 \cdot 11^2 \cdot (3 \cdot 5) \cdot (something)$$

So M must contain at least

$$2^2 \cdot 5^2 \cdot 7^3 \cdot 11^2 \cdot (3 \cdot 5) = 2^2 \cdot 3 \cdot 5^3 \cdot 7^3 \cdot 11^2$$

and this number is the least common multiple of A and B. In general, to calculate the least common multiple of A and B, we take all the primes that are factors of either A or B, and we raise each such prime P to the larger of the P-orders of A and B. Just as in our Logo model for GCF, we use a larger set of "trial factors"; this time, to make sure that we include all primes that divide either A or B, we look at all primes up to the larger of A and B:

```
TO LCM :A :B
 OP L.PROD "MAXTERM (SE :A :B) PRIMES.UPTO (MAX :A :B)
END

TO MAXTERM :A :B :P
 OP (POWER :P (MAX (ORD :P :A) (ORD :P :B)))
END
```

Experiment 12.8 Find the value of each expression. Look for theorems.

1. $\mathrm{LCM}(4, 6)$

2. $\mathrm{LCM}(8, 12)$

3. $\mathrm{LCM}(20, 30)$

4. $\mathrm{LCM}(12, 18)$

5. $\mathrm{LCM}(16, 36)$

6. $\mathrm{LCM}(64, 144)$

7. $\mathrm{LCM}(12^{12}, 18^{18})$

8. $\mathrm{LCM}(15, 8)$

9. $\mathrm{LCM}(63, 20)$

10. $\mathrm{LCM}(8, 27)$

11. $\mathrm{LCM}(12, 16)$

12. $\mathrm{LCM}(12, 16 + 12)$

13. $\mathrm{LCM}(12, 16 + 312)$

14. $\mathrm{LCM}(5, 10)$

15. $\mathrm{LCM}(17, 17^{23})$

16. $\mathrm{GCD}(4, 6) \cdot \mathrm{LCM}(4, 6)$

17. $\mathrm{GCD}(10, 12) \cdot \mathrm{LCM}(1012)$

18. $\mathrm{GCD}(4 + 6, \mathrm{LCM}(4, 6))$

19. $\mathrm{GCD}(15 + 20, \mathrm{LCM}(15, 20))$

20. $\mathrm{GCD}(8 + 12, \mathrm{LCM}(8, 12))$

The Logo model for LCM suggests the following theorem:

Theorem 12.5 If A and B are integers and $M = \mathrm{LCM}(A, B)$, then for all primes P,

$$\mathrm{ORD}_P(M) = \mathrm{MAX}(\mathrm{ORD}_P(A), \mathrm{ORD}_P(B))$$

Notice the similarity with GCF. If P is any prime,

$$\text{ORD}_P(\text{GCF}(A, B)) = \text{MIN}(\text{ORD}_P(A), \text{ORD}_P(B))$$

whereas

$$\text{ORD}_P(\text{LCM}(A, B)) = \text{MAX}(\text{ORD}_P(A), \text{ORD}_P(B))$$

Theorem 12.5 and the local-to-global theorem allow us to establish facts about LCM using the "one prime at a time" local strategy. For example, the last experiment suggests that if A, B and C are positive integers, then $\text{LCM}(CA, CB) = C \cdot \text{LCM}(A, B)$. Let's prove it.

If P is any prime, then

$$\text{ORD}_P(\text{LCM}(CA, CB)) = \text{MAX}(\text{ORD}_P(CA), \text{ORD}_P(CB))$$

$$= \text{MAX}(\text{ORD}_P(C) + \text{ORD}_P(A), \text{ORD}_P(C) + \text{ORD}_P(B))$$

and

$$\text{ORD}_P(C \cdot \text{LCM}(A, B)) = \text{ORD}_P(C) + \text{ORD}_P(\text{LCM}(A, B))$$

$$= \text{ORD}_P(C) + \text{MAX}(\text{ORD}_P(A), \text{ORD}_P(B))$$

So our result follows from a property of MAX,

$$\text{MAX}(X + Y, X + Z) = X + \text{MAX}(Y, Z)$$

and that's an easy thing to establish.

Project 12.9 Prove that if A and B are positive integers, then

$$(\text{LCM}(A, B))^2 = \text{LCM}(A^2, B^2)$$

Hint: Use theorem 12.5 and the local-to-global theorem.

I don't want you to think that the one-prime-at-a-time strategy is the only way to prove facts about LCM. Sometimes it's easier to go right back to the definition of least common multiple (definition 12.4); For example, let's prove that if A and B are relatively prime, then $\text{LCM}(A, B) = AB$.

By definition 12.4, we must show the following:

1. $A \mid AB$ and $B \mid AB$. This is clear.

2. If N is an integer so that $A \mid N$ and $B \mid N$, then $AB \mid N$. This follows because A and B are relatively prime (see project 11.34).

Project 12.10 Use this strategy to show that if A and B are integers, then

$$\text{LCM}(A + B, B) = \text{LCM}(A, B)$$

Also show that if $A \mid B$, then

$$\text{LCM}(A, B) = B$$

The following project establishes something that you probably noticed in experiment 12.8.

Project 12.11 Prove that if A and B are positive integers,

$$\text{LCM}(A, B) \cdot \text{GCD}(A, B) = AB$$

Hint: Use the local-to-global theorem; that is, show that each side of the equation has the same P-order at every prime P. Look at the result from experiment 12.3.

Suppose that $A = 45$ and $B = 525$. When I think of the result in the above project, I think of this diagram

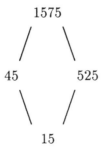

Here, I've placed the GCD beneath A and B and the LCM above them. The fact that $\text{LCM}(A, B) \cdot \text{GCD}(A, B) = AB$ tells us that the product of the numbers at the ends of one diagonal is the same as the product of the numbers at the ends of the other diagonal. This is even more suggestive if you factor everything into primes:

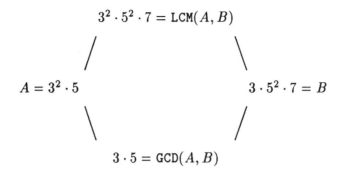

$$3^2 \cdot 5^2 \cdot 7 = \text{LCM}(A, B)$$

$$A = 3^2 \cdot 5 \qquad\qquad 3 \cdot 5^2 \cdot 7 = B$$

$$3 \cdot 5 = \text{GCD}(A, B)$$

You get the GCD by taking the primes common to both factorizations and by raising each prime to the smaller of the exponents to which it occurs. You get the LCM by taking the primes that occur in either factorization and by raising each prime to the largest exponent to which it occurs. Notice that if P^E occurs in either A or in B, then P^E occurs in exactly one of $\text{GCD}(A, B)$ or $\text{LCM}(A, B)$. This explains why $(3^2 \cdot 5^2 \cdot 7) \cdot (3 \cdot 5) = (3^2 \cdot 5) \cdot (3 \cdot 5^2 \cdot 7)$.

The fact that $\text{LCM}(A, B) \cdot \text{GCD}(A, B) = AB$ can be used to give a new model for LCM:

```
TO LCM :A :B
 OP (:A * :B) / (GCD :A :B)
END
```

From now on, when you think about LCM, think of our original Logo model (the product over PRIMES.UPTO(MAX(A, B)),each prime P raised to the MAX of $\text{ORD}_P(A)$ and $\text{ORD}_P(B)$), but when you write a function that uses LCM, you can make it run faster by using this fast version of LCM.

#Project 12.12 Show that if A and B are positive integers,

$$\text{GCD}(A + B, \text{LCM}(A, B)) = \text{GCD}(A, B)$$

Hint: Think of how A and B look when they are factored into primes.

Experiment 12.13 Let F be the arithmetic sequence with first term 5 and common difference 12:

```
TO F :N
 IF :N = 1 [OP 5]
 OP 12 + (F :N - 1)
END
```

Suppose we take the values of F and "reduce" them MOD 42:

```
TO G :N
 OP MOD (F :N) 42
END
```

If you tabulate G, you notice that the outputs repeat. When do they start to repeat? What is the significance of this number? Suppose you have a generic arithmetic sequence with first term A and common difference D:

```
TO F :A :D :N
 IF :N = 1 [OP :A]
 OP :D + (F :N - 1)
END
```

and you reduce the outputs MOD M:

```
TO G :A :D :M :N
 OP MOD (F :A :D :N) :M
END
```

How long does it take for the outputs of G to repeat? Develop a function RETURN so that RETURN(A, D, M) outputs the smallest integer C so that G(A, D, M, C) is the same as G$(A, D, M, 1)$. Play with various values for A, D and M as inputs to RETURN. When is RETURN(A, D, M) the same as M?

    # Is there a simple description of the sum of the outputs of G(A, D, M, N) as N goes from 1 to RETURN$(A, D, M) - 1$? How about this sum MOD M? Hint: In your investigations, you might want to use functions like

```
TO H :A :D :M :N
 OP SIGMA "G (SE :A :B :M) 1 (RETURN :A :D :M) - 1
END
```

and

```
TO K :A :D :M :N
 OP MOD (H :A :D :M :N) :M
END
```

H uses the old version of SIGMA rather that L.SIGMA.

    As another experiment, carry out this experiment using geometric sequences instead of arithmetic sequences.

Factor Lists

Many important functions in number theory are defined using certain interesting lists. We have already built two of these lists: $\text{PRIMES.UPTO}(N)$ (the list of primes that are less than or equal to N) and $\text{FACTOR}(N)$ (the list of pairs $[P \; \text{ORD}_P(N)]$ where P runs over the primes that divide N). Some other lists we'll need are

1. $\text{DIVISORS}(N)$ is the list of divisors of N. So $\text{DIVISORS}(12)$ is

   ```
   [1 2 3 4 6 12]
   ```

2. $\text{PRIME.TO}(N)$ is the list of numbers that are between 1 and N and are relatively prime to N. So $\text{PRIME.TO}(14)$ is

   ```
   [1 3 5 9 11 13]
   ```

3. $\text{MULTIPLES}(M, N)$ is the list of multiples of M that are less than or equal to N. So $\text{MULTIPLES}(3, 31)$ is

   ```
   [3 6 9 12 15 18 21 24 27 30]
   ```

Notice that $\text{MULTIPLES}(M, N)$ is part of the output list of the arithmetic sequence whose first term is 0 and whose common difference is M.

Each of these functions can be viewed as the output of the filter of a predicate over $\text{NUMBERS.UPTO}(N)$:

```
TO NUMBERS.UPTO :N
 IF :N = 0 [OP []]
 OP SE (NUMBERS.UPTO :N - 1) :N
END
```

(Compare this function with the LIST.UPTO function of chapter 10.)
    To be specific,

```
TO DIVISORS :N
 OP FILTER "DIVIS? :N (NUMBERS.UPTO :N)
END

TO PRIME.TO :N
 OP FILTER "RELATIVELY.PRIME? :N (NUMBERS.UPTO :N)
END
```

```
TO MULTIPLES :M :N
 OP FILTER "DIVIS.BY? :M (NUMBERS.UPTO :N)
END
```

The predicate `DIVIS.BY?` is defined like this

```
TO DIVIS.BY? :M :N
 OP DIVIS? :N :M
END
```

Project 12.14 One of my students came up with this method for defining `MULTIPLES`:

```
TO NEW.MULTIPLES :M :N
 IF :N = 0 [OP []]
 IF DIVIS? :N :M [OP SE (NEW.MULTIPLES :M :N - :M) :N]
 OP NEW.MULTIPLES :M :N - 1
END
```

Why is `NEW.MULTIPLES` equal to `MULTIPLES` on all pairs of integers? Is it faster?

Project 12.15 Suppose that A and B are relatively prime. Pick an integer D in `DIVISORS`(A), and pick an integer E in `DIVISORS`(B). Show that D and E are relatively prime. (Hint: If D and E had a common factor, why would A and B also have a common factor?) Suppose you pick two different integers D and D' in `DIVISORS`(A) and you also pick two different integers E and E' in `DIVISORS`(B). Show that DE and $D'E'$ cannot be equal. Hint: Be sure to try this with some concrete examples before you attempt a proof. Since D and D' are not equal, there exists a prime P so that $\text{ORD}_P(D)$ and $\text{ORD}_P(D')$ are not equal. Show that, for this prime P, $\text{ORD}_P(E)$ and $\text{ORD}_P(E')$ are both 0. Conclude that $\text{ORD}_P(DE)$ and $\text{ORD}_P(D'E')$ are not equal.

Project 12.16 If P is a prime, describe `DIVISORS`(P). How about `DIVISORS`(P^2)? `DIVISORS`(P^3)? `DIVISORS`(P^K)? Write a simple function (that uses the theory of geometric series) equal to the following function:

```
TO F :P :K
 OP L.SIGMA "ID [] DIVISORS (POWER :P :K)
END
```

```
TO ID :X
  OP :X
END
```

Project 12.17 If P and Q are distinct primes, describe $\text{DIVISORS}(PQ)$ in terms of $\text{DIVISORS}(P)$ and $\text{DIVISORS}(Q)$. More generally, describe DIVISORS($P^K Q^J$) in terms of $\text{DIVISORS}(P^K)$ and $\text{DIVISORS}(Q^J)$.

Project 12.18 Have you ever thought about multiplying two lists? For example, if $L = $ [1 2 3] and $L' = $ [1 2 5 7 35], we could define the "list product" of L and L' to be the list of all possible products that you get when you take a factor from L and a factor from L':

LIST.PRODUCT(L, L') = [1 2 5 7 35 2 4 10 14 70 3 6 15 21 105]

(This is very much like multiplying polynomials. First I multiplied everything in L by 1, then by 2, then by 5, then by 7, and then by 35.)

Write a Logo model for LIST.PRODUCT. If you get stuck, there's a version in the appendix.

Suppose that the two lists that you "multiply" are lists of divisors for two integers. For example,

LIST.PRODUCT (DIVISORS (15), DIVISORS (6))

= LIST.PRODUCT ([1 3 5 15], [1 2 3 6])

= [1 3 5 15 2 6 10 30 3 9 15 45 6 18 30 90]

Notice that the elements of this list are all factors of 90 (which is $15 \cdot 6$). And (comparing with DIVISORS(90)) every divisor of 90 is on the list. Unfortunately, some divisors show up twice in the LIST.PRODUCT. Why is this? One way around this problem is to write a function that takes a list as input and "reduces" it (that is, outputs the list of distinct elements in the input list with no repeats). Try it if you enjoy this kind of list processing. Another idea is to choose the divisors of 90 more carefully. Would it happen if, instead of 15 and 6, you took, say, 5 and 18? In other words, is

LIST.PRODUCT(DIVISORS(5), DIVISORS(18)) = DIVISORS(90)

(I'm being a little sloppy here. The "equals" sign in the above sentence means that the list on the left-hand side contains the same elements as DIVISORS(90)

with no repeats. So for this project, make believe that order doesn't count in a list; that is, think of two lists with the same elements and the same COUNT as being the same list.) Give some other examples of integers A and B so that

$$\texttt{LIST.PRODUCT(DIVISORS}(A), \texttt{DIVISORS}(B)) = \texttt{DIVISORS}(AB)$$

In general, suppose that A and B are relatively prime. Show that

$$\texttt{LIST.PRODUCT(DIVISORS}(A), \texttt{DIVISORS}(B)) = \texttt{DIVISORS}(AB)$$

Hint: Use project 12.15 to show that the left-hand side contains no repeats. Then it suffices to show that every divisor of AB can be written as a product DE where $D \mid A$ and $E \mid B$. To show this, think of the prime factorizations of A, B, and AB. It might help to write a Logo function SPLIT that takes three inputs: A, B, and C (a divisor of AB). SPLIT(A, B, C) outputs the part of C that divides A, and SPLIT(B, A, C) outputs the part of C that divides B. Check that SPLIT$(A, B, C) \cdot$ SPLIT$(B, A, C) = C$.

Project 12.19 How many divisors does an integer have? Define a function NU (for the Greek letter ν) that outputs the number of divisors of its input. For example NU(36) is 9 because 36 has 9 divisors (DIVISORS(36) is [1 2 3 4 6 9 12 18 36]). Tabulate your Logo model for NU, and try to find a simple formula for NU. In particular, try to describe the output of NU in terms of the prime factorization of its input. You might want to start by looking at values of NU at powers of a single prime. For example, complete the following tables:

N		NU(N)
3		
9	(3^2)	
27	(3^3)	
81	(3^4)	
243	(3^5)	
729	(3^6)	

N		NU(N)
5		
25	(5^2)	
125	(5^3)	
625	(5^4)	
3125	(5^5)	
15625	(5^6)	

If P is a prime and K is a positive integer, what is NU(P^K)? Can you explain your answer?

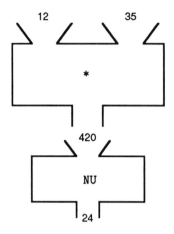

Figure 12.1

If A and B are relatively prime, show that $NU(AB) = NU(A) \cdot NU(B)$. (Hint: Use project 12.17.)

This property (the "multiplicative property") is shared by several other important functions in number theory. It says, for example, that if you want to compute $NU(12 \cdot 35)$ (which would require a fair amount of time on my computer), you can "save" the multiplication until after you have evaluated NU at each factor. Since $NU(12) = 6$ and $NU(35) = 4$, $NU(12 \cdot 35)$ is $6 \cdot 4$ or 24. If you think of functions as machines, the multiplicative property says that the two composites shown in figures 12.1 and 12.2 will produce the same output.

If A and B are not relatively prime, however, is $NU(AB) = NU(A) \cdot NU(B)$? Compare NU to the following function TU

```
TO TU :N
 OP L.PROD "ADJUSTED.ORD :N PRIMES.UPTO :N
END

TO ADJUSTED.ORD :N :P
 OP (ORD :P :N) + 1
END
```

Prove that $TU = NU$ on integers greater than 1.

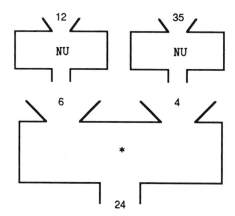

Figure 12.2

Hint: Either use the previous parts of this project or study the following example.

To find the number of divisors of $2^3 \cdot 3^2 \cdot 5$, count all the ways you can build such a divisor. If D is a divisor of this number, D can only be divisible by 2, 3, or 5. In fact, we know that

$$\text{ORD}_2(D) \le 3, \text{ORD}_3(D) \le 2 \text{ and } \text{ORD}_5(D) \le 1$$

This means that the only prime powers that can occur in D are

$2^0 = 1$	$3^0 = 1$	$5^0 = 1$
$2^1 = 2$	$3^1 = 3$	$5^1 = 5$
$2^2 = 4$	$3^2 = 9$	
$2^3 = 8$		

Now, to build D, you must take one factor from each column. For example, one factor is $2^2 \cdot 3^0 \cdot 5$ or 20. Since there are four factors in the first column, three factors in the second column, and two factors in the third column, there are $4 \cdot 3 \cdot 2$ or 24 possible factors.

You can probably use this kind of argument to give a different proof that $\text{NU}(AB) = \text{NU}(A) \cdot \text{NU}(B)$ for relatively prime A and B.

Project 12.20 Consider the function that outputs the product of the divisors of its input:

```
TO PROD.OF.DIVISORS :N
 OP L.PROD "ID [] (DIVISORS :N)
END

TO ID :X
 OP :X
END
```

Tabulate `PROD.OF.DIVISORS`. Can you see anything?

Here's an idea: Suppose that `SQUARE` is the function that squares its input. What is the relation between `PROD.OF.DIVISORS` and the function:

```
TO PROD.OF.SQUARE.DIVISORS :N
 OP L.PROD "SQUARE [] (DIVISORS :N)
END
```

Prove it. Now tabulate `PROD.OF.SQUARE.DIVISORS`. The output is a power of the input. What is the power? (Hint: Look at project 12.19.) Prove that your conjecture is correct.

Hints:

1. Use these hints only if you are stuck.

2. Consider the function:

   ```
   TO BACKWARD.PRODUCT.OF.DIVISORS :N
    OP L.PROD "QUOT :N (DIVISORS :N)
   END
   ```

   Look at the outputs of `BACKWARD.PRODUCT.OF.DIVISORS` and `PRODUCT.OF.DIVISORS` for several different inputs.

   Show that `BACKWARD.PRODUCT.OF.DIVISORS` and `PRODUCT.OF.DIVISORS` are equal on positive integers.

3. Conclude that for any positive integer N,

$$(\text{PRODUCT.OF.DIVISORS}(N))(\text{BACKWARD.PRODUCT.OF.DIVISORS}(N))$$
$$= \text{PROD.OF.SQUARE.DIVISORS}(N)$$

4. Suppose that F is the function that always outputs its first input:

```
TO F :N :K
 OP :N
END
```

Tabulate the function

```
TO MANY :N
 OP L.PROD "F "N (DIVISORS :N)
END
```

MANY simply multiplies N by itself $\text{COUNT}(\text{DIVISORS}(N))$ times, so $\text{MANY}(N)$ outputs $\text{POWER}(N, \text{NU}(N))$. Show that MANY is also equal to the product of

BACKWARD.PRODUCT.OF.DIVISORS and PRODUCT.OF.DIVISORS

For example,

$$(\text{PRODUCT.OF.DIVISORS}(12))(\text{BACKWARDS.PRODUCT.OF.DIVISORS}(12))$$
$$= (1 \cdot 2 \cdot 3 \cdot 4 \cdot 6 \cdot 12) \cdot (12 \cdot 6 \cdot 4 \cdot 3 \cdot 2 \cdot 1)$$
$$= (1 \cdot 12) \cdot (2 \cdot 6) \cdot (3 \cdot 4) \cdot (4 \cdot 3) \cdot (6 \cdot 2) \cdot (12 \cdot 1)$$

(I rearranged the product, multiplying each term in the first parenthesis by the corresponding term in the second parenthesis.)

So

$$(\text{PRODUCT.OF.DIVISORS}(12))(\text{BACKWARDS.PRODUCT.OF.DIVISORS}(12))$$
$$= 12 \cdot 12 \cdot 12 \cdot 12 \cdot 12 \cdot 12 = \text{POWER}(12, \text{NU}(12))$$

Project 12.21 The above project raises an interesting question:

Can $\text{NU}(N)$ ever be odd?

Why does the above project raise this question? Can $\text{NU}(N)$ ever be odd? Justify your answer.

In project 12.19 you showed that

$$\text{NU}(AB) = \text{NU}(A) \cdot \text{NU}(B)$$

if A and B are relatively prime. (You'll be able to give another proof of this fact later in this chapter.) This property would not be very important if it were not for the fundamental theorem, but because of the fundamental theorem, functions with this property can often be described by interesting formulas. Here's why.

If N is any integer, factor N into primes

$$N = P_1^{E_1} \, P_2^{E_2} \, P_3^{E_3} \, \ldots P_T^{E_T}$$

Then, inductively apply the fact $\text{NU}(AB) = \text{NU}(A) \cdot \text{NU}(B)$ for all relatively prime A and B:

$$
\begin{aligned}
\text{NU}(N) &= \text{NU}(P_1^{E_1} \, P_2^{E_2} \, P_3^{E_3} \ldots P_T^{E_T}) \\
&= \text{NU}(P_1^{E_1})\text{NU}(P_2^{E_2} \, P_3^{E_3} \ldots P_T^{E_T}) \\
&= \text{NU}(P_1^{E_1})\text{NU}(P_2^{E_2})\text{NU}(P_3^{E_3} \ldots P_T^{E_T}) \\
&= \text{NU}(P_1^{E_1})\text{NU}(P_2^{E_2})\text{NU}(P_3^{E_3}) \ldots \text{NU}(P_T^{E_T})
\end{aligned}
$$

Here I'm using the fact that, for example, $P_1^{E_1}$ is relatively prime to $P_2^{E_2} \, P_3^{E_3} \ldots P_T^{E_T}$. In other words, we know the value of NU on any integer N if we know its values on powers of primes. It's easy to calculate $\text{NU}(P^K)$. Since

$$\text{DIVISORS}(P^K) = [1 \ P \ P^2 \ P^3 \ P^4 \ldots P^K]$$

we see that $\text{NU}(PK) = K + 1$. This means that for our N above,

$$\text{NU}(N) = (E_1 + 1)(E_2 + 1)(E_3 + 1) \cdots (E_T + 1)$$

(compare this with the TU function of project 12.19).

So, for example, since $2025 = 5^2 \cdot 3^4$, 2025 has $(2 + 1)(4 + 1) = 15$ factors, and

$$2^4 \cdot 3^6 \cdot 7^2$$

has $5 \cdot 7 \cdot 3 = 105$ factors.

Let's call functions that behave like NU "multiplicative" functions.

Multiplicative Functions

Definition 12.6 A function F whose domain is a subset of **Z** is called a "multiplicative function" if, whenever A and B are relatively prime, the following is true:

$$F(AB) = F(A) \cdot F(B)$$

In other words, F is multiplicative if, for all relatively prime pairs of integers A and B, the output is the same whether you

1. first multiply A and B together, and then apply F to this product, or

2. apply F to A, apply F to B, and then multiply these outputs together.

See the discussion of this property in project 12.19 for more details.

As an example, consider the function F so that $F(X) = X^3$. If A and B are any integers,

$$F(AB) = (AB)^3 = A^3 B^3$$

But A^3 is $F(A)$ and B^3 is $F(B)$, so $A^3 B^3 = F(A) \cdot F(B)$. Note that for this F, we didn't even need to assume that A and B are relatively prime; in this case, $F(AB) = F(A) \cdot F(B)$ for all integers A and B.

The notion of multiplicativity has been quite important in number theory. As we'll see, many number-theoretic functions of interest have this multiplicativity property, and, as we'll also see, knowing that a function is multiplicative gives us a valuable method of attack when we investigate it. So for part of the rest of this chapter and for all of the next one, we'll look at some answers to the following questions:

1. Given a function defined on $\mathbf{Z}^+$, how can you tell if it is multiplicative?

2. How can you build your own multiplicative functions?

3. How can you use the fact that a function is multiplicative to gain more insight into it?

Experiment 12.22 Describe each function in words. Which functions seem to be multiplicative? Can you supply any proofs? (To show that a function F is not multiplicative, you just have to find one example of relatively prime integers A and B so that $\text{F}(AB)$ is not the same as $\text{F}(A) \cdot \text{F}(B)$.)

Hint: Spend a good amount of time on this experiment; it will make the rest of our discussion of multiplicative functions seem much more concrete. To test a function for multiplicativity, try it out on, say, ten pairs of relatively prime integers. You might want to customize TAB for this purpose.

1. ```
   TO ID :X
     OP :X
   END
   ```

2. ```
   TO SQUARE :X
     OP :X * :X
   END
   ```

3. ```
   TO F :X
     OP :X + 1
   END
   ```

4. ```
   TO ONE :X
     OP 1
   END
   ```

5. ```
   TO SCALE :X
     OP 3 * :X
   END
   ```

6. ```
   TO REDUCE :N
     OP MOD :N 12
   END
   ```

7. ```
   TO RESIDUE :N
     OP MOD :N 7
   END
   ```
   ```

```
8.  TO FACT :N
     IF :N = 0 [OP 1]
     OP :N * (FACT (:N - 1))
    END

9.  TO HOW.EVEN :N
     OP ORD 2 :N
    END
```

10. The SQRT function

```
11. TO ABS :X
     IF :X > 0 [OP :X]
     OP -1 * :X
    END

12. TO FUNNY.ABS :N
     IF :N = 0 [OP 0]
     OP POWER (1/5) ORD 5 :N
    END

13. TO ADDUP :N
     OP SIGMA "ID [] DIVISORS :N
    END

14. TO MULTUP :N
     OP L.PROD "ID DIVISORS :N
    END

15. TO ADDADDUP :N
     OP L.SIGMA "ADDUP [] DIVISORS :N
    END

16. TO ADDADDADDUP :N
     OP L.SIGMA "ADDADDUP [] DIVISORS :N
    END

17. TO NEWADDUP :N
     OP L.SIGMA "NU [] DIVISORS :N
    END
```

18. TO NEWNEWADDUP :N
      OP L.SIGMA "NEWADDUP [] DIVISORS :N
    END

19. TO ADDUPSCALE :N
      OP L.SIGMA "SCALE [] DIVISORS :N
    END

20. TO ADDUPSQUARE :N
      OP L.SIGMA "SQUARE [] DIVISORS :N
    END

21. TO PHI :N
      OP L.SIGMA "ONE [] PRIME.TO :N
    END

22. TO ADDPHI :N
      OP L.SIGMA "PHI DIVISORS :N
    END

Which of the above functions F have the property that

$$F(AB) = F(A) \cdot F(B)$$

for all A and B (not just for relatively prime A and B)? Such functions are called "strongly multiplicative functions."

There are some properties that hold for all multiplicative functions. For example, suppose that F is a multiplicative function. Then

1. If $F(1) = 0$, then $F(anything) = 0$, because, if A is any integer, since A and 1 are relatively prime, we would have

$$F(A) = F(1 \cdot A) = F(1) \cdot F(A) = 0 \cdot F(A) = 0$$

2. If $F(1)$ isn't 0, it has to be 1, because then we could argue like this:

$$F(1) = F(1 \cdot 1) = F(1) \cdot F(1)$$

Now divide both sides by $F(1)$ (it isn't 0, so you can do this); the result is

$$\frac{F(1)}{F(1)} = \frac{F(1) \cdot F(1)}{F(1)}$$

or

$$1 = F(1)$$

So if F is a multiplicative function, either $F(1) = 0$ (in which case, F always outputs 0) or $F(1) = 1$.

Arguments like this (in which properties of a function are derived by formal logic from an abstract definition) show up throughout mathematics. My students can almost always follow such arguments, but they often complain that such proofs are contrived (how did you know to write A as $1 \cdot A$?). I agree. The only consolation is that everyone gets better at these things as they study more mathematics.

It's easy to build multiplicative functions. Suppose you want to construct a multiplicative function F. Simply define F on prime powers and "extend by multiplicativity." For example, suppose I declare that F is a multiplicative function and, for any prime power P^K (with $K > 0$), $F(P^K) = K$. Then F is automatically defined on all integers greater than 1. In particular,

$F(81) = 4 \qquad (81 = 3^4)$

$F(16) = 4 \qquad (16 = 2^4)$

$F(125) = 3 \qquad (125 = 5^3)$

$F(75) = F(5^2 \cdot 3) = F(5^2) \cdot F(3) = 2 \cdot 1 = 2$

$F(1440) = F(3^2 \cdot 2^4 \cdot 5) = F(3^2) \cdot F(2^4) \cdot F(5) = 2 \cdot 4 \cdot 1 = 8$

Since F outputs numbers other than 0, $F(1)$ must be 1.

A Logo model for F can be built using the FACTOR list. Recall that

$$\text{FACTOR}(12) = [\ [2 \ 2] \ [3 \ 1] \ ]$$

$$\text{FACTOR}(1440) = [\ [2 \ 4] \ [3 \ 2] \ [5 \ 1] \ ]$$

and so on. Think of each element in the output of FACTOR as a power of a prime. Then if we define PRIMITIVE as

```
TO PRIMITIVE :PRIMEPOWER
 OP LAST :PRIMEPOWER
END
```

then F can be modeled as

```
TO F :N
 IF :N = 1 [OP 1]
 OP L.PROD "PRIMITIVE [] FACTOR :N
END
```

Play with this function for a bit. Tabulate it. Can you see anything? If you didn't know where F came from, would you guess from your tabulation that F is multiplicative? If you knew that F is multiplicative but didn't know its definition, could you recover its definition from the tabulation? Try it out on your little sister or brother.

In the next chapter, we'll look at the process of extension by multiplicativity in a slightly different way.

Project 12.23 Build a Logo model, defined on all of $\mathbf{Z}^+$ for each multiplicative function (define the output at 1 to be 1). Then tabulate the function and try to find a simple description of it:

1. $F(P^K) = K - 1$

2. $F(P^K) = P$

3. $F(P^K) = (-1)^K$

4. $F(P^K) = (-1)^{(K+1)} P^{(K-1)}$

5. $F(P^K) = \begin{cases} 0 & \text{if } K > 1 \\ -1 & \text{if } K = 1 \end{cases}$

6. $F(P^K) = \begin{cases} -2 & \text{if } K = 1 \\ 1 & \text{if } K = 2 \\ 0 & \text{if } K > 2 \end{cases}$

The above method of extending by multiplicativity gives you a way to build a multiplicative function from scratch (simply define your function on prime powers). There is another way to build multiplicative functions; this method builds new multiplicative functions from old ones, and it generalizes what you probably noticed in experiment 12.22.

Building New Multiplicative Functions from Old Ones

In part II we constructed some interesting functions by summing simple functions over the integers between 1 and N. What happens if, instead of summing a simple function over NUMBERS.UP.TO(N), we sum it over a number theoretic list like DIVISORS(N)? Well, the simplest function is the one that always outputs 1:

```
TO ONE :X
 OP 1
END
```

If we sum ONE over any list L, we simply obtain the COUNT of L (why?), so the function

```
TO F :N
 OP L.SIGMA "ONE [] DIVISORS :N
END
```

is equal to the function that outputs the COUNT of DIVISORS(N). This function is just our old friend NU. In experiment 12.22 you summed some other functions over DIVISORS(N), and I hope you noticed the following phenomenon:

Conjecture: If F is a multiplicative function and G(N) is defined as the sum of the outputs of F over DIVISORS(N),

```
TO G :N
 OP SIGMA "F [] DIVISORS :N
END
```

then G is also a multiplicative function.

Before reading on, try to convince yourself that this conjecture is really true.

How would you go about proving such a result? You'd have to show that if F is any multiplicative function and G is defined like this:

$$G(N) = \sum_{D \in \text{DIVISORS}(N)} F(D)$$

then, if A and B are relatively prime integers, $G(AB) = G(A) \cdot G(B)$.

Proofs like this are just generic calculations. You work out a few examples for specific functions F and specific numbers A and B, and then you change the function in your calculation to F, and you change the numbers in your calculations to A and B. Let's be "quasigeneric"; let's assume that $A = 12$ and $B = 35$, but let's use a generic multiplicative function F instead of a specific one (like NU or ID). Look at $G(12 \cdot 35)$:

$$G(12 \cdot 35) = \sum_{D \in \text{DIVISORS}(12 \cdot 35)} F(D)$$

Since 12 and 35 are relatively prime, DIVISORS$(12 \cdot 35)$ is the LIST.PRODUCT of DIVISORS(12) and DIVISORS(35) (see project 12.17). This means that

$$G(12 \cdot 35) = \sum_{D \in \text{LIST.PRODUCT}(\text{DIVISORS}(12), \text{DIVISORS}(35))} F(D)$$

$$= \sum_{D \in \text{LIST.PRODUCT}([1\ 2\ 3\ 4\ 6\ 12], [1\ 5\ 7\ 35])} F(D)$$

Think about how you would form

$$\text{LIST.PRODUCT}([1\ 2\ 3\ 4\ 6\ 12], [1\ 5\ 7\ 35])$$

You would take each element in $[1\ 2\ 3\ 4\ 6\ 12]$, and you would multiply it by everything in $[1\ 5\ 7\ 35]$. In other words, a typical D in our LIST.PRODUCT can be written as CE where C is in $[1\ 2\ 3\ 4\ 6\ 12]$ and E is in $[1\ 5\ 7\ 35]$. To be explicit, the above sum can be written as

$$\sum_{E \in [1\ 5\ 7\ 35]} F(1 \cdot E) + \sum_{E \in [1\ 5\ 7\ 35]} F(2 \cdot E)$$

$$+ \sum_{E \in [1\ 5\ 7\ 35]} F(3 \cdot E) + \sum_{E \in [1\ 5\ 7\ 35]} F(4 \cdot E)$$

$$+ \sum_{E \in [1\ 5\ 7\ 35]} F(6 \cdot E) + \sum_{E \in [1\ 5\ 7\ 35]} F(12 \cdot E)$$

But F is multiplicative. Since everything in $[1\ 2\ 3\ 4\ 6\ 12]$ is relatively prime to every E in $[1\ 5\ 7\ 35]$, the above sum can be written as

$$\sum_{E \in [1\ 5\ 7\ 35]} F(1) \cdot F(E) + \sum_{E \in [1\ 5\ 7\ 35]} F(2) \cdot F(E)$$

$$+ \sum_{E \in [1\ 5\ 7\ 35]} F(3) \cdot F(E) + \sum_{E \in [1\ 5\ 7\ 35]} F(4) \cdot F(E)$$

$$+ \sum_{E \in [1\ 5\ 7\ 35]} F(6) \cdot F(E) + \sum_{E \in [1\ 5\ 7\ 35]} F(12) \cdot F(E)$$

Factor a $F(1)$ out of the first sum, an $F(2)$ out of the second sum, an $F(3)$ out of the third sum, and so on:

$$F(1) \left(\sum_{E \in [1\ 5\ 7\ 35]} F(E) \right) + F(2) \left(\sum_{E \in [1\ 5\ 7\ 35]} F(E) \right)$$

$$+ F(3) \left(\sum_{E \in [1\ 5\ 7\ 35]} F(E) \right) + F(4) \left(\sum_{E \in [1\ 5\ 7\ 35]} F(E) \right)$$

$$+ F(6) \left(\sum_{E \in [1\ 5\ 7\ 35]} F(E) \right) + F(12) \left(\sum_{E \in [1\ 5\ 7\ 35]} F(E) \right)$$

But look at G's definition and you'll see that

$$G(35) = \sum_{E \in [1\ 5\ 7\ 35]} F(E)$$

so the above calculation can be written as

$$F(1) \cdot G(35) + F(2) \cdot G(35) + F(3) \cdot G(35)$$
$$+ F(4) \cdot G(35) + F(6) \cdot G(35) + F(12) \cdot G(35)$$

Factor out the $G(35)$ and you have

$$(F(1) + F(2) + F(3) + F(4) + F(6) + F(12))) \cdot G(35)$$

which is

$$\left(\sum_{C \in [1 \ 2 \ 3 \ 4 \ 6 \ 12]} \text{F}(C) \right) \text{G}(35)$$

and (again looking at G's definition) the above sum is just G(12). So if you chase this chain of calculations back to the beginning, you see that

$$\text{G}(12 \cdot 35) = \text{G}(12) \cdot \text{G}(35)$$

Of course, there is nothing special about 12 and 35 in the above argument; I could have picked any two relatively prime integers (can you find at least two places where I needed the fact that 12 and 35 are relatively prime?). Try working out the above calculation if $A = 8$ and $B = 15$. Then try doing it with a generic A and B. You have just proved the following theorem:

Theorem 12.7 If F is a multiplicative function and $\text{G}(N)$ is defined as the sum of the outputs of F over DIVISORS(N),

```
TO G :N
 OP SIGMA "F [] DIVISORS :N
END
```

then G is also a multiplicative function.

If G is defined in terms of F as in the theorem, let's say that G "compiles" F. So NU compiles ONE, and ONE compiles the function E:

```
TO E :N
 IF :N = 1 [OP 1]
 OP 0
END
```

Theorem 12.7 is a useful method for showing that a function is multiplicative (to show that F is multiplicative, simply show that F compiles some multiplicative function G). Once you know that F is multiplicative, what can you do with this information? The point is that if F is multiplicative, F is determined by its outputs at prime powers, and it's often possible to find an interesting formula for these outputs of F. For example, consider the function whose output at N is the sum of N's divisors:

```
TO SIG :N                          TO ID :X
 OP L.SIGMA "ID [] DIVISORS :N      OP :X
END                                END
```

(SIG is short for "sigma"; the Greek lowercase sigma, σ, is often used to denote this "sum of the divisors" function.) In part 14 of experiment 12.22, you saw that SIG seems to be multiplicative. If you try to show that SIG is multiplicative using the definition of multiplicative, you wind up using exactly the kind of lengthy argument that you used to prove theorem 12.7. But since ID is multiplicative (it is even strongly multiplicative), you can apply theorem 12.7 and conclude that SIG is multiplicative. This fact isn't at all obvious, and you should verify it again for several examples. (Is SIG(4 · 15) equal to SIG(4) · SIG(15)?)

The important thing is that once you know that SIG is multiplicative, you can find its output at any integer if you know its output at prime powers. Again, this is because, for example,

$$\text{SIG}(450) = \text{SIG}(2 \cdot 3^2 \cdot 5^2) = (\text{SIG}(2)) \cdot (\text{SIG}(3^2)) \cdot (\text{SIG}(5^2))$$

by multiplicativity.

In other words, it might be possible to find a different (perhaps more efficient, perhaps more elegant, perhaps just different) way to define SIG by finding a formula for the outputs of SIG at prime powers and then by extending this formula by multiplicativity.

Suppose that P is a prime and K is a positive integer. Then

$$\text{DIVISORS}(P^K) = [1 \ P \ P^2 \ P^3 \ P^4 \ldots P^K]$$

so

$$\text{SIG}(P^K) = 1 + P + P^2 + P^3 + P^4 + \cdots + P^K$$

$$= \frac{P^{(K+1)} - 1}{P - 1}$$

To compute SIG(N), factor N into prime powers and apply the above formula to each factor. For example, if $N = 2^3 \cdot 5^2 \cdot 7^6$ (or 23529800),

$$\text{SIG}(N) = \frac{2^4 - 1}{2 - 1} \cdot \frac{5^3 - 1}{5 - 1} \cdot \frac{7^7 - 1}{7 - 1}$$

$$= 63824505$$

and the sum of the divisors of 2329800 is 63824505.

This version of SIG can be modeled in Logo as

```
TO NEWSIG :N
 IF N = 1 [OP 1]
 OP L.PROD "CONVERT [] FACTOR :N
END

TO CONVERT :TERM
 OP ((POWER FIRST :TERM (1 + (LAST :TERM))) - 1) →
           / ((FIRST :TERM) - 1)
END
```

Compare NEW.SIG to SIG for inputs of 1 to 12.

Experiment 12.24 Tabulate SIG. What can you say about N if $SIG(N)$ is odd?

Project 12.25 A number N is called "perfect" if $SIG(N) = 2N$. Perfect numbers are equal to the sum of their "proper" divisors (a proper divisor of N is any divisor of N except N itself). Find all perfect numbers less than 100. Show that 8128 is perfect.

Consider one more example: Suppose that F is the function that outputs the sum of the reciprocals of the divisors of its inputs:

```
TO F :N                           TO RECIP :D
 OP L.SIGMA "RECIP [] DIVISORS :N   OP 1 / :D
END                               END
```

Verify that F is multiplicative with a few examples. Of course, since RECIP is multiplicative, theorem 12.7 guarantees that F is multiplicative. What does F do to primes? If P is a prime,

$$F(P) = \frac{1}{1} + \frac{1}{P} = 1 + \frac{1}{P} = \frac{1+P}{P}$$

Similarly,

$$F(P^K) = 1 + \left(\frac{1}{P}\right) + \left(\frac{1}{P^2}\right) + \left(\frac{1}{P^3}\right) + \cdots + \left(\frac{1}{P^K}\right)$$

Using the common denominator P^K, we have

$$F(P^K) = \frac{P^K + P^{(K-1)} + P^{(K-2)} + \cdots + 1}{P^K}$$

$$= \frac{\frac{P^{(K+1)}-1}{P-1}}{P^K} = \frac{P^{(K+1)} - 1}{P^K(P-1)}$$

This means that, for example,

$$1 + \frac{1}{2} + \frac{1}{3} + \frac{1}{4} + \frac{1}{6} + \frac{1}{12} = F(12) = \frac{2^3 - 1}{2^2(2-1)} \cdot \frac{3^2 - 1}{3(3-1)}$$

(The last equality is because $F(12) = F(2^2 \cdot 3) = F(2^2) \cdot F(3)$.)
Simplifying, we see that

$$1 + \frac{1}{2} + \frac{1}{3} + \frac{1}{4} + \frac{1}{6} + \frac{1}{12} = \frac{7}{4} \cdot \frac{8}{6} = \frac{7}{3}$$

Project 12.26 We have seen the if F compiles G and if G is multiplicative, then F is multiplicative. In the next chapter, we'll show that every multiplicative function is the compilation of some other multiplicative function. Try it for a few multiplicative functions. Hint: Look at project 12.23 for ideas.

1. Find a function E so that ONE could be defined like this:

```
TO ONE :N
 OP COMPILE "E [] :N
END
```

2. Find a function F so that ID could be defined like this:

```
TO ID :N
 OP COMPILE "F [] :N
END
```

3. Let L be the multiplicative function that is defined on prime powers by $L(P^K) = K$. Find a multiplicative function J so that L compiles J. Hint: How must J act on prime powers?

Chapter 12

Other Applications of the Fundamental Theorem

In the next chapter, we'll return to the topic of multiplicative functions. The rest of the problems in this section take up some miscellaneous ways to use the fundamental theorem.

Project 12.27 A function F is called an "additive" function if, whenever A and B are relatively prime, we have

$$F(A \cdot B) = F(A) + F(B)$$

Give an example of an additive function that you have used extensively in your study of number theory. If F is an additive function, show that $F(1)$ must be 0. If F is an additive function, and you know the outputs of F at prime powers, explain how you can "extend F by additivity." Suppose F is additive and

$$F(P^K) = \begin{cases} 1 & \text{if } K = 1 \\ 0 & \text{if } K > 1 \end{cases}$$

Describe the output of $F(N)$ for any integer N.

Is the compilation of an additive function also an additive function? Is there a function that is both additive and multiplicative?

Project 12.28 Recall the factorial function

```
TO FACT :N
 IF :N = 0 [OP 1]
 OP :N * (FACT :N - 1)
END
```

If N is a positive integer, $FACT(N) = 1 \cdot 2 \cdot 3 \cdot 4 \cdots (N-1) \cdot N$. If P is a prime, consider the following function:

```
TO FACT.ORD :P :N
 OP ORD :P (FACT :N)
END
```

Since $FACT(N)$ has every multiple of P (between P and N) as a factor, you might wonder whether or not there is an interesting formula for FACT.ORD. There is.

Let's look at an example. Suppose we want $ORD_3(FACT(31))$. Well, $FACT(31)$ is

$$1 \cdot 2 \cdot 3 \cdot 4 \cdot 5 \cdot 6 \cdot 7 \cdot 8 \cdot 9 \cdot 10 \cdot$$
$$11 \cdot 12 \cdot 13 \cdot 14 \cdot 15 \cdot 16 \cdot 17 \cdot 18 \cdot 19 \cdot 20 \cdot$$
$$21 \cdot 22 \cdot 23 \cdot 24 \cdot 25 \cdot 26 \cdot 27 \cdot 28 \cdot 29 \cdot 30 \cdot 31$$

Now, the ORD of the product is the sum of the ORDs, so $ORD_3(FACT(31))$ is the sum of the 3-orders of each of the numbers between 1 and 31. Of course, the numbers that are not divisible by 3 do not contribute anything to this sum. So

$$ORD_3(FACT(31)) = ORD_3(3) + ORD_3(6) + ORD_3(9) + ORD_3(12) + ORD_3(15)$$
$$+ ORD_3(18) + ORD_3(21) + ORD_3(24) + ORD_3(27) + ORD_3(30)$$

If I tabulate the multiples of 3 together with their contribution to our sum, things look like this:

The multiple of 3	Its 3-order
3	1
6	1
9	2
12	1
15	1
18	2
21	1
24	1
27	3
30	1

So each multiple of 3 contributes 1 to our sum. Each multiple of 9 contributes an additional 1, and each multiple of 27 contributes even another 1. Look at the lists of multiples of powers of 3 that are less than 31:

$$MULTIPLES(3, 31) = [3\ 6\ 9\ 12\ 15\ 18\ 21\ 24\ 27\ 30]$$

$$MULTIPLES(9, 31) = [9\ 18\ 27]$$

$$MULTIPLES(27, 31) = [27]$$

If you add up the number of elements in all of these lists, you get a contribution of 1 for each multiple of 3 that isn't a multiple of 9, a contribution of 2 for each multiple of 9 that isn't a multiple of 27, and a contribution of 3 for 27. This is precisely $\text{ORD}_3(\text{FACT}(31))$. In general, to calculate $\text{ORD}_P(\text{FACT}(N))$, we could simply add up the COUNTs of the lists:

MULTIPLES(P, N)

MULTIPLES(P^2, N)

MULTIPLES(P^3, N)

$\vdots$

MULTIPLES(P^K, N)

Where P^K is the highest power of P that is less than or equal to N. We'll need to determine this K as a function of P and N, so write a function HIGHEST.POWER so that

> HIGHEST.POWER(P, N) is the highest power of P that is less than or equal to N

Then you can build a Logo model of our above method for calculating FACT.ORD like this:

```
TO FACT.ORD :P :N
 OP L.SIGMA "TERM (SE :P :N) NUMBERS.UPTO HIGHEST.POWER :P :N
END

TO TERM :P :N :J
 OP COUNT MULTIPLES (POWER :P :J) :N
END
```

Experiment with TERM. Find a simple function that is equal to TERM but is much faster to output.

In most number theory books, you find a theorem like this:

$$\text{ORD}_P(\text{FACT}(N)) = \sum_{K=1}^{\infty} \text{FLOOR}\left(\frac{N}{P^K}\right)$$

What does this mean? Is it true?

Project 12.29 If P is a prime, N is an integer and K is an integer between 0 and P^N, express $\text{ORD}_P(\text{B}(P^N, K))$ (B is the binomial coefficient function of part II) in terms of N and $\text{ORD}_P(K)$. #Justify your answer.

Hint: Show that if $A \mid C$, then $\text{ORD}_P(\text{QUOT}(C, A)) = \text{ORD}_P(C) - \text{ORD}_P(A)$. Show that if K is between 0 and P^N, $\text{ORD}_P(K) = \text{ORD}_P(P^N - K)$. Write $\text{B}(P^N, K)$ as

$$\frac{P^N \cdot (P^N - 1) \cdot (P^N - 2) \cdot (P^N - 3) \cdots (P^N - (K - 1))}{1 \cdot 2 \cdot 3 \cdots K - 1}$$

(This is the model 3 version of B.) Can you say anything about $\text{ORD}_P(\text{B}(M, K))$ when M is not a power of P?

Project 12.30 This project will, among other things, show you how to give another proof of the fact that there are infinitely many primes. Although this new proof will be considerably more involved than the proof of Euclid that we outlined in chapter 10, it develops an approach that has found widespread use in modern number theory. This approach was used by Dirichlet, for example, to show that an arithmetic sequence whose first term and common difference are relatively prime contains infinitely many primes.

Define the "support" of an integer to be the list of primes that occur in the integer. We can model this support function in Logo:

```
TO SUPPORT :N
 OP FILTER "DIVIS? :N PRIMES.UPTO :N
END
```

Suppose that we want to focus only on those numbers whose support is [3]; these numbers are just the powers of 3, and we can pick them out with the following predicate:

```
TO POWER.OF.THREE? :N
 OP (SUPPORT :N) = [3]
END
```

What is the sum of the reciprocals of these powers of 3? Remember, there are infinitely many such numbers, but if you look at them, you see that they form a geometric sequence with first term 1 and common ratio $1/3$:

$$1, \frac{1}{3}, \frac{1}{9}, \frac{1}{27}, \frac{1}{81}, \cdots, \frac{1}{3^N}, \cdots$$

By the sum of these reciprocals, we mean the limit (as N increases) of the sum of the geometric series:

```
TO SERIES :N
 OP SIGMA "POWER (1/3) 0 :N
END
```

In part II we saw that as N gets larger and larger, SERIES(N) converges to

$$\frac{1}{1 - (1/3)}$$

or 3/2.

Let's generalize a bit. Suppose we want to focus on numbers only divisible by, say, 3 or 5 (or both). Let's call such numbers "special":

```
TO SPECIAL? :N
 OP MEMBERP SUPPORT :N [[3] [5] [3 5]]
END
```

Consider the function

```
TO SPECIAL.RECIP :N
 IF :N = 1 [OP 1]
 IF SPECIAL? :N [OP 1 / :N]
 OP 0
END
```

SPECIAL.RECIP takes a number N as input. If N happens to be divisible only by the primes 3 and 5 (or if $N = 1$), SPECIAL.RECIP outputs the reciprocal of N, but if N is divisible by anything other than 3 or 5, SPECIAL.RECIP outputs 0. Tabulate SPECIAL.RECIP between 1 and 20. You see that the output is 0 except at 1, 3, 5, 9, and 15. What numbers less than 100 produce nonzero outputs?

The function that I really care about is the analogue of SERIES above; it is just the summation of SPECIAL.RECIP:

```
TO Z :N
 OP SIGMA "SPECIAL.RECIP [] 1 :N
END
```

Z(N) is the sum of the reciprocals of all the special numbers between 1 and N. Tabulate Z between 1 and 20. The first thing you notice is that the tabulation takes a long time. Why? The second thing you notice is that the tabulation "steps up" at 3, 5, and 15 and that Z is constant between these numbers. Why?

Notice that the outputs of Z get bigger:

N	Z(N)
1	1
3	1.33333333
5	1.53333333
9	1.64444444
15	1.71111111

Will this always happen? Why? Do the outputs of Z grow without bound? This last question is very interesting; think about it for a while before reading on.

If you want to see if the the outputs of Z eventually get bigger than, say, 4, you'll want to evaluate Z at some big numbers. The model we have is just too slow; we need something that is built along the lines of SERIES. To speed things up, think of integers as they look when they are factored into primes. Since Z doesn't change except at numbers that only contain 3's and 5's, we can think of a "big number" as a number that looks like

$$3^{(high\ power)} \cdot 5^{(high\ power)}$$

For example, what is Z($3^{10} \cdot 5^{10}$)? This calculation would be out of the question with our present model for Z. What we really want to do is to add the reciprocals of all the numbers of the form $3^A \cdot 5^B$ where A ranges from 0 to 10 and B also ranges from 0 to 10 (all the other numbers between 1 and $3^{10} \cdot 5^{10}$ do not contribute to Z's output). Think of it this way:

Imagine a table with 11 rows and 11 columns:

A	0	1	2	3	4	5	6	7	8	9	10
B											
0											
1											
2				$3^3 \cdot 5^2$							
3											
4										$3^9 \cdot 5^4$	
5											
6											
7											
8											
9											
10											

The entry in the B row and the A column is $3^A \cdot 5^B$; I've labeled two entries to show you what I mean. Remember, if a number N between 1 and $3^{10} \cdot 5^{10}$ isn't on the table, then SPECIAL.RECIP(N) is 0. So $Z(3^{10} \cdot 5^{10})$ is just the sum of the reciprocals of the entries in the table. That shouldn't be too hard to model efficiently in Logo; try it before reading on.

We'll need a function that takes A and B and outputs $\dfrac{1}{A^B}$:

```
TO RECIP.POWER :A :B
 OP 1 / (POWER :A :B)
END
```

Now, SINGLE sums the reciprocals of the entries in the Mth column of our table:

```
TO SINGLE :N :M
 OP (SIGMA "RECIP.POWER 5 0 :N) * (RECIP.POWER 3 :M)
END
```

Why is this so?

DOUBLE sums the output of SINGLE:

```
TO DOUBLE :N :M
 OP SIGMA "SINGLE :N 0 :M
END
```

The output of $Z(3^{10} \cdot 5^{10})$ is then the same as the output of DOUBLE(10, 10). Why?

In other words, we can get a relatively quick estimate for Z at big numbers by

```
TO POWER.Z :N
 OP DOUBLE :N :N
END
```

Be careful to notice that POWER.Z(N) is the same as $Z(3^N \cdot 5^N)$. So POWER.Z(10) outputs Z(576650390625); on my computer, this output is 1.874989377.

Now you have a tool that can be used to investigate Z. Tabulate POWER.Z between, say, 10 and 20. Does it ever get bigger than 4? Than 2? Remember, POWER.Z(20) is the output of Z at an extremely large number.

So what do you think? My tabulations suggest that as N increases, $Z(N)$ gets closer and closer to 1.875. Let's see why.

Break the "special" numbers into three types:

Type 1. Powers of 3

Type 2. Powers of 5

Type 3. Mixed

A mixed number is one like $3^4 \cdot 5^2$. Let's agree that 1 is both a type 1 and a type 2 number. Using our results about convergent geometric series, it's easy to find the limit of the sum of the reciprocals of the numbers of type 1 (we did it above) and type 2:

$$1 + \frac{1}{3} + \frac{1}{3^2} + \frac{1}{3^3} + \frac{1}{3^4} + \cdots \text{ converges to } \frac{1}{1 - (\frac{1}{3})} \text{ or } \frac{3}{2}$$

$$1 + \frac{1}{5} + \frac{1}{5^2} + \frac{1}{5^3} + \frac{1}{5^4} + \cdots \text{ converges to } \frac{1}{1 - (\frac{1}{5})} \text{ or } \frac{5}{4}$$

Do you see anything? Could it be?

$$\left(\frac{3}{2}\right) \cdot \left(\frac{5}{4}\right) = \frac{15}{8} = 1.875$$

and this seems to be the limit of Z's outputs. What's going on?

Well, notice that

$$\left(\frac{3}{2}\right)\left(\frac{5}{4}\right) = (1 + \frac{1}{3} + \frac{1}{3^2} + \frac{1}{3^3} + \frac{1}{3^4} + \cdots) \times$$
$$(1 + \frac{1}{5} + \frac{1}{5^2} + \frac{1}{5^3} + \frac{1}{5^4} + \cdots)$$

This equation should be looked at in the proper light. All it means is that $\frac{3}{2}$ is the limit of the first series and $\frac{5}{4}$ is the limit of the second series. To be more precise, we could define

```
TO ONE.THIRD.SERIES :N
  OP SIGMA "POWER (1/3) 0 :N
END

TO ONE.FIFTH.SERIES :N
  OP SIGMA "POWER (1/5) 0 :N
END
```

and

```
TO RIGHT.SIDE :N
  OP (ONE.THIRD.SERIES :N) * (ONE.FIFTH.SERIES :N)
END
```

Then, when we say that

$$\left(\frac{3}{2}\right)\left(\frac{5}{4}\right) = (1 + \frac{1}{3} + \frac{1}{3^2} + \frac{1}{3^3} + \frac{1}{3^4} + \cdots) \times$$
$$(1 + \frac{1}{5} + \frac{1}{5^2} + \frac{1}{5^3} + \frac{1}{5^4} + \cdots)$$

we mean that RIGHT.SIDE(N) converges to $(\frac{3}{2})(\frac{5}{4})$ as N gets large. Why is this so?

Tabulate RIGHT.SIDE. It seems that RIGHT.SIDE is equal to POWER.Z on Z^+. If this is true, then POWER.Z will also converge to $(\frac{3}{2})(\frac{5}{4})$ (that is, to 1.875), and we'll be done.

Well, if you think about it,

$$\texttt{RIGHT.SIDE}(N) = \left(1 + \frac{1}{3} + \frac{1}{3^2} + \frac{1}{3^3} + \frac{1}{3^4} + \cdots + \frac{1}{3^N}\right) \times$$
$$\left(1 + \frac{1}{5} + \frac{1}{5^2} + \frac{1}{5^3} + \frac{1}{5^4} + \cdots + \frac{1}{5^N}\right)$$

Multiply this out. I don't know exactly how you do this kind of thing, but I always take each thing in the first parentheses and run it through the second parentheses. So first I run the 1 through; this yields

$$1 + \frac{1}{5} + \frac{1}{5^2} + \frac{1}{5^3} + \frac{1}{5^4} + \cdots + \frac{1}{5^N}$$

Then I run the 1/3 through and get

$$\frac{1}{3} + \frac{1}{(3 \cdot 5)} + \frac{1}{(3 \cdot 5^2)} + \frac{1}{(3 \cdot 5^3)} + \frac{1}{(3 \cdot 5^4)} + \cdots + \frac{1}{(3 \cdot 5^N)}$$

Then I run the $\frac{1}{3^2}$ through and get

$$\frac{1}{3^2} + \frac{1}{(3^2 \cdot 5)} + \frac{1}{(3^2 \cdot 5^2)} + \frac{1}{(3^2 \cdot 5^3)} + \frac{1}{(3^2 \cdot 5^4)} + \cdots + \frac{1}{(3^2 \cdot 5^N)}$$

If I keep this up, I'll finally run the $\frac{1}{3^N}$ through and get

$$\frac{1}{3^N} + \frac{1}{(3^N \cdot 5)} + \frac{1}{(3^N \cdot 5^2)} + \frac{1}{(3^N \cdot 5^3)} + \frac{1}{(3^N \cdot 5^4)} + \cdots + \frac{1}{(3^N \cdot 5^N)}$$

If I add all of these terms together, I'll get precisely the sum of the entries in our table. In other words, RIGHT.SIDE equals POWER.Z on $\mathbf{Z}^+$, and so POWER.Z (and hence Z) converges to 1.875.

(By the way, what is the sum of the reciprocals of all the mixed numbers —numbers of the form $3^A \cdot 5^B$ where A and B are strictly positive?)

Next, suppose that you only care about numbers whose support is contained in a list of three primes. For example, suppose you only care about numbers divisible by 3, 5, or 7. Modify the predicate SPECIAL?. What do you think the sum of the reciprocals of these special numbers is? Go through the above arguments, adjusting the functions where necessary, and verify your conjecture experimentally and theoretically.

Give an argument to support the following fact:

Suppose that $P_1, P_2, \ldots, P_T$ are primes. The sum of the reciprocals of the positive integers whose support is contained in

$$[P_1 \ P_2 \ldots P_T]$$

is

$$\frac{P_1}{P_1 - 1} \cdot \frac{P_2}{P_2 - 1} \cdot \frac{P_3}{P_3 - 1} \cdots \frac{P_T}{P_T - 1}$$

What does this have to do with the infinitude of primes? The idea is this: Suppose there were only a finite number of primes, say, $P_1, P_2, \ldots, P_T$. Then, by the fundamental theorem, every number would be "special" (that is, every number would have a support contained in $[P_1 \ P_2 \ldots P_T]$ because this would be the complete set of primes). But then the sum of the reciprocals of all positive integers N would be

$$\frac{P_1}{P_1 - 1} \cdot \frac{P_2}{P_2 - 1} \cdot \frac{P_3}{P_3 - 1} \cdots \frac{P_T}{P_T - 1}$$

In other words, the function

```
TO ADD.RECIPS.UPTO :N            TO RECIP :N
 OP SIGMA "RECIP [] 1 :N          OP 1/:N
END                              END
```

would converge to the number Q where

$$Q = \frac{P_1}{P_1 - 1} \cdot \frac{P_2}{P_2 - 1} \cdot \frac{P_3}{P_3 - 1} \cdots \frac{P_T}{P_T - 1}$$

The idea of the proof is to show that this can't happen by showing that the outputs of ADD.RECIPS.UPTO grow without bound (so they can't converge to anything).

Well, what happens if you tabulate ADD.RECIPS.UPTO. Between 1 and 20, you get something like this:

```
 1 . . . 1
 2 . . . 1.5
 3 . . . 1.8333333333333333333
 4 . . . 2.0833333333333333333
 5 . . . 2.2833333333333333333
 6 . . . 2.45
 7 . . . 2.5928571428571428571
 8 . . . 2.7178571428571428571
 9 . . . 2.8289682539682539682
10 . . . 2.9289682539682539682
11 . . . 3.0198773448773448773
12 . . . 3.1032106782106782106
13 . . . 3.1801337551337551337
14 . . . 3.2515623265623265623
15 . . . 3.318228993228993229
16 . . . 3.380728993228993229
17 . . . 3.4395525226407579349
18 . . . 3.4951080781963134905
19 . . . 3.5477396571436819116
20 . . . 3.5977396571436819116
```

Looks like the outputs are getting bigger, but not by much. There certainly is't enough evidence here to decide about the convergence of ADD.RECIPS.UPTO. Let's pick up the action at 50:

```
50 . . . 4.4992053383294250574
51 . . . 4.5188131814666799594
52 . . . 4.5380439506974491902
53 . . . 4.556911875225751077
54 . . . 4.5754303937442695955
55 . . . 4.5936122119260877773
56 . . . 4.6114693547832306344
57 . . . 4.6290132144323534414
58 . . . 4.646254593742698269
59 . . . 4.6632037462850711504
60 . . . 4.6798704129517378171
61 . . . 4.6962638555746886368
62 . . . 4.7123928878327531529
63 . . . 4.7282659037057690259
64 . . . 4.7438909037057690259
65 . . . 4.7592755190903844105
```

66 . . . 4.774427034241899562
67 . . . 4.7893524073762279202
68 . . . 4.8040582897291690967
69 . . . 4.8185510433523575025
70 . . . 4.8328367576380717882

I'm still not convinced. If you start at 100, you find

100 . . . 5.1873775176396202605
101 . . . 5.1972785077386301615
102 . . . 5.2070824293072576125
103 . . . 5.2167911671713352824
104 . . . 5.2264065517867198978
105 . . . 5.2359303613105294216
106 . . . 5.245364323574680365
107 . . . 5.2547101179672037295
108 . . . 5.2639693772264629888
109 . . . 5.2731436891530684934
110 . . . 5.2822345982439775843

Not much growth. Even when you input 1000, the output is only about 7.485470. This is the first example that we've seen where a tabulation doesn't seem to help. The outputs of ADD.RECIPS.UPTO could grow without bound very slowly, or they could always be bounded by, say, 100. The tabulation doesn't seem to hold any clues. Or does it?

Since things seem to be growing very slowly, maybe we'd get a better picture of the growth of the outputs if we speed up the growth of the inputs. Instead of having the inputs increase by 1 in our tabulation, let's have them double. If you focus on the powers of 2 on the tabulation, you see

2 . . . 1.5
4 . . . 2.0833333333333333333
8 . . . 2.7178571428571428571
16 . . . 3.380728993228993229
64 . . . 4.7438909037057690259

This looks promising. It seems that if the input is doubled, the output increases by something like .6. Write a function DIFF that calculates the difference between outputs of ADD.RECIPS.UPTO at successive powers of 2. That is, you want

$$\text{DIFF}(N) = \text{ADD.RECIPS.UPTO}(2^N) - \text{ADD.RECIPS.UPTO}(2^{(N-1)})$$

Now tabulate **DIFF**. My computer produces something like this:

1 ... 0.5
2 ... 0.583333333
3 ... 0.63452381
4 ... 0.66287185
5 ... 0.677766203
6 ... 0.68539571
7 ... 0.689256189
8 ... 0.691197872
9 ... 0.692171571
10 ... 0.692659131

Remember, this tabulates the difference between the outputs of ADD.RECIPS. UPTO at successive powers of 2. For example,

$$\text{ADD.RECIPS.UPTO}(2^9) - \text{ADD.RECIPS.UPTO}(28) = 0.692171571$$

The actual values of the differences do look interesting, but what's important for us is that the differences do not seem to decrease; they seem to be all bigger than, say, .5. (If you know any calculus, notice that the differences seem to be approaching LN(2); can you explain why?). If it's true that the differences never dip below .5, we'd be in good shape with respect to showing that the outputs of ADD.RECIPS.UPTO grow without bound. Here's why:

Suppose that for all integers N, we knew that

$$\text{ADD.RECIPS.UPTO}(2^N) - \text{ADD.RECIPS.UPTO}(2^{(N-1)}) \geq .5$$

Then we could calculate inductively:

$$\text{ADD.RECIPS.UPTO}(2^N) \geq \text{ADD.RECIPS.UPTO}(2^{(N-1)}) + .5$$
$$\geq \text{ADD.RECIPS.UPTO}(2^{(N-2)}) + .5 + .5$$
$$\geq \text{ADD.RECIPS.UPTO}(2^{(N-3)}) + 3 \cdot .5$$
$$\geq \text{ADD.RECIPS.UPTO}(2^{(N-4)}) + 4 \cdot .5$$
$$\vdots$$
$$\geq \text{ADD.RECIPS.UPTO}(2^{(N-N)}) + N \cdot .5$$
$$= 1 + N \cdot .5$$
$$= \frac{2 + N}{2}$$

Now the function

```
TO F :N
 OP (2 + N)/2
END
```

grows without bound as N increases (why?). So if we could prove what our tabulation of DIFF suggests, that is,

$$\text{ADD.RECIPS.UPTO}(2^N) - \text{ADD.RECIPS.UPTO}(2^{(N-1)}) \geq .5$$

then we would know that, for all positive integers N, ADD.RECIPS.UPTO(2^N) would be larger than F(N). This would mean that the outputs of ADD.RECIPS.UPTO would diverge (grow without bound), and this would imply that the list of primes could not be finite. (Notice that the tabulation of DIFF suggests that the difference between successive powers of 2 is (for the most part) considerably bigger than .5; compare ADD.RECIPS.UPTO(210) to $(2 + 10)/2$.) Before you continue, go over the above argument again. The basic ideas are the following three:

1. If there were only a finite number of primes, then the function

   ```
   TO ADD.RECIPS.UPTO :N
    OP SIGMA "RECIP [] 1 :N
   END
   ```

   would converge (to a number that could be written down explicitly).

2. The function DIFF suggests (and we'll prove it below) that, for all positive integers N,

$$\texttt{ADD.RECIPS.UPTO}(2N) \geq \texttt{F}(N) \quad \text{where} \quad \texttt{F}(N) = \frac{(2+N)}{2}$$

3. Since $\texttt{F}(N)$ diverges, so does $\texttt{ADD.RECIPS.UPTO}$. This is a contradiction, so there can't be only a finite number of primes. In other words, there are infinitely many primes.

The argument will be complete once we establish that

$$\texttt{ADD.RECIPS.UPTO}(2^N) \geq \texttt{F}(N) \quad \text{where} \quad \texttt{F}(N) = \frac{(2+N)}{2}$$

for all positive integers N. Prove this by induction on N.

Hints:

1. Show that, for positive integer inputs N, $\texttt{F}$ can be defined this way:

```
TO F :N
 IF :N = 1 [OP 1.5]
 OP (F :N - 1) + .5
END
```

2. Then calculate like this:

If $N = 1$,

$$\texttt{ADD.RECIPS.UPTO}(2^1) = 1.5 = \texttt{F}(1)$$

If $N = 2$,

$$\texttt{ADD.RECIPS.UPTO}(2^2) = 1 + \frac{1}{2} + \frac{1}{3} + \frac{1}{4}$$

$$= \texttt{ADD.RECIPS.UPTO}(2^1) + (\frac{1}{3} + \frac{1}{4})$$

$$\geq \texttt{F}(1) + (\frac{1}{3} + \frac{1}{4})$$

$$\geq \texttt{F}(1) + (\frac{1}{4} + \frac{1}{4}) = F(1) + \frac{1}{2} = \texttt{F}(2)$$

393

If $N = 3$,

$$\texttt{ADD.RECIPS.UPTO}(2^3) = 1 + \frac{1}{2} + \frac{1}{3} + \frac{1}{4} + \frac{1}{5} + \frac{1}{6} + \frac{1}{7} + \frac{1}{8}$$

$$= \texttt{ADD.RECIPS.UPTO}(2^2) + (\frac{1}{5} + \frac{1}{6} + \frac{1}{7} + \frac{1}{8})$$

$$\geq \texttt{F}(2) + (\frac{1}{5} + \frac{1}{6} + \frac{1}{7} + \frac{1}{8})$$

$$\geq \texttt{F}(2) + (\frac{1}{8} + \frac{1}{8} + \frac{1}{8} + \frac{1}{8}) = \texttt{F}(2) + \frac{1}{2} = \texttt{F}(3)$$

Keep going.

The key ingredient in the above proof is the fact that the outputs of `ADD.RECIPS.UPTO` grow without bound. A stronger result (that also implies that there are infinitely many primes) is that the sum of the reciprocals of the primes diverges. That is, if you define the function `RECIP` so that $\texttt{RECIP}(N) = 1/N$, then the outputs of

```
TO Z.PRIMES :N
 OP L.SIGMA "RECIP [] PRIMES.UPTO :N
END
```

has outputs that do not converge. Check it out.

Using the notion of convergence to discuss the distribution of primes is the central technique of what is known as "analytic number theory," a branch of number theory that uses the techniques of analysis (limits and series) to investigate properties of integers.

Chapter 13

Descendants and Ancestors of ONE and ID

In the last chapter we constructed several multiplicative functions that gave us some information about the divisors of an integer. For example, NU outputs the number of positive factors of its input, and SIG outputs the sum of these factors. Then we discovered a method, compilation, for building new multiplicative functions from old ones. G compiles F if

$$G(N) = \sum_{D \in \text{DIVISORS}(N)} F(D)$$

This notion of compilation brings out many relationships among multiplicative functions. For example, NU and SIG are the just two functions in a sequence of compilations of power functions. NU compiles the function ONE, where $\text{ONE}(X) = 1 \ (= X^0)$, and SIG compiles the function ID, where $\text{ID}(X) = X \ (X^1)$.

Think of compilation as a higher-order function that takes one multiplicative function and outputs another; if you input ID, you get back SIG:

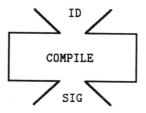

Figure 13.1

Actually, our Logo model for COMPILE is somewhat different:

```
TO COMPILE :F :E :N
 IF :N = 1 [OP 1]
 OP L.SIGMA :F :E DIVISORS :N
END
```

The difference is that this model for COMPILE outputs a number (not a function). It is possible to coax a Logo model for COMPILE that actually outputs a function, but the fussy programming details involved in such a project would obscure some very beautiful mathematical ideas.

Check that typing

```
SHOW COMPILE "ONE [] 12
```

produces the same thing as typing

```
SHOW NU 12
```

Let's look at our current stash of multiplicative functions. So far, we have considered the following functions:

```
TO ONE :N
 OP 1
END
```

```
TO ID :N
 OP :N
END
```

Of course, ID and ONE are special cases of EXPONENT.

```
TO EXPONENT :E :N
 OP POWER :N :E
END
```

in the sense that $ONE(N) = EXPONENT(0, N)$ and $ID(N) = EXPONENT(1, N)$. For a fixed exponent E, $EXPONENT(E, N)$ is a strongly multiplicative function of N. Recall that this means that

$$EXPONENT(E, AB) = EXPONENT(E, A) \cdot EXPONENT(E, B)$$

(or that $(AB)^E = A^E \cdot B^E$) for all integers A and B

We have some other multiplicative functions. For example,

```
TO NU :N
 OP COUNT DIVISORS :N
END
```

NU can be defined as

```
TO NU :N
 OP COMPILE "ONE [] :N
END
```

We also have

```
TO SIG :N
 OP COMPILE "ID [] :N
END
```

(Note: SIG will always stand for the "sum of the divisors" function. Don't confuse it with the higher-order functions SIGMA and L.SIGMA.)

In this chapter, we'll see how all these functions are related to each other with respect to the COMPILE function. These relationships will suggest some other interesting multiplicative functions.

I came up with many of the ideas in this section by playing with our Logo COMPILE function. I started with a simple function like ONE, and I repeatedly COMPILEd it:

```
TO NU :N
 OP COMPILE "ONE [] :N
END
```

```
TO NU2 :N
 OP COMPILE "NU [] :N
END
```

```
TO NU3 :N
 OP COMPILE "NU2 [] :N
END
```

and so on. At each stage, I tabulated the current function, looking for a pattern. Of course, each of my functions is multiplicative, so I only had to look at the outputs at prime powers. So, for example, I looked at NU_3's outputs at $1, 3, 9, 27, 81, \ldots$, and then at $5, 25, 125, \ldots$. A pattern emerged that was very pleasing.

Then I wondered if it was possible to go in the other direction; NU compiles ONE, but does ONE compile some other function? Does this function compile yet another function? Is there a pattern to the outputs at these "negative" levels? Is there a simple formula that describes the outputs of each function in this infinite stream of functions? What if I change the "zeroth" level from ONE to, say, ID? But I'm getting ahead of the story.

Parents and Children

The above game of repeated compilation suggests the following vocabulary: Suppose that F and G are multiplicative functions so that F compiles G:

$$F(N) = \sum_{D \in \text{DIVISORS}(N)} G(D)$$

Then we'll say that G is the "parent" of F and that F is the "child" of G. So NU is the child of ONE, and ID is the parent of SIG. Notice that I say "the" parent. This is because a multiplicative function can have only one parent, as you'll see when you do the next two projects.

Project 13.1

1. If G and H are multiplicative functions so that $G(P^K) = H(P^K)$ for all primes P and for all nonnegative integers K, show that $G = H$ on $\mathbf{Z}^+$. (Hint: If N is any integer, factor N into prime powers and use the multiplicativity of G and H to show that $G(N) = H(N)$.)

2. If F is the child of the multiplicative function G, show that

$$F(P^K) = G(1) + G(P) + G(P^2) + G(P^3) + \cdots + G(P^K)$$

(Hint: What is $\text{DIVISORS}(P^K)$?)

Project 13.2 If G and H are two multiplicative functions that are parents of the same multiplicative function F, show that $G = H$ on $\mathbf{Z}^+$. Hints: Since G and H are multiplicative functions, it's enough to show that G and H are equal on prime powers (why?). If F is not the zero function, then F, G, and H all output 1 at 1 (why?). Since F compiles both G and H, if P is any prime, then

$$F(P) = G(1) + G(P)$$

and

$$F(P) = H(1) + H(P)$$

Conclude that $G(P) = H(P)$ for all P. Now proceed by induction; suppose that $G(P^K) = H(P^K)$ for all primes P and some positive integer K. Use this to prove that $G(P^{(K+1)}) = H(P^{(K+1)})$ for all primes P by noting that

$$F(P^{(K+1)}) = G(1) + G(P) + G(P^2) + \cdots + G(P^K) + G(P^{(K+1)})$$

and

$$F(P^{(K+1)}) = H(1) + H(P) + H(P^2) + \cdots + H(P^K) + H(P^{(K+1)})$$

The above project is typical of the approach we'll take in this chapter. We will investigate a particular multiplicative function by determining its output at nonnegative powers of primes; the function can then be extended to $\mathbf{Z}^+$ by multiplicativity. For example, consider the function G so that

$$G(P^K) = \begin{cases} 1 & \text{if } K = 0 \text{ (that is, } G(1) = 1) \\ P^{(K+1)} & \text{for all primes } P \text{ and all positive integers } K \end{cases}$$

G can be thought of as a function of two variables:

```
TO G :P :K
 IF :K = 0 [OP 1]
 OP POWER :P (:K + 1)
END
```

Of course, you can input any number for P (not just a prime), but the understanding here is that P is a prime and K is a non-negative integer. This "PK" version of G is useful when we want to investigate the outputs of G at prime powers, but, when we extend G to a function on $\mathbf{Z}^+$ by multiplicativity, we'll want a function of one input N, and we'll want to know how G acts on numbers that have more than one prime in their support.

Recall that the "support" of an integer is the list of primes that actually divide it. The support for a positive integer N can be obtained by using this Logo function:

```
TO SUPPORT :N
 OP FILTER "DIVIS? :N (PRIMES.UPTO :N)
END
```

For example, what is G(72)? By multiplicativity,

$$G(72) = G(2^3 \cdot 3^2) = G(2^3) \cdot G(3^2) = 2^4 \cdot 3^3 = 432$$

This extension of G to a "real" function on $\mathbf{Z}^+$ can be modeled in Logo (see project 12.23). To find $G(N)$, construct the FACTOR list for N, calculate the output of G at the FIRST and LAST element of each pair, and then multiply all these numbers together. For example, suppose you want G(600). Well,

$\text{FACTOR}(600) = [\ [2\ 3]\ [3\ 1]\ [5\ 2]\ ]$

$G(2, 3) = 2^4 = 16$

$G(3, 1) = 3^2 = 9$

$G(5, 2) = 5^3 = 125$

To find G(600), take the PRODuct of each of these terms:

$$G(600) = 16 \cdot 9 \cdot 125 = 18000$$

In Logo,

```
TO REAL.G :N
 IF :N = 1 [OP 1]
 OP PROD "G [] FACTOR :N
END
```

Can you explain why the input G to PROD is correctly APPLYed to the elements of FACTOR(N) even though these elements are lists of the form $[P\ K]$ while G is a function of two distinct inputs?

This extension by multiplicativity can be captured in the following higher-order function EXTEND that takes a function F of two inputs P and K (and some possible extra inputs E) and an integer N, and outputs the extension of F applied to N:

```
TO EXTEND :F :E :N
 IF :N = 1 [OP 1]
 OP PROD :F :E FACTOR :N
END
```

The EXTEND function should convince you that we really do "know" a multiplicative function once we know what it does to prime powers. In the above example, typing

```
SHOW EXTEND "G [] 12
```

should produce the same thing as typing

```
SHOW REAL.G 12
```

One word of caution: Suppose you have a multiplicative function modeled as a function of P and K; for example, suppose you have

```
TO H :P :K
 IF :K = 0 [OP 1]
 OP POWER :P (:K - 1)
END
```

If you want to tabulate the extension of H, you might try

```
TAB "EXTEND SE "H [] 1 10
```

thinking of H as the "extra" input to EXTEND. It doesn't work. There are two easy fixes. One is to simply give the extension of H a name,

```
TO REAL.H :N
 OP EXTEND "H   [] :N
END
```

and then to tabulate REAL.H:

```
TAB "REAL.H [] 1 10
```

The other fix is to use the QUOTE function

```
TO QUOTE :NAME
 OP WORD "" :NAME
END
```

and to `TAB` like this:

```
TAB "EXTEND LIST QUOTE "H [] 1 10
```

I like this way better because it doesn't clutter up the workspace with extraneous functions like `REAL.H`, but the necessity of a function like `QUOTE` makes me very annoyed with Logo (though only for a little while). Why do I have to use `LIST` instead of our usual `SE`? Do you see that the "extra" input list to `EXTEND` is `["H [] ]`? You can also use this method to tabulate `COMPILE`s, `SIGMA`s and `PROD`s.

Of course, once you extend a multiplicative function to $\mathbf{Z}^+$, you might discover a new (maybe more efficient, maybe more beautiful, maybe just different) way to define the extension. For example, if we think of `NU` as a function of two inputs

```
TO PKNU :P :K
 OP :K + 1
END
```

then the extension of `NU` to $\mathbf{Z}^+$

```
TO REAL.NU :N
 OP EXTEND "PKNU [] :N
END
```

can also be defined as

```
TO REAL.NU :N
 OP COUNT DIVISORS :N
END
```

These alternate forms are often useful.

Experiment 13.3 Tabulate the extension of the function F:

```
TO F :P :K
 IF :K = 0 [OP 1]
 OP POWER :P (:K - 1)
END
```

Is there a simple definition for this extension?

Descendants of ONE

Let's return to the parents and children idea. Suppose we start with ONE:

```
TO ONE :N
 OP 1
END
```

ONE's child is NU:

```
TO NU :N
 OP COMPILE "ONE [] :N
END
```

If you tabulate NU, you see that at prime powers, NU has a predictable behavior:

$NU(3) = 2$ $NU(5) = 2$
$NU(9) = 3$ $NU(25) = 3$
$NU(27) = 4$ $NU(125) = 4$

This shouldn't be a surprise; since

$$\text{DIVISORS}(P^K) = [\,1\ P\ P^2\ P^3\ \ldots\ P^K\,]$$

we see that

$$\begin{aligned}
\text{NU}(P^K) &= \text{ONE}(1) + \text{ONE}(P) + \text{ONE}(P^2) + \cdots + \text{ONE}(P^K) \\
&= 1 + 1 + 1 + \cdots + 1 \\
&= K + 1
\end{aligned}$$

So, viewed as a function of P and K, NU is especially simple:

```
TO PKNU :P :K
 OP :K + 1
END
```

Note that this model gives the right output at 1 (that is, when $K = 0$) without using a special case.

This method of defining NU at prime powers gives an alternate formulation for NU:

```
TO ALT.NU :N
 OP EXTEND "PKNU [] :N
END
```

This gives us three Logo models for NU, and hence three ways to think about it. The three models and their interpretations are

```
TO ORIG.NU :N
 OP COUNT DIVISORS :N
END
```

Interpretation: NU counts its input's factors.

```
TO NEW.NU :N
 OP COMPILE "ONE [] :N
END
```

Interpretation: NU is the child of ONE; it COMPILEs ONE's outputs.

```
TO ALT.NU :N
 OP EXTEND "PKNU [] :N
END

TO PKNU :P :K
 OP :K + 1
END
```

Interpretation: See the next exercise.

Exercise 13.4 The definition of ALT.NU translates into the following algorithm that is sometimes taught in elementary school:

To find the number of factors of N, factor N into prime power factors, add 1 to each of the exponents that show up, and multiply all these "augmented exponents" together.

Use this method to find the number of factors of 36, 72, 1400, 63, 64, 37, 3737, 1024, 3969, and 144169.

Exercise 13.5 Show that if you double an odd number, you double the number of factors. Is the same thing true if you double an even number?

Suppose we let NU_2 be the child of NU:

```
TO NU2 :N
 OP COMPILE "NU [] :N
END
```

A tabulation yields a rather chaotic picture:

$N \ldots NU_2(N)$
1 ... 1
2 ... 3
3 ... 3
4 ... 6
5 ... 3
6 ... 9
7 ... 3
8 ... 10
9 ... 6
10 ... 9
11 ... 3
12 ... 18
13 ... 3
14 ... 9
15 ... 9
16 ... 15
17 ... 3
18 ... 18
19 ... 3
20 ... 18
21 ... 9
22 ... 9
23 ... 3
24 ... 30
25 ... 6
26 ... 9
27 ... 10
28 ... 18
29 ... 3
30 ... 27

Look at this before you read on; can you see anything?

The key is to remember that $\mathrm{NU_2}$ is a multiplicative function, so it is determined by what it does at prime powers. Look at some subtables of the above tabulation:

```
1  ... 1
2  ... 3
4  ... 6
8  ... 10
16 ... 15

1  ... 1
3  ... 3
9  ... 6
27 ... 10

1  ... 1
5  ... 3
25 ... 6
```

You should check that the rest of the tabulation is consistent with these facts (and the multiplicativity of $\mathrm{NU_2}$). Is $\mathrm{NU_2}(18)$ the same as $\mathrm{NU_2}(2) \cdot \mathrm{NU_2}(9)$?

Do the above numbers look familiar to you? Do you get the feeling that something is going on? Take the numbers 1, 3, 6, 10; what would be the next one? Where have we seen these numbers before? Think about this before you read on.

An analysis of the output of $\mathrm{NU_2}$ at prime powers tells the story. Since $\mathrm{NU_2}$ compiles NU,

$$\mathrm{NU_2}(P^K) = \sum_{D \in \mathrm{DIVISORS}(P^K)} \mathrm{NU}(D)$$

$$= \mathrm{NU}(1) + \mathrm{NU}(P) + \mathrm{NU}(P^2) + \mathrm{NU}(P^3) + \cdots + \mathrm{NU}(P^K)$$

But $\mathrm{NU}(P^K) = K + 1$, so this last sum is

$$1 + 2 + 3 + 4 + \cdots + (K + 1)$$

Once again, we meet Gauss' formula. We have the following result:

$$NU_2(PK) = \frac{(K+2)(K+1)}{2}$$

Notice that the outputs of NU_2 at prime powers depend only on the power and not on the prime. So $NU_2(27) = NU_2(125) = (5 \cdot 4)/2 = 10$. Also notice that the outputs of NU_2 are entries in Pascal's triangle. (Isn't it eerie how Pascal's triangle keeps showing up?)

$$
\begin{array}{ccccccccccccc}
 & & & & & & 1 & & & & & & \\
 & & & & & 1 & & 1 & & & & & \\
 & & & & 1 & & 2 & & 1 & & & & \\
 & & & 1 & & 3 & & 3 & & 1 & & & \\
 & & 1 & & 4 & & 6 & & 4 & & 1 & & \\
 & 1 & & 5 & & 10 & & 10 & & 5 & & 1 & \\
1 & & 6 & & 15 & & 20 & & 15 & & 6 & & 1
\end{array}
$$

Using the notation of part II, we have two ways to write $NU_2(P^K)$:

$$NU_2(P^K) = \binom{K+2}{2}$$

or

$$NU_2(P^K) = \binom{K+2}{K}$$

Make sure that you understand why these two expressions for NU_2 define the same function. We'll use both expressions for $NU_2(P^K)$.

Since the triangle is making its presence felt again, we might as well recall the fast (model 4) version for generating the binomial coefficients:

```
TO B :N :K
 OP B.HELPER :N :K 0 1
END

TO B.HELPER :N :K :C :T
 IF :C = :K [OP :T]
 OP B.HELPER :N :K :C + 1 :T * (:N - :C) / (:C + 1)
END
```

We can write a model of NU_2 as a function of P and K:

```
TO PKNU2 :P :K               or               TO PKNU2 :P :K
 OP B :K + 2 :K                                 OP B :K + 2 2
END                                            END
```

(Again, notice that the case $K = 0$ works without special attention.)

Of course, we should be able to recover NU_2 by EXTENDing PKNU_2:

```
TO ALT.NU2 :N
 OP EXTEND "PKNU2 [] :N
END
```

Tabulate both NU_2 and ALT.NU_2 to check that everything works.

Well, how about NU_2's child:

```
TO NU3 :N
 OP COMPILE "NU2 [] :N
END
```

Tabulate NU_3 to see if you can find anything. Don't forget to concentrate on prime powers.

I'm assuming that you've now worked at this for a while. Look at what happens at prime powers:

$$\text{NU}_3(P^K) = \sum_{D \in \text{DIVISORS}(P^K)} \text{NU}_2(P^K)$$
$$= \text{NU}_2(1) + \text{NU}_2(P) + \text{NU}_2(P^2) + \text{NU}_2(P^3) + \cdots + \text{NU}_2(P^K)$$
$$= \binom{2}{2} + \binom{3}{2} + \binom{4}{2} + \binom{5}{2} + \cdots + \binom{K+2}{2}$$

When I first saw this, I was amazed. This is precisely the sum that we first met in project 5.22 and later revisited in project 7.20. By the "hockey stick" theorem, this sum is

$$\binom{K+3}{3} \quad \text{or} \quad \binom{K+3}{K}$$

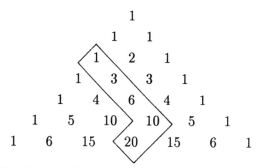

So we have the following result:
    If PKNU$_3$ is defined by either the model

```
TO PKNU3 :P :K
 OP B :K + 3 3
END
```

or the model

```
TO PKNU3 :P :K
 OP B :K + 3 :K
END
```

and ALT.NU$_3$ is the function

```
TO ALT.NU3 :N
 OP EXTEND "PKNU3 [] :N
END
```

then ALT.NU$_3$ equals NU$_3$ on $\mathbf{Z}^+$. Check it out.
    A pattern emerges. If NU$_3$'s child is NU$_4$, convince yourself that NU$_4$ can be modeled as ALT.NU$_4$, the extension of PKNU$_4$:

```
TO PKNU4 :P :K
 OP B :K + 4 4
END
```

or

```
TO PKNU4 :P :K
 OP B :K + 4 :K
END
```

which EXTENDs as

```
TO ALT.NU4 :N
 OP EXTEND "PKNU3 [] :N
END
```

Of course, the sequence of functions ONE, NU, NU_2, NU_3, ... can be thought of as a function of two inputs:

$$NU(0, N) = ONE(N) = 1$$

$$NU(1, N) = NU(N)$$

$$NU(2, N) = NU_2(N)$$

$$NU(3, N) = NU_3(N)$$

$$NU(4, N) = NU_4(N)$$

$$\vdots$$

In Logo we can model this more general NU:

```
TO NU :LEVEL :N
 IF :LEVEL = 0 [OP ONE :N]
 OP COMPILE "NU :LEVEL - 1 :N
END
```

Now, the sequence of functions

$$PKNU(0, P^K) = ONE(P^K) = 1 = B(K, K)$$

$$PKNU(1, P^K) = NU(P^K) = K + 1 = B(K + 1, K)$$

$$PKNU(2, P^K) = NU_2(P^K) = B(K + 2, K)$$

$$PKNU(3, P^K) = NU_3(P^K) = B(K + 3, K)$$

$$PKNU(4, P^K) = NU_4(P^K) = B(K + 4, K)$$

$$\vdots$$

can also be modeled in Logo:

```
TO PKNU :LEVEL :P :K
  OP B :LEVEL + :K :K
END
```

So we can EXTEND PKNU to $\mathbf{Z}^+$:

```
TO ALT.NU :LEVEL :N
  OP EXTEND "PKNU :LEVEL :N
END
```

Now, we come to the punch line:

Theorem 13.1 If L and N are nonnegative integers, then

$$\text{ALT.NU}(L, N) = \text{NU}(L, N)$$

Project 13.6 Prove this theorem. Hint: Induct in L, and use project 7.20.

We now have an infinite stream of multiplicative functions:

$$\cdots \to \text{NU}_L \to \text{NU}_{(L-1)} \to \cdots \to \text{NU}_3 \to \text{NU}_2 \to \text{NU}_1 \to \text{NU}_0$$

In this stream, each function points to its parent. It's helpful to think of each function in two ways. Each function compiles its parent, and each function outputs a binomial coefficient at prime powers:

$$\text{NU}(L, P^K) = \binom{K + L}{K}$$

Experiment 13.7 Tabulate NU at various levels. Since ALT.NU is faster to output than NU (can you explain why?), you might study the results of

```
TAB "ALT.NU 1 1 30

TAB "ALT.NU 2 1 30

TAB "ALT.NU 3 1 30

TAB "ALT.NU 4 1 30

TAB "ALT.NU 5 1 30

TAB "ALT.NU 6 1 30
```

Make some conjectures, and see if you can prove them. For example,

1. Is NU(L, 14) always equal to NU(L, 15)?

2. Is NU(L, 30) always a perfect cube?

3. Is NU(4, N) always divisible by 5? Is NU(5, N) ever divisible by 5?

##4. Describe all pairs (L, N) so that NU$(L, N) = N$.

There are many other possible theorems hidden in the tabulations; take some time to look for them.

Experiment 13.8 Suppose I define a function F on $\mathbf{Z}^+$ like this: $F(1) = 1$, and to find $F(N)$ for N bigger than 1, I write down all of N's divisors in a row, and beneath each divisor, I write down all the divisors of the divisor. $F(N)$ is the total number of integers that I write down. For example, to find $F(12)$, I proceed like this:

$$1\ 2\ 3\ 4\ 6\ 12$$
$$1\ 1\ 2\ 3\ 6$$
$$1\ 2\ 4$$
$$1\ 3$$
$$2$$
$$1$$

Since there are 18 integers in the array, $F(12) = 18$. Find a Logo model for F and relate F to our current discussion.

Ancestors of ONE

So ONE has some interesting descendants. How about its ancestors? Does ONE have a parent? Let's use a common method of mathematical attack: We'll suppose that ONE has a parent, we'll give this hypothetical parent a name, say E, and then we'll try to figure out some of E's properties.

> This technique of naming a thing before you have established its existence is an extremely useful device in mathematics, but you have to be careful when you use it. What does it mean for a mathematical object to exist? Can any grammatically correct definition bring a mathematical object into existence? What if I say, "Let N be the smallest positive odd

integer that is divisible by 2"? To what extent the things we talk about in mathematics really "exist" has occupied the work of many philosophers. A readable account of some of this work is in Davis (1981); a somewhat more difficult but fascinating book is Wittgenstein (1983). Mathematics is full of anecdotes about people who have defined a certain notion, proved several theorems about its properties, and then discovered that no mathematical object of any interest could ever satisfy the definition. This is sometimes amusing, but it is very dangerous in situations that have an influence on people's lives. An account of one ongoing tragedy that resulted from this "reification" in psychology is given in Gould (1981).

Well, E is multiplicative, so we need only worry about what E does to prime powers P^K. Since E isn't the function that always outputs 0 (because ONE is the child of E, and ONE isn't the zero function), E(1) must be 1. If P is any prime,

$$\text{ONE}(P) = \text{E}(1) + \text{E}(P)$$

because DIVISORS$(P) = [1 \; P]$, and ONE(P) is the sum of the outputs of E over DIVISORS(P).

But ONE$(P) = 1$, and E$(1) = 1$. So E$(P) = 0$. Things don't get much better:

$$1 = \text{ONE}(P^2) = \text{E}(1) + \text{E}(P) + \text{E}(P^2)$$

(because DIVISORS$(P^2) = [1 \; P \; P^2]$, and ONE(P^2) is the sum of the outputs of E over DIVISORS(P^2)).

Since E$(1) = 1$ and E$(P) = 0$, we must have that E$(P^2) = 0$. Inductively, we must have that E$(P^K) = 0$ if $K > 0$. So E is a rather dull function:

$$\text{E}(P^K) = \begin{cases} 1 & \text{if } K = 0 \\ 0 & \text{if } K > 0 \end{cases}$$

This function is easy to model in Logo; here's a PK version:

```
TO PKE :P :K
 IF :K = 0 [OP 1]
 OP 0
END
```

If you EXTEND this function to $\mathbf{Z}^+$,

```
TO ALT.E :N
 OP EXTEND "PKE [] :N
END
```

and you tabulate it, you come up with the more conventional model for E:

```
TO E :N
 IF :N = 1 [OP 1]
 OP 0
END
```

ONE *is* in fact the child of E. You can check this by tabulating the COMPILE of E; do you always get 1? It's not hard to see why:

If N is any nonnegative integer, DIVISORS(N) is the list containing 1 and all the other factors of N. If we COMPILE E at N, we evaluate E at 1 and at all the other divisors of N, and we add the outputs. But E(1) = 1, and E(any other number) = 0. So the sum of the outputs of E at the divisors of N is 1. That is, the COMPILE of E is ONE.

What about E's parent? Let's give it the temporary name TEMP. Then, because E isn't the zero function, TEMP(1) = 1. Proceeding as above, let P be any prime. Then E(P^K) is the sum of the outputs of TEMP at the divisors of P^K. But for $K > 0$, E(P^K) = 0. So

$$E(P) = 0 = \text{TEMP}(1) + \text{TEMP}(P)$$
$$= \quad 1 \quad + \text{TEMP}(P) \qquad\qquad (\text{so TEMP}(P) = -1)$$
$$E(P^2) = 0 = \text{TEMP}(1) + \text{TEMP}(P) + \text{TEMP}(P^2)$$
$$= \quad 1 \quad + \quad -1 \quad + \text{TEMP}(P^2) \qquad (\text{so TEMP}(P^2) = 0)$$
$$E(P^3) = 0 = \text{TEMP}(1) + \text{TEMP}(P) + \text{TEMP}(P^2) + \text{TEMP}(P^3)$$
$$= \quad 1 \quad + \quad -1 \quad + \quad 0 \quad + \text{TEMP}(P^3) \quad (\text{so TEMP}(P^3) = 0)$$

and, inductively, TEMP(P^K) = 0 if $K > 2$.

The multiplicative function that extends TEMP to $\mathbf{Z}^+$ is known as the *Möbius* function, and it is usually called MU (for the Greek letter μ):

```
TO PKMU :P :K
 IF :K = 0 [OP 1]
 IF :K = 1 [OP -1]
 OP 0
END
```

```
TO ALT.MU :N
 OP EXTEND "PKMU [] :N
END
```

Tabulate `ALT.MU`, and look carefully at the tabulation:

N	$\mathtt{ALT.MU}(N)$
1 ...	1
2 ...	−1
3 ...	−1
4 ...	0
5 ...	−1
6 ...	1
7 ...	−1
8 ...	0
9 ...	0
10 ...	1
11 ...	−1
12 ...	0
13 ...	−1
14 ...	1
15 ...	1
16 ...	0
17 ...	−1
18 ...	0

$\vdots$

Before you read on, see if you can find a pattern in this tabulation. (Hint: Think of how a number looks when it is factored into primes.)

The idea is this: To find `ALT.MU`(N), factor N into primes. Since `ALT.MU` is multiplicative, you can apply `PKMU` to each prime power and multiply the outputs. If one of the prime powers contains an exponent bigger than 1, `PKMU` outputs 0, so the whole product collapses to 0. For example,

$$\mathtt{ALT.MU}(18) = \mathtt{PKMU}(2) \cdot \mathtt{PKMU}(3^2) = -1 \cdot 0 = 0$$

In other words, `ALT.MU`$(N) = 0$ if N is divisible by two or more factors of the same prime. Put another way, `ALT.MU`$(N) = 0$ if N is divisible by a perfect square. A number that isn't divisible by a perfect square is called

415

"squarefree"; 6 is squarefree and so is 210. If a number is squarefree, it is a product of distinct primes. Since PKNU outputs -1 at each of these primes, ALT.MU will output 1 at a squarefree number if its support contains an even number of primes and -1 if this support contains an odd number of primes. For example,

$$\text{ALT.MU}(6) = \text{PKMU}(2) \cdot \text{PKMU}(3) = -1 \cdot -1 = 1$$
$$\text{ALT.MU}(30) = \text{PKMU}(2) \cdot \text{PKMU}(3) \cdot \text{PKMU}(5) = -1 \cdot -1 \cdot -1 = -1$$

In summary,

$$\text{MU}(N) = \begin{cases} 1 & \text{if } N \text{ is squarefree and } \text{COUNT}(\text{SUPPORT}(N)) \text{ is odd} \\ -1 & \text{if } N \text{ is squarefree and } \text{COUNT}(\text{SUPPORT}(N)) \text{ is even} \\ 0 & \text{if } N \text{ is not squarefree} \end{cases}$$

The first two cases of MU's definition can be neatly combined into one:

$$\text{MU}(N) = \begin{cases} -1^{\text{COUNT}(\text{SUPPORT}(N))} & \text{if } N \text{ is squarefree} \\ 0 & \text{if } N \text{ is not squarefree} \end{cases}$$

A Logo model for MU might look like this:

```
TO MU :N
 IF :N = 1 [OP 1]
 IF SQUAREFREE? :N [OP (POWER -1 COUNT SUPPORT :N)]
 OP 0
END
```

The predicate SQUAREFREE? can be defined in many ways. One way is to scan the FACTOR list of the input, looking for exponents bigger than 1:

```
TO SQUAREFREE? :N
 OP SF.HELPER FACTOR :N
END

TO SF.HELPER :L
 IF EMPTYP :L [OP "TRUE]
 IF (LAST FIRST :L > 1 [OP "FALSE]
 OP SF.HELPER BF :L
END
```

Tabulate MU, and compare it to ALT.MU. Are the functions equal on $\mathbf{Z}^+$?

The function MU, in spite of its simple definition, is one of the most important and mysterious functions in number theory. Some of the mystery can be seen by tabulating MU. The tabulation exhibits a seemingly chaotic behavior; the outputs oscillate among the numbers 1, 0, and -1 with no simple pattern that depends only on the size of the number. Tabulate MU for a while to see what I mean.

In spite of MU's erratic behavior, "in the long run" there seems to be some regularity in its outputs. For example, if N is any integer greater than 1, the sum of the outputs of MU at the divisors of N is 0. If $N = 18$,

$$MU(1) + MU(2) + MU(3) + MU(6) + MU(9) + MU(18)$$

This should come as no surprise, since the above sum is just the COMPILE of MU applied to N, and MU's child is E, which outputs 0 at all integers greater than 1.

The situation is much more mysterious if, instead of summing MU over DIVISORS(N), you sum it over NUMBERS.UPTO(N). Call this function M:

```
TO M :N
 OP L.SIGMA "MU [] NUMBERS.UPTO :N
END
```

So

$$M(6) = MU(1) + MU(2) + MU(3) + MU(4) + MU(5) + MU(6)$$
$$= \quad 1 \quad + \quad -1 \quad + \quad -1 \quad + \quad 0 \quad + \quad -1 \quad + \quad 1 \quad = -1$$

If you tabulate M you'll see something like this:

```
1 ...  1
2 ...  0
3 ... -1
4 ... -1
5 ... -2
6 ... -1
7 ... -2
8 ... -2
9 ... -2
10 ... -1
11 ... -2
```

12 . . . −2
13 . . . −3
14 . . . −2
15 . . . −1
16 . . . −1
17 . . . −2
18 . . . −2
19 . . . −3
20 . . . −3

What does M actually measure? $M(N)$ measures the difference between the number of squarefree integers between 1 and N that have an even number of primes in their support and the number of squarefree integers between 1 and N that have an odd number of primes in their support. One of the most famous unproved conjectures in mathematics was made by Georg Riemann in 1859. Roughly, Riemann conjectured that the absolute value of $M(N)$ would never be much greater than $SQRT(N)$. In 1897, Franz Mertens conjectured that $M(N)$ was never greater than $SQRT(N)$ itself, and this was verified for very large values of N. In 1985, A.M. Odlyzko showed that Mertens was wrong; there are infinitely many N for which $M(N) > SQRT(N)$. Furthermore $M(N)$ can be greater than $SQRT(N)$ in both (positive and negative) directions. But never by very much, if the "Riemann hypothesis" is true. A very readable account of the Riemann hypothesis and the tricks that Z can play on our intuition is in Wilf (1987).

What about MU's parent? Let's give it a name. If we think of NU as NU_1 and ONE as NU_0, we should think of E as NU_{-1}, MU as NU_{-2}, and MU's parent as NU_{-3}. Recall what MU does to prime powers:

$$\text{MU}(P^K) = \begin{cases} 1 & \text{if } K = 0 \\ -1 & \text{if } K = 1 \\ 0 & \text{if } K > 1 \end{cases}$$

So we can go through our usual calculation:

$NU_{-3}(1) = 1$, and because NU_{-3} is MU's parent, NU_{-3}'s outputs at prime powers can be calculated:

$$MU(P) = -1 = NU_{-3}(1) + NU_{-3}(P)$$
$$= 1 + NU_{-3}(P) \qquad \text{(so } NU_{-3}(P) = -2)$$

$$MU(P^2) = 0 = NU_{-3}(1) + NU_{-3}(P) + NU_{-3}(P^2)$$
$$= 1 + -2 + NU_{-3}(P^2) \qquad \text{(so } NU_{-3}(P^2) = 1)$$

$$MU(P^3) = 0 = NU_{-3}(1) + NU_{-3}(P) + NU_{-3}(P^2) + NU_{-3}(P^3)$$
$$= 1 + -2 + 1 + NU_{-3}(P^3) \qquad \text{(so } NU_{-3}(P^3) = 0)$$

$$MU(P^4) = 0 = NU_{-3}(1) + NU_{-3}(P) + NU_{-3}(P^2) + NU_{-3}(P^3) + NU_{-3}(P^4)$$
$$= 1 + -2 + 1 + 0 + NU_{-3}(P^4)$$
$$\text{(so } NU_{-3}(P^4) = 0)$$

and, inductively, $NU_{-3}(P^K) = 0$ if $K \geq 3$.

That is,

$$NU_{-3}(P^K) = \begin{cases} 1 & \text{if } K = 0 \\ -2 & \text{if } K = 1 \\ 1 & \text{if } K = 2 \\ 0 & \text{if } K > 2 \end{cases}$$

In Logo,

```
TO PKNU_3 :P :K
 IF :K = 0 [OP 1]
 IF :K = 1 [OP -2]
 IF :K = 2 [OP 1]
 OP 0
END
```

Notice that I used the underscore "_" instead of the minus sign "−" to keep Logo from thinking that I am doing arithmetic. We get MU's parent by EXTENDing PKNU$_3$:

```
TO ALT.NU_3 :N
 OP EXTEND "PKNU_3 [] :N
END
```

#Project 13.9 Tabulate ALT.NU$_3$, and find a Logo model for it that is similar to our model for MU.

Hints:

1. You might want a predicate CUBEFREE?.

2. Write a function that outputs the product of the primes in the SUPPORT of its input. If this function is S, describe $N/S(N)$.

How about NU_{-4}? Well, since NU_{-3} compiles NU_{-4},

$NU_{-4}(1) \;\; = \;\; 1$

$NU_{-3}(P) \;\; = -2 = NU_{-4}(1) + NU_{-4}(P)$

$\qquad\qquad = \quad 1 \quad + NU_{-4}(P)$ $\qquad\qquad\qquad\qquad$ (so $NU_{-4}(P) = -3$)

$NU_{-3}(P^2) = \;\; 1 \;\; = NU_{-4}(1) + NU_{-4}(P) + NU_{-4}(P^2)$

$\qquad\qquad = \quad 1 \quad + \quad -3 \quad + NU_{-4}(P^2)$ $\qquad\qquad$ (so $NU_{-4}(P^2) = 3$)

$NU_{-3}(P^3) = \;\; 0 \;\; = NU_{-4}(1) + NU_{-4}(P) + NU_{-4}(P^2) + NU_{-4}(P^3)$

$\qquad\qquad = \quad 1 \quad + \quad -3 \quad + \quad 3 \quad + NU_{-4}(P^3)$ $\quad$ (so $NU_{-4}(P^3) = -1$)

$NU_{-3}(P^4) = \;\; 0 \;\; = NU_{-4}(1) + NU_{-4}(P) + NU_{-4}(P^2) + NU_{-4}(P^3) + NU_{-4}(P^4)$

$\qquad\qquad = \quad 1 \quad + \quad -3 \quad + \quad 3 \quad + \quad -1 \quad + NU_{-4}(P^4)$

$\qquad\qquad\qquad\qquad\qquad\qquad\qquad\qquad\qquad\qquad$ (so $NU_{-4}(P^4) = 0$)

$NU_{-3}(P^5) = \;\; 0 \;\; = NU_{-4}(1) + NU_{-4}(P) + NU_{-4}(P^2) + NU_{-4}(P^3) + NU_{-4}(P^4) + NU_{-4}(P^5)$

$\qquad\qquad = \quad 1 \quad + \quad -3 \quad + \quad 3 \quad + \quad -1 \quad + \quad 0 \quad + NU_{-4}(P^5)$

$\qquad\qquad\qquad\qquad\qquad\qquad\qquad\qquad\qquad\qquad$ (so $NU_{-4}(P^5) = 0$)

and, inductively, $NU_{-4}(P^K) = 0$ if $K \geq 4$.
That is,

$$NU_{-4}(P^K) = \begin{cases} 1 & \text{if } K = 0 \\ -3 & \text{if } K = 1 \\ 3 & \text{if } K = 2 \\ -1 & \text{if } K = 3 \\ 0 & \text{if } K > 3 \end{cases}$$

In Logo,

```
TO PKNU_4 :P :K
 IF :K = 0 [OP 1]
 IF :K = 1 [OP -3]
 IF :K = 2 [OP 3]
 IF :K = 3 [OP -1]
 OP 0
END
```

Project 13.10 Write ALT.NU_4 by EXTENDing PKNU_4 to Z^+. #Tabulate ALT.NU_4, and find a Logo model for it similar to the one for MU.

I'm sure you realize that a most amazing pattern is emerging. Look at ONE's ancestors:

```
TO PKNU_1 :P :K        (PKNU_1 is what we called PKE above)
 IF :K = 0 [OP 1]
 OP 0
END
```

```
TO PKNU_2 :P :K        (PKNU_2 is  PKMU)
 IF :K = 0 [OP 1]
 IF :K = 1 [OP -1]
 OP 0
END
```

```
TO PKNU_3 :P :K
 IF :K = 0 [OP 1]
 IF :K = 1 [OP -2]
 IF :K = 2 [OP 1]
 OP 0
END
```

```
TO PKNU_4 :P :K
 IF :K = 0 [OP 1]
 IF :K = 1 [OP -3]
 IF :K = 2 [OP 3]
 IF :K = 3 [OP -1]
 OP 0
END
```

Check that NU_5 can be modeled as the extension of

```
TO PKNU_5 :N
 IF :K = 0 [OP 1]
 IF :K = 1 [OP -4]
 IF :K = 2 [OP 6]
 IF :K = 3 [OP -4]
 IF :K = 4 [OP 1]
 OP 0
END
```

In general, it seems as if, at prime powers P^K, ONE's ancestors take on the alternating entries in a row of Pascal's triangle for a while, and then they stay constant at 0. Let's be more precise about what we think happens (I say "we" because I hope that your thoughts about this are the same as mine). Go back to our infinite stream of multiplicative functions (this time the stream includes negative levels):

$$\cdots \to NU_3 \to NU_2 \to NU_1 \to NU_0 \to NU_{-1} \to NU_{-2} \to NU_{-3} \cdots$$

where each function points at its parent. Some of the functions have aliases: NU_1 is NU, NU_0 is ONE, NU_{-1} is E, and NU_{-2} is MU. For nonnegative levels (that is, for NU_0, NU_1, NU_2, ...), we were able to find a formula for the functions at prime powers:

```
TO PKNU :LEVEL :P :K
 OP B :LEVEL + :K :K
END
```

Now, we suspect that we have a formula at negative levels as well. Look at the evidence:

LEVEL	OUTPUTS AT PRIME POWERS
-1	$1, 0, 0, 0, \ldots$
-2	$1, -1, 0, 0, 0, \ldots$
-3	$1, -2, 1, 0, 0, 0, \ldots$
-4	$1, -3, 3, -1, 0, 0, 0, \ldots$
-5	$1, -4, 6, -4, 1, 0, 0, 0, \ldots$

It seems that if the level is J, and J is a negative number, then we get the alternating entries in the $-J - 1$ row of Pascal's triangle. For example, if $J = -4$, we get the entries in the $-(-4) - 1$ ($= 4 - 1 = 3$) row of Pascal's triangle. Notice also that the output at P^0 is positive (it is always 1), the output at P^1 is negative, the output at P^2 is positive, and, in general, the output of P^K is positive if K is even and negative if K is odd. Before you read on, see if you can pull all this together into a nice formula (it might help to write a Logo model for NU at negative levels). Just a hint: you can make things alternate in sign by multiplying them by consecutive powers of -1.

You probably ended up with a formula like this:

```
TO PKNEGNU :NEG.LEVEL :P :K
 IF :K < -1 * :NEG.LEVEL →
    [OP (POWER -1 :K) * (B (-1 * :NEG.LEVEL - 1) :K)]
 OP 0
END
```

Project 13.11 Verify that the above version of PKNEGNU agrees with our calculations at levels -1, -2, -3, -4 and -5. EXTEND PKNEGNU to ALT.NEGNU, a function of *LEVEL* and *N*. #Prove that for all negative values of *LEVEL*,

$$\text{ALT.NEGNU}(LEVEL, N) = \text{COMPILE}(\text{ALT.NEGNU}, LEVEL - 1, N)$$

In other words, prove that ALT.NEGNU is a correct model for the ancestors of ONE.

Hints:

1. The best way to prove this is to continue the pattern of calculations that we began above (say, through *LEVEL* -8); then try to capture the essence of what you are doing in a generic calculation. If you like more formal proofs, read the following hints.

2. Since all functions are multiplicative, it's enough to establish our claim at prime powers P^K. That is, all you have to do is to show that for all primes P and all nonnegative integers K,

$$\text{ALT.NEGNU}(LEVEL, P^K) = \text{COMPILE}(\text{ALT.NEGNU}, LEVEL - 1, P^K)$$

Now, COMPILE(ALT.NEGNU, $LEVEL - 1, P^K$) is given by

$$\text{ALT.NEGNU}(LEVEL - 1, 1) + \text{ALT.NEGNU}(LEVEL - 1, P)$$
$$+ \text{ALT.NEGNU}(LEVEL - 1, P^2) + \text{ALT.NEGNU}(LEVEL - 1, P^3)$$
$$+ \cdots + \text{ALT.NEGNU}(LEVEL - 1, P^K)$$

At prime powers, ALT.NEGNU equals PKNEGNU, so it's enough to show that

$$\text{PKNEGNU}(LEVEL, P, K)$$
$$= \text{PKNEGNU}(LEVEL - 1, 1) + \text{PKNEGNU}(LEVEL - 1, P)$$
$$+ \text{PKNEGNU}(LEVEL - 1, P^2) + \text{PKNEGNU}(LEVEL - 1, P^3)$$
$$+ \cdots + \text{PKNEGNU}(LEVEL - 1, P^K)$$

To do this, notice that the alternating sum of a certain number of entries along any row of Pascal's triangle is (up to a sign) the entry above where you stop adding:

$$
\begin{array}{ccccccccccccc}
 & & & & & & 1 & & & & & & \\
 & & & & & 1 & & 1 & & & & & \\
 & & & & 1 & & 2 & & 1 & & & & \\
 & & & 1 & & 3 & & 3 & & 1 & & & \\
 & & 1 & & 4 & & 6 & & \boxed{4} & & 1 & & \\
 & \boxed{1} & & 5 & & 10 & & 10 & & 5 & & 1 & \\
1 & & 6 & & 15 & & 20 & & 15 & & 6 & & 1
\end{array}
$$

For example, $1 - 6 + 15 - 20 = -10$, $1 - 5 + 10 - 10 = -4$, and $1 - 6 + 15 = 10$. State this as a fact about binomial coefficients (getting the sign right), and prove that it always works. Then use this fact and the definition of PKNEGNU. If you like even more formality, read on.

3. To establish the equality

$$\begin{aligned}
\text{PKNEGNU}(LEVEL, P, K) = {} & \text{PKNEGNU}(LEVEL - 1, 1) \\
& + \text{PKNEGNU}(LEVEL - 1, P) \\
& + \text{PKNEGNU}(LEVEL - 1, P^2) \\
& + \text{PKNEGNU}(LEVEL - 1, P^3) \\
& + \cdots + \text{PKNEGNU}(LEVEL - 1, P^K)
\end{aligned}$$

Use "backward induction" on $LEVEL$; that is, show that, if for some value M of $LEVEL$, we have

$$\begin{aligned}
\text{PKNEGNU}(M, P^K) = {} & \text{COMPILE}(\text{PKNEGNU}, M - 1, P^K) \\
= {} & \text{PKNEGNU}(M - 1, 1) + \text{PKNEGNU}(M - 1, P) \\
& + \text{PKNEGNU}(M - 1, P^2) + \text{PKNEGNU}(M - 1, P^3) \\
& + \cdots + \text{PKNEGNU}(M - 1, P^K)
\end{aligned}$$

for all P and K, then we also have

$$\begin{aligned}
\text{PKNEGNU}(M - 1, P^K) = {} & \text{COMPILE}(\text{PKNEGNU}, M - 2, P^K) \\
= {} & \text{PKNEGNU}(M - 2, 1) + \text{PKNEGNU}(M - 2, P) \\
& + \text{PKNEGNU}(M - 2, P^2) + \text{PKNEGNU}(M - 2, P^3) \\
& + \cdots + \text{PKNEGNU}(M - 2, P^K)
\end{aligned}$$

for all P and K. Do this by using the definition of PKNEGNU and facts about binomial coefficients.

Then, since we have established our claim for $M = 0$, -1, -2 and -3 (at least), it will then hold for all negative values of M.

When I was working out the details of these calculations, I got to this point and thought that I knew the whole story about ONE's family tree. I knew that ONE's descendants were given at prime powers by

$$\text{NU}(L, P^K) = \begin{pmatrix} L + K \\ K \end{pmatrix}$$

(L is supposed to be a nonnegative integer)

or, in Logo,

```
TO PKNU :LEVEL :P :K
 OP B :LEVEL + :K :K
END
```

I also knew that ONE's ancestors were given by

$$\text{NU}(L, P^K) = \begin{cases} (-1)^K \begin{pmatrix} -L-1 \\ K \end{pmatrix} & \text{if } K < -L \text{ (and } K \geq 0) \\ 0 & \text{otherwise} \end{cases}$$

(L is supposed to be a negative integer)

or, in Logo,

```
TO PKNEGNU :NEG.LEVEL :P :K
 IF :K < -1 * :NEG.LEVEL →
    [OP (POWER -1 :K) * (B (-1 * :NEG.LEVEL - 1) :K)]
 OP 0
END
```

I was all set to write a general NU that allowed for positive and negative levels, using an IF to distinguish the two cases and the above formulas. Before doing this, I tried (just to see what would happen) giving my function PKNU (the one for positive levels) a negative level. I fully expected things to crash because the definition of my function is

```
TO PKNU :LEVEL :P :K
 OP B :LEVEL + :K :K
END
```

and, if *LEVEL* is, for example, -2 and K is 1, I'd be asking for B$(-1, 1)$. Since this would call for something like

$$\frac{-1!}{1!\,(-2)!}$$

I expected problems. Let me show you what actually happened; what follows is an actual transcript of the dialogue that I had with my machine.

First, I TABbed PKNU at some proper levels to make sure it was working:

```
?TAB "PKNU [2 5] 0 7
0 . . . 1
1 . . . 3
2 . . . 6
3 . . . 10
4 . . . 15
5 . . . 21
6 . . . 28
7 . . . 36
```

This looks fine. The [2 5] tells me that I'm at the second level and that the prime is 5 (any other choice for the prime will do just as well). How about *LEVEL* 0? (This should yield ONE itself.)

```
?TAB "PKNU [0 5] 0 7
0 . . . 1
1 . . . 1
2 . . . 1
3 . . . 1
4 . . . 1
5 . . . 1
```

This is right. How about *LEVEL* −1?

```
?TAB "PKNU [-1 5] 0 7
0 . . . 1
1 . . . 0
2 . . . 0
3 . . . 0
4 . . . 0
5 . . . 0
6 . . . 0
7 . . . 0
```

This works too (*LEVEL* −1 is E). Surely it will crash at *LEVEL* −2:

```
?TAB "PKNU [-2 5] 0 7
0 . . . 1
1 . . . -1
2 . . . 0
3 . . . 0
4 . . . 0
5 . . . 0
6 . . . 0
7 . . . 0
```

Something's going on. Maybe there's a bug in my functions. Well,

```
?TAB "PKNU [-3 5] 0 7
0 . . . 1
1 . . . -2
2 . . . 1
3 . . . 0
4 . . . 0
5 . . . 0
6 . . . 0
7 . . . 0
```

```
?TAB "PKNU [-4 5] 0 7
0 . . . 1
1 . . . -3
2 . . . 3
3 . . . -1
4 . . . 0
5 . . . 0
6 . . . 0
7 . . . 0
```

```
?TAB "PKNU [-5 5] 0 7
0 . . . 1
1 . . . -4
2 . . . 6
3 . . . -4
4 . . . 1
5 . . . 0
6 . . . 0
7 . . . 0
```

```
?TAB "PKNU [-6 5] 0 7
0 . . . 1
1 . . . -5
2 . . . 10
3 . . . -10
4 . . . 5
5 . . . -1
6 . . . 0
7 . . . 0
```

Try it for yourself.

How can this happen? B doesn't crash at negative inputs, and PKNU outputs *exactly the right thing* for negative levels!

The reason that B accepts a negative first input without complaining is not surprising. My problem was that I was thinking of the following model for B:

```
TO B :N :K
 OP (FACT :N) / ((FACT :K) * (FACT (:N - :K)))
END
```

and this would certainly balk at a first input of, say, -2. However, for reasons of speed, we used the "model 4" version of B:

```
TO B :N :K
 OP B.HELPER :N :K 1 0
END

TO B.HELPER :N :K :T :C
 IF :C = :K [OP :T]
 OP B.HELPER :N :K :T * (:N - :C) / (:C + 1) :C + 1
END
```

If you think about how this calculates $B(N, K)$, you see that it describes the following calculation:

$$B(N, K) = \frac{N}{1} \cdot \frac{N-1}{2} \cdot \frac{N-2}{3} \cdot \frac{N-3}{4} \cdot \frac{N-4}{5} \cdots \frac{N-K+1}{K}$$

and this makes sense if N is negative. For example,

$$B(-5,2) = \frac{-5}{1} \cdot \frac{-6}{2} = 15,$$

$$B(-6,3) = \frac{-6}{1} \cdot \frac{-7}{2} \cdot \frac{-8}{3} = -56, \text{ and}$$

$$B(-4,6) = \frac{-4}{1} \cdot \frac{-5}{2} \cdot \frac{-6}{3} \cdot \frac{-7}{4} \cdot \frac{-8}{5} \cdot \frac{-9}{6} = 84$$

Of course, this opens up a whole new area for investigation. In preparation for the important question ("why does the PKNU for positive levels seem to work for negative levels?") look at the next set of problems; they are designed to develop an intuition about these strange new objects.

Experiment 13.12 Tabulate B for some negative levels, and develop some conjectures about B. Then prove your conjectures using the model 4 version of B. For example, is $B(N,0)$ always 1 even if N is negative? Is $B(N,1)$ always N? How about $B(0,K)$? How can you determine when $B(N,K)$ is negative?

Project 13.13 Notice that the model 4 version for B not only allows for negative first inputs, but it also allows for a second input that is greater than the first input. What is $B(5,7)$? What can you say about $B(N,K)$ if N is positive and $K > N$? Prove it using the model 4 version of B.

Even though we are now thinking of B as a purely algebraic object, don't forget that, in the beginning, $B(N,K)$ stood for the number of K-element subsets of an N-element set. This makes no sense if N is -3, but how many 7-element subsets should a 5-element set have?

Experiment 13.14 Tabulate B holding the first input at -1 between 0 and 10. Then tabulate B if the first input is -2. Do the same for -3, -4, -5, and -6. Notice that the outputs of B at negative "levels" seem to be (up to a sign) entries from Pascal's triangle. If N and K are nonnegative integers, develop a conjecture that expresses $B(-N,K)$ in terms of $B(?,??)$ where "?" and "??" are nonnegative integers. Can you prove it? If you can, it will settle a nagging doubt that bothered me when I first started thinking about B at negative levels: How can you be sure that $B(N,K)$ is an integer if N is negative? The model 4 formula

$$B(N,K) = \frac{N}{1} \cdot \frac{N-1}{2} \cdot \frac{N-2}{3} \cdot \frac{N-3}{4} \cdot \frac{N-4}{5} \cdots \frac{N-K+1}{K}$$

expresses $B(N,K)$ as a product of fractions; couldn't $B(N,K)$ be a fraction? Not if it is equal in absolute value to an entry of Pascal's triangle.

Project 13.15 Many people look at Pascal's triangle in this way:

Row 0:	1						
Row 1:	1	1					
Row 2:	1	2	1				
Row 3:	1	3	3	1			
Row 4:	1	4	6	4	1		
Row 5:	1	5	10	10	5	1	
Row 6:	1	6	15	20	15	6	1

$\vdots$

Suppose that we "fill out" the zeroth row with zeros:

Row 0:	1	0	0	0	0	0	0	0	0	...
Row 1:	1	1								
Row 2:	1	2	1							
Row 3:	1	3	3	1						
Row 4:	1	4	6	4	1					
Row 5:	1	5	10	10	5	1				
Row 6:	1	6	15	20	15	6	1			

(Why does this make sense?) Then we force Pascal's identity

$$B(N, K) = B(N - 1, K - 1) + B(N - 1, K)$$

(which says that any entry is the sum of the two above it) to work even if K is greater than or equal to N. So $B(1, 1)$ (which is 1) would equal $B(0, 0) + B(0, 1) = 1 + 0$, and this works. $B(1, 2)$ would equal $B(0, 1) + B(0, 2)$ which is $0 + 0$, so $B(1, 2)$ would equal 0. Inductively, convince yourself that the rest of "Pascal's array" would fill out like this:

Row 0:	1	0	0	0	0	0	0	0	0	...
Row 1:	1	1	0	0	0	0	0	0	0	...
Row 2:	1	2	1	0	0	0	0	0	0	...
Row 3:	1	3	3	1	0	0	0	0	0	...
Row 4:	1	4	6	4	1	0	0	0	0	...
Row 5:	1	5	10	10	5	1	0	0	0	...

$\vdots$

Now suppose that we allow "negative rows," and that we start off each row with a 1:

$\vdots$

Row −4:	1								
Row −3:	1								
Row −2:	1								
Row −1:	1								
Row 0:	1	0	0	0	0	0	0	0	0 ...
Row 1:	1	1	0	0	0	0	0	0	0 ...
Row 2:	1	2	1	0	0	0	0	0	0 ...
Row 3:	1	3	3	1	0	0	0	0	0 ...
Row 4:	1	4	6	4	1	0	0	0	0 ...
Row 5:	1	5	10	10	5	1	0	0	0 ...

$\vdots$

If we insist that each row will be constructed by the same Pascal's identity that we have come to admire (every entry is the sum of the two above it), then working backward from the zeroth row, we can inductively fill in the generalized Pascal array:

$\vdots$

Row −4:	1	−4	10	−20	35	−56	84	−120	165 ...
Row −3:	1	−3	6	−10	15	−21	28	−36	45 ...
Row −2:	1	−2	3	−4	5	−6	7	−8	9 ...
Row −1:	1	−1	1	−1	1	−1	1	−1	1 ...
Row 0:	1	0	0	0	0	0	0	0	0 ...
Row 1:	1	1	0	0	0	0	0	0	0 ...
Row 2:	1	2	1	0	0	0	0	0	0 ...
Row 3:	1	3	3	1	0	0	0	0	0 ...
Row 4:	1	4	6	4	1	0	0	0	0 ...
Row 5:	1	5	10	10	5	1	0	0	0 ...

$\vdots$

This is an extremely appealing array. Notice how diagonals show up as rows in other places. Find some other interesting properties.

Model this array in Logo; that is, try to find a Logo function P so that P(N, K) is the Kth entry (starting with the zeroth entry) in the Nth row of Pascal's array. Hint: Break your function up into four cases:

1. If $K = 0$, output 1.

2. If $N = 0$ and $K > 0$, output 0.

3. If $N > 0$, use Pascal's identity.

4. If $N < 0$, solve Pascal's identity for B($N - 1, K$), replace $N - 1$ by N (so that N becomes $N + 1$), and use "backward recursion."

Finally, tabulate P and the model 4 version of B. Can you prove what you see? Hint: Because of the way that P is constructed, break you proof up into four cases. Show that Pascal's identity still holds for B even with its new domain. Make heavy use of informal induction.

What if you fill out the zeroth row to the left with 0's and work down and up using Pascal's identity. Does anything interesting happen? What if you change the zeroth row to something else (say, all 1's), and let Pascal's identity propagate the rest of the array?

If you have played with the above problems, you have all the equipment to explain our riddle. Notice that in Pascal's array

$\vdots$

Row −4:	1	−4	10	−20	35	−56	84	−120	165 ...
Row −3:	1	−3	6	−10	15	−21	28	−36	45 ...
Row −2:	1	−2	3	−4	5	−6	7	−8	9 ...
Row −1:	1	−1	1	−1	1	−1	1	−1	1 ...
Row 0:	1	0	0	0	0	0	0	0	0 ...
Row 1:	1	1	0	0	0	0	0	0	0 ...
Row 2:	1	2	1	0	0	0	0	0	0 ...
Row 3:	1	3	3	1	0	0	0	0	0 ...
Row 4:	1	4	6	4	1	0	0	0	0 ...
Row 5:	1	5	10	10	5	1	0	0	0 ...

$\vdots$

there is an enchanting quasi-symmetry. Certain diagonals are alternating versions of rows. I've circled two examples to show you what I mean. If we write down what seems to happen, we have relations like

$$B(-4,0) = B(3,0)$$
$$B(-3,1) = -B(3,1)$$
$$B(-2,2) = B(3,2)$$
$$B(-1,3) = -B(3,3)$$
$$B(0,4) = B(3,4)$$
$$B(1,5) = -B(3,5)$$

$$\vdots$$

I've included the alternating signs in the last equation (even though the output is 0) to stress the pattern. Also, because I'm using Pascal's array, I should be using the function P of project 13.15 instead of B, but you proved in that project that B and P are equal for all integers N and all nonnegative integers K. Look at another example:

$$B(-5,0) = B(4,0)$$
$$B(-4,1) = -B(4,1)$$
$$B(-3,2) = B(4,2)$$
$$B(-2,3) = -B(4,3)$$
$$B(-1,4) = B(4,4)$$
$$B(0,5) = -B(4,5)$$
$$B(1,6) = B(4,6)$$
$$B(2,7) = -B(4,7)$$

$$\vdots$$

Look at this, and see if you can find a formula that expresses the relationship.

We are looking for something like

$$B(?,K) = \pm B(N,K)$$

The sign is easy:

$$B(?, K) = (-1)^K B(N, K)$$

The "?" depends on N and K, and a tabulation shows what's going on:

N	K	?
4	7	2
4	6	1
4	5	0
4	4	−1
4	3	−2
4	2	−3

Expressing "?" in terms of N and K produces

$$? = -N + K - 1$$

So our identity becomes

$$B(-N + K - 1, K) = (-1)^K B(N, K)$$

because the $(-1)^K$ is just 1 or −1, we can put it on either side of the equation (or, if you like to be formal, multiply both sides of the above equation by $(-1)^K$ and note that $(-1)^K \cdot (-1)^K = (-1)^{2K} = 1$), so we have

$$(-1)^K B(-N + K - 1, K) = B(N, K)$$

Try this out for several values of N and K. Notice that it seems to work if N is positive or negative. We have the following result:

Theorem 13.2 For all integers N and all nonnegative integers K,

$$(-1)^K B(-N + K - 1, K) = B(N, K)$$

Project 13.16 Prove this theorem. Hint: Use either the model 4 version of B and a generic calculation, or use Pascal's identity and induction.

We can now explain why, if given a negative first input, the function

```
TO PKNU :LEVEL :P :K
  OP B :LEVEL + :K :K
END
```

produces the same thing as

```
TO PKNEGNU :NEG.LEVEL :P :K
  IF :K < -1 * :NEG.LEVEL →
      [OP (POWER -1 :K) * (B (-1 * :NEG.LEVEL - 1) :K)]
  OP 0
END
```

First, notice that there is no need for the IF in PKNEGNU; that is, we could have defined PKNEGNU as

```
TO PKNEGNU :NEG.LEVEL :P :K
  OP (POWER -1 :K) * (B (-1 * :NEG.LEVEL - 1) :K)
END
```

The reason is that if K is greater than or equal to $-NEG.LEVEL$, then K is strictly greater than the positive number $-NEG.LEVEL - 1$, and the binomial coefficient $B(-NEG.LEVEL - 1, K)$ is 0. So we don't need to break up the negative levels into two special cases. We have reduced our problem to showing that the following two functions are equal:

```
TO PKNU1 :LEVEL :P :K
  OP (POWER -1 :K) * (B (-1 * :LEVEL - 1) :K)
END
```

and

```
TO PKNU :LEVEL :P :K
  OP B :LEVEL + :K :K
END
```

In other words, we must show that

$$(-1)^K B(-L - 1, K) = B(L + K, K)$$

This follows easily from theorem 13.2 which asserts that

$$(-1)^K B(-N + K - 1, K) = B(N, K)$$

for all N and K. Simply replace N by $L + K$, and you find that

$$(-1)^K \mathbf{B}\left(-(L + K) + K - 1, K\right) = \mathbf{B}\left(L + K, K\right)$$

But $-(L + K) + K - 1 = -L - K + K - 1 = -L - 1$, so we have a very simple description of ONE's family tree:

Theorem 13.3 The stream

$$\cdots \to \mathtt{NU}_4 \to \mathtt{NU}_3 \to \mathtt{NU}_2 \to \mathtt{NU}_1 \to \mathtt{NU}_0 \to \mathtt{NU}_{-1} \to \mathtt{NU}_{-2} \to \cdots$$

where $\mathtt{NU}_0$ is ONE and each function points at its parent can be modeled in Logo like this:

```
TO PKNU :LEVEL :P :K
 OP B :LEVEL + :K :K
END

TO NU :LEVEL :N
 OP EXTEND "PKNU :LEVEL :N
END
```

I've dropped the "ALT" prefix in NU. From now on, this is the model for NU that we'll use. The theorem amounts to the statement that, using the above model, NU at any level COMPILEs NU at one lower level.

What's Behind the Formula?

Before we go on, think about the previous discussion. We started off looking for ONE's descendants. Because we insisted that these children be multiplicative, we only had to develop formulas at prime powers P^K (EXTEND took care of arbitrary inputs). It soon became apparent that these formulas resulted from our earlier formula that described the hockey-stick theorem

$$\sum_{J=0}^{K} \binom{L + J}{J} = \binom{L + 1 + K}{K}$$

Happy with our success, we looked for ONE's ancestors. Again focusing our attention on prime powers, we constructed the functions E and MU, and then, pushing down to lower levels, we discovered another pattern that involved rows of Pascal's triangle modified by alternating signs. This led to another function that handled the negative levels.

But then we discovered that our model 4 version of B accepted negative first inputs and that, without modification, our function for ONE's descendants could also be used to generate ONE's ancestors.

Why does this happen? I don't mean "why" in the mathematical sense. We supplied a proof over the course of the above discussion, so there should be no question in your mind that, for example, theorem 13.3 is true. One of my friends once said about a certain result, "I know how to prove it, but I don't know why it's true." That's the "why" I'm talking about. Why do binomial coefficients turn up in a discussion of multiplicative functions? Why does a Logo model for B, when fed inputs that we never thought about when we wrote the model, produce exactly the right function to model our stream of ONE's ancestors?

Here's one explanation: Long before the idea occurred to us, ONE had a family tree. NU was its child and MU was its grandparent, and the whole stream of functions was laying around waiting to be discovered. And that's exactly what we did; little by little we discovered properties of these functions. One of these discoveries, made (like so many discoveries) by accident, was that a single very simple formula can be used to describe all the functions in ONE's family tree. This formula (the one in PKNU) was always there, and through our cleverness, we stumbled upon it. There are probably many other beautiful facts about this family tree that we do not yet know. The idea that abstractions have a genuine existence is reflected in many aspects of our language. For example, in this book we often offer several Logo "models" for the same function; the idea is that there is an abstract function F that is really "out there"; we can construct mechanical and concrete machines that, when implemented on a computer, behave like this "real" F. Pushed to the extreme, this point of view, called Platonism, implies the existence of a world of ideas that is independent of, but that can be partially understood by, us.

Here's another explanation: There *is* no "why" except the mathematical "why"; a statement is true when it has been proved, and the only reason that something is true is that a proof for it exists. Any confusion on our part about why a proved statement is true stems from a lack of understanding of the proof at some level. The wonderful properties of NU, the fact that binomial coefficients give the right answer in an unexpected situation, the fact that binomial coefficients show up at all in a discussion of multiplicative functions; these things are all implicit in the questions that we ask. Theorem 13.3 and everything that led up to it was already built into the definitions of multiplicative function and compilation. All that is required to extract the theorems from the definitions is a more or less mechanical process of logic, and that process has been hard-wired into our brains through centuries of evolution. Pleasing results come from asking questions that will produce these results, and productive mathematicians have had years of experience learning how to ask questions that logic will transform into striking theorems. If you don't take the right path in the first place, logic will lead you to a tangle of unrelated facts. When this happens, the typical thing to do is to start over, trying a different approach. In other words, we impose our own structure on our calculations. Given any set of hypotheses, there are many possible conclusions; coming up with the ones that produce beautiful results is a large part of doing mathematics. For example, if we hadn't concentrated on prime powers, we would have been looking for a formula for NU at all positive integers, and without using the fundamental theorem of arithmetic, it's unlikely that we would have come up with anything. Mathematical objects do not exist independently from us; we invent them. There is no function F; there are simply many machines that act the same way. Pushed to the extreme, this point of view turns mathematics into a game of logic in which we state some initial assumptions, define some symbols, and then spend our days drawing up the logical consequences of what we have invented. Any impression that mathematical objects actually exist is an illusion.

These two explanations are part of a debate that has intrigued mathematicians for centuries. It extends, of course, beyond mathematics into philosophy, and it is concerned with some very delicate questions about existence and knowledge. A provocative account of some positions in the debate is in Davis (1981).

What do you think? When you do mathematics, are you acting like a scientist, discovering facts about things that exist, or are you like a musician, creating new things simply because they are beautiful?

In this book, we often act as if we were working with something real, but, equally as often, we play with our ideas, changing our functions a bit to see what will happen. That's probably the way most mathematicians work. If the fact that the model 4 version of B can be used to give a coherence to ONE's family tree is inherent in its definition, that doesn't make our sense of discovery any less striking. If our impression that we are working with something real is an illusion, then it is a very powerful illusion, and illusions are often useful.

Besides, when it's 3 A.M. and you are trying to derive a relationship among a family of functions, but the thing you are looking for seems to be playing games with you, you *know* that mathematical objects are real.

Project 13.17 You can think of our COMPILE function as a higher order function that takes a multiplicative function as input and outputs its child. This isn't quite right, because COMPILE is a function of several inputs, but what I mean is that if F is the child of G, then (ignoring the "extra inputs" in our Logo model)

$$F(N) = \text{COMPILE}(G, N)$$

Write a higher-order function PARENT that transforms a multiplicative function into its parent.

Hint: Mimic the process that we used to model ONE's ancestors. Suppose that we have a nonzero multiplicative function G modeled as a function of P and K (you might want to write a generic PK function that takes a multiplicative function and outputs its PK version). Show that if G's parent is H, then $G(1) = H(1)$, and for all primes P and positive integers K,

$$H(P^K) = G(P^K) - G(P^{(K-1)})$$

To do this, proceed inductively (again, look at how we built E or MU above). To be precise, induct on K, using the fact that

$$G(P^K) = H(1) + H(P) + H(P^2) + \cdots + H(P^K)$$

ID's Family Tree

Theorem 13.3 gives a simple function NU that describes all the ancestors and descendants of ONE:

```
TO PKNU :LEVEL :P :K
 OP B :LEVEL + :K :K
END
```

```
TO NU :LEVEL :N
 OP EXTEND "PKNU :LEVEL :N
END
```

> Notice that PKNU doesn't even use the value of the prime P when it describes its output. This means that the output of NU at any level does not depend on the primes that divide the input; all that matters is the ORD at these primes.

This especially simple formulation for NU might be due to the fact that we started with an especially simple function: ONE. Suppose we start with a function different from ONE and investigate descendants and ancestors. What happens if we start with ID?

Remember, $ID(N) = N$, so if you compile ID, you get the function that adds the divisors of its inputs. In other words, ID's child is SIG. Suppose we compile SIG:

```
TO SIG2 :N
 OP COMPILE "SIG [] :N
END
```

A tabulation of SIG2 looks something like this:

```
1 ... 1
2 ... 4
3 ... 5
4 ... 11
5 ... 7
6 ... 20
7 ... 9
8 ... 26
9 ... 18
10 ... 28
11 ... 13
12 ... 55
13 ... 15
14 ... 36
15 ... 35
16 ... 57
17 ... 19
18 ... 72
19 ... 21
20 ... 77
```

Before you read on, try to find a pattern in the above table.

STOP

Because things worked out so nicely for ONE, I was certain that there must be a simple and elegant formulation for ID's descendants and ancestors. Furthermore it seemed clear that the approach that we used to look at the ONE family should apply here as well, so I decided to look at prime powers (just look at the prime inputs in the above table). Things started to fall into place almost immediately.

If we are going to look at prime powers, we should look at the PK versions of our functions:

```
TO PKID :P :K
 OP POWER :P :K
END
```

Since the divisors of P^K are just the smaller powers of P, we have

```
TO PKSIG :P :K
 OP SIGMA "POWER :P 0 :K
END
```

In other words,

$$\text{SIG}(P^K) = 1 + P + P^2 + P^3 + \cdots + P^K$$

But this is just the sum of some terms in a geometric sequence, and in part II we developed a simple closed form for such things. In this case we have the following:

$$\text{SIG}(P^K) = \frac{P^{(K+1)} - 1}{P - 1}$$

This means that we can model SIG like this

```
TO PKSIG :P :K
 OP ((POWER :P :K + 1) - 1) / (:P - 1)
END

TO ALT.SIG :N
 OP EXTEND "PKSIG [] :N
END
```

Looking at SIG this way allows you to quickly find the sum of the divisors of an integer once you know its prime factorization. For example,

$$\text{SIG}(5^2 \cdot 3^4 \cdot 7) = \frac{5^3 - 1}{5 - 1} \cdot \frac{3^5 - 1}{3 - 1} \cdot \frac{7^2 - 1}{7 - 1}$$

What about SIG's child? Let's call it SIG_2. My first attempt was to use the above model for PKSIG, and to calculate like this:

Since SIG_2 compiles SIG,

$$\text{SIG}_2(P^K) = \text{SIG}(1) + \text{SIG}(P) + \text{SIG}(P^2) + \text{SIG}(P^3) + \cdots + \text{SIG}(P^K)$$

$$= 1 + \frac{P^2 - 1}{P - 1} + \frac{P^3 - 1}{P - 1} + \frac{P^4 - 1}{P - 1} + \cdots + \frac{P^{(K+1)} - 1}{P - 1}$$

To simplify this expression, I wrote 1 as $(P - 1)/(P - 1)$ so that it becomes

$$\frac{P - 1 + P^2 - 1 + P^3 - 1 + P^4 - 1 + \cdots + P^{(K+1)} - 1}{P - 1}$$

$$= \frac{P + P^2 + P^3 + P^4 + \cdots + P^{(K+1)} - (1 + 1 + 1 + 1 + \cdots + 1)}{P - 1}$$

$$= \frac{P(1 + P + P^2 + P^3 + \cdots + P^K) - (K + 1)}{P - 1}$$

$$= \frac{\frac{P(P^{(K+1)} - 1)}{P - 1} - (K + 1)}{P - 1}$$

$$= \frac{P(P^{(K+1)} - 1) - (K + 1)(P - 1)}{(P - 1)^2}$$

At this point, it wasn't clear what to do. There are dozens of ways for rewriting the above expression, and all of them look equally "simple." Should we write it as

$$\frac{P^{(K+2)} - (K + 2)P + 1}{(P - 1)^2}$$

or

$$\frac{P(P^{(K+1)} - 1)}{(P - 1)^2} - \frac{K + 1}{P - 1}$$

or

$$\frac{P^{(K+2)}}{(P - 1)^2} - \frac{P}{(P - 1)^2} - \frac{K + 1}{P - 1}$$

All of these expressions are "correct"; the problem is to choose one that will lead somewhere. In this case, "lead somewhere" means that we will be able to use it to find a simple formula that captures the whole family tree for ID. This is clearly a case where we are imposing our own structure on our calculations, and in fact it's not at all clear which structure we should impose.

I played a little with the last expression. That is, I looked at SIG_2 like this:

```
TO PKSIG2 :P :K
 OP ((POWER :P :K+2) / (POWER :P-1 2)) →
          - (:P / (POWER :P-1) 2) - (:K+1) / (:P-1)
END

TO SIG2 :N
 OP EXTEND "PKSIG2 [] :N
END
```

Experiment 13.18 Tabulate SIG_2. Replace K by 0 in the formula for PKSIG2. What do you get? Make sure that SIG_2's PARENT agrees with SIG. Are there any interesting patterns in SIG_2's outputs?

The above expression for SIG_2 just didn't feel right to me, but I carried out one more compilation to see if anything interesting would happen. So suppose SIG_3 is SIG_2's child. Then

$$\text{SIG}_3(P^K) = \text{SIG}_2(1) + \text{SIG}_2(P) + \text{SIG}_2(P^2) + \text{SIG}_2(P^3) + \cdots + \text{SIG}_2(P^K)$$

$$= \frac{P^2}{(P-1)^2} - \frac{P}{(P-1)^2} - \frac{1}{(P-1)} \qquad (\text{this is } \text{SIG}_2(1))$$

$$+ \frac{P^3}{(P-1)^2} - \frac{P}{(P-1)^2} - \frac{2}{(P-1)} \qquad (\text{SIG}_2(P))$$

$$+ \frac{P^4}{(P-1)^2} - \frac{P}{(P-1)^2} - \frac{3}{(P-1)} \qquad (\text{SIG}_2(P^2))$$

$$+ \frac{P^5}{(P-1)^2} - \frac{P}{(P-1)^2} - \frac{4}{(P-1)} \qquad (\text{SIG}_2(P^3))$$

$$+ \cdots + \frac{P^{(K+2)}}{(P-1)^2} - \frac{P}{(P-1)^2} - \frac{(K+1)}{(P-1)} \qquad (\text{SIG}_2(P^K))$$

Now add up the expressions in each "column"; the result is

$$\frac{P^2 + P^3 + P^4 + P^5 + \cdots + P^{(K+2)}}{(P-1)^2}$$

$$- \frac{P + P + P + P + \cdots + P}{(P-1)^2}$$

$$- \frac{1 + 2 + 3 + 4 + \cdots + (K+1)}{(P-1)}$$

and this becomes

$$\frac{P^2(1 + P + P^2 + P^3 + \cdots + P^K)}{(P-1)^2}$$

$$- \frac{P(1 + 1 + 1 + 1 + \cdots + 1)}{(P-1)^2}$$

$$- \frac{1 + 2 + 3 + 4 + \cdots + (K+1)}{(P-1)}$$

Using formulas for geometric series and arithmetic series, this becomes

$$\frac{P^2 \dfrac{P^{(K+1)} - 1}{P - 1}}{(P-1)^2} - \frac{P(K+1)}{(P-1)^2} - \frac{\binom{K+2}{2}}{(P-1)^2}$$

Simplifying the first expression and writing $K + 1$ in the second expression as the more suggestive $\binom{K+1}{1}$, this whole thing becomes

$$\frac{P^{(K+3)}}{(P-1)^3} - \frac{P^2}{(P-1)^3} - \binom{K+1}{1}\frac{P}{(P-1)^2} - \binom{K+2}{2}\frac{1}{(P-1)}$$

Yuck. A pattern is emerging, but it's not a very simple one. Of course, simplicity is a relative term, so perhaps you can see something here that I can't. It looks to me that the next compilation will yield a formula for SIG_4 that looks something like

$$SIG_4(P^K) = \frac{P^{(K+4)}}{(P-1)^4} - \frac{P^3}{(P-1)^4} - \binom{K+1}{1}\frac{P^2}{(P-1)^3}$$

$$- \binom{K+2}{2}\frac{P}{(P-1)} - \binom{K+3}{3}\frac{1}{(P-1)}$$

but I don't see a way to simplify this further (I see plenty of ways to rewrite it, but that's not the same thing as simplifying it). Take some time now and see what you can do.

STOP

What I did at this point was to move to the other side of the family tree. Perhaps by looking at the ancestors of ID, we can find a formula that will work for our whole stream of functions. Let's fix our notation for this whole stream of functions in the usual way:

$$\cdots \to SIG_2 \to SIG_1 \to SIG_0 \to SIG_{-1} \to SIG_{-2} \to SIG_{-3} \to \cdots$$
$$\text{(SIG)} \quad \text{(ID)}$$

Using a result from project 13.17, finding ID's ancestors is straightforward. The result I'm thinking of is this:

If G is a nonzero multiplicative function, and if G's parent is H, then

$$H(P^K) = \begin{cases} 1 & \text{if } K = 0 \\ G(P^K) - G(P^{(K-1)}) & \text{if } K > 0 \end{cases}$$

This means that since SIG_{-1} is ID's parent, then

$$SIG_{-1}(P^K) = \begin{cases} 1 & \text{if } K = 0 \\ ID(P^K) - ID(P^{(K-1)}) & \text{if } K > 0 \end{cases}$$

or

$$\text{SIG}_{-1}(P^K) = \begin{cases} 1 & \text{if } K = 0 \\ P^K - P^{(K-1)} & \text{if } K > 0 \end{cases}$$

A Logo model for our SIG_{-1} is

```
TO PKSIG_1 :P :K
 IF :K = 0 [OP 1]
 OP (POWER :P :K) - (POWER :P :K - 1)
END

TO SIG_1 :N
 OP EXTEND "PKSIG_1 [] :N
END
```

I've named the model SIG_1 instead of our usual ALT.SIG_1 because, for now, this is the only way we have to think about SIG_{-1}. Sometimes the formula for SIG_{-1} at prime powers is written as

$$\text{SIG}_{-1}(P^K) = P^{(K-1)}(P - 1)$$

So, if you want to calculate $\text{SIG}_{-1}(72)$, the calculation would look like:

$$\text{SIG}_{-1}(72) = \text{SIG}_{-1}(2^3 \cdot 3^2) = \text{SIG}_{-1}(2^3) \cdot \text{SIG}_{-1}(3^2)$$
$$= 2^2 \cdot (2 - 1) \cdot 3 \cdot (3 - 1) = 24$$

It turns out that SIG_{-1} is an extremely important function in number theory, and we'll derive some of its properties in the next two chapters. However, before we continue with our investigation, take some time to work on the following problems; they'll give you a preview of things to come.

Exercise 13.19 Make sure that SIG_1 is indeed the parent of ID. One way to increase your confidence is to COMPILE SIG_1 at several integers. For example, check that

COMPILE "SIG_1 [] 3 outputs 3,
COMPILE "SIG_1 [] 6 outputs 6,
COMPILE "SIG_1 [] 12 outputs 12, and
COMPILE "SIG_1 [] 18 outputs 18.

If you have the time, try TAB "COMPILE (LIST QUOTE "SIG_1 []) 1 20.

Experiment 13.20 Tabulate SIG_1 itself and look for interesting proper-ties. Can $\text{SIG}_{-1}(N)$ ever be odd? List all values of N so that $\text{SIG}_{-1}(N)$ is equal to 2. Can you prove that your list is complete? List all values of N so that $\text{SIG}_{-1}(N)$ is equal to 4. Can you prove that your list is complete? Explain why, for a given integer M, there cannot be an infinite number of N so that $\text{SIG}_{-1}(N) = M$. Are there any integers M so that there are no values of N with $\text{SIG}_{-1}(N) = M$? If so, find two such M; if not, explain why SIG_{-1} is an "onto" function. If you triple certain numbers, the output of SIG_{-1} is also tripled. For example, $\text{SIG}_{-1}(9)$ is 6 and $\text{SIG}_{-1}(27)$ is 18. If you triple other numbers, the output of SIG_{-1} is doubled. For example, $\text{SIG}_{-1}(11)$ is 10 and $\text{SIG}_{-1}(33)$ is 20. What is the difference between a number whose triple causes the output of SIG_{-1} to triple and a number whose triple cause the output of SIG_{-1} to double? Are there any numbers that, when tripled, cause the output of SIG_{-1} to quadruple? It seems that, for many numbers N, $\text{SIG}_{-1}(N)$ and N have a common factor bigger than one. When is this true? When is it false? Look at the function

```
TO F :N
 OP GCD :N (SIG_1 :N)
END
```

Describe those numbers N for which $\text{F}(N) > 1$.

We know that SIG_{-1} is multiplicative. Is it strongly multiplicative? Are there any integers A and B that are not relatively prime but still have the property that

$$\text{SIG}_{-1}(AB) = \text{SIG}_{-1}(A)\text{SIG}_{-1}(B)?$$

There are intimate connections between $\text{SIG}_{-1}(N)$ and the integers be-tween 1 and N that are relatively prime to N. The following problems give you a start at discovering some of these connections. The best way to treat these results theoretically is through the language of congruence, which we'll discuss in the next chapter. Of course, I say "the best way to treat these results theoretically is through the language of congruence" because that's the way I learned to look at things. Perhaps you can find other "better" ways.

Project 13.21 Recall that PRIME.TO(N) is the list of integers between 1 and N that are relatively prime to N. In chapter 12, we constructed PRIME.TO(N) by FILTERing the predicate RELATIVELY.PRIME? over NUMBERS.UPTO(N).

Euler (1707–1783) was very fond of the following function, which is now known as the Euler PHI (for the Greek letter φ) function:

```
TO PHI :N
 OP COUNT PRIME.TO :N
END
```

Tabulate PHI, and compare it to SIG_{-1}. What is happening? Prove that what you see is true for the special case of prime powers. Hint: The numbers between 1 and P^K that have a factor bigger than 1 in common with P^K are

$$P, \ 2P, \ 3P, \ 4P, \ 5P, \ \ldots, \ P^{(K-1)}P$$

#In chapter 15 we'll prove that PHI equals SIG_{-1} on all positive integers. You have just shown that PHI equals SIG_{-1} on all prime powers P^K (including the case when $K = 0$), and we know that SIG_{-1} is multiplicative (that's how we built it). If we can show that PHI is also multiplicative, then, by project 13.1, PHI and SIG_{-1} will be equal (two multiplicative functions that are equal on prime powers are equal on all integers). So, to prove that PHI is ID's parent, it's enough to show that PHI is multiplicative, and the cleanest way I can see to do this is to use the techniques of the next chapter. But why don't you try to find a way to prove it using the techniques that we have right now. That is, try to prove that if A and B are relatively prime, then

$$PHI(AB) = PHI(A) \cdot PHI(B)$$

You might start by using a specific example, say, $A = 12$ and $B = 35$. Look at the corresponding PRIME.TO lists:

PRIME.TO(12)   is [1 5 7 11]

PRIME.TO(35)   is

[1 2 3 4 6 8 9 11 12 13 16 17 18 19 22 23 24 26 27 29 31 32 33 34]

Now look at PRIME.TO($12 \cdot 35$); make sure that it has 96 elements in it, and try to find a way to transform the above two lists into PRIME.TO($12 \cdot 35$) (unfortunately, you can't simply take the LIST.PRODUCT).

The fact that $SIG_{-1}(N)$ can be thought of as the number of integers less than N that are relatively prime to N allows you to look at some facts about SIG_{-1} in a new light. For example, thinking of SIG_{-1} as PHI, why do the following statements make good sense?

1. $\mathrm{SIG}_{-1}(P) = P - 1$ for all primes P.

2. If $\mathrm{SIG}_{-1}(N) = N - 1$, then N must be a prime.

3. $\mathrm{SIG}_{-1}(N) < N$ for all integers $N > 1$.

4. $\mathrm{SIG}_{-1}(N!) < N! - N + 1$ for all integers $N > 1$.

Experiment 13.22 We defined $\mathrm{PHI}(N)$ as the COUNT of $\mathrm{PRIME.TO}(N)$, but you could also think of it as

```
TO PHI :N
 OP L.SIGMA "ONE [] PRIME.TO :N
END
```

Why?

Even if you haven't proved it yet, it seems that PHI is the same function as SIG_{-1}. Suppose we sum a slightly more complicated function over $\mathrm{PRIME.TO}(N)$ (I bet you know what's coming next). Consider, for example, the function F:

```
TO F :N
 OP L.SIGMA "ID [] PRIME.TO N
END
```

In other words, $F(N)$ is the sum of all the integers between 1 and N that are relatively prime to N. Tabulate F and find a simple formula for it. Don't forget, SIG_{-1} is the function currently under consideration.

This last experiment suggests a modification of the ideas in this chapter. Suppose you redefine COMPILE so that the sum in its definition is taken over $\mathrm{PRIME.TO}(N)$ instead of $\mathrm{DIVISORS}(N)$. Is the child of a multiplicative function still multiplicative? Do family trees still make sense? Are there any interesting results? You might want to come back to this idea when you finish working through this chapter.

Experiment 13.23 Consider (with Euler) the following function:

```
TO EU :M :N
 OP MOD (POWER :N (SIG_1 :M)) :M
END
```

Think of M as a constant and EU as a function of N. Keep M at 5, and tabulate EU between 1 and 16. Change M to 12, and repeat the experiment. Try various values for M. What happens?

Let's return to ID's family tree. Since SIG_{-2} is SIG_{-1}'s parent, then, by project 13.17,

$$\text{SIG}_{-2}(P^K) = \begin{cases} 1 & \text{if } K = 0 \\ \text{SIG}_{-1}(P^K) - \text{SIG}_{-1}(P^{(K-1)}) & \text{if } K > 0 \end{cases}$$

If K is 1 in the above formula, $K - 1$ is 0, so we should break up the second case into two cases:

$$\text{SIG}_{-2}(P^K) = \begin{cases} 1 & \text{if } K = 0 \\ \text{SIG}_{-1}(P) - \text{SIG}_{-1}(1) & \text{if } K = 1 \\ \text{SIG}_{-1}(P^K) - \text{SIG}_{-1}(P^{(K-1)}) & \text{if } K > 1 \end{cases}$$

Using the definition of SIG_{-1}, this becomes

$$\text{SIG}_{-2}(P^K) = \begin{cases} 1 & \text{if } K = 0 \\ (P - 1) - 1 & \text{if } K = 1 \\ (P^K - P^{(K-1)}) - (P^{(K-1)} - P^{(K-2)}) & \text{if } K > 1 \end{cases}$$

This simplifies to

$$\text{SIG}_{-2}(P^K) = \begin{cases} 1 & \text{if } K = 0 \\ P - 2 & \text{if } K = 1 \\ P^K - 2P^{(K-1)} + P^{(K-2)} & \text{if } K > 1 \end{cases}$$

It looks like something interesting and familiar is developing.

Experiment 13.24 Build a Logo model for SIG_{-2}. Tabulate it and see if you can find anything interesting in the tabulation. For what numbers N is $\text{SIG}_{-2}(N)$ equal to 0? If N is a perfect square, is $\text{SIG}_{-2}(N)$ a perfect square?

Let's keep going for another level. Since SIG_{-3} is SIG_{-2}'s parent, we have

$$\text{SIG}_{-3}(P^K) = \begin{cases} 1 & \text{if } K = 0 \\ \text{SIG}_{-2}(P^K) - \text{SIG}_{-2}(P^{(K-1)}) & \text{if } K > 0 \end{cases}$$

Looking at the definition of SIG_{-2}, we see that it breaks up into three parts, so we should also break up the second half of the above formula into three parts:

$$\text{SIG}_{-3}(P^K) = \begin{cases} 1 & \text{if } K = 0 \\ \text{SIG}_{-2}(P) - \text{SIG}_{-2}(1) & \text{if } K = 1 \\ \text{SIG}_{-2}(P^2) - \text{SIG}_{-2}(P) & \text{if } K = 2 \\ \text{SIG}_{-2}(P^K) - \text{SIG}_{-2}(P^{(K-1)}) & \text{if } K > 2 \end{cases}$$

Now, use the formulas for SIG_{-2}, and conclude that

$$\text{SIG}_{-3}(P^K) = \begin{cases} 1 & \text{if } K = 0 \\ (P - 2) - 1 & \text{if } K = 1 \\ (P^2 - 2P + 1) - (P - 2) & \text{if } K = 2 \\ (P^K - 2P^{(K-1)} + P^{(K-2)}) \\ \quad - (P^{(K-1)} - 2P^{(K-2)} + P^{(K-3)}) & \text{if } K > 2 \end{cases}$$

Simplifying, this becomes

$$\text{SIG}_{-3}(P^K) = \begin{cases} 1 & \text{if } K = 0 \\ P - 3 & \text{if } K = 1 \\ P^2 - 3P + 3 & \text{if } K = 2 \\ P^K - 3P^{(K-1)} + 3P^{(K-2)}) - P^{(K-3)} & \text{if } K > 2 \end{cases}$$

Model SIG_{-3} in Logo, and see if you can find any theorems about it.

The pattern that is emerging leads me to think that SIG_{-4} will turn out to be defined at prime powers like this:

$$\text{SIG}_{-4}(P^K) = \begin{cases} 1 & \text{if } K = 0 \\ P - 4 & \text{if } K = 1 \\ P^2 - 4P + 6 & \text{if } K = 2 \\ P^3 - 4P^2 + 6P - 4 & \text{if } K = 3 \\ P^K - 4P^{(K-1)} + 6P^{(K-2)} - 4P^{(K-3)} + P^{(K-4)} & \text{if } K > 3 \end{cases}$$

Is this true?

How can we capture this pattern in a simple formula? Right now, we are not looking for proofs; we are simply looking for a concise description of the above pattern. Before reading on, try to find one on your own.

STOP

My attempt to find a simple description of what's going on here developed like this:

First, I was bothered that the pattern took a while to "get going." For example, in SIG_{-4}, the formula you get seems to depend on K. If K is 1, you get $P - 4$, whereas if K is 2, you get $P^2 - 4P + 6$, and so on, until K is greater than 3, when you get the "full" formula

$$P^K - 4P^{(K-1)} + 6P^{(K-2)} - 4P^{(K-3)} + P^{(K-4)}$$

In order to eliminate this need for cases, I decided to look at the output at P^K as a sum of all the powers of P from K down to 0. That is, I looked for a formula of the form:

$$\text{SIG}_L(P^K) = P^K + (?)P^{(K-1)} + (??)P^{(K-2)} + (???)P^{(K-3)}$$
$$+ \cdots + (?????? \ldots ?)P + (???????? \ldots ??)$$

Here L is supposed to be a negative integer. For example, if our pattern really does describe things correctly for negative levels, $\text{SIG}_{-4}(P^6)$ is given by

$$\text{SIG}_{-4}(P^6) = P^6 - 4P^5 + 6P^4 - 4P^3 + P^2$$

and I looked at this as

$$\text{SIG}_{-4}(P^6) = P^6 - 4P^5 + 6P^4 - 4P^3 + P^2 + 0P + 0$$

Of course, the missing coefficients (all the question marks in the above expression) *must* come from Pascal's array; look where the coefficients for $\text{SIG}_{-4}(P^6)$ sit:

Row −5:	1	−5	.	.	.	.	.	.	...
Row −4:	1	−4	10	−20	35	−56	84	−120	165	...
Row −3:	1	−3	6	−10	15	−21	28	−36	45	...
Row −2:	1	−2	3	−4	5	−6	7	−8	9	...
Row −1:	1	−1	1	−1	1	−1	1	−1	1	...
Row 0:	1	0	0	0	0	0	0	0	0	...
Row 1:	1	1	0	0	0	0	0	0	0	...
Row 2:	1	2	1	0	0	0	0	0	0	...

A formula was at hand, but before I tried to fit an expression involving binomial coefficients to this pattern, I returned to the positive side of ID's family tree; I was still intent on finding a single formula that described both the ancestors and descendants.

On the negative side, I got some clarity by looking at the output of SIG at prime powers as an expression like

$$\text{SIG}_L(P^K) = P^K + (?)P^{(K-1)} + (??)P^{(K-2)} + (???)P^{(K-3)}$$
$$+ \cdots + (?????? \ldots ?)P + (???????? \ldots ??)$$

What if I do the same thing for nonnegative levels. Here are some special cases.

Level 0

$$\text{ID}(P^K) = P^K = P^K + 0P^{(K-1)} + 0P^{(K-2)} + 0P^{(K-3)} + \cdots + 0P^0$$

The coefficients are

$$1\,0\,0\,0\,0\ldots0$$

Level 1

$$\text{SIG}(P^K) = \text{ID}(P^K) + \text{ID}(P^{(K-1)}) + \text{ID}(P^{(K-2)}) + \text{ID}(P^{(K-3)}) + \cdots + \text{ID}(P^0)$$
$$= P^K + 1P^{(K-1)} + 1P^{(K-2)} + 1P^{(K-3)} + \cdots + 1P^0$$

The coefficients are

$$1\,1\,1\,1\,1\ldots1$$

(Maybe the trick was not to use the formula for the sum of a geometric series, but to leave this expression as a sum of powers; we'll see.)

Level 2

$$\text{SIG}_2(P^K) = \text{SIG}(P^K) + \text{SIG}(P^{(K-1)}) + \text{SIG}(P^{(K-2)})$$
$$+ \text{SIG}(P^{(K-3)}) + \cdots + \text{SIG}(P^0)$$

$$= P^K + P^{(K-1)} + P^{(K-2)} + P^{(K-3)} + \cdots + P^0 \qquad (\text{SIG}(P^K))$$

$$+ P^{(K-1)} + P^{(K-2)} + P^{(K-3)} + \cdots + P^0 \qquad (\text{SIG}(P^{(K-1)}))$$

$$+ P^{(K-2)} + P^{(K-3)} + \cdots + P^0 \qquad (\text{SIG}(P^{(K-2)}))$$

$$+ P^{(K-3)} + \cdots + P^0 \qquad (\text{SIG}(P^{(K-3)}))$$

$$\vdots$$

$$+ P^0 \qquad (\text{SIG}(P^0))$$

Adding columns, the output of SIG_2 becomes

$$\text{SIG}_2(P^K) = P^K + 2P^{(K-1)} + 3P^{(K-2)} + 4P^{(K-3)} + \cdots + (K+1)P^0$$

and the coefficients are

$$1\ 2\ 3\ 4\ \ldots\ K + 1$$

This is much more promising. Circle the coefficients for $\text{SIG}_L(P^6)$ where L is -2, -1, 0, 1, and 2 on Pascal's array to see what I mean. The search for a unifying formula is leading somewhere.

So, what was complicating things in our first calculation was all the summing of geometric series. We should have let each prime power stand on its own; then we get an expression for SIG's output that seems to be consistent across levels.

All that remains is to express what we have found in terms of binomial coefficients and to encapsulate our calculations in a proof. Before reading on, try to do these things on your own.

The situation at level 3 is worth looking at. By a calculation exactly like the ones we have been doing (keeping the powers of P separate), you can check that

$$\text{SIG}_3(P^K) = P^K + 3P^{(K-1)} + 6P^{(K-2)} + \cdots + \frac{(K+1)(K+2)}{2}P^0$$

$$= P^K + \binom{3}{1}P^{(K-1)} + \binom{4}{2}P^{(K-2)} + \binom{5}{3}P^{(K-3)}$$

$$+ \cdots + \binom{K+2}{K}$$

How can we describe the coefficients? The $\binom{3}{1}$ seems to be the key. Now 3 is the level, and 1 is what you subtract from K to get the current power of P. And notice that this is always true about the second input to the binomial coefficient: it adds together with the exponent of P to give K. So, if the level is L, we have something like this:

$$P^K + \binom{L}{1}P^{(K-1)} + \binom{L+1}{2}P^{(K-2)} + \binom{L+2}{3}P^{(K-3)}$$

$$+ \cdots + \binom{L+?}{K-J}P^J + \cdots + \binom{L+??}{K}$$

The coefficient of P^K can be written as $\binom{L-1}{0}$, so that fits. What about the question marks? Notice that in the terms where we have no question marks, what's added to L is one less than the second input to the binomial coefficient. So perhaps we should have this:

$$\binom{L-1}{0}P^K + \binom{L}{1}P^{(K-1)} + \binom{L+1}{2}P^{(K-2)} + \binom{L+2}{3}P^{(K-3)}$$

$$+ \cdots + \binom{L+K-J-1}{K-J}P^J + \cdots + \binom{L+K-1}{K}$$

The generic term for P^J can be modeled in Logo as

```
TO SIG.TERM :L :P :J
 OP (B (:L + :K - :J - 1) (:K - :J)) * (POWER :P :J)
END
```

and this can be summed as J goes from 0 to K to model the above expression:

```
TO PK.SIG :L :P :K
 OP SIGMA "SIG.TERM SE :L :P 0 :K
END
```

Well, we haven't proved a thing, and most of what we *have* done is to capture a pattern in a formula. Does it work? In other words, is

```
TO HOPEFUL.SIG :L :N
 OP EXTEND "PK.SIG :L :N
END
```

a function that is equal to `SIG` for all levels? It's time to find out.

Project 13.25 You currently have Logo models for `SIG` at all positive levels (just keep `COMPILE`ing `SIG` at one lower level), and you also have a model at levels -1, -2, and -3. Build a few more models at negative levels. For example, SIG_{-4} can be obtained from SIG_{-3} by the formula

$$SIG_{-4}(P^K) = \begin{cases} 1 & \text{if } K = 0 \\ SIG_{-3}(P^K) - SIG_{-3}(P^{(K-1)}) & \text{if } K > 1 \end{cases}$$

and then by `EXTEND`ing this to all of $\mathbf{Z}^+$. When you have a stash of Logo models for `SIG` at various levels, compare them with `HOPEFUL.SIG` using tabulations. Does `SIG_2` tabulate the same as `HOPEFUL.SIG` when the first input to `HOPEFUL.SIG` is kept at 2? Does `SIG_2` tabulate the same as `HOPEFUL.SIG` when the first input to `HOPEFUL.SIG` is kept at -2? Try various other levels. Also `COMPILE HOPEFUL.SIG` at one level and check that you get the same outputs as `HOPEFUL.SIG` produces at the next higher level.

Project 13.26 `HOPEFUL.SIG` is built upon the following formula:

$$PK.SIG(L, P, K) = \binom{L-1}{0}P^K + \binom{L}{1}P^{(K-1)} + \binom{L+1}{2}P^{(K-2)}$$

$$+ \binom{L+2}{3}P^{(K-3)} + \cdots + \binom{L+K-J-1}{K-J}P^J$$

$$+ \cdots + \binom{L+K-1}{K}$$

Describe how to locate these binomial coefficients in Pascal's array. Why, at negative levels, does the formula only contain a few powers of P, whereas at positive levels, it contains all the powers of P from P^K down to 1? At negative level L, how many powers of P show up with nonzero coefficients in the formula? (Hint: The answer for small values of K is different from the answer if $K > |L| - 1$.) In the above formula, P is supposed to be a prime. Suppose, by mistake, you input 1 for P. Give a simple description of the following function:

```
TO F :L :K
 OP PK.SIG :L 1 :K
END
```

Project 13.27 Prove that HOPEFUL.SIG is equal to SIG. That is, prove that for all integers L and for all positive integers N,

$$\text{HOPEFUL.SIG}(L, N) = \text{SIG}_L(N)$$

Hints: Since the functions are multiplicative, it's enough to prove the theorem when N is a prime power, say, P^K. But then, because of the way the functions are defined, it's enough to prove that

$$\text{PK.SIG}(L, P, K) = \text{SIG}_L(P^K)$$

To do this, mimic our proof for ONE's family tree. Essentially, you want to use an inductive argument to show that PK.SIG at one level is the COMPILE of PK.SIG at one lower level. This amounts to giving generic versions of the calculations in this section. Of course, Pascal's identity and our favorite generalization of it,

$$\sum_{J=0}^{M} \binom{H + J}{J} = \binom{H + 1 + M}{M}$$

will play a part in your proof.

Once you have completed the above project, you can change HOPEFUL.SIG's name to SIG.

Experiment 13.28 We saw in project 13.21 that $\text{SIG}_{-1}(N)$ seems to have a connection to the integers less than N that are relatively prime to N. We also know that $\text{SIG}_1(N)$ is the sum of the divisors of N. See if you can find a similar number-theoretic interpretation for some other levels of SIG. You might want to concentrate on one other level, say, -2.

Project 13.29 Discuss the family tree for SQUARE

```
TO SQUARE :N
 OP :N * :N
END
```

Hint: Carefully mimic what we did for SIG. In particular, keep the powers of P separate. Don't worry about formal proofs at this stage; just try to find a formula similar to the one for PK.SIG.

Family Trees for Other Functions

At the beginning of this chapter, I mentioned that ID and ONE are special cases of the function

```
TO EXPONENT :E :N
 OP POWER :N :E
END
```

Similarly, SQUARE in the previous project is EXPONENT with the first input kept at 2. So, imagine the following diagram of functions

$$\vdots$$

$$\cdots \rightarrow NU_2 \rightarrow NU_1 \rightarrow \quad ONE \quad \rightarrow NU_{-1} \rightarrow NU_{-2} \rightarrow NU_{-3} \rightarrow \cdots$$
$$\cdots \rightarrow SIG_2 \rightarrow SIG_1 \rightarrow \quad ID \quad \rightarrow SIG_{-1} \rightarrow SIG_{-2} \rightarrow SIG_{-3} \rightarrow \cdots$$
$$\cdots \rightarrow SQ_2 \rightarrow SQ_1 \rightarrow SQUARE \rightarrow SQ_{-1} \rightarrow SQ_{-2} \rightarrow SQ_{-3} \rightarrow \cdots$$
$$\cdots \rightarrow CU_2 \rightarrow CU_1 \rightarrow CUBE \rightarrow CU_{-1} \rightarrow CU_{-2} \rightarrow CU_{-3} \rightarrow \cdots$$

$$\vdots$$

The rows in our diagram represent the family trees of particular cases of EXPONENT. Let's call the first input to EXPONENT its "height," so that ONE is EXPONENT with height 0, ID is EXPONENT with height 1, SQUARE is EXPONENT with height 2, and CUBE is EXPONENT with height 3. For each height, there is a whole stream of functions corresponding to the levels in the family tree of EXPONENT at that height.

Project 13.30 Write a general function DIAGRAM that captures all of these functions. DIAGRAM takes three inputs: the height of EXPONENT, the level in the family tree, and the actual input to the function. So DIAGRAM$(0, 1, 32)$ is

$NU(32)$, $DIAGRAM(1, -2, 67)$ is $SIG_{-2}(67)$, $DIAGRAM(3, 2, 13)$ is CUBE's grandchild evaluated at 13, and so on.

Hints: Write a function PK.DIAGRAM that takes four inputs: the height, the level, the prime, and the power. To do this, modify the formula for SIG's family tree (keep the powers of P separate).

When you get PK.DIAGRAM, simply EXTEND it to get DIAGRAM:

```
TO DIAGRAM :HEIGHT :LEVEL :N
 OP EXTEND "PK.DIAGRAM SE :HEIGHT :LEVEL :N
END
```

Check that TAB "DIAGRAM [0 -2] 1 10 agrees with the first ten outputs of MU, and try some other heights and levels.

Suppose that we call functions at the same level but different heights of our diagram "cousins." So NU and SIG are cousins, as are MU and SIG_{-2}. Is there a simple formula that gives all the cousins at the same level? #Do cousins have any common number-theoretic description? (For example, level 1 cousins give the sums of the various powers of the divisors of their inputs.) You might want to concentrate on one level, say, -1 or -2.

DIAGRAM gives us a general framework for thinking about some concrete functions. It took quite a bit of work to come up with the central formula that provides this framework:

$$
\begin{aligned}
DIAGRAM(H, L, P^K) = & \binom{L-1}{0} P^{HK} + \binom{L}{1} P^{H(K-1)} + \binom{L+1}{2} P^{H(K-2)} \\
& + \binom{L+2}{3} P^{H(K-3)} + \cdots + \binom{L+K-J-1}{K-J} P^{HJ} \\
& + \cdots + \binom{L+K-1}{K}
\end{aligned}
$$

and there are several important questions about what we have done here. For example, consider these:

1. Did we discover this formula, or did we impose our own structure on our calculations? At the beginning (when we were considering ONE), it seemed as if things we falling together in an almost magical fashion. As the base function became more complicated, it wasn't at all clear that the family

trees had a "natural" structure, and we had to fiddle with our calculations until we found something that fit.

2. DIAGRAM is very pleasing because it is both general and abstract. It is general because it describes many special cases (the actual functions in the diagram) with one formula, and it is abstract because it hides the differences among these many functions and stresses their similarities. Is DIAGRAM a simple description of these functions? Look at the above formula. We know where it comes from, and we can appreciate its power, but suppose you were new to this discussion. Would the formula be especially appealing? Would it be a simple description of all these functions? Is it as simple as you can get without sacrificing generality?

3. Do you really want to hide the differences among these functions? There are some extremely useful functions in this diagram. Especially important are NU, SIG, E, MU, and what we have called SIG_{-1}. When you want to think about, say, SIG, DIAGRAM tells you to start with

$$SIG(P^K) = P^K + P^{(K-1)} + P^{(K-2)} + P^{(K-3)} + \cdots + 1$$

Wouldn't it be easier to think of

$$SIG(P^K) = \frac{P^{(K+1)} - 1}{P - 1}$$

Or, is the DIAGRAM method for thinking about SIG important because it makes the relation between SIG and SIG_2 clear, and perhaps this connection can be used to transport some of SIG's properties (say, obtained by looking at SIG in the "traditional" way) to SIG_2?

4. Can you have too much generality? Remember our wonderful formula for ONE's family tree? It was based upon PKNU:

```
TO PKNU :LEVEL :P :K
  OP B :LEVEL + :K :K
END
```

DIAGRAM outlines a much more complicated formula for this calculation (it keeps the "powers of P" separate, even though all these powers are P^0), and so it hides a delightful identity that was in fact the very thing that motivated us to look for family trees at heights larger than 0.

Once again, is the fact that DIAGRAM stresses the similarities among trees at various heights (at the expense of hiding an interesting fact about a particular height) the reason that DIAGRAM is important?

In the end, questions like these are usually answered on utilitarian grounds. DIAGRAM is important if you can use it to discover new facts about the functions in the actual diagram. It is important if it helps you find new insights about old functions or if it helps you discover (invent?) new and interesting functions. Of course, you can't tell in advance if a construction like DIAGRAM will prove useful. That's why so much mathematics is developed by simply looking for similarities among seemingly unrelated ideas.

Experiment 13.31 What does DIAGRAM do if you give it a negative height? Experiment with this phenomenon. Describe in words the function

```
TO F :N
 OP DIAGRAM -1 1 :N
END
```

Project 13.32 Return to ID's family tree. Look at the following baroque collection of functions:

```
TO CRAZY :M :D :X :J
OP (POWER -1 :J) * ( FACT :M ) * ( B :D :M ) →
     * ( B :M - 1 :J ) * (POWER :X :D - :J) / (:D - :J)
END

TO I :M :D :X
 OP ((SIGMA "CRAZY (SE :M :D :X) 0 (:M - 1)) →
     + (POWER -1 :M) * (FACT :M - 1) ) / (POWER (:X - 1) :M)
END

TO PK.CRAZYSIG :L :P :K
 OP ((POWER :P :K) * ( I :L :K + :L - 1 (1 / :P)) →
     / FACT (:L - 1) ) + ( B :L + :K - 1 :K )
END
```

```
TO CRAZY.SIG :L :N
 OP EXTEND "PK.CRAZYSIG :L :N
END
```

Does CRAZY.SIG agree with SIG at any levels? Can you prove it? Is CRAZY.SIG a "simple" model for SIG in any sense? Can CRAZY.SIG be modified to give a model for SIG at all levels?

Chapter 14

Modular Arithmetic

The topics from number theory that we have so far considered all depend explicitly on the fundamental theorem of arithmetic. For example, our treatment of multiplicative functions would have been impossible if we hadn't known that such functions could be defined on prime powers and then extended uniquely by multiplicativity.

In this chapter, the fundamental theorem won't play such a central role (although we will have to use it from time to time). Instead, we'll use some basic ideas about arithmetic in **Z** (like theorem 10.1) and our results about greatest common divisor and least common multiple. Accordingly, the topics we discuss will be concerned with questions of divisibility, so they will have a slightly different flavor. Some of our discussion will be about questions that you may have already seen ("when is a number divisible by 11?"), while others will probably be new. Our major tool will be the idea of congruence.

The notion of *congruence* for integers (it doesn't mean the same thing as geometric congruence) is extremely simple, but it wasn't formalized until Gauss gave the definition in *Disquisitiones Arithmeticae*. Many times in number theory, the situation at hand becomes easier to understand if you neglect all multiples of a given integer (most often, the neglected integer is a prime or a power of a prime), and congruence gives a precise way to do this.

In Logo's geometry certain inputs to RT produce the same effect on the turtle's heading. For example, all of the following commands are equivalent to each other:

RT 32, RT 392, RT 752, and RT -328

It's easy to come up with other inputs that produce the same results. Try to find a few.

We say that 752 and −328 are "congruent modulo 360." In fact, the numbers 32, 392, 752, and −328 are all congruent modulo 360.

This is just new vocabulary for a simple idea. If you ask a turtle geometer (even a very young one) to describe the relationship between two numbers that cause RT to produce the same effect, you'll probably hear something like

> *Two inputs to RT produce the same effect on the turtle's heading if they differ by 360*

So, for example, RT 43 will have the same effect on the turtle's heading as RT 403 because 403 is just $43 + 360$, so a right turn of 403 can be thought of as a pair of right turns, one of magnitude 43 and the other of magnitude 360. Since a right turn of 360 has no effect on the turtle's heading, RT 403 is the same as RT 43.

In fact, since a right turn of any multiple of 360 (for example, -720 or 1080) has no effect on the turtle's heading, more is true:

> *Two inputs to RT produce the same effect on the turtle's heading if they differ by a multiple of 360*

This "differing by a multiple of" is precisely the condition that defines congruence:

> *Two numbers are congruent modulo 360 if they differ by a multiple of 360*

Look, for example, at the numbers we considered above, and their respective differences:

$-$	32	392	752	-328
32	0	-360	720	360
392	360	0	-360	720
752	720	360	0	1080
-328	-360	-720	-1080	0

Every difference is a multiple of 360. Notice that I can pick any of the numbers, say, 392, and I can represent each of the other numbers in the form $392 + 360K$ for some integer K. For example, $32 = 392 + 360 \cdot (-1)$, and $-328 = 392 + 360 \cdot (-2)$. If you start with 392 and calculate $392 + 360K$ where K is allowed to be any integer, you get the stream of integers

$$\ldots, 392 + 360 \cdot (-4), \ 392 + 360 \cdot (-3), \ 392 + 360 \cdot (-2),$$
$$392 + 360 \cdot (-1), \ 392 + 360 \cdot 0, \ 392 + 360 \cdot 1,$$
$$392 + 360 \cdot 2, \ 392 + 360 \cdot 3, \ 392 + 360 \cdot 4, \ \ldots$$

or

$$\ldots, \; -688, \; -328, \; 32, \; 392, \; 752, \; 1112, \; 1472, \; 1832, \; \ldots$$

This is like an arithmetic sequence with common difference 360, except that there is no first term. This stream of integers has two properties:

1. Any two numbers in the stream are congruent modulo 360.

2. If a number A is congruent modulo 360 to one of the numbers in the stream, then A itself must be in the stream.

The second property isn't completely obvious, but here's a short proof: Suppose that A is an integer that is congruent modulo 360 to one of the numbers, say 1112, in the stream. This means that A and 1112 differ by a multiple of 360, so there is an integer J such that

$$A - 1112 = 360J$$

But then we could calculate like this:

$$A = 1112 + 360J = (392 + 360 \cdot 2) + 360J = 392 + 360(2 + J)$$
$$= 392 + 360 \cdot (something)$$

So A is 392 plus a multiple of 360, and this is precisely what it means for A to be in the stream.

A stream of integers like the one above is called a "congruence class" modulo 360. A congruence class modulo 360 contains precisely all the integers that are congruent to each other modulo 360. There are, of course, other congruence classes modulo 360. Write down a few numbers that are in the same class as 25. How many congruence classes modulo 360 are there? Is every integer in one of these? Is there an integer that is in more than one of them? Write down a few integers in the congruence class modulo 360 that contains 0.

Of course, there is nothing special about 360. Suppose that, instead of dividing a complete rotation into 360 degrees, we decided that a complete rotation consisted of five bigger units, say "begrees." Then a begree would be 72 degrees, and we could redefine RT so that a right turn of 5 would be a complete rotation:

```
TO NEW.RT :N
 RT 72 * :N
END
```

Then the following commands would have the same effect on the turtle:

NEW.RT 3, NEW.RT 8, NEW.RT 18

NEW.RT −2, NEW.RT 253, and NEW.RT −17

We say that 3 and 18 are "congruent modulo 5." In fact, the numbers 3, 8, 18, −2, 253, and −17 are all congruent modulo 5.

See if you can find four other integers that are congruent modulo 5 to the above integers. Can you list seven numbers that are each congruent modulo 5 to 13?

If this is the first time you are seeing the notion of congruence, you may as yet be unimpressed. The point of this section and the next is to convince you that this idea can be extremely useful in number theory. Be patient.

Just some notation and terminology: If A and B are congruent modulo M (that is, if A and B differ by a multiple of M), it is customary to write

$$A \equiv B \text{ (MODULO } M)$$

For example, $253 \equiv -2$ (MODULO 5) and $42 \equiv 0$ (MODULO 6). The number M is called the "modulus," and it is always taken as a positive integer. Remember in chapter 10 we used the word "modulo" when we constructed the function MOD, and I mentioned then that a common usage of the word is to express the idea "except for." The current contex is consistent with that usage. In fact one way to think of statement $253 \equiv -2$ (MODULO 5) is

253 and −2 are equal except for a multiple of 5

More precisely, 253 and −2 are equal except for 255, which is $5 \cdot 51$.

Think of a measuring stick exactly 5 units long. Then, on a number line, you could place one end of the stick at −2 and keep marking off "stick lengths" 255 times, and you'd end up exactly at 253. 253 and −2 are equal "in the measure" 5.

So, whenever you see the phrase "congruent modulo," you can think of the phrase "equal except for a multiple of."

Experiment 14.1 Build a Logo predicate CONGRUENT.MODULO? that takes three inputs M, A, and B. CONGRUENT.MODULO? outputs TRUE if A and B are congruent modulo M, and FALSE otherwise. (If, and only if, you want a hint, look at the next theorem, but you should be able to do this using the functions that we already have.)

We haven't yet written down a formal definition of what it means for two integers to be congruent modulo a third, so here it is.

Definition 14.1 If M is a positive integer, we say that two integers A and B are congruent modulo M if $M \mid (B - A)$ (or, if $B - A$ is a multiple of M). That is, A and B are congruent modulo M if you can find an integer K so that

$$B - A = KM$$

The above definition simply formalizes the ideas that we used in the above examples, but formal definitions allow people to make sure that they are talking about the same thing. For example, the next theorem models the congruence idea in several different ways, and you can use the above definition to see that these different models are equivalent.

Theorem 14.2 The following predicates are equal, and they each output TRUE precisely when the last two inputs are congruent modulo the first:

```
TO X.CONGRUENT.MODULO? :MODULUS :A :B
 OP DIVIS? (:B - :A) :MODULUS
END

TO Y.CONGRUENT.MODULO? :MODULUS :A :B
 OP (MOD (:B - :A) :MODULUS) = 0
END

TO Z.CONGRUENT.MODULO? :MODULUS :A :B
 OP (MOD :A :MODULUS) = (MOD :B :MODULUS)
END
```

Project 14.2 Prove theorem 14.2.

Hints:

1. Look first at X.CONGRUENT.MODULO?. If A and B are congruent modulo M (in the sense of definition 14.1), then

$$M \mid (B - A)$$

This is exactly what it means for DIVIS?$(B - A, M)$ to output TRUE. So X.CONGRUENT.MODULO? faithfully models the mathematical notion of congruence. Hence it's enough to show that the three Logo predicates are equal.

2. To see that X.CONGRUENT.MODULO? is equal to Y.CONGRUENT.MODULO?, recall the definition of DIVIS?:

```
TO DIVIS? :N :K
 OP MOD :N :K = 0
END
```

3. Finally (this is the hard part), show that Z.CONGRUENT.MODULO? is equal to Y.CONGRUENT.MODULO?.

Think of MOD(A, M) as the nonnegative remainder when A is divided by M (you might want to look over the part of chapter 10 where we defined MOD and QUOT). Then saying that Z.CONGRUENT.MODULO? is equal to Y.CONGRUENT.MODULO? amounts to saying

A and B have the same remainder when they are divided by
M precisely when B − A has remainder 0 when divided by M

This sentence says two things:

Thing 1. If A and B have the same remainder when they are divided by M, then $B - A$ has remainder 0 when it is divided by M.

Thing 2. If $B - A$ has remainder 0 when it is divided by M, then A and B have the same remainder when they are each divided by M.

If you think about this long enough, it makes perfect sense. Look at two examples.

Example 1 (*How thing 1 might be proved in a special case*) Suppose that $M = 6$, and A and B are two integers that have the same remainder, say, 5, when divided by 6. We want to show that $B - A$ is divisible by 6 (if you like, think of A as 11 and B as 53). Now, $\mathtt{MOD}(A, 6) = 5$ and $\mathtt{MOD}(B, 6) = 5$. This really means that

$$A = 6Q + 5 \quad \text{and} \quad B = 6Q' + 5$$

for some integers Q and Q'. (If you are thinking of $A = 11$ and $B = 53$, then Q is 1 and Q' is 8, so that $B = 6 \cdot 8 + 5$ and $A = 6 \cdot 1 + 5$.)

Subtract these two equations, and find that

$$B - A = (6Q' + 5) - (6Q + 5)$$

This can be written as

$$B - A = (6Q' - 6Q) + (5 - 5)$$

or

$$B - A = 6Q' - 6Q = 6(Q' - Q) = 6 \cdot (something)$$

so $B - A$ is divisible by 6.

Example 2 (*How thing 2 might be proved in a special case*) Suppose that B and A are integers so that $B - A$ has remainder 0 when divided by 6 (in other words, so that $\mathtt{Y.CONGRUENT.MODULO?}(B, A)$ outputs $\mathtt{TRUE}$). Then $B - A$ is divisible by 6 so that $B - A = 6K$ for some integer K. This means that $B = 6K + A$. Now, suppose that $\mathtt{QUOT}(A, 6)$ is Q and $\mathtt{MOD}(A, 6)$ is R. Then Q and R are the unique integers with the properties that

$$A = 6Q + R$$
$$0 \le R < 6$$

(see project 10.5). Since $A = 6Q + R$ and $B = 6K + A$, we have

$$B = 6K + 6Q + R = 6(K + Q) + R$$

Now, apply the result of project 10.5 to B (if you didn't do project 10.5 yet, just assume its result for now and work on it after this project). Since

$$B = 6(K + Q) + R$$

and

$$0 \leq R < 6$$

it must be true that $K + Q$ is QUOT($B, 6$) and, more importantly, that R is MOD($B, 6$). This means that MOD($B, 6$) equals MOD($A, 6$).

Now use these two examples as templates for the general proof. Simply replace 6 by M, and fill in the details.

The last predicate in theorem 14.2 is the one that I find most useful, so for now let's adopt it as our official test for congruence:

```
TO CONGRUENT.MODULO? :MODULUS :A :B
 OP (MOD :A :MODULUS) = (MOD :B :MODULUS)
END
```

Check it out. Try, for example,

```
SHOW CONGRUENT.MODULO? 8 12 3
```

```
SHOW CONGRUENT.MODULO? 8 12 4
```

or

```
SHOW CONGRUENT.MODULO? 8 17 (17 + 8 * 1988)
```

One reason that I like this way of thinking about congruence is that this predicate makes it clear that there are only a finite number of congruence classes for a given modulus. Let me explain with an example.

Suppose that we take 8 as the modulus. According to the definition of congruence, if we want to see if two integers are congruent modulo 8, we should subtract them and see if their difference is divisible by 8. So, 651 is congruent modulo 8 to 899 because $651 - 899$ is -248, which is divisible by 8. In practice, this is the way most people do it. Our official predicate CONGRUENT.MODULO? outlines a slightly different process (which leads, by theorem 14.2, to the same result): To decide if two integers are congruent modulo 8, we divide each by 8 and take the remainder. If the remainders are equal, the numbers are congruent modulo 8, and if the remainders are not equal, the numbers are not congruent modulo 8. Since 899 and 651 both leave a remainder (or a "residue") of 3 when they are divided by 8, 899 is congruent modulo 8 to 651. In fact, CONGRUENT.MODULO? shows that any number that leaves a remainder of 3 when divided by 8 is congruent modulo 8 to any *other* number that leaves a remainder of 3 when divided by 8. Similarly, the numbers that are congruent modulo 8 to 77 can be described as the numbers that leave a remainder of 5 when divided by 8. In other words, there is one "congruence class modulo 8" of integers for each possible remainder that can show up when you divide by 8. But there are precisely eight such remainders

$$0, 1, 2, 3, 4, 5, 6, \text{ and } 7$$

because, when you divide by 8, the remainder must be strictly less than 8.

Look at some integers in each congruence class:

The congruence class containing 0:

$$\ldots, -24, -16, -8, 0, 8, 16, 24, 32, 40, 48, 56, \ldots$$

The congruence class containing 1:

$$\ldots, -23, -15, -7, 1, 9, 17, 25, 33, 41, 49, 57, \ldots$$

The congruence class containing 2:

$$\ldots, 22, -14, -6, 2, 10, 18, 26, 34, 42, 50, 58, \ldots$$

The congruence class containing 3:

$$\ldots, -21, -13, -5, 3, 11, 19, 27, 35, 43, 51, 59, \ldots$$

The congruence class containing 4:

$$\ldots, -20, -12, -4, 4, 12, 20, 28, 36, 44, 52, 60, \ldots$$

The congruence class containing 5:

$$\ldots, -19, -11, -3, 5, 13, 21, 29, 37, 45, 53, 61, \ldots$$

The congruence class containing 6:

$$\ldots, -18, -10, -2, 6, 14, 22, 30, 38, 46, 54, 62, \ldots$$

The congruence class containing 7:

$$\ldots, \ -19, \ -11, \ -1, \ 7, \ 15, \ 23, \ 31, \ 39, \ 47, \ 55, \ 63, \ \ldots$$

These 8 congruence classes are disjoint (no integer is in two of them), and their union is all of **Z** (every integer is in one of them).

Notice that, for example, the congruence class modulo 8 determined by 5 is the set of all integers of the form $8Q+5$, where Q is allowed to be any integer. This simple observation can be used to prove many facts about congruence. For example, if you square each of the numbers in the congruence class modulo 8 that contains 7, the squares seem to all be in the class that contains 1. So we have a conjecture:

> If a number is in the congruence class modulo 8 determined by 7, then its square is in the congruence class modulo 8 determined by 1

Put another way, it says:

> If a number is congruent modulo 8 to 7, then its square is congruent modulo 8 to 1

The proof amounts to showing:

> If a number is of the form $8Q+7$ for some integer Q, then its square is of the form $8Q'+1$ for some integer Q'

That's not hard at all:

$$\begin{aligned}
(8Q+7)^2 &= 64Q^2 + 112Q + 49 \\
&= 64Q^2 + 112Q + 48 + 1 \\
&= 8(8Q^2 + 14Q + 6) + 1 \\
&= 8 \cdot (something) + 1
\end{aligned}$$

In general, if M is any positive integer, there are M distinct congruence classes modulo M, each one containing exactly one of the integers between 0 and $M-1$ (these are the possible remainders that you can get when you divide by M). The congruence classes can be described as follows:

The congruence class containing 0 is the set of all integers of the form $MQ + 0$, where Q is allowed to be any integer (this class contains all the multiples of M).

The congruence class containing 1 is the set of all integers of the form $MQ + 1$, where Q is allowed to be any integer.

The congruence class containing 2 is the set of all integers of the form $MQ + 2$, where Q is allowed to be any integer.

The congruence class containing 3 is the set of all integers of the form $MQ + 3$, where Q is allowed to be any integer.

$\vdots$

The congruence class containing $M - 1$ is the set of all integers of the form $MQ + M - 1$, where Q is allowed to be any integer.

These M congruence classes are disjoint (no integer is in two of them), and their union is all of **Z** (every integer is in one of them).

Arithmetic with Congruences

Our `CONGRUENT.MODULO?` predicate makes the following shorthand for our notation very suggestive:

Instead of writing $17 \equiv 32$ (MODULO 5), we'll write $17 \equiv 32$ (MOD 5)

After all, our `CONGRUENT.MODULO?` predicate says that 17 and 32 are congruent modulo 5 precisely if $\text{MOD}(17, 5) = \text{MOD}(32, 5)$.

Exercise 14.3 True or false? Look for theorems.

1. $12 \equiv 2$ (MOD 10)

2. $12 \equiv 2$ (MOD 5)

3. $12 \equiv 2$ (MOD 2)

4. $12 \equiv 2 \;(\mathrm{MOD}\;4)$

5. $123 \equiv 0 \;(\mathrm{MOD}\;123)$

6. If N is a positive integer, $N \equiv 0 \;(\mathrm{MOD}\;N)$

7. If N is a positive integer, $N \equiv -N \;(\mathrm{MOD}\;N)$

8. If N is a positive integer, $4N \equiv N \;(\mathrm{MOD}\;N)$

9. If N is a positive integer, $4N \equiv N \;(\mathrm{MOD}\;3)$

10. $743 \equiv 7 + 4 + 3 \;(\mathrm{MOD}\;9)$

11. $743 \equiv 7 - 4 + 3 \;(\mathrm{MOD}\;11)$

12. $5623 \equiv 5 + 6 + 2 + 3 \;(\mathrm{MOD}\;9)$

13. $5623 \equiv 5 - 6 + 2 - 3 \;(\mathrm{MOD}\;11)$

14. $5^7 \equiv 5 \;(\mathrm{MOD}\;7)$

15. $4^7 \equiv 4 \;(\mathrm{MOD}\;7)$

16. $3^7 \equiv 3 \;(\mathrm{MOD}\;7)$

17. $2^6 \equiv 2 \;(\mathrm{MOD}\;6)$

18. If K is an integer between 1 and 6, $B(7, K) \equiv 0 \;(\mathrm{MOD}\;7)$

19. If K is an integer between 1 and 10, $B(11, K) \equiv 0 \;(\mathrm{MOD}\;11)$

20. If K is an integer between 1 and 7, $B(8, K) \equiv 0 \;(\mathrm{MOD}\;8)$

21. $6! \equiv -1 \;(\mathrm{MOD}\;7)$

22. $4! \equiv -1 \;(\mathrm{MOD}\;5)$

23. $8! \equiv -1 \;(\mathrm{MOD}\;9)$

Exercise 14.4

1. Prove that if A is congruent modulo 8 to 5, then A^2 is congruent modulo 8 to 1.

2. Prove that if A is congruent modulo 8 to 5, then A^3 is also congruent modulo 8 to 5.

3. Prove that if A is in the congruence class modulo 8 determined by 6, then $3A$ is in the congruence class modulo 8 determined by 2.

4. Every integer is in one of eight congruence classes modulo 8. These classes are determined by the remainders 0, 1, 2, 3, 4, 5, 6 and 7 (let's call these integers the "labels" for the eight classes). For each of these classes, describe the class that contains the squares of the integers in the class. For example, if A is in the class determined by 5, A^2 is in the class determined by 1. Write a Logo function S that takes the label for a class and outputs the label for the class that contains the squares from the input class.

Project 14.5 Use the definition of congruence or our CONGRUENT.MODULO? predicate to explain why the following statements are true:

1. Any multiple of M is congruent modulo M to 0. That is, if $A = M \cdot (something)$, then $A \equiv 0 \ (\text{MOD } M)$.

2. If A and B are integers so that $A = B + MK$, then $A \equiv B \ (\text{MOD } M)$.

3. If A is an integer, $A + M \equiv A \ (\text{MOD } M)$.

4. If $X \equiv Y \ (\text{MOD } M)$ and X and Y are between 0 and $M - 1$, then $X = Y$.

5. If A is an integer, $A \equiv \text{MOD}(A, M) \ (\text{MOD } M)$.

Hints: To prove 1–3, use definition 14.1. To prove 4, explain why it is impossible for two different integers between 0 and $M - 1$ to differ by a multiple of M (try it with, say, $M = 10$). To prove 5, either use definition 14.1 and the fact that

if R is $\text{MOD}(A, M)$, then $A = QM + R$ for some integer Q,

or use CONGRUENT.MODULO? and the fact that

$$\text{MOD}(\text{MOD}(A, M), M) = \text{MOD}(A, M)$$

Project 14.6 Suppose that M is a fixed positive integer. Prove the following theorems:

1. If $A \equiv B \ (\text{MOD } M)$ and $C \equiv D \ (\text{MOD } M)$, then $A + C \equiv B + D \ (\text{MOD } M)$.

2. If $A \equiv B \ (\text{MOD } M)$ and $C \equiv D \ (\text{MOD } M)$, then $AC \equiv BD \ (\text{MOD } M)$.

3. If $A \equiv B \,(\text{MOD } M)$ and $B \equiv C \,(\text{MOD } M)$, then $A \equiv C \,(\text{MOD } M)$.

4. If $A \equiv B \,(\text{MOD } M)$ and N is a positive divisor of M, then $A \equiv B \,(\text{MOD } N)$.

Hint: Use definition 14.1 when you think about congruence. For example, look at the first theorem. You are given that $M \mid (B - A)$ and that $M \mid (D - C)$. Then you can find integers K and J so that

$$B - A = MK \text{ and } D - C = MJ$$

Add these two equations and conclude that

$$(B + D) - (A + C) = M(something), \text{ so that}$$
$$A + C \equiv B + D \,(\text{MOD } M)$$

The other statements are proved similarly, but the proof of the second fact might give you some trouble. Here again, you know that

$$B - A = MK \quad \text{and} \quad D - C = MJ$$

for some integers K and J. This time, you want to show that

$$BD - AC = M \cdot (something)$$

To find the value of "*something*" (in terms of A, B, C, D, K, and J), work out some examples. For example, suppose that M is 7. In the following table, A and B are congruent modulo 7, C and D are congruent modulo 7, and you can check that AC and BD are congruent modulo 7.

A	B	K	C	D	J	AC	BD	"*something*"
3	10	1	5	12	1	15	120	15
4	11	1	2	9	1	8	99	13
−3	4		5	12				
10	17		6	13				
17	10		13	6				
11	4		2	9				
4	18		2	16				
5	19	2	6	27	3	30	513	69

The properties that you proved in the previous project can be used to solve problems in arithmetic like this:

> Show that if A has remainder 5 when divided by 6 and B has remainder 3 when divided by 6, then $A + B$ has remainder 2 when divided by 6 and AB has remainder 3 when divided by 6.

You could probably figure this out without any knowledge of congruence, but I just want to show you how to use congruence in this very simple situation before we move on to more complicated things. Make sure that the result is true in some special cases; for example, try $A = 11$ and $B = 15$, or even $A = 17$ and $B = -3$.

Now, for the proof, we know that $A \equiv 5$ (MOD 6) and $B \equiv 3$ (MOD 6). So, by part 1 of project 14.6, $A + B \equiv 8$ (MOD 6). But $8 \equiv 2$ (MOD 6), so by part 3 of the same project, $A + B \equiv 2$ (MOD 6). By part 5 of project 14.5, $A + B$ is also congruent modulo 6 to $\text{MOD}(A + B, 6)$. It follows (again by part 5 of project 14.5) that $2 \equiv \text{MOD}(A + B, 6)$ (MOD 6). But $\text{MOD}(A + B, 6)$ is between 0 and 5, and so is 2. So, by part 4 of project 14.5, $\text{MOD}(A + B, 6) = 2$. In other words, if $A + B$ is divided by 6, the remainder is 2.

No one goes through all these gymnastics to prove such things. A more typical argument leaves out most of the details; for example, to prove the second part of the statement, we might argue like this:

> Since $A \equiv 5$ (MOD 6) and $B \equiv 3$ (MOD 6), then $AB \equiv 15 \equiv 3$ (MOD 6). So the remainder when AB is divided by 6 is 3.

It is just understood that if a number is congruent modulo M to R, and R is between 0 and $M - 1$, then R is the remainder when the number is divided by M. Furthermore, "reducing modulo M" is usually done in the midst of arithmetic calculations. For example, suppose you wanted the remainder when $123 \cdot 326 \cdot 3 + 1009 \cdot 41$ is divided by 7. One way, of course, is to do the calculation, and to then reduce the answer MOD 7:

$$123 \cdot 326 \cdot 13 + 1009 \cdot 41 = 562643$$

and

$$\text{MOD}(562643, 7) = 4$$

so the remainder is 4.

Another way is "reduce mod 7" whenever the numbers get bigger than 6; in other words, we can calculate like this:

$$123 \cdot 326 \cdot 13 + 1009 \cdot 41 \equiv 4 \cdot 4 \cdot 6 + 16 \equiv 5 + 6 \equiv 4 \text{ (MOD 7)}$$

Here I replaced 123 by 4 (123 is congruent modulo 7 to 4), 326 by 4 ($326 \equiv 4$ (MOD 7)), 13 by 6 ($13 \equiv 6$ (MOD 7)), 1009 by 1, and 41 by 6. Then I multiplied $4 \cdot 4 \cdot 6$ to get 96, which is congruent modulo 7 to 5, and added 5 to 6 to get 11, which can finally be replaced by 4 (because $11 \equiv 4$ (MOD 7)). Try it with a few examples.

Exercise 14.7

1. Find the remainder when $123 \cdot 452 + 201 \cdot 3998$ is divided by 7. What is the remainder if this same number is divided by 2? By 4?

2. Find the remainder when $127 \cdot 31 + 4228$ is divided by 14. By 7. By 6. By 31.

3. What is the remainder when 1425 is divided by 10? When 3,567,198 is divided by 10? When 100,007 is divided by 10? What is the units digit of

$$431 \cdot 2373 + 1032 \cdot 2989 \cdot 47$$

Project 14.8 Show that if M is a positive integer and A and B are integers that are congruent modulo M, then $\text{GCD}(A, M) = \text{GCD}(B, M)$. Hint: Apply theorem 3.2.2 to A and M and to B and M.

Project 14.9 Suppose that M is a positive integer and that A is any integer. Show that no two of the integers

$$A, A + 1, A + 2, A + 3, \ldots, A + M - 1$$

are congruent modulo M (this is sometimes expressed by saying, "Any M consecutive integers are incongruent modulo M.")

Hint: Suppose that $A + J$ were congruent modulo M to $A + K$ where K and J are between 0 and $M - 1$. That is, suppose that

$$A + J \equiv A + K (MOD\ M)$$

Then "subtract A from both sides" of the congruence to conclude that

$$J \equiv K(MOD\ M)$$

Now use part 4 of exercise 14.5.

Explain why, since the numbers

$$A, A+1, A+2, A+3, \ldots, A+M-1$$

are not congruent modulo M, that these numbers must be congruent modulo M to

$$0, 1, 2, 3, \ldots, M-1$$

in some order.

The method of constantly reducing modulo M in a calculation is often useful in modular arithmetic. For example, suppose that you wanted the remainder when 5^8 is divided by 7. Rather than calculating 5^8 and reducing modulo 7, you could reduce mod 7 at each stage of the recursive process that defines exponentiation:

$$5^1 = 5 \equiv 5\ (\text{MOD } 7)$$

$$5^2 = 5 \cdot 5 = 25 \equiv 4\ (\text{MOD } 7)$$

$$5^3 = 5 \cdot 5^2 \equiv 5 \cdot 4 = 20 \equiv 6\ (\text{MOD } 7)$$

$$5^4 = 5 \cdot 5^3 \equiv 5 \cdot 6 = 30 \equiv 2\ (\text{MOD } 7)$$

$$5^5 = 5 \cdot 5^4 \equiv 5 \cdot 2 = 10 \equiv 3\ (\text{MOD } 7)$$

$$5^6 = 5 \cdot 5^5 \equiv 5 \cdot 3 = 15 \equiv 1\ (\text{MOD } 7)$$

$$5^7 = 5 \cdot 5^6 \equiv 5 \cdot 1 = 5 \equiv 5\ (\text{MOD } 7)$$

$$5^8 = 5 \cdot 5^7 \equiv 5 \cdot 5 = 25 \equiv 4\ (\text{MOD } 7)$$

So $5^8 \equiv 4$ (MOD 7), and we never had to use numbers bigger than 30 in our calculations. (Notice that we could have taken shortcuts. For example, since $5^4 \equiv 2$ (MOD 7), we could have reasoned like this:

$$5^8 = (5^4)^2 \equiv 2^2 \equiv 4\ (\text{MOD } 7))$$

We can model the above method for modular exponentiation in Logo. Of course, one way to calculate the remainder when N^E is divided by M is to use brute force:

```
TO BRUTE.FORCE.POWERMOD :N :E :M
 OP MOD (POWER :N :E) :M
END
```

This will work fine for small numbers, but if N or E is large enough, POWER will round off its output. A more delicate process (modeled after the above calculation of 5^8 modulo 7) is reminiscent of our original POWER function. Recall that POWER was defined like this:

```
TO POWER :N :E
 IF :E = 0 [OP 1]
 OP :N * POWER :N (:E - 1)
END
```

POWERMOD is built along these lines, but it reduces the output at every stage of the recursive process:

```
TO POWERMOD :N :E :M
 IF :E = 0 [OP 1]
 OP MOD (:N * POWERMOD :N (:E - 1)) :M
END
```

Project 14.10 POWERMOD can be very slow to execute. Write a function FPOWERMOD that is equal to POWERMOD, but that uses the shortcut that we employed above when we calculated 5^8 as $(5^4)^2$.

Hints: Write a function SQUAREMOD that takes two inputs N and M and outputs $MOD(N^2, M)$. Then, in FPOWERMOD, if E isn't 0, test to see if it is even. If it is, apply SQUAREMOD to the inputs N, $E/2$, and M. If it isn't, proceed as in POWERMOD.

Experiment 14.11 Consider the calculation outlined in POWERMOD. What happens to 3 at the various levels in the calculation of POWERMOD$(3, 10, 7)$? Since no numbers are ever bigger than 6, 3 must take on values between 0 and 6. Does it take on all of them? Does it take on some more than others? Let's see:

$\texttt{POWERMOD}(3,0) = 1$

$\texttt{POWERMOD}(3,1) = \texttt{MOD}(3 \cdot \texttt{POWERMOD}(3,0),7) = \texttt{MOD}(3,7) = 3$

$\texttt{POWERMOD}(3,2) = \texttt{MOD}(3 \cdot \texttt{POWERMOD}(3,1),7) = \texttt{MOD}(9,7) = 2$

$\texttt{POWERMOD}(3,3) = \texttt{MOD}(3 \cdot \texttt{POWERMOD}(3,2),7) = \texttt{MOD}(6,7) = 6$

$\texttt{POWERMOD}(3,4) = \texttt{MOD}(3 \cdot \texttt{POWERMOD}(3,3),7) = \texttt{MOD}(18,7) = 4$

$\texttt{POWERMOD}(3,5) = \texttt{MOD}(3 \cdot \texttt{POWERMOD}(3,4),7) = \texttt{MOD}(12,7) = 5$

$\texttt{POWERMOD}(3,6) = \texttt{MOD}(3 \cdot \texttt{POWERMOD}(3,5),7) = \texttt{MOD}(15,7) = 1$

$\texttt{POWERMOD}(3,7) = \texttt{MOD}(3 \cdot \texttt{POWERMOD}(3,6),7) = \texttt{MOD}(3,7) = 3$

$\texttt{POWERMOD}(3,8) = \texttt{MOD}(3 \cdot \texttt{POWERMOD}(3,7),7) = \texttt{MOD}(9,7) = 2$

$\texttt{POWERMOD}(3,9) = \texttt{MOD}(3 \cdot \texttt{POWERMOD}(3,8),7) = \texttt{MOD}(6,7) = 6$

$\texttt{POWERMOD}(3,10) = \texttt{MOD}(3 \cdot \texttt{POWERMOD}(3,9),7) = \texttt{MOD}(18,7) = 4$

There's plenty to think about here. The remainders when the powers of 3 are divided by 7 are 1, 3, 2, 6, 4, 5, 1, and then the whole pattern repeats. Why will the sequence of powers repeat once some power is 1? So, $3^6 \equiv 1 \ (\text{MOD } 7)$. That means that $3^{24} = (3^6)^4 \equiv (1)^4 = 1 (\text{MOD } 7)$, and $3^{26} = 3^{(24+2)} = 3^{24} \cdot 3^2 \equiv 1 \cdot 2 = 2 \ (\text{MOD } 7)$. What is the remainder when 3^{435} is divided by 7?

The set $\{1 \ 3 \ 2 \ 6 \ 4 \ 5\}$ can be called the "orbit of 3 modulo 7", and because 3^6 is the smallest positive power of 3 that is congruent modulo 7 to 1, we can call 6 the "order of 3 modulo 7." Some questions that come to mind are:

Does the orbit of N modulo M contain all the integers between 0 and $M - 1$? If not, can we describe the orbit? Or, can we describe those integers that have a "full" orbit? Or, can we describe those moduli M for which there is a "primitive element" (an element whose orbit uses up all the integers between 0 and $M - 1$)? Does every element have an order (that is, given any integer N, is there a number E so that $N^E \equiv 1 \ (\text{MOD } M)$)?

One way to experiment with these questions is to TAB POWERMOD against the value E while holding N and M fixed. To do this using our standard TAB tool, we'll need to permute the inputs to POWERMOD:

```
TO MODPOWER :N :M :E
 OP POWERMOD :N :E :M
END
```

Then, to see the first 10 powers of 2 modulo 5, we could type

```
TAB "MODPOWER [2 5] 0 10
```

and we'd see

```
0  . . . 1
1  . . . 2
2  . . . 4
3  . . . 3
4  . . . 1
5  . . . 2
6  . . . 4
7  . . . 3
8  . . . 1
9  . . . 2
10 . . . 4
```

So 2 is a "primitive element" modulo 5, and its order is 4. What is the remainder when 2^{3451} is divided by 5? How does 2 behave modulo 7?

```
?TAB "MODPOWER [2 7] 0 10
0  . . . 1
1  . . . 2
2  . . . 4
3  . . . 1
4  . . . 2
5  . . . 4
6  . . . 1
7  . . . 2
8  . . . 4
9  . . . 1
10 . . . 2
```

Well, it has an order (3), but it isn't a primitive element. What is the remainder when 2^{3451} is divided by 7?

Experiment with these ideas. Write down the orbits and the order (if there is one) for all the numbers between 0 and $M - 1$ if M is 5. Then do the same thing if M is 6, then 7, then 8, then 9, then 10, all the way until M is 17. Try to develop some conjectures. Do even moduli act differently than odd ones? Do prime moduli act differently than composite ones? Are there always primitive elements? For a given modulus, which elements have orders?

Exercise 14.12 Use the ideas from the previous project to find the units digit in $(1409)^{23}$.

Exercise 14.13 Look at the congruence classes modulo 8. Which class contains 32577? Which class contains -90? Are there classes that contain only even numbers? Are there primes in every class? Are there perfect squares in every class? Perfect cubes? Which class contains -1?

Exercise 14.14 Do the same thing as in exercise 14.13, except use the congruence classes modulo 7 instead of 8. Then answer the same questions for the classes modulo 12.

Exercise 14.15 If M is any positive integer, give a simple description of the congruence class modulo M that contains 0. Which class (using the labels $0, 1, 2, 3, \ldots, M - 1$) contains -1? -2?

Exercise 14.16 Describe all the integers that are congruent modulo 1 to 17. Describe all the integers that are congruent modulo 2 to 17.

Project 14.17 Suppose that you have a three-digit number, and you form a new number by adding the digits of your number. Show that this new number is congruent modulo 9 to your original number.

Hint: Look at some examples first. If you start with 421, the sum of the digits is 7, and 421 is congruent modulo 9 to 7. To see why, note that

$$421 = 4 \cdot 100 + 2 \cdot 10 + 1$$

while

$$7 = 4 \qquad + 2 \qquad + 1$$

Now subtract these equations and "factor out a 9."

Is this result true for four-digit numbers? How can you tell if a number is divisible by 9? Look at parts 11 and 13 of exercise 14.3. How can you tell if a number is divisible by 11?

Exercise 14.18 Describe the integers that are common to the congruence class modulo 5 that contains 4 and the congruence class modulo 8 that contains 3. Give your description as a single congruence class.

Representing Congruence Classes in Logo

When you think of a congruence class mod M (I'm using "congruence class mod M" as a shorthand for "congruence class modulo M"), you probably think of an infinite stream of integers, all differing by M. For example, here's a congruence class mod 7:

$$\ldots, -5, 2, 9, 16, 23, 30, 37, 44, 51, 58, \ldots$$

This stream of integers is completely determined if you know the modulus and just one integer in the stream. For example, I could describe it as the congruence class mod 7 that contains 23, or as the congruence class mod 7 that contains -12. A more common use of language is to call the stream something like "the class of 16 mod 7" or simply "16 mod 7." So when I speak of 23 mod 5, I'm thinking of the whole class:

$$\ldots, -7, -2, 3, 8, 13, 18, 23, 28, 33, 38, \ldots$$

Another name for this class is 8 mod 5, so it makes sense to say:

$$8 \bmod 5 \text{ equals } 23 \bmod 5$$

Of course, this sentence can be given at least two meanings. One interpretation could be that

$$\text{MOD}(8, 5) = \text{MOD}(23, 5)$$

and another interpretation (the one we have in mind here) is that

> The congruence class modulo 5 of 8 and the congruence class modulo 5 of 23 are the same.

The fact that the same sentence can stand for two different twists on the same idea makes it delightfully expressive.

Think of a congruence class mod 7, say,

$$\ldots, -5, 2, 9, 16, 23, 30, 37, 44, 51, 58, \ldots$$

Any integer in the class is called a "representative" of the class. So, if I describe the class as "44 mod 7," 7 is the modulus of the class and 44 is the representative of the class. Now, every class mod 7 has a representative between 0 and 6; this is just another way to say that every number is congruent modulo 7 to one of the integers 0, 1, 2, 3, 4, 5, or 6. Let's call this representative the "distinguished representative" for the class. So, the distinguished representative for the above class is 2, and the distinguished representative for 16 mod 5 is 1.

All of the above machinery translates naturally into Logo. First, let's build a Logo representation for congruence classes.

> Many computer scientists would say that this should be the last thing that we do; first we should build the functions that operate on congruence classes (like REPRESENTATIVE and MODULUS), and then we should construct the actual representation for our data objects. Carrying out such a program makes for an interesting way to spend an afternoon, but I find it unnatural to design functions that operate on objects that do not have a concrete representation. A convincing argument against my point of view is in Abelson (1985).

We have seen that a congruence class is completely determined by one representative and its modulus. In other words, a congruence class is determined by two integers, and we can represent a pair of integers as a list. So we could think of the class "16 mod 5" as [16 5], and use the following Logo function as a first try at describing congruence classes:

```
TO CLASS :N :MODULUS
 OP LIST :N :MODULUS
END
```

Using this method for describing congruence classes, it's easy to make the mistake of thinking that there are infinitely many congruence classes for a given modulus. For example, look at all the different CLASSes mod 5:

$$...,[-3\ 5],[-2\ 5],[-1\ 5],[0\ 5],[1\ 5],[2\ 5],...$$
$$[21\ 5],[22\ 5],[23\ 5],...$$

But [22 5] stands for the same congruence class as [-3 5], and [-1 5] stands for the same congruence class as [4 5]. In fact there are only five distinct congruence classes modulo 5; we could describe them as

CLASS 0 5, CLASS 1 5, CLASS 2 5, CLASS 3 5, and CLASS 4 5

Every other description of a congruence class mod 5 is "equal" to one of these in the sense that it describes the same class as one of these. Of course, I could pick other names for the five distinct classes modulo 5, say,

CLASS 5 5, CLASS 11 5, CLASS − 3 5, CLASS 13 5, and CLASS 2094 5

but most of the time we'll think of the distinct congruence classes classified by their distinguished representatives. So why don't we fix our labels once and for all and agree to label the congruence classes mod M by their distinguished representatives? In other words, we'll change our CLASS function so that

CLASS 23 5 outputs [3 5]

CLASS -2 7 outputs [5 7]

To do this, we can modify CLASS:

```
TO CLASS :N :MODULUS
 OP LIST (MOD :N :MODULUS) :MODULUS
END
```

Make sure that CLASS does the right thing. Make sure that each of the following produce [5 7]:

SHOW CLASS 12 7

SHOW CLASS 5 7

SHOW CLASS 19 7

SHOW CLASS -2 7

It might take a while to get used to this representation, but it will become very natural once you do. Just practice thinking about

$$\ldots, -8, -3, 2, 7, 12, 17, 22, 27, 32, 37, \ldots$$

whenever you see CLASS 2 5. Of course, you should think of the same congruence class when you see CLASS -3 5. Notice that if you type

SHOW (CLASS 2 5) = (CLASS -3 5)

you'll see **TRUE**.

We'll say that "CLASS 2 5" describes (or represents, or stands for) the congruence class

$$\ldots, -8, -3, 2, 7, 12, 17, 22, 27, 32, 37, \ldots$$

Later on, I might get sloppy and refer to **CLASS 2 5** as a congruence class. You'll know what I mean.

When you are calculating with your computer, you'll always type

```
CLASS 12 5
```

when you are thinking of the congruence class modulo 5 that contains 12. As usual, when I am writing for you, I may also use the more conventional mathematical notation

$$\text{CLASS}(12, 5)$$

for the same thing. When you are speaking to someone, you can say

$$12 \bmod 5$$

for this same class. Finally, it will also be convenient (especially when we do arithmetic with congruence classes) to introduce one more notation for the same idea:

$$\{12\ 5\}$$

will stand for the congruence class modulo 5 that contains 12.

So **CLASS 12 5** (when working in Logo), CLASS(12,5) or {12 5} (when writing for people), and "12 MOD 5" (when talking to people) all stand for

$$\ldots, -8, -3, 2, 7, 12, 17, 22, 27, 32, 37, \ldots$$

We'll need two "selectors" that operate on our **CLASS**es; one gives the representative of a **CLASS** and the other gives the modulus:

```
TO REP :CLASS
 OP FIRST :CLASS
END
```

```
TO MODULUS :CLASS
 OP LAST :CLASS
END
```

Notice that REP outputs the distinguished representative of a class, so that

```
REP CLASS 12 7
```

outputs 5. Notice the difference between

```
SHOW CONGRUENT.MODULO? 5 (REP CLASS 13 5) 13
```

and

```
SHOW (REP CLASS 13 5) = 13
```

You may wonder why I bother to use REP and MODULUS. Why not simply use FIRST and LAST? The reason is that I don't want you to think of $CLASS(2, 5)$ as the list [2 5], and that is precisely what would happen if we kept the names FIRST and LAST for our selectors. Once you start thinking of $CLASS(2, 5)$ as [2 5], you'll start using [2 5] as an input to our functions when you really should input CLASS 2 5. This can cause trouble. For example, even though REP [2 5] outputs the right thing, REP [12 5] does not. Another example: Compare the output of

```
(CLASS 2 5) = (CLASS 12 5)
```

with that of

```
[2 5] = [12 5]
```

So now that we have CLASS, REP, and MODULUS to experiment with, forget that they have anything to do with lists. When you see the pair [2 3] on the computer's screen, just think of it as a symbol for the stream of integers that are congruent modulo 3 to 2.

> In fact, the tendency to confuse objects with their Logo representations is one of the reasons that computer scientists would object to our defining CLASS, REP, and MODULUS at the beginning of our project. On the other hand, it would be difficult to experiment with congruence classes without some way to represent them in Logo.

Experiment 14.19 You have probably noticed that CLASS is not a "one-to-one" function of its first input. For example, CLASS$(4,5)$ has the same value as CLASS$(29,5)$. Describe the relationship between A and B if

$$\text{CLASS}(A,M) = \text{CLASS}(B,M)$$

Project 14.20 Suppose that M is a positive integer. Explain why the following statement is true:

If $A \equiv B \ (\text{MOD } M)$ then CLASS$(A,M) = $ CLASS(B,M)

Also explain why the converse is true:

If CLASS$(A,M) = $ CLASS(B,M), then $A \equiv B \ (\text{MOD } M)$

Hint: When you see "$A \equiv B \ (\text{MOD } M)$", think of our official CONGRUENT.MODULO? predicate. It says that A and B are congruent mod M precisely when

$$\text{MOD}(A,M) = \text{MOD}(B,M)$$

Now look at the definition of our CLASS function.

Project 14.21 Write a Logo function LOCATE.NEAR that takes two inputs, an integer SOURCE and a congruence class C. LOCATE.NEAR outputs the smallest integer that is greater than or equal to SOURCE and in the congruence class represented by C. For example,

```
LOCATE.NEAR 17 CLASS 3 4
```

outputs 19, because 19 is the smallest integer greater than or equal to 17 that is in the class represented by CLASS$(3,4)$
    Another example:

```
LOCATE.NEAR -34 CLASS 5 8
```

outputs -27, because -27 is the smallest integer that is greater than or equal to -34 and congruent modulo 8 to 5.
    One final example:

```
LOCATE.NEAR -34 CLASS 6 8
```

outputs -34, because -34 is itself in the class represented by $\text{CLASS}(6, 8)$.

Note that calling "LOCATE.NEAR -34 CLASS 5 8" is the same as calling "LOCATE.NEAR -34 CLASS 13 8"

Hint: Start searching at $SOURCE$ for a number that is congruent modulo the $MODULUS$ of C to the REPresentative of C. If you find one, output it. If not, add 1 and try again. Project 14.9 guarantees that your search will stop in at most M tries where M is the modulus of your input class.

Suppose our modulus is 8. Then we have seen that there are exactly eight congruence classes mod 8, that every integer is in one of them, and that no integer is in more than one of them. Mathematicians have another way of looking at this fact that has proved to be very useful in number theory (and elsewhere).

CLASS has only eight possible outputs; these outputs look like lists on the computer screen, but they stand for the congruence classes:

$$\{0\ 8\}, \{1\ 8\}, \{2\ 8\}, \{3\ 8\}, \{4\ 8\}, \{5\ 8\}, \{6\ 8\}, \text{ and } \{7\ 8\}$$

The set of these 8 objects is called "the integers mod 8", and it is written as "$\mathbf{Z}/8\mathbf{Z}$" (I'll explain why shortly). So in symbols,

$$\mathbf{Z}/8\mathbf{Z} = \Big\{ \{0\ 8\}\ \{1\ 8\}\ \{2\ 8\}\ \{3\ 8\}\ \{4\ 8\}\ \{5\ 8\}\ \{6\ 8\}\ \{7\ 8\} \Big\}$$

Now, viewed as a function of its first input (with the second input kept fixed at 8), CLASS is simply a function that takes an integer as input and outputs an element of $\mathbf{Z}/8\mathbf{Z}$.

Of course, CLASS is not one-to-one; it maps an infinite set ($\mathbf{Z}$) onto a set with only eight elements ($\mathbf{Z}/8\mathbf{Z}$). But it's easy to describe the integers that end up at the same place under CLASS. For example, what integers have a CLASS of $\{3\ 8\}$? Precisely the integers that are congruent modulo 8 to 3; that is, the "pull-back" of $\{3\ 8\}$ under CLASS is

$$\ldots, -13, -5, 3, 11, 19, 27, 35, \ldots$$

which is the congruence class modulo 8 with distinguished representative 3. (Try typing

```
SHOW CLASS -13 8
SHOW CLASS -5 8
SHOW CLASS 3 8
```

and so on.)

In other words, CLASS is a means for treating an entire congruence class as a single object. CLASS takes the set of integers, breaks it up into eight disjoint sets, and treats all the integers in the same set as if they were identical. Mathematicians call this process of applying CLASS "reducing the integers modulo 8."

Of course, there is nothing special about 8. We could "reduce the integers mod 7," and that would mean that we would apply CLASS with a second input of 7 to every integer. Every integer would then end up looking like one of the elements in $\mathbf{Z}/7\mathbf{Z}$:

$$\{0\ 7\}, \{1\ 7\}, \{2\ 7\}, \{3\ 7\}, \{4\ 7\}, \{5\ 7\}, \text{ or } \{6\ 7\}$$

The reason that this collapsing of an entire congruence class into a single object is so useful is that it's possible (we'll do it momentarily) to define addition and multiplication on $\mathbf{Z}/M\mathbf{Z}$ for any modulus M. This arithmetic is very simple (there are only M different objects to combine), but we will be able to use this arithmetic to discover some wonderful facts about divisibility and congruence in $\mathbf{Z}$. Moreover $\mathbf{Z}/M\mathbf{Z}$ itself gives us a new place to look for interesting problems.

> Why do they use the notation $\mathbf{Z}/M\mathbf{Z}$ for the integers mod M? This is an example of a very general and flexible notation. Fix M at, say, 9. Then 9$\mathbf{Z}$ stands (quite suggestively) for all multiples of 9. (Take every integer, and multiply it by 9; you get all multiples of 9.) $\mathbf{Z}/9\mathbf{Z}$ stands for the set that you get when you start with $\mathbf{Z}$ and think of two integers as "equal" if they differ by an element of 9$\mathbf{Z}$. So 5 equals 23 in $\mathbf{Z}/9\mathbf{Z}$ because 5 and 23 differ by an element of 9$\mathbf{Z}$. If you think about it for a minute, this is just another way to look at the set of congruence classes mod 9. The idea can be used in other situations. For example, if R stands for the real numbers, then $R/\mathbf{Z}$ is the set that you get by starting with R and "identifying" two real numbers when they differ by an integer. So in $R/\mathbf{Z}$, .5 is the same as 23.5, .789 is the same as 45.789, and 0 is the same as 6. Some people think of $R/\mathbf{Z}$ as a circle with circumference 1. Do you see why? So roughly S/T means the creature that you get when you start with S and "identify" any two elements of S that "differ" by an element of T. The precise meaning of "differ" depends on the kind of binary operations that make sense in S.

You may have already noticed the following phenomenon:

Fix a modulus, say, 9, and look at two congruence classes, say, CLASS$(4, 9)$,

$$\ldots, -14, -5, 4, 13, 22, 31, 40, \ldots$$

and CLASS$(16, 9)$,

$$\ldots, -11, -2, 7, 16, 25, 34, 43, \ldots$$

If you take any integer in CLASS$(4, 9)$ and you add it to any integer in the CLASS$(16, 9)$, you get an integer in CLASS$(4+16, 9)$, or CLASS$(20, 9)$,

$$\ldots, -7, 2, 11, 20, 29, 38, 45, \ldots$$

For example, $-5 + 16 = 11$, $31 + -11 = 20$, $7 + 4 = 11$, and $13 + 16 = 29$, and part 1 of project 14.6 guarantees that this will happen for any choice of integers, one from CLASS$(4, 9)$, and one from CLASS$(16, 9)$. It is also true that every integer in CLASS$(20, 9)$ is the sum of two integers, one from CLASS$(4, 9)$, and one from CLASS$(16, 9)$. For example, if N is in CLASS$(20, 9)$, then $N = 20 + 9K$ for some integer K. This means that N can be written as $(4 + 9K) + 16$. But $4 + 9K$ is in CLASS$(4, 9)$ and 16 is in CLASS$(16, 9)$, so N is the sum of two integers, one from CLASS$(4, 9)$ and one from CLASS$(16, 9)$.

So it makes sense to say that the sum of CLASS$(4, 9)$ and CLASS$(16, 9)$ is CLASS$(20, 9)$. If you look at the actual output of CLASS,

CLASS$(4, 9)$ outputs [4 9], which stands for $\{4\ 9\}$

CLASS$(16, 9)$ outputs [7 9], which stands for $\{7\ 9\}$

CLASS$(20, 9)$ outputs [2 9], which stands for $\{2\ 9\}$

So, looking at $\mathbf{Z}/9\mathbf{Z}$, we want to say that

The sum of $\{4\ 9\}$ and $\{7\ 9\}$ is $\{2\ 9\}$

or even

$$\{4\ 9\} + \{7\ 9\} = \{2\ 9\}$$

The representative for the sum (2) is obtained by adding 4 and 7 (you get 11) and then "reducing" this sum mod 9. We can model this addition in Logo. If C and C' are congruence classes with the same modulus, then we have

```
TO ADD :C :C'
 OP CLASS ((REP :C) + (REP :C')) MODULUS :C
END
```

Notice how **CLASS** takes care of the details of reducing, so that we can describe **ADD**'s instructions as

> To add two classes, form the class whose representative is the sum of the representatives of the addends

or even

> The sum of the classes is the class of the sum

For example, if you type

```
SHOW ADD CLASS 4 5 CLASS 3 5
```

you should see

```
[2 5]
```

which stands for $\{2\ 5\}$ (the congruence class modulo 5 that contains 2). Make sure that you understand that we can write "$\{4\ 5\} + \{3\ 5\}$," but that we have to type "**ADD CLASS 4 5 CLASS 3 5**" in Logo.

One of the nice things about $\mathbf{Z}/9\mathbf{Z}$ is that it contains only nine elements. That means I can write down the complete addition table for $\mathbf{Z}/9\mathbf{Z}$. Table 14.1 shows the addition table for $\mathbf{Z}/9\mathbf{Z}$.

Check that your **ADD** function generates the same sums; make sure, for example, that when you type

```
SHOW ADD CLASS 7 9 CLASS 6 9
```

you see

```
[4 9]
```

which stands, of course for $\{4\ 9\}$ (which stands for, of course, the congruence class modulo 9 that contains 4).

	{0 9}	{1 9}	{2 9}	{3 9}	{4 9}	{5 9}	{6 9}	{7 9}	{8 9}
{0 9}	{0 9}	{1 9}	{2 9}	{3 9}	{4 9}	{5 9}	{6 9}	{7 9}	{8 9}
{1 9}	{1 9}	{2 9}	{3 9}	{4 9}	{5 9}	{6 9}	{7 9}	{8 9}	{0 9}
{2 9}	{2 9}	{3 9}	{4 9}	{5 9}	{6 9}	{7 9}	{8 9}	{0 9}	{1 9}
{3 9}	{3 9}	{4 9}	{5 9}	{6 9}	{7 9}	{8 9}	{0 9}	{1 9}	{2 9}
{4 9}	{4 9}	{5 9}	{6 9}	{7 9}	{8 9}	{0 9}	{1 9}	{2 9}	{3 9}
{5 9}	{5 9}	{6 9}	{7 9}	{8 9}	{0 9}	{1 9}	{2 9}	{3 9}	{4 9}
{6 9}	{6 9}	{7 9}	{8 9}	{0 9}	{1 9}	{2 9}	{3 9}	{4 9}	{5 9}
{7 9}	{7 9}	{8 9}	{0 9}	{1 9}	{2 9}	{3 9}	{4 9}	{5 9}	{6 9}
{8 9}	{8 9}	{0 9}	{1 9}	{2 9}	{3 9}	{4 9}	{5 9}	{6 9}	{7 9}

Table 14.1

In spite of its simplicity the table stores quite a bit of information. For example, from the fact that the sum of {6 9} and {5 9} is {2 9}, we know that if A is congruent modulo 9 to 6 and B is congruent modulo 9 to 5, then $A + B$ is congruent modulo 9 to 2. In more elementary language, it says that if A leaves a remainder of 6 when it is divided by 9 and B leaves a remainder of 5 when it is divided by 9, then $A + B$ will leave a remainder of 2 when divided by 9. It also says that if a number leaves a remainder of 8 when divided by 9, then its double leaves a remainder of 7 when divided by 9 ({8 9} + {8 9} = {7 9}).

At the risk of being repetitive, remember that when I write

$$\{6\ 9\} + \{5\ 9\} = \{2\ 9\}$$

I mean that the sum of the classes {6 9} and {5 9} is the class {2 9}. If you want to check this in Logo, you'd look at the output of

```
ADD (CLASS 6 9) (CLASS 2 9)
```

It's just because of the way we were all brought up that

$$\{6\ 9\} + \{5\ 9\} = \{2\ 9\}$$

seems more natural than

`ADD (CLASS 6 9) (CLASS 2 9)` outputs `[2 9]`

I could also use the hybrid functional notation:

$$\texttt{ADD}(\{6\ 9\}, \{5\ 9\}) = \{2\ 9\}$$

Using "+" in this slightly incorrect way (as in "$\{12\ 4\} + \{2\ 4\} = \{14\ 4\}$") will cause no trouble to us because we can figure out its meaning from its context. It would be very difficult (but not impossible) to make use of such context clues when you are working in Logo.

Before playing with this new addition, let me show you a simple way to think about these new sums. Suppose we are working in $\mathbf{Z}/5\mathbf{Z}$. Arrange the elements of $\mathbf{Z}/5\mathbf{Z}$ in a "ring":

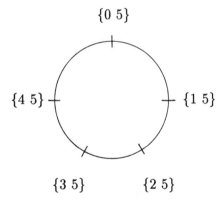

To add say $\{1\ 5\}$ to $\{3\ 5\}$, start at $\{1\ 5\}$ and move around the ring 3 spaces. You'll end up at $\{4\ 5\}$, so the sum of $\{1\ 5\}$ and $\{3\ 5\}$ is $\{4\ 5\}$. Suppose you want to add $\{2\ 5\}$ to $\{4\ 5\}$. Start at $\{2\ 5\}$ and move around 4 spaces. You'll come to $\{1\ 5\}$, so $\{2\ 5\} + \{4\ 5\} = \{1\ 5\}$. This method of adding in $\mathbf{Z}/M\mathbf{Z}$ used to be taught in elementary school (under the name of "clock arithmetic"); unfortunately, few people made the connection between what seemed like a silly game and the underlying facts about remainders.

Exercise 14.22 Use the addition table for $\mathbf{Z}/9\mathbf{Z}$ and your Logo function ADD to answer the following questions (look for theorems):

1. What is $\{2\ 9\} + \{8\ 9\}$?

2. What is $(\{2\ 9\} + \{8\ 9\}) + \{3\ 9\}$?

3. What is $\{2\ 9\} + (\{8\ 9\} + \{3\ 9\})$?

4. Is $C + C'$ the same as $C' + C$ for all classes C and C'?

5. What is $\{0\ 9\} + C$ for any class C?

6. Is $(C + C') + C''$ the same as $C + (C' + C'')$ for all classes C, C' and C''?

7. What is C if $\{5\ 9\} + C = \{0\ 9\}$?

8. What is C if $\{7\ 9\} + C = \{2\ 9\}$?

9. Is there a class C so that $C + C = \{1\ 9\}$?

10. Is there a class C so that $C + C + C + C = \{1\ 9\}$?

11. Is there a class C so that $C + C + C = \{1\ 9\}$?

12. I have a number A that, when divided by 9, leaves a remainder of 3. I have another number B, that, when divided by 9, leaves a remainder of 2. What is the remainder when $4A + 7B$ is divided by 9? What is the remainder when $A + B + 234$ is divided by 9? What is the remainder when $10A$ is divided by 9?

Exercise 14.23 Write out the addition tables for $\mathbf{Z}/2\mathbf{Z}$, $\mathbf{Z}/3\mathbf{Z}$, $\mathbf{Z}/4\mathbf{Z}$, $\mathbf{Z}/5\mathbf{Z}$, $\mathbf{Z}/6\mathbf{Z}$, $\mathbf{Z}/7\mathbf{Z}$ and $\mathbf{Z}/12\mathbf{Z}$.

Fix a positive modulus M. Then, keeping the second input to CLASS at M, CLASS is a function that takes an integer as input and outputs an element of $\mathbf{Z}/M\mathbf{Z}$.

Once again, CLASS is not one-to-one; it sends an entire congruence class to the same place, so that, if M is 9, for example, $\ldots, -2, 7, 16, 25, \ldots$ ends up at $\{7\ 9\}$. CLASS is, of course, "onto"; that just means that every element of $\mathbf{Z}/M\mathbf{Z}$ is the output of CLASS for at least one integer.

Now, $\mathbf{Z}$ and $\mathbf{Z}/M\mathbf{Z}$ are not simply sets of objects. $\mathbf{Z}$ has a very rich structure; you can add in $\mathbf{Z}$, you can multiply in $\mathbf{Z}$, and addition and multiplication enjoy some deep properties (like the fundamental theorem of arithmetic).

Right now, all we can do in $\mathbf{Z}/M\mathbf{Z}$ is add. If you look at how we defined addition in $\mathbf{Z}/M\mathbf{Z}$,

```
TO ADD :C :C'
 OP CLASS ((REP :C) + (REP :C')) MODULUS :C
END
```

you'll see that addition in $\mathbf{Z}/M\mathbf{Z}$ is simply the shadow of addition in $\mathbf{Z}$. That is, we add two classes by looking at the representatives for these classes. These representatives are integers, so we add them in $\mathbf{Z}$. Then we form the class whose representative is this sum. In other words, we defined addition in $\mathbf{Z}/M\mathbf{Z}$ to ensure that the CLASS function has the following property.

Theorem 14.3 If M is a positive integer and A and B are integers, then

$$\text{CLASS}(A + B, M) = \text{ADD}(\text{CLASS}(A, M), \text{CLASS}(B, M))$$

or more suggestively,

$$\text{CLASS}(A + B, M) = \text{CLASS}(A, M) + \text{CLASS}(B, M)$$

or even

$$\{A + B M\} = \{A\ M\} + \{B\ M\}$$

Notice that in the statement

$$\{A + B\ M\} = \{A\ M\} + \{B\ M\}$$

the "+" stands for different things on each side of the equation; on the left-hand side, it stands for addition in $\mathbf{Z}$, and on the right-hand side, it stands for addition in $\mathbf{Z}/M\mathbf{Z}$.

Theorem 14.3 guarantees that the following two instructions will produce the same thing on your screen:

```
SHOW CLASS 5 + 17 6
```

and

```
SHOW ADD CLASS 5 6 CLASS 17 6
```

This theorem says that CLASS is more than a function between the sets **Z** and **Z**/M**Z**; it also respects the "additive structures" of **Z** and **Z**/M**Z**. Think of it this way:

Suppose that A and B are integers (and, as usual, M is a fixed positive integer). Then we can add A and B as integers and form the CLASS of the sum, as shown in figure 14.1. We can also form the CLASS of A and of B and ADD the results (in **Z**/M**Z**), as shown in figure 14.2.

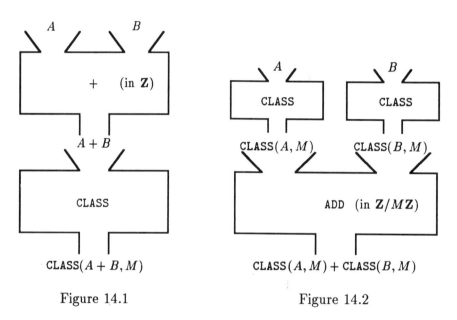

Figure 14.1   Figure 14.2

The theorem says that the result will be the same in both cases.

Another way to visualize this is to think of the diagram shown in figure 14.3. This diagram is "commutative" in the sense that if you follow the arrows that start at A and B to the right and down, you get the same result as if you follow the arrows from A and B moving first down and then to the right.

Earlier, we wrote out a more cryptic way to express this fact:

The CLASS of the sum is the sum of the CLASSes

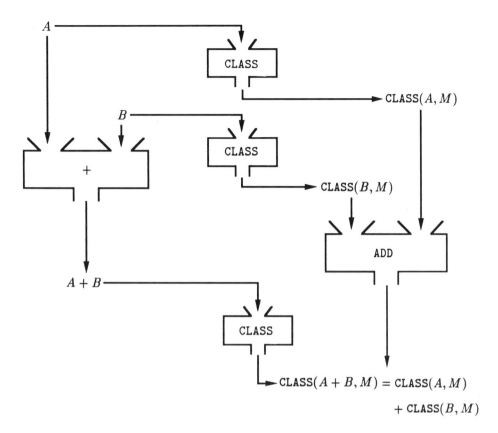

Figure 14.3

Once again, in this sentence the word "sum" is used in two different senses. The first instance of "sum" refers to addition in $\mathbf{Z}$, the second instance refers to addition in $\mathbf{Z}/M\mathbf{Z}$.

Theorem 14.3 isn't especially deep; it merely describes the way we defined addition on $\mathbf{Z}/M\mathbf{Z}$. It's not as if we are given $\mathbf{Z}/M\mathbf{Z}$ complete with a method for adding, and we then discover that the class of the sum is the sum of the classes; we invented our own addition on $\mathbf{Z}/M\mathbf{Z}$, and we did so by simply defining the sum of two classes to be the class of the sum. Because we add in $\mathbf{Z}/M\mathbf{Z}$ by simply borrowing $\mathbf{Z}$'s addition, most of the properties of addition in $\mathbf{Z}$ can be transported to $\mathbf{Z}/M\mathbf{Z}$. For example, addition in $\mathbf{Z}/M\mathbf{Z}$ is commutative. This means that if C and C' are elements of $\mathbf{Z}/M\mathbf{Z}$, then $C + C'$ is the same as $C' + C$. The proof of this fact is almost trivial:

Suppose that $C = \text{CLASS}(A, M)$ and $C' = \text{CLASS}(B, M)$ for some integers A and B. Then

$$C + C' = \text{CLASS}(A, M) + \text{CLASS}(B, M)$$

$$= \text{CLASS}(A + B, M) \quad \text{(by theorem 14.3)}$$

$$= \text{CLASS}(B + A, M) \quad \text{(because addition is commutative in } \mathbf{Z},$$
$$\text{so } A + B = B + A)$$

$$= \text{CLASS}(B, M) + \text{CLASS}(A, M) \quad \text{(again by theorem 14.3)}$$

$$= C' + C$$

Exercise 14.24 Write out proofs similar to the one above for the following facts about $\mathbf{Z}/9\mathbf{Z}$'s addition:

1. Addition in $\mathbf{Z}/9\mathbf{Z}$ is associative. That is, if C, C' and C'' are classes in $\mathbf{Z}/9\mathbf{Z}$, then $C + (C' + C'') = (C + C') + C''$. Using the ADD notation, this says that

    $$\text{ADD}(C, \text{ADD}(C'C'')) = \text{ADD}(\text{ADD}(C, C'), C'')$$

    For example,

    `SHOW ADD (CLASS 4 15) ADD (CLASS 3 15) (CLASS 19 15)`

    should produce the same thing on your screen as

    `SHOW ADD ADD (CLASS 4 15) (CLASS 3 15) (CLASS 19 15)`

2. $\text{CLASS}(0, M)$ is the identity for addition in $\mathbf{Z}/M\mathbf{Z}$. That is, if C is any class in $\mathbf{Z}/M\mathbf{Z}$, then

    $$C + \text{CLASS}(0, M) = C$$

    For example, `SHOW ADD (CLASS 3 7) (CLASS 0 7)` should produce the same thing on your screen as `SHOW (CLASS 3 7)`.

In your proofs, replace classes like C by outputs of CLASS (like $\text{CLASS}(A, M)$), and use theorem 14.3.

Look at all the addition tables you constructed for $\mathbf{Z}/M\mathbf{Z}$ in exercise 14.21. Notice that just below the diagonal that runs from the upper right-hand corner of the table to the lower left-hand corner of the table, you'll find $\{0 \ M\}$. This means that every element of $\mathbf{Z}/M\mathbf{Z}$ has a "negative" (or an additive inverse). In other words, for every class C there is a class C' so that $C + C' = \{0 \ M\}$, the identity for addition in $\mathbf{Z}/M\mathbf{Z}$. For example, in $\mathbf{Z}/6\mathbf{Z}$,

$$\{0 \ 6\} + \{0 \ 6\} = \{0 \ 6\}$$

$$\{1 \ 6\} + \{5 \ 6\} = \{0 \ 6\} \qquad \text{(check that \texttt{ADD CLASS 1 6 CLASS 5 6}}$$
$$\text{outputs the same thing as \texttt{CLASS 0 6})}$$

$$\{2 \ 6\} + \{4 \ 6\} = \{0 \ 6\}$$

$$\{3 \ 6\} + \{3 \ 6\} = \{0 \ 6\}$$

So $\{0 \ 6\}$ is its own negative, $\{1 \ 6\}$ and $\{5 \ 6\}$ are negatives, $\{2 \ 6\}$ and $\{4 \ 6\}$ are negatives, and $\{3 \ 6\}$ is its own negative. You can probably figure out a method for finding the negative of an element of $\mathbf{Z}/M\mathbf{Z}$, but theorem 14.3 says that you don't have to bother:

```
TO NEG :C
 OP CLASS (-1 * REP :C) MODULUS :C
END
```

In other words, you can negate before you reduce modulo M. So `NEG` works like this:

```
?SHOW NEG CLASS 4 5
[1 5]
```

(which stands for $\{1 \ 5\}$).

Experiment 14.25 Suppose that A is an integer between 0 and $M - 1$. Describe the connection between

$$\text{REP}(\text{CLASS}(A, M)) \text{ and } \text{REP}(\text{NEG}(\text{CLASS}(A, M)))$$

You can experiment by comparing the output of REP to the output of F:

```
TO F :C
 OP REP NEG :C
END
```

Now suppose that you allow A to be any integer (not just an integer between 0 and $M - 1$). Find a simple description of the connection between A and REP(NEG(CLASS(A, M))) (Hint: Your description might involve outputs of MOD.)

Multiplication in Z/MZ

How about multiplication in Z/MZ? It should be fairly clear how we should proceed. By part 2 of project 14.6, if you take an integer in CLASS(A, M) and multiply it by an integer in CLASS(B, M), you get an element of CLASS(AB, M). So we'll simply transport Z's multiplication to Z/MZ:

```
TO MULT :C :C'
 OP CLASS (REP :C) * (REP :C') MODULUS :C
END
```

So, for example, the following two instructions should produce the same thing on the screen:

```
SHOW MULT (CLASS 13 4) (CLASS 3 4)
```

and

```
SHOW CLASS 13 * 3 4
```

Because multiplication in Z is so closely related to questions of divisibility, multiplication in Z/MZ will be more important than addition for us. It is also considerably more complicated, and its properties will require that we look carefully at arithmetic in Z. It is probably useful for you to generate a few multiplication tables by hand, but for more extensive experiments, it will be handy to have Logo generate the tables for you. This is a straightforward task, and I've included one way to do it in the appendix.

Look at the multiplication table for $Z/6$Z:

	{0 6}	{1 6}	{2 6}	{3 6}	{4 6}	{5 6}
{0 6}	{0 6}	{0 6}	{0 6}	{0 6}	{0 6}	{0 6}
{1 6}	{0 6}	{1 6}	{2 6}	{3 6}	{4 6}	{5 6}
{2 6}	{0 6}	{2 6}	{4 6}	{0 6}	{2 6}	{4 6}
{3 6}	{0 6}	{3 6}	{0 6}	{3 6}	{0 6}	{3 6}
{4 6}	{0 6}	{4 6}	{2 6}	{0 6}	{4 6}	{2 6}
{5 6}	{0 6}	{5 6}	{4 6}	{3 6}	{2 6}	{1 6}

Also, for reference, here's the table for $\mathbf{Z}/7\mathbf{Z}$:

	{0 7}	{1 7}	{2 7}	{3 7}	{4 7}	{5 7}	{6 7}
{0 7}	{0 7}	{0 7}	{0 7}	{0 7}	{0 7}	{0 7}	{0 7}
{1 7}	{0 7}	{1 7}	{2 7}	{3 7}	{4 7}	{5 7}	{6 7}
{2 7}	{0 7}	{2 7}	{4 7}	{6 7}	{1 7}	{3 7}	{5 7}
{3 7}	{0 7}	{3 7}	{6 7}	{2 7}	{5 7}	{1 7}	{4 7}
{4 7}	{0 7}	{4 7}	{1 7}	{5 7}	{2 7}	{6 7}	{3 7}
{5 7}	{0 7}	{5 7}	{3 7}	{1 7}	{6 7}	{4 7}	{2 7}
{6 7}	{0 7}	{6 7}	{5 7}	{4 7}	{3 7}	{2 7}	{1 7}

Notice that the tables are symmetric with respect to the diagonal that runs from upper left to lower right. In other words, multiplication is commutative in $\mathbf{Z}/M\mathbf{Z}$. That's just a consequence of the way we defined multiplication; just like for addition, we have the following theorem:

Theorem 14.4 If M is a positive integer and A and B are integers, then:

$$\text{CLASS}(AB, M) = \text{MULT}(\text{CLASS}(A, M), \text{CLASS}(B, M))$$

or more suggestively

$$\text{CLASS}(AB, M) = \text{CLASS}(A, M) \cdot \text{CLASS}(B, M)$$

or even

$$\{AB\ M\} = \{A\ M\} \cdot \{B\ M\}$$

Of course, in the second statement in the theorem the multiplication on the right-hand side of the equation ("AB") means something different from the one on the left-hand side ("CLASS(A,M) · CLASS(B,M)"). When we are talking among ourselves, we can say:

The CLASS of the product is the product of the CLASSes

You can visualize this fact by thinking of the commutative diagram shown in figure 14.4.

Exercise 14.26 Use the method of exercise 14.23 to show the following things:

1. If C and C' are classes in $\mathbf{Z}/M\mathbf{Z}$, then $CC' = C'C$.

2. If C, C' and C'' are classes in $\mathbf{Z}/M\mathbf{Z}$, then $C(C'C'') = (CC')C''$.

3. If C is any class in $\mathbf{Z}/M\mathbf{Z}$, then $C \cdot \{1\ M\} = C$.

So multiplication in $\mathbf{Z}/M\mathbf{Z}$ behaves just like multiplication in $\mathbf{Z}$. Or does it?

A look at the table for $\mathbf{Z}/6\mathbf{Z}$ shows some disturbing products. I'm thinking, for example, of the fact that $\{3\ 6\}\{4\ 6\} = \{0\ 6\}$. Remember, I'll write $\{3\ 6\}\ \{4\ 6\}$, but in Logo, you'll have to type the following:

```
SHOW MULT (CLASS 3 6) (CLASS 4 6)
```

This bothers me because such things cannot happen in $\mathbf{Z}$. For ordinary integers, in order for a product AB to be 0, one of the factors, either A or B, must also be 0. Can you think of a proof of this fact?

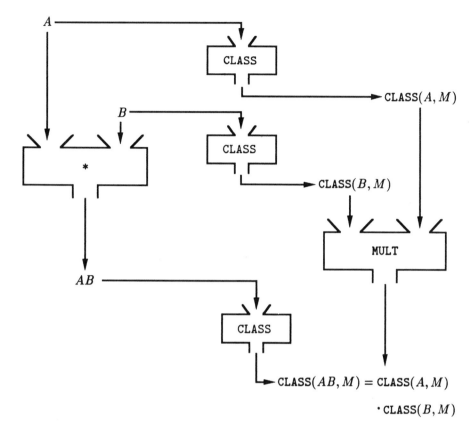

Figure 14.4

Of course, when translated into a fact about congruences, the troublesome equation

$$\{3\ 6\}\ \{4\ 6\} = \{0\ 6\}$$

is no longer mysterious. It says:

> If A is congruent modulo 6 to 3, and B is congruent modulo
> 6 to 4, then AB is divisible by 6

In fact, all statements about addition and multiplication in $\mathbf{Z}/M\mathbf{Z}$ can be translated into statements about congruence in $\mathbf{Z}$, and all statements about congruence give rise to properties of $\mathbf{Z}/M\mathbf{Z}$. A fruitful line of investigation is to take a fact about ordinary arithmetic in $\mathbf{Z}$, to see how that fact has to be modified to hold in $\mathbf{Z}/M\mathbf{Z}$ (this modification often depends on M), and to take this new property and translate it back into a statement about divisibility or congruence in **Z**. Looking at the same statement in two ways, once as a statement about congruence in **Z** and again as a statement about equality in **Z**/*M***Z**, will give us an insight that is difficult to gain using a single point of view.

We'll call classes like $\{4\ 6\}$ "zero divisors"; a zero divisor is a class that is not $\{0\ M\}$ but that can be multiplied by another nonzero class to give $\{0\ M\}$. So $\{2\ 6\}$ is a zero divisor in **Z**/6**Z** because

$$\{2\ 6\} \cdot \{3\ 6\} = \{0\ 6\}$$

and $\{6\ 24\}$ is a zero divisor in **Z**/24**Z** because

$$\{6\ 24\} \cdot \{8\ 24\} = \{0\ 24\}$$

(Check that SHOW MULT (CLASS 6 24) (CLASS 8 24) outputs the same thing as SHOW (CLASS 0 24).)

Notice that there are no zero divisors in **Z**/7**Z**. Can you explain why? Also **Z**/7**Z** has the interesting property that every non-zero element in **Z**/7**Z** has a "reciprocal" in **Z**/7**Z**. By the reciprocal of a class C, I mean a class C' so that $CC' = \{1\ 7\}$. To be specific,

$$\{1\ 7\}\{1\ 7\} = \{1\ 7\}$$
$$\{2\ 7\}\{4\ 7\} = \{1\ 7\} \qquad (\text{try SHOW MULT CLASS 2 7 CLASS 4 7})$$
$$\{3\ 7\}\{5\ 7\} = \{1\ 7\}$$
$$\{6\ 7\}\{6\ 7\} = \{1\ 7\}$$

So $\{1\ 7\}$ is its own reciprocal, $\{2\ 7\}$ and $\{4\ 7\}$ are reciprocals, $\{3\ 7\}$ and $\{5\ 7\}$ are reciprocals, and $\{6\ 7\}$ is its own reciprocal. Nothing like that happens in **Z**; The only integers that have integer reciprocals are 1 and -1. Of course all nonzero integers have reciprocals in the rational numbers **Q**; in fact all nonzero elements of **Q** have reciprocals in **Q**. In this respect **Z**/7**Z** resembles Q more than it does **Z**.

Which elements of **Z**/6**Z** have reciprocals in **Z**/6**Z**? Well, $\{1\ 6\}$ is its own reciprocal and so is $\{5\ 6\}$, and these are the only two elements of **Z**/6**Z** that have reciprocals. Notice that all the other nonzero elements of **Z**/6**Z** are zero divisors. Is there a theorem in the wings?

The elements in $\mathbf{Z}/M\mathbf{Z}$ that have reciprocals in $\mathbf{Z}/M\mathbf{Z}$ are called the "units" of $\mathbf{Z}/M\mathbf{Z}$. $\mathbf{Z}/6\mathbf{Z}$ has two units, while every nonzero element of $\mathbf{Z}/7\mathbf{Z}$ is a unit. Why is $\{0\ M\}$ never a unit in $\mathbf{Z}/M\mathbf{Z}$?

Clearly, quite a bit is going on here. Before we develop all these fragments into a full arithmetic for $\mathbf{Z}/M\mathbf{Z}$, you should take some time to experiment on your own. Write down any conjectures that you have. If you want some direction for your investigations, work on the next experiment. In fact it is a very bad idea for you to read on unless you work on the next experiment.

Experiment 14.27 Look at the multiplication tables for $\mathbf{Z}/M\mathbf{Z}$ where M runs from 2 to 12. Then tackle these problems.

1. Which elements of $\mathbf{Z}/M\mathbf{Z}$ are zero divisors? Write a Logo predicate ZERO.DIVISOR? that takes a class as input and tells whether or not that class is a zero divisor (so that ZERO.DIVISOR? CLASS 2 6 outputs TRUE, while ZERO.DIVISOR? CLASS 2 7 outputs FALSE). Hint: Don't forget GCD and RELATIVELY.PRIME?.

2. Which elements of $\mathbf{Z}/M\mathbf{Z}$ are units? Write a Logo predicate UNIT? that takes a class as input and tells whether or not that class is a unit (so that UNIT? CLASS 3 16 outputs TRUE, while UNIT? CLASS 3 15 outputs FALSE). Hint: See the hint for part 1 above.

3. What seems to be the connection between units and zero divisors?

4. For what values of M is every nonzero element of $\mathbf{Z}/M\mathbf{Z}$ a unit? Can you explain why?

5. For some classes C, every element of $\mathbf{Z}/M\mathbf{Z}$ can be written as $C \cdot (something)$. In other words, given any class D, you can find a class C' so that $CC' = D$. For example, look at $\{9\ 10\}$ in $\mathbf{Z}/10\mathbf{Z}$:

$\{0\ 10\}$ is $\{9\ 10\} \cdot \{0\ 10\}$

$\{1\ 10\}$ is $\{9\ 10\} \cdot \{9\ 10\}$

$\{2\ 10\}$ is $\{9\ 10\} \cdot \{8\ 10\}$

$\{3\ 10\}$ is $\{9\ 10\} \cdot \{7\ 10\}$

$\{4\ 10\}$ is $\{9\ 10\} \cdot \{6\ 10\}$

$\{5\ 10\}$ is $\{9\ 10\} \cdot \{5\ 10\}$

$\{6\ 10\}$ is $\{9\ 10\} \cdot \{4\ 10\}$

$\{7\ 10\}$ is $\{9\ 10\} \cdot \{3\ 10\}$

$\{8\ 10\}$ is $\{9\ 10\} \cdot \{2\ 10\}$

$\{9\ 10\}$ is $\{9\ 10\} \cdot \{1\ 10\}$

Put another way, you can solve the equation $\{9\ 10\} \cdot X = D$ for every class D in $\mathbf{Z}/10\mathbf{Z}$. Some elements of $\mathbf{Z}/10\mathbf{Z}$ do not enjoy this property. For example, you can't solve $\{4\ 10\} \cdot X = \{3\ 10\}$ in $\mathbf{Z}/10\mathbf{Z}$.

Call an element C of $\mathbf{Z}/M\mathbf{Z}$ "good" if you can solve the equation $C \cdot X = D$ for all elements D of $\mathbf{Z}/M\mathbf{Z}$. Give a precise description of the elements in $\mathbf{Z}/M\mathbf{Z}$ that are good.

#6. Write a function that takes an input M and outputs the number of units in $\mathbf{Z}/M\mathbf{Z}$. Verify that this function seems to be multiplicative. Hint: Look at chapter 13 again.

#7. Write a Logo function RECIP that takes a unit in $\mathbf{Z}/M\mathbf{Z}$ as input and outputs its reciprocal. Hint: Think of what it means to be a unit in terms of GCD, and then look at theorem 11.4.

8. Explain how to solve the equation $\{4\ 9\} \cdot X = \{7\ 9\}$ in $\mathbf{Z}/9\mathbf{Z}$ without using the multiplication table for $\mathbf{Z}/9\mathbf{Z}$. Hint: $\{4\ 9\}$ is a unit, so it has a reciprocal. How do you solve the equation $4X = 56$ in elementary algebra?

More generally, if C is a unit in $\mathbf{Z}/M\mathbf{Z}$ and D is any element of $\mathbf{Z}/M\mathbf{Z}$, explain how to solve the equation $CX = D$ for X in $\mathbf{Z}/M\mathbf{Z}$.

9. Verify that if C and C' are units in $\mathbf{Z}/M\mathbf{Z}$, then CC' is also a unit in $\mathbf{Z}/M\mathbf{Z}$. For example, $\{3\ 8\}$ and $\{7\ 8\}$ are units in $\mathbf{Z}/8\mathbf{Z}$. Verify that

UNIT? MULT CLASS 3 8 CLASS 7 8

outputs TRUE. Try lots of other combinations.

Describe the reciprocal of CC' in terms of the reciprocals of C and C'.

10. Write a power function for $\mathbf{Z}/M\mathbf{Z}$. That is, write a function EXPMOD that takes two inputs: a class C and an integer E. The output is the Eth power of the class C. For example,

```
SHOW EXPMOD (CLASS 5 7) 3
```

should output the same thing as

```
SHOW MULT (CLASS 5 7) (MULT (CLASS 5 7) (CLASS 5 7))
```

and also the same thing as

```
SHOW CLASS 125 7
```

Hint: Use the POWERMOD function of this section, or mimic the definition of POWER, replacing "*" by MULT.

11. Show that the fourth power of any nonzero element in $\mathbf{Z}/5\mathbf{Z}$ is $\{1\ 5\}$. For example,

```
SHOW EXPMOD CLASS 3 5 4
```

should produce the same thing as

```
SHOW CLASS 1 5
```

Show that the tenth power of any nonzero element in $\mathbf{Z}/11\mathbf{Z}$ is $\{1\ 11\}$. Suppose that the function you constructed in part 6 above is called P, so that $P(M)$ is the number of units in $\mathbf{Z}/M\mathbf{Z}$. Verify that, in $\mathbf{Z}/M\mathbf{Z}$ (for M between 2 and 12), the $P(M)$ power of every unit is $\{1\ M\}$. For example, EXPMOD (CLASS 4 6) P 6 should output the same thing as CLASS 1 6.

12. Investigate the powers of elements in $\mathbf{Z}/M\mathbf{Z}$. For example, if I tabulate the EXPMOD function in part 9 above, I can look at the powers of $\{2\ 7\}$ in $\mathbf{Z}/7\mathbf{Z}$:

```
?TAB "EXPMOD (LIST "CLASS 2 7) 0 6
0 . . . [1 7]
1 . . . [2 7]
2 . . . [4 7]
3 . . . [1 7]
4 . . . [2 7]
5 . . . [4 7]
6 . . . [1 7]
```

(Why do I have to input the "extra" input to TAB as (LIST "CLASS 2 7)?)

Notice that {2 7} has "order 3," (its third power is {1 7}), so it will only have three distinct powers. Can we do better? Look at the powers of {3 7} in **Z**/7**Z**:

```
?TAB "EXPMOD (LIST "CLASS 3 7) 0 6
0 . . . [1 7]
1 . . . [3 7]
2 . . . [2 7]
3 . . . [6 7]
4 . . . [4 7]
5 . . . [5 7]
6 . . . [1 7]
```

Here, the order is 6, so we get six distinct powers of {3 7}.

Look at the other elements of **Z**/7**Z**. What kinds of orders show up? How about in **Z**/9**Z**? Does every element even have an order? Can powers ever be {0 M}? Can the order of an element in **Z**/M**Z** ever be M? Greater than M? Can any integer between 0 and $M - 1$ be the order for some element of **Z**/M**Z**? Describe the orders that do show up by their relationship with M.

13. If A is a perfect square in **Z**, is CLASS(A, M) a perfect square in **Z**/M**Z**? Justify your answer. Is every perfect square in **Z**/M**Z** of the form CLASS(A, M) where A is a perfect square in **Z**?

14. Is CLASS($-1, M$) ever a perfect square in **Z**/M**Z**?

15. Use the multiplication table for **Z**/10**Z** to determine the only possible units digits for perfect squares in **Z**. What are the only possible units digits for perfect cubes in **Z**?

16. Describe the product of all the nonzero elements in **Z**/M**Z** for $M = 2, 3, 5, 7,$ and 11. Describe the same product for $M = 4, 6, 8, 9, 10$ and 12.

Project 14.28 This project is an example of the interplay between **Z** and **Z**/M**Z**. Show that if N is any integer not divisible by 7, then $N^7 - N$ is divisible by 42.

Hints: By direct calculation with the EXPMOD function of the previous experiment, show that the sixth power of every nonzero element in **Z**/7**Z** is

$\{1\ 7\}$. Show that the seventh power of every element in $\mathbf{Z}/6\mathbf{Z}$ is itself. In the language of congruence, this means that if N is any integer, two things are true:

$$N^6 \equiv 1 \ (\text{MOD } 7) \text{ if } N \text{ isn't divisible by } 7$$

and

$$N^7 \equiv N \ (\text{MOD } 6) \text{ without restriction}$$

Suppose that N is any integer not divisible by 7. Then $N^7 - N$ is divisible by 6. Also, since $N^7 - N = N(N^6 - 1)$, and since $N^6 - 1$ is divisible by 7, $N^7 - N$ is divisible by 7. Now, 6 and 7 are relatively prime, so use project 11.34.

Project 14.29 Show that if N is any integer, $N^{13} - N$ is divisible by 5.

Hint: Verify that if C is any nonzero class in $\mathbf{Z}/5\mathbf{Z}$, then $C^4 = \{1\ 5\}$. It follows that $C^{12} = (C^4)^3 = \{1\ 5\}^3 = \{1\ 5\}$. Translating to $\mathbf{Z}$, this implies that if N is not divisible by 5, $N^{12} \equiv 1 \ (\text{MOD } 5)$. Now multiply both sides by N. Why does this remove the need to insist that N is not divisible by 5?

Similarly, use arithmetic in $\mathbf{Z}/7\mathbf{Z}$ to show that, for any integer N, $N^{13} - N$ is divisible as well by 7.

Project 14.30 Show that there are infinitely many primes that are congruent modulo 4 to 3.

Hint: Any power of $\{1\ 4\}$ is $\{1\ 4\}$ in $\mathbf{Z}/4\mathbf{Z}$. This means that if you have several numbers each congruent modulo 4 to 1, then their product is also congruent modulo 4 to 1. Suppose that N is an integer so that $\text{CLASS}(N, 4) = \{3\ 4\}$. Think of the prime factorization of N. Why must it be true that at least one of the primes in the support of N is congruent modulo 4 to 3? Now, following Euclid, suppose that there are only finitely many positive primes congruent modulo 4 to 3. List them according to size, say $P_1, P_2, P_3, \ldots, P_K$ (so that $P_1 = 3$, $P_2 = 7$, $P_3 = 11$, $\ldots$), and consider the integer N:

$$N = 4P_2P_3 \ldots P_K + 3$$

(Notice that we are leaving out 3.) Show that $\text{CLASS}(N, 4) = \{3\ 4\}$, so that N has a prime factor P congruent modulo 4 to 3. Also show that $\text{CLASS}(N, P_J) = \{3\ P_J\}$ for $J = 2, 3, \ldots, K$. Finally, show that $\text{CLASS}(N, 3)$ is not $\{0\ 3\}$. Deduce that P is different from $P_1, P_2, P_3, \ldots$, and P_K.

Multiplication, Units and Zero Divisors

I'm assuming that you have already worked on experiment 14.26. If you have, you've probably discovered many of the following theorems.

First, let's take care of the zero divisors. A zero divisor in $\mathbf{Z}/12\mathbf{Z}$ is a class like $\{8\ 12\}$ which is not $\{0\ 12\}$, but which when multiplied by another nonzero class (like $\{3\ 12\}$) yields $\{0\ 12\}$. Why does this happen? The reason is that 8 is not divisible by 12, 3 is not divisible by 12, but 8 3 is divisible by 12. Another "partner" for $\{8\ 12\}$ is $\{9\ 12\}$; neither 8 nor 9 is divisible by 12, but their product is. In $\mathbf{Z}/M\mathbf{Z}$ a class C will be a zero divisor if its representative is not divisible by M, but has a common factor with M. This pathological factor can be combined with another factor to yield a multiple of M; in $\mathbf{Z}/M\mathbf{Z}$ this translates into the fact that you can find a nonzero class C' so that $CC' = \{0\ M\}$. How can you tell if a nonzero class has a representative that has a common factor with its modulus? Simply see if they are not relatively prime. In other words, we have the following test:

Theorem 14.5 The following predicate outputs TRUE precisely when its input is a zero divisor:

```
TO ZERO.DIVISOR? :C
 OP NOT RELATIVELY.PRIME? REP :C MODULUS :C
END
```

Exercise 14.31 Because of the way we have defined zero divisors, this predicate has a slight bug in it. It pronounces $\{0\ M\}$ a zero divisor, while we insist that a zero divisor be a nonzero class. Fix ZERO.DIVISOR? so that it tests its input to make sure that it isn't the zero class.

Project 14.32 Show that ZERO.DIVISOR? doesn't depend on the fact that we are picking representatives between 0 and $M - 1$ for our classes in $\mathbf{Z}/M\mathbf{Z}$. That is, ZERO.DIVISOR? pronounces $\{20\ 12\}$ a zero divisor because the distinguished representative for $\{20\ 12\}$ is 8, and 8 and 12 have a common factor. And of course, I'll see TRUE if I type any of these things:

```
SHOW ZERO.DIVISOR? CLASS 8 12

SHOW ZERO.DIVISOR? CLASS 20 12

SHOW ZERO.DIVISOR? CLASS -4 12

SHOW ZERO.DIVISOR? CLASS 32 12

SHOW ZERO.DIVISOR? CLASS 44 12
```

because **CLASS** is constructed in such a way that all the above calls to **CLASS** produce the same output. Now, I could have constructed **CLASS** differently by taking the distinguished representatives for the classes modulo 12 to be, say,

$$0, 13, 14, 15, 16, 17, 18, 31, 32, 33, 34, \text{ and } 35$$

If I did that, it would have been a shame if **ZERO.DIVISOR?** didn't still work. Show that it would. That is, show that any element of the congruence class represented by {8 12} also has a factor in common with 12. Hint: See project 14.8.

Project 14.33 The discussion before the theorem shows that if **ZERO.DIVISOR?** outputs TRUE, then its input is a zero divisor. Finish the proof of the theorem by showing that if C is a zero divisor, then **ZERO.DIVISOR?**(C) must output TRUE.

Hint: Suppose that $C = $ **CLASS**(A, M) is a zero divisor in $\mathbf{Z}/M\mathbf{Z}$, but that A and M are relatively prime, and derive a contradiction. Argue this by assuming three things:

1. A and M are relatively prime.

2. There is a class **CLASS**(B, M) so that **CLASS**$(A, M) \cdot$ **CLASS**$(B, M) = $ **CLASS**$(0, M)$.

3. **CLASS**(B, M) is not **CLASS**$(0, M)$.

The second thing implies (by theorem 14.4) that

$$\text{CLASS}(AB, M) = \text{CLASS}(0, M), \text{ so } AB \equiv 0 \ (\text{MOD } M)$$

Translating into statements about divisibility, we have

1. M and A are relatively prime.

2. $M \mid AB$.

3. M does not divide B.

Now apply project 14.21.

Suppose that the modulus is a prime P. Then every integer that is not divisible by P is relatively prime to P, so none of the classes in $\mathbf{Z}/P\mathbf{Z}$ are zero divisors:

Theorem 14.6 If P is a prime, $\mathbf{Z}/P\mathbf{Z}$ has no zero divisors.

A glance at the multiplication tables for the various $\mathbf{Z}/M\mathbf{Z}$ shows that the units seem to be the nonzero elements that are not zero divisors. Let's see why.

First, suppose that C is a unit in $\mathbf{Z}/M\mathbf{Z}$. We want to show that C is not a zero divisor in $\mathbf{Z}/M\mathbf{Z}$. To do this, it's enough to show that the only number you can multiply C by to get the zero class is the zero class itself. Suppose that there is a class C' so that

$$CC' = \{0 \ M\}$$

The idea is to multiply both sides of this equation by the reciprocal of C to conclude that C' is $\{0 \ M\}$. More precisely, because C is a unit in $\mathbf{Z}/M\mathbf{Z}$, there is a class C'' so that $C''C = \{1 \ M\}$. Take the equation:

$$CC' = \{0 \ M\}$$

and multiply both sides by C''; you get

$$C''(CC') = C''\{0 \ M\} = \{0 \ M\}$$

Since multiplication is associative, this implies that

$$(C''C)C' = \{0 \ M\}$$

But $C''C = \{1 \ M\}$, and $\{1 \ M\}C' = C'$, so

$$C' = \{0\ M\}$$

In other words, if $CC' = \{0\ M\}$, then C' must be $\{0\ M\}$. So, C is not a zero divisor.

Next, suppose that C is a nonzero element of $\mathbf{Z}/M\mathbf{Z}$ that not a zero divisor in $\mathbf{Z}/M\mathbf{Z}$. We want to show that C is a unit in $\mathbf{Z}/M\mathbf{Z}$. That is, we want to show that there is a class D so that $CD = \{1\ M\}$. There are several ways to see this; here's a proof that not only shows that C is a unit but also gives a method for constructing D:

Suppose that $\text{REP}(C) = A$ (so that $C = \text{CLASS}(A, M)$), and that C is not a zero divisor. Then A and M are relatively prime. This means that the GCD of A and M is 1. Now look at theorem 11.3. If X is $\text{FIRST.COEFF}(A, M)$ and Y is $\text{SECOND.COEFF}(A, M)$, then

$$AX + MY = 1$$

This means that $\text{CLASS}(AX + MY, M) = \text{CLASS}(1, M)$. Then in $\mathbf{Z}/M\mathbf{Z}$,

$$
\begin{aligned}
\{1\ M\} = \{AX + MY\ M\} &= \{AX\ M\} + \{MY\ M\} \\
&= \{A\ M\} \cdot \{X\ M\} + \{M\ M\} \cdot \{Y\ M\} \\
&= \{A\ M\} \cdot \{X\ M\} + \{0\ M\} \cdot \{Y\ M\} \\
&= \{A\ M\} \cdot \{X\ M\} \\
&= C \cdot \{X\ M\}
\end{aligned}
$$

If we call D $\{X\ M\}$, then $\{1\ M\} = CD$, so C is a unit.

You should be able to fill in the reasons for each step of the above calculation. If this calculation is too terse, or if you want more details and references, start with

$$\text{CLASS}(AX + MY, M) = \text{CLASS}(1, M)$$

Using experiment 14.18, we know that since $AX + MY \equiv AX\ (\text{MOD}\ M)$, $\text{CLASS}(AX + MY, M) = \text{CLASS}(AX, M)$. Also by theorem 14.4,

$$\text{CLASS}(AX, M) = \text{CLASS}(A, M) \cdot \text{CLASS}(X, M)$$

This means that $\text{CLASS}(A, M) \cdot \text{CLASS}(X, M) = \text{CLASS}(1, M)$. If $D = \text{CLASS}(X, M)$, then $CD = \{1\ M\}$, so C is a unit in $\mathbf{Z}/M\mathbf{Z}$.

We have proved the following theorem:

Theorem 14.7 The units in $\mathbf{Z}/M\mathbf{Z}$ are precisely the nonzero elements of $\mathbf{Z}/M\mathbf{Z}$ that are not zero divisors.

A Logo model of the criteria in the above theorem is

```
TO UNIT? :C
  OP AND (NOT ZERO? :C) (NOT ZERO.DIVISOR? :C)
END
```

Where the predicate ZERO? tests a class to see if it is the zero class:

```
TO ZERO? :C
  OP REP :C = 0
END
```

(Once again, make sure that you input your classes in the right form; ZERO? CLASS 28 4 will output TRUE and ZERO? CLASS 29 4 will output FALSE.)

We can simplify UNIT? a bit. Look at ZERO.DIVISOR?; a zero divisor is a class that is not the zero class and whose REP is not relatively prime to its modulus. So something is not a zero divisor if either it is the zero class or its REP is relatively prime to its modulus. But a unit can't be the zero class, so we can test a class to see if a class is a unit by taking the condition:

> Either it is the zero class or its REP is relatively prime to its modulus

and forgetting about the "it is the zero class" part. In other words, a simpler predicate that is equal to the above version of UNIT? is

```
TO UNIT? :C
  OP REL.PRIME? REP :C MODULUS :C
END
```

Of course, if P is a prime, every integer not divisible by P is relatively prime to P, so we have the following theorem:

Theorem 14.8 If P is a prime, every nonzero element of $\mathbf{Z}/P\mathbf{Z}$ is a unit.

Project 14.34 This is very similar to project 14.32. Show that UNIT? doesn't depend on the fact that we are picking representatives between 0 and $M - 1$ for our classes in $\mathbf{Z}/M\mathbf{Z}$. That is, UNIT? pronounces {23 12} a unit because the distinguished representative for {23 12} is 11, and 11 and 12 are relatively prime. Of course, I'll see TRUE if I type any of these things:

```
SHOW UNIT? CLASS 11 12
SHOW UNIT? CLASS 23 12
SHOW UNIT? CLASS -1 12
SHOW UNIT? CLASS 35 12
SHOW UNIT? CLASS 47 12
```

This is because CLASS is constructed in such a way that all the above calls to CLASS produce the same output. Now, I could have constructed CLASS differently by taking the distinguished representatives for the classes modulo 12 to be, say,

$$0, 13, 14, 15, 16, 17, 18, 31, 32, 33, 34, \text{ and } 11$$

If I did that, it would have been a shame if UNIT? didn't still work. Show that it would. That is, show that any element of the congruence class represented by {11 12} is also relatively prime to 12. Hint: See project 14.8.

Project 14.35 This project outlines a different proof of the fact that if C is a nonzero class that is not a zero divisor in $\mathbf{Z}/M\mathbf{Z}$ then C is a unit in $\mathbf{Z}/M\mathbf{Z}$. There are $M - 1$ nonzero classes in $\mathbf{Z}/M\mathbf{Z}$; C is one of them. Construct a function F that takes an input class D and outputs CD. For example, suppose that C is {4 9}. Then F is this function:

```
TO F :D
 OP MULT (CLASS 4 9) :D
END
```

Try typing

```
SHOW F CLASS 1 9
SHOW F CLASS 2 9
SHOW F CLASS 3 9
SHOW F CLASS 4 9
```

```
SHOW F CLASS 5 9
SHOW F CLASS 6 9
SHOW F CLASS 7 9
SHOW F CLASS 8 9
```

The point is that the outputs of F are all different (that is, F is one-to-one). Show that this happens in general. That is, if C is not a zero divisor in $\mathbf{Z}/M\mathbf{Z}$, and $\mathrm{F}(D) = CD$, show that the outputs

$$\mathrm{F}(\{1\ M\}), \mathrm{F}(\{2\ M\}), \mathrm{F}(\{3\ M\}), \mathrm{F}(\{4\ M\}), \ldots, \mathrm{F}(\{M-1\ M\})$$

are all different.

Hint: If $\mathrm{F}(D) = \mathrm{F}(D')$ for different elements D and D', then

$$CD = CD'$$

so

$$C(D - D') = \{0\ M\}$$

Why would this mean that C is a zero divisor?

If the outputs of F are all different and there are $M - 1$ of them, one of the outputs must be $\{1\ M\}$. Why does this show that C is a unit?

The above project outlines a clever proof of half of theorem 14.7, but the first proof was far more informative. Briefly, it went like this:

Suppose that C is not a zero divisor and $C = \mathrm{CLASS}(A, M)$. Then $\mathrm{GCD}(A, M) = 1$. So, using functions from chapter 11,

$$A \cdot \mathrm{FIRST.COEFF}(A, M) + M \cdot \mathrm{SECOND.COEFF}(A, M) = 1$$

Applying CLASS to both sides, this became

$$\mathrm{CLASS}(A, M) \cdot \mathrm{CLASS}(\mathrm{FIRST.COEFF}(A, M), M) = \mathrm{CLASS}(1, M)$$

and this gives us an efficient method for calculating the reciprocal of a unit.

Theorem 14.9 The following function takes a unit as input and outputs its reciprocal:

```
TO RECIP :C
 OP CLASS (FIRST.COEFF REP :C MODULUS :C) MODULUS :C
END
```

For example,

```
SHOW RECIP (CLASS 4 9)
```

should produce the same thing as

```
SHOW (CLASS 7 9)
```

and, indeed, {4 9} and {7 9} are reciprocals. What will you see if you type
SHOW MULT CLASS 31 17 RECIP CLASS 31 17 ?

Project 14.36 Show that if C is a unit in $\mathbf{Z}/M\mathbf{Z}$, the output of RECIP(C) is the only reciprocal that C has in $\mathbf{Z}/M\mathbf{Z}$. That is, show that reciprocals are unique; if

$$CC' = \{1 \ M\}$$

and

$$CC'' = \{1 \ M\}$$

show that $C' = C''$.

Hint: It would follow that $CC' = CC''$. Multiply both sides by, say, C'.

The RECIP function can be used to solve simple equation in $\mathbf{Z}/M\mathbf{Z}$, just as ordinary reciprocals can be used to solve equations in algebra. Suppose you want to solve the equation $\{2 \ 9\} \cdot X = \{6 \ 9\}$ in $\mathbf{Z}/9\mathbf{Z}$. Since $\{2 \ 9\}$ is a unit, we can multiply both sides of our equation by the reciprocal of 2 9 and we'll find that $X = \text{RECIP}(\{2 \ 9\}) \cdot \{6 \ 9\}$. To find the solution in Logo, simply type

```
SHOW MULT RECIP (CLASS 2 9) (CLASS 6 9)
```

Experiment 14.37 But what if the coefficient of X isn't a unit? For example, consider the equation $\{3 \ 9\} \cdot X = \{6 \ 9\}$. A solution by inspection is $\{2 \ 9\}$. However, some equations, like $\{3 \ 9\} \cdot X = \{4 \ 9\}$, or certainly $\{3 \ 9\} \cdot X = \{1 \ 9\}$, have no solutions. Investigate this phenomenon. If C is a nonunit (a zero divisor) in $\mathbf{Z}/M\mathbf{Z}$, for what classes D can you solve $CX = D$.

Experiment 14.38 In project 14.25 we saw that if C is a nonzero class in $\mathbf{Z}/M\mathbf{Z}$, its negative is the class that is "symmetric with respect to the middle" of the nonzero elements of $\mathbf{Z}/M\mathbf{Z}$. For example, I've connected each element of $\mathbf{Z}/8\mathbf{Z}$ to its negative:

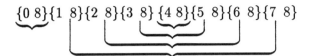

Suppose that P is a prime, so that every nonzero element of $\mathbf{Z}/P\mathbf{Z}$ has a reciprocal. Given a class, can you predict what its reciprocal will look like? For example, in $\mathbf{Z}/7\mathbf{Z}$, we have the following data:

```
?SHOW RECIP CLASS 1 7
[1 7]
?SHOW RECIP CLASS 2 7
[4 7]
?SHOW RECIP CLASS 3 7
[5 7]
?SHOW RECIP CLASS 4 7
[2 7]
?SHOW RECIP CLASS 5 7
[3 7]
?SHOW RECIP CLASS 6 7
[6 7]
```

Generate the data for other primes, and see if you can find a pattern.

Suppose that C and C' are units in $\mathbf{Z}/M\mathbf{Z}$; for example, suppose that C is $\{4\ 9\}$ and C' is $\{2\ 9\}$. Then the sum of C and C' is $\{6\ 9\}$, a zero divisor, but the product is $\{8\ 9\}$, another unit. In general, the sum of two units need not be another unit, but the product of two units is a unit:

Theorem 14.10 If C and C' are units in $\mathbf{Z}/M\mathbf{Z}$, then CC' is a unit in $\mathbf{Z}/M\mathbf{Z}$.

Project 14.39 Prove this theorem in two ways:

1. Show that CC' is not a zero divisor. Hint: If A is REP(C) and B is REP(C'), then CC' is CLASS(AB, M), where M is the modulus of C and C'. Since A and M are relatively prime and B and M are relatively prime, AB and M must also be relatively prime (why?).

2. Show that CC' has a reciprocal in $\mathbf{Z}/M\mathbf{Z}$. Hint: Experiment with several units and their products. See if you can predict the reciprocal of the product from the reciprocals of the factors.

Experiment 14.40 So, the product of two units is another unit. This means that the units in $\mathbf{Z}/M\mathbf{Z}$ are "closed" under multiplication. Still, can a nonunit ever "break in"? That is, is it possible to find a nonunit C and another class D so that CD is a unit? Look around in $\mathbf{Z}/6\mathbf{Z}$, $\mathbf{Z}/8\mathbf{Z}$, $\mathbf{Z}/9\mathbf{Z}$, and $\mathbf{Z}/12\mathbf{Z}$.

Theorem 14.9 suggests that it might be interesting to focus on the units in $\mathbf{Z}/M\mathbf{Z}$, and such attention has indeed led to some important results in number theory. In $\mathbf{Z}/14\mathbf{Z}$, for example, the units are

$$\{1\ 14\}\{3\ 14\}\{5\ 14\}\{9\ 14\}\{11\ 14\}\{13\ 14\}$$

and the set of these classes is closed under multiplication; this means that the product of two units is another unit:

	{1 14}	{3 14}	{5 14}	{9 14}	{11 14}	{13 14}
{1 14}	{1 14}	{3 14}	{5 14}	{9 14}	{11 14}	{13 14}
{3 14}	{3 14}	{9 14}	{1 14}	{13 14}	{5 14}	{11 14}
{5 14}	{5 14}	{1 14}	{11 14}	{3 14}	{13 14}	{9 14}
{9 14}	{9 14}	{13 14}	{3 14}	{11 14}	{1 14}	{5 14}
{11 14}	{11 14}	{5 14}	{13 14}	{1 14}	{9 14}	{3 14}
{13 14}	{13 14}	{11 14}	{9 14}	{5 14}	{3 14}	{1 14}

(Remember, it is not closed under addition; find two units whose sum is not a unit.)

The set of units in $\mathbf{Z}/M\mathbf{Z}$ is usually denoted by $(\mathbf{Z}/M\mathbf{Z})^\times$ (the superscript "$\times$" is to remind us that the set of units are closed under multiplication) or sometimes by $U(\mathbf{Z}/M\mathbf{Z})$ ("the units in $\mathbf{Z}/M\mathbf{Z}$"). We'll study the structure of $(\mathbf{Z}/M\mathbf{Z})^\times$ in detail in chapter 15, but for now, let's make three elementary observations:

1. If P is a prime, it's easy to describe $(\mathbf{Z}/P\mathbf{Z})^{\times}$: $(\mathbf{Z}/P\mathbf{Z})^{\times}$ is simply the set of nonzero elements in $\mathbf{Z}/P\mathbf{Z}$. So there are $P-1$ elements in $(\mathbf{Z}/P\mathbf{Z})^{\times}$.

2. For nonprime moduli, the situation is more complicated. Here an element of $\mathbf{Z}/M\mathbf{Z}$ is in $(\mathbf{Z}/M\mathbf{Z})^{\times}$ precisely when its representative is relatively prime to M. This means that the number of units in $\mathbf{Z}/M\mathbf{Z}$ (or the number of elements in $(\mathbf{Z}/M\mathbf{Z})^{\times}$) is precisely the number of integers between 1 and M that are relatively prime to M. We discussed this function in chapter 13; it is Euler's PHI function,

```
TO PHI :N
 OP COUNT PRIME.TO :N
END
```

where PRIME.TO(N) is the list of integers that are less than or equal to N but relatively prime to N:

```
TO PRIME.TO :N
 OP FILTER "RELATIVELY.PRIME? :N (NUMBERS.UPTO :N)
END
```

Recall that in chapter 13, we conjectured that PHI was equal to the parent of ID, and we showed that, to prove this, it is enough to show that PHI is multiplicative. We'll do this in the next chapter, and a major tool in our proof will be that PHI(M) is the number of elements in $(\mathbf{Z}/M\mathbf{Z})^{\times}$.

3. Suppose that C is a unit in $\mathbf{Z}/M\mathbf{Z}$. Then by Theorem 14.9, CC is also a unit, and inductively, any power of C is also a unit. Now, consider the powers of C:

$$C, C^2, C^3, C^4, C^5, \ldots$$

These classes can't all be distinct; any power of C is a unit, and there are only a finite number (in fact, PHI(M)) of units, so two of them have to be the same. That is, for two distinct integers J and K, we must have

$$C^J = C^K$$

Suppose, for example, that $J > K$. Then since $C^J = CC^{(J-1)}$ and $C^K = CC^{(K-1)}$ (look at the definition of EXPMOD), our equation can be written as

$$CC^{(J-1)} = CC^{(K-1)}$$

Multiply both sides by the reciprocal of C and conclude that

$$C^{(J-1)} = C^{(K-1)}$$

Canceling a C from both sides again, we see that

$$C^{(J-2)} = C^{(K-2)}$$

Do this for a total of K times, and you have

$$C^{(J-K)} = C^0 = \{1\ M\}$$

So, some power of C is 1. If C is in $(\mathbf{Z}/M\mathbf{Z})^\times$, we define the order of C to be the smallest integer E so that $C^E = \{1\ M\}$. Right now, all we know is that such an E exists for each unit. In the next chapter, we'll investigate the possible values that E can assume.

Experiment 14.41 Can a nonunit ever have a power equal to $\{1\ M\}$? Why or why not?

Experiment 14.42 Investigate the possible orders that a unit can have in the simplest case: the case when the modulus is prime. Look at $\mathbf{Z}/5\mathbf{Z}$, $\mathbf{Z}/7\mathbf{Z}$, $\mathbf{Z}/11\mathbf{Z}$, $\mathbf{Z}/13\mathbf{Z}$, and $\mathbf{Z}/23\mathbf{Z}$. Then look at cases when the modulus is not prime.

#Project 14.43 In the proof that every unit has an order, I would have liked to say something like this:

Suppose that $C^J = C^K$ and $J > K$. Then multiply both sides by C^{-K} and conclude that $C^{(J-K)} = \{1\ M\}$, so some power of C is $\{1\ M\}$.

The reason that I couldn't do this is that I was talking about powers in $\mathbf{Z}/M\mathbf{Z}$, not in $\mathbf{Z}$, and EXPMOD only allows for nonnegative exponents. Let's fix that and at the same time show that exponentiation in $\mathbf{Z}/M\mathbf{Z}$ enjoys many of the same properties as ordinary exponentiation in $\mathbf{Z}$.

First, prove that if C and D are classes in $\mathbf{Z}/M\mathbf{Z}$ and that K and J are positive integers, then

1. $(CD)^K = C^K D^K$

2. $C^{(K+J)} = C^K C^J$

3. $(C^K)^J = C^{(KJ)}$

To do this, write C as CLASS(A, M) and D as CLASS(B, M), and use theorems 14.3 and 14.4 to borrow these properties from $\mathbf{Z}$.

Next, prove that the reciprocal of the Kth power of C is the Kth power of the reciprocal of C:

$$\text{RECIP}(C^K) = (\text{RECIP}(C))^K$$

To check this in Logo, compare

```
SHOW RECIP (EXPMOD (CLASS 5 14) 9)
```

with

```
SHOW EXPMOD (RECIP (CLASS 5 14)) 9
```

Show that this always happens.

Hint: Show, using the properties of exponents derived above, that:

$$C^K(\text{RECIP}(C))^K = \{1 \ M\}$$

So $(\text{RECIP}(C))^K$ is a class which when multiplied by C^K, yields $\{1 \ M\}$. By project 14.36, $(\text{RECIP}(C))^K$ must be the reciprocal of C^K.

Finally, if we represent the reciprocal of C^K symbolically by C^{-K}, show that the same rules of exponents that you derived above hold for positive and negative exponents. For example, to show that

$$(CD)^K = C^K D^K \text{ even if } K \text{ is negative}$$

argue like this: Suppose that K is a negative number, say, $K = -J$ where J is a positive number. Then

$$(CD)^K = (CD)^{(-J)} = \text{RECIP}(CD)^J = \text{RECIP}(C^J D^J)$$

$$= (\text{RECIP}(C^J))(\text{RECIP}(D^J))$$

$$= C^{(-J)} D^{(-J)}$$

$$= C^K D^K$$

Make sure that you can give a reason for every step in this calculation.

The other properties:

2. $C^{(K+J)} = C^K C^J$ and

3. $(C^K)^J = C^{(KJ)}$

are proved similarly, although they are more tedious because they involve two exponents (so you have to check the cases when K is positive and J is negative, when they're both negative, and so on).

The results of the above project suggests the following extension of the domain of EXPMOD so that it handles negative exponents:

```
TO EXPMOD :C :E
  IF :E < 0 [OP RECIP EXPMOD :C -1 * :E]
  IF :E = 0 [OP CLASS 1 MODULUS :C]
  OP MULT :C EXPMOD :C :E - 1
END
```

We can now type

```
SHOW EXPMOD (CLASS 5 14) -9
```

and this produces the same thing as

```
SHOW EXPMOD (RECIP (CLASS 5 14)) 9
```

Chapter 15

Some Applications of Modular Arithmetic

In the previous chapter, we introduced the notion of congruence and its more formal companion, the ring $\mathbf{Z}/M\mathbf{Z}$. In this chapter, we'll apply these ideas to obtain some results in arithmetic. These results are interesting on their own, but they have also been extremely useful in modern number theoretic research.

Let's begin with a "number trick." Suppose I ask you to pick a number between 1 and 100 (your age, say), and I tell you not to give me the number, but to give me the remainder when the number is divided by 3, the remainder when the number is divided by 5 and the remainder when the number is divided by 7. Then I can tell you what number you chose. Here's how.

I have four numbers that I always use; they are 70, 21, 15 and 105. Suppose you picked 29. Then you would tell me that the remainder when you divide your number by 3 is 2, the remainder when you divide your number by 5 is 4, and the remainder when you divide your number by 7 is 1. So, your remainders are 2, 4, and 1. I calculate with my magic numbers as

$$2 \cdot 70 + 4 \cdot 21 + 1 \cdot 15 = 239$$

and

$$\texttt{MOD}(239, 105) = 29$$

So your number is 29.

Let's try it again. Suppose that you pick 49. Then the remainder when you divide 49 by 3 is 1, the remainder when you divide 49 by 5 is 4, and the remainder when you divide 49 by 7 is 0. So, the remainders are 1, 4 and 0, and I do my calculation

$$1 \cdot 70 + 4 \cdot 21 + 0 \cdot 15 = 154$$

and

$$\text{MOD}(154, 105) = 49$$

The trick can easily be modeled in Logo:

```
TO AGE :REM.BY.3 :REM.BY.5 :REM.BY.7
 OP MOD (:REM.BY.3 * 70 + :REM.BY.5 * 21 + :REM.BY.7 * 15) 105
END
```

To use this function, suppose someone picks 17. Then they'll give you the remainders 2, 2, and 4. You type

```
SHOW AGE 2 2 4
```

and you'll have 17. If you ask a very young person to play the game, you have to remember that the remainder when you divide 4 by 7 is 4 (and the quotient is 0). So, if someone happens to pick 4, the correct remainders are 1, 4, and 4.

Well, how does it work? Where do the numbers 70, 21, 15, and 105 come from? Before reading on, try to figure it out for yourself.

In the language of modular arithmetic, what's going on is this: A number N is picked between 1 and 100 (actually, we'll see that the number could be between 0 and 104), and the following information about the number is known:

$\text{REP}(\text{CLASS}(N, 3))$ (or $\text{MOD}(N, 3)$); let's call it A,

$\text{REP}(\text{CLASS}(N, 5))$ (or $\text{MOD}(N, 5)$); let's call it B, and

$\text{REP}(\text{CLASS}(N, 7))$ (or $\text{MOD}(N, 5)$); let's call it C.

From this information, you can find the number N.

Well, that's not completely right, because there are plenty of numbers that produce the same three remainders A, B and C when divided by 3, 5, and 7. For example, the remainders when you divide 49 by 3, 5, and 7 are 1, 4, and 0. But 154 has this same property, and so does 259. Notice that 49, 154, and 259 are all congruent modulo 105. What is true is that there is exactly one congruence class modulo 105 that contains the complete set of integers R that have the property that

$$R \equiv 1 \ (\text{MOD } 3)$$
$$R \equiv 4 \ (\text{MOD } 5)$$
$$R \equiv 0 \ (\text{MOD } 7)$$

This class is CLASS(49, 105) (or CLASS(154, 105) or CLASS(259, 105)); its distinguished representative is 49, so 49 is the only number between 0 and 104 that is in the "solution class."

So what's the theorem? It may be something like this:

> For any three remainders A (between 0 and 2), B (between 0 and 4), and C (between 0 and 6), there is a unique congruence class C modulo 105 so that C contains precisely all the numbers R that have the following properties:
>
> $$R \equiv A \ (\text{MOD } 3), \quad R \equiv B \ (\text{MOD } 5), \quad \text{and} \quad R \equiv C \ (\text{MOD } 7)$$

That's very awkward (it's even hard to say it). Let's take a closer look at my numbers 70, 21, 15, and 105, and let's take a slightly different perspective on the problem. Consider the following two questions:

1. Is it true that given any three remainders A, B, and C, I can find a number R so that $R \equiv A$ (MOD 3), $R \equiv B$ (MOD 5), and $R \equiv C$ (MOD 7)?

2. If the answer to question 1 is yes, what can you say about the set of all numbers R so that $R \equiv A$ (MOD 3), $R \equiv B$ (MOD 5), and $R \equiv C$ (MOD 7)?

Question 1 is the hard question, so let's focus on it first.

If our Logo function AGE does what it's supposed to do, the answer to the first question should certainly be yes. In fact I should be able to find an R that does the trick by the formula

$$R = A \cdot 70 + B \cdot 21 + C \cdot 15$$

(Notice that I haven't yet reduced modulo 105.) Does this work? Well, using theorems 14.3 and 14.4, look at the situation modulo 3:

$$\begin{aligned} \text{CLASS}(R, 3) &= \text{CLASS}(A \cdot 70 + B \cdot 21 + C \cdot 15, 3) \\ &= \text{CLASS}(A \cdot 70, 3) + \text{CLASS}(B \cdot 21, 3) + \text{CLASS}(C \cdot 15, 3) \end{aligned}$$

But $B \cdot 21$ and $C \cdot 15$ are each divisible by 3, so both CLASS($B \cdot 21, 3$) and CLASS($C \cdot 15, 3$) are the same as CLASS(0, 3), and these terms disappear from our sum. That means that

$$\text{CLASS}(R, 3) = \text{CLASS}(A \cdot 70, 3) = \text{CLASS}(A, 3) \cdot \text{CLASS}(70, 3)$$

but $\text{CLASS}(70,3) = \text{CLASS}(1,3)$. We finally have that

$$\text{CLASS}(R,3) = \text{CLASS}(A,3)$$

and this means that

$$R \equiv A \ (\text{MOD } 3)$$

How fortunate that $\text{CLASS}(21,3)$ and $\text{CLASS}(15,3)$ are both the zero class and that $\text{CLASS}(70,3)$ is the same as $\text{CLASS}(1,3)$. I think you know what's coming next. Look at the situation modulo 5:

$$\begin{aligned}
CLASS(R,5) &= \text{CLASS}(A \cdot 70 + B \cdot 21 + C \cdot 15, 5) \\
&= \text{CLASS}(A \cdot 70, 5) + \text{CLASS}(B \cdot 21, 5) + \text{CLASS}(C \cdot 15, 5) \\
&= \text{CLASS}(0, 5) + \text{CLASS}(B \cdot 21, 5) + \text{CLASS}(0, 5) \\
&= \text{CLASS}(B \cdot 21, 5) \\
&= \text{CLASS}(B, 5) \cdot \text{CLASS}(21, 5) \\
&= \text{CLASS}(B, 5) \cdot \text{CLASS}(1, 5) \\
&= \text{CLASS}(B, 5)
\end{aligned}$$

So $R \equiv B \ (\text{MOD } 5)$. How fortunate that $\text{CLASS}(70,5)$ and $\text{CLASS}(15,5)$ are both the zero class and that $\text{CLASS}(21,5)$ is the same as $\text{CLASS}(1,5)$.

Finally, look at the situation modulo 7:

$$\begin{aligned}
\text{CLASS}(R,7) &= \text{CLASS}(A \cdot 70 + B \cdot 21 + C15, 7) \\
&= \text{CLASS}(A \cdot 70, 7) + \text{CLASS}(B \cdot 21, 7) + \text{CLASS}(C \cdot 15, 7) \\
&= \text{CLASS}(0, 7) + \text{CLASS}(0, 7) + \text{CLASS}(C \cdot 15, 7) \\
&= \text{CLASS}(C \cdot 15, 7) \\
&= \text{CLASS}(C, 7) \cdot \text{CLASS}(15, 7) \\
&= \text{CLASS}(C, 7) \cdot \text{CLASS}(1, 7) \\
&= \text{CLASS}(C, 7)
\end{aligned}$$

So $R \equiv C \ (\text{MOD } 7)$. How fortunate that $\text{CLASS}(70,7)$ and $\text{CLASS}(21,7)$ are both the zero class and that $\text{CLASS}(15,7)$ is the same as $\text{CLASS}(1,7)$.

Now you see why the numbers 70, 21, and 15 work so well. We have the three moduli 3, 5, and 7 and three magic numbers 70, 21, and 15. Modulo the moduli, and the magic numbers behave like this:

Modulus	Magic number		
	70	21	15
3	1	0	0
5	0	1	0
7	0	0	1

This means that for any integers A, B, and C, if we form the number $R = A \cdot 70 + B \cdot 21 + C \cdot 15$, then R will be congruent modulo 3 to A, modulo 5 to B, and modulo 7 to C. Notice that there are no restrictions on A, B, and C so that we do not have to insist that A is between 0 and 2, or that B is between 0 and 4, or that C is between 0 and 6. For example, to find a number that is congruent modulo 3 to 13 and modulo 5 to 8 and modulo 7 to 4, simply take

$$70 \cdot 13 + 2 \cdot 8 + 15 \cdot 4$$

or 1138. Check it out:

$$1138 - 13 \quad \text{is divisible by 3}$$
$$1138 - 8 \quad \text{is divisible by 5}$$
$$1138 - 4 \quad \text{is divisible by 7}$$

Before we go any further, let me show you how I found the magic numbers. What I did is very much in the spirit of the BEAST function of chapter 3. Suppose that the numbers A, B, and C are given. Then my solution will be the number

$$(A \cdot 5 \cdot 7 \cdot ?) + (B \cdot 3 \cdot 7 \cdot ??) + (C \cdot 3 \cdot 5 \cdot ???)$$
$$= (A \cdot 35 \cdot ?) + (B \cdot 21 \cdot ??) + (C \cdot 15 \cdot ???)$$

where the question marks will be filled in in a minute. Now, modulo 3, this becomes $(A \cdot 35 \cdot ?$ because 21 and 15 each contain a factor of 3. I want it to be (modulo 3) just A. But $\text{CLASS}(35, 3) = \text{CLASS}(2, 3)$, which is a unit in $\mathbf{Z}/3\mathbf{Z}$, and the inverse class is (by coincidence) also $\text{CLASS}(2, 3)$. Simply put,

$$\text{RECIP}(\text{CLASS}(35, 3)) = \text{CLASS}(2, 3)$$

becomes

$$\{35\ 3\} \cdot \{2\ 3\} = \{1\ 3\}$$

or

$$\{70\ 3\} = \{1\ 3\}$$

So I put "?" equal to 2.

I have constructed the first magic number: 70. It came from wanting a number that is 0 modulo 5 and 7, so I used 35 as a start, and from wanting this same number to be 1 modulo 3, so I multiplied 35 by REP(RECIP(CLASS(35, 3))), or 2.

Now my solution looks like this:

$$(A \cdot 70) + (B \cdot 21 \cdot\ ??) + (C \cdot 15 \cdot\ ???)$$

Now, look modulo 5. Well, the $A \cdot 70$ and the $C \cdot 15 \cdot\ ???$ vanish, so we are left with $B \cdot 21 \cdot\ ??$. But, in $\mathbf{Z}/5\mathbf{Z}$, CLASS(21, 5) = CLASS(1, 5), so I don't even have to worry about finding the reciprocal; I can take ?? to be 1, and the second magic number is 21.

Modulo 7, the story is the same. The expression

$$(A \cdot 70) + (B \cdot 21) + (C \cdot 15 \cdot\ ???)$$

becomes $C \cdot 15 \cdot\ ???$, and (as luck would have it), CLASS(15, 7) = CLASS(1, 7), so I don't have to modify 15. I can take ??? to be 1 and the last magic number is 15. Now, I have a theorem that is much easier to state:

> If A, B and C are any integers, and $R = A \cdot 70 + B \cdot 21 + C \cdot 15$, then $R \equiv A$ (MOD 3), $R \equiv B$ (MOD 5), and $R \equiv C$ (MOD 7).

An Example with Different Moduli

Before we worry about the role of 105 in all this, let's see if we can apply this same method to three other moduli. Suppose the moduli are 13, 5, and 46.

Suppose further that three "residues" A, B, and C are given, and we seek a number R so that

$$R \equiv A \text{ (MOD 13)}, \quad R \equiv B \text{ (MOD 5)}, \quad \text{and} \quad R \equiv C \text{ (MOD 46)}$$

I begin with the expression

$$(A \cdot 5 \cdot 46 \cdot ?) + (B \cdot 13 \cdot 46 \cdot ??) + (C \cdot 13 \cdot 5 \cdot ???)$$
$$= (A \cdot 230 \cdot ?) + (B \cdot 598 \cdot ??) + (C \cdot 65 \cdot ???)$$

where the question marks will be filled in in a minute.

Now modulo 13, this expression becomes $A \cdot 230 \cdot ?$, and we want it to be just A. Well, CLASS$(230, 13) = \{9\ 13\}$, and $\{9\ 13\}$ is a unit in $\mathbf{Z}/13\mathbf{Z}$, with reciprocal $\{3\ 13\}$. This means that $\{230\ 13\} \cdot \{3\ 13\} = \{1\ 13\}$, or $\{230 \cdot 3\ 13\} = \{1\ 13\}$, so that $230 \cdot 3 \equiv 1$ (MOD 13). So I make "?" equal to 3. Then our expression will reduce modulo 13 to

$$A \cdot 230 \cdot 3 = A \cdot 690 \equiv A \text{ (MOD 13)}$$

and the first magic number is $5 \cdot 46 \cdot 3$, or 690.

690 is 0 modulo 5 and 46, and it is 1 modulo 13.

It is 0 modulo 5 and 46 because it contains a factor of $5 \cdot 46$.

It is 1 modulo 13 because the reciprocal of $\{5 \cdot 46\ 13\}$ in $\mathbf{Z}/13\mathbf{Z}$ is $\{3\ 13\}$, so $5 \cdot 46 \cdot 3$ is congruent modulo 13 to 1.

The "solution" is now

$$(A \cdot 690) + (B \cdot 598 \cdot ??) + (C \cdot 65 \cdot ???)$$

Modulo 5, this becomes $B \cdot 598 \cdot ??$. CLASS$(598, 5) = \{3\ 5\}$, a unit in $\mathbf{Z}/5\mathbf{Z}$. RECIP(CLASS$(3, 5)$) is $\{2\ 5\}$, so I make ?? equal to 2, and the second magic number is $13 \cdot 46 \cdot 2$, or 1196.

1196 is 0 modulo 13 and 46, and it is 1 modulo 5.

It is 0 modulo 13 and 46 because it contains a factor of $13 \cdot 46$.

It is 1 modulo 5 because the reciprocal of {13 · 46 5} in **Z**/5**Z** is {2 5}, so 13 · 46 · 2 is congruent modulo 5 to 1.

The solution is now

$$(A \cdot 690) + (B \cdot 1196) + (C \cdot 65 \cdot ???)$$

Modulo 46, this becomes $C \cdot 65 \cdot ???$. CLASS(65, 46) = {19 46}, a unit in **Z**/46**Z**, and RECIP(CLASS(19, 46)) = {17 46}. So I put ??? equal to 17, and the final magic number is 13 · 5 · 17, or 1105.

1105 is 0 modulo 13 and 5, and it is 1 modulo 46.

It is 0 modulo 13 and 5 because it contains a factor of 13 · 5.

It is 1 modulo 46 because the reciprocal of {13 · 5 46} in **Z**/46**Z** is {17 36}, so 13 · 5 · 17 is congruent modulo 46 to 1

The final solution is

$$(A \cdot 690) + (B \cdot 1196) + (C \cdot 1105)$$

The numbers 690, 1196, and 1105 behave like this modulo 13, 5, and 46:

	Magic number		
Modulus	690	1196	1105
13	1	0	0
5	0	1	0
46	0	0	1

Try it out. Suppose I want a number that is 6 modulo 13, 4 modulo 5, and 23 modulo 46. I simply form: $6 \cdot 690 + 4 \cdot 1196 + 23 \cdot 1105$, or 34339, and 34339 does the trick. Of course, there are other numbers that also do the trick (like 1449), but it looks like we have a method to find at least one solution to our problem.

Exactly what is "our problem"? Essentially, we are taking three moduli, say, M, N, and Q, and three integers, say, A, B, and C. We think that we have a method for finding an integer R so that $R \equiv A$ (MOD M), $R \equiv B$ (MOD N), and $R \equiv C$ (MOD Q). In other words, we have a method for finding a simultaneous solution to the three congruences:

$$X \equiv A \ (\mathrm{MOD}\ M)$$
$$X \equiv B \ (\mathrm{MOD}\ N)$$
$$X \equiv C \ (\mathrm{MOD}\ Q)$$

There are several nagging questions in the background ("Will it always work?" "Can you find all solutions?" "What is the smallest positive solution?" "What about more than three moduli?" and so on). There are also other ways to word our problem ("Find an integer that is in all three of the following classes: {6 13}, {4 5} and {23 46}."). We'll worry about these things eventually, but right now, let's see if we can pin down exactly what we have. The best way to do this is to model our method in Logo, and I'm about to give one way to write such a model. So, a good thing to do is to close the book for a while and to try to find a Logo function that takes six inputs A, B, C, M, N, and Q, and outputs a number R so that

$$R \equiv A \ (\mathrm{MOD}\ M)$$
$$R \equiv B \ (\mathrm{MOD}\ N)$$
$$R \equiv C \ (\mathrm{MOD}\ Q)$$

Here's a function that captures our algorithm

```
TO SOLUTION :A :B :C :M :N :Q
 OP :A * (MAGIC :M :N*:Q) + :B * (MAGIC :N :M*:Q) →
     + :C * (MAGIC :Q :M*:N)
END

TO MAGIC :L :P
 OP :P * REP RECIP (CLASS :P :L)
END
```

Try it out; type

```
SHOW SOLUTION 6 4 23 13 5 46
```

and you should see 34339. So, as above,

$$34339 \equiv 6 \ (\text{MOD } 13)$$
$$34339 \equiv 4 \ (\text{MOD } 5)$$
$$34339 \equiv 23 \ (\text{MOD } 46)$$

Here are some things to notice and some questions:

1. We haven't yet proved that SOLUTION outputs the right thing.

2. If (or when) SOLUTION works for three moduli, it should work for more than three, and the extension of SOLUTION to handle more than three moduli is an exercise in list processing.

3. The AGE function that started this whole thing can be modeled as

```
TO AGE :REM.BY.3 :REM.BY.5 :REM.BY.7
 OP MOD (SOLUTION :REM.BY.3 :REM.BY.5 :REM.BY.7 3 5 7) 105
END
```

Why is it necessary to reduce the answer at the end, and why 105?

When Does the Method Work?

Well, why shouldn't SOLUTION output the right thing? If you look at MAGIC, you see that, for example, MAGIC(Q, MN) outputs a number that is divisible by both M and N and that is also congruent to 1 modulo Q; it outputs

$$MN \cdot \text{REP}(\text{RECIP}(\text{CLASS}(MN, Q)))$$

This number is 0 modulo M and N because it contains a factor of MN. And, it is 1 modulo Q because, if the reciprocal of $\{MN \cdot Q\}$ in $\mathbf{Z}/Q\mathbf{Z}$ is $\{J \ Q\}$, then $(MN) \cdot J$ is congruent modulo Q to 1.

So the outputs of MAGIC behave like this with respect to our three moduli

Modulus	Magic number		
	MAGIC(M, NQ)	MAGIC(N, MQ)	MAGIC(Q, MN)
M	1	0	0
N	0	1	0
Q	0	0	1

and that's exactly what we need. It guarantees that

$$A \cdot (\text{MAGIC}(M, NQ)) + B \cdot (\text{MAGIC}(N, MQ)) + C \cdot (\text{MAGIC}(Q, MN))$$

will be congruent modulo M to A, modulo N to B, and modulo Q to C.

Except that sometimes it *can't* work. For example, there is no number R that satisfies these congruences:

$R \equiv 3$ (MOD 8)

$R \equiv 2$ (MOD 4)

$R \equiv 1$ (MOD 5)

The reason is that if R is congruent modulo 8 to 3, it is also congruent modulo 4 to 3, so it can't be congruent modulo 4 to 2. Now, SOLUTION outputs *something* when you input 3, 2, 1, 8, 4, and 5, but it is certainly *not* a number R that is congruent modulo 8 to 3 and congruent modulo 4 to 2 and congruent modulo 5 to 1. (It is an interesting project to try to figure out exactly what SOLUTION outputs in these cases.) The problem shows up when you look at what MAGIC is describing. Suppose we ask for the output of SOLUTION(3, 2, 1, 8, 4, 5). Then we are asking for a computation of

$$3 \cdot (\text{MAGIC}(8, 4 \cdot 5)) + 2 \cdot (\text{MAGIC}(4, 8 \cdot 5)) + 1 \cdot (\text{MAGIC}(5, 8 \cdot 4))$$

Now MAGIC($8, 4 \cdot 5$) is computed as

$$4 \cdot 5 \cdot \text{REP}(\text{RECIP}(\text{CLASS}(8, 4 \cdot 5)))$$

or

$$4 \cdot 5 \cdot \text{REP}(\text{RECIP}(\text{CLASS}(8, 20)))$$

But CLASS(20, 8) is {4 8}, which is not a unit in $\mathbf{Z}/8\mathbf{Z}$, so it doesn't have a reciprocal. (When we wrote RECIP, we just assumed that it would take a unit as input; we could have built in a check to make sure that its input was a unit, but we have not included such "domain checking" in our functions.)

So the only time our algorithm will not work is when one of the classes:

$$\{MN\ Q\},\ \{MQ\ N\},\ \text{or}\ \{NQ\ M\}$$

is not a unit. To ensure that each of the above classes is a unit, it's enough to insist that the representatives (distinguished or not) are relatively prime to the moduli, and for that, it's enough to insist that M, N, and Q are relatively prime in pairs. For example, if M and Q are relatively prime and N and Q are relatively prime, then MN is relatively prime to Q. Now we have this theorem:

> *If M, N and Q are relatively prime in pairs and A, B and C are integers, then* SOLUTION(A, B, C, M, N, Q) *outputs an integer R that is congruent modulo M to A, modulo N to B and modulo Q to C.*

Experiment 15.1 Extend SOLUTION so that it handles four moduli. So

```
SHOW SOLUTION 1 2 3 4 5 6 7 11
```

will produce a number that is congruent modulo 5 to 1, modulo 6 to 2, modulo 7 to 3, and modulo 11 to 4. Use this SOLUTION to generate many integers that are congruent modulo 5 to 1, modulo 6 to 2, and modulo 7 to 3 by varying the class modulo 11. For example, type

```
SHOW SOLUTION 1 2 3 1 5 6 7 11
SHOW SOLUTION 1 2 3 2 5 6 7 11
SHOW SOLUTION 1 2 3 3 5 6 7 11
SHOW SOLUTION 1 2 3 4 5 6 7 11
SHOW SOLUTION 1 2 3 5 5 6 7 11
```

and so on. The numbers you get will all be congruent modulo 5 to 1, modulo 6 to 2, and modulo 7 to 3 (and modulo 11 to something). How are the various outputs connected?

Experiment 15.2 Sometimes, even if the moduli are not relatively prime, there is a solution to the congruences. For example, if $R = 3$, then

$R \equiv 8 \ (\text{MOD } 5)$

$R \equiv 0 \ (\text{MOD } 3)$

$R \equiv 9 \ (\text{MOD } 6)$

Does `SOLUTION` produce a correct solution in these cases? #If it does, explain why; if it doesn't, fix it.

Suppose that M, N, and Q are relatively prime and that A, B, and C are integers. We now have a way to find an integer R so that

$R \equiv A \ (\text{MOD } M)$

$R \equiv B \ (\text{MOD } N)$

$R \equiv C \ (\text{MOD } Q)$

We have seen that there are other solutions as well. For example,

$29 \equiv 2 \ (\text{MOD } 3)$

$29 \equiv 4 \ (\text{MOD } 5)$

$29 \equiv 1 \ (\text{MOD } 7)$

and we also have

$134 \equiv 2 \ (\text{MOD } 3)$

$134 \equiv 4 \ (\text{MOD } 5)$

$134 \equiv 1 \ (\text{MOD } 7)$

I got 134 by adding $3 \cdot 5 \cdot 7$ (the famous 105) to 29. In fact, if I add any multiple of 105 to 29, I'll get another solution to the three congruences. That's just because

$29 \equiv 29 + 105K \ (\text{MOD } 3)$

$29 \equiv 29 + 105K \ (\text{MOD } 5)$

$29 \equiv 29 + 105K \ (\text{MOD } 7)$

for any integer K.

In general, if R is an integer so that

$R \equiv A \;(\text{MOD } M)$

$R \equiv B \;(\text{MOD } N)$

$R \equiv C \;(\text{MOD } Q)$

and K is any integer, then $R + (K \cdot MNQ)$ is another integer that is congruent modulo M to A, modulo N to B, and modulo Q to C.

Exercise 15.3 Use this method to generate six solutions to the system of congruences:

$X \equiv 3 \;(\text{MOD } 5)$

$X \equiv 12 \;(\text{MOD } 17)$

$X \equiv 8 \;(\text{MOD } 14)$

It turns out that this is the only way to generate new solutions from old ones. Here's why.

Suppose that R and R' are two integers that are congruent modulo M to A, modulo N to B, and modulo Q to C

$$R \equiv A \;(\text{MOD } M) \qquad R' \equiv A \;(\text{MOD } M)$$
$$R \equiv B \;(\text{MOD } N) \qquad R' \equiv B \;(\text{MOD } N)$$
$$R \equiv C \;(\text{MOD } Q) \qquad R' \equiv C \;(\text{MOD } Q)$$

Then, subtracting, we have

$R - R' \equiv 0 \;(\text{MOD } M)$

$R - R' \equiv 0 \;(\text{MOD } N)$

$R - R' \equiv 0 \;(\text{MOD } Q)$

This means that

$$M \mid (R - R')$$
$$N \mid (R - R')$$
$$Q \mid (R - R')$$

But M, N and Q are relatively prime, so by project 11.34, MNQ is also a factor of $R - R'$; that is,

$$R - R' \equiv 0 \; (\text{MOD } MNQ)$$

so

$$R \equiv R' \; (\text{MOD } MNQ)$$

and that means that R and R' differ by a multiple of MNQ.

Now we're getting somewhere. If M, N, and Q are pairwise relatively prime positive integers, and A, B, and C are any integers, then $\text{SOLUTION}(A, B, C, M, N, Q)$ outputs a number R so that $R \equiv A \; (\text{MOD } M)$, $R \equiv B \; (\text{MOD } N)$, and $R \equiv C \; (\text{MOD } Q)$. Furthermore, any other number that satisfies these congruences is congruent modulo MNQ to R, and, conversely, any number in the class $\{R \; MNQ\}$ satisfies the congruences. So the complete solution to the system of congruences:

$$X \equiv A \; (\text{MOD } M)$$
$$X \equiv B \; (\text{MOD } N)$$
$$X \equiv C \; (\text{MOD } Q)$$

"is" the congruence class $\text{CLASS}(R, MNQ)$ in the sense that this class contains precisely those integers that satisfy the congruences. So why don't we modify SOLUTION so that it outputs the Logo representation for the whole class of solutions:

```
TO SOLUTION :A :B :C :M :N :Q
  OP CLASS(:A * (MAGIC :M :N*:Q) + :B * (MAGIC :M :M*:Q) →
                    + :C * (MAGIC :Q :M*N)) :M * :N * :Q
END
```

```
TO MAGIC :L :P
 OP :P * REP RECIP CLASS :P :L
END
```

Now, SOLUTION outputs the representation for a class; from this you can write down as many solutions as you like. So, for example, if you type

```
SHOW SOLUTION 5 4 2 13 5 46
```

you'll see

```
[1474 2990]
```

This means that {1474 2990} is the class of solutions to

$$X \equiv 5 \ (\mathrm{MOD} \ 13)$$
$$X \equiv 4 \ (\mathrm{MOD} \ 5)$$
$$X \equiv 2 \ (\mathrm{MOD} \ 13)$$

1474 satisfies these congruences, and every other solution can be obtained from 1474 by adding multiples of 2990. Notice that 1474 is the smallest positive solution to the system; our AGE function could be modeled as

```
TO AGE :REM.BY.3 :REM.BY.5 :REM.BY.7
 OP REP (SOLUTION :REM.BY.3 :REM.BY.5 :REM.BY.7 3 5 7)
END
```

Exercise 15.4 Find six solutions to the system of congruences

$$X \equiv 3 \ (\mathrm{MOD} \ 12)$$
$$X \equiv 10 \ (\mathrm{MOD} \ 11)$$
$$X \equiv 1 \ (\mathrm{MOD} \ 35)$$

Exercise 15.5 If my age is divided by 3, the remainder is 2, if it is divided by 5, the remainder is 1, and if it is divided by 7, the remainder is 6. How old am I?

Exercise 15.6 Describe the set of all integers that are common to the classes {2 13}, {3 4}, and {6 9}.

Exercise 15.7 Find the smallest positive integer that is 2 modulo 3, 3 modulo 4, and 4 modulo 5. Find the smallest positive integer that is 3 modulo 4, 4 modulo 5, and 2 modulo 3.

Exercise 15.8 Give the solution to

$X \equiv 12$ (MOD 13)
$X \equiv 12$ (MOD 14)
$X \equiv 12$ (MOD 15)

without using SOLUTION. Check it with SOLUTION.

Experiment 15.9

1. If my age is divided by 3, the remainder is 1; if it is divided by 5, the remainder is 2; if it is divided by 7, the remainder is 0. How old am I?

2. If my age is divided by 3, the remainder is 1; if it is divided by 5, the remainder is 2; if it is divided by 7, the remainder is 1. How old am I?

3. If my age is divided by 3, the remainder is 1; if it is divided by 5, the remainder is 2; if it is divided by 7, the remainder is 2. How old am I?

4. If my age is divided by 3, the remainder is 1; if it is divided by 5, the remainder is 2; if it is divided by 7, the remainder is 3. How old am I?

5. If my age is divided by 3, the remainder is 1; if it is divided by 5, the remainder is 2; if it is divided by 7, the remainder is 4. How old am I?

6. If my age is divided by 3, the remainder is 1; if it is divided by 5, the remainder is 2; if it is divided by 7, the remainder is 5. How old am I?

7. If my age is divided by 3, the remainder is 1; if it is divided by 5, the remainder is 2; if it is divided by 7, the remainder is 6. How old am I?

What's going on here? State a theorem.

Exercise 15.10 Explain how you could find a solution to

$X \equiv 2$ (MOD 6) and
$X \equiv 3$ (MOD 13)

using SOLUTION. #How could you use SOLUTION to find all of the solutions to this pair of congruences?

We have proved the following theorem.

Theorem 15.1 If M, N, and Q are pairwise relatively prime positive integers, and if A, B, and C are any integers, then the three congruences:

$$X \equiv A \ (\text{MOD } M)$$
$$X \equiv B \ (\text{MOD } N)$$
$$X \equiv C \ (\text{MOD } Q)$$

have a common solution. In fact the complete set of solutions forms a single congruence class modulo MNQ, and the following function outputs this class:

```
TO SOLUTION :A :B :C :M :N :Q
 OP CLASS(:A * (MAGIC :M :N*:Q) + :B * (MAGIC :N :M*:Q)  →
                 + :C * (MAGIC :Q :M*:N)) :M * :N * :Q
END

TO MAGIC :L :P
 OP :P * REP RECIP (CLASS :P :L)
END
```

More Than Three Moduli

The above theorem can be extended to any number of moduli (a project that we'll undertake shortly and that requires only notational technicalities), and this extension is known as the Chinese remainder theorem (we'll use CRT as a shorthand for it). Essentially, the CRT says that if you have a collection of pairwise relatively prime moduli, then any system of congruences modulo these moduli can be solved, that the complete set of solutions forms a congruence class modulo the product of the moduli, and that the "diagonalization" technique that produces the magic numbers will generate the solution for you. The theorem holds true in many other arithmetic systems besides **Z**, and it is fundamental to the study of abstract number theory. Ireland and Rosen (1982) note that Hardy and Wright (1960) note that R. Bachman (1902) notes that Sun Tsu was aware of the theorem in the first century A.D.

The best way to extend the CRT so that it can handle any number of moduli is to think of it as a function of two lists: the list of constants (the A, B, and C in SOLUTION), and the list of moduli. So, we envision a function CRT that starts off this way:

```
TO CRT :CONSTANTS :MODULI
   ⋮
END
```

so that when I type

```
SHOW CRT [1 4 0] [3 5 7]
```

I'll see the Logo representation for $\{49\ 105\}$, because this class is the set of solutions to the congruences

$$X \equiv 1 \ (\text{MOD } 3)$$
$$X \equiv 4 \ (\text{MOD } 5)$$
$$X \equiv 0 \ (\text{MOD } 7)$$

This general CRT will also allow us to call

```
CRT [1 2 3 0] [4 5 7 11]
```

What would be the output? Let's see how we could systematically figure this out by hand. We want a number R so that

$$R \equiv 1 \ (\text{MOD } 4)$$
$$R \equiv 2 \ (\text{MOD } 5)$$
$$R \equiv 3 \ (\text{MOD } 7)$$
$$R \equiv 0 \ (\text{MOD } 11)$$

once we find R, our output will be CLASS$(R, 4 \cdot 5 \cdot 7 \cdot 11)$. The number $4 \cdot 5 \cdot 7 \cdot 11$ will certainly be important in our calculation (let's call it the "modulus" of the problem). What worked before is that we were able to construct the magic numbers; each magic number was congruent modulo one of the moduli to 1 and congruent modulo the rest of the moduli to 0. We can get the "congruent modulo the rest of the moduli to 0" part by simply taking all "partial products" of the moduli:

$5 \cdot 7 \cdot 11$ is 0 modulo 5, 7, and 11

$4 \cdot 7 \cdot 11$ is 0 modulo 4, 7, and 11

$4 \cdot 5 \cdot 7$ is 0 modulo 4, 5, and 7

$5 \cdot 7 \cdot 11$ is 0 modulo 5, 7, and 11

These numbers $5 \cdot 7 \cdot 11$, $4 \cdot 7 \cdot 11$, $4 \cdot 5 \cdot 7$, and $5 \cdot 7 \cdot 11$ will certainly be important in our calculations; let's call them the "partials." Each partial is congruent modulo all but one of the moduli to 0.

Before we go on, here's a way to think about what we are doing that might be helpful.

Imagine that we start off with two lists (the constants and the moduli), and we transform them in different ways to form new and interesting data. For example, so far we have used them to pick up two new pieces of information: the "modulus" and the "partials." Think of it as a sequence of transformations:

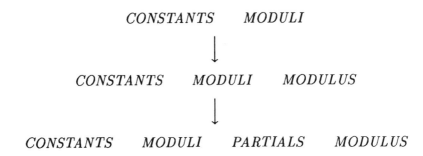

$$CONSTANTS \quad MODULI$$
$$\downarrow$$
$$CONSTANTS \quad MODULI \quad MODULUS$$
$$\downarrow$$
$$CONSTANTS \quad MODULI \quad PARTIALS \quad MODULUS$$

In our case we have

$$[1\ 2\ 3\ 0] \quad [4\ 5\ 7\ 11]$$
$$\downarrow$$
$$[1\ 2\ 3\ 0] \quad [4\ 5\ 7\ 11] \quad 4 \cdot 5 \cdot 7 \cdot 11$$
$$\downarrow$$
$$[1\ 2\ 3\ 0] \quad [4\ 5\ 7\ 11] \quad [5 \cdot 7 \cdot 11\ 4 \cdot 7 \cdot 11\ 4 \cdot 5 \cdot 11\ 4 \cdot 5 \cdot 7] \quad 4 \cdot 5 \cdot 7 \cdot 11$$

We may not need to carry each piece of data all along our journey. Notice that it is easy to compute each new piece of information from the previous ones. The modulus is simply the product of the moduli, and we could calculate the partials by dividing the modulus by each of the moduli in turn ($5 \cdot 7 \cdot 11$ is the modulus divided by 4, $4 \cdot 7 \cdot 11$ is the modulus divided by 5, and so on). We could also calculate the moduli by dividing the modulus by each of the partials in turn (4 is obtained by dividing the modulus by $5 \cdot 7 \cdot 11$, 5 is obtained by dividing the modulus by $4 \cdot 7 \cdot 11$, and so on). So we can safely drop one of our pieces of data at this stage; let's drop the moduli (we can always get them back if we need them), and look at our transformation as

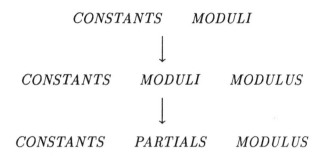

or in our case

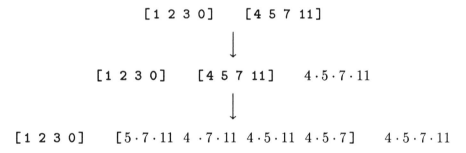

The next step is to turn the partials into the magic numbers. Right now, each partial is 0 modulo each of its factors; we also want to make it 1 modulo the "missing factor." Since the moduli are pairwise relatively prime, each partial is a unit modulo the missing factor. So we can transform $5 \cdot 7 \cdot 11$ into a magic number by replacing it by

$$5 \cdot 7 \cdot 11 \cdot \text{REP}(\text{RECIP}(\text{CLASS}(5 \cdot 7 \cdot 11, 4)))$$

This number is 0 modulo 5, 7 and 11 and 1 modulo 4.

Let's call this function MAGIC (as before). MAGIC takes two inputs: a partial and the corresponding missing factor. But we threw the missing factors away when we dropped the list of moduli. Well, we'll look at this version of MAGIC as a function of the modulus and a partial; after all, if P is a partial and M is the modulus, then M/P is the missing factor. So, if we define MAGIC as

```
TO MAGIC :M :P
 OP :P * (REP RECIP (CLASS :P :M/:P))
END
```

then we can replace the list of partials by the list of magic numbers:

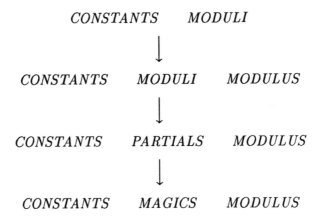

$$CONSTANTS \quad MODULI$$

$$\downarrow$$

$$CONSTANTS \quad MODULI \quad MODULUS$$

$$\downarrow$$

$$CONSTANTS \quad PARTIALS \quad MODULUS$$

$$\downarrow$$

$$CONSTANTS \quad MAGICS \quad MODULUS$$

In our example we have

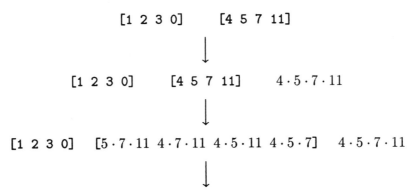

$$[1\ 2\ 3\ 0] \quad [4\ 5\ 7\ 11]$$

$$\downarrow$$

$$[1\ 2\ 3\ 0] \quad [4\ 5\ 7\ 11] \quad 4\cdot5\cdot7\cdot11$$

$$\downarrow$$

$$[1\ 2\ 3\ 0] \quad [5\cdot7\cdot11\ \ 4\cdot7\cdot11\ \ 4\cdot5\cdot11\ \ 4\cdot5\cdot7] \quad 4\cdot5\cdot7\cdot11$$

$$\downarrow$$

$$[1\ 2\ 3\ 0]\ [\texttt{MAGIC}(M,5\cdot7\cdot11)\ \texttt{MAGIC}(M,4\cdot7\cdot11)\ \texttt{MAGIC}(M,4\cdot5\cdot11)\ \texttt{MAGIC}(M,4\cdot5\cdot7)]\ 4\cdot5\cdot7\cdot11$$

Here I'm using M to stand for $4 \cdot 5 \cdot 7 \cdot 11$. If you work out all of these calculations, the actual numbers look like this:

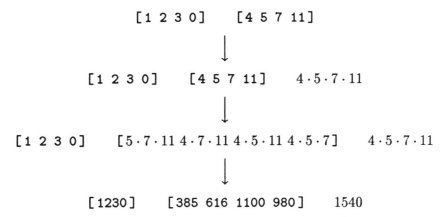

Here I've replaced $4 \cdot 5 \cdot 7 \cdot 11$ by 1540 and $\mathtt{MAGIC}(M, 5 \cdot 7 \cdot 11)$ by 385, and $\mathtt{MAGIC}(M, 4 \cdot 7 \cdot 11)$ by 616, and so on. (You can check that 385 is 1 modulo 4 and 0 modulo 5, 7, and 11, and that 616 is 1 modulo 5 and 0 modulo 4, 7, and 11.)

All that's left to do is to combine the constants with the magic numbers and to output the class of the resulting combination modulo the modulus. In our case, we simply output

$$\mathtt{CLASS}(1 \cdot 385 + 2 \cdot 616 + 3 \cdot 1100 + 0 \cdot 980, 1540)$$

If we call this "combining" function $\mathtt{COMBINE}$, we could model it as

```
TO COMBINE :LIST1 :LIST2 :MODULUS
 OP CLASS (L.SIGMA "ID [] LISTPROD :LIST1 :LIST2) :MODULUS
END
```

where $\mathtt{L.SIGMA}$ is our list summer, $\mathtt{LISTPROD}$ is the function

```
TO LISTPROD :A :B
 IF EMPTYP :A [OP []]
 OP FPUT (FIRST :A) * (FIRST :B) LISTPROD BF :A BF :B
END
```

and $\mathtt{ID}$ is the function that outputs its input

```
TO ID :X
 OP :X
END
```

Of course, you can write COMBINE from scratch, but I like to recycle old functions. So the whole process can be thought of as a series of transformations:

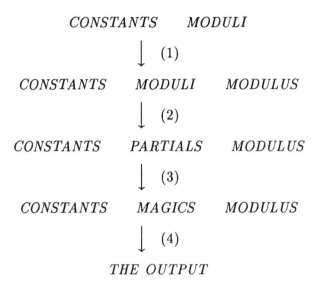

$$CONSTANTS \quad MODULI$$

$$\downarrow \;\; (1)$$

$$CONSTANTS \quad MODULI \quad MODULUS$$

$$\downarrow \;\; (2)$$

$$CONSTANTS \quad PARTIALS \quad MODULUS$$

$$\downarrow \;\; (3)$$

$$CONSTANTS \quad MAGICS \quad MODULUS$$

$$\downarrow \;\; (4)$$

$$THE\ OUTPUT$$

I've numbered the steps for reference. In our example, the transformations look like this:

$$[1\ 2\ 3\ 0] \quad [4\ 5\ 7\ 11]$$

$$\downarrow \;\; (1)$$

$$[1\ 2\ 3\ 0] \quad [4\ 5\ 7\ 11] \quad 4\cdot5\cdot7\cdot11$$

$$\downarrow \;\; (2)$$

$$[1\ 2\ 3\ 0] \quad [5\cdot7\cdot11\ 4\cdot7\cdot11\ 4\cdot5\cdot11\ 4\cdot5\cdot7] \quad 4\cdot5\cdot7\cdot11$$

$$\downarrow \;\; (3)$$

$$[1\ 2\ 3\ 0] \quad [385\ 616\ 1100\ 980] \quad 1540$$

$$\downarrow \;\; (4)$$

CLASS (L.SIGMA "ID [ ] LISTPROD [1 2 3 0] [385 616 1100 980]) 1540

(What is the final output?)

Now all we have to do is to figure out how to take the data at one step and transform it to the data at the next step. Well, in step 1 all we do is introduce the modulus, and keep everything else the same. The modulus is just the product of the MODULI, and we can multiply the elements of a list together by simply using our L.PROD function together with ID.

```
TO LISTMULT :L
 OP L.PROD "ID [] :L
END
```

Notice the difference between LISTMULT and LISTPROD. So we can start off our calculation like this:

```
TO CRT :CONSTANTS :MODULI
 OP CRT1 :CONSTANTS :MODULI (LISTMULT :MODULI)
END
```

Here I've created a dummy function CRT1 whose only purpose is to hold onto the old values of *CONSTANTS* and *MODULI* while keeping the new object that we have called "the modulus" (it is the product of the integers in the list *MODULI*).

So assume that we have the constants, the individual moduli, and their product at our disposal. How can we carry out step 2? In this step, the constants and the modulus stay the same, but the moduli get replaced by the "partials." How can we compute the list of partials from what we know? We simply divide the modulus in turn by each element in the list moduli. In our example, we could get the partials from [4 5 7 11] and $4 \cdot 5 \cdot 7 \cdot 11$ by forming the list

$$[\,(4 \cdot 5 \cdot 7 \cdot 11/4)\ (4 \cdot 5 \cdot 7 \cdot 11/5)\ (4 \cdot 5 \cdot 7 \cdot 11/7)\ (4 \cdot 5 \cdot 7 \cdot 11/11)\,]$$

I'm sure that you can figure out a way to do this in Logo. It can be accomplished neatly by using the following general list-processing strategy:

Suppose you have a function F and a list L; say, $F(X) = X + 2$, and $L = $ [3 5 2 6 8]. You want to construct the list that you get by applying F to each element of L; you want to construct [5 7 4 8 10]. The process is called "mapping F over L". There is a Logo model in the appendix for this higher-order function that maps a function over a list; it works like this: if S is the function that squares its input, then

```
SHOW MAP "S [] [2 4 1 6]
```

will produce

[4 16 1 36]

MAP allows you to map a function of more than one input over a list if you tell it what the "extra" inputs are. If $H(X, Y, Z) = X + 2Y - Z$, then

```
SHOW MAP "H [3 2] [1 2 3 4]
```

will produce

[6 5 4 3]

Here $6 = H(3, 2, 1), 5 = H(3, 2, 2), 4 = H(3, 2, 3)$, and $3 = H(3, 2, 4)$. If your Logo allows you to use "+" like any other procedure (so that SHOW + 5 6 produces 11), then typing

```
SHOW MAP "+ 3 [6 7 8 9]
```

produces

[9 10 11 12]

MAP is useful whenever you want to transform one list into another by doing the same thing to each of its elements. That's exactly what we want to do here. We want to take [4 5 7 11] and construct the list whose elements are obtained from these by dividing each one into $4 \cdot 5 \cdot 7 \cdot 11$. In other words, if I define DIVIDE as

```
TO DIVIDE :A :B
 OP :A / :B
END
```

then MAP "DIVIDE 1540 [4 5 7 11] will output the list whose elements are 5 7 11, 4 7 11, 4 5 11, and 4 5 7. Check it out. If your Logo allows you to use "/" like any other procedure, you don't even need DIVIDE. You can simply use

```
MAP "/ 1540 [4 5 7 11]
```

So, creating a new dummy function to hold on to all our lists, we can write CRT1 like this:

```
TO CRT1 :CONSTANTS :MODULI :MODULUS
 OP CRT2 :CONSTANTS (MAP "DIVIDE :MODULUS :MODULI) :MODULUS
END
```

Now we have the constants, the partials, and the modulus, and we want to carry out transformation 3. We have already seen how to transform each partial into the corresponding magic number; in our example, the list of partials is [385 308 220 280], and the modulus is 1540. To get the first magic number, simply calculate MAGIC(1540, 385), to get the second, calculate MAGIC(1540, 308), and so on. In other words, to get the list of magic numbers, simply MAP MAGIC over the PARTIALS, using MODULUS as the "extra" input:

```
TO CRT2 :CONSTANTS :PARTIALS :MODULUS
 OP CRT3 :CONSTANTS (MAP "MAGIC :MODULUS :PARTIALS) :MODULUS
END
```

CRT3 can simply COMBINE its inputs, and we are done:

```
TO CRT3 :CONSTANTS :MAGICS :MODULUS
 OP COMBINE :CONSTANTS :MAGICS :MODULUS
END
```

Of course, there was no need for CRT3 at all (CRT3 is the same as COMBINE), but the extra dummy function makes the set of Logo functions a more faithful model of our four steps above.

The whole routine is outlined like this:

```
TO CRT :CONSTANTS :MODULI
 OP CRT1 :CONSTANTS :MODULI (LISTMULT :MODULI)
END
```

```
TO CRT1 :CONSTANTS :MODULI :MODULUS
 OP CRT2 :CONSTANTS (MAP "DIVIDE :MODULUS :MODULI) :MODULUS
END
```

```
TO CRT2 :CONSTANTS :PARTIALS :MODULUS
 OP CRT3 :CONSTANTS (MAP "MAGIC :MODULUS :PARTIALS) :MODULUS
END
```

```
TO CRT3 :CONSTANTS :MAGICS :MODULUS
 OP COMBINE :CONSTANTS :MAGICS :MODULUS
END
```

Again, notice that the "CRT" functions do no work at all; the work is done by the functions LISTMULT, DIVIDE, MAGIC and COMBINE, and the higher-order function MAP. The dummy functions exist only to help us clarify our thoughts; I could, if I wanted to be especially baroque, eliminate all the dummy functions and lump the whole algorithm into one function like this:

```
TO CRT :CONSTANTS :MODULI
  OP COMBINE :CONSTANTS (MAP "MAGIC(LISTMULT :MODULI)  →
          (MAP "DIVIDE (LISTMULT :MODULI) :MODULI))  →
                (LISTMULT :MODULI)
  END
```

This works (try it), but it is in extremely bad taste. It is impossible to read, and it gives no hint at the beautiful method that we use to solve our congruences. The whole idea of using Logo to help us do mathematics is that Logo code is a natural model of mathematical language. Functions like the above beast might just as well be written in machine code.

Another technique that would eliminate the need for the CRT functions would be to use (local) assignments. We haven't had to use LOCAL and MAKE so far in this book, so there is no need to interrupt our functional style at this late stage.

So now we have it. The function CRT inspires our theorem:

Theorem 15.2 (*The Chinese remainder theorem*) If the elements of the list *MODULI* are relatively prime in pairs, and if *CONSTANTS* is any list of integers (with the same size as *MODULI*), then CRT(*CONSTANTS, MODULI*) outputs a congruence class whose modulus is the product of the elements in *MODULI* and that contains precisely all the integers that are congruent modulo any element of *MODULI* to the corresponding element of *CONSTANTS*.

More precisely, if *MODULI* is the list [M_1 M_2 M_3 M_4 ... M_K], and *CONSTANTS* is [A_1 A_2 A_3 A_4 ... A_K], and the elements of *MODULI* are relatively prime in pairs, then CRT(*CONSTANTS, MODULI*) outputs a class CLASS(R, M) that has the following two properties:

1. M is $M_1 \cdot M_2 \cdot M_3 \cdots M_K$

2. CLASS(R, M) consists of the entire set of numbers that satisfy the congruences

$$X \equiv A_1 \ (\text{MOD } M_1)$$
$$X \equiv A_2 \ (\text{MOD } M_2)$$
$$X \equiv A_3 \ (\text{MOD } M_3)$$
$$X \equiv A_4 \ (\text{MOD } M_4)$$
$$\vdots$$
$$X \equiv A_K \ (\text{MOD } M_K)$$

Exercise 15.11 Find a number that is congruent modulo 9 to 7, modulo 19 to 17, modulo 29 to 27 and modulo 49 to 47.

Project 15.12 Make sure that you understand the proof of the CRT in the general case. Why does REP(CRT(CONSTANTS,MODULI)) give one solution to our congruences? (Hint: What properties do the outputs of MAGIC enjoy?) Why are any two solutions congruent modulo the product of the moduli? Why is every number in the class output by CRT a solution? (Hint: Look at the arguments that we used for three moduli. The proof in general uses exactly the same ideas as the proof for three moduli, so this is not a hard project. Just make sure that you know why the final COMBINE gives us something that works, and make sure you know why all the solutions form a congruence class modulo the product of the moduli.)

Exercise 15.13 Suppose that I have two numbers R and R' that are both congruent modulo 9 to 1 and modulo 7 to 5. How small can $R - R'$ be?

Exercise 15.14 In the age trick, I use the moduli 3, 5, and 7. You give me the remainders when your age is divided by 3, 5, and 7, and I essentially apply CRT and take the REP of the output. Why is it unlikely that the correct answer might be something else in the class output by CRT? What are some other good moduli that could be used in an age trick? What are three good moduli to be used in a trick that starts off "Pick a year in this century ..."?

Experiment 15.15 Find the smallest integer that is 1 modulo 3, 5 and 7. Modulo 3, 5, 7, and 11. Modulo 3, 5, 7, 11, and 13.

Exercise 15.16 Without actually finding them, determine how many integers between 0 and 1000 are congruent modulo 15 to 3 and modulo 34 to 67.

Experiment 15.17 Find the smallest positive number that is congruent to -1 modulo 2, 3, and 5. Find the smallest positive number that is congruent to -1 modulo 2, 3, 5, and 7.

The next project is important for an understanding of the rest of this section.

Project 15.18 Show that if R is any integer, and M and M' are relatively prime moduli, then

$$\text{CRT}([R\ R], [M\ M']) = \text{CLASS}(R, MM')$$

Hints:

1. To see what this is really saying, first try some examples. Try, for example, typing each of the following pairs

   ```
   SHOW CRT [2 2] [3 5]
   SHOW CLASS 2 15
   ```

   ```
   SHOW CRT [5 5] [4 7]
   SHOW CLASS 5 28
   ```

   ```
   SHOW CRT [12 12] [3 7]
   SHOW CLASS 12 21
   ```

   ```
   SHOW CRT [8 8] [4 7]
   SHOW CLASS 8 28
   ```

   ```
   SHOW CRT [37 37] [5 7]
   SHOW CLASS 37 35
   ```

   ```
   SHOW CRT [231 231] [4 7]
   SHOW CLASS 231 28
   ```

2. What does $\text{CRT}([R\ R], [M\ M'])$ really output? It outputs a class modulo MM' that consists of all the numbers which are congruent modulo M to R and modulo M' to R. Doesn't R itself satisfy these two congruences?

3. So, if $\text{CRT}([R\ R], [M\ M'])$ outputs $\text{CLASS}(A, MM')$, isn't R in this class? Then isn't $\text{CLASS}(A, MM')$ the same as $\text{CLASS}(R, MM')$?

Exercise 15.19 Use CRT to find the intersection of the following sets of congruence classes:

1. $\{1\ 4\}$, $\{2\ 7\}$ and $\{5\ 15\}$

2. $\{3\ 13\}$ and $\{7\ 12\}$

3. $\{3\ 11\}$ and $\{7\ 17\}$

4. $\{2\ 3\}$ and $\{4\ 10\}$

5. $\{12\ 13\}$ and $\{15\ 16\}$

Applying the Chinese Remainder Theorem: PHI **Revisited**

The last exercise suggests an interesting line of investigation that will eventually bring us back to the ideas in chapter 13. The CRT gives us a chance to work with various different moduli; perhaps we can use it to see if there are any connections between $\mathbf{Z}/M\mathbf{Z}$ and $\mathbf{Z}/M'\mathbf{Z}$ for different moduli M and M'. For example, we can use the CRT to find the numbers that are common to two congruence classes; it tells us that if M and M' are relatively prime, the intersection of a class in $\mathbf{Z}/M\mathbf{Z}$ and a class in $\mathbf{Z}/M'\mathbf{Z}$ is a class in $\mathbf{Z}/MM'\mathbf{Z}$. To find the intersection of $\{2\ 3\}$ and $\{4\ 10\}$, for example, simply type

```
SHOW CRT [2 4] [3 10]
```

Notice that you have to separate the representatives from the moduli before you use CRT. Or, we can write a function that intersects two classes for us:

```
TO INTERSECT :C :C'
 OP CRT (LIST REP :C REP :C') (LIST MODULUS :C MODULUS :C')
END
```

INTERSECT is a function that takes two classes as input, and if the moduli of the classes are relatively prime, it outputs a class that is contained in each of the input classes (in fact, the output is the "largest" class that is contained in the input classes). For the rest of this discussion, we'll keep the moduli of the classes constant. That is, we'll assume that the first input to INTERSECT comes from $\mathbf{Z}/M\mathbf{Z}$, that the second input comes from $\mathbf{Z}/M'\mathbf{Z}$, and that M and M'

are fixed (relatively prime) moduli. Then INTERSECT is a function from pairs of classes (one from $\mathbf{Z}/M\mathbf{Z}$ and the other from $\mathbf{Z}/M'\mathbf{Z}$) to $\mathbf{Z}/MM'\mathbf{Z}$.

For example, let's suppose that we are working in $\mathbf{Z}/3\mathbf{Z}$ and $\mathbf{Z}/4\mathbf{Z}$, and let's write out exactly what INTERSECTION does. To get the information in this table, I used INTERSECT like this:

SHOW INTERSECT (CLASS 1 3) (CLASS 2 4)

As you can see, there are twelve possible combinations for inputs to IN-TERSECT, and here's the output table:

	{0 3}	{1 3}	{2 3}
{0 4}	{0 12}	{4 12}	{8 12}
{1 4}	{9 12}	{1 12}	{5 12}
{2 4}	{6 12}	{10 12}	{2 12}
{3 4}	{3 12}	{7 12}	{11 12}

What does this tell us? There are several things to notice.

1. On the simplest level, looking at the entry under {1 3} and beside {3 4} we know that the intersection of the class {1 3} and {3 4} is the class {7 12}. This means that if a number is congruent modulo 3 to 1 and modulo 4 to 3, that number is congruent modulo 12 to 7, and, conversely, any number congruent modulo 12 to 7 is congruent modulo 3 to 1 and modulo 4 to 3. So, asking for the output of INTERSECT({1 3}, {3 4}) is the same thing as asking for the solution set of the two congruences:

    $$X \equiv 1 \ (\text{MOD } 3)$$
    $$X \equiv 3 \ (\text{MOD } 4)$$

    This solution set is {7 12}.

2. Every element in $\mathbf{Z}/12\mathbf{Z}$ is an entry in the table.

3. No element of $\mathbf{Z}/12\mathbf{Z}$ is an entry in the table more than once.

The last two properties are especially important. Let's see why they hold.

Why does every element in $\mathbf{Z}/12\mathbf{Z}$ show up as an element in the table? The question is really this:

Given a class $\text{CLASS}(R, 12)$ in $\mathbf{Z}/12\mathbf{Z}$, is there a class C in $\mathbf{Z}/3\mathbf{Z}$ and a class C' in $\mathbf{Z}/4\mathbf{Z}$ so that $\text{INTERSECT}(C, C')$ is $\text{CLASS}(R, 12)$?

Look at this for a minute before reading on.

If you translate the question back to the language of congruences, it almost disappears. What's really going on is that we are trying to "invert" our INTERSECT function. If we input $\{1\ 3\}$ and $\{2\ 4\}$ to INTERSECT, it outputs $\{10\ 12\}$. Why? Because

$$10 \equiv 1\ (\text{MOD } 3)$$
$$10 \equiv 2\ (\text{MOD } 4)$$

Now, however, we are given a class in $\mathbf{Z}/12\mathbf{Z}$, say $\{9\ 12\}$, and we are trying to find two classes $\{A\ 3\}$ and $\{A'\ 4\}$ so that $\{9\ 12\}$ is their intersection. That is, we are trying to find A and A' so that

$$9 \equiv A\ (\text{MOD } 3)$$
$$9 \equiv A'\ (\text{MOD } 4)$$

In other words, we wonder if $\text{CLASS}(9, 12)$ is the output of $\text{CRT}([\,A\ A'\,], [\,3\ 4\,])$ for any integers A and A'. Look at project 15.17; it tells us that $\text{CRT}([\,9\ 9\,], [\,3\ 4\,])$ outputs $\text{CLASS}(9, 12)$. Translating back to a statement about INTERSECT, this says that

$$\text{INTERSECT}((\text{CLASS}(9, 3)), (\text{CLASS}(9, 4))) = \text{CLASS}(9, 12)$$

But $\text{CLASS}(9, 3) = \text{CLASS}(0, 3)$ and $\text{CLASS}(9, 4) = \text{CLASS}(1, 4)$, so

$$\text{INTERSECT}((\text{CLASS}(0, 3)), (\text{CLASS}(1, 4))) = \text{CLASS}(9, 12)$$

If you look on the table under $\{0\ 3\}$ and beside $\{1\ 4\}$, you'll find $\{9\ 12\}$.

Another example: without looking at the table, let's figure out where $\{10\ 12\}$ comes from. *This* is the same as trying to find two classes $\{A\ 3\}$ and $\{A'\ 4\}$ so that $\text{INTERSECT}(\{A\ 3\}, \{A'\ 4\}) = \{10\ 12\}$. This is the same as trying to find A and A' so that $\text{CRT}([\,A\ A'\,]\,[\,3\ 4\,]) = \text{CLASS}(10, 12)$. Project 15.17 says that $\text{CRT}([\,10\ 10\,], [\,3\ 4\,]) = \text{CLASS}(10, 12)$, and this means that

$$\text{INTERSECT}((\text{CLASS}(10,3)),(\text{CLASS}(10,4))) = \text{CLASS}(10,12)$$

But $\text{CLASS}(10,3) = \text{CLASS}(1,3)$ and $\text{CLASS}(10,4) = \text{CLASS}(2,4)$, so

$$\text{INTERSECT}((\text{CLASS}(1,3)),(\text{CLASS}(2,4))) = \text{CLASS}(10,12)$$

If you look on the table under {1 3} and beside {2 4}, you'll find {10 12}. You should check this fact with more examples; try typing

```
SHOW CLASS 7 3, and
SHOW CLASS 7 4, and
SHOW INTERSECT(CLASS 7 3) (CLASS 7 4)
```

or

```
SHOW CLASS 8 3, and
SHOW CLASS 8 4, and
SHOW INTERSECT(CLASS 8 3) (CLASS 8 4)
```

or

```
SHOW CLASS 5 3, and
SHOW CLASS 5 4, and
SHOW INTERSECT(CLASS 5 3) (CLASS 5 4)
```

or

```
SHOW CLASS 11 3, and
SHOW CLASS 11 4, and
SHOW INTERSECT(CLASS 11 3) (CLASS 11 4)
```

or

```
SHOW CLASS 2 3, and
SHOW CLASS 2 4, and
SHOW INTERSECT(CLASS 2 3) (CLASS 2 4)
```

More generally, we have the following result:

Theorem 15.3 The function INTERSECT is onto. That is, if M and M' are relatively prime moduli and R is any integer, the class $\text{CLASS}(R, MM')$ is the output of INTERSECT for some pair of inputs C (from $\mathbf{Z}/M\mathbf{Z}$) and C' (from $\mathbf{Z}/M'\mathbf{Z}$). In fact,

$$\text{INTERSECT}((\text{CLASS}(R, M)), (\text{CLASS}(R, M'))) = \text{CLASS}(R, MM')$$

so that we can take C to be $\text{CLASS}(R, M)$ and C' to be $\text{CLASS}(R, M')$.

The proof in general is the same as in our special case: To say that $\text{INTERSECT}((\text{CLASS}(A, M)), (\text{CLASS}(A', M'))) = \text{CLASS}(R, MM')$ is to say that $\text{CRT}([\,A\ A'\,], [\,M\ M'\,]) = \text{CLASS}(R, MM')$. But project 15.17 says that

$$\text{CRT}([\,R\ R\,], [\,M\ M'\,]) = \text{CLASS}(R, MM')$$

and this says that

$$\text{INTERSECT}((\text{CLASS}(R, M)), (\text{CLASS}(R, M'))) = \text{CLASS}(R, MM')$$

This theorem tells us that if M and M' are relatively prime, every element of $\mathbf{Z}/MM'\mathbf{Z}$ is the intersection of two classes, one from $\mathbf{Z}/M\mathbf{Z}$ and one from $\mathbf{Z}/MM'\mathbf{Z}$. In how many ways can this happen?

That is, suppose that $\text{CLASS}(R, MM')$ is an element of $\mathbf{Z}/MM'\mathbf{Z}$. Then we know that this class is the output of

$$\text{INTERSECT}((\text{CLASS}(R, M)), (\text{CLASS}(R, M')))$$

But couldn't there be two other classes D (from $\mathbf{Z}/M\mathbf{Z}$) and D' (from $\mathbf{Z}/M'\mathbf{Z}$) so that $\text{INTERSECT}(D, D')$ also outputs $\text{CLASS}(R, MM')$? In our example where $M = 3$ and $M' = 4$, this doesn't happen. Can you see why it can't happen in general?

One way to see it is to start with our special case ($M = 3$ and $M' = 4$). We know that $\mathbf{Z}/3\mathbf{Z}$ has 3 elements and $\mathbf{Z}/4\mathbf{Z}$ has 4 elements. There are therefore 12 pairs (C, C') that can be input to INTERSECT. Suppose that two of the pairs caused INTERSECT to output the same thing. That would mean that INTERSECT could have at most 11 distinct outputs. But we have seen that INTERSECT has 12 distinct outputs because, by theorem 15.3, every element of $\mathbf{Z}/12\mathbf{Z}$ is the output of INTERSECT for some choice of inputs, and there are 12 distinct elements in $\mathbf{Z}/12\mathbf{Z}$. So no two pairs can cause INTERSECT to output the same class in $\mathbf{Z}/12\mathbf{Z}$.

The argument in general is exactly the same: Just take the above paragraph and replace 3 by M and 4 by M'. We have the following result:

Theorem 15.4 The function INTERSECT is one-to-one. That is, if the moduli M and M' are relatively prime, then any element in $\mathbf{Z}/MM'\mathbf{Z}$ is the output of INTERSECT for exactly one pair of classes (one from $\mathbf{Z}/M\mathbf{Z}$ and the other from $\mathbf{Z}/M'\mathbf{Z}$).

Project 15.20 The proof that we gave for theorem 15.4 rests on the fact that we know how many elements are in $\mathbf{Z}/N\mathbf{Z}$ for any modulus N. Give another proof of this theorem that does not rely on such "counting." Hints: Suppose that $C = \text{CLASS}(A, M)$, $D = \text{CLASS}(B, M)$, $C' = \text{CLASS}(A', M)$, $D' = \text{CLASS}(B', M)$, and

$$\text{INTERSECT}(C, C') = \text{INTERSECT}(D, D') = \text{CLASS}(R, MM')$$

Show that $C = C'$ and $D = D'$. To do this, note that the definition of INTERSECT implies that the above equation gives us the following congruences:

$R \equiv A \ (\text{MOD } M)$

$R \equiv A' \ (\text{MOD } M')$

$R \equiv B \ (\text{MOD } M)$

$R \equiv B' \ (\text{MOD } M')$

Why does this show that $C = C'$ and $D = D'$?

What happens if I only allow units to be input to INTERSECT? That is, suppose I restrict the domain of INTERSECT to pairs (C, C') where C comes from $(\mathbf{Z}/M\mathbf{Z})^\times$ and C' comes from $(\mathbf{Z}/M'\mathbf{Z})^\times$. The following questions arise right away:

1. If C and C' are units, is $\text{INTERSECT}(C, C')$ a unit in $\mathbf{Z}/MM'\mathbf{Z}$?

2. If D is a unit in $\mathbf{Z}/MM'\mathbf{Z}$, we know that there is exactly one pair (C, C') so that $\text{INTERSECT}(C, C') = D$. Is C a unit in $\mathbf{Z}/M\mathbf{Z}$, and is C' a unit in $\mathbf{Z}/M'\mathbf{Z}$?

Look at our example ($M = 3$ and $M' = 4$). Since 3 is prime, every nonzero element of $\mathbf{Z}/3\mathbf{Z}$ is a unit; $(\mathbf{Z}/3\mathbf{Z})^\times$ consists of CLASS$(1, 3)$ and CLASS$(2, 3)$. In $\mathbf{Z}/4\mathbf{Z}$ the only units are the classes whose representatives are relatively prime to 4 CLASS$(1,4)$ and CLASS$(3,4)$. So the restricted INTERSECT table looks like this:

	$\{1\ 3\}$	$\{2\ 3\}$
$\{1\ 4\}$	$\{1\ 12\}$	$\{5\ 12\}$
$\{3\ 4\}$	$\{7\ 12\}$	$\{11\ 12\}$

Every output is a unit in $\mathbf{Z}/12\mathbf{Z}$ (the representatives are relatively prime to 12). Furthermore, you can check that there are precisely four units in $\mathbf{Z}/12\mathbf{Z}$ (the classes in the body of the table). In this case, the answer to both of the above questions is yes.

Exercise 15.21 Answer these questions if $M = 12$ and $M' = 35$. That is, take the INTERSECT of all pairs of units, one from $\mathbf{Z}/12\mathbf{Z}$ and one from $\mathbf{Z}/35\mathbf{Z}$. Is the output always a unit in $\mathbf{Z}/12 \cdot 35\mathbf{Z}$? Is every unit in $\mathbf{Z}/12 \cdot 35\mathbf{Z}$ the intersect of two units (one from $(\mathbf{Z}/12\mathbf{Z})^\times$ and one from $(\mathbf{Z}/35\mathbf{Z})^\times$)?

Let's see what's going on in general. Suppose that M and M' are relatively prime moduli, and that C is in $(\mathbf{Z}/M\mathbf{Z})^\times$ and C' is in $(\mathbf{Z}/M'\mathbf{Z})^\times$. Then any representative of C is relatively prime to M, and any representative of C' is relatively prime to M'. Suppose that $C = \text{CLASS}(A, M)$, that $C' = \text{CLASS}(A', M')$, and that

$$\text{INTERSECT}(C, C') = \text{CLASS}(R, MM')$$

Once again, this simply means that

$R \equiv A \ (\text{MOD } M)$
$R \equiv A' \ (\text{MOD } M')$

This implies (see project 14.8) that R is relatively prime to M (because A is relatively prime to M and $R \equiv A \ (\text{MOD } M)$) and that R is also relatively prime to M'. But M and M' are relatively prime, so by project 11.35, R and MM' are relatively prime. This means that $\text{CLASS}(R, MM')$ is a unit in $\mathbf{Z}/MM'\mathbf{Z}$.

> I'm referring back to previous projects here just to show you that we *did* establish these results earlier; you should be able to visualize the reasons by simply picturing facts about congruence and prime factorizations.

For example, since $R \equiv A$ (MOD M), there is an integer K so that $R - A = MK$. Now if R and M had a common factor Q, wouldn't Q be a common factor of A and M? But A and M are relatively prime. Another example: To visualize the proof of the statement that R and MM' are relatively prime, imagine the prime factorizations of R, M, M', and MM'. If R and M have no primes in common and R and M' have no primes in common, can R and MM' have any primes in common?

So units end up at units. Do units come from units? That is, if CLASS(R, MM') is a unit in $\mathbf{Z}/MM'\mathbf{Z}$, and if CLASS(R, MM') is the INTERSECT of classes C (in $\mathbf{Z}/M\mathbf{Z}$) and C' (in $\mathbf{Z}/M'\mathbf{Z}$), are C and C' units? Well, thanks to theorem 15.3, we have explicit formulas for C and C':

$C = $ CLASS(R, M)
$C' = $ CLASS(R, M')

Now to say that CLASS(R, MM') is a unit in $\mathbf{Z}/MM'\mathbf{Z}$ is to say that R and MM' are relatively prime. This implies that R and M are relatively prime and that R and M' are relatively prime (why?). And this implies that CLASS(R, M) is a unit in $\mathbf{Z}/M\mathbf{Z}$ and that CLASS(R, M') is a unit in $\mathbf{Z}/M'\mathbf{Z}$.

We have proved the following theorem.

Theorem 15.5 If M and M' are fixed relatively prime moduli, the function INTERSECT sets up a one-to-one correspondence between pairs of units (from $(\mathbf{Z}/M\mathbf{Z})^{\times}$ and $(\mathbf{Z}/M'\mathbf{Z})^{\times}$ and the units in $(\mathbf{Z}/MM'\mathbf{Z})^{\times}$:

1. If C is a unit in $\mathbf{Z}/M\mathbf{Z}$ and C' is a unit in $\mathbf{Z}/M'\mathbf{Z}$, then INTERSECT(C, C') is a unit in $\mathbf{Z}/MM'\mathbf{Z}$.

2. If D is a unit in $\mathbf{Z}/MM'\mathbf{Z}$, then there is exactly one pair (C, C') (C from $(\mathbf{Z}/M\mathbf{Z})^{\times}$ and C' from $(\mathbf{Z}/M'\mathbf{Z})^{\times}$) so that INTERSECT($C, C'$) = D.

Theorem 15.5 has many applications; the most important one for us concerns the function PHI.

In the last chapter, we realized that the number of units in $\mathbf{Z}/M\mathbf{Z}$ is the number of integers that are less than or equal to M and relatively prime to M. This number is given by Euler's PHI function

```
TO PHI :M
 OP COUNT PRIME.TO :M
END
```

So, the number of elements in $(\mathbf{Z}/M\mathbf{Z})^{\times}$ is PHI(12), or 4. Similarly, the number of elements in $(\mathbf{Z}/35\mathbf{Z})^{\times}$ is PHI(35), or 24. How many elements are there in $(\mathbf{Z}/12 \cdot 35\mathbf{Z})^{\times}$? Well, there are PHI($12 \cdot 35$) elements. On the other hand, the number of units in $\mathbf{Z}/12 \cdot 35\mathbf{Z}$ is the same as the number of pairs of units (C, C') where C is from $(\mathbf{Z}/12\mathbf{Z})^{\times}$ and C' is from $(\mathbf{Z}/35\mathbf{Z})^{\times}$. There are PHI(12) elements in $(\mathbf{Z}/12\mathbf{Z})^{\times}$ and PHI(35) elements in $(\mathbf{Z}/35\mathbf{Z})^{\times}$, so there are $(\text{PHI}(12)) \cdot (\text{PHI}(35))$ possible pairs. In other words,

$$(\text{PHI}(12)) \cdot (\text{PHI}(35)) = \text{PHI}(12 \cdot 35)$$

This technique works in general. If M and M' are relatively prime, then, on one hand, there are PHI(MM') units in $(\mathbf{Z}/MM'\mathbf{Z})^{\times}$, and on the other hand there are as many units in $(\mathbf{Z}/MM'\mathbf{Z})^{\times}$ as there are pairs (C, C'), C from $(\mathbf{Z}/M\mathbf{Z})^{\times}$ and C' from $(\mathbf{Z}/M'\mathbf{Z})^{\times}$. But there are PHI($M$) possible values for C and PHI(M') possible values for C', so there are $(\text{PHI}(M)) \cdot (\text{PHI}(M'))$ possible pairs. We have at last proved the following theorem:

Theorem 15.6 The Euler function PHI is multiplicative. That is, if M and M' are relatively prime, then

$$\text{PHI}(MM') = (\text{PHI}(M))(\text{PHI}(M'))$$

This theorem allows us to wrap up some unfinished business from chapter 13. In project 13.19 we introduced Euler's PHI function and showed that it agrees on prime powers with the parent of ID, SIG_{-1}. Indeed, both functions behave at prime powers like this:

$$\text{PHI}(P^K) = P^K - P^{(K-1)}$$
$$\text{SIG}_{-1}(P^K) = P^K - P^{(K-1)}$$

Of course, these values are correct for different reasons. The formula for PHI holds because the right-hand side gives the number of integers less than or equal to P^K that have no common factor with P^K. The formula for SIG_{-1} holds because we want SIG_{-1} to be the parent of ID, and we saw that if we define SIG_{-1} at prime powers this way, then the COMPILE of SIG_{-1} is ID; that is, for any positive integer N,

$$\sum_{D \in \text{DIVISORS}(N)} \text{SIG}_{-1}(D) = \text{ID}(N) = N$$

We now know that both functions are multiplicative (we always knew that SIG_{-1} is multiplicative, and we suspected that PHI is multiplicative, but now we can *say* that PHI is multiplicative without feeling nervous). But, as we saw in chapter 13, two multiplicative functions that agree on prime powers are equal, and we have the following theorem.

Theorem 15.7 The functions PHI and SIG_{-1} are equal on positive integers. That is, the Euler PHI function is the parent of ID.

So ID has an interesting child (SIG), and an even more interesting parent (PHI).

This theorem gives us two ways to think about PHI, and this duality allows us to state some theorems that would otherwise be rather startling.

Theorem 15.8 If N is any positive integer,

$$\sum_{D \in \text{DIVISORS}(N)} \text{PHI}(D) = N$$

Of course, this is obvious in light of the fact that PHI is the parent of ID; it just says that if you COMPILE ID's, parent you get ID. But think of what it would say if we didn't know that PHI was ID's parent; imagine all that we knew was that $\text{PHI}(N)$ is the number of integers less than or equal to N that are relatively prime to N. Then, for example, if we take N to be 21, the theorem says that

(the number of integers less than or equal to 1 and relatively prime to 1)

+ (the number of integers less than or equal to 3 and relatively prime to 3)

+ (the number of integers less than or equal to 7 and relatively prime to 7)

+ (the number of integers less than or equal to 21 and relatively prime to 21)

= 21

This works $(1 + 2 + 6 + 12 = 21)$, but without theorem 15.6, it would take a contrived proof to establish the result in general.

The fact that PHI is multiplicative can also be used to quickly calculate the values of PHI. For example, if I want to know the value of $\text{PHI}(35)$, I don't have to list the numbers between 1 and 35 and count all the ones that are relatively prime to 35; instead, I can just calculate $\text{PHI}(7) \cdot \text{PHI}(5)$. Now 7 is a prime, so $\text{PHI}(7) = 6$ (every integer between 1 and 6 is relatively prime to

7), and similarly, PHI(5) = 4. So PHI(35) = 6 · 4, or 24. Twenty-four of the integers between 1 and 35 have no factor in common with 35.

We can extend PHI by multiplicativity, just as we did for SIG$_{-1}$. Since we know what PHI does to prime powers, we have the following theorem.

Theorem 15.8 If N is a positive integer whose prime factorization is

$$N = P_1^{E_1} P_2^{E_2} \cdots P_K^{E_K}$$

then

$$\text{PHI}(N) = (P_1^{E_1} - P_1^{(E_1-1)})(P_2^{E_2} - P_2^{(E_2-1)})(P_3^{E_3} - P_3^{(E_3-1)}) \cdots (P_K^{E_K} - P_K^{(E_K-1)})$$

This method of calculating the outputs of PHI gives rise to another interesting formula. Suppose we take the formula in the theorem and factor a "P^E" out of every parentheses; that is, we write the first term

$$\left(P_1^{E_1} - P_1^{(E_1-1)} \right)$$

as

$$P_1^{E_1} \left(1 - \frac{1}{P_1} \right)$$

and we write the second term

$$\left(P_2^{E_2} - P_2^{(E_2-1)} \right)$$

as

$$P_2^{E_2} \left(1 - \frac{1}{P_2} \right)$$

and so on. Then we have

$$\text{PHI}(N) = P_1^{E_1}(1 - \frac{1}{P_1}) P_2^{E_2}(1 - 1/P_2) P_3^{E_3}(1 - \frac{1}{P_3}) \cdots P_K^{E_K}(1 - \frac{1}{P_K})$$

$$= P_1^{E_1} P_2^{E_2} \cdots P_K^{E_K}(1 - \frac{1}{P_1})(1 - \frac{1}{P_2})(1 - \frac{1}{P_3}) \cdots (1 - \frac{1}{P_K})$$

$$= N(1 - \frac{1}{P_1})(1 - \frac{1}{P_2})(1 - \frac{1}{P_3}) \cdots (1 - \frac{1}{P_K})$$

This formula

$$\text{PHI}(N) = N \prod_{\substack{P \text{ a prime} \\ P \in \text{DIVISORS}(N)}} \left(1 - \frac{1}{P}\right)$$

is sometimes called the *product formula* for PHI; we can model it in Logo like this

```
TO PROD.PHI :N
 OP :N * (PROD "P.TERM [] SUPPORT :N)
END

TO P.TERM :P
 OP 1 - (1/P)
END
```

Recall that the support of N can be calculated as

```
TO SUPPORT :N
 OP FILTER "DIVIS? :N PRIMES.UPTO :N
END
```

In this version of PHI, all we need to know about the input is its support (you don't need to know the *p*-orders for the primes that divide the input), but be careful when using this version of PHI; because it introduces fractions into the calculation, roundoff might creep into the outputs (PHI should output an integer).

Exercise 15.22 Use the multiplicativity of PHI to evaluate

1. PHI(120)

2. PHI(1213)

3. PHI(210)

4. PHI(8!)

Exercise 15.23 If N is an odd number, why is the number of integers less than or equal to N that are relatively prime to N the same as the number of integers less than or equal to $2N$ that are relatively prime to $2N$? Is the same thing true if N is even?

Exercise 15.24 How many units are there in **Z**/1440**Z**?

Project 15.25 Suppose that F is the function defined on positive integers like this:

```
TO F :N
 OP (PROD "P.TERM [] SUPPORT :N)
END
```

where P.TERM is defined as above. Tabulate F between 1 and 30, and verify that F seems to be multiplicative (F need not output integers). Prove that F is multiplicative by showing that the function

```
TO G :N
 OP (PHI :N) / :N
END
```

is multiplicative.

Experiment 15.26 Suppose that we define the function T as

```
TO T :N
 OP (MU :N) / :N
END
```

where MU is the Möbius function of chapter 13.

```
TO MU :N
 IF :N = 1 [OP 1]
 IF SQUAREFREE? :N [OP POWER -1 COUNT SUPPORT :N]
 OP 0
END
```

Tabulate T, and look for patterns. Then let S be the child of T:

```
TO S :N
 OP COMPILE "T [] :N
END
```

Tabulate S, and express S in terms of well-known functions.

Project 15.27 Suppose that M and N are two integers with the same support. Show that

$$\frac{\text{PHI}(N)}{\text{PHI}(M)} = \frac{N}{M}$$

Hint: Use the product formula for PHI.

Fields and Arithmetic in $\mathbf{Z}/P\mathbf{Z}$

In the last chapter, we saw that every unit in $\mathbf{Z}/M\mathbf{Z}$ has an order. That is, if C is a unit in $\mathbf{Z}/M\mathbf{Z}$, there is an integer E so that $C^E = \{1\ M\}$. Let's look at this phenomenon more closely.

The simplest place to start is in $\mathbf{Z}/P\mathbf{Z}$ where P is a prime. The reason is that every nonzero element of $\mathbf{Z}/P\mathbf{Z}$ is a unit. As I mentioned before, this means that $\mathbf{Z}/P\mathbf{Z}$ resembles the rational numbers much more than it resembles $\mathbf{Z}$. $\mathbf{Z}/P\mathbf{Z}$ and the rational numbers are examples of what mathematicians call "fields." A field is a set of objects that can be added and multiplied and that obey the usual laws of algebra (including the one that says that nonzero elements have reciprocals). Examples of fields are $\mathbf{Z}/P\mathbf{Z}$, the rational numbers, the real numbers, and the complex numbers. Nonexamples are $\mathbf{Z}/12\mathbf{Z}$ (not every nonzero element has a reciprocal), and $\mathbf{Z}$ (3 doesn't have a reciprocal in $\mathbf{Z}$). A field either has infinitely many elements (like the rational numbers) or a finite number of elements (like $\mathbf{Z}/5\mathbf{Z}$), and a theorem from algebra says that every field contains either the rational numbers or $\mathbf{Z}/P\mathbf{Z}$ for some prime P. Field theory (it doesn't mean the same thing as in physics) is that branch of algebra that studies properties that are common to whole classes of fields.

The thing about fields is that you can do algebra in them. By that, I mean that you can forget what the objects you are working with look like, and you can manipulate them according to the rules of elementary algebra. These rules assume that you have two operations, addition and multiplication, and they simply say that addition is commutative and associative, that there is a zero element for addition, that every element has a negative, that multiplication is commutative and associative, that there is an identity element for multiplication, that every nonzero element has a reciprocal, and that multiplication distributes over addition. Let me give you some examples.

Example 1 In any field, $(X + A)(X - A) = X^2 - A^2$. (Do you remember how this identity is derived from the rules of algebra?) Since this is true in any field, it is true in $\mathbf{Z}/5\mathbf{Z}$. So, in $\mathbf{Z}/5\mathbf{Z}$,

$$(\{2\ 5\} + \{4\ 5\})(\{2\ 5\} - \{4\ 5\}) = \{2\ 5\}^2 - \{4\ 5\}^2$$

To see this, look at the left-hand side:

$$\{2\ 5\} + \{4\ 5\} = \{1\ 5\}$$
$$\{2\ 5\} - \{4\ 5\} = \{3\ 5\}$$
$$\{1\ 5\}\{3\ 5\} = \{3\ 5\}$$

Now, look at the right-hand side:

$$\{2\ 5\}^2 = \{4\ 5\}$$
$$\{4\ 5\}^2 = \{1\ 5\}$$
$$\{4\ 5\} - \{1\ 5\} = \{3\ 5\}$$

Check that the identity holds in $\mathbf{Z}/7\mathbf{Z}$ as well. (Actually, because the derivation of this identity in algebra never makes use of the fact that nonzero elements have reciprocals, it will also hold in $\mathbf{Z}/M\mathbf{Z}$ where M is not a prime.)

Example 2 In any field, if A is not zero, the solution to $AX = B$ is $X = B/A$. Of course, by B/A we mean "B times the reciprocal of A." So, in $\mathbf{Z}/11\mathbf{Z}$, if I want to solve $\{3\ 11\}X = \{7\ 11\}$, I multiply both sides by the reciprocal of $\{3\ 11\}$ (which exists because $\mathbf{Z}/11\mathbf{Z}$ is a field), or $\{4\ 11\}$. My solution is then

$$X = \{7\ 11\} \cdot \{4\ 11\}, \text{ or } X = \{6\ 11\}$$

(Check that $\{6\ 11\}$ satisfies the original equation.)

Example 3 In any field, if $AD - BC$ is not zero, then the solution to the system of two equations in two unknowns:

$$AX + BY = E$$
$$CX + DY = F$$

is:

$$X = \frac{ED - BF}{AD - BC} \quad \text{and} \quad Y = \frac{AF - EC}{AD - BC}$$

This is called *Cramer's rule*. Suppose we had the system of equations in $\mathbf{Z}/7\mathbf{Z}$:

$$\{2\ 7\}X + \{4\ 7\}Y = \{3\ 7\}$$
$$\{1\ 7\}X + \{5\ 7\}Y = \{6\ 7\}$$

According to Cramer's rule,

$$X = \frac{\{3\ 7\} \cdot \{5\ 7\} - \{4\ 7\} \cdot \{6\ 7\}}{\{2\ 7\} \cdot \{5\ 7\} - \{4\ 7\} \cdot \{1\ 7\}} \quad \text{and} \quad Y = \frac{\{2\ 7\} \cdot \{6\ 7\} - \{3\ 7\} \cdot \{1\ 7\}}{\{2\ 7\} \cdot \{5\ 7\} - \{4\ 7\} \cdot \{1\ 7\}}$$

Of course, this has to be interpreted as

$$X = (\{3\ 7\} \cdot \{5\ 7\} - \{4\ 7\} \cdot \{6\ 7\})\texttt{RECIP}(\{2\ 7\} \cdot \{5\ 7\} - \{4\ 7\} \cdot \{1\ 7\})$$

$$Y = (\{2\ 7\} \cdot \{6\ 7\} - \{3\ 7\} \cdot \{1\ 7\})\texttt{RECIP}(\{2\ 7\} \cdot \{5\ 7\} - \{4\ 7\} \cdot \{1\ 7\})$$

The calculation is then mechanical (working in the arithmetic of $\mathbf{Z}/7\mathbf{Z}$); try it and check that your result actually satisfies the system. In fact, you can get Logo to do the work for you.

Project 15.28 Write a Logo function **CRAMER** that takes six classes from $\mathbf{Z}/P\mathbf{Z}$ as input. $\texttt{CRAMER}(A, B, C, D, E, F)$ will output the solution to

$$AX + BY = E$$
$$CX + DY = F$$

For example,

```
SHOW CRAMER CLASS 2 7 CLASS 4 7 CLASS 1 7 CLASS 5 7 →
          CLASS 3 7 CLASS 6 7
```

will produce the solution to

$$\{2\ 7\}X + \{4\ 7\}Y = \{3\ 7\}$$
$$\{1\ 7\}X + \{5\ 7\}Y = \{6\ 7\}$$

Hint: You might want to use the determinant function:

```
TO DET :R :S :T :U
 OP ADD (MULT :R :T) (NEG (MULT :S :U))
END
```

Remember, all the algebra is in $\mathbf{Z}/P\mathbf{Z}$, so you have to use ADD, MULT, NEG, and RECIP instead of $+$, $*$, $-$, and $/$.

Example 4 The usual theorems from the theory of equations carry over to any field. For example, we have

1. If an equation has degree N, it has at most N roots. This means that

$$\{1\ 5\}X^3 + \{3\ 5\}X^2 + \{2\ 5\}X + \{4\ 5\} = \{0\ 5\}$$

has at most three roots in $\mathbf{Z}/5\mathbf{Z}$. (How many does it have?)

2. If A is a root of a polynomial equation in the variable X, then $X - A$ is a factor of that polynomial. In the above example, $\{1\ 5\}$ is a root of the equation. This means that

$$\begin{aligned}
\{1\ 5\}X^3 + \{3\ 5\}X^2 &+ \{2\ 5\}X + \{4\ 5\} \\
&= (\{1\ 5\}X - \{1\ 5\}) \cdot (something)
\end{aligned}$$

In fact,

$$\begin{aligned}
\{1\ 5\}X^3 + \{3\ 5\}X^2 &+ \{2\ 5\}X + \{3\ 5\} \\
&= (\{1\ 5\}X - \{1\ 5\})(\{1\ 5\}X^2 + \{4\ 5\}X + \{1\ 5\})
\end{aligned}$$

To get the factorization, I used "synthetic division in $\mathbf{Z}/5\mathbf{Z}$":

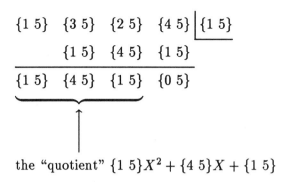

the "quotient" $\{1\ 5\}X^2 + \{4\ 5\}X + \{1\ 5\}$

3. If two polynomials have the same degree, the same zeros, and the same leading coefficients, then the polynomials are exactly the same. For example, in $\mathbf{Z}/11\mathbf{Z}$, suppose that

$$\mathbf{F}(X) = \{1\ 11\}X^3 + \{3\ 11\}X^2 + \{8\ 11\}X + \{10\ 11\}$$

and

$$\mathbf{G}(X) = (\{1\ 11\}X - \{1\ 11\})(\{1\ 11\}X - \{3\ 11\})(\{1\ 11\}X - \{4\ 11\})$$

then both polynomials have degree 3, both polynomials have leading coefficient $\{1\ 11\}$, and both polynomials have the same zeros: $\{1\ 11\}$, $\{3\ 11\}$ and $\{4\ 11\}$. (You can check that these classes are zeros of $\mathbf{F}$. Why are they the only zeros of $\mathbf{F}$?) So $\mathbf{F}(X)$ and $\mathbf{G}(X)$ are identical; that is, if you multiply out the three terms in $\mathbf{G}$, you'll get a polynomial of degree 3 with exactly the same coefficients as $\mathbf{F}$. You should try it; remember that all the arithmetic is done modulo 11.

In the above example it was cumbersome to write the coefficients as classes. Since we all knew that the modulus was 11, we could have written

$$\{1\ 11\}X^3 + \{3\ 11\}X^2 + \{8\ 11\}X + \{10\ 11\}$$

as

$$1X^3 + 3X^2 + 8X + 10$$

or even as

$$X^3 + 3X^2 + 8X + 10$$

Let's do this from now on; if we are working in $\mathbf{Z}/P\mathbf{Z}$ and the value of P is clear from the context (or is constant and doesn't make a difference in our discussion), we'll write A instead of $\mathtt{CLASS}(A, P)$ or $\{A, P\}$. So, here's how the discussion in 2 would look if we employed this shorthand:

2'. If A is a root of a polynomial equation in the variable X, then $X - A$ is a factor of that polynomial. In the above example (keeping the modulus at 5), 1 is a root of the equation. This means that

$$X^3 + 3X^2 + 2X + 4 = (X - 1) \cdot (something)$$

In fact

$$X^3 + 3X^2 + 2X + 3 = (X - 1)(X^2 + 4X + 1)$$

To get the factorization, I used "synthetic division in $\mathbf{Z}/5\mathbf{Z}$":

$$
\begin{array}{ccc|c}
1 & 3 & 2 & 4 \,\rule{0.5pt}{20pt}\, 1 \\
  & 1 & 4 & 1 \\
\hline
1 & 4 & 1 & 0
\end{array}
$$

$$\underbrace{}$$
$$\uparrow$$

the "quotient" $X^2 + 4X + 1$

Example 5 The binomial theorem is true in $\mathbf{Z}/5\mathbf{Z}$. For example, in $\mathbf{Z}/5\mathbf{Z}$,

$$\begin{aligned}
(X + Y)^4 &= X^4 + 4X^3 + 6X^2 + 4X + 1 \\
&= X^4 + 4X^3 + 2X^2 + 4X + 1
\end{aligned}$$

(I should be writing

$$\begin{aligned}
(\{1\ 5\}X + \{1\ 5\}Y)^4 &= \{1\ 5\}X^4 + \{4\ 5\}X^3 + \{6\ 5\}X^2 + \{4\ 5\}X + \{1\ 5\} \\
&= \{1\ 5\}X^4 + \{4\ 5\}X^3 + \{2\ 5\}X^2 + \{4\ 5\}X + \{1\ 5\}
\end{aligned}$$

but remember, we've agreed to leave off the "{ 5}" decoration.)

Take another example:

$$(X + Y)^5 = X^5 + 5X^4Y + 10X^3Y^2 + 10X^2Y^3 + 5XY^4 + Y^5$$

All of the middle coefficients belong to the class {0 5} in $\mathbf{Z}/5\mathbf{Z}$, so this simplifies to

$$(X + Y)^5 = X^5 + Y^5$$

That's interesting; it says that in $\mathbf{Z}/5\mathbf{Z}$, $(X + Y)^5 = X^5 + Y^5$. Is this true for any prime P? For any modulus M?

Experiment 15.29 For what values of M between 2 and 29 is it true that

$$(X + Y)^M = X^M + Y^M \text{ in } \mathbf{Z}/M\mathbf{Z}$$

To do this experiment, remember that the coefficients of $(X + Y)^M$ can be read off from the Mth row of Pascal's triangle, so generate 29 rows of the triangle and reduce the Mth row modulo M for each M between 2 and 29. In fact, you can easily modify the functions that we wrote to generate Pascal's triangle so that the Mth row is output already reduced mod M.

Project 15.30 Show that if P is a prime, then

$$(X + Y)^P = X^P + Y^P \text{ in } \mathbf{Z}/P\mathbf{Z}$$

Hint: By the binomial theorem, it's enough to show that the "interior" elements of the Pth row of Pascal's triangle are divisible by P. For example, the seventh row of the triangle is

$$1 \quad 7 \quad 21 \quad 35 \quad 35 \quad 21 \quad 7 \quad 1$$

and, modulo 7, this is

$$1 \quad 0 \quad 0 \quad 0 \quad 0 \quad 0 \quad 0 \quad 1$$

The Kth entry in the Pth row is simply $\mathrm{B}(P, K)$. So show that if K is any integer between 1 and $P - 1$, $\mathrm{B}(P, K) \equiv 0 \ (\mathrm{MOD} \ P)$. For this, use the model 3 version of B.

```
TO B :N :K
 OP (FACT :N) / ((FACT :K) * (FACT (:N - :K)))
END
```

This says that $B(P, K) = \dfrac{P!}{K! * (P - K)!}$

Now $B(P, K)$ is an integer (why?), so the denominator must be a factor of the numerator. But if K is between 2 and $P - 1$, every factor of the denominator is less than P (why?). Therefore (and *this* is because P is prime) every factor of the denominator is relatively prime to P. Conclude that the denominator must be a factor of $(P - 1)!$ (it is a factor of $P!$ and it is relatively prime to P). In other words,

$$B(P, K) = \frac{P \cdot (something)}{1} = P \cdot (something)$$

Why does this argument break down if P is not a prime? Are there special cases when it works for nonprime moduli?

The result of the above project is important enough to state as a theorem:

Theorem 15.9 If P is a prime, then

$$(X + Y)^P = X^P + Y^P \text{ in } \mathbf{Z}/P\mathbf{Z}$$

So, in $\mathbf{Z}/7\mathbf{Z}$, $(5 + 4)^7 = 5^7 + 4^7$. This means, of course, that

$$(\{5\ 7\} + \{4\ 7\})^7 = \{5\ 7\}^7 + \{4\ 7\}^7$$

or

$$\{2\ 7\}^7 = \{5\ 7\}^7 + \{4\ 7\}^7$$

To check this in Logo, make sure that the following produce the same result:

```
SHOW EXPMOD (ADD CLASS 5 7 CLASS 4 7) 7
```

```
SHOW ADD (EXPMOD (CLASS 5 7) 7) (EXPMOD (CLASS 4 7) 7)
```

```
SHOW EXPMOD (CLASS 2 7) 7
```

Did you notice that

SHOW EXPMOD (CLASS 2 7) 7

produces the same thing as

SHOW CLASS 2 7

Does this always happen?

Experiment 15.31 Look at the seventh power of every element in $\mathbf{Z}/7\mathbf{Z}$:

SHOW EXPMOD (CLASS 0 7) 7

SHOW EXPMOD (CLASS 1 7) 7

SHOW EXPMOD (CLASS 2 7) 7

SHOW EXPMOD (CLASS 3 7) 7

SHOW EXPMOD (CLASS 4 7) 7

SHOW EXPMOD (CLASS 5 7) 7

SHOW EXPMOD (CLASS 6 7) 7

Check the eleventh power of all the elements in $\mathbf{Z}/11\mathbf{Z}$.

One way to see that this always works is to use the binomial theorem in $\mathbf{Z}/P\mathbf{Z}$. Let's fix our prime P and identify classes with their representatives (so that 2 means $\{2\ P\}$). Then, in $\mathbf{Z}/P\mathbf{Z}$,

$$0^P = 0$$

$$1^P = 1$$

$$2^P = (1+1)^P = 1^P + 1^P = 1 + 1 = 2$$

$$3^P = (1+2)^P = 1^P + 2^P = 1 + 2 = 3$$

$$4^P = (1+3)^P = 1^P + 3^P = 1 + 3 = 4$$

$$\vdots$$

$$K^P = (1+(K-1))^P = 1^P + (K-1)^P = 1 + K - 1 = K$$

$$\vdots$$

and inductively we have the following result:

Theorem 15.10 For any element C in $\mathbf{Z}/P\mathbf{Z}$, $C^P = C$.

Suppose that C is a nonzero element on $\mathbf{Z}/P\mathbf{Z}$. Then $C^P = C$, and C has a reciprocal. Multiplying both sides of this equation by the reciprocal of C, we have the following celebrated result.

Theorem 15.11 (*Fermat's little theorem*) If C is a nonzero element of $\mathbf{Z}/P\mathbf{Z}$, then $C^{(P-1)} = 1$.

Exercise 15.32 Verify this result for several primes. For example, in $\mathbf{Z}/5\mathbf{Z}$, what happens if you type

```
SHOW EXPMOD (CLASS 1 5) 4

SHOW EXPMOD (CLASS 2 5) 4

SHOW EXPMOD (CLASS 3 5) 4

SHOW EXPMOD (CLASS 4 5) 4
```

Try it for 7, 11, 13, and 23.

Experiment 15.33 Is Fermat's little theorem true for any non-prime moduli? If it isn't true for all the classes in $\mathbf{Z}/M\mathbf{Z}$ for a particular value of M, can you describe those classes C in $\mathbf{Z}/M\mathbf{Z}$ for which $C^{(M-1)} = 1$? #Can you find a modulus M that is not prime, but so that $C^{(M-1)} = 1$ for all units C in $\mathbf{Z}/M\mathbf{Z}$?

Fermat's little theorem is often translated into the language of congruence in $\mathbf{Z}$:

'Theorem 15.11 (*Fermat's little theorem—congruence version*) If A is an integer not divisible by a prime P, then $A^{(P-1)} \equiv 1 \ (\mathrm{MOD} \ P)$.

This version can be used to speed up the exponentiation of classes in $\mathbf{Z}/P\mathbf{Z}$. For example, suppose we are in $\mathbf{Z}/7\mathbf{Z}$, and we want the 346th power of $\{3 \ 7\}$. Well, first look at the twelfth power of $\{3 \ 7\}$:

$$\{3 \ 7\}^6 = \{1 \ 7\}, \text{ so } \{3 \ 7\}^{12} = (\{3 \ 7\}^6)^2 = \{1 \ 7\}^2 = \{1 \ 7\}$$

Similarly, if $E = 6K$ for some integer K,

$$\{3 \ 7\}^E = (\{3 \ 7\}^6)^K = \{1 \ 7\}^K = \{1 \ 7\}$$

Now 346 isn't divisible by 6; if E is 346, $E \equiv 4 \ (\mathrm{MOD} \ 6)$ So, $E = 6K + 4$ for some integer K, and

$$\{3\ 7\}^E = \{3\ 7\}^{(6K+4)} = \{3\ 7\}^{6K}\{3\ 7\}^4 = \{1\ 7\}\{3\ 7\}^4 = \{3\ 7\}^4 = \{4\ 7\}$$

The last step was calculated by actually raising $\{3\ 7\}$ to the fourth power.

So, in $\mathbf{Z}/P\mathbf{Z}$, The value of C^E only depends on the remainder when E is divided by $P - 1$, that is on $\text{MOD}(E, P - 1)$. To calculate $\{5\ 11\}^{3452}$, I simply reduce the exponent modulo 10 ($10 = 11 - 1$), and because every 10th power of $\{5\ 11\}$ is 1 in $\mathbf{Z}/11\mathbf{Z}$, $\{5\ 11\}^{3450}$ is 1. This means that $\{5\ 11\}^{3542}$ is the same as $\{5\ 11\}^2$ or $\{3\ 11\}$. In other words,

$$\{5\ 11\}^{3452} = \{5\ 11\}^{(\text{MOD}(3452,10))} = \{5\ 11\}^2 = \{3\ 11\}$$

Think of how efficient this is. Raising a class in $\mathbf{Z}/P\mathbf{Z}$ to any power amounts to a calculation with an exponent of at most $P - 1$. We can modify our EXPMOD function to take advantage of this fact.

```
TO EXPMOD.P :C :E
  IF :E < 0 [OP RECIP EXPMOD.P :C -1 * :E]
  IF :E = 0 [OP CLASS 1 MODULUS :C]
  IF :E < MODULUS :C [OP  MULT :C (EXPMOD.P :C :E - 1)]
  OP EXPMOD.P :C (MOD :E ((MODULUS :C) - 1))
END
```

Compare this to EXPMOD for a few calculations:

```
SHOW EXPMOD CLASS 5 7 23

SHOW EXPMOD.P CLASS 5 7 23

SHOW EXPMOD CLASS 5 7 53

SHOW EXPMOD.P CLASS 5 7 53
```

and so on.

Be very careful that you only use the fast EXPMOD.P when the modulus is prime. Of course, you could write a generic EXPMOD.G that first checked the modulus for primality and then called EXPMOD.P or EXPMOD as a result of the test. From the standpoint of efficiency, why is this a silly idea?

Exercise 15.34 Show that if P is a prime and $E \equiv E'$ (MOD $(P - 1)$), then for all classes C in $\mathbf{Z}/P\mathbf{Z}$, $C^E = C^{E'}$.

Fermat's little theorem has many interesting implications. For example, it says that every nonzero element in $\mathbf{Z}/P\mathbf{Z}$ is a solution to the equation:

$$X^{(P-1)} - 1 = 0$$

(Remember, this stands for $\{1\ P\}X^{(P-1)} - \{1\ P\} = 0$.)

There are precisely $P - 1$ nonzero elements in $\mathbf{Z}/P\mathbf{Z}$, so these must be all of the solutions to the above equation (its degree is only $P - 1$). This means that the polynomial $X^{(P-1)} - 1$ must factor (as a polynomial with coefficients in $\mathbf{Z}/P\mathbf{Z}$) as

$$X^{(P-1)} - 1 = (X - 1)(X - 2)(X - 3)(X - 4) \cdots (X - (P - 1))$$

Make sure that you understand what this means. I'm not saying that this is true as a statement about polynomials with integer coefficients; it certainly isn't true that

$$X^4 - 1 = (X - 1)(X - 2)(X - 3)(X - 4)$$

in the ordinary algebra of high school. But if I interpret the coefficients as standing for the classes that they represent in $\mathbf{Z}/5\mathbf{Z}$, then it is true that

$$\{1\ 5\}X^4 - \{1\ 5\} =$$
$$(\{1\ 5\}X - \{1\ 5\})(\{1\ 5\}X - \{2\ 5\})(\{1\ 5\}X - \{3\ 5\})(\{1\ 5\}X - \{4\ 5\})$$

You should check this by multiplying out the right-hand side (using arithmetic in Z/5Z) exactly as you would in algebra:

$$(\{1\ 5\}X - \{1\ 5\})(\{1\ 5\}X - \{2\ 5\})$$
$$= (\{1\ 5\}\{1\ 5\})X^2 - (\{1\ 5\} \cdot \{1\ 5\} + \{1\ 5\} \cdot \{2\ 5\})X + \{1\ 5\} \cdot \{2\ 5\}$$
$$= \{1\ 5\}X^2 - \{3\ 5\}X + \{2\ 5\}$$
$$= \{1\ 5\}X^2 + \{2\ 5\}X + \{2\ 5\}$$

Multiply this by the next term $\{1\ 5\}X - \{3\ 5\}$, and finally by the fourth term $\{1\ 5\}X - \{4\ 5\}$.

An easier way to do this algebra (because we were all brought up in the algebra of $\mathbf{Z}$ rather than in that of $\mathbf{Z}/5\mathbf{Z}$) is to multiply out

$$(X - 1)(X - 2)(X - 3)(X - 4)$$

as you usually do and reduce the coefficient modulo 5 (either as you go or at the end). So, you could do something like this:

$$
\begin{aligned}
(X - 1)(X - 2)(X - 3)(X - 4) &= (X^2 - 3X + 2)(X - 3)(X - 4) \\
&\equiv (X^2 + 2X + 2)(X - 3)(X - 4) \\
&= (X^3 - X^2 - 4X - 6)(X - 4) \\
&\equiv (X^3 + 4X^2 + X + 4)(X - 4) \\
&= X^4 - 15X^2 - 16 \\
&\equiv X^4 - 1
\end{aligned}
$$

Here I multiplied things out via usual algebra and then replaced coefficients by their distinguished representatives modulo 5 (so that -6 becomes 4). There are other styles of calculating; some people multiply the whole thing out and then reduce, while others only reduce numbers whose absolute values are bigger that 4.

I realize that this discussion is very much like a crash course, but the topic of algebra over finite fields could easily fill up another book (one that would benefit from a use of functional programming). Here we'll simply use several of its techniques and results to get some information about $\mathbf{Z}/P\mathbf{Z}$.

For example, in the algebra of $\mathbf{Z}/P\mathbf{Z}$,

$$X^{(P-1)} - 1 = (X - 1)(X - 2)(X - 3)(X - 4) \cdots (X - (P - 1))$$

Look at the constant term on both sides. On the left, it is simply -1. On the right, it is the product of all the constant terms from the factors

$$(-1)(-2)(-3)(-4)(-5) \cdots (-(P - 1)) = (-1)^{(P-1)}(P - 1)!$$

Now if P is odd (and all primes except 2 are odd), $P - 1$ is even, so the constant term on the right is just $(P - 1)!$.

Of course, this doesn't mean that $-1 = (P - 1)!$; it means that

$$\text{CLASS}(-1, P) = \text{CLASS}((P - 1)!, P)$$

Since this is clearly true if $P = 2$, we have the following theorem.

Theorem 15.12 (*Wilson's theorem*)   If P is a prime,

$$\mathtt{CLASS}(-1, P) = \mathtt{CLASS}((P-1)!, P)$$

or

Theorem 15.12′ (*Wilson's theorem—congruence version*)   If P is a prime,

$$(P-1)! \equiv -1 \ (\mathrm{MOD} \ P)$$

Experiment 15.35   If P is bigger than 2, what can you say about $\mathtt{CLASS}((P-2)!, P)$?

Project 15.36   Calculating factorials leads to big numbers very quickly. Write a function FACT.MOD that takes two inputs N and M and outputs $\mathtt{MOD}(N!, M)$. Have it outline a process that never uses numbers bigger than M. Then write FACT.MOD.P that does the same thing as FACT.MOD for prime moduli, but takes advantage of Wilson's theorem to make the calculation even faster. Hints: Use EXPMOD and EXPMOD.P as models for FACT.MOD and FACT.MOD.P. If you tabulate FACT.MOD for a given modulus, things become uninteresting rather quickly. Why? Why is FACT.MOD.P pointless?

Project 15.37   Show that if M is not prime and is greater than 4, then $(M-1)! \equiv 0 \ (\mathrm{MOD} \ M)$.
   Hints: Check this out for a few examples; try

```
SHOW CLASS (FACT 5) 6

SHOW CLASS (FACT 7) 8

SHOW CLASS (FACT 9) 10
```

and so on.

   Think of the prime factorization of M. If M is not a power of a prime, and P^E occurs in the factorization, then P^E will be a factor of $(M-1)!$ because P^E is strictly smaller than M. This means that M will be a factor of $(M-1)!$.
   #If M is a power of a prime, you have to do a bit more work. Suppose that $M = P^E$. Then E is bigger than 1 (why?). In fact, since $M > 4$, if $P = 2$, $E \geq 3$, and if $P > 2$, $E \geq 2$. Calculate $\mathtt{ORD}_P(M-1)!$ (that is, $\mathtt{ORD}_P(P^E - 1)!$) using the result of project 12.28.
   Why does this argument break down if $M = 4$?

In light of the above project, we can say that

$$(M-1)! \equiv \begin{cases} -1 \,(\mathrm{MOD}\ M) & \text{if } M \text{ is prime} \\ 0 \,(\mathrm{MOD}\ M) & \text{if } M \text{ is not prime and } M > 4 \\ 2 \,(\mathrm{MOD}\ M) & \text{if } M = 4 \end{cases}$$

Project 15.38 In experiment 10.23, we met a strange function that was supposed to produce only primes (and every prime); it was defined like this:

```
TO F :N
 OP :N * (TERM :N) + 2 * (1 - TERM :N)
END

TO TERM :N
 OP MOD (POWER (FACT.MOD :N - 1 :N) 2) :N
END

TO FACT.MOD :N :M
 IF :N = 0 [OP 1]
 OP MOD :N * (FACT.MOD :N - 1 :M) :M
END
```

It turned out that F was a "cruel joke"; F seemed to be equal to the following function

```
TO G :N
 IF PRIME? :N [OP :N]
 OP 2
END
```

Prove that F = G for all integers greater than 1.

Hint: In our current terminology, we could write

$$F(N) = N \cdot \mathrm{REP\ CLASS}((N-1)!^2, N) + 2(1 - (\mathrm{REP\ CLASS}((N-1)!^2, N)))$$

Now consider three cases: If N is prime, if N is composite and bigger than 4, and if $N = 4$.

Could this function be of any practical use in primality testing?

Project 15.39 Develop a conjecture about the sum of all the nonzero elements in $\mathbf{Z}/P\mathbf{Z}$ and prove your conjecture.

Hints: One way to do this is to use Gauss' formula for the sum of the numbers between 1 and $P-1$ and to reduce it modulo P. Another way is to use the identity:

$$X^{(P-1)} - 1 = (X-1)(X-2)(X-3)(X-4)\cdots(X-(P-1))$$

in $\mathbf{Z}/P\mathbf{Z}$ and to calculate the sum of the zeros on both sides (for the left-hand side, use the fact that the sum of the zeros of a polynomial with coefficients in any field is the negative of the coefficient of the next to highest power of X).

Can anything be said if the modulus is *not* prime?

Let's look at the orders of elements in $\mathbf{Z}/P\mathbf{Z}$. To do this, it will be helpful to have a function that computes the order of an element in $\mathbf{Z}/P\mathbf{Z}$ for us. Recall that the order of C is E if $C^E = \{1\ P\}$ and no smaller power of C is the class $\{1\ P\}$. So we can start looking for the order of C at 1, and keep adding 1 to the "trial" order until we find the real thing:

```
TO ORDER :C
 OP ORDER.H :C 1
END

TO ORDER.H :C :N
 IF EXPMOD :C :N = (CLASS 1 (MODULUS :C)) [OP :N]
 OP ORDER.H :C :N + 1
END
```

Let's start in $\mathbf{Z}/7\mathbf{Z}$:

```
SHOW ORDER CLASS 1 7
1
SHOW ORDER CLASS 2 7
3
SHOW ORDER CLASS 3 7
6
SHOW ORDER CLASS 4 7
3
SHOW ORDER CLASS 5 7
6
SHOW ORDER CLASS 6 7
2
```

So the elements have orders of 1, 2, 3, and 6. The elements of order 6 are especially interesting. If you raise {5 7} to the powers 0, 1, 2, 3, 4, 5, and 6, the classes will all be distinct (why?). This means that the powers of {5 7} generate all the units in $\mathbf{Z}/7\mathbf{Z}$ before coming to rest at {1 7}. Such a class is called a *primitive* for $\mathbf{Z}/7\mathbf{Z}$.

Let's look at $\mathbf{Z}/13\mathbf{Z}$.

```
SHOW ORDER CLASS 1 13
1
SHOW ORDER CLASS 2 13
12
SHOW ORDER CLASS 3 13
3
SHOW ORDER CLASS 4 13
6
SHOW ORDER CLASS 5 13
4
SHOW ORDER CLASS 6 13
12
SHOW ORDER CLASS 7 13
12
SHOW ORDER CLASS 8 13
4
SHOW ORDER CLASS 9 13
3
SHOW ORDER CLASS 10 13
6
SHOW ORDER CLASS 11 13
12
SHOW ORDER CLASS 12 13
2
```

So the elements have orders 1, 2, 3, 4, 6, and 12. Something is going on. Could it be that the order of a nonzero element in $\mathbf{Z}/P\mathbf{Z}$ is a factor of $P - 1$?

Take some time to experiment with this phenomenon before reading on. Check the fields $\mathbf{Z}/11\mathbf{Z}$ (10 only has 2 factors) and $\mathbf{Z}/37\mathbf{Z}$ (36 has lots of factors). Is it true? Does every factor of $P - 1$ show up as an order? Is there always a primitive element?

STOP

Well, it's true. We have the following theorem:

Theorem 15.13 The order of any nonzero element in $\mathbf{Z}/P\mathbf{Z}$ is a factor of $P-1$.

To see why, suppose that C is a class in $\mathbf{Z}/P\mathbf{Z}$ and that the order of C is E. This means that $C^E = 1$ ("1" means $\{1\ P\}$), and no smaller power of C has this property. Suppose that $P-1$ were not divisible by E. Then $P-1$ would be congruent modulo E to some number E' between 1 and $E-1$. But then, by exercise 15.33 (which is very easy to prove if you haven't looked at it yet),

$$C^{(P-1)} = C^{E'}$$

But by Fermat's little theorem, the left-hand side of this is 1, so we would have

$$1 = C^{E'}$$

and that can't happen because E is the smallest power of C that gives 1.

Theorem 15.13 just scratches the surface. Still unresolved is the question of whether or not there is always a primitive element in $\mathbf{Z}/P\mathbf{Z}$ and which factors of $P-1$ can show up as orders. A famous theorem of Gauss is that $\mathbf{Z}/P\mathbf{Z}$ always has a primitive element, and an easy consequence of that result is that every factor of $P-1$ shows up as an order. I wish we could discuss these things, but the book is already too long, and we have yet to look at the units in $\mathbf{Z}/M\mathbf{Z}$ where M is not a prime. Maybe another time. Well, the next experiment might give you some ideas.

Experiment 15.40 Find a primitive element in $\mathbf{Z}/P\mathbf{Z}$ for $P = 3$, 5, 7, 11, 13, 17, 19, and 23. For each of these primitive elements C, investigate the orders of the various powers C^E as E goes from 1 to $P-1$.

Nonprime Moduli

Think about how we proved theorem 15.13. We first used the binomial theorem modulo P to prove Fermat's little theorem, then we used the fact that the $P-1$ power of any unit is $\{1\ P\}$ to show that the order of a unit has to divide $P-1$. In other words, we started with the fact that $P-1$ would serve as a "temporary" order for every element of $\mathbf{Z}/P\mathbf{Z}$, and then it followed that every element has an order that divides $P - 1$. If we could show that the Rth power of an element is $\{1\ P\}$, then the order of that element would be a factor of R. In $\mathbf{Z}/P\mathbf{Z}$, we have an "R" of $P - 1$ for every element. In $\mathbf{Z}/M\mathbf{Z}$, we don't have a little Fermat at the outset, so we can't use the same argument. We'll have to work from the "bottom up"; we'll determine what kind of orders can show up without knowing a global number R so that $C^R = 1$ for every class.

If M is not a prime, we wonder about the kinds of numbers that can show up as orders for units. Let's look at some examples:

Example 1 $\mathbf{Z}/10\mathbf{Z}$ has 4 units, and their orders are

```
SHOW ORDER CLASS 1 10
1
SHOW ORDER CLASS 3 10
4
SHOW ORDER CLASS 7 10
4
SHOW ORDER CLASS 9 10
2
```

The possible orders are 1, 2, and 4. Notice that there are two primitives.

Example 2 In $\mathbf{Z}/15\mathbf{Z}$, there are 8 units; their orders are

```
SHOW ORDER CLASS 1 15
1
SHOW ORDER CLASS 2 15
4
SHOW ORDER CLASS 4 15
2
SHOW ORDER CLASS 7 15
4
SHOW ORDER CLASS 8 15
4
SHOW ORDER CLASS 11 15
2
SHOW ORDER CLASS 13 15
4
SHOW ORDER CLASS 14 15
2
```

The possible orders are 1, 2, and 4. This time there are no primitives.

Example 3 In $\mathbf{Z}/21\mathbf{Z}$ there are 12 units, and

```
SHOW ORDER CLASS 1 21
1
SHOW ORDER CLASS 2 21
6
SHOW ORDER CLASS 4 21
3
SHOW ORDER CLASS 5 21
6
SHOW ORDER CLASS 8 21
2
SHOW ORDER CLASS 10 21
6
SHOW ORDER CLASS 11 21
6
SHOW ORDER CLASS 13 21
2
SHOW ORDER CLASS 16 21
3
SHOW ORDER CLASS 17 21
6
SHOW ORDER CLASS 19 21
6
SHOW ORDER CLASS 20 21
2
```

The orders 1, 2, 3, and 6 show up; there are no elements of order 12. We have the following conjecture:

> In $\mathbf{Z}/M\mathbf{Z}$, the order of an unit is a factor of the number of units. In other words, the order of a unit is a factor of PHI(M).

This will be our last major result; we'll prove the following theorem:

Theorem 15.14 If C is a unit in $\mathbf{Z}/M\mathbf{Z}$, then ORDER(C) is a factor of PHI(M).

This is a special case of a theorem (due to Lagrange) from a branch of algebra known as "group theory."

The proof involves extending the notion of modular arithmetic to one more level of abstraction. This time, for a given unit C, we'll want to look at $(\mathbf{Z}/M\mathbf{Z})^{\times}$ modulo the orbit of C. Let me explain.

Take for example $\mathbf{Z}/21\mathbf{Z}$. Here there are 12 units:

$$\{1\ 21\}, \{2\ 21\}, \{4\ 21\}, \{5\ 21\}, \{8\ 21\}, \{10\ 21\}, \{11\ 21\},$$
$$\{13\ 21\}, \{16\ 21\}, \{17\ 21\}, \{19\ 21\}, \text{ and } \{20\ 21\}$$

Let's pick one of these units, say, $\{16\ 21\}$ and call it C. Now, C has a certain order (make believe you didn't know that it is 3), and if that order is E, we have E different classes in the orbit of C:

$$C, C^2, C^3, C^4, \ldots, C^E$$

Let S be this set of units that are powers of C:

$$S = \{C, C^2, C^3, C^4, \ldots, C^E\}$$

Notice that C^E is 1 and that every power of C is in S (this is clear for positive powers of C, but it is true even for negative powers of C because, for example, C^{-1} is the same as $C^{(E-1)}$). Now, if $E = 12$, then clearly, E is a factor of 12. So suppose that $E < 12$. (E couldn't be bigger than 12 because there are only 12 distinct units, and the power of a unit is a unit. So C^{13} must be the same as C^K for some K less than 12. This means that $C^{(13-K)} = 1$.)

Suppose that D is any unit not in S (that is, D is not a power of C). Then the set DS defined as

$$DS = \{DC, DC^2, DC^3, DC^4, \ldots, DC^E\}$$

In our example,

$$S = \left\{\{16\ 21\}, \{4\ 21\}, \{1\ 21\}\right\}$$

so D can be any element in $(\mathbf{Z}/21\mathbf{Z})^{\times}$ that is not in S, say, $D = \{3\ 21\}$. Then DS is simply the set of units obtained by multiplying every element of S by D (the product of a unit and a unit is another unit):

$$DS = \left\{\{3\ 21\} \cdot \{16\ 21\}, \{3\ 21\} \cdot \{4\ 21\}, \{3\ 21\} \cdot \{1\ 21\}\right\}$$

or

$$DS = \Big\{ \{6 \ 21\}, \ \{12 \ 21\}, \ \{3 \ 21\} \Big\}$$

Notice that $D = DC^E$, so D is a member of DS.

In general, I claim that the elements of DS are different from the elements of S and that there are E distinct elements in DS. To see this, suppose first that there is an element common to S and DS. Then, because the element is in S, it can be written as C^K for some exponent K between 1 and E. Because the element is in DS, it can be written as DC^J for some exponent J between 1 and E. Then we would have that

$$DC^J = C^K, \text{ or } D = C^{(K-J)}$$

But this would say that D is a power of C (positive or negative). So D would be in S, and that's silly (we picked D so that it is not in S). Similarly, if two elements of DS were equal, then we would have

$$DC^K = DC^J$$

for some positive integers J and K between 1 and E. But if J and K were not equal, we could assume that J is bigger than K, and our equation would become (after dividing both sides by D)

$$1 = C^{(J-K)}$$

So some power of C that is less than E (the "$J - K$" power) would be 1, and that's silly because E is the order of C.

So the elements of S and DS are all distinct. Since both sets contain E units, we have used up $2E$ units so far. If this is all there is, then

$$2E = \text{the number of units}$$

(in our case 12, and in general PHI(M)), so E is a factor of the number of units. If there is another unit, say, D', that is not in S or in DS, then we can construct $D'S$ just as we constructed DS:

$$D'S = \{D'C, D'C^2, D'C^3, D'C^4, \ldots, D'C^E\}$$

In our example, we could take D' to be any unit not in S or DS; since

$$S = \Big\{ \{16\ 21\},\ \{4\ 21\},\ \{1\ 21\} \Big\}$$

$$DS = \Big\{ \{6\ 21\},\ \{12\ 21\},\ \{3\ 21\} \Big\}$$

we could take D' to be $\{5\ 21\}$. Then $D'S$ would be

$$D'S = \Big\{ \{5\ 21\} \cdot \{16\ 21\},\ \{5\ 21\} \cdot \{4\ 21\},\ \{5\ 21\} \cdot \{1\ 21\} \Big\}$$

or

$$D'S = \Big\{ \{17\ 21\},\ \{20\ 21\},\ \{5\ 21\} \Big\}$$

Once again, you could prove that the elements of $D'S$ are distinct, and that they are also distinct from from the elements of S and from the elements of DS. I'll leave the details to you, but here's an example of how you would proceed.

Suppose that an element of $D'S$ were the same as an element of DS. Then for some integers J and K between 1 and E, we would have

$$D'C^J = DC^K$$

Then $D' = DC^{(K-J)}$, so D' would be in DS, a contradiction. So the elements of $D'S$ and DS are distinct.

If we have used up all the units, then

$$3E = \text{the number of units}$$

and E is again a factor of $\mathrm{PHI}(M)$. If we have not used up all the units, we pick a unit D'' that is not in S, DS, or $D'S$, and we prove that the elements of $D''S$ are distinct form each other and from all previous elements of S, DS, and $D'S$. In our example, there is a unit not in our three sets. For example, we could take D'' to be $\{2\ 21\}$. Then $D''S$ would be

$$D''S = \Big\{ \{2\ 21\} \cdot \{16\ 21\},\ \{2\ 21\} \cdot \{4\ 21\},\ \{2\ 21\} \cdot \{1\ 21\} \Big\}$$

or

$$D'S = \Big\{ \{11\ 21\},\ \{8\ 21\},\ \{2\ 21\} \Big\}$$

So in this example, we have used up all the elements of $(\mathbf{Z}/M\mathbf{Z})^\times$, and $4E = 12$, so E is a factor of 12.

Inductively, we can keep picking units $D'''\cdots'$ not in the previous sets, and prove that $D'''\cdots'S$ is a set of E units, all different from the previous ones. Eventually, we'll run out of units. If this is when we have Q distinct "multiples" of S, then QE must be the number of units. That is, E is a factor of $\text{PHI}(M)$.

> If you stand back and look at what we are doing, you see that we are starting off with $(\mathbf{Z}/M\mathbf{Z})^\times$, picking a unit C, forming the orbit of C, S, and noting that S is a subset of $(\mathbf{Z}/M\mathbf{Z})^\times$ that contains 1 $(1 = C^E)$ and is closed under multiplication (any power of C is another power of C). We then lump together all the elements of $(\mathbf{Z}/M\mathbf{Z})^\times$ that are equal except for a power of C. For example, D and DC^3 are in the same "lump" because one is obtained from the other by multiplying by a power of C. In our example, S is all the powers of $\{16\ 21\}$, so $\{20\ 21\}$ and $\{5\ 21\}$ are in the same lump because
>
> $$\{20\ 21\} = \{5\ 21\} \cdot \{4\ 21\} = \{5\ 21\} \cdot \{16\ 21\}^2$$
>
> What we are constructing, then, is $(\mathbf{Z}/M\mathbf{Z})^\times/S$, the units in $\mathbf{Z}/M\mathbf{Z}$ modulo the orbit of one unit.

Project 15.41 Prove Euler's theorem: If C is any element in $(\mathbf{Z}/M\mathbf{Z})^\times$, then $C^{(\text{PHI}(M))} = 1$ in $\mathbf{Z}/M\mathbf{Z}$. Hints: Check this out in $\mathbf{Z}/21\mathbf{Z}$; type

```
SHOW EXPMOD CLASS 2 21 PHI 21
```

and so on for each unit.

Suppose that C is in $(\mathbf{Z}/M\mathbf{Z})^\times$. Then if the order of C is E, $E \mid (\text{PHI}(M))$, so there is an integer K so that $EK = \text{PHI}(M)$.

Why is Fermat's little theorem a special case of Euler's theorem?

Project 15.42 Modify the ORDER function so that it only tries divisors of $\text{PHI}(M)$ as trial orders. Hint: Modify it so that it takes trial orders from any list, and then give it the list $\text{DIVISORS}(\text{PHI}(M))$.

Experiment 15.43 What familiar function is equal to F:

```
TO F :CLASS
 OP EXPMOD :CLASS ((PHI MODULUS :CLASS) - 1)
END
```

Appendix: Logo Tools

The point of this appendix is to write down some Logo functions and procedures that are used throughout the book. These "tools" are not the object of our study; they are the means by which we conduct our investigations. Most of them are "higher order" in the sense that they operate on ordinary mathematical functions. This appendix also includes a very brief description of some Logo functions that are used to manipulate lists.

I hope that the reason you are reading this is that you were reading the book, came to something unfamiliar (like SIGMA or TAB), and looked here for an explanation. I tried to include a phrase like "see the appendix" whenever I used something that is explained here.

If what's puzzling you isn't discussed here, you'll most certainly find it explained in Volume 1 of *Computer Science Logo Style* (Harvey 1985).

List Processing

The discussion here is far from complete; it considers only the topics that show up in the book. It is also far from rigorous; for a precise discussion of "compound data," see chapter 2 of Abelson-Sussman (1985).

Think of a list as a collection of objects placed between square brackets "[" and "]." The objects can be words (like numbers or names of functions), or they can be other lists. So examples of lists are

[1 3 -3], [F 4 7], [[2 3] [1 3] [0 3]], and [[1] [2 3] [4]]

The Logo functions SE (for SEntence) and LIST can be used to build a new list from existing ones:

```
SHOW SE [1 3] [2 4 5]
[1 3 2 4 5]

SHOW LIST [1 3] [2 4 5]
[[1 3] [2 4 5]]
```

Both of these functions take two inputs. The inputs can be lists, as in the above examples, or they can be words:

```
SHOW SE 5 [6 7]
[5 6 7]

SHOW LIST 5 [6 7]
[5 [6 7]]

SHOW SE "F [3 4]
[F 3 4]

SHOW LIST "F [3 4]
[F [3 4]]
```

SE outputs a list whose objects are the objects in the first input and the objects in the second input. LIST outputs a list whose objects are its inputs. If L and M are lists, $COUNT(SE(L, M)) = COUNT(L) + COUNT(M)$, while $COUNT(LIST(L, M)) = 2$.

Both SE and LIST can take more than two inputs if we use their "greedy" form. To do this, enclose the function and all its inputs in parentheses:

```
SHOW (SE [1 2] [3 4 5] [6 7 8])
[1 2 3 4 5 6 7 8]

SHOW (LIST [1 2] [3 4 5] [6 7 8])
[[1 2] [3 4 5] [6 7 8]]
```

For most of our applications, we use SE because its "flattening" effect is to our advantage. For example, when we build higher-order functions, it is important to form lists like this:

```
[F 2 3]
```

Here, I'm thinking of F as the name of a function and 2 and 3 as its inputs. The reason that lists like this are important is that they can be input to RUN. If [F 2 3] is input to RUN, the output will be $F(2, 3)$. For example, if F is defined like this:

```
TO F :X :Y
  OP :X + 2 * :Y
END
```

then

```
SHOW RUN [F 2 3]
```

produces 8.

Our functions will sometimes take three or five inputs or just one input, and we don't want to adjust our workspace for each of these changes. SE behaves like this:

```
SHOW SE "F SE 2 3
[F 2 3]

SHOW SE "F SE [3 4] 5
[F 3 4 5]

SHOW SE "F SE [] 5
[F 5]

SHOW (SE "G [4 5] 6)
[G 4 5 6]
```

Try replacing SE by LIST in the above examples.

Sometimes (as in chapters 9 through 15) we need to define a list inductively. For example, suppose we want to construct the list of whole numbers between *A* and *B*. One way to do this is

```
TO INTERVAL :A :B
 IF :A > :B [OP []]
 OP SE :A INTERVAL :A + 1 :B
END
```

If you type SHOW INTERVAL 3 6, you see [3 4 5 6]. What happens if you change SE to LIST?

This flattening effect of SE is occasionally inappropriate. For example, suppose we want a function Z that acts like this:

```
SHOW Z 5
[[0 5] [1 5] [2 5] [3 5] [4 5]]

SHOW Z 6
[[0 6] [1 6] [2 6] [3 6] [4 6] [5 6]]
```

We might start like this:

```
TO Z :N
 OP Z.HELPER :N 0
END

TO Z.HELPER :N :START
 IF :START > :N - 1 [OP []]
 OP SE (LIST :START :N) Z.HELPER :N :START + 1
END
```

If you type SHOW Z 6, you see [0 6 1 6 2 6 3 6 4 6 5 6]. Suppose we change the *combiner* to LIST:

```
TO Z.HELPER :N :START
 IF :START > :N - 1 [OP []]
 OP LIST (LIST :START :N) Z.HELPER :N :START + 1
END
```

What is the output of Z 6 now?

There are many ways to fix the bug, but the easiest thing to do is to use another combiner: FPUT ("FrontPUT"). It works like this:

```
SHOW FPUT 3 [5 6]
[3 5 6]

SHOW FPUT [7 8] [6 8 0]
[[7 8] 6 8 0]

SHOW FPUT [7 8] []
[[7 8]]
```

It's this last example that makes FPUT such a useful tool when building lists of lists inductively. Try

```
SHOW SE [7 8] []
```

and

```
SHOW LIST [7 8] []
```

to see an important difference among SE, LIST, and FPUT. So a fix for Z is

```
TO Z.HELPER :N :START
 IF :START > :N - 1 [OP []]
 OP FPUT (LIST :START :N) Z.HELPER :N :START + 1
END
```

The Logo function LPUT (LastPUT) behaves similarly.

The Logo functions FIRST and BF (ButFirst) can be used to take lists apart. The following examples explain how they work:

```
SHOW FIRST [1 2 3 4]
1
SHOW BF [1 2 3 4]
[2 3 4]

SHOW FIRST [[2 3] [4 6][8 9]]
[2 3]
SHOW BF [[2 3][4 6][8 9]]
[[4 6][8 9]]

SHOW FIRST [[2 3] [4 6]]
[2 3]
SHOW BF [[2 3][4 6]]
[[4 6]]
```

There are also functions LAST and BL (ButLast). Convince yourself that if a list has two elements, applying LAST to it produces something different from applying BF to it.

Using FIRST and BF, you can locate any element in a list. Most Logos have a function ITEM that does this for you, so that if you type SHOW ITEM 3 [2 4 6 8 10], you'll see 6. If your Logo doesn't have an ITEM, you can build your own like this:

```
TO ITEM :N :L
 IF :N = 1 [OP FIRST :L]
 OP ITEM :N - 1 BF :L
END
```

The built-in ITEM probably runs faster than this model, and it might produce different error messages than this model if N is bigger than the COUNT of *L*. By the way, if you didn't have a COUNT, you could use this:

```
TO COUNT :L
 IF EMPTYP :L [OP 0]
 OP 1 + (COUNT BF :L)
END
```

Some Logos have a SETITEM. It works like this:

```
SHOW SETITEM 3 [5 6 7 8 9 0] -1
[5 6 -1 8 9 0]
```

So SETITEM(N, L, X) outputs the list obtained from L by replacing its Nth element by X. If you don't have a SETITEM, you can build one:

First write a function FRONT that outputs the first N elements of a list L:

```
TO FRONT :N :L
 OP FRONT.HELPER :L [] :N 0
END
```

```
TO FRONT.HELPER :I :O :N :C
 IF :C > :N - 1 [OP :O]
 OP FRONT.HELPER BF :I (LPUT FIRST :I :O) :N :C + 1
END
```

It works like this:

```
SHOW FRONT  4 [6 7 8 9 10 11]
[6 7 8 9]
```

Similarly, write a function TAIL:

```
TO TAIL :N :L
 OP TAIL.HELPER :L [] :N 0
END
```

```
TO TAIL.HELPER :I :O :N :C
 IF :C > :N - 1 [OP :O]
 OP TAIL.HELPER BL :I (FPUT LAST :I :O) :N :C + 1
END
```

SETITEM(N, L, X) simply tucks X between the two pieces of L that are sheared off by FRONT and TAIL:

```
TO SETITEM :N :L :X
 OP (SE (FRONT :N - 1 :L) :X (TAIL (COUNT :L) - :N :L))
END
```

APPLY and Tabulations

Suppose you were working on a project that required you to take several dozen numbers, double them, and add 3 to each of the doubles. You'd probably make use of the function

```
TO F :X
 OP 2 * :X + 3
END
```

It often happens that we have several functions on hand, and we want to repeatedly perform the same kind of process to each of them. For example, we might want to tabulate them, or to sum their outputs between, say, 1 and 10. In order to encapsulate these operations on functions into actual procedures that can be modeled in Logo, we'll make heavy use of APPLY.

```
TO APPLY :FUNCTION :X
 OP RUN SE :FUNCTION :X
END
```

It works like this:

```
SHOW APPLY "F 4
11
```

In other words, APPLY "F 4 produces the same thing as F 4. So why bother with APPLY? An example might help.

Consider the interesting problem: Given a function F, find a formula for the function G so that $G(X) = F(X + 1) - F(X)$. If $F(X) = X^2$, then

$$
\begin{aligned}
G(X) &= F(X + 1) - F(X) \\
&= (X + 1)^2 - X^2 \\
&= 2X + 1
\end{aligned}
$$

If $F(X) = X^3$, then

$$G(X) = F(X + 1) - F(X)$$
$$= (X + 1)^3 - X^3$$
$$= 3X^2 + 3X + 1$$

In general, you might want to write a Logo model for G, and this model should include the function F as one of its inputs; a first attempt might be

```
TO G :FUNC :X
 OP (:FUNC (:X + 1)) - (:FUNC :X)
END
```

If F is defined like this:

```
TO F :X
 OP 2 * :X + 3
END
```

you would want to type SHOW G "F 4; it doesn't work, and a fix is

```
TO G :FUNC :X
 OP (APPLY :FUNC (:X + 1)) - (APPLY :FUNC :X)
END
```

The point of this function G is that it works for any function FUNC. If H is defined like this:

```
TO H :X
 OP :X * :X * :X
END
```

then G "H 4 would output $(4 + 1)^3 - 4^3$. Using G as part of a systematic investigation might lead you to conjectures about this "difference" process.

APPLY can be used to generate tabulations. The following procedure gives a simple method for tabulating a function at all the integers between A and B:

```
TO TAB :F :A :B
 IF :A > :B [STOP]
 (SHOW :A ". ". ". APPLY :F :A)
 TAB :F :A + 1 :B
END
```

Notice that the greedy form of SHOW is used. If H is defined as above, then typing

```
TAB "H 1 4
```

produces

```
1 . . . 1
2 . . . 8
3 . . . 27
4 . . . 64
```

TAB can be modified in several useful ways. One way is to allow the function that you are tabulating to take more than one input. For example, suppose that R is the function so that $R(X, Y) = X + 3Y$. You might want to tabulate R keeping X fixed at, say, 7, and letting Y range from 1 to 5. To tabulate a function F "against its last input" while keeping the other inputs fixed, we can use this generalized version of TAB:

```
TO TAB :F :E :A :B
 IF :A > :B [STOP]
 (SHOW :A ". ". ". APPLY :F SE :E :A
 TAB :F :E :A + 1 :B
END
```

Here, think of E as the "extra" inputs to F. If R is defined as above, then typing TAB "R 3 1 4 produces

```
1 . . . 6      (R(3, 1))
2 . . . 9      (R(3, 2))
3 . . . 12     (R(3, 3))
4 . . . 15     (R(3, 4))
```

If you have a function that takes more than two inputs, like

```
TO J :X :Y :Z
 OP :X - :Y + 2*:Z
END
```

you can tabulate J, keeping its first two inputs at 4 and 6 and letting its last input range from 3 to 10 by typing

```
TAB "J [4 6] 3 10
```

SE makes sure that the [4 6] is combined with the last input and correctly handed over to APPLY.

This generalized TAB can do the work of our old TAB. If H is a function (as above) that only takes one input, then you can tabulate H between 1 and 7 by typing

```
TAB "H [] 1 10
```

Sometimes, you want to tabulate a function over a list. That is, instead of seeing the outputs of F as its input goes from 1 to 10, you want to see its outputs as its input takes on the values in [1 3 5 7 8]. TAB can be modified like this:

```
TO L.TAB :F :L
 IF EMPTYP :L [STOP]
 (SHOW (FIRST :L) ". ". ". APPLY :F FIRST :L)
 L.TAB :F BF :L
END
```

If you want F to take extra inputs, simply modify L.TAB:

```
TO L.TAB :F :E :L
 IF EMPTYP :L [STOP]
 (SHOW (FIRST :L) ". ". ". APPLY :F SE :E FIRST :L)
 L.TAB :F :E BF :L
END
```

If J is defined as above, then typing

```
L.TAB "J [2 4] [1 -1 4 10]
```

produces

1 ... 0	$(J(2, 4, 1))$
-1 ... -4	$(J(2, 4, -1))$
4 ... 6	$(J(2, 4, 4))$
10 ... 18	$(J(2, 4, 10))$

Using the `INTERVAL` function of 1. above, `L.TAB` can do the work of `TAB`.

Accumulations

Suppose we have several functions on hand, and for each function, we want to find the sum of the outputs as the inputs range from 1 to 10. That is, if `F` is any one of our functions, we want to find

$$F(1) + F(2) + F(3) + F(4) + F(5) + F(6) + F(7) + F(8) + F(9) + F(10)$$

We can capture this idea of summing a function between integers A and B in Logo with `SIGMA`:

```
TO SIGMA :F :A :B
 IF :A > :B [OP 0]
 OP (APPLY :F :A) + (SIGMA :F :A + 1 :B)
END
```

If `SQUARE` is the function that squares its input, we can add up the first twenty squares by typing

```
SHOW SIGMA "SQUARE 1 20
```

The Greek letter Σ (pronounced "sigma") is the equivalent of the letter "S" in the Roman alphabet, and it is often used in mathematics to denote a sum. If `G` is any function, then the notation

$$\sum_{K=1}^{8} G(K)$$

is read "the sum of the $G(K)$ as K goes from 1 to 8." It means

$$G(1) + G(2) + G(3) + G(4) + G(5) + G(6) + G(7) + G(8)$$

If `G` is defined as

```
TO G :X
 OP 2 * :X + 3
END
```

then

$$\sum_{K=1}^{8} \text{G}(K)$$

means

$$(2 \cdot 1 + 3) + (2 \cdot 2 + 3) + (2 \cdot 3 + 3) + (2 \cdot 4 + 3) + (2 \cdot 5 + 3)$$
$$+ (2 \cdot 6 + 3) + (2 \cdot 7 + 3) + (2 \cdot 8 + 3)$$

You can find the value of this sum by typing

```
SHOW SIGMA "G 1 8
```

SIGMA can be modified in many ways. For example, suppose you have a function H that takes three inputs, and you want the sum

$$\text{H}(1,3,4) + \text{H}(1,3,5) + \text{H}(1,3,6) + \text{H}(1,3,7) + \text{H}(1,3,8) + \text{H}(1,3,9)$$

Then you can modify SIGMA so that it sums a function of several inputs "against the last input":

```
TO SIGMA :F :E :A :B
 IF :A > :B [OP 0]
 OP (APPLY :F SE :E :A) + (SIGMA :F :E :A + 1 :B)
END
```

The above sum involving H can be evaluated by typing

```
SHOW SIGMA "H [1 3] 4 9
```

If you want to sum a function over a list, use

```
TO L.SIGMA :F :E :L
 IF EMPTYP :L [OP 0]
 OP (APPLY :F SE :E FIRST :L) + (SIGMA :F :E BF :L)
END
```

It's also easy to modify SIGMA so that it sums a function between A and B with increments of, say, .1.

Suppose you want to multiply the outputs of a function together instead of summing them. You can build a higher-order function PROD that looks very much like SIGMA:

```
TO PROD :F :A :B
 IF :A > :B [OP 0]
 OP (APPLY :F :A) * (PROD :F :A + 1 :B)
END
```

So, if G is defined as above, you can find the value of

$$G(2) \cdot G(3) \cdot G(4) \cdot G(5) \cdot G(6) \cdot G(7) \cdot G(8)$$

by typing

```
SHOW PROD "G 2 8
```

The mathematical notation for the above product is

$$\prod_{K=2}^{8} G(K)$$

The Greek letter π (pi) stands for product. I wanted to call PROD PI, but many Logos have a built-in function PI (it outputs the ratio of the circumference of a circle to its diameter).

PROD can be modified to accept functions of more than one input

```
TO PROD :F :E :A :B
 IF :A > :B [OP 0]
 OP (APPLY :F SE :E :A) * (PROD :F :E :A + 1 :B)
END
```

and to multiply over lists:

```
TO L.PROD :F :E :L
 IF EMPTYP :L [OP 0]
 OP (APPLY :F SE :E FIRST :L) * (PROD :F :E :BF :L)
END
```

For example, if H is a function that takes three inputs,

```
SHOW L.PROD "H [2 5] [1 3 -2 9]
```

produces the value of

$$H(2,5,1) \cdot H(2,5,3) \cdot H(2,5,-2) \cdot H(2,5,9)$$

Predicates and Filters

A predicate is a function that outputs TRUE or FALSE. For example, the following predicate outputs TRUE if a number is bigger than 10:

```
TO BIG? :N
 IF :N > 10 [OP "TRUE]
 OP "FALSE
END
```

Ending predicates with a "?" is suggestive; typing

```
SHOW BIG? 20
```

suggests that you are asking a question ("is 20 big?"). Logo has some built-in predicates, and most versions don't use a "?" in their names. In some Logos, some built-in predicates end in a "P" (for "predicate"), whereas in other Logos, some predicates end in a "Q" (for "question"). For example, in LCSI logo, if you type

```
SHOW EMPTYP [1 2 3]
```

you'll see FALSE. Another built-in predicate is MEMBERP; typing

```
SHOW MEMBERP 5 [3 4 5 6]
```

produces TRUE.

EQUALP is a very useful predicate. It takes two inputs and outputs TRUE precisely when its inputs are the same. So EQUALP 5 4 + 1 outputs TRUE. There is another name for EQUALP that is often more expressive. The following three lines are equivalent (again, in LCSI Logo):

```
SHOW EQUALP 5 4 + 1
```

```
SHOW = 5 4 + 1
```

```
SHOW 5 = 4 + 1
```

In other words, the mathematical symbol "=" is the name of a Logo predicate that is the same predicate as EQUALP. Moreover it can be placed between its inputs rather than before them. There are several other Logo predicates that behave this way. Try typing

```
SHOW > 5 4 + 1
SHOW 5 > 4 + 1
SHOW < 4 5
SHOW 4 < 5
```

The fact that > is a predicate means that the above predicate BIG? could have a very simple Logo model

```
TO BIG? :N
 OP :N > 10
END
```

The point here is that the expression ":N > 10" will output TRUE or FALSE. Here are some other predicates defined in this style:

```
TO SMALL :N
 OP :N < 11
END

TO NEG? :N
 OP :N < 0
END

TO EVEN? :N
 OP (REMAINDER :N 2) = 0
END

TO DIVIS.BY.3? :N
 OP (REMAINDER :N 3) = 0
END

TO BIG.AND.EVEN? :N
 OP AND (:N > 10) ((REMAINDER :N 2) = 0)
END
```

```
TO BIG.AND.EVEN? :N
 OP AND (BIG? :N) (EVEN? :N)
END
```

Predicates are used with **IF**. **IF** is a procedure that takes two inputs; its first input must be **TRUE** or **FALSE** (precisely the outputs from a predicate) and its second input is a list of instructions. If the first input is **TRUE**, **IF** runs the list of instructions; if the first input is **FALSE**, it does nothing. For example, in the expression

```
IF :N = 10 [OP 3]
```

the first input to **IF** is the result of ":N = 10"; it is either **TRUE** or **FALSE**. If this outputs **TRUE**, **IF** outputs 3; otherwise, it does nothing (and the next line of the function containing the **IF** is evaluated).

So our first version of **BIG?** was somewhat wordy:

```
TO BIG? :N
 IF :N > 10 [OP "TRUE]
 OP "FALSE
END
```

It says: If ":N > 10" outputs **TRUE**, output **TRUE**, otherwise (if ":N > 10" outputs **FALSE**) output **FALSE**. In other words, it says to output the output of ":N > 10."

Suppose you have a list of numbers and you want to construct the sublist containing all the numbers that are bigger than 10. You could "filter" the predicate **BIG?** over your list:

```
TO FILTER :L
 IF EMPTYP :L [OP []]
 IF (BIG? (FIRST :L)) [OP SE (FIRST :L) (FILTER (BF :L))]
 OP FILTER (BF :L)
END
```

Since predicates are functions, you can **APPLY** them to inputs, so you can write a generic **FILTER** function that filters any predicate over any list:

```
TO FILTER :PRED :L
 IF EMPTYP :L [OP []]
 IF (APPLY :PRED (FIRST :L)) →
    [OP SE (FIRST :L) (FILTER :PRED (BF :L))]
 OP FILTER :PRED (BF :L)
END
```

So, to pick out all the numbers greater than 10 in the list

[1 2 4 6 10 23 3 15 18]

simply type

SHOW FILTER "BIG? [1 2 4 6 10 23 3 15 18]

Sometimes predicates take more than one input. You can generalize FILTER so that it allows for predicates with extra inputs:

```
TO FILTER :PRED :E :L
 IF EMPTYP :L [OP []]
 IF (APPLY :PRED SE :E (FIRST :L)) →
    [OP SE (FIRST :L) (FILTER :PRED :E (BF :L))]
 OP FILTER :PRED :E (BF :L)
END
```

Filtering out the big numbers from the above list could be accomplished by typing

SHOW FILTER "< 10 [1 2 4 6 10 23 3 15 18]

Why do I use "<" instead of ">" as my predicate?

Mappings, LIST.PRODUCT, and Multiplication Tables in $\mathbf{Z}/_M\mathbf{Z}$

Suppose you have a function F and a list L; say $\mathrm{F}(X) = X + 2$, and $L = $ [3 5 2 6 8]. You want to construct the list that you get by applying F to each element of L; you want to construct [5 7 4 8 10]. The process is called "mapping F over L," and for this particular F, we could write the Logo model as

```
TO MAP :L
 IF EMPTYP :L [OP []]
 OP FPUT F (FIRST :L) MAP BF :L
END
```

We can make our MAP function much more flexible if we are allowed to input any function:

```
TO MAP :F :L
 IF EMPTYP :L [OP []]
 OP FPUT APPLY :F (FIRST :L) MAP :F BF :L
END
```

While we're at it, we might as well allow F to take some extra inputs:

```
TO MAP :F :E :L
 IF EMPTYP :L [OP []]
 OP FPUT APPLY :F (SE :E (FIRST :L)) MAP :F :E BF :L
END
```

So, if S is the function that squares its input, then

```
SHOW MAP "S [] [2 4 1 6]
```

will produce

```
[4 16 1 36]
```

MAP is useful whenever you want to transform one list into another by doing the same thing to each of its elements.

In chapter 12 we want to form the LIST.PRODUCT of two lists. For example, if we type

```
SHOW LIST.PRODUCT [1 2 3] [4 5]
```

we want to see

```
[4 5 8 10 12 15]
```

LIST.PRODUCT can be modeled from scratch, but it can also be thought of as an iterated mapping of multiplication over the second list. Here are the details:

```
TO LIST.PRODUCT :L :L'
 IF EMPTYP :L [OP []]
 OP SE (MAP "* (FIRST :L) :L') LIST.PRODUCT BF :L :L'
END
```

If your version of Logo doesn't allow you to use * like any other function, change the "*" to PRODUCT, where, if PRODUCT isn't defined, you can define it like this:

```
TO PRODUCT :A :B
 OP :A * :B
END
```

In chapter 15, we need a tool to generate multiplication tables for $Z/M Z$. One way to do it is to use another instance of the "list product" idea. First, we need a function that outputs the list of classes in $Z/M Z$:

```
TO ZMOD :M
 OP ZMOD.HELPER :M 0 []
END

TO ZMOD.HELPER :N :C :T
 IF :C > :N - 1 [OP :T]
 OP ZMOD.HELPER :N :C + 1 LPUT (CLASS :C :N) :T
END
```

If you type

```
SHOW ZMOD 5
```

you'll see

```
[[0 5] [1 5] [2 5] [3 5] [4 5]]
```

which is supposed to stand for the list of the five classes in $Z/5Z$.

Next, we define a variant of LIST.PRODUCT, where * is replaced by MULT and there is no flattening of the outputs:

```
TO LIST.PRODUCT1 :L :L'
 IF EMPTYP :L [OP []]
 OP FPUT MAP1 "MULT (FIRST :L) :L' LIST.PRODUCT1 BF :L :L'
END
```

```
TO MAP1 :F :E :L
 IF EMPTYP :L [OP []]
 OP FPUT APPLY :F LIST :E FIRST :L MAP1 :F :E BF :L
END
```

If you type

```
SHOW LIST.PRODUCT1 (ZMOD 5) (ZMOD 5)
```

you'll see the multiplication table for $Z/5Z$ in a particularly unattractive form (it is a list of 5 lists, each of which is a list of 5 classes). All we have to do is to use the DISPLAY tool from chapter 9:

```
TO DISPLAY :L
 IF EMPTYP :L [STOP]
 SHOW FIRST :L
 DISPLAY BF :L
END
```

To see the multiplication table for $Z/6Z$, just type SHOW TABLE 6, where TABLE is defined like this:

```
TO TABLE :M
 DISPLAY LIST.PRODUCT1 (ZMOD :M) (ZMOD :M)
END
```

References

Abelson, Harold, and Gerald Jay Sussman. 1985. *Structure and Interpretation of Computer Programs.* Cambridge, MA: The MIT Press.

Bachman, P. 1902. *Niedere Zahlentheorie.* Leipzig: Teubner.

Birch, Alison. 1988. *Logo Probability.* Malden, MA: Terrapin.

Bourbaki, Nicolas. 1968. *Theory of Sets.* Volume 1 of *Elements of Mathematics.* Reading, MA: Addison Wesley.

Conway, John B. 1978. *Functions of One Complex Variable.* New York: Springer-Verlag.

Cuoco, Albert A. 1984. "Making a Divergent Series Converge." *The Mathematics Teacher* 77(9):715.

Davis, Philip J., and Reuben Hersh. 1981. *The Mathematical Experience.* Boston, MA: Houghton Mifflin.

Dewdney, A.K. 1984. "Yin and Yang: Recursion and Iteration, the Tower of Hanoi and the Chinese Rings." *Scientific American* 251(5):19.

Gauss, Carl Friedrich. 1965. *Disquisitiones Arithmeticae.* Translated by Arthur A. Clarke. New Haven, CT: Yale University Press.

Goetgheluck, P. 1987. "Computing Binomial Coefficients." *The American Mathematical Monthly* 94(4):360.

Gould, Steven Jay. 1981. *The Mismeasure of Man.* New York, NY: W.W. Norton.

Hardy, G.H., and E.M. Wright. 1960. *An Introduction to the Theory of Numbers.* New York, NY: Oxford University Press.

References

Harvey, Brian. 1985. *Computer Science Logo Style. Intermediate Programming.* Cambridge, MA: The MIT Press.

Harvey, Brian. 1987. *Computer Science Logo Style.* Volume 3: *Advanced Topics.* Cambridge, MA: The MIT Press.

Hayes, Brian. 1984. "On the Ups and Downs of Hailstone Numbers." *Scientific American* 250(1):10.

Hilton, Peter, and Jean Pedersen. 1987. "Looking into Pascal's Triangle: Combinatorics, Arithmetic, and Geometry." *Mathematics Magazine* 60(5):305.

Ireland, Kenneth, and Michael Rosen. 1982. *A Classical Introduction to Modern Number Theory.* New York, NY: Springer-Verlag.

Koblitz, Neal. 1987. *A Course in Number Theory and Cryptography.* New York, NY: Springer Verlag.

Korec, I., and S. Znam. 1987. "A Note on the 3x + 1 Problem." *The American Mathematical Monthly* 94(8):771.

Lagarias, Jeffery C. 1985. "The $3x+1$ Problem and Its Generalizations." *The American Mathematical Monthly* 92(1):3.

Logothetti, Dave. 1987. "Proof without Words." *Mathematics Magazine* 60(5):291.

Polites, George W. 1988. "Prime Desert n-Tuplets." *The American Mathematical Monthly* 95(2):98.

Stewart, Ian. 1986. "Frog and Mouse Revisited." *The Mathematical Intelligencer* 8(4). *Also see*: Richman, Fred. 1987. "The Frog Replies." *The Mathematical Intelligencer* 9(3):22.

Wagon, Stan. 1986. "Fermat's Last Theorem." *The Mathematical Intelligencer* 8(1):59.

Wilf, Herbert S. 1987. "A Greeting; and a View of Riemann's Hypothesis." *The American Mathematical Monthly* 94(1):3.

Wittgenstein, Ludwig. 1983. *Remarks on the Foundations of Mathematics.* Cambridge, MA: The MIT Press.

Index

The MIT Press, with Peter Denning as general consulting editor, publishes computer science books in the following series:

ACM Doctoral Dissertation Award and Distinguished Dissertation Series

Artificial Intelligence
Patrick Winston, Founding editor
Michael Brady, Daniel Bobrow, and Randall Davis, editors

Charles Babbage Institute Reprint Series for the History of Computing
Martin Campbell-Kelly, editor

Computer Systems
Herb Schwetman, editor

Explorations with Logo
E. Paul Goldenberg, editor

Foundations of Computing
Michael Garey and Albert Meyer, editors

History of Computing
I. Bernard Cohen and William Aspray, editors

Information Systems
Michael Lesk, editor

Logic Programming
Ehud Shapiro, editor; Fernando Pereira, Koichi Furukawa, Jean-Louis Lassez, and David H. D. Warren, Associate editors

The MIT Press Electrical Engineering and Computer Science Series

Research Monographs in Parallel and Distributed Processing
Christopher Jesshope and David Klappholz, editors

Scientific and Engineering Computation
Janusz Kowalik, editor

Technical Communication
Ed Barrett, editor

BUILDING
SHANGHAI

BUILDING
SHANGHAI

The Story of China's Gateway

EDWARD DENISON

GUANG YU REN

WILEY-ACADEMY

Other Wiley Editorial Offices
John Wiley & Sons Inc., 111 River Street, Hoboken, NJ 07030, USA
Jossey-Bass, 989 Market Street, San Francisco, CA 94103-1741, USA
Wiley-VCH Verlag GmbH, Boschstr. 12, D-69469 Weinheim, Germany
John Wiley & Sons Australia Ltd, 42 McDougall Street, Milton, Queensland 4064, Australia
John Wiley & Sons (Asia) Pte Ltd, 2 Clementi Loop #02-01, Jin Xing Distripark,
     Singapore 129809
John Wiley & Sons Canada Ltd, 22 Worcester Road, Etobicoke, Ontario, Canada M9W 1L1

ISBN-13 978 0 470 01637 4 (HB)
ISBN-10 0 470 01637 X (HB)

Executive Commissioning Editor: Helen Castle
Development Editor: Mariangela Palazzi-Williams
Content Editor: Louise Porter
Publishing Assistant: Calver Lezama

Page design and layouts by Liz Sephton
Printed and bound by Saik Wah Press, Singapore

CONTENTS

Notes about Spelling and Grid References

The spelling of Chinese names historically causes an insolvable transliteration problem. We have chosen to use the spelling by which particular words are most commonly understood or referred to, and have therefore not adhered exclusively to the contemporary system of pinyin. Road names are a particular source of confusion. The contemporary map on page 13 contains most versions of street names since 1843.

Both contemporary maps on pages 11-12 and page 13 and the aerial photograph on page 190 contain a grid reference system to assist the reader to locate sites on the map more easily. The grid reference is referred to in the text at the first mention of each key site or building and appears as a bracketed double-digit code, e.g.: (A1).

ACKNOWLEDGEMENTS

Too many people have contributed to this book for us to be able to thank them all individually. We will forever be indebted to all those Shanghainese who, against a prevailing trend, shared their time, stories and spaces with us. Our sincere gratitude goes also to so many other individuals and organisations that have supported, guided and corrected us along the way. Any errors remaining in the text are of our own making. Space does not allow us to mention everyone individually, but the following people will be aware of their contributions, though maybe unaware of the extent of our sincere appreciation and gratitude: Nick and Jocelyn Atkinson, Joanna Burke, Patrick Conner and the Martyn Gregory Gallery, Malcolm Cooper, Stella Dong, Robert Elwall and the staff at the RIBA, Arlene Fleming, Michelle Garnaut, Bruno vanderBerg, Marcus Ford, and all the staff at M-on-the-Bund, Edwin Green, Lenore Heitkamp, Alan Hollinghurst, Jim Hollington, Tess Johnston, Professor Luo Xiao Wei, Pan Lynn, Fred Manson, Qian Zong Hao, Professor Ruan Yi San, Richard Rogers, Robert Torday, Selahadin Abdullah, Semira Ibrahim and Heden, and Wu Jiang. We are grateful also to the British Council and their China Studies programme for providing invaluable financial and institutional support in the early stages of research; and to the Graham Foundation for their generous support of research and use of materials, many of which would not be featured in this book had it not been for their generous consideration. The following are among the many other institutions that have helped to make this book as comprehensive and informative as possible: the British Library, the HSBC Archives, the Library of Congress, the National Archive of Great Britain, the Royal Institute of British Architects, the Shanghai Library, the Shanghai Municipal Archives, and the University of Victoria (Canada). We also wish to extend a very special thank you to all those at and associated with Wiley-Academy and John Wiley & Sons who have worked so hard to complete this book with such dedicated professionalism: Helen Castle, Jenny McCall, Mariangela Palazzi-Williams, Famida Rasheed, Liz Sephton, Louise Porter, Lorna Skinner, Rowan Stanfield, Vivien Ng, Kaycee Tan, Lucy Isenberg and Abigail Grater. Our greatest debt of gratitude is to Hou Ji Xing, Ren He Tian, friends and family in Shanghai, Eleanor and John, whose patience, understanding, contributions and support have been beyond measure. Last and not least, to Phil Ochs for being a constant source of light in dark times – 'I won't be laughing at the lies when I'm gone'.

Above View of the Bund from the mid-1860's

Below View of the Bund today

SHANGHAI

Legend:

First delineation of the British Settlement 20.09.1846

Second delineation of the British Settlement 27.11.1848

Informal early American Settlement area

Informal Boundary of American Settlement amalgamated with British Settlement in 1863

International Settlement extension 1899

First delineation of the French Concession 06.04.1849

Extension of the French Concession 29.10.1861

Extension of the French Concession 27.01.1900

Extension of the French Concession 20.07.1914

Former Walled City

Former Park

Park

Waterway

Boundary of the Jewish area

Subway Station

Subway Line

Railway Line

Site Name — Historic Building

Site Name — Contemporary Building

Building

Gate

Church

Mosque

Cemetery

CENTRAL SHANGHAI

	City Block & Road
	Road pre-1941
••••••	Road, 1850s
	Current Park
	Former Park
	Waterway
	Former Major Creek
Nanjing Road	Current Road Name
Nanjing Road	Road Name pre-1941
Park Lane	Road Name pre-1860s
Land Renters	Major Bund Firm, 1850s
	Building
	Church
	Gate
	Military Position
	Cemetery
★	Bomb, 1937

The Story of China's Gateway

In this city the gulf between society's two halves is too grossly wide for any bridge …And we ourselves though we wear out our shoes walking the slums, though we take notes, though we are genuinely shocked and indignant, belong, unescapably, to the other world. We return, always, to Number One House for lunch.

In our world, there are garden-parties and the night-clubs, the hot baths and the cocktails, the singsong girls and the Ambassador's cook. In our world, European business men write to the local newspapers, complaining that the Chinese are cruel to pigs, and saying that the refuges should be turned out of the Settlement because they are beginning to smell.

And the well-meaning tourist, the liberal and humanitarian intellectual, can only wring his hands over all this and exclaim: 'Oh dear, things are so awful here – so complicated. One doesn't know where to start.'

WH Auden and Christopher Isherwood, *Journey to a War*, 1939.

Right Flying kites on Shanghai's historic Bund

We shape our buildings – thereafter they shape us.

Winston Churchill, House of Commons Speech, 28 October 1943

Shanghai is an inimitable city. In the past, no other city was more heterogeneous, more autonomous, or more iniquitous. Today, no other city is undergoing such massive change. For the future, no other city has such ostentatious designs. Infamous for its depravity and famed for its autonomy, Shanghai's celebrated prosperity between the two world wars spawned a renowned impiety that would have appalled even the depraved inhabitants of Sodom and Gomorrah. Sex, drugs and organised crime underpinned the city's social life as much as greed, power and decadence defined its architecture and urban growth. However, this illustrious chapter represents only a snippet of the story. For centuries, Shanghai has navigated highs and lows, and lured millions who came to make their fortune or steal others'. While rapaciously consuming everything that has come its way, by attracting powerful people and appalling conflict, which resulted in unparalleled misery, debauched hedonism and immeasurable wealth, Shanghai has become greater than the sum of its parts – a peculiar urban form, a mega-metropolis, an irrepressible and abstract entity. As one journalist put it: 'Shanghai has had many conquerors, but Shanghai conquers the conquerors.'[1] Foreign and Chinese architectural firms are once again flocking to Shanghai to take part in the largest urban transformation in history, driven by China's burgeoning economy. A new battle for Shanghai is taking place, as the city's unprecedented development looks either to undermine or to enhance Shanghai's distinguished heritage.

Standing at the gateway to the Yangtze River, the backbone of China and the world's entry point to the vast trading potential of the country's interior, Shanghai has evoked many things to many people, garnering an extensive list of epithets which depict an almost absurdly schizophrenic character: 'Whore of the Orient', 'Paris of the East', 'Queen of Eastern Settlements', 'Paradise of Adventurers', 'New York of the Far East', 'City of Palaces', 'Yellow Babylon of the Far East', and the former Duke of Somerset's 'Sink of Iniquity'. However, behind the vacuous sobriquets, the city's eminence and consequent international importance derive solely from its outstanding geographical location for trade. This is as important today as it always was and always will be: trade provides the stimulus driving this dynamic mercantile city; it is trade that has engendered the lust for wealth which is synonymous with Shanghai and with the character of its residents –

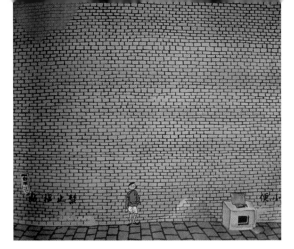

industrious people renowned for their capacity to flourish in the shadow of the skyscraper.

International trade has permeated every layer of Shanghai's rich history and left its mark on the city's urban form and diverse architectural composition. Its vibrant mix of colonial structures, Modernist piles, Art Deco motifs, eclectic styles and postmodern towers makes the city a treasure trove for both the idle wanderer and the discerning professional. Inscribed in the streets and buildings are the legacies of every major event that has taken place within the city's boundaries. The first Opium War (1840–3) and Britain's subsequent government-sponsored drug smuggling that led to Shanghai's foundation (1843) and the West's rape of China shaped the opulent facades along Shanghai's famous Bund and downtown. China's bitter domestic conflicts (from the 1850s) and myriad refugees forged the street plan of the former British Settlement. The narrow-mindedness and greed of early settlers and of subsequent administrations were responsible for Shanghai's tortuous road network and its infamously paltry pavements. The rise of Chinese republicanism in the early 20th century can be read in the absence of the ancient city wall, whose silhouette appears as an annular scar in an otherwise linear street pattern. The Russian revolutions are manifested in apartment buildings and in the domes of former Orthodox churches. Japanese aggression and the origins of the Second World War emerge through the underprivileged suburbs that witnessed the world's first urban aerial bombing campaign. Nazi persecution is unveiled in former ghettos that became the world's last safe refuge for European Jews. The tragedy of the Cultural Revolution and China's global isolation appear in faded Maoist slogans, tired facades and ill-considered urban programmes.

It is remarkable enough that so many disparate international events swept over Shanghai, but that these historical events are recorded in the surviving buildings and streets after decades of isolation is almost miraculous. However, the longevity of Shanghai's hibernation is matched only by the velocity of its recent resurgence. The most comprehensive and revolutionary urban metamorphosis in history has transformed the city's skyline with its 4,000 high-rise buildings sprouting from Shanghai's alluvial terrain since the mid-1980s. The scale of the city's regeneration is characterised by the duel between the past and the future that

so blatantly evades the present, a duel in which developers and preservationists have become the new protagonists in a conflict over Shanghai's future – not for political or economic gain, but for the continuity of its famously rich urban texture.

Shanghai offers a unique case study in which many contemporary urban problems are conspicuous by their exaggeration and through which much can be learned. This book sets out to contextualise contemporary Shanghai by illustrating its history through its architecture and urban landscape. By exploring the city's remarkable past, from its ancient origins, through foreign dominance, to China's resurgence, one gains a startlingly clear picture of Shanghai's unique physical character. A close examination of Shanghai's architecture and urbanism reveals, perhaps more than anywhere else in the world, all the facets of human nature, from its altruistic best to its debauched worst, helps make sense of the overwhelming changes taking place in modern China and sheds light on an enigmatic future.

While most cities develop almost imperceptibly as their fortunes ebb and flow with time, where fresh ideas inject vitality, where the recent past is condemned and where the old is deified or destroyed, Shanghai flouts these perceived norms and defies established principles of urban development and preservation. The eyes of the world are on Shanghai's illustrious plans for the 21st century and beyond, yet few have stopped to ponder the origin of this phenomenal transformation or questioned its price. Behind Shanghai's headline-grabbing superlatives, history is not in the making, but being repeated.

THE ORIGINS OF SHANGHAI

The Origins of Shanghai

CHAPTER ONE

[The native city] is traversed by lanes or streets which might better be termed fetid tunnels, seething with filth and teeming with miserable and vicious looking humanity. Odours are suffocating and the eyes can find nothing attractive or beautiful to rest upon: squalor, indigence, misery, slush, stench, depravity, dilapidation, and decay prevail everywhere. One almost fears to enter a place of so many repugnant scenes.

J Ricalton, *China through the Stereoscope*, 1901, p 77

Previous pages The Yuyuan gardens and teahouse

The story of Shanghai and its environs, contrary to many early settler accounts, does not start with a desolate swamp formed by the Yangtze's eternal effluent, or with a nondescript fishing village struggling to survive on China's coast. It begins with a settlement formed many hundreds of years ago that evolved into an illustrious merchant community and a unique Chinese city. Early foreign descriptions rarely allude to this; instead, they disparage the nature of the land and people they encountered, so exalting their own contribution. The 'waste land without houses',[1] from which foreigners built the settlements that became the 'stronghold of civilisation in the Far East',[2] was actually a clearly defined area, highly regarded by local Chinese and subject to strict land ownership for centuries. The foreigner did not transform a 'sedgy swamp'[3] into a magnificent city through self-ordained civilising brilliance, but invaded the gateway to China and exploited a well-established mercantile community by exposing it to international trade. The consequent growth of a settlement from this fusion of two disparate trading groups in such a prime location was inevitable.

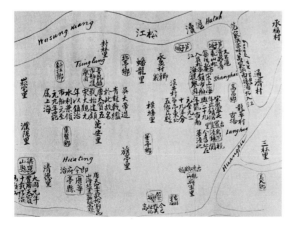

Right Administrative map of the Shanghai region in the 1700s

Location and meaning

Shanghai stands 15 miles south of the mouth of the Yangtze River – the backbone of China that divides the country almost equally and has an estimated 400 million people living in its catchment. The former walled city sat close to the intersection of two important waterways, the Whuangpu River and the Woosung River, which provide access to the sea and the hinterland respectively. Few cities on earth are so advantageously located for the pursuit of domestic and international trade.

The topography of the surrounding area is central to Shanghai's eminence. The traditionally affluent neighbouring provinces of Jiangsu and Zhejiang include the wealthy Yangtze Triangle, an area containing the prosperous silk and tea region of the Hang-Jia-Hu Plain.[4] This area alone has made China famous throughout the world for those two primary exports, and at the start of the 21st century, with 6 per cent of China's population, accounts for 18 per cent of the country's production. Despite appalling if sporadic incidence of flooding and famine that have caused untold misery, over the centuries the normally auspicious conditions have created a region that, characterised by abundant agricultural activity, has been described as the Garden of China.

Many diverse accounts attest to the etymology of *Shanghai*. In Chinese, 'Shanghai' is made up of two characters, *Shang* and *Hai*, the former meaning 'up', 'upper', or 'above', and the latter meaning 'sea'. The name *Shanghai* therefore has various possible interpretations. Two straightforward suggestions are derived from the city being 'up from the sea' or 'above the sea'. Another possibility arises from the location relative to an area called Xia Hai Pu, *Xia* being the opposite to *Shang* and *Pu* meaning 'by the water', often referring to a river bank. Historical records suggest that two of the Woosung River's tributaries were called Shang Hai Pu, or 'Upper Sea', and Xia Hai Pu, or 'Lower Sea'. Shang Hai Pu once flowed into the area of Pudong, across the Whuangpu from Shanghai, while on the opposite bank Xia Hai Pu flowed into what later became Shanghai's northern suburb of Hongkou. It is believed that the ruins of the temple of Xia Hai existed up until the mid-20th century.

Shanghai is also referred to as Hu and Shen. Hu originates from a 4th-century settlement called Hu Tu Lei, located approximately one mile north of the old city of Shanghai. The Hu derives from a method of tidal fishing with nets strung on bamboo poles that was very common on the waterways around the region. *Tu* refers to a single stream leading to the sea, while *Lei* refers to a mound, in this case a fortification. The name *Shen* derives from the title, *Chuen Shen*, given to Huang

Xie, who was awarded this land during the reign of the Kingdom of Chu in the 4th century BC.

The Shanghai region

The earliest records of the region around Shanghai date from the era of Chinese history called 'Spring and Autumn' (Chun Qiu) between 770 BC and 476 BC which was named after one of the five Confucian Classics written in this period. Together with the 'Warring States' period, this disunited and turbulent time was considered the golden age of Chinese philosophy, which also saw the establishment of the doctrines of Taoism. The Shanghai region was then a dominion of the Wu Kingdom, whose people frequently fought with their neighbours, the Yue Kingdom. To afford protection to his kingdom, the king of Wu built a city in his own name, He Lu, between 514 BC and 494 BC on the banks of the Woosong River a few miles from present-day Shanghai.

The boundaries of the Yue and the Wu Kingdoms varied constantly during the Warring States, or Zhan Guo, period of Chinese history (between 475 BC and 221 BC), which ended when China was united under the famous Emperor Qin Shi Huang, who built much of the Great Wall and the Terracotta Army. In the turmoil characterising this period, the administration of the Shanghai region shifted from Wu to Yue, then in 355 BC to the Chu Kingdom, under whose rule the region became known as Lou from 207 BC.

Later, in the epoch known as 'Three Kingdoms' (AD 220–80), the first phase of an era of bitter disunity in China that lasted until the 7th century AD and is often compared to Europe's Dark Ages, the primary settlement in the Shanghai region was a town called Qin Long, or 'Blue Dragon'. This city acquired its name when Sun Quan, the emperor of one of the Three Kingdoms, built a warship on the banks of the Woosung and called the ship *Qin Long*. Qin Long, 25 miles up the Woosung from present-day Shanghai, was used by the emperor as a military port and the site of the customs office, serving as the region's gateway for goods into and out of the interior.

During the Eastern Jin Dynasty (AD 317–420), a settlement called Hu Tu Lei was established a few miles east of Qin Long on the bank of the Woosong River, close to the former settlement of He Lu. Hu Tu Lei comprised two separate fortifications near the site of the British Consulate in the British Settlement which was formed over one and a half thousand years later. These sites, being so close to the future foreign settlements in Shanghai, assume an important role in the ancient history of Shanghai. In the 1850s it was suggested that the new foreign settlement in Shanghai should be called Lu Zi Cheng ('City of Reeds'), after an ancient settlement constructed close to the forts of Hu Tu Lei, but the name was not adopted.

The regional administration around Shanghai altered considerably from the 6th century. In AD 507, the region of Lou was renamed Xin Yi, which itself was subdivided in AD 535. Present-day Shanghai was located in the southern portion

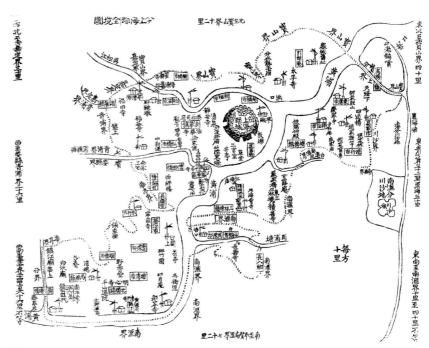

Above Regional map of Shanghai before foreign settlement

of this subdivision, named Kun Shan, part of which was absorbed in AD 751 into a new administration called Hua Ting. Shanghai evolved in the region of Hua Ting, and became administratively independent by the end of the Song Dynasty (AD 960–1279) between AD 1265 and 1267.

The first recorded mention of the name 'Shanghai' remains ambiguous. There is a trend for later records to quote earlier dates, while older records quote later ones. Records from the Ming Dynasty (AD 1368–1644) suggest that Shanghai was formed in the late Song Dynasty (AD 1127–1279), but records from the later Qing Dynasty (AD 1644–1911) claim Shanghai was established in the early Song Dynasty (AD 960–1127).[5] Foreign interpretations veer towards the date AD 1074, perhaps because the first mention of this in an English language publication appears in AD 1850,[6] which itself is likely to have derived from a Chinese record of AD 1814.

Despite the numerous discrepancies, most authorities concur that Shanghai was founded in the Song Dynasty, but more important is its independence from the region of Hua Ting. Shanghai's illustrious recent history began in AD 1291,[7] when it became a 'Xian' or district administration, making it an important centre administratively, culturally and commercially. Its eminence as a port was boosted by the relocation of the local customs office to Shanghai from Qin Long, which had silted up and become unnavigable for large ships.

The city of Shanghai

After becoming a Xian, Shanghai's institutions were augmented significantly in keeping with its new status. Four years after

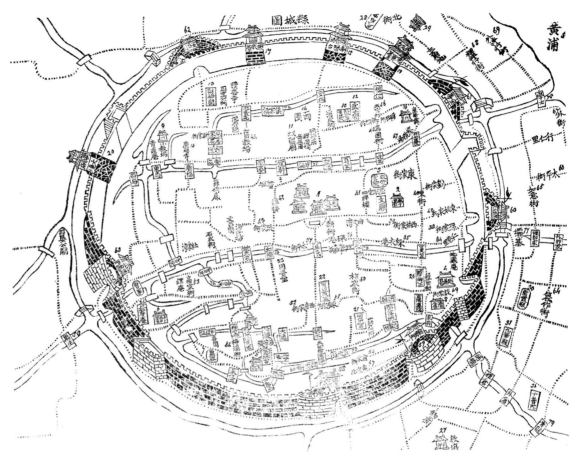

its administrative promotion, Shanghai established official centres of learning, known as Xian Xue, after which many other schools were built in Shanghai. These state schools taught Confucianism based on a method of 'question and debate', a system that relied on rhetorical teaching as opposed to deductive reasoning and instruction.

Shanghai is said once to have been a 'secluded place', whose inhabitants were 'rude and simple'[8] and travelled no further than the neighbouring provinces, but by the time it had become a Xian it was 'a large town, celebrated for its press of business, and not for its sea port alone'.[9] Towards the end of the 15th century, Shanghai is said to have become culturally rich, with poets, musicians and eminent scholars and politicians making it a place of renown.

The ascendancy of Shanghai as a significant Chinese trading and cultural centre soon attracted unwelcome attention internationally. Japanese forces and complicit Chinese pirates, who for centuries had plagued the coast of China, attacked the city with increasing frequency. Between April and June 1553,[10] the Japanese launched five assaults on the region, looting, sacking villages and towns and raping and killing the hapless residents. Having discovered the source of rich pickings, these marauding troops returned in 300 ships and routed Shanghai, which 'was set on fire and burnt to the ground'.[11] In response to these series of massacres, the residents of Shanghai contributed generously to the construction of a city wall to prevent further attacks.[12]

The city wall was the largest physical change to affect Shanghai until foreigners arrived in the mid-19th century. The annular wall was 2.5 miles in circumference, 24 feet high and surrounded by a 30 foot ditch. Along it four arrow towers were constructed with 20 smaller bastions and 3,600 embrasures to augment the defence. Six gates provided for ingress and egress: Chaozong (Big East Gate), Baodai (Small East Gate), Kualong (Big South Gate), Chaoyang (Small South Gate), Yifeng (West Gate), and Yanghai (North Gate). When peace was restored, the arrow towers were converted into temples, and in 1607 the wall was raised by five feet.

Later, four water gates were built adjoining four of the six land gates. These four water gates provided access into and out of the city for the city's three largest canals, only one of which, Zhao Jia Bang, traversed the city from the Whuangpu on the east side and penetrated the west wall. The four gates were: Baodai water gate across the Fang Bang, Chaozong water gate

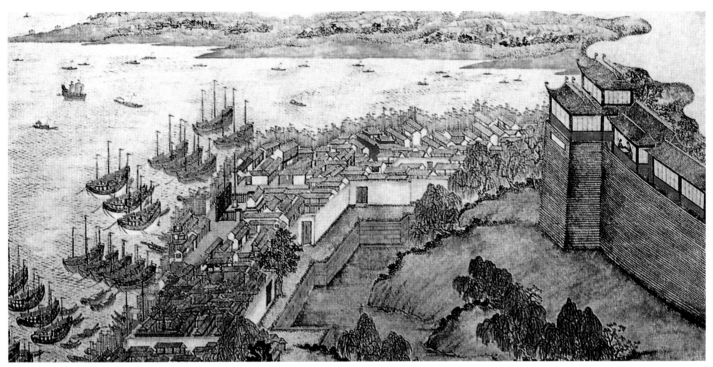

across East Zhaojia Bang, Yifeng water gate across West Zhaojia Bang, and Chaoyang water gate across Xiujia Bang, which, in 1598, was the last of the water gates to be added. These waterways, connected to the moat and the Whuangpu, served as the lifeblood of the city, providing defence, a means of transportation, waste disposal and drinking water.

Within the city, there were five major creeks with many smaller tributaries. The footpaths and roads tended to follow the line of these waterways, with over a hundred bridges crossing them throughout the city. The city's tidal waterways caused several problems. If a fire broke out during low tide and the creeks were dry, it could easily develop into a

conflagration; conversely, heavy winter rains combined with high tides could flood the city. On one occasion in the Qing Dynasty the city drowned under 5 feet of water and boats were seen 'travelling in the fields'.[13] The tide also brought silt and sand, blocking the creeks and increasing salinity in the water table. By the early 20th century, the condition had deteriorated so much that the creeks were filled in or covered over and replaced by roads.

During the Ming Dynasty (AD 1368–1644), there were five main streets in Shanghai, crossing the city from east to west and north to south. Ten street names are recorded, echoing the names of prominent residents of the time. Much later, in the early 19th century, the street layout had become considerably more dense. From 1805, 63 streets are recorded, 27 of which are named after important families, a concrete reflection of the city's feudal structure. The centre of the city was called Xian Shu (the Office of Xian)(H6), and was situated west of the existing City God Temple (Cheng Huang Miao). The significance of the Xian Shu's location at the core of the city was further emphasised by the arrangement and proliferation of public, religious and academic institutions around this core and reflected in the surrounding street names such as 'Left of Xian Street' and 'Behind Xian Street'.

Street names traditionally played an important role in Shanghai, often denoting some landmark area such as a religious site, place of historical interest or important personage. Many street names also denoted waterways, creeks and bridges which they followed or crossed, or indicated the trades and types of activity that predominated in a particular street. Commercial areas were arranged according to specific activities so that similar trades or produce could be found along one street. This organisation significantly influenced Shanghai's character and was evidenced through many of its street names, such as Fish Street and Fruit Street, some of which still exist, though most have become extinct with the advent of modern town planning.

After 1681, when during the Qing Dynasty the threat from pirates and other enemies was considered passed, the ban on using the sea for transportation and commerce was lifted and some of Shanghai's most important streets developed along the river bank outside the city wall, where commercial activities flourished. The area of land between the Whuangpu and the southeast portion of the city wall soon became a centre of trade, where the Chinese customs duties office, Jiang Hai Guan, was built and a prestigious suburb grew up containing eleven main streets, five running north to south and six running east to west.

The street nearest the Whuangpu had many wharfs and jetties but was often submerged or flooded during heavy rains or high tides. This street was called Wai Ma Lu (Outside Road), the 'Ma Lu' portion literally meaning 'Horse Road', which was always used to denote a road in Chinese. Foreigners in Shanghai commonly referred to this term as 'Maloo'. To combat the recurring problem caused by flooding, the construction of larger public and commercial wharfs connected to the mainland above the high-water mark improved the area, which in its prime boasted over 20 wharfs and the only vehicle ferry to Pudong, on the opposite bank of the Whuangpu. Parallel to Wai Ma Lu was Li Ma Lu (Inside Road), now connected to the Bund via South Zhongshan Road. The third and fourth streets were notable for selling all manner of foodstuffs and served the important Bean Market Street near the Big East Gate, around which wholesale businesses were concentrated, particularly in staples such as rice, flour, wheat and oil. Further to the south, near the suburb of Dong Jia Du (often referred to by foreigners as Tunkadoo), bamboo and wood for the construction industry were among the primary imports. The fifth street, today Zhong Hua Lu, was built when the city wall was destroyed in 1913–14.

North of this riverside suburb was a smaller suburb containing one of the most important streets in Shanghai from the 18th century – Yang Hang Jie (Foreign Hong Street, now called Yangshuo Road). Yang Hang Jie, over 300 metres long, contained many 'hongs' (warehouses) belonging to merchants who bought and sold foreign goods. Spanish silver from Canton and Fujian was the standard currency. This

Below The 'forest of masts' on the Whuangpu in the mid-19th century

area outside Little East Gate was the most prosperous in Shanghai during the Qing Dynasty, dealing in imported goods such as sandalwood, turtle shell, birds' nests, and export goods such as cloth, pottery, silk, tobacco and dried fruit. It spawned many restaurants and shops and attracted wealthy merchants from all over China, especially from Canton and Fujian provinces.

These merchants established guilds called *huiguan* or *gongsuo* based on their region or trade. Huiguan supported resident communities and their families, protecting the rights of members and providing medical and charitable services, religious temples, education and sometimes guesthouses or cemeteries. Those huiguan that served professional interests sought to resolve trade disputes and promoted the vocation of their members. Shanghai was both renowned and unique for its large variety of huiguan, often being described as the original expression of multiculturalism in China, preceding international multiculturalism in Shanghai by over a century.

Architecturally huiguan were often very elaborate,

reflecting the craftsmanship and religious and vernacular styles of the region they represented. Their spatial arrangement varied depending on the size and influence of the community. The smaller ones comprised an office, a shrine and perhaps a guesthouse, whereas the larger ones might also include stages for theatrical performances, schools, teahouses, hospitals and even a cemetery. Their architectural style changed throughout the 19th century particularly in response to Western influence. Before the Opium Wars they tended to be larger and more elaborate, but after the arrival of foreigners in Shanghai they became smaller and less sophisticated. By the end of the 19th century, Western architectural motifs were used, representing a fusion of Eastern and Western styles and depictions. The Wood Merchants' Huiguan was decorated with woodcarvings depicting foreigners walking their dogs and ladies riding rickshaws. Shanghai once had over 30 huiguan representing different communities and over 100 representing different trades, including pig slaughtering, hat manufacturing, wine making and shipping.

Boat owners were among the most prosperous and numerous merchants in Shanghai at the time, commonly owning 30 to 50 boats each. Only the largest merchant ships serving the China coast dared to navigate the treacherous currents at the mouth of the Whuangpu and Yangtze, while most boats plied the local rivers and waterways. In Shanghai's prime there were over 3,500 registered boats, appearing like a 'forest of masts'[14] to the first foreign visitors. The huiguan belonging to the Commercial Boat Association (Shang Chuan Huiguan), built in 1715, was the earliest and one of the largest in Shanghai – its design so elaborate that foreigners often mistook it for a temple.

Shanghai possessed many temples and shrines honouring various gods, individuals and philosophers such as Lao-Tzi (Taoism) and Kong-Tzi (Confucianism). As a commercial centre, Shanghai tolerated many different religious beliefs, which endowed the city with a diverse spiritual character that embraced Buddhism, Islam, Christianity and various local religions. Religion, philosophy and other forms of worship were central to life in China until the mid-20th century.

Among the most important temples was Cheng Huang Miao, or City God Temple, on the northern bank of the Fang Creek. Built at the start of the 15th century, this temple was devoted to Huo Guang, a man who had succeeded, at least temporarily, in protecting the city from the ravages of the sea. Soon after it was built, it was enlarged and improved, though it was destroyed by fire in 1606 and despoiled by various insurgents over the centuries, including the British who used it as an army base when they invaded Shanghai in 1842. Two uprisings against Chinese imperial rule in the mid-19th century wrought further havoc on the city and on the City God Temple. The first, in 1853, saw it looted and destroyed by a band of rebels called the Small Swords; and a little over ten years later it was again ravaged, this time by the infamous Taipings, whose four-year spree of violence brought unmitigated devastation across China. Fire again destroyed the temple twice in the 20th century, soon after which the compound was converted into a school and factory during the Cultural Revolution. Since 1994, it has resumed its original function.

A temple to Confucius (Wen Miao (G7)) was located inside the East Gate, but the Small Swords occupied it in 1853 and destroyed it during their retreat in 1855. The temple complex was then moved to the West Gate, where it remains, though it became a park in 1931 and a public library has been added.

Another renowned Shanghai landmark is the Hu Xin Ting (H6), a pavilion that became known among foreigners as the 'Willow-Patterned Teahouse' because of its resemblance to the famous willow pattern pottery. The pavilion stands in a small lake next to the Yu Yuan Gardens near the City God Temple and is connected to the bank by a distinctive zigzag walkway, designed to fox evil spirits who are believed to travel only in straight lines. Built in 1784, it was originally a pavilion and meeting place for merchants dealing in the local blue-dyed

Left The City God Temple

Above The Yuyuan gardens and teahouse

Opposite The region around Shanghai showing other walled settlements and their dependence on the abundant waterways. The Yangtze River is visible bottom left

cotton, but in 1855 it was converted into a teahouse. These were popular venues for conducting business in an informal environment – a customary activity throughout China. Benefiting from its prime location, the teahouse prospered and was extended. Originally square in plan, two small additions were made to make it semi-hexagonal. Later extensions completed the hexagonal floor plan. The various stages of development are evident in the supporting columns and internal structure. The British 'occupied' the pavilion compound when they invaded Shanghai, 'delighted with the curious bridges, gateways, gigantic lamps, grottoes, shady alcoves, and…the rockery'.[15]

Major waterways

Historically, waterways have always played an integral part in the life and development of the region around Shanghai. Early maps of Shanghai illustrate clearly the dependence on waterways for transport and the notable scarcity of significant roads and footpaths, due to the preponderance of creeks, canals and rivers that interlace the region, but these vital arteries have altered considerably over the past two millennia. Tracing the exact location of settlements is therefore challenging, as the position of these ephemeral markers shifts considerably over time. Settlements are relocated and waterways oscillate with countless tides and floods or through human intervention.

Shanghai's link to the sea is the broad Whuangpu River, which winds in a generally north–south direction. Legend has it that this river is named after Huang Xie of the Chu Kingdom in the 4th century BC. The much smaller Woosung River, which joins the Whuangpu in the heart of the present-day city, runs in an east–west direction, linking Shanghai to the ancient city of Suzhou. Maps dating from the 11th

century show the Woosung to be 'an immense sheet of water', up to 5 miles wide and unconnected to the Whuangpu, which was then an 'insignificant canal' flowing due east from the village of Lunghua directly into the sea.[16]

These two waterways were both tidal, but the Woosung especially was prone to flooding, which caused immense devastation. In AD 1403, an enormous inundation so overwhelmed the region that the then Emperor was compelled to send a representative to try solve the problem. Much effort was expended on building dykes and constructing dams so that from 1403 a small tributary linking the Whuangpu and the Woosung was widened in an attempt to regulate the flow of these rivers. The canal was known as the Fan Jia Bang (often referred to as the Van Ka Pang) named after a family called Fan who lived in the area. Over time the Fan Jia Bang attracted the flow of the Whuangpu, while the upper Woosung contracted. With the volume of the Whuangpu now flowing to the sea via the Fan Jia Bang and the lower Woosung, the watercourse widened and became a large river. In 1569 the Woosung was modified by a man named Hai Rui, who reduced its flow drastically, transforming it into the diminutive tributary that it is today. After foreigners arrived in Shanghai, the Woosung became known as Soochow (Suzhou) Creek.

The unique city

Shanghai can claim to be unique among ancient Chinese cities. The annular wall reflected the city's relatively minor political status among China's larger imperial cities that employed rectangular walls and linear street patterns. Lacking a systematised street layout and with its irregular street plan originating in age-old methods of transportation along the rivers and creeks that traversed the city, Shanghai's design was distinct from that of traditional Chinese urban centres that observe formalised rectilinear street patterns and the strict arrangement of individual components, such as courtyard houses, temples and state buildings. As Johnson observes, the pattern of Shanghai's development 'was one of organic growth rather than structured design'.[17] The more conservative, accustomed to the formal delineation of urban spaces, frowned upon Shanghai's atypical form and its unusual buildings designed for mixed use which predominated over the stereotypical arrangement of courtyard dwellings popular elsewhere in China.

These particularities of layout and building confirmed Shanghai's cultural and commercial diversity long before foreigners arrived. Its physical characteristics reflected the city as a melting pot of new ideas – its buildings, their function, style and setting. Shanghai's predilection for trade is largely responsible for its renowned tolerance of cultural diversity and demonstrates an important departure from traditional Chinese urban design. This was a factor that remained evident throughout Shanghai's history.

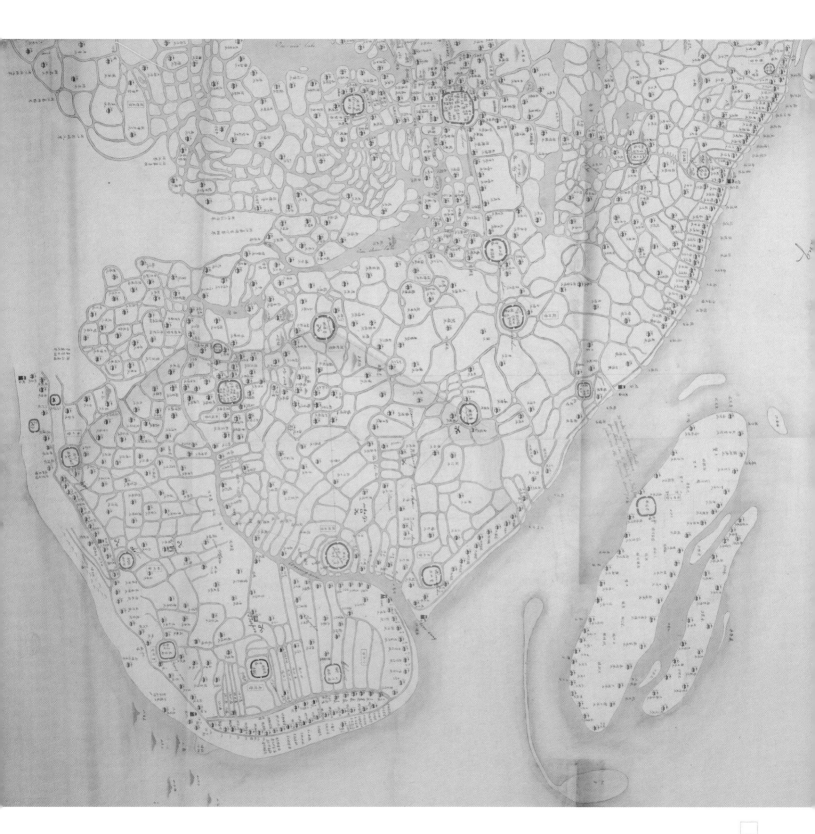

ESTABLISHING AND LEGALISING THE FOREIGN SETTLEMENTS

Establishing and Legalising
the Foreign Settlements

Shanghae is by far the most important station for foreign trade on the coast of China. No other town with which I am acquainted possesses such advantages: it is the great gate – the principal entrance, in fact, to the Chinese empire … there can be no doubt that in a few years it will not only rival Canton, but become a place of far greater importance.

Robert Fortune, *Three Years' Wanderings in the Northern Provinces of China*, 1847

Previous pages The first Custom House on the foreign Bund

Foreign contact with China extends back thousands of years, but with the advent of the Industrial Revolution and advances in maritime trade, China's relationship with the outside world changed fundamentally in the 19th century. The British occupation of Shanghai in 1842 can be traced to earlier encounters with the Chinese administration and previous attempts by foreigners to avoid integration with the Chinese while seeking preferential terms of trade and to establish a permanent settlement in China, whereas the Chinese endeavoured in vain to flush foreign influence from their closeted kingdom. This clash of cultures over the pursuit of trade proved an unavoidable catalyst to the development of Shanghai from a Chinese city to Asia's largest foreign enclave and one of the largest cities in the world.

Early foreign contact with China

The roots of foreign settlement in Shanghai extend to the southern port of Canton and were nourished by the desire among foreign nations to conduct trade with the impervious Chinese empire. In 1757, the Emperor declared Canton the sole port open to foreigners, and so created the city's monopoly of trade with the West, while the equally monopolistic East India Company exercised its exclusive rights to British trade in China. This situation was far from perfect and a grudging acceptance of the status quo evolved into dissent and corruption among both the British and the Chinese. Britain aspired to fill the wardrobes of China with its cotton and wool, but succeeded instead in extracting far greater quantities of tea and silk, troubling the British Exchequer with a growing balance of payments deficit. However, the answer to all of Britain's problems and the cause of most of China's arrived from India in the form of the poppy seed.

The European aristocracy now enjoyed the luxuries of green tea and silk thread, bought and paid for by China's addiction to opium. Through a sustained campaign of international drug dealing of vast proportions, the British Empire employed narcotics to prise open the door that had until the 19th century so successfully barred access to the Chinese Empire. Despite the opium ban by imperial decree in 1800, trade in the drug continued through unofficial channels, lining the pockets of Cantonese officials who had much to lose from its prohibition and amassing untold wealth in influential foreign trading firms, many of which later dominated Shanghai. Corruption and unfair trading fuelled a rapidly deteriorating relationship between the Chinese and foreigners in Canton, providing the impetus for foreign merchants to seek alternative inroads into China's vast and untapped commercial potential. Addicted to opium and paying for this expensive craving in silver, China was forced to succumb.

Foreign merchants were prohibited from dealing directly with the native population in Canton, doing business instead through a syndicate of 14 middlemen known as the 'Co-hong'. Enjoying the privileges of this oligopoly, the Cantonese authorities subjected the constrained foreign merchants to all manner of 'extortion and intimidation',[1] while for their part the foreigners objected to being answerable to the seemingly heavy-handed Chinese criminal law that dictated that foreign sailors could be beheaded or strangled for crimes committed during their stay. A Parliamentary Act of 1833 put an end to this practice by granting the establishment of a Seaman's Court in Whampoa, near Canton, so denying the Chinese jurisdiction over foreign merchants and laying the foundation of 'extraterritoriality', a principle later adopted in Shanghai and other Treaty Ports that proved fundamental to their growth and central to their downfall.

These attempts coincided with a loosening of trade restriction laws in Britain, which now permitted private involvement in the China trade. In 1828, William Jardine and James and Alexander Matheson, three merchants from the East India Company, one of the leading opium peddlers, had started to petition Parliament to encourage private trade, which had been growing steadily under the American flag. In 1834, the East India Company's monopoly was abolished and the first private merchants to trade with China were quick to reap the spoils.

The first European to recognise Shanghai's suitability for trade was Frederick Pigou of the East India Company, who visited Shanghai in 1756. The report he compiled for the company's head office in Canton extolled the city as a desirable place to trade, but his superiors were unmoved, since their position in Canton had not yet become untenable. By the 1830s the situation had changed. In 1831, the Reverend Charles Gutzlaff visited Shanghai in a junk and was impressed enough to return the following year as interpreter to Hugh Hamilton Lindsay on the East India Company's ship the *Lord Amherst*, arriving at 4.30 pm on 20 June.[2] Mr Lindsay, to avoid the wrath of Cantonese officials, travelled in disguise as a man named Hoo-Hea-Me, destined for Japan, but his alter ego failed to convince the Chinese officials, who snubbed him in each of the ports he visited.

Upon his arrival in Shanghai, the reception appeared no less hostile. Passing the forts at Woosung at the mouth of the Whuangpu and Yangtze Rivers and 15 miles from Shanghai, the *Lord Amherst* received a volley of 'vigorous but blank fire'.[3] Further alarm was assuaged when what looked like extensive troop encampments along the banks of the Whuangpu turned out to be whitewashed mounds of soil. On reaching Shanghai, the party disembarked and, passing thronging crowds with placards repudiating trade with foreigners, made their way to the office of the city's representative or 'Taotai', who was appointed by the government to oversee the administration of the city, and with whom their encounters were a farce.

When he found the Taotai's office door closed, Mr Lindsay, devoid of diplomatic savoir faire, allowed two members of his party, Messrs Simpson and Stevens, to break it down 'with a great clatter'. According to Mr Lindsay, the Chinese officials received his party warmly and with 'great politeness', but it seems more likely that such intemperate behaviour incurred the wrath of the city's magistrate, Wan Lun Chan, who apparently scolded Mr Lindsay for his actions. Nonetheless, Mr Wan listened to 'the tales of woe undergone at Canton',[4] only for the brief discussion to come to an abrupt halt when Mr Lindsay joined Mr Wan in being seated. In the eyes of the Chinese officials, these guests were merchants and according to etiquette should deliver their petition standing. Mr Wan, objecting vigorously to his guests' faux pas, stormed out of the room, demanding later that Mr Lindsay and Mr Gutzlaff retire to the Temple of the Queen of Heaven, where the Taotai would meet them in due course.

With the question of being seated now a point of principle for Mr Lindsay, and with the Taotai refusing to provide seats for his guests, both parties agreed to compromise by standing to discuss the matter. However, on arriving to deliver his petition, Mr Lindsay was confronted by six seated Chinese officials. Feeling utterly deceived, he remonstrated until the Taotai stood to receive his letter. The Taotai countered by expressing disgust at the suggestion of trading with foreign 'barbarians', and reminded Mr Lindsay that if any Chinese vessels should arrive at British ports, they too should be refused anchorage. The impasse was only broken when he eventually accepted a copy of the petition and then banished the foreigners to the temple for the night. Escaping from their temporary confines, Mr Lindsay and Mr Gutzlaff spent the evening strolling Shanghai's streets, where they were impressed by the kindliness of the local population, who, unlike their masters, appeared receptive to the idea of trade with foreigners.

The following morning the two returned to their ship, where they received a stout refusal from the Taotai. Mr Lindsay delivered his petition again, this time threatening to take up the matter with higher officials in Nanjing, which immediately elicited a more conciliatory tone from the Taotai. Two weeks passed, during which time the delegation enjoyed very amiable relations with the local population, who appeared 'of a more peaceful type than the turbulent Cantonese'.[5]

Local merchants were forbidden to enter into negotiations with the foreigners, and although a few hundred dollars' worth of silk and gauze purchased by Mr Lindsay 'constituted the first ever transaction a foreign merchant entered into in Shanghai',[6] it also remained the only trade authorised during the visit. The currency used in this momentous transaction would likely have been Mexican silver dollars. These had been in use in China for centuries and their importation reached its peak in 1597 when 345 tons of silver were shipped to China from Acapulco. In China, various international and regional currencies were used in transactions, as well as silver, gold and even goods such as rice. The Shanghai officials begged the foreigners to leave, recommending instead that their embassy make a formal approach to the Emperor, since only he had the authority to amend the imperial laws forbidding trade with foreigners. Accepting that trade was not feasible, the *Lord Amherst* withdrew and, having passed Woosung, received a symbolic volley of cannon fire from the Chinese fleet 6 miles away.

In October of the same year, the ship *Huron* visited Shanghai, this time with Mr Medhurst and Mr Stevens onboard. Their reception seemed 'altogether more hostile' than before, though the Chinese merchants sent them 'secret messages' in the hope of establishing trade relations,[7] proving that Shanghai could be swayed on the issue of trade.

The report from Mr Lindsay's unsuccessful trip was lodged with the East India Company, prompting investigations into alternatives to Canton. Shanghai, despite its enviable location, had proved difficult, and as a consequence of the *Lord Amherst*'s visit the city's defences were improved significantly. The ageing forts at Woosung were rebuilt in granite and extended to over 3 miles long, while the city's arsenal manufactured hundreds of guns cast with awesome titles that would soon need to be lived up to: Shanghai now owed its protection to armaments with

sombre sobriquets like 'Tamer and Subduer of Barbarians', 'The Robbers' Judgement' and 'The Barbarian'.[8]

Invasion of Shanghai

During the infamous 'Opium War' with China (1840–3) brought about by the Emperor's attempt to halt the illegal smuggling of opium into Canton by foreign ships, Britain occupied and devastated the island of Chusan in 1840, after some in Britain considered it a more desirable trading post than Hong Kong and Shanghai. An article in the *India Gazette* from 1840 described the savagery of the attack: 'A more complete pillage could not be conceived than took place. Every house was broken open, every drawer and box ransacked, the streets strewn with fragments of furniture, pictures, tables, chairs, grain of all sorts – the whole set off by the dead or the living bodies of those who had been unable to leave the city from the wounds received from our merciless guns ... The plunder ceased only when there was nothing to take or destroy.'

Despite Chusan's potential – had it become the major trading post, Shanghai's future would have been uneventful – the decision was made to invade and settle in Shanghai. The East India Company, in collusion with the British Royal Navy, moved on Shanghai on 16 June 1842. At 6 am the fighting started. The upgraded Woosung forts resisted the aggressors resolutely, their fire power breaching the hulls of several

ships and killing and wounding a number of men. It took two hours of 'incessant fire'[9] before the main battery was silenced and troops could be landed, whereupon a fierce land battle ensued between Chinese and British. By noon, the Chinese began their retreat to Paoshan, pursued by British troops. From Paoshan the Chinese retreated further, some to Suzhou while others disbanded. Their resistance against the more organised and better equipped invading forces, in what became eulogised as 'The Battle of Woosung', is widely accepted as heroic.

A notably brave character in this battle was the Chinese Admiral and General, Chin Chung-Min. Then 76 years of age, he had spent 50 years at sea and was undaunted by the superior enemy forces, whose ships 'stood lofty as mountains' and 'projected high over our defences ... to the terror of the whole country'.[10] He commanded his men in the Woosung fort to the last, even handling the guns himself, until finally he received a mortal blow and consequently bowed in the direction of Beijing and 'expired'.[11] His remains were buried at the military temple in Shanghai and a life-size effigy was made for the City God Temple. In death, he was reputed to have been elected second in command on the Board of Thunder, from where he could continue his lifetime's struggle against foreign aggressors.

On 19 June, the British forces headed south towards Shanghai, 1,000 men marching overland,[12] while the navy

proceeded up the Whuangpu. Chaos reigned in Shanghai, where residents fled for Suzhou or further up the Whuangpu. When crossing the Woosung River at the stone 'Sinza' (Xin Zha) bridge (F4), the British were fired upon by the batteries on the site of the future British Consulate, which the Royal Navy's *Nemesis* and *Tenasserim* silenced, allowing the troops to proceed to the gates of Shanghai unopposed. British troops scaled the city wall near the north gate, which they opened, allowing the rest of the army to enter Shanghai, while the native population fled through the other gates.

The British established their military headquarters in the 'picturesque' City God Temple, 'a sort of Palais Royal, larger than that at Paris',[13] next to the famous willow-patterned teahouse. Until additional troops arrived to restore order, the foreign 'barbarians' lived up to their moniker by tearing down 'exquisite wood carvings for fuel', 'revell[ing] in furs and silk' and plundering the city's remaining gold and silver in a looting frenzy abetted by bands of disreputable Chinese to whom they sold their pickings by lowering them on ropes over the city walls.[14] Public buildings, according to the British

Plenipotentiary, Sir Henry Pottinger, also suffered from wanton destruction, including the richly adorned huiguan belonging to the boat merchants, which was used as a British army barracks. Shanghai – not for the first time – was in turmoil.

The British proceeded to state their claim for a formal opening of trade relations with the Chinese, who sent various minor officials to discuss the matter. Weary from their lack of progress, the British forces left Shanghai on 23 June 1842, ransoming the city for 300,000 dollars. With newly arrived reinforcements, 73 ships set sail for Nanjing to force an audience with the imperial commissioner. These contacts concluded with the signing of the Treaty of Nanking, outlining the Treaty Ports to be granted to Britain. A new chapter of Chinese history and Shanghai's ascendancy was about to begin. Through force, sponsored by the illicit trade in narcotics, Britain had gained a foothold in China.

The Treaty of Nanking

Sir Henry Pottinger and the Chinese High Commissioners, Kiying, Elepoo and Niukien, signed the Treaty of Nanking on board HMS *Cornwallis* on 29 August 1842, marking the beginning of official foreign intervention in China and legitimising foreign trade in five key ports.[15] Though it was a treaty of trade, not conquest, the terms were nonetheless ignominious for the Chinese, whose increasingly enfeebled empire was too frail to counter foreign demands, which it tried in vain to 'minimise and resist'.[16] While the details of these subsequent treaties are highly complex, certain key points are critical in their bearing on Shanghai's subsequent growth.

The Treaty of Nanking, designating Canton, Amoy, Foochow, Ningpo and Shanghai (present-day Guangzhou, Xiamen, Fuzhou, Ningbo and Shanghai) open for trade with Britain, is important both in shaping Shanghai's development

Below The official painting of the signing of the Treaty of Nanking on board HMS *Cornwallis*

and in its inadequacy in anticipating future scenarios – the most obvious of which was the settlement and jurisdiction of foreigners wishing to conduct trade. Provisions were stipulated in a series of Articles, the first three of which were most significant. Article 1 required that subjects of Britain and China 'enjoy full security and protection for their persons and property within the dominions of the other territory'. Article 2 stipulated for the opening of five ports to British subjects, where they 'shall be allowed to reside, for the purpose of carrying on their mercantile pursuits, without molestation or restraint' with their families and their establishments, and with consular officials, who would be the 'medium of communication' and responsible for collection of duties. Article 3 required that Hong Kong be ceded to Britain as a base for repairing ships and maintaining stores. Other Articles dealt with such matters as war reparations and compensation, the release of prisoners, abolition of the co-hong and establishment of fair customs duties. The matter of settlement remained ambiguous and its omission in these early stages of negotiation served as a veil under which the Chinese were coerced into extending settlement rights to foreigners.

Queen Victoria's ratification of the Treaty of Nanking arrived in Hong Kong on 6 June 1843 and was signed by the Chinese Commissioner for Foreign Affairs, Kiying, on 26 June. With the opening of five ports and the loss of a strategic island, China had been dragged with great reluctance from its solitary ancient slumber onto the world stage, where the glare of the international spotlight would over the years prove irksome at best to this reticent empire.

Foreign occupation and land regulations

On the night of 8 November 1843 the 36-year-old Captain George Balfour, the first appointed British Consul to Shanghai, arrived on the Medusa.[17] The following day he met the Taotai and, after an amicable exchange, the British officials, their families and the crew of the Medusa, including an interpreter, Dr WH Medhurst, who had previously visited Shanghai in 1831, his son, WH Medhurst (later British Consul to Shanghai), a surgeon, Dr F Hale, and clerk, Mr AF Strachan, sought temporary accommodation.

The walled city, known locally as Xian Cheng, served as a home to the first British Consul and many foreigners for several years, while the acquisition of appropriate land in the area of the proposed British Settlement could be negotiated. The priority in these early days was trade and not civic development. The concept of creating or even planning a city was utterly absent. As one foreign resident later noted, 'Commerce was the beginning, middle and end of our life in China. If there were no trade, not a single man, except missionaries, would have come there at all.'[18] International trade began on 17 November 1843 when Consul Balfour declared Shanghai open. By the end of 1843, 25 British

subjects resided at Shanghai. Mr White, Mr Mackrill Smith and Mr Gibb of Gibb, Livingston & Co, AG Dallas of Jardine & Matheson, Mr Wise of Holliday, Wise & Co, and Mr Beale of Dent & Co were among the first merchants to settle in Shanghai, and many went on to build up the city's most illustrious businesses.

In these embryonic days, the need to establish a legal code defining the rights of land rental became apparent. Although the Treaty of Nanking attempted to define general principles under which the British could operate in China, they were insufficient to deal with the many specific issues that emerged from the settlement of merchants in Shanghai.

Acquiring and building on land exposed the first of many problems with the treaty arrangements, not least because nobody had the right to buy land, since all land belonged to the emperor. Consul Balfour had 'insular pretensions'[19] that all land titles be registered through the British Consulate, but this proved impractical in relation to non-British subjects. Although it 'was an established principle that the English [British] claimed no exclusive privileges' and the settlement was 'open to all', the practice was considerably less clear cut.[20] Formalisation of the land issue was urgently required and was concluded with the 'crude and amateurish in the extreme'[21] Land Regulations, compiled by the Taotai Gong Mu Jiu and Consul Balfour and ratified on 29 November 1845. Up to this point Taotai and British Consul had enjoyed the exercise of a mutual authority once described as 'benevolent despotism'.[22]

There were 23 Land Regulations which attempted to clarify a range of existing and potential issues concerning settlement of foreigners. Those renting land would be responsible for the upkeep of the settlement, in which Chinese were forbidden domicile, and both foreigners and Chinese were forbidden to build houses to rent to Chinese.

The regulations which had the most serious consequences were Articles 14 and 20. Article 14 required land renters of any nation to submit first a 'distinct application to the British Consul, to know whether such can be acceded to, so as to prevent misunderstanding'. Though not intended to create a British colony by stealth, this regulation caused considerable contention, as it was unrealistic to assume that foreign subjects should have to gain permission from the British Consul before renting land in China. Article 20 recommended the election of 'three upright British merchants' to oversee the repair and construction of roads and jetties, expediting the formation of the Committee of Roads and Jetties, which, through extraneous issues, evolved into the Municipal Council, Shanghai's unique form of quasi-government that in practice was more of an autocratic business cartel.

Other nations were quick to follow Britain into China and their presence soon exposed the frailty of the Land Regulations, particularly of Article 14. The Americans entered into formal relations with China for the first time with the

Custom House

A new Custom House (H5), designed by Mr Chambers of Cory & Chambers in 1893, was built on the same site as the Chinese-style Custom House, using red brick and facings of green Ningbo stone. The new structure was conspicuous for its 110 foot clock tower and two adjacent wings with their high-pitched roofs. The four-faced clock, supplied by Pott of Leeds, was famed for striking the Westminster chime. In the months after the clock started ringing its chimes, there were very few fires in Shanghai, which delighted the Chinese, who believed that the fire god had been deceived into thinking the ring at each quarter of the hour was a fire bell and that the city was having enough fires. The revenue collected at this one building was usually between a third and a half of all customs receipts in China, making it a vitally important institution to the country's rulers. It was demolished in the early 1920s to make way for the present Custom House (see pages 139–40).

Above The Custom House designed by Chambers and built in 1893

Above The previous Custom House

Treaty of Wanghia on 3 July 1844. In the same year, an American called Henry Wolcott arrived in Shanghai. Mr Wolcott settled first outside the British Settlement, north of Suzhou Creek in the area of Hongkou, then moved into the Settlement, from where he applied to Mr Cushing, the American Plenipotentiary in Beijing, to become Acting Consul. In June 1846 his request was granted and he became America's first Consul to Shanghai. Shortly after his inauguration, Mr Wolcott was wont to fly the American flag from his house, which drove a minor wedge between American and British relations, as it was the first and only national flag flying in the British Settlement. Consul Balfour and the Taotai protested in vain against his actions, but the issue remained unresolved until after Consul Balfour's departure from Shanghai on 7 October 1846. Consul Wolcott departed from Shanghai soon after Balfour, whereupon the Stars and Stripes were struck and the issue laid to rest, at least temporarily.

This event was important for questioning British jurisdiction over foreigners in the Settlement, which remained ambiguous and led the Americans to discuss acquiring land elsewhere, including an area between the British Settlement and the Chinese city, which they eventually declined. In 1848, a new American Acting Consul, Mr John Griswold, who was

also fond of flying his national flag, arrived in Shanghai and rekindled the ensign argument, which he claimed to be a protest against Britain's 'principle of exclusive privilege and exclusive rights' outlined in Article 8 of the Treaty of the Bogue in 1843. To circumvent the bickering over bunting, the simple answer seemed to be the establishment of a separate settlement.

Mr Griswold continued a more critical discussion with the Taotai than his former colleague had started, which concerned America's right to the direct acquisition of land titles through its own consul. This conflicted with Article 14 of the Land Regulations but forced the hands of Britain and China, necessitating the complete revision of the Land Regulations in the 1850s. The matter came to a head in March 1852 when Mr Griswold's successor, Mr Cunningham, issued a statement in Shanghai's newly established newspaper, the *North-China Herald*, stating that land purchases could be effected 'through the consulate of the United States without the intervention in any manner of any foreign authority'.

The Americans were not the only foreigners to object to the elevated position Britain assumed in the 1845 Land Regulations. The French were quick to establish ties with Shanghai, signing the Treaty of Whampoa on 24 October 1844. In November the following year, the French Plenipotentiary, M Théodose de Lagrené, his family and accompanying officials arrived in Shanghai and by January 1847 the first regularly appointed French Consul, M Charles de Montigny, had taken up residence. With the help of a Catholic priest, he rented a house between the Chinese city and the Yang King Pang (Yang Jin Bang) for $400 per year, about which M Montigny proudly stated that although 'it was small … it was a little piece of France'.[23] 'In the course of 1848' he opened the French Consulate.[24]

The Imperial Maritime Customs, the Shanghai Municipal Council and the Mixed Court

In September 1853 an unruly group of disenchanted Cantonese and Fujianese, called the 'Small Swords', conquered the Chinese city 'without fuss or noise'[25] and established their headquarters in the former British Consulate, which had relocated to the British Settlement in 1851. The consequence of this insurgence was the formation of three pillars of Shanghai's dubious constitution: the Imperial Maritime Customs, the Shanghai Municipal Council and the Mixed Court.

On 8 September, the rebels looted and sacked the Custom House on the Bund, which had been established in 1846 to collect duties from foreign trade. This event ended the notably corrupt and ineffective Chinese custom service and provided the impetus for the establishment of a new customs authority supervised by foreigners. While Chinese officials tried vainly to resurrect a system of collecting customs dues, including establishing an office on a boat in the Whuangpu, Shanghai was effectively a free port. Suggestions were made to remove the Custom House to Hongkou, away from the centre of the Settlement, but a temporary location was set up in a warehouse on the corner of Nanjing and Jiangsu Roads. After the Small Swords' rebellion, the Custom House was relocated to the Bund, where it was rebuilt in a Chinese style in 1857. On 6 July 1854, the opening of the foreign-managed Imperial Maritime Customs was announced, and later became the standard throughout China. China was now reliant on foreigners for the collection of import duties, which represented a significant proportion of imperial revenue.

Below Panorama of the Bund and Whuangpu from the tower of Trinity Cathedral c.1860. This remarkable view from behind the Bund facing eastwards shows the dense, but spacious compounds of the many trading houses on and behind the Bund.

The second institutional development concerned the Shanghai Municipal Council's Land Regulations, which for a number of reasons had been ineffective. This was underlined further when the ban on Chinese living in the British Settlement proved inoperable after tens of thousands of Chinese residents fled there from the walled city to escape the Small Swords. Although the last Chinese buildings were removed from the Settlement by the end of 1853, and despite the fact that the regulations 'completely failed as the means of purging the Settlement of the disreputable Chinese',[26] it would have been unacceptable, even by the standards of the foreign community of Shanghai at that time, to deny asylum to Chinese citizens in the 'neutral' foreign settlements abutting the occupied city. The foreign community was powerless to resist this flood of needy souls, and so, while 20,000 Chinese, comprising 'the offscouring [sic] of Chinese society'[27] and 'mostly bad characters',[28] settled on the northern banks of the Yang Jin Bang, yet another Land Regulation languished.

Another matter that exposed the fragility of the Settlement's administrative structure was defence. In the course of an attempt to oust the rebels from the city, the imperialist forces threatened the British Settlement's western boundary, forcing the British and Americans to compose a makeshift defence force out of sailors and volunteers from the recently established Shanghai Volunteer Corps (SVC) in an event that became eulogised in Shanghai legend as the 'Battle of Muddy Flat'. Though more of an incompetent romp than a battle, the skirmish proved to be a 'baptism of fire'[29] for the SVC and confirmed that the Chinese government was unable to honour its treaty obligations by providing protection to foreigners residing in the settlements.

The incident represented a conflict of authority between the consuls and the captains of the British and American ships that provided men and arms. The navies were under the authority of their respective Admiralties, while consular jurisdiction came from their respective Foreign Offices. This potential fissure was illustrated clearly in early 1855 when a

decision was made to construct a barrier along the Yang Jin Bang to stop the flood of arms and resources entering the walled city from the foreign settlements. When the consuls called upon their respective navies to protect the barrier, the American Navy after hesitation supported the request. The British Admiral, however, refused on the principle of maintaining neutrality, leaving the French, who always had opposed the rebels, to protect the barrier with the Americans. This proved highly effective and forced the rebels to leave the city in February 1855.

External conflict had exposed the frailty of the Land Regulations and the impotence of the existing foreign settlement. The ineffective Committee for Roads and Jetties proved inadequate for the settlements' changing and growing needs, and the decision-making process under three separate treaty powers was proving inefficient. A representative body for all three foreign settlements was required. This concurred with the need for a new system of governance by the navies of numerous foreign nations, who had no responsibility to act on consular orders and required instruction from a united authority if they were to involve themselves in settlement defence. Above all, the foreign settlements had to provide for their own protection, and the Chinese, given their sheer numbers and needs, could no longer be excluded from the settlement.

In a meeting held at the British Consulate on 11 July 1854, the Committee of Roads and Jetties was dissolved and the new British Consul, Mr Alcock, inaugurated the Shanghai Municipal Council, which was made up of five councillors (Messrs Kay, Cunningham, King, Fearon and Medhurst) elected from a select group of eligible land renters. In his inaugural speech, he called for the 'cosmopolitan elements' to 'be welded so as to ensure unity in constitution, purpose and government'.[30]

The three treaty powers approved a new set of Land Regulations. Revision of the controversial Article 14 from the first set of regulations concerning the acquisition and registration of land was the most significant modification. The new article required that the land renter 'must first apply to the Consul of his nation, or, if none be appointed, to the Consul of any friendly power'. The terms of these new regulations extended jurisdiction of land to the consuls rather than local or native governments, and the question of Britain's tenuous authority over the Settlement was clarified. Importantly, the new regulations also omitted any restriction on Chinese residing, renting or building in the foreign settlements.

The new legislative arrangement proved effective through the rest of the 1850s, but in 1860 a new threat appeared in the form of the Taiping Rebellion. Notorious for their barbarism, the Taipings caused regional panic and half a million Chinese flocked into the foreign settlements. Just as it had done after the troubles in 1853–5, Shanghai's transformation through years of local unrest until 1864 altered the city dramatically. The Settlement was now populated largely by Chinese, and the Land Regulations of 1854, like those before them, had become 'defective, inconsistent and inadequate'.[31] The Municipal Council had to ensure the safe and effective operation of the Settlement, but with proportionally fewer resources. The Settlement's governance had to change with the times, but the views of the residents differed greatly from those of the consuls or of the governments of the treaty powers, the former arguing strongly for autonomy from China and the latter insisting on honouring the treaties.

A plan advocating a new Municipal Council was proposed by the British Consul, Walter Medhurst, in which the head would be elected by the community and nine councillors would be paid by the Chinese government – a form of semi-independent civil service doubtless modelled on the successful Imperial Maritime Customs. In an atmosphere of overblown confidence among the foreign communities, other proposals were suggested, some advocating an amalgamation of all foreign settlements, others wishing to maintain the present boundaries, and one, proposed by the Shanghai Defence Committee in a letter to the Municipal Council on 20 June 1862, calling for a 'free-city' under the protectorate of the four great powers, which would have been tantamount to the international annexation of part of China. The British Minister in Beijing, Sir Frederick Bruce, rejected the idea, believing it 'unjustifiable in principle' and fearing that it 'would be attended with endless embarrassments and responsibility ... which the Chinese government would never submit to willingly'.[32] Instead, he chose to adhere to the treaties, insisting that although China was unable to provide necessary protection to foreigners on its soil, it had never abandoned its rights over its subjects or land. He preferred to see a reduction of the Settlement's area and an exclusion of the Chinese, rather than a larger settlement area with Chinese residents, claiming 'There is no more fertile source of friction than Chinese within our limits'.[33] To some, especially the community of foreign merchants seeking independence, the opportunity for a new beginning in Shanghai was lost and it remained only 'to patch up the unsatisfactory régime'.[34] The new Municipal Council, composed of nine members, who again were elected land renters, comprised the system of government with which Shanghai would muddle along until the early 1940s.[35]

Amid all this, in 1862 the French withdrew from the municipal agreements of 1854, claiming that they had never been ratified by their home government. This caused a flurry of protest, but little surprise, since the French, fearing they had too much to lose from being part of a combined International Settlement, had clearly favoured autonomy. The French consul maintained absolute authority over the French Concession, though on 9 May 1862, just over a week after its inception, the Conseil d'Administration Municipale held its first meeting attended by its five newly appointed French members. Despite the illusion of elected representation, no resolutions formulated by the French Municipal Council were operative until approved by the consul. In the face of consular autocracy, the French municipal body was largely cosmetic. On one occasion in 1865, the consul dissolved it for 'arrogating consular powers'.[36]

Extraterritoriality

The final crooked pillar of Shanghai's constitution concerned legal jurisdiction of those without consular representation, the most numerous group of whom were the Chinese. Foreigners enjoyed a peculiar position in Shanghai whereby they were under the legal jurisdiction of their representative consul and not the Chinese courts. This principle, called extraterritoriality, proved more significant and more consequential than the Land Regulations, since it allowed Shanghai to become, in essence, an autonomous republic that resulted in the creation of 'one of the most remarkable places in the world', wherein, in the eyes of an optimist, 'men of all colours and classes and creeds are found, unitedly living in harmonious intercourse'.[37] In reality, extraterritoriality provided the basis for the legal immunity of foreigners and so turned the foreign settlements into impenetrable islands of sanctuary on Chinese soil in which citizens of various nations tried in vain to establish an effective governmental framework. The lack of consensus between the various communities administering the separate parts of Shanghai over the years resulted in the city's disjointed and irregular development.

No explicit mention of extraterritoriality exists in the Treaty of Nanking, though it is implied. However, it does appear in the American Treaty of Wanghia, which was considered an improvement on the Treaty of Nanking. Articles 21 and 25 of the Treaty of Wanghia established the pretext for extraterritoriality, stipulating:

> citizens of the United States who may commit any crime in China shall be subject to be tried and punished only by the consul … according to the laws of the United States.
>
> All questions in regards to rights, whether of property or person, arising between citizens of the United States in China shall be subject to the jurisdiction of and regulated by the authorities of their own Government.

The French, being the last of the initial three nations to establish treaty agreements with China, made sure their treaty was an improvement on previous ones. While the British treaty had laid down the principle and the American treaty had defined it, the French treaty 'was more emphatic'[38] about the extraterritorial question. Problems arose when dealing with those without extraterritorial privileges living in the settlements. In an attempt to address this anomaly, the Mixed Court was established in 1863 in the grounds of the British Consulate specifically for the trial of unrepresented residents,

including Chinese. It later moved to a permanent site in Hongkou and, as an institution, became the cause of considerable antagonism among the Chinese.

At the end of the same year, the British and American communities agreed to combine their settlements to form an 'International Settlement'. From this date on until the Second World War Shanghai functioned as three separate cities within a city: the International Settlement, the French Concession, and the area administered by the Chinese.

In 1868 the 'bureaucratic autocracy'[39] represented by the Conseil d'Administration Municipale published their Règlement, followed in 1869, after much procrastination, by Britain, America, France, Prussia and Russia signing the new Land Regulations that served as the 'Magna Carta or Bill of Rights'[40] for the 'representative oligarchy'[41] of the International Settlement. Further amendments were made to the regulations in 1898. Unlike the previous two sets of Land Regulations, Chinese approval or disapproval was never given. Additionally, although a despatch from Bruce in 1863 stated that 'there shall be a Chinese element in the municipal system',[42] the issue of Chinese representation on the council was mysteriously neglected, something that caused grave repercussions in the 20th century. Foreign dominance had increased in the face of a weakened Chinese empire. Constitutionally, Shanghai changed less in the next 70 years than it did in its first 25 years. There were several attempts in subsequent years to revise and add to the Regulations, which collectively represented a legal mine-field and led one prominent British lawyer to claim he 'had never had a case of greater difficulty presented to him nor one for which it was more hopeless to look for a prece-dent'.[43] While Shanghai had been founded on trade and thrived on trade, it had always been poor in administration. Though its merchant governors had created a constitutional abomination, the system functioned well enough for trade to flourish, at least for the time being.

Within the first 25 years of foreign settlement in Shanghai, foreigners had established a legal and institutional framework that would support the city's subsequent development and sow the seeds of its destruction. The city's course was set, though few paid much attention to the direction as long as trade could be conducted along the way. Although the treaty powers were proud of their creation and considered their actions to be lawful and just, it is worth noting that if the roles were reversed, Britain, America or France would have opened, among other ports on their mainland, Liverpool, San Francisco and Marseilles respectively to China and allowed the Chinese to reside there with legal immunity, while Britain would also have further ceded to China in perpetuity one of its nearby islands. International trade had prised the gateway to China wide open, and the ensuing flood of business would profoundly affect China and the world far into the future.

CONSTRUCTING SHANGHAI, 1843–1899

Constructing Shanghai, 1843–1899

Shanghai is undoubtedly a great ruin. Like many young and rising aspirants it has been carried away by the magnificence of its prospects. People believed so thoroughly in its growing importance and in the certainty of its becoming the grand central emporium of trade in China, that speculation could not run rife sufficiently, and land and property of all sorts reached prices which we now may look upon as absurd.

PG Laurie, *The Model Settlement*, 1866, p 4

Previous pages A sketch of the Bund c.1860 showing the Custom House left of centre.

Right The Lunghua pagoda, south of Shanghai

The Shanghai that confronted the first foreign settlers in the 1840s, with a walled city and suburbs surrounded by orchards and cultivated fields dotted with hamlets, and with the Lunghua pagoda the only structure to pierce the horizon, is an unimaginable picture compared to the city at the turn of the new millennium with its 20 million inhabitants and thousands of skyscrapers. Life then was undoubtedly hard. Interaction between the 'loathsome, dirty'[1] Chinese and the foreign 'barbarians' was inevitable but not favoured. The determination of foreigners to settle, irrespective of their motive and disposition, was matched only by the scale of mutual cultural intolerance. Ironically, what forced these disparate groups to cohabit were the unforeseen and sometimes threatening external events that had to be overcome or endured by both sides. These events shaped the physical character of the city more than foreigners were able or willing to do themselves, and the character of Shanghai today owes itself largely to these earliest engagements.

The growth of the Settlement and Settlement life up to the 1850s

British merchants and missionaries wasted no time in exploiting the new freedoms tendered them through the Treaty of Nanking. With little purpose beyond trading or moralising, one of the primary concerns of new arrivals was finding a place to live and do business. Although it was an uncomfortable necessity, most foreigners coped with living inside the walled city until it was possible to move into the proposed British Settlement. Letters home bewailed the rain pouring in through leaking roofs and walls and snow in winter blowing in through the windows and drifting on the floor, such hardship compounded in the summer by insufferable heat, extreme humidity and plagues of mosquitoes.

Differences in living standards and habits provided fertile ground for discrimination. For many decades the Chinese considered Western buildings unsuited to the local environment and pitiful compared to their own, which were constructed with local materials and traditional techniques. Foreigners eyed the Chinese city with equal contempt, regarding it as 'a wilderness of low, one-storey buildings … traversed by lanes or streets which might better be termed fetid tunnels, seething with filth'[2] and 'a mean place …

actually not important enough to justify the dignity of a wall'.[3] Even the once venerated teahouse had lost its charm in the eyes of foreigners, becoming 'filthy, dirty and neglected'.[4]

The character of the Chinese city remained sharply distinct, contrasting strongly with the Western version of urban modernity that subsequent settlers attempted to create nearby. The walled city's streets were narrow, seldom over 6 feet wide, hardly broad enough for two sedan chairs to pass one another and often muddy and slippery. Open-fronted shops lined the streets on both sides and advertised their names on large vertical signs that hung in the street 'giving the place very much the appearance of a bazaar'.[5]

Some foreigners ventured to claim that the larger streets of the walled city were 'really very picturesque',[6] but the distinct dichotomy between the perception of the 'repugnant'[7] Chinese city and the 'magnificent'[8] foreign settlements illustrates the cultural conflict manifested through perceptions of the built environment. Generally, the Chinese spurned the uncivilised methods of the foreigners that emerged beyond the city walls and foreigners resisted the life and ways of the Chinese inside the city.

Nonetheless, foreign settlers did face many adversities, the most intractable of which related to drinking water and sewage. Obtained from muddy wells or the Whuangpu,

'probably the most polluted sources of water supply in the world,'[9] the water in Shanghai could almost be cut with a knife and a hefty dose of alum was needed to clear its one-twentieth solids. The life cycle of sewage dumped into the river and creeks or collected by appreciative peasant farmers was short enough for it soon to find its way back into the house, either on the vegetables fertilised by this eternal resource or on the laundry that was washed in the rivers and creeks. Gruelling though life inevitably was, sympathy for the foreigners would be unwarranted, for they endured this 'horrible place' because it 'was a good place to make money'.[10] Everyone who came to Shanghai in these early days did so in pursuit of wealth or for the propagation of religious dogma, and they were often far from respectable characters. Shanghai was a frontier land and attracted adventurers, opium dealers, smugglers and vagabonds, many of whom made their fortunes in their dubious trades and later became seemingly honourable gentlemen of the British Empire. As one resident 'honest and outspoken enough to tell the truth' stated: 'In two or three years at farthest I hope to realise a fortune and get away; and what can it matter to me, if all Shanghai disappear in fire or flood? You must not expect men in my situation to condemn themselves to years of prolonged exile in an unhealthy climate for the benefit of posterity. We

Below Shanghai in 1853 showing the four distinct settlements (left to right): the Chinese City, the French Concession, the British Settlement, and the American Settlement

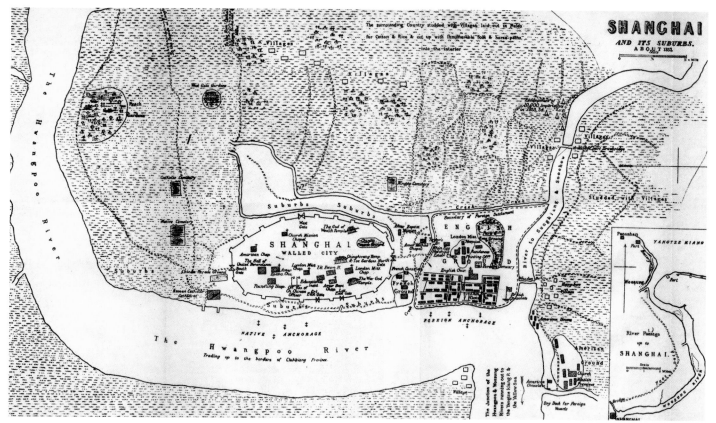

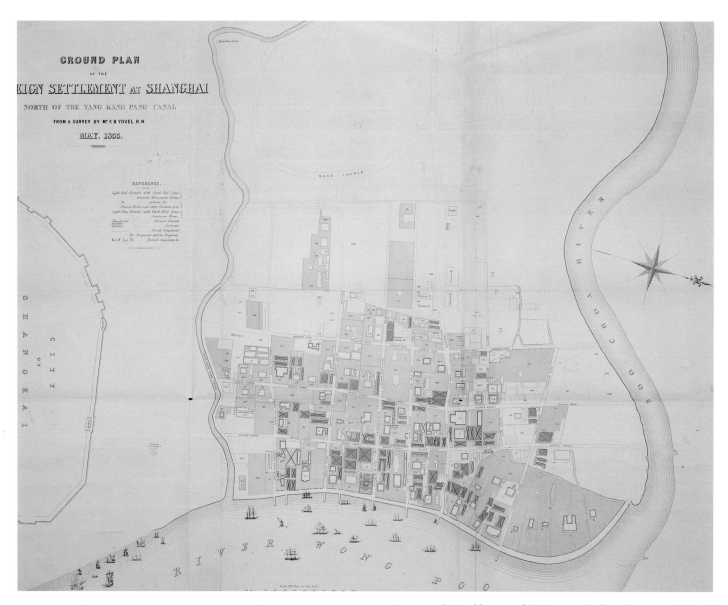

GROUND PLAN
OF THE
EIGN SETTLEMENT AT SHANGHAI
NORTH OF THE YANG KANG PANG CANAL
FROM A SURVEY BY Mr F. B. YOUEL, R. N.
MAY, 1855.

Top and above Map of Shanghai, 1855. This map shows the extent of development in the British Settlement in little over a decade after foreigners arrived in Shanghai

are money-making, practical men. Our business is to make money, as much and as fast as we can.'[11]

The British Settlement

Many accounts describe the area of land on which the British Settlement would later stand, most of which evoke a 'miserable morass'.[12] However, the 'marshy, unoccupied and undeveloped'[13] land 'intersected with smelly ditches and reedy ponds'[14] was subject to complex ownership, subdivided between and used by numerous Chinese families. Described by foreigners as 'a miserable semi-aquatic sort of Chinese population',[15] these families lived on land owned by the Chinese government, which meant it could not be cultivated privately. However, high population densities south of the Yangtze permitted the cultivation of river banks under a system called Lu Ke Tan Di ('Reeds Tax') whereby the occupant paid tax on the land and the resources used from or grown on it. Such land around Shanghai was very common and many Chinese records exist attesting to the history of the

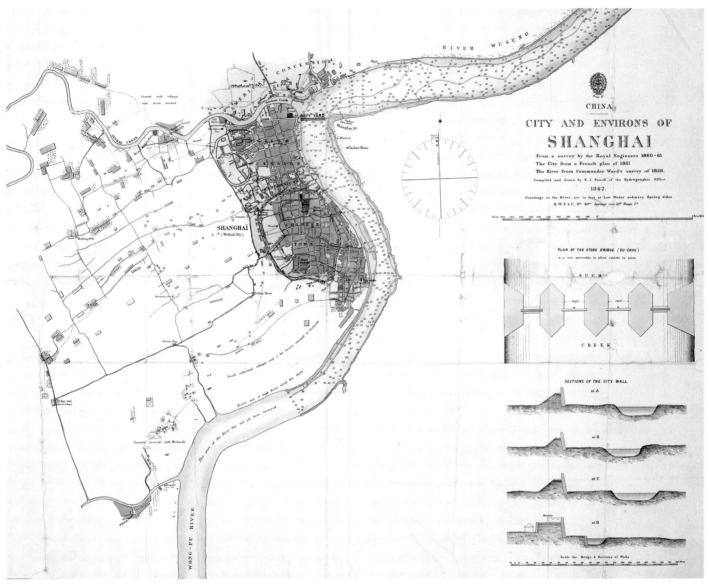

and 'nothing seems to have been done'[17] during this visit, leaving the issue of foreign residence to evolve naturally. Consul Balfour's criteria for suitable boundaries were 'lines of country creek and river, which might, if necessary, be rendered easily defensible'.[18] The Yang Jin Bang to the south and the Li Jia Chang, an area of land on the south bank of Suzhou Creek, owned by a family named Li, were the first two Settlement limits, formally approved in 1845. The Whuangpu was not designated the eastern boundary as the towpath remained a public thoroughfare. The western boundary was defined as Barrier Road (later Henan Road) in an agreement dated 20 September 1846. The Li Jia Chang was eventually purchased for the British Consulate, thus

Above Map of Shanghai, 1858-62. The many waterways extending into the hinterland later became main roads

families living and working the river banks of the Whuangpu and Woosung. Montalto de Jesus accurately describes the land as 'mostly under cultivation, intersected by several small creeks, with a small hamlet nestled here and there among its shady turf, while far and wide the turf heaved in many a mouldering heap over generations of peasants there resting for ever … Along the foreshore lay the dilapidated towing path of old.'[16]

This towpath later formed the central component of the British Settlement, whose formal delineation took some time. Although Sir Henry Pottinger returned from Nanjing via Shanghai to select the ground on which British merchants were to settle, British procrastination got the better of him

extending the Settlement to Suzhou Creek in the north. On 27 November 1848, the western boundary was carried to Defence Creek as a means of compensating for the broken pride of three Englishmen, Messrs Medhurst, Lockhart and Muirhead, who had been ambushed by a large mob of unruly locals while sauntering in the countryside distributing Christian texts. The episode became known as the Qingpu Incident, which demonstrated Britain's willingness to employ her navy to gain political and material advantage. As a result of Britain's threat to use force to bring the culprits to trial, the Chinese were coerced into increasing the Settlement area from 180 acres to 470 acres.

After partially defining the Settlement, the next problem was constructing buildings. Consul Balfour had originally intended to purchase outright the proposed site of the British Settlement 'in the name of Her Britannic Majesty', but the Taotai rejected the idea. Foreigners only had the right to rent land but not to buy it so it was left to the merchants to negotiate the sale of rights over individual plots. This loose arrangement made it impossible to control or coordinate planning, which was left to the British Vice Consul, Mr Brooke Robertson, who was responsible for 'surveying the ground, drawing the plans, marking out the roads, defining the boundaries of lots, etc'.[19]

Many a tussle ensued between foreign merchants and local land renters who were understandably resistant to foreign occupation of their ancestral land. After they had won the Battle of Woosung in a morning, the appropriation of land required for foreigners to 'carry on their mercantile transactions', as stated in the Treaty of Nanking, 'went on very slowly'.[20]

Land renters often failed to relinquish their land, while farmers refused to vacate the parcels they had sold and family members returned to pay respects to their ancestors buried under the newly rented plots, causing many problems for hopeful foreign merchants. One particularly notorious old woman, who owned the plot on which would later stand the Cathay Hotel, one of the most luxurious hotels in the world,

poured a bucket of muck over the head of the negotiating party and spat at the Taotai, claiming 'she would never sell her patrimony to foreign devils!'[21] 'If abused, she resorted to language far more expressive and violent; if touched, she shrieked to such an extent that there was no going near her.'[22] Another obdurate woman, nicknamed 'the Island Queen', owned a house surrounded by water near the centre of what is now the Bund. At the sight of any foreigner, she would retreat into her home and haul up the drawbridge, earning from the large Scottish community the title 'Lady of the Lake'.

The early Bund

Only the brave or the obdurate acquired the plots they desired, while most chose to remain inside or near to the Chinese city until conditions for the appropriation of land became less arduous. Those who did succeed in acquiring land and building in the British Settlement, such as the illustrious trading houses of Jardine, Matheson & Co and Gibb, Livingston & Co, were rewarded handsomely for their perseverance. They occupied the prime sites along the river front at just $15–35 per mow (six mow = one acre). This river front, later known as the Bund, was once a muddy and malodorous towpath reserved for towing large junks and dumping sewage and refuse, but the Taotai insisted that it should remain a public right of way, preventing it from being developed or obstructed.

The term 'Bund' derived from India where it referred to an embankment and so in the early years there were many 'bunds' in Shanghai, including the Suzhou Creek Bund, the Yang Jin Bang Bund and the Defence Creek Bund, the latter being known as the 'West Bund'. These names gradually fell out of use as the Whuangpu Bund grew in stature. An attempt to name the Bund 'Yangtze Road' proved unpopular, so 'the Bund' remained. Today, this 'billion dollar skyline',[23] the symbol of Shanghai, is characterised by its irregular layout, narrow streets and awkwardly positioned buildings – all a result of the ad hoc purchase of land titles in its first days and the failure of subsequent administrations to organise this system effectively.

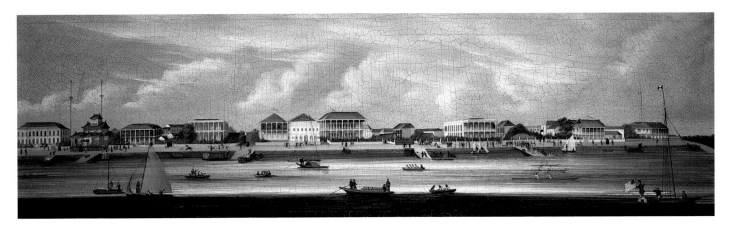

Above The Bund during the 1850s showing only the section from the plot adjacent to the Custom House (Turner & Co) to the British Consulate. Note the rowing boat on the Whuangpu.

Early land renters had to cordon off 30 feet of land for private use behind the towpath, an early intervention that was fundamental to the present Bund's admirable public frontage. By 1920, Darwent, a longtime resident of Shanghai, eulogised: 'Had commerce had its way, we should not have been able to boast that our Bund is one of the handsomest streets in the world. Shanghai owes an incalculable debt to the men of past generations who fought and won the battle for this freedom of the Bund foreshore from all-devouring commerce'.[24] The Taotai's resolve was lost in history, but the result was not.

The acquisition of land along the Bund started in the north, farthest from the walled city, and extended south to Canton Road (now Guangdong Road), beyond which, on the last plot before the Yang Jin Bang, was a chandlery and wood store that jutted out on stilts over the creek, owned by a Mr Hiram Fogg. The area around the Bund at the time was very low lying, causing serious problems for the roads, which could 'not be kept in repair from the sinking away of the banks',[25] and for the construction of buildings, the land below which first had to be raised considerably.

Eleven foreign 'mercantile houses' were built on the Bund by the end of 1843, but it was not until 1846 that the first buildings designed in a foreign style started to appear. By 1847, there were 24 mercantile firms' premises, 25 private residences, five stores, a hotel and a clubhouse, the land value of which averaged £85 per acre. The scarcity of foreign-looking dwellings, 'except for a few houses on the Bund', was due to the scarcity of foreign builders in Shanghai until after the 1850s, making Shanghai 'from an architectural point of view, very backwards'.[26]

The style of the first buildings along the Bund 'had little claim to architectural beauty',[27] often being described disparagingly as 'compradoric', since they were designed by merchants, not architects, and were constructed by Chinese contractors, requiring the comprador to do much of the liaising. A comprador was a Chinese middleman whom foreign firms hired to deal with Chinese counterparts. It was said by one of Shanghai's leading architects of the 19th century, Thomas Kingsmill, that the compradoric style originated from a Cantonese contractor by the name of Chop Dollar who 'developed a style of compradoric architecture peculiar to the place'.[28] As compradors, the Cantonese became influential in the development of Shanghai, particularly through their relationship with foreign merchants. Although 'simple in the extreme'[29] in the eyes of some, for others the 'compradoric' buildings had a 'grand and imposing appearance'.[30] The first buildings were usually constructed from imported designs and materials from Canton and reflected the British Colonial style with wide verandas skirting the ground and first floors, though the earliest buildings tended to be single storey. The veranda was an idea imported from tropical climates, but inappropriate for Shanghai's bitterly cold and damp winters.

A typical 19th-century Shanghai *hong*, a warehouse or foreign merchant's house, was between one and three storeys high and roughly square in plan, with a room occupying each corner. A central hallway connected the front entrance to the back door, linked by a covered walkway to an external kitchen. Two corridors, left and right, would run perpendicular to the central hallway, providing access to the rooms and sometimes a side exit. A staircase facing the main entrance and doubling to the first floor would be located in the centre of the building, where the corridors intersected. The ground floor plan was replicated on the upper floors with the exception that bathrooms occupied some corridor space. A veranda of wood or brick would skirt the building or its front and sides.

The main building served as both a residence and an office. The upper floors or the rear of the building were reserved for accommodation, while the ground floor or a covered veranda provided office space. Kitchens and staff quarters were always located in separate buildings to the rear of the compound. The warehouses, or godowns, were often to the side or rear of each compound, around which the employees would reside in accommodation arranged

Top, right and below Early houses at Shanghai showing typical examples and variations of the Compradoric style of architecture

hierarchically according to seniority and race. In the early years, every compound had abundant gardens that attracted wild pheasants and contained flowerbeds full of English flowers and subtropical specimens such as aloes, yuccas, palms and wisteria.

Roads

By 1850, 'the Bund lots were pretty well built upon'[31] forcing subsequent development westwards, away from the Whuangpu. This necessitated the construction of roads and paths to link the river with the dispersed houses and businesses. Responsibility for the development of a system of roads in Shanghai rested with the remarkably shortsighted Committee of Roads and Jetties, who championed the line of least resistance. Their policy was largely responsible for creating Shanghai's 'narrow and tortuous streets'.[32] Though fondly regarded in the annals of Shanghai, rarely has a committee been so undeserving of its title. Despite excuses that it faced 'many difficulties' and overcame 'most obstacles', the sole committee responsible for the construction of a system of roads in the British Settlement until the mid 1850s 'did not plan much for the future' and 'saw no great need for roads'.[33] Only where the need was demonstrably evident were roads constructed, by adapting towpaths or following creeks and dykes, creating a system of streets 'not in the fashion of other contemporary cities in the New World'.[34] Shanghai's woeful street layout today owes many of its failings to the early oversights of these visionless merchants.

The committee can claim a minor success in building four jetties along the northern Bund opposite the main tracks leading to the river. Jetties were more important in the early years as cargo was transported in boats, while coolies, the lowest stratum in China's endless labour market, hauled goods from the river to warehouses on their backs or on Shanghai's renowned single-wheeled wheelbarrows, carving up the dirt tracks separating the hongs and making them impassable after the rains. Responsibility for repairing and replacing private roads rested with individual trading houses, used clinker or gravel to construct tracks wide enough for this purpose. Consul Balfour's suggestion that roads should be at least 25 feet wide was deemed exaggerated by the committee. 'What do we want more than a road broad enough to ship a bale of silk by?' they exclaimed naively.[35] Maclellan mused reasonably about the 22 foot compromise: 'How many hundreds of thousands of taels would a more liberal spirit have saved subsequent generations?'[36] (The tael was a monetary unit representing approximately 38 grams of pure silver.)

The 25 foot wide road along the Bund was the first and widest in Shanghai, and was widened in the early 1850s. Four other roads running in an east–west direction from the Bund were planned by the committee: Beijing Road, Nanjing Road, Jiujiang Road and Hankou Road (then named

Consulate Road, Park Lane, Rope Walk Road and Custom House Road respectively). Jiujiang Road, at 25 feet wide, was the broadest of the four, while the others were all 20 feet wide. Thereafter, Shanghai's roads radiated westwards from the Bund like veins of germinating blight. In 1862, with significant assistance from the Chinese-speaking Medhurst, the nomenclature of all the roads in the British Settlement changed from English to Chinese: all east–west roads were named after Chinese cities and all north–south roads after provinces. However, the Chinese largely ignored the changes

Above The palatial offices of the illustrious American firm Russell & Co on the Bund between Fuzhou and Canton Roads. The flag represents Sweden and Norway, since a partner of the firm was the acting consul.

Below The Bubbling Well

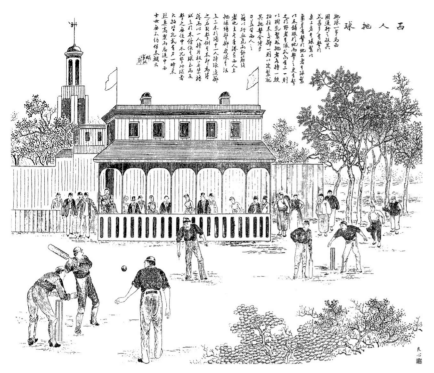

西 人 抛 球 地

地球一事為西國通行之故其
或謂水手頭皮球其一人抛之
上亦以水本挡地者一人接之
其所接者西人謂之接球斗女
老幼無不仿與觀云

Above Playing cricket in Shanghai, described by the Chinese cartoonist as 'Foreigners throwing balls'

Opposite The former Shandong Road Hospital built between 1927 and 1929 by Lester, Johnson & Morris, replacing several earlier buildings dating back to 1845

and continued to classify the roads according to the main thoroughfare, Nanjing Road, known as Da Ma Lu, or Big Horse Road. The names of parallel roads were defined by their position in relation to Nanjing Road, so Fuzhou Road, the fourth road south of and inclusive of Nanjing Road, is called 'Si Ma Lu', or 'Fourth Horse Road'. Other roads retained their old title, but with Chinese pronunciation, so Barrier Road was referred to by Chinese as 'Jie Lu', meaning literally 'Barrier Road'.

The longest road in Shanghai was named after and terminated at the famous 'Bubbling Well' (C5), a spring revered for its continuous emission of gas. Previously referred to as 'Gurgling Well', this spring used to cover a wider area including two reed marshes, which were popular among bathers who believed in the curative properties of the spring's tepid water. In 1778 the Taotai built a pavilion nearby on which an inscription read: 'The fountain that bubbles towards Heaven'. Bubbling Well Road, a rough track formed around 1850, was for many years Shanghai's favourite recreational throughfare, and provided residents with the opportunity for an extended country stroll. Years later it was one of the most sought-after residential roads 'shaded with trees for almost its entire length, and bordered by the lawns and gardens of the many charming houses that lie along its course'.[37] A significant number of Chinese graves and coffins had to be removed when it was widened and became a private toll road in 1862. This was the time when carriages appeared in Shanghai and they made the two-mile

ride Shanghai's favoured route, a status it retained into the 20th century with the advent of the motorcar. Until 1866, all settlement roads were manned by watchmen and had wooden gates where they met the settlement boundary.

While the Bund was the unchallenged face of the infant Settlement, the plots behind it became its heart, attracting the more humble but lively establishments, such as sporting facilities, entertainment venues and missions. Until the end of the 19th century, this area as far as Henan Road constituted the city centre beyond which was a 'rural scene of cotton and paddy fields',[38] where people considered themselves in the country if they ventured beyond Bridge Street (later Sichuan Road).

Such a pastoral scene inevitably evoked a yearning for recreation among the British, who rarely occupied a place for long before seeking solace in sporting pursuits, quite unlike the Chinese to whom sports generally caused considerable bemusement. Fives was one of the first sports in which Shanghai's British residents indulged, even having a street named after it – Fives Court Lane (later Tianjin Road), on which two courts were built some time in the late 1840s, along with a bowling alley and later a rackets court (H5). Being on the outskirts of town at the time, these courts were easy targets for disgruntled Chinese. In 1851, an incident involving some unruly Fujianese and foreigners near the fives courts led to the formation of a vigilante band of foreign residents that two years later went on to form the nucleus of the Shanghai Volunteer Corps, on whose shoulders Shanghai's defence rested until its capitulation to the Japanese in 1941. The bowling alley remained in use until the 1920s, when its 24 members boasted it was the most exclusive club in Shanghai.

Although fives and bowling were deemed idiosyncratic British sports, horseracing was embraced fervently by the Chinese, becoming a major institution and the mainstay of the city's social life. Shanghai's first racecourse was located behind the Bund on eight mow of land south of Nanjing Road between Henan and Jiangxi Roads, incorporating what later became the Holy Trinity Church compound. The growth of the Settlement and the need for a larger course caused its relocation in 1854 to an area east of Defence Creek, leaving in evidence only its grandstand, which became part of the bowling alley and survived to become one of the oldest buildings in Shanghai in the 1920s. The new venue, also called the New Park, provided a place where the wealthier residents could be seen 'gyrating daily',[39] while also serving as a venue for the Shanghai Cricket Club. The large area of land is still clearly visible on a contemporary Shanghai map, fossilised in the urban grain by the rapid expansion of the city during the Taiping Rebellion in the early 1860s. The eastern straight and the southern bend form what is now Zhejiang Road.

Despite claims that 'very careful provision was made for the protection of Chinese graves' when the new racecourse was being laid out, it contained land occupied by the temple and graves of Fujianese, who offered stiff resistance to having their ancestors disturbed by foreigners' equine pleasures. Graves are sacrosanct in Chinese culture and at the time 'were thickly placed all over the settlement'. Although it was said that foreigners 'must not offer the natives any hindrance which would offend their feelings'[40] when the latter were visiting or offering sacrifices at these graves, it was clear that the settlements' development would prevail over native sentiment. Native offence was most violently expressed in 1874 when the French tried to carve a road through the cemetery of the Ningbo Guild (G6), causing a major uprising among the Chinese residents.

So rural was the Settlement in the 1840s that the fields between the London Mission and the foreign cemetery were said to contain coffins of Chinese lying around awaiting burial. The lease for the London Mission was obtained by Rev Medhurst in 1845, and though it was only two blocks west of the Bund the Mission was still considered 'so far from the foreign settlement' that he was advised to build in a Chinese style in case foreign houses should 'excite popular discontent' among the Chinese community in the area.[41] The Mission was a large and important compound. Purchased for $1,080, it contained residences, a printing press and a chapel and was adjacent to a hospital, known to this day as Shandong Road Hospital (H5). The hospital was the first for Chinese in Shanghai and was founded by the highly respected Dr Lockhart, the first British medical missionary in China, who arrived in Shanghai from Canton on 5 November 1843. Dr Lockhart's wife, Catherine Parkes, the first foreign woman to arrive in Shanghai, was considered by foreigners as the 'Mother of Shanghai'. She was also the sister of Harry Parkes, who, as a 14-year-old boy, witnessed the signing of the Treaty of Nanking and later became British Consul to Shanghai. Their uncle was the Reverend Charles Gutzlaff who had been among the first foreign visitors to Shanghai in 1831.

Dr Lockhart and Rev Medhurst settled first in the Chinese city, just outside the Great East Gate, where they started work in February 1844, before the Medical Missionary Society purchased the present site in December 1845 to provide medical assistance to the Chinese workers of the foreign firms. The first hospital was built in 1846 in a style befitting a Chinese building, on a single floor and with oyster shell windows. Between 1861 and 1863 this building was replaced by a new one, which itself only lasted a decade before a 'splendid building' supplanted it that lasted until 1927.[42] The present six-storey building was designed between 1927 and 1929 by Lester, Johnson & Morris and opened on 1 January 1932.

The London Mission's chapel that was the embryonic Union Church, for all Christian denominations, was the earliest church in the British Settlement and opened its doors for worship when Rev Medhurst started services in 1845. It

was not until 1864 that the first purpose-built Union Church was constructed, lasting until 1885, when a new church, designed by William Macdonnell Mitchell Dowdall, began services in July 1886 (H4). Dowdall, born in the year Shanghai was opened to international trade, never received professional architectural training but worked with many architects from 1870 and practised in Shanghai from 1883. He became an Associate of the Royal Institute of British Architects (RIBA) in 1882 and a Fellow in 1891. His cruciform design for the Union Church on Suzhou Road behind the British Consulate was in an English Gothic style and was once described as an 'ungainly structure',[43] incorporating an open-timbered roof and a 108 foot octagonal spire (see page 207). In 1899 a church hall was built next door.

Church services for the British community were held in the British Consulate until Mr Beale of Dent & Co purchased a site as a gift for the construction of the Anglican Church, which opened for worship on 10 April 1847 having cost $6,000 to build. The structure was not famed for its quality and when the roof collapsed at 5.30 am on 24 June 1850, causing $5,000 worth of damage, it closed for repairs until 4 May 1851. The church was eventually pulled down in 1862.

Proposals were made for a grandiose church designed by the eminent British architect Sir George Gilbert Scott.

Scott was born in Buckinghamshire, England, in 1811 and became one of the most renowned architects of the Victorian era, specialising in Gothic Revival, and was President of RIBA from 1873 to 1875. His designs for Holy Trinity Church were made around the time he was producing one of his most famous works, St Pancras Station and Hotel in London. Unfortunately for Shanghai, the fortunes amassed by its wealthy residents were not for dispensing on refined religious structures despite the swelling ranks of foreigners seeking salvation. To accommodate the meagre budget of Shanghai's Christian community the plan was modified to such an extent that it barely resembled the divine intentions of its creator (others claimed the modifications were made to meet the climatic conditions). William Kidner (1841–1900), Shanghai's only resident member of the RIBA at the time, carried out the modification in 1866, the same year he emigrated to Shanghai. He went into partnership with John Myrie Cory until 1878 when he returned to England. Cory (1846–93) was a graduate of Pembroke College, Cambridge, and worked as improver to Sir George Gilbert Scott from 1867 to 1869. He arrived in Shanghai as an assistant to Kidner with whom he was in partnership from 1875 to 1879 and who nominated him for his successful application as Associate of the RIBA in 1880. He became a Fellow of the RIBA in 1886.

Below View of the American Settlement across Suzhou Creek from the grounds of the British Consulate (far left) c.1860. Note the Episcopal Mission church on the banks of the Whuangpu and the absence of the Public Gardens

Holy Trinity Cathedral

The church (**H5**), which became a cathedral in 1875, was constructed with red brick and stone dressings, designed in an 'early thirteenth century Gothic style'.[44] It contained a nave, aisles, transepts, chancel and two chapels for organ and vestry. It was 152 feet long, 58 feet 6 inches wide and 54 feet high. Since Shanghai is east of Jerusalem the altar was at the west end. The organ was made by Walkers of London. Many of the windows were finished in stained glass over the course of its lifetime, one depiction being donated by the Shanghai Cricket Club in memory of the Hong Kong Cricket Team, who drowned on their return home in October 1892. The church shared its compound with other buildings including the deanery and parish rooms. The foundation stone of the 165 foot spire was laid in 1901, though it was removed later in the century. The former cathedral was used by the local government intil 2005 and is due to be restored as a church.

Left The Anglican Church

Right Holy Trinity Cathedral

Bottom left Interior of the Cathedral

Bottom right Morning exercises at the Cathedral School

While the new church was being planned by Kidner, a temporary structure was erected in the northwest corner of the spacious compound and the foundation stone of the new church was laid on 24 May 1866. The new church, named Holy Trinity Church, opened on 1 August 1869, and despite the lack of funds to build the spire it was claimed to be 'by far the most sumptuous building in the settlement'[45], praise that by 1920 had been inflated to 'the most magnificent church in the East'[46]. In 1875, the Bishop of North China, Reverend Russell, accepted the church as his seat and so it became Holy Trinity Cathedral.

The British Consulate

The scramble for suitable plots in Shanghai bypassed the city's primary site, which had been eyed by British officials for several years as a fitting location for their consulate. Although Shanghai for miles around is flat, affording no great vistas and offering little inspiration to the visionary, Consul Balfour recognised that the jewel in this rather drab crown was the plot at the northern end of the Bund where Suzhou Creek meets the Whuangpu. The site which Sir Henry Pottinger had earmarked for the consulate was partly occupied by the family Li and partly by the imperial military, including the half-destroyed fort whose defenders had fired on the invading British army in 1842. However, many complications prevented the purchase from proceeding smoothly.

When Balfour arrived in Shanghai in 1843, the options for a temporary consulate and suitable accommodation appeared to be scant. Unperturbed, he told the Chinese that, as a former soldier, he would happily sleep on a boat or pitch his tent. This proved unnecessary, as a guide appeared and offered to show him a suitable house 'very well situated' in the city, on Se Yaou Kea Street. For $400 per year, the house, 'with a northern and southern aspect consisting of four buildings that contain 52 upper and lower rooms, with wells and reservoirs behind in proper order',[47] appeared to be suited to the bachelor consul's needs. The guide later turned out to be the landlord appointed by the Chinese officials to keep an eye on the 'foreign devils', in the hope of rekindling the co-hong arrangement that so blighted relations in Canton. Balfour rejected outright such monopolistic predilections and banished the landlord from his compound.

The first British Consulate (H4) was declared open on 14 November 1843, three days before the official commencement of foreign trade. Three years later and with $1,300 spent on furnishings, the wife of Mr Rutherford Alcock, the new consul in Shanghai, provided the first feminine opinion of Shanghai's first British Consulate, claiming it would 'always resemble a dilapidated or half-finished barrack more than a habitable residence for Europeans'.[48] Unfortunately for her, it would also be her home until 1849, when the British Consulate moved outside the walled city.

Although it was the policy of the British government not to purchase or build consulates overseas, Balfour felt that the Bund's popularity among the foreign merchants and obstreperous sailors in the early days of Shanghai made it clear that the British Consul should be located nearer to

Right Former British Consulate compound in the 1920s. The buildings behind were built on land sold by Consulate in the 1860s property boom.

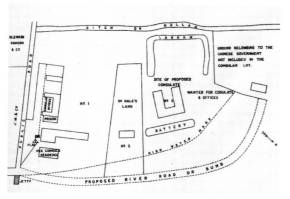

his subjects and the city gaol should be within the consulate grounds. The desired plot was bounded on the north by Suzhou Creek, on the east by the Whuangpu, on the west by Museum Road and on the south by a road separating it from the premises of Jardine, Matheson & Co, later Beijing Road.

However, Balfour's request for $17,000 to complete the purchase of the land title and buildings was refused by Sir John Davies, the British Plenipotentiary, who instead referred the matter to London, where the issue festered. In the meantime, Balfour paid $4,000 out of his own pocket towards the sale and when he left his post in 1846 he gave Mr Beale of Dent & Co power of attorney. The new Consul, Mr John Rutherford Alcock, inherited this problem upon his arrival, and despite the opposition of Lord Aberdeen took the matter up with Lord Palmerston, who in turn brought pressure to bear on the Treasury.

The sale of the land title was further complicated by the need to speak persuasively to the 30 Chinese whose land, covered with 'all manner of ditches and quagmires',[49] was incorporated in the designated plot. It was necessary also to arrange for the adequate exchange of land for parts of the area owned by the Chinese government and the British surgeon, Dr Hale, who had previously purchased a portion of the plot. After negotiating with the parsimonious lordly clique that controlled the British Treasury, whose coffers were lined each year by £3 million in tea duties alone, Shanghai's most desirable site was secured by Consul Alcock for the British Consulate, and the offices formally opened on 21 July 1849, followed in 1852 by the consulate itself.

The consulate foundations were laid by an American, Mr Hetherington, in 1846, and completed by Mr Strachan, the consulate's clerk and Shanghai's first architect by profession, who designed many of Shanghai's early buildings. Mr Strachan developed a style which reflected 'a version of the so-called Greek at the period fashionable in England'.[50] The consulate compound for many years carried the name of its previous owners, Li Jia Chang, and was originally extensive, stretching westwards 300 metres from the Whuangpu. During Shanghai's absurdly frenetic building boom in the early 1860s, the British government sold the western half of the compound (between Museum and Yuan Min Yuan Roads) and a portion of its southeast corner. Eight years later, the money was needed to rebuild the consulate, which burned down on 23 December 1870, the insurance having expired the week before. The greatest loss was the destruction of all the Settlement records stored in the building. The new consulate, designed like the first, though a few feet lower, remained operational on this site until 24 May 1967, when it was evicted by the Shanghai Revolutionary Committee 'to meet the needs of municipal construction and the demands of the broad revolutionary masses'.[51]

The American Settlement

Other nations besides Britain were eager to establish formal representation in Shanghai. America's growing interest in trade raised the question of whether an area of land should be set aside for an American settlement. Though there was never any formal designation of land and America opposed the principle of exclusive rights and privileges for nations, the American Episcopal Mission (14) under Bishop William Boone had moved from the corner of Fuzhou Road on the Bund to 'a newly built house, school and chapel' in Hongkou in 1848. The cheap land on the north side of Suzhou Creek was accessible by a ferry until 1856. Ship repair shops that were suited to the river banks downstream from the merchants' quarter also set up business here. A year later, the first official American consul chose to build his residence on the northern bank of Suzhou Creek, where it empties into the Whuangpu, facing the British Consulate compound. The American Settlement, therefore, 'just growed [sic]' rather than being the result of any formal treaty or contract.

Hongkou was an old settlement, marked by a small port at the point where the former Woosung River joins the Whuangpu, once called 'Whuangpu Kou' meaning 'mouth of the Whuangpu' and also known as 'Hong Kou', 'mouth of the flood'. The concentration of paths leading to this point can still be discerned on a map, where the roads tend to radiate from the river front between Suzhou and Hongkou Creeks. When the Americans settled there, the area was very rural, with 'wild duck, teal, and snipe found in the ponds and marshes out of which rose squalid Chinese villages',[52] but it would become Shanghai's most densely populated suburb –

far removed from the lone village between the mission buildings and Suzhou Creek, and a bamboo copse providing a home for abundant woodcock. The main thoroughfare, a muddy track following the high-water line, became Broadway – Hongkou's equivalent of the Bund.

In 1862, the American area was for the first time defined and agreed between Taotai Hwang and the American Consul, Mr Seward. The delineation at this time extended from a point opposite Defence Creek, along the Suzhou Creek and three 'li' up the Whuangpu, then back in a straight line to the point facing Defence Creek. These boundaries were contested by the Chinese and not formally delineated until May 1893. Nonetheless in 1863, this area was combined with the British Settlement to become the International Settlement.

The French Concession

The establishment of a French settlement in Shanghai followed a different path to British and American areas, not least because their original priority was religious rather than mercantile.

In 1847, the Jesuit missionaries had purchased a site in the hamlet of Xu Jia Hui several miles southwest of the foreign settlements. Xu Jia Hui was named after the resident family 'Xu' and is often referred to by foreigners as 'Siccawei'. The mission's meagre chapel quickly proved too small, so, on 23 March 1851,[53] the foundation stone of the first mission church was laid. This too was replaced, by the much larger St Ignatius Cathedral (A8), which opened on 30 October 1910 with a space for a congregation of 1,200. Designed by Dowdall, 'in the early English Gothic style inclining towards mediaeval French',[54] the 250 foot long and 81 feet high church was constructed with granite doorjambs and arches and sandstone mouldings and dressings. The transepts were 142 foot wide and the nave, aisles and chapels were 93 feet wide. The most conspicuous elements were the two towers with spires, each 129 feet high, which were destroyed during the Cultural Revolution and have since been rebuilt.

Father Heude, a renowned naturalist who arrived in Shanghai in 1868, established a Natural History Museum in the mission compound in 1883, which in 1930 moved to the Aurora University campus. The Cathedral was built on a small zoological garden where Father Heude kept his stags and deer. Also in the mission compound were an orphanage for girls and boys, the premises of the Helpers of Souls in Purgatory, a Carmelite convent, a high school and an internationally renowned observatory. This last was established through the endeavours of Father Henri le Lec from 1871, and was rebuilt in 1900. Commencing operations on 1 January 1901, the station was responsible for the weather reports that were relayed to shipping via the signal station on the French Bund.

The district of Xu Jia Hui is famous locally as it was the family home of, and named after, the revered Xu Guang Qi

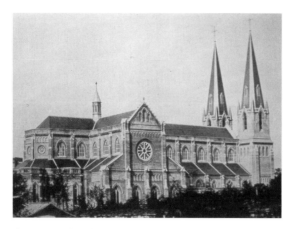

(1562–1633), who became an imperial minister during the reign of Ming Emperor Shen Tsung (1573–1620). A devout Catholic, he was responsible for the establishment of several important Catholic institutions in Shanghai, including a church outside the north gate and one inside the city. Xu's conversion to Catholicism was initiated in 1582 by Matthew Ricci, a member of the second Catholic mission to China,

who followed in the footsteps of a mission under Monte Corvino in 1291. This first mission had built a church in Beijing, but its members were later massacred.

Another important French religious institution was the St Francis Xavier Cathedral (18) in Dong Jia Du, one of the oldest churches in Shanghai. The land on which this church was built was given to the French by the Chinese as compensation for the latters' refusal to allow the French to restore a 17th-century Roman Catholic missionary church that had been converted into a temple of the God of War (the former church was in fact restored to its original use in 1860). Father Nicholas Massa designed the Dong Jia Du church in an Ionic style under the supervision of Father Hélot Louis,[55] and though it was to be 'very high and to have many windows, the original design could not be carried out from want of funds'.[56] The Roman Catholic Bishop of Nanjing laid the foundation stone on 21 November 1849. The church was '210 feet long, 100 feet wide and cost £30,000 less than it would have done in Europe',[57] and served a small community of Catholic converts. After being converted into a factory during the Cultural Revolution, the Cathedral has since been restored as a place of worship. A similar fate befell another of

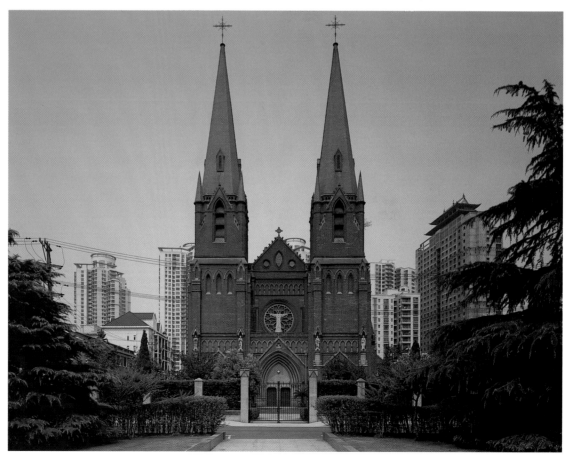

the former French Concession' sold churches. The Catholic church of St Joseph (H6), designed by Hélot Louis and built between 1859 and 1862, was once said to be 'the finest in the Mission in this part of the world'.

In spite of their prolific missionary work the French were keen to remain autonomous in Shanghai, requesting from the Taotai that a separate piece of land be made available for the exclusive interests of French nationals. Accordingly, on 6 April 1849, the Taotai designated 164 acres of land between the British Settlement and the Chinese city on which 'all Frenchmen should be permitted to rent houses and factories, and also ground on which they could build houses, churches, hospitals, almshouses, colleges, and set apart cemeteries'. The French Concession was bound to the south by the moat of the Chinese city, to the north by the Yang Jin Bang, to the east by the Whuangpu from the Yang Jin Bang to the Canton Guild, and to the west by the creek adjoining the Temple of the God of War (Guan Di Miao). The 'French Ground' was small in comparison to the British Settlement, but although underdeveloped for many years and almost exclusively Chinese in appearance until well into the 20th century, it was strategically important. The first French

Consulate, on the Quai de France (the French Bund) (H6) at the end of Rue du Consulat, was opened in 1867 and replaced on 14 January 1896, when a new consulate opened, the foundation stone having been laid on 22 August 1894. Designed by MJ Chollot, the new consulate was in a Colonial style with open verandas. Behind the consulate and near to St Joseph's Church was the French Post Office and the Hotel des

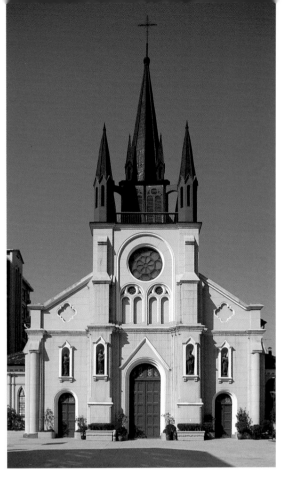

Colonies, the primary hotel in the French Concession and one of the first proper hotels in Shanghai. The other prominent 19th-century foreign buildings in the French Concession included the French Municipal offices, designed by FH Knevitt, built in 1864 and extended in 1877. The building was set in formal gardens overlooked by a bronze statue of Admiral Protet who died during the Taiping Rebellion, and a Parisian lamppost gave it the impression of being 'a little piece of France transplanted to China'. The nearby fire station has been built in a similar style, using red brick 'in a modern colonial style'.[58]

The French and American areas contrasted with the British Settlement by dint of their relative lack of activity in the early years of Shanghai. Nearly all the foreign trade, development and accommodation were confined to the British area, regardless of the nationality of its resident population and ensuring the Settlement's swift development.

The leisurely life with plenty of time 'for pleasure and peace and quiet' that characterised the late 1840s was soon swept away by events in the early 1850s. A general improvement in trade conditions created a minor boom by 1852, resulting in what the records of the Mission Hospital show to be a dramatic rise in injuries caused by the growing number of unruly visitors to Shanghai, as well as a marked increase in patients with injuries received while

Right St Joseph's Church

Right Map of the French Concession, 1870

PLAN DE LA CONCESSION FRANÇAISE, A SHANGHAI, LEVE EN 1865. RECTIFIE EN 1870.

Left Panorama of the Bund, showing the French Concession far left.

engaged in construction work. It was 'a year of great prosperity when new buildings of a private and commercial character were springing up on every side'.[59] Always an accurate barometer of activity in Shanghai, the autumn races were postponed in 1852, as nobody had time to enter a pony. However, such trifling affairs were insignificant compared with the events about to take place and which proved far beyond the control of the foreign settlements. These events would redefine the emerging settlements and force them to accept their place in China and to cope with the consequences.

The Small Swords and the Battle of Muddy Flat

Numerous uprisings have interrupted Shanghai's desire to trade, but have never extinguished it. This historical certainty remained unchanged in spite of the newly established foreign settlements, but the sanctuary that these neutral areas provided added an extra dimension to the internal strife which characterised China's provinces. The earliest upheaval witnessed by the foreign settlements mirrored similar events over the subsequent century.

Since 1851, a rebel army originating from the south of China and opposed to the Emperor had been busy fomenting turmoil, so familiar and so wearisome to the Chinese peasantry. Known as the Taipings, this group had captured Nanjing, but by 1853 a band of soldiers claiming to be their affiliates were close to Shanghai, where their presence was unsettling the community. Though the Taipings disowned them and denounced their 'immoral habits and vicious propensities', the 'Small Swords', or 'Triads' as they were also known, breached the gates of Shanghai shortly before 4 am on 7 September and successfully occupied it.

Although the foreign settlement claimed neutrality, the foreign residents maintained their bias for profiteering by building houses and renting them to over 20,000 Chinese refugees. High-density terrace houses constructed in wood sprang up on the northern banks of the Yang Jin Bang around what is today Fujian Road, near the Shandong Road Hospital, which treated the wounded and dispensed rice to civilians affected by the ensuing famine. The Taotai proclaimed: 'Those persons who have erected houses can only rent them to foreigners for their own occupation; the under letting of

Left A plan of the centre of the French Concession from the late 19th century

houses or land to Chinese subjects is sanctioned by no Regulation. Foreigners in doing so have acted on their own accord, very improperly, and this proceeding on their part must be put a stop to.' But his appeals fell on deaf ears, as Shanghai listened only to the sound of money changing hands, instituting the city's real estate market. The arms trade was also thriving, selling both to the rebels and to the huge Imperialist army that had arrived to try to oust them. These provisions, shipped into the city through Hongkou via the Settlement, sustained the rebel presence in the besieged city for 17 months. In late 1853, an attempt by Imperial forces to capture one such consignment of arms led to the first significant breach of the Settlement by the Chinese, who reached the Custom House, but were repelled by foreign volunteers and sailors from the British navy.

Taotai Wu was the first in a long line of political figures to benefit from the Settlement's neutrality. Trapped inside the city when the Small Swords overran it, two foreigners, Dr Hall and Mr Caldecott-Smith, hatched an elaborate plan to free him. On 9 September, having first lost their way among the Chinese city's disorientating streets, they successfully located Wu and secured his freedom by lowering him over the walls of the city by a rope, in the same manner that the plundering British soldiers had used to disperse their booty 11 years earlier.

On 7 December, during one of the attempts by the Imperialists to recapture the city, described as 'ludicrous in their ineffectiveness',[60] the entire suburb between the city wall and the Whuangpu, including 1,500 houses and the famous merchant area around Yang Hang Jie, was razed in a devastating fire. The loss of life and property was estimated at $3 million.

The foreign community found the siege frightfully jolly, flocking to the tower of the Anglican Church, the tallest structure in the Settlement at the time, to watch fate unfolding on their hapless Chinese neighbours. A note in the *North China Herald* on 1 April 1854 attempted to curb this popular entertainment, stating: 'We have been requested to caution the community against ascending in large numbers on the Church Tower, in order to watch the attack of the Imperialists against the rebels in the City. The upper portion of the tower is very slightly built, and if it be crowded as on Wednesday night last, and again on Thursday, a catastrophe too painful to contemplate may result.' Needless to say, the pain caused in the walled city by the unfolding catastrophe which the foreign voyeurs climbed the tower to witness was, in the minds of the foreign community, insignificant by comparison to the possibility of injury to several of their own falling from a shoddy church tower.

Two days later the Imperialists did attack, but not the Chinese city. Instead, and no doubt to the considerable alarm of those in the church tower, the Imperialists menaced the western boundary of the British Settlement, resulting in a 'battle' that has since been said to have crowned Shanghai's

proudest moments, but in reality was a comic sham. The Battle of Muddy Flat, as it became known after a misprint in the local press altered the original title of the 'Battle of Muddy Foot', was the first real test for Shanghai's recently established Volunteer Corps. With up to 30,000 imperial troops surrounding Shanghai, it was inevitable that a few unruly individuals would use the opportunity to harass the unpopular foreigners. Various incidents were reported of foreigners being fired on, in or around the new racecourse, but a tense situation culminated with two people being attacked with swords near the northern bend of the course on 3 April 1854. Though they survived the ordeal, Consul Alcock issued an ultimatum to the Chinese general in charge of the imperial forces, demanding a full withdrawal of troops west of the racecourse by 4 pm the following day, or the foreign troops would be forced to attack.

No reply arrived so the foreign troops assembled in the grounds of the Anglican Church. At 3.30 pm, the Shanghai Volunteer Corps and an estimated 250 British and 130 American troops from warships in the Whuangpu marched from the church along Park Lane (later Nanjing Road) towards the racecourse. At what was later Zhejiang Road, the forces split and, with trepidation, the Americans headed south along the line of the racecourse, while the British continued along Park Lane. At 4 pm, both contingents started firing at the Imperial troops in an event tantamount to a declaration of war on China by Britain and America.

Having been ordered to 'charge!', the American troops advanced 'hurrahing as if it were the greatest fun imaginable', but were brought to an abrupt halt by the 30 feet wide and 4 feet deep Zhao Jia Bang, later called Defence Creek, that Captain Kelly, commander in charge of their troops, had failed to notice was separating his men from the enemy. Displaying only a fraction more ingenuity, the British troops crossed the creek by way of a bridge and forced the Imperialists to retreat towards the south, helped almost entirely by the involvement of the rebels, who, not wishing to miss a brawl with their enemy, advanced from the walled city to join in the farce. With the Americans stuck behind their own defences and pinned back by 'one Chinaman that was firing at them', and the British force consisting of little more than 200 troops, 'not half of whom knew anything about fighting', it is generally accepted that the two-hour 'Battle' was won by the rebels, to whom the Settlement was 'chiefly indebted for our easy victory'.[61] It is equally likely that some sort of deal was struck with the Imperial general, who ordered his numerically superior army to retreat at the sight of a motley bunch of foreign troops, half of whom were rendered impotent by a ditch while half of the remainder knew nothing of the intricacies of armed combat. More than 30 Imperial troops and four foreigners were killed in the battle, while the earthworks from the Imperialist camps were much appreciated by the foreign merchants, who had them shipped to the Bund to raise the level of the foreshore. The names of the foreign fallen – Pearson, Brine, Blackman and McCorkle – were commemorated on a plaque that hung in the Anglican Church.

Later that year, tired of their unruly neighbours and without support from their neutral foreign allies, the French launched an assault on the rebel-held city. At the time, only four foreign buildings were said to have existed in the French area, two of which belonged to American missionaries, the other two to a Parisian watchmaker and the French Consulate. However, since the French felt compelled to protect the Catholic community around Dong Jia Du outside the south gate of the city, they attacked the city's northeast side, supported by an Imperialist attack on the west gate. Though both forces inflicted heavy losses, they were repelled at the cost of 2,200 Imperial troops and 64 French killed or wounded. The assault did reap certain dividends. The French, as a reward for their involvement, were later granted a 23 acre extension to their concession on 29 October 1861, including much of the land formerly occupied by the suburb destroyed in the conflagration of 1853. The highly prized riverfront extension, paid for with the lives of many young men, took in the suburbs between the Chinese city and the river frontage along the Whuangpu as far as the Little East Gate, including the wealthy mercantile suburb which incorporated Yang Hang Jie. This lengthened the French river frontage from 180 metres to 630 metres.

The rebel occupation lasted until early 1855, when the erection of a barrier between the British Settlement and the walled city starved them of the resources and weapons that once flowed into the city from the hands of unscrupulous foreign businessmen. On 17 February, coinciding with Chinese New Year's Day, the rebels finally left the city. The incoming Imperialists decapitated 300 rebels and 1,500 'sympathisers' left inside the city and by beheading the occupants of coffins awaiting burial, denied even the dead eternal union with their heads. 'Immense mounds of heads and headless bodies were everywhere about the city and suburbs, and the unfortunate people who were found alive were ruthlessly pillaged.'[62] The city was again set alight and half of it was destroyed in the fire.

The Taiping Rebellion

After the defeat of the Small Swords, life in the foreign settlements soon returned to relative normality and the rest of the decade saw a continual increase in Shanghai's trade and development, encouraged by the Treaty of Tientsin in June 1858 allowing foreign trade up the Yangtze River, which opened up China's vast interior. It seemed that Shanghai's time had really come, but another external threat appeared in 1860, this time from the Taipings. The Taiping Rebellion, regarded by some as one of the 'greatest uprisings of Chinese history', was founded on 'dynastic decline,

agrarian distress, overpopulation, foreign penetration, failure to provide an adequate officialdom, and Chinese resentment against the misrule of alien Manchu overlords'.[63] One of the more curious facets of the rebellion was its leader, Hong Xiu Quan. Hong was a farmer's son from Canton who, having failed his civil service exams and been introduced to Christianity, proclaimed himself the second son of God and founded a movement bent on bringing down the Qing Dynasty. He christened his movement the Taipings ('Universal Peace') with himself as the leader, Tien Wang ('Heavenly King'). The Taipings' tenuous affiliation to Christianity made them invulnerable to foreign opposition during their march northwards from southern China. This changed following their successful overthrow of Nanjing in March 1853, which provided a foretaste of the chaos to come in which 20 million Chinese are said to have died during the Taiping campaign. By the time the nearby city of Suzhou had fallen on 29 June 1860, defensive measures in Shanghai were hastily arranged and the previously disbanded Shanghai Volunteer Corps was resurrected. On 18 August the Taipings had reached the walled city, which was now defended by the British and a battalion of Sikh troops, under Captain Budd, and the French, under Colonel Fauré, as well as the Imperialist forces.

Mounting their attack from their newly established headquarters in the Jesuit Mission in Xu Jia Hui, and killing and maiming several of the residents while occupying and pillaging the compound, the Taipings approached the west and south gates of the city, only to be repelled by fire from the ramparts. That night, in an attempt to deny the Taipings any cover, the Imperialists razed all the houses surrounding the city. The French also cleared the area between their settlement and the city walls and, not for the first time, burned 'an immense quantity of valuable property in the most wanton and useless manner'. The rebels' attempt to settle near the racecourse was denied when the Royal Navy's *Nimrod* and *Pioneer* fired over the Settlement at them, forcing their retreat to Xu Jia Hui, from which they departed 'amidst ghastly vestiges of barbarities'.

The Taiping threat subsided in late 1860 and through 1861, but reappeared in early 1862. In Hangzhou, the besieged capital city of the neighbouring Zhejiang province, the situation was so desperate that human flesh was being sold in the streets, and in the besieged city of Nanjing wayfarers captured by the rebels were 'tied up to trees and devoured slice by slice'.[64] Such atrocities caused half a million Chinese refugees to flock to the foreign settlements. So terrified were these new residents that on one occasion when a rumour circulated that the Taipings had reached Bubbling Well, it triggered a mad dash to the Bund. Several woman and children were trampled to death in the insane stampede. Many even failed to stop at the water's edge, but continued their frantic charge into the Whuangpu and drowned.

The physical character of Shanghai altered irrevocably during these troubled times, as the city became 'an enormous bivouac'. Half a million Chinese refugees bringing with them all their valuables precipitated a construction boom in the foreign settlements and an absurd escalation in land prices, and covered former rural areas of the Settlement in 'a maze of new streets and alleyways with thousands of new tenements'.[65] Just as they had done when selling arms and renting shelter during the Small Swords' uprising 10 years earlier, the foreign community, while bemoaning the influx of Chinese, were eager to amass fortunes from their woes, selling land which they had purchased for as little as £46 per acre for as much as $12,000 an acre. The swathes of wooden tenement houses now filling the Settlement posed a serious fire risk (and because of the frequent conflagrations they were banned in the 1870s). This gave rise to a new building type, called a Shi Ku Men, which comprised a form of terrace housing that contained a stone firewall separating each unit, and these emerged in the 1870s (see page 159 onwards).

In January 1862, 3 feet of snow fell on Shanghai, checking the Taiping advance and giving the foreigners time to complete their defences. A public meeting was held on 13 January, in which it was decided to construct three lines of defence. The outer line was Defence Creek, where the American troops had been forced to halt during the Battle of Muddy Flat. This creek was to be widened to 50 feet and extended to Suzhou Creek from the Yang Jin Bang, with fortifications along its length. As with the nearby Imperialist forts in 1854, the earth from these excavations was sold to grateful land renters on the Bund, who desperately needed the soil to stop their properties from sinking into the Whuangpu. The second line of defence was Fujian Road, which was also to be extended to Suzhou Creek. The third line was the former Barrier Road, now Henan Road, and the outer limit of the British Settlement in the 1840s. These lines of defence, though designed to secure the city's safety from the rebels, were intended also to curb the movement of Chinese refugees within the Settlement.

The Taipings got within a few hundred yards of Shanghai on occasions, causing considerable alarm among the residents, but the threat was limited and so the foreigners switched from the defensive to the offensive. A 30-mile exclusion zone was established around Shanghai, but the plan proved difficult to enforce. Attempts to halt the seemingly eternal carnage in China's provinces were undermined yet again by the morally immune commercial minds of Shanghai's merchants, who were keener to profit from smuggling arms than securing the peace of the wider community. In April 1862, one vessel alone supplied the rebels with over 5 tons of gunpowder and 3,000 firearms.

In response to the marauding rebel army, a composite army of Chinese and foreigners set out to restore peace to the region and to China. It was led by a 30-year-old American

Above The Shanghai Volunteer Corps marching out in defence of Shanghai on one of many occasions, here in 1894

vigilante named Frederick Ward, and his success on the battlefield made him a hero of the Chinese and one of Shanghai's most legendary adventurers. Though originally mocked by the foreigners in Shanghai and cursed by the foreign navies for tempting away too many of their poorly paid conscripts, Ward's celebrated 'Ever Victorious Army' was Shanghai's redeemer in the face of the Taiping threat. Ward was killed 'by a stray bullet' on 21 September 1862, and after two unsuccessful appointments General Charles Gordon was appointed on 24 March to lead this legendary band of men. Gordon's military genius was far too great for the Taipings, whose movement, for various reasons, quickly crumbled. Gordon resigned in May 1864 and the Ever Victorious Army was disbanded. A plaque was laid inside the Public Gardens of Shanghai in memory of the 48 'officers of the Ever Victorious Army who were killed in action' fighting the Taipings from 1862 to 1864. The threat of bloodshed inside the Settlement was extinguished and from May 1864 Shanghai was left to get on with what it did best – business.

The growth of the Settlement from the 1860s

The opening of the Yangtze River to trade as far as Hankou in 1861 boosted trade in Shanghai, but it was the Taiping threat, which had imposed a virtual siege on the city, that fuelled an unprecedented economic boom. While the cities and ports in the neighbouring regions were disabled by rebel occupation, giving Shanghai a monopoly on trade, affluent and desperate Chinese willing to pay any price for safety sought refuge and offloaded their wealth in the settlements, where 'the wildest speculation was in land'.[66] Every inch of land in the

Settlement was bought, sold, bought again and resold, each time accruing scandalous profit. While land renters inside the Settlement amassed vast fortunes in months, they bought land titles beyond the Settlement at a fraction of the price, and roads built for military use, such as the road to Jessfield Park, encouraged development beyond the boundaries of the Settlement. With opulent villas, model farms and country roads being built in the western districts beyond the Settlement, Shanghai's urban sprawl had begun. The city 'had gone perfectly mad'.[67]

This prosperous age attracted all sorts of merchants and adventurers to Shanghai, such that it was 'infested by foreign and Chinese scoundrels, who committed all kinds of outrages', and its condition had become 'scandalous'.[68] The British Consul, Sir Harry Parkes, stated to the land renters in a meeting, that out of 10,000 Chinese houses constructed in the Settlement, 668 were brothels, while gambling houses and opium dens were 'beyond counting'. However, the newly established Shanghai Municipal Council, charged with tackling the city's problems, was also to blame. As it represented and was composed largely of land renters, it was willing to overlook the wider concerns of urban development, while reaping the vast profits to which land renters were accustomed in those days from renting land and property. The Shanghai resident saw it as his 'business to make a fortune with the least possible loss of time by letting land to Chinese'.[69] Sir Frederick Bruce, the British Minister in Beijing, gave an apposite appraisal of the matter: 'The character of the concession has been entirely changed by the acts of the foreigners themselves.' Although crime, sanitation,

Above The Shanghai Paper Hunt

plumbing, fire hazards and planning were major concerns, there were serious fortunes to be made, and Shanghai's focus, as ever, was on money. 'For good or for ill the die was cast, and the character of the Settlement became what it is today.'[70]

Shocking though the influx of Chinese may have appeared to the foreign community, it proved incomparable to their exodus when they returned to their towns and villages following the defeat of the Taipings. The Chinese population in the British Settlement fell from over 500,000 to just 77,000 in less than a year and to just 51,421 by 1870. Development halted almost instantly, leaving entire streets unfinished, new buildings abandoned, warehouses and wharfs deserted, and countless private investors facing bankruptcy, demonstrating an important historical lesson in the interdependence of Chinese and foreigners in Shanghai. The city's prospects seemed apocalyptic:

> Everybody appears to run wild, nobody has any money and the bulk of the population is composed of a number of lively spirits who call themselves brokers, but whose occupation is apparently gone. The Settlement itself is a very apt illustration of its inhabitants. It is tumble down, rickety, and in many parts desolate and in ruin. California in its worst days could not have been worse than the Shanghae of to-day ... Everyone and everything was by force of circumstance turned topsy-turvy, struggling, broken, and wrecked. The city, the people, and the institutions all partook in the general ruin.[71]

During the same period, *The Times* published a glowing article in 1864 about the booming trade and fabulous Settlement 'in which a merchant could attach a deer park to his house', but the timing could not have been worse, attracting a 'great number of adventurers and seekers of fortune, only to be bitterly disappointed'.[72] In 1865, a global depression coincided with the American war, and the reckless speculation in land and business caused an immediate recession in Shanghai.

By 1866, settlement life in the early years was reflectively recalled. After just two decades, nostalgia was painting a picture of bygone settlement life 'composed of magnificent palatial residences', where 'streets were wide and each house was situated in its own compound with fine gardens and shrubberies surrounding' and, vitally but mistakenly, 'there were then no Chinese inhabitants, and no struggling Europeans'.[73] By 1867, life in the settlements was 'pleasanter', and the opening of the Suez Canal in 1869 helped to improve trade, but the pace of development remained unhurried for much of the remainder of the century. Shanghai was 'imperceptibly but surely growing, a house, a few buildings, a block at a time'.[74]

Social life

While construction remained slow throughout the century's closing decades, Shanghai's society did its best to alleviate the problems of living an exiled existence deprived of home amenities. The British, whose numbers accounted for over half of the foreign population in the International Settlement in 1870, dominated social activities, though many were Scottish, whose 'assertiveness chiefly consisted in ramming the kingdom of Scotland down our throats on every occasion [and] did not put forward their countrymen as models of sobriety'.[75] The St Andrew's Society, founded on 30 November 1865, had over 700 members by 1912 and continued to host Shanghai's largest ball until the Settlement's dying days. In 1870, the Americans 'exercised more influence than their numbers warranted',[76] while the Germans only numbered 138l.[77] Other groups included Portuguese, Spanish, and a small number of very influential Baghdadi Jews who made their fortunes in the opium trade, and whose roots in Shanghai can be traced to the first settlers. At this time, social clubs and other activities were emerging and the life of the Shanghailander was encapsulated most appositely by former British Consul Walter Medhurst in his book *The Foreigner in Far Cathay* (1872):

> He builds himself a mansion in the handsomest style that his firm or himself can afford, and he furnishes it as a rule with homemade furniture, plate, glass, etc., all of the best quality. For the business requirements through the day the Shanghae resident generally keeps a Norwich car, brougham, or some other convenient kind of vehicle, in which to traverse the settlement in all its parts. For evening exercise, if a subordinate, he goes to cricket or rackets, or bowls, or takes a gallop on a pet pony, or trots out his dog-cart or phaeton. If a head of house or a married man, he drives out some more pretentious vehicle with a pair of Cape, Australian, or Californian horses; nearly everybody drives or rides, and he must be a struggling creature who cannot muster an animal or vehicle of some kind. After the evening airing comes dinner, and it is at this meal that the foreign resident in China concentrates his efforts to forget that he is an exile from home.

Below Painting depicting a rowing regatta on the Whuangpu River

Above The interior of the former Lyceum Theatre, 1910s

Such wistful longing was often assuaged in sporting pursuits. An alternative to foxhunting imported from the playing fields of Eton and Rugby via the Crimea and India arrived in Shanghai in 1863: the Paper Hunt. Its motto 'Sport for the sake of Sport' sums up its futility, and the sport was described by an avid proponent as 'rank madness', replacing the fox with pieces of paper strewn by a lead huntsman along a given route. The 'hunt' would then proceed by chasing these quiescent leaves about the neighbouring countryside, showing scant regard for the often furious peasant farmers who could only stand and observe their sustenance wantonly destroyed by this ludicrous gambol. Such activities cultivated bitter resentment between local Chinese and foreigners, who saw it as their divine right to frolic on horseback all over Shanghai's breadbasket. The absurdity of this spectacle was topped only by an 'on-foot' version of the Paper Hunt, which proved too daft even by Shanghai's standards, and so was disbanded in 1868. Rowing was the first outdoor sport in Shanghai. A boathouse was built in 1860 on part of the British Consulate compound on the banks of Suzhou Creek (I4). A clubhouse was added in 1904, followed by a 100 foot swimming pool in 1905. The first regatta was held in 1859 on the upper reaches of the Suzhou Creek, but owing to the increased traffic on this waterway it was later moved to the Whuangpu.

The backbone of Shanghai's sporting scene was the Race Club (F5), which relocated west of Defence Creek following the sale of the old racecourse on 19 February 1863. In 1860, a Recreation Fund had been established by four residents who felt it critical that a piece of land be set aside for sporting pursuits, but 'more especially for a cricket ground', so they purchased a 5 acre plot for this purpose inside the old racecourse, where the Town Hall would later stand. This land was then bought from the four residents by the fund's shareholders for Tls 4,421. Within months, owing to the escalating land prices at the time, the shareholders were advised to sell the land and relocate to inside the new racecourse, west of Defence Creek. The Recreation Fund's shareholders raised Tls 49,425 from the sale and purchased 70 acres of land inside the new racecourse for just Tls 10,750. This accommodated the new public Recreation Ground, forming the only significant open space in the centre of Shanghai and providing an invaluable venue for a wide range of sports. The profit from the sale of the old ground was also used to fund emerging sporting clubs and cultural institutions.

The new racecourse had two tracks, an outer grass track for the racecourse shareholders (44 yards short of a mile and a quarter) and an inner mud track for the public, owned by the Recreation Fund. The Race Club's clubhouse and grandstand were built in the 1860s, but were later extensively adapted and modified, and a clock tower constructed around 1890. By the 1930s, after a new clubhouse had been built, it was claimed optimistically that the new course 'probably compares well with any in the world'.[78]

Apart from sport, Shanghai's social scene was expanding with an increasing range of clubs and societies, whose proliferation would eventually surpass any city for 'their glamorous heights of prestige, power and influence'.[79] National clubs were one of the mainstays, but non-sporting special interests were also catered for by societies such as the Amateur Dramatic Club of Shanghai that put on regular performances in the Lyceum Theatre (see page 171), the Société Dramatique Française, Shanghai Society for the Prevention of Cruelty to Animals, the Shanghai Benevolent Society and even a Smoking Concert Club. Masonic lodges were quick to take root in Shanghai and established a school that became Shanghai Public School when its administration was handed to the Municipal Council in 1893 and moved near to Hongkou Park in 1895. The headquarters of the North China Branch of the Masons was built on one of the sites sold by the British Consulate in the 1860s. The foundation stone of the Renaissance style Masonic Hall (I4) was laid on 3 July 1865 and the building opened in 1867. It was rebuilt in 1909–10 according to designs by Christie & Johnson and opened in November 1910. Only the large hall, a room central to Shanghai's social life and used for all manner of balls, concerts and theatrical performances, was retained from the original structure. At the other end of the Bund, the highly exclusive and shamelessly pompous Shanghai Club (H5), serving the British residents of Shanghai, was built on the grounds of Hiram Fogg's chandlery and wood store and was opened in 1864 (see page 70). The club's construction nearly bankrupted the Recreation Fund, which advanced a dubious loan for the purpose. The influential German community were quick to follow the British and on 20 October 1865 founded their own club, the Club Concordia (H5) on Fuzhou Road, entry to which was restricted to German speakers (see also pages 103–4). The club moved and was reopened on 1 January 1881 in new 'unpretentious' premises on the corner of Sichuan and Canton Roads, boasting a small ballroom, a stage for theatrical performances, billiard rooms, a card-room and a bowling alley, which even played host to Prince Henry of Prussia when he visited Shanghai in April 1898.

Hongkou

With the French Concession and International Settlement playing host to fanciful social activities and institutions, the less salubrious former American Settlement, on the north banks of Suzhou Creek, hosted the city's nascent industrial base. Hongkou, being the poor neighbour to the city centre, was thus an attractive location for less affluent communities and establishments, such as emerging industrial facilities, missions and schools. The Fearon Road power station, the concrete factory, steel manufacturers, cotton mills, gasworks, waterworks and Shanghai's docklands, including the premises of the Shanghai Dock & Engineering Co Ltd, which began in 1862 as Farnham, Boyd & Co Ltd, were among the first industrial facilities in Shanghai and most were based in Hongkou. A predecessor to all of these, also located in Hongkou before it was removed to the south of the Chinese city, was the Kiangnan Arsenal, the Chinese foundry which produced so many of the arms that supplied the various warring factions over the years. In 1875, after it had moved to the suburb of Lunghua in 1869, it was said to be 'perhaps the highest development of Chinese technical industry'.[80]

Predating industry by two decades, missionaries were the first foreigners to exploit Hongkou's inexpensive land, following Bishop Boone's lead in 1848. Mission churches included the Mission for Seamen's St Andrew's Church on Broadway, designed by Atkinson & Dallas, and the Catholic community's Church of the Sacred Heart of Jesus (14) on the

Right The original Shanghai Club built in 1864

banks of Hongkou Creek, which opened on 12 June 1874, having previously conducted services in a godown. The American Episcopal Mission's Church of Our Saviour (I4), built in 1853 and demolished in 1916, had a 'modest steeple rising from the midst of embowering trees' that was described in the late 19th century as 'the one redeeming feature of that otherwise unpicturesque neighbourhood'.[81] It is interesting to note the words of Walter Medhurst, concerning church steeples in China from the 1870s, which all denominations were guilty of erecting:

> There is a propensity to erect pretentious churches after the foreign style of architecture with tall steeples or towers that show out obtrusively over the uniformly low roofs of a Chinese city. These towers are apt to create ill-will in an entire population, the Chinese idea being that any erection pointing upwards unless it be done of their own propitiatory pagodas, is calculated to bring down evil influences productive of ill-fortune, disease, and death upon the entire neighbourhood.

The American Episcopal Mission was responsible for establishing several major institutions in Shanghai. In 1879, they founded what became Shanghai's first and most prestigious university, St John's University in Jessfield, beyond the city's western boundary (A3). Initially a secondary school, St John's became a university in 1906 and expanded quickly, while educating some of the wealthiest and best scholars in China. It was among the first to construct buildings in a style combining Western and Chinese motifs, 'wittily called "Eurasian"'[82] and the main building was designed by Atkinson & Dallas (see page 71). In 1869, the Episcopal Mission founded Hongkou's first hospital, St Luke's (I4), which was first sited near the West Gate of the Chinese City before removing to the Bund in 1864 and then relocating to Hongkou, opposite the Catholic Church. The Catholics established a hospital in 1877 on the banks of Suzhou Creek, which later became the General Hospital (H4). They also built the St Francis Xavier School (see page 72), which started out with Father Desjacques giving 'private lessons to foreign little boys in his own room' in 1857.[83] In

1874, Father Twrdy started giving formal lessons to four pupils in the grounds of St Joseph's Church in the French Concession. At that time it was for foreign pupils only, but it later accepted Chinese and moved to Hongkou in 1884, the foundation stone having been laid in November 1882.

Another educational establishment to settle in Hongkou was the renowned Thomas Hanbury School and Children's Home (I4), an amalgamation of the Children's Home for Chinese and the Eurasian School which had stood on the same site (see page 72). A 'fine new building' went up on the corner of Boone and Miller Roads, next to the Catholic Church, which opened its doors in 1891. The five-storey building, designed by Cory, was once the highest in Shanghai, commanding 'one of the most comprehensive views in the Settlement' and 'magnificent' vistas from the attic.[84] Each dormitory had 14 beds and the school accommodated 84 children. The school later moved further north in Hongkou and divided into separate campuses for girls and boys.

On the other side of the Woosung (Wusong) Road was the China Inland Mission (I3), the 'handsome premises' of which, built in the 1890s, served as their headquarters. Though not 'having much claim to architectural beauty', soon after their construction the buildings were described as 'substantial, effective-looking and admirably suited to the purposes for which they were built'.[85] Opposite the mission compound was the huge Hongkou Market (I4), Shanghai's best stocked and most renowned market.

The modest cost of living in Hongkou also attracted less charismatic municipal departments such as the mental hospital, nursing home, slaughterhouse and Mixed Court (G3) (after it was removed from the British Consulate compound) as well as accommodating the lower classes, who, like the Chinese refugee, sustained Shanghai's property market. The Shanghai Land Investment Company was one of the first companies to take advantage of this market, starting their business in Hongkou from 1888 with a number of major residential developments that 'totally changed the appearance of some quarters of the town'.[86] These types of estate served the poorer communities such as the Chinese, Portuguese and Japanese, who began to settle in Hongkou in the 1870s.

In 1870, there were just three Japanese men living in Hongkou and seven in the International Settlement, but this had increased to 736 by the end of the century. At this point, the Japanese occupied a relatively lowly rung in the foreign hierarchy in Shanghai – the male population ran minor businesses while the female population worked restaurant tables and sexually deprived men. This changed dramatically in 1894 when China and Japan went to war over Korea. The consequences of the Sino–Japanese conflict were instrumental to the expansion of Japanese interests in China and the development of Shanghai. The Japanese established the Tong Wen College in Shanghai, designed to prime young students

Right The 'Eurasian' style of St John's University, here illustrated in the new Science Laboratory and, **opposite**, in the main University building

Schools

St Francis Xavier School

The four-storeyed brick building was designed by Brother Moirot in a 'plain style of French architecture' and cost $40,000. Thirteen tall windows provided the school with excellent light and ventilation so that the building 'receives the benefit of the breezes from whatever quarter they may blow'.[87] The building was 190 feet long and 60 feet deep, behind which was a large square playground. The centre of the facade boasted an $800 clock, donated by the Taotai, which chimed on the hour, day and night (the clock was made by Gourdin and came from Mayet in France). The first floors contained classrooms for charity boys and Chinese pupils, a dining hall and tiffin rooms. The second floor contained four classrooms and study rooms, with staff accommodation, infirmary and library on the third floor. A dormitory and music room occupied the top floor.

Thomas Hanbury School

The school building was 73 feet high, with a depth of 55 feet and a 92 foot facade on Boone Road. No funds were wasted on 'unnecessary exterior ornamentation', the 'plain, bold' exterior being simply finished in red and grey brick. The main entrance was located in the centre of the building and housed in a porch, flanked by two smaller side entrances. Inside the main entrance a 10 foot wide teak-floored lobby provided access to the classrooms and a large staircase provided access to the upper floors. Classrooms were located on the ground floor and staff quarters and dormitories on the upper floors – boys on the west side of the building and girls on the east. The roof was tiled in French tiles supplied by Mr Hanbury and at the time was predicted to 'endure for generations as a solid evidence of the noble generosity of its founders and endowers'.[88]

Above St Francis Xavier School

Above The new boys' boarding block of the Thomas Hanbury School

for business in China. In little over a decade, this investment brought tremendous dividends. The three-year college course had turned out 900 students by 1910 and by 1915 Japan's trade with China had doubled, making Japan the leading trading nation in Shanghai. These achievements were consequent on the signing of a commercial treaty between China, Japan and Britain in Beijing on 21 July 1896, which was attached to the peace treaty of Shimonoseki, by which Japanese subjects had the right to 'carry on trade, industry and manufactures' at any of the treaty ports. The article automatically applied to other treaty nations through the 'Most Favoured Nation' clause. From hereon, industrial growth in Shanghai was unstoppable and within 30 years outstripped Glasgow, Manchester or Birmingham. The rapidly expanding Japanese community bought land along the Woosung Road, much of which was being sold by the

nigh-bankrupt comprador of Dent & Co, Xu Run. With new-found confidence, the Japanese even sought their own settlement in Shanghai, but their request fell on deaf ears.

Nonetheless, following the Japanese treaty, foreign industrial development was set in motion. Factories and mills sprouted in Hongkou's distant suburbs, occupying the northern bank of the Whuangpu in the Eastern District of the International Settlement, far from the downtown areas and with minimal rents. Cotton, flour and silk mills were among the first and most prosperous industries, followed by supporting industries, such as machine shops, stores and transportation, all of which nurtured an emergent labour force. Hongkou became the industrial heart of Shanghai and the engine of China.

Industrial development relied on important technological innovations, all of which had to be imported. The Chinese,

who were deeply suspicious of the foreigners' motives and contraptions, accepted grudgingly the introduction of new processes and products. In 1866, the firm Russell & Co laid Shanghai's first telegraph connecting Hongkou with the French Concession, and its immediate success excited demand for a regional system. However, the Taotai forbade it because a man had died under the shadow of a telegraph pole, and this was blamed for fatally upsetting his feng shui. A similar fate befell electricity. Shanghai's first gas street lighting appeared in 1865, but it soon faced competition from electricity, which was first demonstrated in Shanghai in the Public Gardens bandstand in June 1882. Confounded by the fireless light that could kill a man or burn down a house, the Taotai outlawed its use by Chinese, but, as with the telegraph, he was powerless to prevent its eventual proliferation and today few countries in the world use electrical light as brilliantly as China.

The worst excesses of Chinese distrust of Western innovation were directed at the railways. Although Shanghai was home to China's first railway, its introduction was a depressing affair. Foreign merchants attempted to build the first railway in China in 1863 linking Shanghai with Suzhou, but their proposal was refused. In 1864 Sir Macdonald Stephenson visited China with the stated intention of averting the ills of haphazard development which had so afflicted Britain, and submitted a proposal to build a vast network of railways throughout China. This too was refused. In the face of such tenacious opposition, the foreigners resorted to subterfuge. They requested first to reconstruct and reroute a

military road built during the Taiping Rebellion, and then they announced their plan to lay tramlines along the road. Without the Taotai's permission, the 30 inch gauge railway was completed along a distance of 5 miles towards Woosung and opened on 30 June 1876. Six trains ran daily for passengers until August, when a man was killed on the tracks

Right The first railway journey in China

Far right The Town Hall

through either 'extremely dense stupidity, or a malicious intention to commit suicide and thereby create a prejudice against railways'.[89] The service was stopped and negotiations for the sale of the track and rolling stock ended with the Chinese buying them for Tls 285,000 on 21 October 1877. The new owners promptly tore up the track and shipped it to Taiwan, where it was dumped on a beach to rot.

Municipal improvements

The remainder of the 19th century was not a period of significant architectural activity. Instead, progress was being made in municipal areas, which, like the escalation of industrial activity at the close of the century, helped lay the foundation for Shanghai's growth at the start of the 20th century. One of the Municipal Council's most perennial problems was drainage. The settlement had been built on an alluvial plain so there was a constant battle to stop the ground from consuming what was built above it, a task that required

a 'triumph of mind over mud'. Providing a system of drainage to ensure that waste water was carried away from instead of transferred between abodes was one of Shanghai's 'chief difficulties'.[90] The situation became so bad by the 1860s that a major epidemic broke out, blamed of course on the 'naturally filthy habits'[91] of the Chinese and their 'utter disregard of sanitary conditions ... giving Shanghai hygiene, over most of the civilized world, a bad reputation'.[92] Others blamed municipal incompetence for wasting Tls 85,000 'in trying to make water run uphill'. Whatever the reason, it was not acceptable for Shanghai to be described as 'disgusting in the extreme, offensive to the eye and a pesthole in warm weather – simply filthy and highly dangerous'.[93] If Shanghai was going to mature, standards of living, provided by an enhanced infrastructure, had to improve, but it would have to get worse before getting better.

While the Council's less attractive problems would not go away, it nevertheless found the resources to build

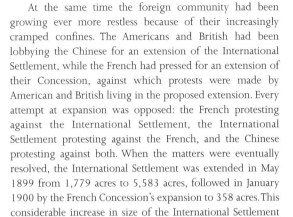

Left FM Gratton's Chinese Market behind the Town Hall

Shanghai's first Town Hall (G5) on Nanjing Road in 1896. With red brick and Ningpo stone dressing, the building and its 'heavy gables' were said to give 'a very dignified appearance'.[94] Inside the Town Hall was a large room with a solid concrete floor, 154 feet by 80 feet, used for a drill hall by the Shanghai Volunteer Corps and for social functions. Replaced by the new municipal offices opened in 1922 (see page 96–8), the Town Hall was demolished in 1929. Behind the Town Hall, a large Chinese market, designed by Frederick Montague Gratton of Morrison & Gratton and using 575 tons of steel shipped from London, was opened on 1 January 1899 and was one of the first steel-framed structures in Shanghai. Gratton (1859– 1918) studied engineering from 1872 to 1875, starting professional work in 1877 and becoming an Associate of the RIBA in 1881 and a Fellow two years later. He arrived in Shanghai in 1882 to take charge of the architectural portion of GJ Morrison's engineering firm, with whom he formed a partnership, Morrison & Gratton, in 1885.

At the same time the foreign community had been growing ever more restless because of their increasingly cramped confines. The Americans and British had been lobbying the Chinese for an extension of the International Settlement, while the French had pressed for an extension of their Concession, against which protests were made by American and British living in the proposed extension. Every attempt at expansion was opposed: the French protesting against the International Settlement, the International Settlement protesting against the French, and the Chinese protesting against both. When the matters were eventually resolved, the International Settlement was extended in May 1899 from 1,779 acres to 5,583 acres, followed in January 1900 by the French Concession's expansion to 358 acres. This considerable increase in size of the International Settlement represented its last extension, despite persistent pressure on the Chinese in the first decades of the 20th century. Shanghai's International Settlement had reached its limits.

A city emerges

In little over half a century the foreign settlements had emerged and, despite numerous obstacles, had prospered. With the Chinese city witnessing the first semblances of a municipal administration, Shanghai had evolved from a single unit comprising a Chinese mercantile city into a tripartite urban form. The creation of a settlement, with all the trappings of an emerging city, was lauded by its ruling caste: 'We have seen the wretched swamp, the fields of paddy, and the dank marshes develop into a handsome city, with fine roads, stately buildings, a smoothly working form of civil government, and all, or nearly all, the accompaniments of Western civilization'.[95] Inevitably, fond retrospection overlooked the contributions of the native population, whose cheap labour, skills and local knowledge had provided the means to realise such achievements.

Below The newly established Public Garden (opened in 1868) photographed here between 1876 and 1878 showing the impressive frontage of the Bund and its 'compradoric' facades

Right A typical example of an early foreign merchant's premises

Below An example of the crude style of architecture that characterised Shanghai's sense of permanence towards the end of the 19th century

This unacknowledged reliance on native talents applied particularly to the building industry, where for several decades the fanciful plans of untrained foreigners were carried out by Chinese craftsmen and master builders, whose disciplines served as an alternative to architecture, which the Chinese did not embrace until the early 20th century. The synthesis of Western and Chinese construction techniques

and working practices, combined with a dependence on local materials, had evolved from an amateur building industry, the products of which were often defined stylistically as 'compradoric'(see page 47–8), to a more regulated system. In these promising circumstances a growing number of professional architects arriving in Shanghai in the years before the close of the 19th century were able to take advantage of the city's new-found sense of permanence. Residents and businesses were investing in larger, lasting structures, exemplified by the construction of the city's first major buildings designed by foreign architects, such as Holy Trinity Cathedral and the French Municipal offices.

The system of tenders for these larger buildings demanded the formalisation of the building industry and put pressure on the Chinese to modernise their practices in order to compete with foreign companies. This transitional process is evident in the design of the first building of the Hongkong and Shanghai Banking Corporation by William Kidner in 1877 (see page 136), which 'apart from its architectural merit is of considerable interest as showing the manner in which Chinese workmen can adapt themselves to the carrying out of European requirements'.[96] The result of this process was the establishment of foreign architectural firms and Chinese contractors adopting Western working practices, and the cultivation of the expertise of regional Chinese workers, particularly from Ningbo, whose consummate skills in stone carving and carpentry commanded a wage almost double that of Chinese workers from other towns and provinces.

Shanghai's embryonic industrial facilities were now able to supply and manufacture building materials that previously had to be imported, and supported innovations that transformed construction techniques. The proliferation of stone, brick and mortar was being challenged by concrete and steel. Underpinning this evolving industry was the rampant demand for housing in the British Settlement during the various disturbances, creating a real estate market that became as important to Shanghai as trade and industry.

These forces 'threw open the hitherto closed doors of

China with her hundreds of millions of able, industrious, and intelligent people', and laid the foundations for the growth of one of the most important cities in the world, while its emergent industrial capacity would cause 'many and varied social and economical changes, affecting deeply the mode of life of both Chinese and foreigners'.[97] However, at the close of the century the conspicuousness of the city's visible progress masked other events that proved significant for Shanghai 'more so than people realised at the time',[98] and served as a precursor to the major events that befell the city in the 20th century. China had fought and lost a war with Japan and rumblings of discontent over foreign occupation fuelled a growing sense of national identity as China's final dynasty tottered on the brink of collapse. Shanghai's role in these events and their consequences over the course of the 20th century would affect not just 'a single continent, but the whole world, Europe, Asia, Africa, America, and Australia'.[99]

Above left One of the oldest buildings on the Bund, reflecting the 19th-century architectural style

Above Chinese carpenters and other craftsmen were vital in providing the skills to build Shanghai

Below The Bund, 1889

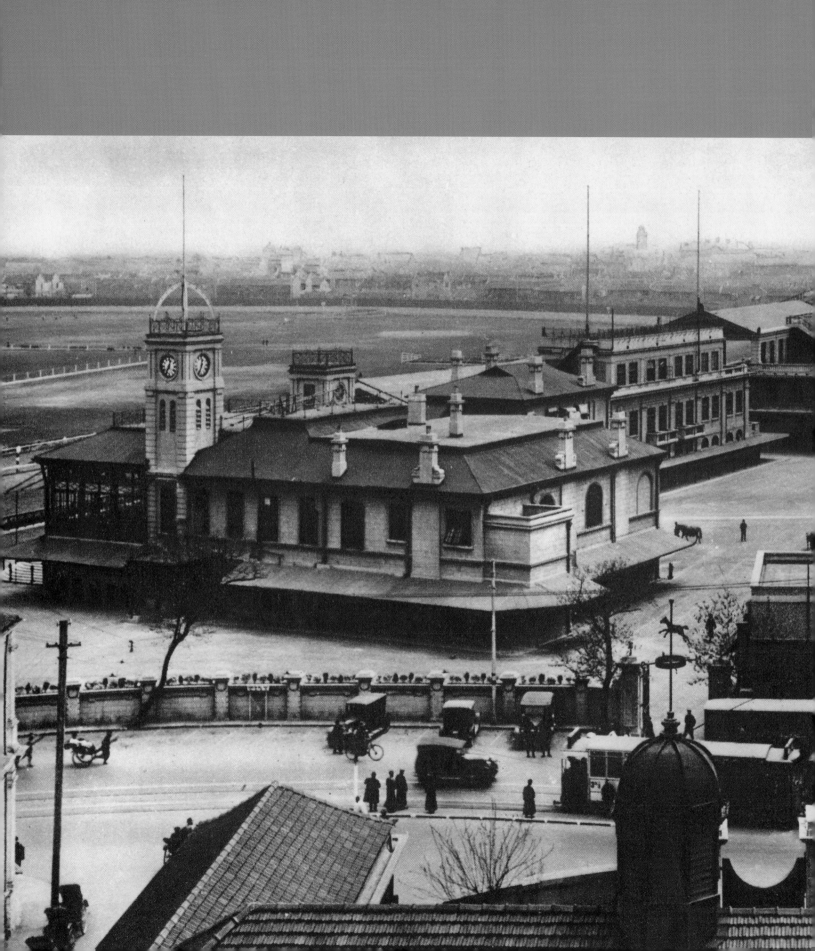

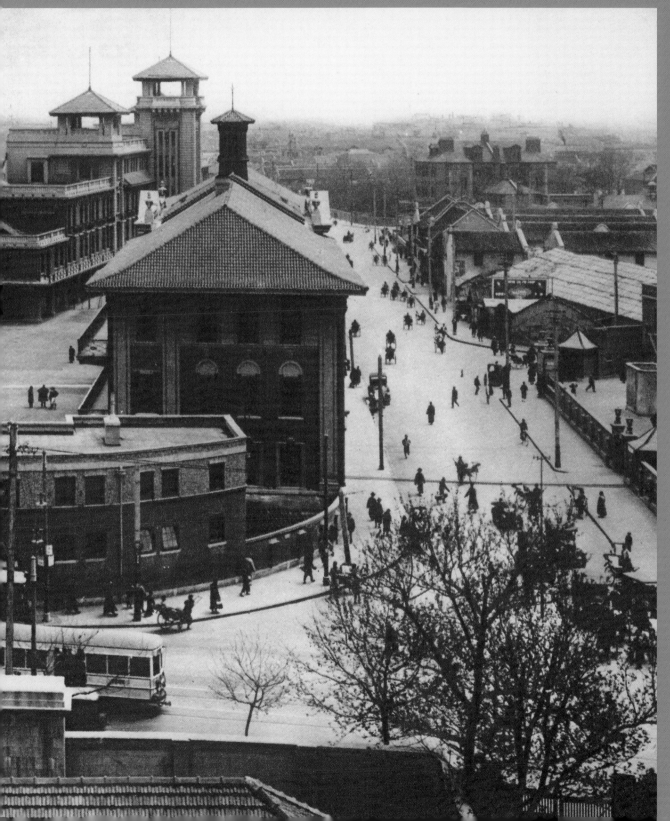

Becoming a City, 1900–1920

Changes are going on continually all over the city. Day by day old buildings are disappearing and modern ones rising in their place. It is to be feared that many of the ancient landmarks will soon be gone.

Mary Ninde Gamewell, *The Gateway to China*, 1916

Above Panorama from behind the Bund. Note the densification of the central district compared with the painting on pages 36–7 painted from the same position.

In 1893, the jubilee had been celebrated sumptuously by a cosmopolitan foreign community united in collective self-congratulation for their achievements in building the 'Model Settlement'. Little did they know that extraterritorial Shanghai was halfway through its life. In exactly the same time it took to reach this significant milestone, Shanghai would grow beyond their wildest dreams and be lost forever to them and their children – true 'Shanghailanders', those born in the city and who considered it home. By the 1900s, new developments were transforming the recently expanded settlements. The consequent loss of structures once variously ridiculed, belittled or praised by the city's founding fathers invited mournful reminiscences from nostalgic sections of a foreign community in 1914: 'It is only a question of a few years before the last remaining landmarks of British Shanghai fifty years ago will have disappeared'.[1] The next fifty years saw Shanghai disappear completely from the foreigner's gaze – through which time it flourished and was damned.

A speech given to Shanghai's Society of Engineers and Architects during the 'dark and difficult' days of 1940 fondly recounted the Settlement's condition in 1901, providing an apposite overview:

> There were then no railways in Shanghai (other than the ill-started line to Woosung); the harbour was in a very bad state; practically all building construction was in brickwork and timber; all roads were either waterbound macadam, chip-paving or plain mud; and there was no water borne sewage

system. There were no motor cars, trams or buses, few bicycles and only a few semi-privately operated telephones … electrical power was in its infancy … and the ordinary man was little affected or concerned by the international storm clouds which were already beginning to gather over Shanghai in particular and the world in general.

Internationally, though design innovation was prolific, technological change and the Industrial Revolution were yet to yield the great design movements of the 20th century, which would begin redefining Shanghai after the city's own industrial transformation in the first two decades of the century.

Beyond the realm of design, the death of Queen Victoria in January 1901 brought to an end Britain's illustrious Victorian era of empire, innovation and expansion – the factors that had been instrumental in the genesis of Shanghai. Conversely, America's share of trade was increasing, and Japan was a growing influence, contributing to Shanghai's rise and fuelling its destruction. In 1911, the revolution in China replaced 5,000 years of dynastic rule with virtual anarchy before a central government emerged in the 1920s. Britain and Japan maintained vigilance over Russia's inroads into Manchuria which ended in the Russo-Japanese War of 1904, while Germany, France and the rest of Europe eyed one another distrustfully, before embarking on the First World War that, following China's entry in 1917, caused the expulsion of the thriving German and Austrian communities

Previous pages The Race Club and Racecourse looking south from its northwest corner

from China and the confiscation of their property. Over 1,460 were deported from Shanghai from 6 to 10 March 1919, followed by nearly 1,000 more in April. Europe's collective interests were undermined in Shanghai and in the world, leaving Japan, America and, for a short while, Shanghai to reap the spoils.

Urban Transformation

The 20th century started ominously for China with the onset of the Boxer Rebellion, an uprising aimed at menacing foreigners and foreign sympathisers in the north of China. United under the motto 'Preserve the Dynasty, Exterminate the Foreigners', the Boxers' stated intention was unambiguous. Shanghai's viceroy gave assurances to the foreign community that Shanghai would not be attacked as long as foreign troops remained confined to the north of China. Britain was not willing to take a chance. On 17 August 1900, 3,000 Indian troops were sent from Hong Kong to defend Shanghai. Their presence unsettled other treaty powers, who in turn sent their own contingents and turned the city into a military camp with over 8,000 troops from all over the world. The attack never materialised, and Shanghai was affected only by the absence of many of its workers and artisans who answered their country's call. Nonetheless, another feather was added in the cap of the Shanghai Volunteer Corps, who, although their 'enthusiasm and numbers had never been higher', felt sorely 'cheated' by the Boxers' absence[2] and managed only to parade their multinational 'motley crowd'[3] on the recreation ground in the centre of the racecourse.

Anti-foreign sentiment in China and a more articulate opposition presented by a budding Chinese-educated class were growing, but had yet to mature. For now, the disorganised rebellion created only chaos as the rebels besieged the foreign legations in Beijing and executed foreign missionaries in the outlying areas. A multinational assortment of troops sent to Beijing to liberate the legations routed the Boxers and went on to sack the city with brutal abandon, inflicting the gravest dishonour on the Chinese empire. As China's last dynasty lay in ruins, foreign powers imposed further humiliating demands on the broken country in the form of indemnities. Signed by China and 11 foreign powers on 7 September 1901, the agreement demanded swingeing financial reparations.

The consequences of this crippling agreement were far reaching politically and economically, but in the field of architecture also they were profound. In 1908, America agreed to return a portion of its share of the Boxer Indemnity in exchange for the education of Chinese in America. The money allocated to America therefore went instead into educational programmes, including the establishment of Tsing Hua College (later University) in Beijing in 1911, designed to prepare students for their American education. Through Tsing Hua's doors passed the first ranks of foreign-trained Chinese architects who later returned to China and built some of the country's, and Shanghai's, most significant modern buildings. This coincided with the Chinese revolution, which heralded the birth of a new, progressive generation of Chinese intent on learning about and acquiring Western skills and methods.

With the Boxer threat consigned to history, commercial activity improved. Trade figures were rising, with Shanghai accounting for more than half of foreign trade with China. From 1895 to 1905, trade had doubled, increasing by 30 per cent between 1904 and 1905. The majority of this was

Below Map of Shanghai, 1904, showing the separate Municipal Districts and Settlement extensions of 1899 with proposed road layouts.

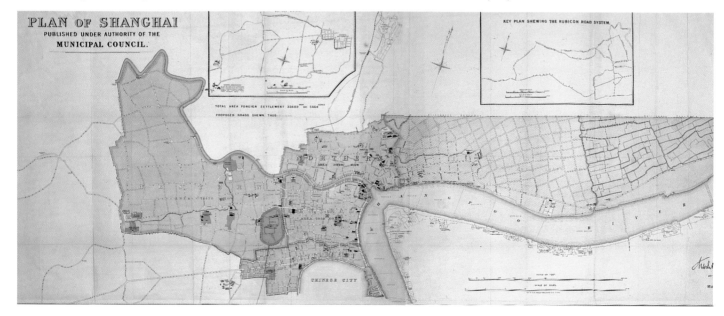

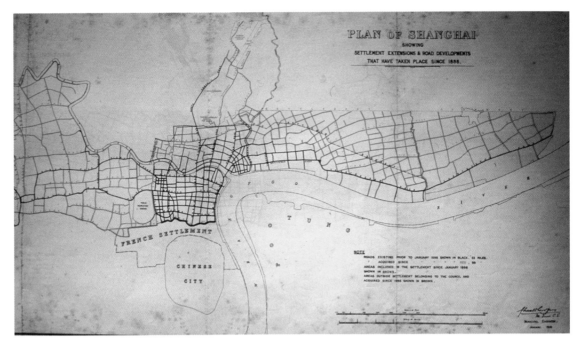

shared by the major European powers, America and Japan, though British interests still dominated shipping, banking, insurance, tea, cotton and silk.

Booming trade stimulated urban development, with the number of plans for new buildings submitted to Shanghai's Municipal Council increasing from 5,672 in 1903 to 6,599 in 1904.[4] The increased building activity was due in part to the settlement extensions of 1899 and 1900. In 1899 the International Settlement grew to 5,583 acres after gaining 1,908 and 1,896 acres in the Western and Eastern Districts respectively, while on 27 January 1900, the French Concession grew to 358 acres after 152 acres was added along with an additional 19 acres adjacent to the Chinese city which they had already occupied and developed, but which had not been officially recognised. This added an extra 3,975 acres of countryside on which to build. These extensions also improved trade by increasing the water frontage and therefore the limits of the harbour.

Affluent from recent economic gains, Shanghai's newly established Western District sprouted magnificent villas and clubs on a scale, in an abundance and of a grandeur unfamiliar to the now 'vast and heterogeneous city'.[5] A worldwide depression ended this boom in 1907, worsening in 1910 with the collapse of the global rubber industry, which stifled construction activity until 1913. The Municipal Council's engineers blamed it on 'over building in previous years combined with depressed trade and the Revolutionary movement',[6] while Shanghai's business community vociferously demanded reductions in rent. Vacancies reached an all-time high of 15 per cent for foreign buildings and 8 per

cent for Chinese buildings, demand for which was traditionally infinite. Confidence was rattled severely.

In a time of domestic turmoil, the foreign settlements again provided a sanctuary for political refugees from Russia, Korea and, not least, for the leader of China's republican movement and the founding father of modern China, Dr Sun Yat Sen, who returned from exile to Shanghai on 24 December 1911. Corrupt and inefficient, China's last dynasty had bowed out on 4 November 1911 to be replaced by an ineffectual republicanism that heralded a return of China's habitual warlords. The foundation of the Republic of China was proclaimed by Dr Sun from Nanjing on 1 January 1912.

In Shanghai, the major casualty of this transition was the city wall, which had been considered a hindrance to trade by the city's residents and the Chinese City Council (Tsung Kung Chi), established in 1905, and was now seen as representing the feudal past. Its removal had been discussed for several years and, despite extra gates in the west, north and east of the wall being added after 1909 and existing gates widened, from 1912 it started to be pulled down. A British cemetery (G6) at the foot of the wall on the northwest side containing approximately 300 graves of soldiers who had died fighting the Taipings removed in exchange for land elsewhere, but ownership of the new road that replaced the wall and its moat caused a greater stir. Since it was the border of the French Concession and the Chinese city, both the French and the Chinese staked their claims on a title, eventually compromising with 'Boulevard des Deux Républiques'. For the ever nostalgic foreigner, the removal of this much maligned structure and its long-condemned waterways 'choked with all manner of debris'[7] prompted instant pining for the past: 'but for interest and picturesqueness [sic] the change is ruinous. Somehow there was more art possibility along the old Yang-king-pang and the old city moat than there is in all the foreign streets put together with all their expensive and pretentious architecture. None can deny that – who wants to paint a reinforced concrete block of offices?'.[8] For such blinkered conservatives, there was still the willow pattern teahouse, which, even in the 1920s, boasted 'a stagnant, putrid pond, covered with an unwholesome green scum'.[9]

Ironically, Shanghai, the epitome of much despised foreign power and dominance in China, became the cradle of the new republic and China's future, while foreign contempt for the Chinese stimulated a growing sense of national identity. As Ransome described: 'Every blow struck by foreigners in China is a blow in the welding of a nation. And just as one of the motives for the old wars between the Western Powers and China was foreign resentment of the contemptuous attitude of the Chinese, so now one of the forces uniting the Chinese is their resentment of the contemptuous attitude of the foreigners.'[10] Unfortunately for Dr Sun and for China, his republican dreams were premature and his country slid back into a fractured and embattled assortment of provinces, ruled over by warring leaders and desperate peasant soldiers. For a further 15 years, only turmoil characterised China's provinces, with Shanghai hosting its bitter and bloody conclusion.

As was the case in the 19th century, China's loss was Shanghai's gain. After the 1911 revolution, Chinese flocked to the settlements, where they bought houses and established businesses. When the Great War started in 1914, Europe's loss too became Shanghai's gain, as the war consumed the wares of an emerging class of Chinese capitalists and industrialists. Shanghai 'made more material progress in the past three years [1914–16] than in any other six years of its history … Building activity has been so rapid that former residents, returning, say that they scarcely can believe that the city is that which they left only a few years ago.'[11] In the first quarter of 1914, 2,394 houses were constructed, compared with 1,350 during the same months in 1906, when the previous record was set over the same period. In 1914–15 alone, over 23,000 building permits were issued.

Shanghai's rapid growth during this period was boosted by the introduction of trams, which opened up and accelerated development in the suburbs and made them easily accessible to downtown. Tenders for a tram network had been invited in the 1890s, but it was not until 1906 that Bruce, Peebles & Co Ltd of Edinburgh started constructing the International Settlement's network, which was officially opened on 5 March 1908, followed on 8 May by the French Concession's network. Although built independently, the two networks used the same gauge track and were designed to

connect, which they finally did in 1912. There was some doubt about the financial viability of the service, as jinrikisha, two-wheeled vehicles drawn by a person and introduced to Shanghai from Japan in the 1873, were an established, abundant and cheap means of transport whose numbers had increased by 55 per cent between 1903 and 1907. These fears appeared well founded when the first 18 months of tram service produced a deficit of $200,000 owing to an 'unprecedentedly large service of cheap rickshaws'.[12] However, by the 1910s, the trams appeared to be gaining ground on Shanghai's time-honoured jinrikisha, whose numbers fell as dramatically as the life expectancy of their drivers, who were described as short-lived 'miserable looking wretches'[13]. In 1916, there were 8,920 jinrikisha licensed in the International Settlement whereas in the French Concession, where licensing was never restricted, their numbers grew to over 17,000 by the 1930s. Passenger numbers on the International Settlement's 16.5 mile tramway increased from 11.8 million in 1909 to over 90 million in 1919, while the number using the French Concession's 12.5 mile network increased from 4.5 million in 1909 to 14.7 million in 1913.

The phenomenal success of these networks and the removal of the city wall heralded the construction of the Chinese city's tramway. After being postponed due to the late delivery of the rails (caused by a fire on board the ship carrying them from Hamburg and a Chinese rebellion in July that destroyed areas of the Chinese city through which the tram was supposed to operate), China's first domestically financed and built tramway was inaugurated on 11 August

Above Municipal transport improvements showing the laying of tramlines and **above right** woodblocks for roads

1913. With an expanding tram network and an increase in electricity usage, the first threads were being woven in what would become Shanghai's renowned tapestry of overhead electrical wires.

In many cases, especially in the downtown area behind the Bund, trams were impossible because the roads were too narrow, but the laying of new tramlines necessitated improvements to Shanghai's notorious roads, which had suffered from want of planning and funding since the days of the Committee of Roads and Jetties. In 1889, the International Settlement had just 36 miles of roads, most of which were dirt roads. Only the major thoroughfares were gravelled or macadamised, both of which required continuous maintenance to prevent them from disappearing

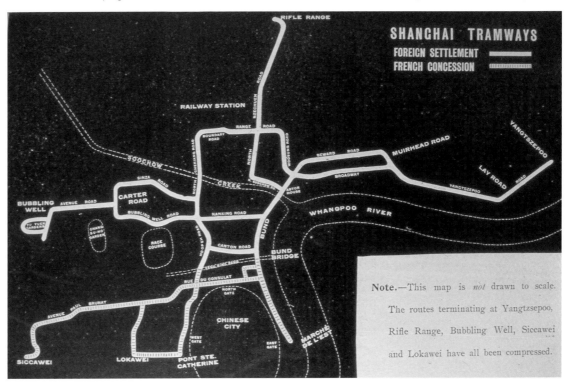

Right Map showing Shanghai's tram network

beneath Shanghai's moist subsoil or from being 'torn apart by the forceful currents of the flood waters'[14] during the typhoon season. They also had to cope with one of the most diverse ranges of vehicular use anywhere in the world. Shanghai's infamous one-wheeled wheelbarrow, 'one of the most ruinous contraptions conceivable in its action on asphalt',[15] along with iron-rimmed handcarts, *jinrikisha*, bicycles, buses, trucks and pneumatic car tyres presented the Municipal Council with an unprecedented headache, made worse by Shanghai's peculiar climate, where temperature differential throughout the year can be as much as 130 degrees Fahrenheit.

By 1909, the extent of the International Settlement's roads had increased gradually to 102 miles, 37 of which were macadamised and 16 were gravel. In contrast, the French were consistently more active in laying roads, building proportionally more of them at a faster pace. A growing network inside and beyond the foreign settlements did much to encourage motorcar use, which started with the introduction of Oldsmobiles in 1902, causing 'quite a stir, frightening horses and rousing much curiosity among the pedestrians'[16]. So successful was the motorcar that 'no other industry made more noticeable progress in the orient',[17] as residents in a rare display of rescinding national allegiances selected their ideal car from among those marketed by the 70 international manufacturers represented in Shanghai in 1912, when Shanghai had 500 licensed motorcars.

The motorcar also encouraged the development of 'extra-settlement roads' – roads extending beyond the settlement boundaries. Foreigners had built country villas on the cheap land along extra-settlement roads even before Bubbling Well Road, the first extra-settlement road, was sold to the Municipal Council in 1866, but the scale of development in the first decades of the 20th century was altogether different. Shanghai's growth and improved transportation encouraged the construction of more and more extra-settlement roads, both sides of which were swiftly occupied by foreigners' houses. The Chinese grudgingly accepted that the land these roads and buildings occupied was subject to treaty agreements, though this form of annexation by stealth caused much dispute between the foreign and Chinese authorities that was never resolved.

The western suburbs

The prospect of a huge area of rural residential land becoming available to the foreign community within the settlement boundaries was realised on 20 July 1914 when the expansion of the French Concession was ratified, extending the settlement as far as, but not including, their Catholic Mission in Xu Jia Hui. In this year, the Shanghai Municipal Council's annual report claimed 60 per cent of development was on agricultural land. As had happened from 1899 along the International Settlement's Bubbling Well (Nanjing Xi Lu) and Avenue (Beijing Xi Lu) Roads, the French Concession's main

roads such as Avenue Paul Brunat (later Avenue Joffre and Huai Hai Lu) soon were lined by the residences of 'merchant-princes, the home of the taipan and banker, where strings of tiny palaces, brilliantly lit and high-walled, stood out in magnificent evidence of a great city's wealth'.[18] Huai Hai Lu was laid out in the early 20th century and named after Paul Brunat, the Chairman of the French Municipal Council at the time of the extension of the French Concession. The road changed name after the Great War in honour of a visit to Shanghai by Marshall Joffre, the Frenchman charged with trying to resist the German invasion of France. Bubbling Well Road and Avenue Joffre presented the perfect picture of suburban geniality and vied for superiority, residents on each fiercely promoting their own patch. Bubbling Well Road, described in 1886 as the 'Rotten Row drive, utterly devoid of beauty',[19] was claimed by one British resident in 1920 to be 'the prettiest road in Shanghai, the foliage is rich and full … Being curved according to British taste, not dead straight as French roads are, it is much more beautiful.'[20]

In 1916, so great was 'the demand for residence sites that many roads which were once dismissed as being too far out for such use now are fringed with handsome structures of brick, concrete and stucco, many of them surrounded by beautiful lawns and gardens where only two years ago the Chinese agriculturalist pursued the even tenor of his truck farming'.[21] The symbiotic and enduring relationship between land use inside and outside the settlements was mutually

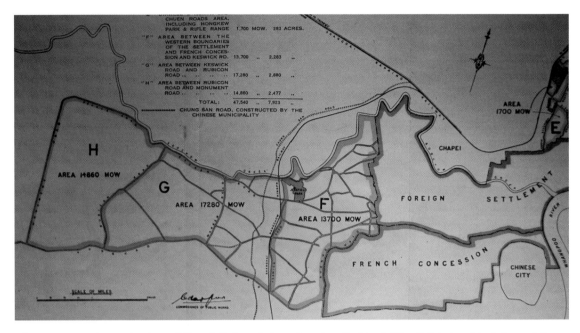

Right Map showing the extent of land covered by extra-settlement roads by 1930

advantageous, as destruction beyond Shanghai's boundaries fuelled development inside. As the city devoured more land and materials, one foreigner commented: 'Many a Bubbling Well villa is founded on the remains of what was once a Chinese bourgeois home.'[22]

Supreme among these colossal villas stood the McBain family villa set in 10 acres of land on Bubbling Well Road (see also the McBain Building on the Bund, pages 104 and 106) and described as 'the most sumptuous private residence in Shanghai'. Like all things in Shanghai, it did not last long: in 1924 it was demolished to be replaced by the lavish Majestic Hotel (E4), the city's 'newest and most luxurious Residential Hotel',[23] designed by Lafuente & Yaron. Another sumptuous building nearby was the Country Club (F5) on Bubbling Well Road, Shanghai's 'great social rendezvous' and 'pleasantest club'. Opened in July 1880, the first club was a modest venue set in 2 acres of land, but it grew steadily and by the turn of the century 'resembled a large country residence'[24] in 11 acres of exquisite gardens replete with lawns, flowerbeds and ornamental water that, by the 1940s, 'were packed with skyscrapers'.[25] Inside, six billiard tables, a card-room, a miniature theatre, ballroom and four ping-pong tables provided its 175 members with every leisurely pursuit they desired. On the same road but several

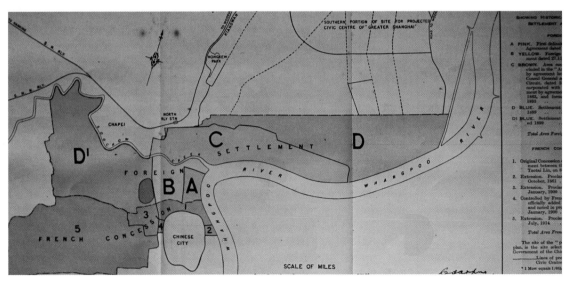

Right Chronological map showing the expansion of Shanghai's boundaries

blocks west was the 100-room, air-conditioned Burlington Hotel (D5) designed by Moorhead & Halse. Robert Moorhead was an engineer who had come to China to work in railway construction 20 years earlier before settling in Shanghai. In 1895, he joined William Dowdall before going independent in 1900. In 1907, he joined Sidney Halse, a former employee of Scott & Carter and Associate of the RIBA from 1901, who became a Fellow in 1932. The district was also popular for consulates, including the Portuguese, Swedish, Belgian, and Italian consulates. The Italian Consulate, designed by Atkinson & Dallas under the supervision of FA Pearson, was among the first to relocate to this area. Brenan Atkinson joined Arthur Dallas to form the influential architectural firm Atkinson & Dallas in 1898, which designed many commercial, industrial and residential buildings, as well as the Mixed Court (1899) and many of the early projects for the Shanghai Land Investment Company. Dallas was Chief Municipal Engineer before joining Atkinson, who died in 1907, but his name lived on in the company through his brother, GB Atkinson, who joined in 1908. The Italian Consulate was opened in mid-1904 and, entitled to extraterritorial rights, the new consulate contained a 'large and commodious' courtroom, at the front of which stood a life-size bust in Carrara marble of King Victor Emmanuel III with a somewhat paradoxical inscription reading 'Justice for All' in Italian.

The Chinese area

Sandwiched between these new salubrious suburbs and the Central District and behind the Bund, and flanked by Henan Road and Defence Creek, was an area 'more weird and

WINTER GARDEN. MAJESTIC HOTEL. DESIGNED & EXECUTED BY ARTS & CRAFTS. L™ SHANGHAI

thought-provoking'[26] than the Central District and 'just as much Chinese as the Chinese City itself'.[27] Originally occupied by the Chinese during the Taiping Rebellion, this quarter was on the outskirts of the Settlement at the time and therefore retained the cheapest land values. It became densely populated with over 40,000 dwellings typifying 'the Chinese ideas of domestic comfort'[28] and commercial enterprise and where, according to the Shanghai Municipal Council, 'overcrowding was deplorable'. The Chinese tradition of assigning certain streets to the sale of specific products was characterised here, with Foochow (Fuzhou) Road specialising in books and ornaments, Canton (Guangdong) Road in shoes, Honan (Henan) Road in silks and embroideries, Shantung (Shandong) Road in clothing and pottery, Sunkiang Road in curios and second-hand wares and Fokien (Fujian) Road in jinrikisha and coffins.

Distinguished among these streets was Fuzhou Road, 'one long series of restaurants, sing-song houses, theatres, lights, laughter and colour' and regarded as the 'Chinaman's Paradise'.[29] In the ritual manner by which colonials endowed their overseas domains with names from 'home', Fuzhou Road was tagged the 'Piccadilly of China' or what 'Fifth Avenue is to New York'. Fuzhou Road never had any false pretensions towards aesthetic beauty or architectural ascendancy. Instead, it was the epicentre of Shanghai's opium dens and possessed 'but very few fair specimens of semi-Chinese architecture'.[30] Yet, when the opium dens in the International Settlement were forced to close in 1909, nostalgic foreigners pined their loss. Following the 'pulling down of the quaint Chinese buildings and the erection of stores and hotels of concrete', it was 'not as picturesque as it was twenty years ago'.[31] Several theatres and teashops vitalised the street and surrounding area, including the 2,000 seat Da Wu Tai, or 'Grand Stage', the appropriately named Free and Easys music hall and the three-storeyed Louen-Yuen Billiard Saloon. The size of this structure made it a rarity for the early 20th century and 'a good specimen of Chinese architecture'.[32] The lower storey, built of brick, housed the billiard tables and bowling alley, while the upper two storeys, constructed of wood and decorated with 'grotesque' woodcarvings on the facade, were reserved for tea drinkers and, formerly, for opium smokers.

While Fuzhou Road and its neighbouring alleys, lanes and streets presented an intimate commercial experience, **Below** The former Country Club

Right Fuzhou Road in the 1910s

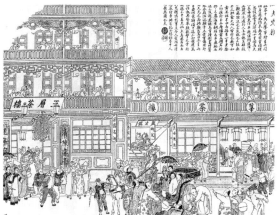

Far right Chinese depiction of the activities on Fuzhou Road in the early 20th century

Shanghai's retail colossus, Nanjing Road, was altogether different. While foreigners had long extolled their own 'examples of the highest type in business architecture'[33] in downtown Shanghai, the Chinese had learned fast. Nanjing Road, or 'Da Ma Lu' (Big Horse Road) to the Chinese, had catered only for small shops interspersed with residential dwellings but by the turn of the century it looked 'as if before long the Ma Lu [would] rival Fuzhou Road'.[34] By the 1910s, on every side of Nanjing Road 'rose clouds of dust from the demolition of residences that had lain just outside the beaten track of commercial activity'.[35] By 1920, it was described in

Darwent's guide to Shanghai as 'certainly one of the most interesting streets in the world'. An article in the *Far Eastern Review* applauded: 'No other business street in the Far East shows such activity by day or such a blaze of brilliancy by night (with the possible exception of the Ginza in Tokyo). Its entire length is lined with handsome buildings of brick and concrete. 20 new blocks have been built in the past two years and half a dozen of magnitude are in progress.'[36] The retail phenomenon had arrived in China. No city greeted it more readily than Shanghai, and no street in Shanghai embraced it more fervently than Nanjing Road. In the 1910s, apart from

Right Nanjing Road, west of Henan Road, in 1907

Left Nanjing Road looking east from the corner of Tibet Road, showing the unmistakable spires of China's first department stores of (left to right) Sun Sun (1926), Sincere (1917) and Wing On (1918)

Wing On Department Store

On the south side, occupying 215 feet of Nanjing Road and 200 feet of Zhejiang Road, Wing On Department Store and the Great Eastern Hotel leased 36,300 square feet of land from the businessman Hardoon for 35 years for $40,000 per year to provide unparalleled service to a Chinese clientele 'accustomed to Occidental manners and customs'. The department store was opened to the public in September 1918. The six-storey building had a roof garden 97 feet above the pavement and a 68 foot tower, which the original design shows to be a prominent landmark on the corner of Nanjing and Zhejiang Roads, but this had to be repositioned because the leaseholder on this corner site refused to relinquish the lease. The entrances to the hotel and to the department store were on separate sides of the building, the department store's main entrance being in the centre of the Nanjing Road facade, behind which were spacious stairways and lifts leading to the upper floors. The architect boasted of the many innovative features employed in the building, including flush toilets, an arcaded main entrance and copper shop fronts and doors. Designed in a Renaissance style, the building was constructed in reinforced

Illustrations of the Wing On Department Store showing the southern elevation and the entrance to the Great Eastern Hotel (*top left*), the north-eastern corner and northern facade facing Nanjing Road (*bottom left*) and the eastern elevation (*right*).

concrete with brick walls on a ribbed reinforced concrete raft 164 feet by 174 feet and 4.5 foot 6 inches below street level. The fire escapes were deliberately inside the building rather than having 'unsightly' metal stairways on the exterior of the building. The exterior was finished in artificial granite, which was arranged on the facade in vertical panels and pilasters to bear unobtrusively the Chinese characters for Wing On and a list of what they sold to avoid 'the usual haphazard plastering of characters all over the front and consequent disfigurement'. As was a customary requirement among Chinese businesses on Nanjing Road, the exterior was finished with a resplendent display of electric lights which proved to be 'no small item in the cost'.[38]

the Town Hall, Nanjing Road west of Henan Road was entirely Chinese in character, its endless rows of open shop fronts ablaze with bright lights, gaudy colours and frantic activity. Every shop vied to surpass its neighbour, with their fronts presenting fantastic concoctions of extravagant carved wooden ornamentation gilded in gold leaf, lit by coloured electric lanterns and adorned with streamers and banners. Nowhere did a street use colour so liberally, sustained at night by 'coloured electric sky signs' unsurpassed 'in brilliance and intricacy of design'. Nanjing Road was among the first to nurture 'the Chinese delight in brilliant light',[37] which has today become synonymous with Asian urban centres.

Two unprecedented buildings vied for supremacy on Nanjing Road in the late 1910s. Wing On and Sincere department stores (G5) and their associated modern class of hotel, massive, ostentatious and the first of their kind in China, marked the beginning of a retail and hotel revolution

in Shanghai. Wing On was designed by the eminent architectural firm Palmer & Turner, who later dominated the architectural field in Shanghai, while Sincere was designed by Lester, Johnson & Morris. Henry Lester was born in England in 1840 and arrived in Shanghai in 1867, where he found work with the Municipal Council and in real estate. In 1913, three years before he retired, he joined George A Johnson and Gordon Morris to form the architectural firm Lester, Johnson & Morris. The firm continued after his retirement, designing, most significantly, the North-China Daily News Building (1924), Shandong Road Hospital (1932), the Lester School (1932) and the Lester Institute of Technical Education (1934).

The intersection of Nanjing and Zhejiang Roads in the heart of the Chinese community and theatre district had been carefully selected by the owners and provided an ideal site on which these two architectural firms could design these landmark department stores. The recent construction of the

tramway in Shanghai made this the city's busiest intersection with an estimated 200,000 people passing every day in the years before the stores opened. No site had greater retail potential. Facing one another across Nanjing Road, these two mega-stores marched into business.

Not far from these two giants was another innovation in building type that became one of Shanghai's primary leisure institutions. The fusion of various Western and Chinese amusement buildings such as theatres and teahouses had evolved into a form of Chinese entertainment complex originating in the Chinese theatre, which was common either as an independent building or as part of a teahouse where performances provided complementary entertainment. The Chinese theatre synthesised with Western theatre, well established in Shanghai for many years, and assumed various manifestations in which traditional Chinese theatres replaced their square stages with semicircular stages lit from above.

The Xin Wu Tai (The New Stage), built in 1908, was the first Chinese theatre to adopt this Western model, though many others followed suit. Socially, this served as a modern adaptation of the teahouse, where people could spend a day chatting, eating and drinking, and functioned also as a venue for Chinese theatrical performances in a contemporary Western setting.

This theatre concept evolved further when in 1913 the New Stage relocated to the corner of Zhejiang and Hubei Roads in the heart of the Chinese quarter, and was renamed Lou Wai Lou (Building Beyond the Buildings). Financed by Huang Chu Jiu, a pharmaceutical mogul and renowned businessman, the two-storeyed building was constructed in reinforced concrete and comprised a theatre on the ground and first floors, called the Xin Xin Wu Tai (the New New Stage), and a roof-top garden with open-air cinema. The building type, where a number of forms of entertainment

Top left Nanjing Road in the 21st century, pedestrianised and just as busy and colourful as it always has been. Note the tower on Sun Sun (top left) has been removed

Above left Nanjing Road at night, still retaining its characteristic spectacularly illuminated signage

Above The recently refurbished former Wing On and Sincere Department Stores

Sincere Department Store

On the north side of Nanjing Road stood the Sincere Department Store, opened in October 1917. Comprising four buildings on one block joined by overhead bridges, this development occupied approximately 340 feet on Nanjing Road and 240 feet on Zhejiang Road. Designed in an 'English Renaissance' style, the southwest corner of the block, with a 150 foot frontage to Nanking Road, was divided into two parts, one occupied by the four-storeyed Sincere Store, the other occupied by a hotel five storeys high. Like the Great Eastern Hotel, the Sincere's Oriental Hotel was designed to provide for Chinese 'accustomed to foreign manners and customs'.[39] The hotel's ground floor was occupied by a lounge, with

bedrooms on the upper four floors and a tea garden on the roof. The second building, five storeys high, on the junction of Nanjing and Zhejiang Roads, was entered via a large teashop and foreign shops occupied the remainder of the ground floor. Sincere succeeded with a corner tower where Wing On failed, building a 150 foot high tower on the corner of Nanjing and Zhejiang Roads. The remaining two buildings were located behind the first two, and provided three floors of shops and a roof garden with an open-air cinema in one building, while the other building had four floors for Chinese shops and the Sincere staff.

Above The former Sincere Store (looking west) before renovation in 2005

Left The Nanjing Road facade of Sincere Store in the 1920s

Below An artist's impression of Sincere from the 1930s

were housed under one roof, represented a radical development in China inspired by Western forms of entertainment complexes. Commercially it was a triumph. On the success of this first venture, Huang sold it and built the 'New World' on the corner of Nanjing and Tibet Roads (G5). Regarded as the 'Earl's Court' or 'Crystal Palace' of Shanghai, the New World was designed by Atkinson & Dallas and had two wings, one completed in 1914, the other in 1916. Inside was 'an amazing agglomeration of halls, theatres, menageries, distorting glasses, refreshment rooms … roof gardens on different levels where hundreds of people drink tea and eat and there is always something new. Changing China is indeed seen here; and the crowd is sober, good natured and happy!'⁴⁰ Another first for China was the subway dug under Nanjing Road to provide access to the building.

The instant success of the New World proved insufficient to Huang, who sold it to build the 'Great World' (G5). Designed by Zhou Hui Nan, considered to be Shanghai's first Chinese architect, the building opened in 1917 and occupied the southeast corner of Tibet Road and King Edward VII Avenue. It became one of Shanghai's great institutions, providing the Chinese public with a cheap and unsurpassed amusement venue. Replete with every conceivable form of entertainment, the Great World housed commercial stalls, a miniature racecourse, roller-skating rink, aviary (with a resident tiger!), 50 foot big wheel, aerial runway, a free cinema, Chinese garden and goldfish pond, and a newspaper press. The building also contained Shanghai's largest theatre, seating 5,000, and providing free performances, until it was discovered that coolies used to turn up before the show and settle into the prime seats for the entire night's performances. Every weekday 8,000 people would visit the Great World, increasing to 10,000 at the weekend and over 40,000 on public holidays.

The central area

'Demolition of old buildings and the erection of new premises going on all over the Foreign Settlements'⁴¹ defined the prosperity in the Chinese area of the International Settlement during the Great War period, but the previous boom in the early 1900s heralded the most conspicuous development in the emerging Central District, east of Henan Road. Despite land values increasing by 1,000 per cent since the 1890s, this area started to resemble the downtown of any modern city in Europe or America, and was predicted to extend beyond Henan Road by the mid-1920s. The three- or four-storeyed structures 'towering to the skies'⁴² in this district represented a 'complete revolution'⁴³ from previous commercial structures in this area, using the latest materials and technologies, employing modern spatial configurations and usually decorated externally 'in a monotonous fashion'⁴⁴ with terracotta brick and ornamentation and Ningbo mottled agglomerate – once described collectively and disparagingly

The Great World

The Great World was built in March 1917 in time for opening on the day of the French National Fete and occupied 2.5 acres of land. The land could not be bought outright, since it was leased for 25 years. The building was two storeys high with three roof gardens and a two-storey tower above a main entrance at the corner of the site. The ground floor, arranged in galleries, contained small market stalls and two courtyards, one housing the aviary, the other incorporating the small racecourse and roller-skating rink.

Above The Great World

as the 'Shanghai Renaissance' style. The three-storey offices of the trading house, Gibb, Livingston & Co located behind the site of their former offices on the Bund, the five-storey Kahlee Hotel (H5) or the neighbouring offices of Carlowitz & Co (H5) (1898), opposite Holy Trinity Cathedral, were among the first of this type, the latter being for some time the largest building in the Settlement. Offices or shops usually occupied the ground and first floors and accommodation for foreign staff occupied the upper floors. Native staff and servants' accommodation was usually confined to the attic.

On the opposite side of the Cathedral, construction of the new **Municipal Council offices** (H5) started in 1914, after they had outgrown the Town Hall on Nanjing Road. The Municipal Council's architect, Robert Charles Turner (1875–1950), presented a number of proposals for a site on the corner of Jiangxi and Fuzhou Roads. Turner started his professional training in 1892 and became a Licentiate of the RIBA in 1911. During his time as the city architect for the

Municipal Council (1904–25), he designed many buildings, including police and fire stations and the public swimming pool. He retired in 1925 and became a Fellow of the RIBA the following year. The council's choice of design for their new offices was sent to the president of the RIBA in London for a review, the result of which suggested the building should be completed in granite rather than artificial stone. The site, occupied by offices and Chinese houses, was cleared and the new council offices were erected in reinforced concrete and Suzhou granite, and officially opened on 16 November 1922. They were later claimed to have 'symbolized the growth of the Settlement and mirrored the confidence of the residents in the future of their fast-risen city'.⁴⁵ The style of the building has been described as 'English classic Renaissance', a style that according to Darwent's 1912 guide was 'unsurpassed for dignity, strength and beauty' and which was used for most buildings of this period in this district. The four-storey building contained the new Town Hall, department offices,

Below The corner of Henan and Nanjing Roads in the early 20th century

Far left Office of Mitsubishi, designed by a Japanese architect

Left The Kahlee Hotel (now demolished)

Below A richy decorated downtown doorway

Far left and left Former offices of Gibb, Livingston & Co in 2005 (**far left**) and in the 1910s (**left**)

Below The former Carlowitz Building

council committee rooms and the headquarters for the Shanghai Volunteer Corps and their drill hall. The original design intended a 158 foot tower to stand above the main entrance, but the poor soil proved too yielding. After tests showed the structure to sink 18 inches, it was decided that it could not bear such a weight. The main entrance was located on the corner of Hankou and Jiangxi Roads, outside Trinity Cathedral. A second entrance was located on the junction of Jiangxi and Fuzhou Roads and was composed of a large convex arc. This presented the opportunity for the creation of a formal circus at this junction, a prospect that was later realised when the remaining three sides of the junction were developed in the 1930s.

Behind this building, on Henan Road, was the **Central Police Station**, 'a dignified building of red brick in the Early Renaissance style erected during 1891–94 from competitive designs', with the project awarded to TW Kingsmill and B Atkinson. This architectural partnership presented an important linkage in Shanghai's architectural history. Thomas Kingsmill was among the first professionally trained architects to work in Shanghai and was joined by Atkinson, who became his assistant and went independent the year the Central Police Station was finished.

Next to the Central Police Station stood the **Central Fire Station**, built in 1902, a four-storey Renaissance style building of red brick, Ningbo green stone dressings and Suzhou granite lintels. Their imaginative motto above the entrance read 'We Fight the Flames', but nothing could combat the station's dangerous list causing it to lean towards the Council offices after they were built. A quirk of Shanghai's malleable soil acted like a giant weighing scales –

the weight of a heavy building beside a lighter structure caused the latter to lean amorously towards the former. The Council Health Department, designed in a similar style, was built in the same year adjacent to the Fire Station.

One of the most prominent buildings in this district was the **China Mutual Life Assurance Co** building (H5), the new headquarters of which, designed in an English Renaissance style by Atkinson & Dallas and proudly just 'a stone's throw from the Bund', was claimed to be 'one of the most attractive buildings in Shanghai' and housed an extraordinarily lavish interior.

Nearby, the four-storey 'solid and satisfying' **North China Insurance Company** building (H5), built in 1916 on the southeast junction of Jiujiang and Sichuan Roads and designed by RE Stewardson, is another typical example of a building of this period in this district.

China Mutual Life Assurance Co

Above Celebrating the coronation of King George V

Above right The glass dome that once adorned the main hall

Below One of several stained-glass windows that miraculously survived the Cultural Revolution

The building stands at the junction of Guangdong and Sichuan Roads on the site of the former German Club. Above the curved entrance were the white marble statues of Prudence and Abundance, which have since been removed. The exterior conforms to the Ionic order, with a rusticated first floor containing large round-arched windows, above which bold columns support a weighty cornice giving the overall impression of 'solidity'. Hammer-dressed Qingdao granite has been used throughout the exterior walls, contrasting with the polished two-storey columns. No expense has been spared on the interior. Inside the main entrance, the vestibule has been designed to dumbfound the visitor. The walls are made of marble, encrusted in the Italian style and decorated with moulded architraves, cornice arches, caps and bases in white statuary marble. The flat-domed ceiling, inlaid with Salviati gold mosaic, and detached columns are in transparent green Mexican onyx, protruding from sunken panels of Paonazzo marble, while the marble floor has been finished in a geometric design. Two 'exquisite carvings in high relief in white Carrara

marble, having for their subjects the "Three Fates" and "Relieving the Aged", occupy the spaces over the main doorways'. Inside the main hall, 18 columns of red marble standing on white statuary marble bases support the roof, which once contained a central stained-glass dome made of 16 panels representing the virtues: truth, wisdom, prudence, courage, prosperity, knowledge, perseverance, mercy, justice, discretion, hope, charity, faith, fortitude, peace and industry(146). The building's interior was lined entirely with Burmese teak and 'replete with every detail tending towards efficient administration.'[47] Miraculously, the splendid interior of the vestibule, having been boxed in – perhaps deliberately – by its former owners, survived the Cultural Revolution. It has since been restored.

Above The exquisitely decorated vestibule shortly after completion

Above An artist's impression of the China Mutual Life Assurance Co

Right The former North China Insurance Company building

Far right The new premises of the distinguished Whiteaway, Laidlaw & Co

The Insurance Company occupied the ground floor, accessed by a main entrance on the corner of the building. The upper floors contained further office space, access to which was provided by a separate entrance on Sichuan Road. The exterior was constructed entirely of granite, which was rusticated on the corner and part of the principal elevations, the remaining recessed portion comprising eight 40 foot Corinthian columns supporting the dentilled entablature and third floor, on top of which two floors have since been added. As was the norm at the time, 'due regard given to the sanitary arrangements' meant that foreigners and Chinese used separate lavatories.[48]

This area contained not only offices but also higher-class shops and retail outlets. Shanghai's first department stores, Huiluo (Whiteaway, Laidlaw & Co Ltd), designed by Walter Scott, Fuhlee (Hall and Holtz), and Lane Crawford, stocked a wide range of international brands. Walter Scott (1860–1917) was another of Shanghai's renowned architects of the period and an Associate of the RIBA from 1883. Born in India and educated in England, Scott qualified as an architect in 1882 and studied further at University College, London. He arrived in Shanghai in 1889 and worked as an assistant to Morrison & Gratton, which became Morrison, Gratton & Scott from 1899 to 1902. In 1902, he left to join WJB Carter and formed Scott & Carter before going independent after Carter died in 1907. Their last major project together was the Palace Hotel on the Bund (see page 105). Behind the Palace Hotel on Nanjing Road was the Fuhlee department store, a unique building, not just in terms of building type, but also for its use of firewalls throughout. Fire had always been a major problem in Shanghai, particularly in the dense Chinese neighbourhoods where myriad terraces of low-cost housing were constructed predominantly from wood. Following a major fire in Fuhlee, the renowned establishment was extensively redeveloped in 1904 and fitted with a firewall between the 'drapery and provision departments', as well as ten automatic fire doors throughout the three-storey building. The store contained a furnishings department, brasswork room, tailor's, a shipping office and a printing office. The whole building was panelled in cedar with fire-resistant floors made of 2 inch thick Australian oak laid in a herringbone pattern. The exterior was designed in a 'classic style', using carved green Ningbo stone and with an entrance in the centre of the Nanjing Road facade.

The Bund

While these multistoreyed piles, many of which were faced with conspicuous red brick, abutted the narrow streets behind the Bund, they did not compare to the larger solid granite structures posturing along the river front. If all the world is a stage, Shanghai's Bund provided front row seats where the business and social elite busily jostled for position in order to be as much a part of the performance as a witness to its unfolding. Always more blustering and giving an 'impression of majesty',[49] the Bund's Neoclassical and 'British Renaissance' facades were designed to boast of status, projecting the outward pretensions of civic pride, while inwardly coveting unbridled wealth.

Few institutions were better at or more proud of boasting than the **Shanghai Club** (H5). The vilified former home of this club was once described as 'execrable'[50] architecture in 'the true debased and carpenteresque style'[51], but the new building was lauded, like the 'extravagant' furniture of its former home which was reportedly the 'finest found anywhere in the East', as being 'without exception the most imposing club house in the Far East'.[52] At No 3 the Bund, the new building, on the same site as the previous club, was designed by BH Tarrand and opened on 6 January 1910 by Sir Pelham Warren. The building's sober exterior belied the intoxicated constitution of the members inside, who forbade women or Chinese in the club unless serving their needs. Forming the epicentre of British society in Shanghai, it embodied the worst traits of empire: discrimination, egotism

Left The original premises of Lane Crawford on Nanjing Road from the 1860s

Below The Bund in June 1911. Note the decoration to celebrate the Coronation of George V

Shanghai Club

Costing Tls 600,000 and weighing 17,000 tons, the five-storey Shanghai Club was among the first buildings in Shanghai to use reinforced concrete. The 'English Renaissance' design, including a facade of artificial stone and columns of Suzhou granite, was chosen from an open competition, but Tarrand died before the building was finished. AG Bray, who was responsible for the 'sumptuous' interior, finished the work. Access was provided by a flight of wide granite steps from the street into the main entrance, in the centre of the symmetrical facade. Owing to Shanghai's notorious soil, these steps have long since disappeared into the mud and now the street is higher than the front door. Inside the main entrance was the Grand Hall (90 feet by 39 feet and 41 feet high), with its black and white marble floor and a fine barrelled ceiling of glass held up by 17 foot high Ionic columns that supported entablatures and arches surmounted by a heavy dentilled cornice. To the south of the hall was the renowned 'longest bar in the world' (110 feet by 39 feet), designed in a Jacobean style of panelled oak and serving as an accurate but strict barometer of Shanghai's social hierarchy – the nearer to the front of the building a member could sit, the higher his status. Also on the ground floor were the medieval-styled billiard room with oak-panelled walls, raftered ceiling and leaded windows, a reading room in the Adam style, a smoking room and news room, waiting rooms, and a domino room. A stairway of Sicilian marble provided access from the Grand Hall to a balcony on the first floor and 'one of the most splendidly appointed dining rooms in Shanghai'.[53] Overlooking the Whuangpu, this red teak-lined dining room (102 feet by 43 feet) was watched over by the portraits of King Edward and Queen Alexandra that overhung a grand fireplace at each end of the room. The very latest in modern conveniences and luxury was provided by 1,000 electrical lights (among the first interior electrical lights in Shanghai), 100 steam radiators, and five electric service lifts delivering food from the kitchens on the top floor. Also on the first floor were three other dining rooms, a card room, a library, a second oak-panelled billiard room and another reading room, while 40 en-suite bedrooms occupied the second and third floors. The basement housed a bowling alley, barber's shops, dressing rooms, cold storage rooms and a wine cellar.

Left The Shanghai Club in the 1940s
Below An artist's impression of the new Shanghai Club, opened in 1910

and a rabid arrogance, providing a fitting mainstay among Shanghai's social institutions.

Only the German community's **Club Concordia**, 'one of the most handsome structures on the Bund',[54] rivalled the Shanghai Club's overt extravagance with its idiosyncratic 'German Renaissance' style and 'graceful corner tower' making it a 'decided addition to the architectural beauty of the city'.[55] An open competition to design the Club Concordia had been won by H Becker, later of Becker & Baedecker, one of the few non-English architects in Shanghai at the time. Becker was a graduate of Munich University and worked in Egypt for five years before arriving in Shanghai in 1899. In 1905, he joined C Baedecker and together they designed many buildings in China, including many residences along Bubbling Well Road and Avenue Paul Brunat and the nearby German Post Office in 1905. The Club Concordia's foundation stone was laid by Prince Albert of Prussia on 22 October 1904 in the presence of the entire German colony of Shanghai. It opened in February 1907. Unfortunately for those attending the ceremony, their tenancy on this prestigious site was not to last long, as Germany and Austria's role in the First World War caused their expulsion from Shanghai and the seizure by China of all their assets. The building was later bought by the Bank of China and demolished in the 1930s.

Left and below The former Club Concordia

Right The former German Post Office

Below The former Central Hotel (right) and The Chartered Bank (left)

The land was purchased for Tls 225,000 and with a 98 foot frontage on the Bund and a depth of 166 feet, and renowned for its exquisite stained glass, the Club Concordia matched the Shanghai Club for its facilities and surpassed most buildings for its elaborate interior. It was decorated in rich terracotta shades with green and ivory, carved wood and stonework with fountains and murals of Berlin and Bremen in the bar. Facilities included a large bar and refreshment room, billiard rooms, reading rooms, a dining hall on the first floor overlooking the Whuangpu with murals of Berlin, Vienna and Munich on the facing wall, a library, meeting rooms, and even 'a fine modern sanitary toilet room'.[56] Bedrooms for members and their guests were located on the top floor.

In the centre of the Bund, on the south corner of Nanjing Road, the Central Hotel, formerly the Victoria Hotel, had occupied one of the Settlement's prime locations for many years. By the turn of the century, it was obvious that the site could easily support a larger business. In its place, the new six-storey **Palace Hotel** (H5) designed by Scott & Carter and built by the contractors Wong Fah Ki, had its foundation stone laid at noon on 21 January 1905 and became the largest building in the Settlement at the time, providing the very highest standards in hotel accommodation. Its roof garden was renowned for being the most refreshing place in Shanghai to enjoy a revitalising drink on a blistering summer's afternoon, despite its lacklustre white tiling giving it the appearance of a 'disused lavatory'.[57]

Clubs and hotels were the rare exceptions to occupy sites along Shanghai's most expensive street. The big earners such as banks, insurance companies and trading houses could more easily afford the exorbitant price tag of these exclusive plots. Since new structures had to reflect the prestige of their prime location, old diminutive buildings were pulled down and the original small plots along the Bund were amalgamated or spacious gardens were built on to accommodate more imposing structures. In 1913–16, the 'Renaissance styled' **McBain Building (Asia Petroleum Company)** (H5) was built on No 1 the Bund, overshadowing its neighbour, the Shanghai Club. The massive structure was seven storeys high, containing 180 rooms for offices and apartments, and was designed by Robert Moorhead of Moorhead & Halse. A Swiss civil engineer, Emil Luthy, who specialised in reinforced concrete construction and went on to open his own office in Shanghai in 1926, supervised the construction. The building's owner, George McBain, was an English businessman who arrived in Shanghai in 1870 and established his own trading company in 1879 with an office at No 1 the French Bund, and became a member of the French Municipal Council on which he served for six years. In 1899, he bought the plot at No 1 The Bund, previously owned by Hogg Bros, and demolished the existing building to make way for the new offices. The building was later

The Palace Hotel

The Palace Hotel was constructed in two parts so that business could start once the first portion was complete in 1907. The site was long and narrow, with the longest side running 290 feet along Nanjing Road and with the main entrance in its centre. Also on the ground floor were six shops with five show windows, setting a trend for modern display windows in Shanghai. To maximise internal space, the building was tall for the number of storeys, with six storeys accounting for the 90 feet height from the pavement to the eaves. The building also had a basement and a roof garden. From the reception area, a staircase and two passenger elevators (among the first to be used in China) led to the bar, billiard rooms, the 3,000 square foot restaurant on the top floor overlooking the whole of Shanghai and the 110 private rooms, all of which had en-suite bathrooms 'with every modern convenience'. All the public rooms were partially panelled in teak. The building's exterior was designed in the 'Victorian Renaissance' style, and built using 'a judicious choice' of local materials, including Ningbo stone and terracotta brick, providing colour to the exterior.

Above An artist's impression of the Palace Hotel

Right The Palace Hotel in 2005

Right The former China Telegraph Building on the Bund

Far Right An artist's impression of the Russo-Chinese Bank

rented to the Asia Petroleum Company and an extra storey was added in 1919.

Other early 20th-century structures along the Bund were the offices of the **Oriental Bank** (1911–14), the **China Telegraph** building, and the **Union Assurance Company of Canton Limited** on the corner of the Bund and Guangdong Road. Commissioned in 1913, the Union Assurance

Company building was designed by Palmer & Turner. It was the first office building in Shanghai to use a steel frame, though various steel structures predated it such as the 1898 Public Market behind the Town Hall, various bridges across Suzhou Creek and the Yang Jin Bang, and several factories. These important milestones reflected also the growth of the city's steel manufacturing industry. Companies such as the

Right The former McBain Building

Shanghai Dock & Engineering Company were able to satisfy the building industry's structural and decorative requirements and were involved in the construction of many of Shanghai's later buildings. Although the steel frame represented a major development in construction in Shanghai, the engineering principles behind it mirrored Chinese building practice, which for millennia had erected buildings using a load-bearing wooden frame. Therefore, with the advent of the steel frame, Western theory, rather than making an evolutionary leap, had actually moved closer to ancient Eastern construction methods.

The site of the **Union Assurance Company** building (H5) was formerly owned by Dodwell & Co Ltd, next to the Shanghai Club, and had a 100 foot frontage on the Bund and a 240 foot frontage on Guangdong Road. The six-storey structure was 105 foot high from the ground to the top of the sixth floor and 150 foot to the top of the 'golden argosy' that once formed a weather vane on top of the cupola and square tower. Designed in a Renaissance style, the building's lightness and verticality expressed through the soaring lines and tall windows hinted at the steel skeletal structure. One entrance was at the corner of the building, but the main entrance occupied the centre of the Guangdong Road facade. The building's steel frame was infilled with brick and reinforced concrete and the exterior was faced in stone. The first three floors were designed for offices, with the ground floor intended for a bank, offering Shanghai's largest single office space without supporting walls. The fourth and fifth floors contained residential flats.

Steel was not the only material to provide innovations in construction techniques in Shanghai at this time. Reinforced concrete was widely used from the early 1900s, following the emergence of concrete manufacturing in Shanghai from the 1890s. Shanghai's first factory for the production of concrete was opened in 1890, supplying the city with concrete pipes for drainage and, later, sewers, as well as for such purposes as the construction of floors, pavements and roads. One of the first buildings in Shanghai to use concrete and steel in its construction is the 1902 squat 'Greek renaissance' former **Russo-Chinese Bank** (H5), established to finance and administer the expansion of the Russian railways in northern and eastern China, which began in the late 19th century. Despite being 'too short for the breadth',[58] the building was the first major job for Becker, who designed it with R Steel of Yokohama. Once described as being all that a bank should be, 'massiveness and beauty blended',[59] it remains one of the oldest buildings on the Bund and was among the first in Shanghai to use elevators. While the first reinforced concrete building on the Bund was the Shanghai Club, the first in Shanghai was the **Shanghai Mutual Telephone Company** building (H5), built in 1908 and designed by Davies & Thomas, a prominent architectural firm founded originally by Gilbert Davies in 1896 before Thomas joined in

1899. The firm designed many Shanghai residences and other larger buildings, including the offices of Butterfield & Swire, 'one of the most handsome structures on the French Bund'.[60]

The advent of reinforced concrete heralded a new era of larger, taller structures. These presented considerable problems because of Shanghai's infamously boggy soil, which was unable to support the heavy loads imposed by

such buildings, causing 'the architect and engineer a few
sleepless nights'.[61] One structure that illustrates this problem is
the **Yangtse Insurance Association** building (H5), at the north
end of the Bund. The Yangtse Insurance Company was started
in 1862 by the American firm Russell & Co to insure the hulls
and cargoes of ships and became one of the major insurance
companies in Shanghai. The headquarters, designed by Palmer
& Turner and constructed in 1918, are listing quite severely.

Characteristic of many Bund plots, the Yangtse Insurance
Association occupied a site with a narrow frontage of 50 feet,
but a considerable depth of 117 feet. To exploit the relatively
small site, the building was designed to be seven storeys and
115 foot tall. The ground floor was leased to a bank, while
the insurance company occupied the first floor and rented
out the second, third and fourth floors. Lavish apartments
occupied the top two floors, above which was a roof garden.
The facade was faced entirely in granite, with the exception
of the marble entrance, and the entire structure was
constructed on a concrete raft.

The gleaming face of the Bund, the 'redeeming feature of a town otherwise devoid of beauty',[62] with its regimented buildings resembling a toothy grin appears a century later like an aged gawk, crooked, soiled and sunken as its buildings list and descend slowly into thousands of years of saturated alluvial deposits. The Municipal Council conducted various studies throughout the 20th century to determine the depth of mud on which Shanghai stands. Samples from as far down as 900 foot showed no signs of bedrock, so with nothing but mud for hundreds of foot below the city, engineers devised a solution whereby buildings were constructed on reinforced concrete rafts, allowing them to float. Rafts were first employed on the Bund when it was believed that six storeys was the city's height limit. Sidney Powell, a local expert on the matter claimed: 'Shanghai can only stand six floors, London sixty floors, New York and Hong Kong any number'. Consequently, Powell believed the land value to have peaked, as the soil 'will only bear a weight of three quarters of a ton per square foot'.[63] As technologies improved and rafts were

introduced, the number of floors increased and land values rose. The raft was designed to spread the weight evenly over the site, while piles were sunk into the soil to prevent subsidence by increasing the friction between their surface and the mud. To counter settling, buildings were routinely constructed 1 foot higher than their anticipated level, pleasing the engineers of the day with their ingenuity, but today the semi-submerged buildings along the Bund reveal the failure of the calculations to account for the duration of the building.

Among the first buildings to use a raft was the **Banque de l'Indo Chine** (14), built by contractors Chang Yi Zung and designed by Atkinson & Dallas, and formally opened on 13 June 1914.

The building's symmetrical Renaissance facade was faced in Suzhou granite to a height of 23 feet and thereafter artificial stone to the roof. The ground floor was finished in rusticated granite, as were the corners of the building facing the Bund. The centre portion had two Qingdao polished granite pilasters and two polished three-quarter Qingdao granite columns between the windows and extending two storeys to the cornice, topped with Ionic caps and entablature in the same order. The windows in the centre of the main elevation had detached columns, entablature and cornice in Doric order with a small balustrade forming a balcony. The name of the bank was incised into the central architrave and gilded over, above which a balustrade to the flat roof was flanked by copings in the form of carved swags and shields. The side elevations were in exactly the same style as the main elevation, but finished in artificial stone. In the centre of the building, detached polished Qingdao granite columns stood astride the main entrance, which comprised a massive teak door with elaborate wrought iron gates. Inside the entrance, the manager and deputy manager's offices were to the right and left, with the main 4,290 square foot banking hall in the centre of the building, above which was a glass dome

supported by six Ionic columns. The entire building was fitted out in teak, including all the column surrounds and parquet flooring. The first and second floors were reserved for accommodation for foreign staff, while native staff lived in detached units behind the building. The structure was built on a 2 foot 6 inch thick concrete raft, though the ground floor once stood 4 feet above street level, accessed by a marble staircase.

The Public Garden

Innovations and rapid development in building coincided with gradual improvements in the public realm. Whether their existence was the result of a genuine urge to cater for the public's needs or of a selfish desire to enhance the environment around the properties of the city's most influential land renters, the Bund foreshore and the Public Garden opposite the British Consulate were Shanghai's most treasured public spaces (14). For this, the population of Shanghai should thank the Taotai of the 1840s, whose insistence on preserving the sanctity of the ancient towpath along the Whuangpu safeguarded the foreshore of the former British Settlement from the type of maritime development that deprived the French Concession and the former American Settlement of a river frontage. However, although the foreshore was conserved, it was many years before the Bund resembled anything like an attractive park or promenade;

instead, it was a place to dump refuse and sewage. During the giddy years of the early 1860s, a plan was devised to widen the Bund to the low-water mark. This substantial extension would have provided an 8 foot pavement behind a 30 foot wide thoroughfare and a 30 foot public park overlooking the river, but such public-mindedness manifest in this 'delightful vision' was quickly curtailed by 'the stern necessity for retrenchment'[64] among Shanghai's benefactors. Incremental improvements continued until 1919 when the growing volume of traffic on this, one of the 'most interesting, famous and handsome thoroughfares in the world',[65] forced the issue. Some 35 feet of the Whuangpu were reclaimed to allow

Right Plans for the extension of the Public Garden

Below Plans for the improvement and widening of the Bund, 1919–20

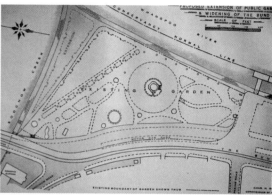

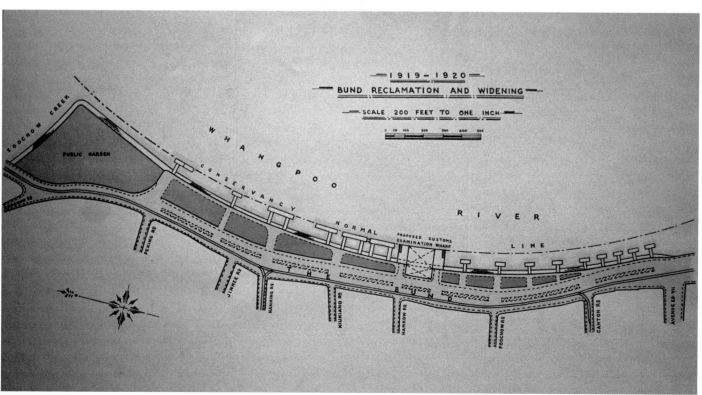

the road to be widened from 85 feet to 115 feet, while extensive landscaping beautified the foreshore.

At the Bund's northern end, there remained an equally unfulfilled opportunity for improvements in the foreshore, which petered out unexceptionally at Suzhou Creek. This prime location once accommodated the fort from which the British were fired upon when they invaded Shanghai, but after many years of wrangling it was incorporated into the British Consulate site, the abandoned foreshore becoming known as 'the Consular Flats'. A few metres from the shoreline, a boat wreck accumulating silt had created an artificial island, and suggestions were made to consolidate this islet with the mainland and turn it into a public park. In 1864, the British Consulate agreed to donate its foreshore to the public on the understanding that if it ever ceased to be a public space, ownership would revert to the consulate. These events gave rise to the birth of Shanghai's **Public Garden**, elevated from the waterline by mud dredged from the Yang Jin Bang and gifted to the Municipal Council on 8 April 1868. However, the park's position at the junction of the Whuangpu and Suzhou Creek caused considerable problems with the two waterways, particularly Suzhou Creek. This creek, and the Whuangpu from this junction to the sea, once formed the Woosung River, but over time the Whuangpu had grown and the creek had shrunk. The construction of the Public Garden, on the southern corner where these two waterways meet, directed the water leaving the creek southwards. Since this was upstream of the Whuangpu, it prevented the free entrance of flood tides and the free exit of ebb tides, and caused treacherous currents. In 1905, a solution was devised whereby the gardens would be extended to the north and east, to force the direction of Suzhou Creek downstream of the Whuangpu. This coincided with the need to reduce the park along its western edge to enlarge the Bund by 60 feet in June of the same year. Five and a half mow of land were added to the Public Garden from 40,000 tons of mud excavated from bunding works in front of the German Consulate in Hongkou, on the opposite banks of Suzhou Creek. The mud was carried over Garden Bridge at night to complete 'one of the greatest improvements carried out in Shanghai for some years'.[66]

The Public Garden attempted to represent the quintessence of conviviality. This exclusive patch of foreign soil was the Municipal Council's answer to a metropolitan park, and, like Shanghai's other paltry parks, it provided a segregated environment where Shanghailanders could revel in their own company until 1928, before which the 'miserable and vicious looking'[67] Chinese were 'rigorously excluded'[68] from this 'parody of a garden'.[69] Chinese nannies were allowed access to the Public Garden and a small strip of land nearby on the south bank of Suzhou Creek served as a Chinese Garden (H4), though it was hardly revered. In 1910, the Shanghai Volunteer Corps requested it to be converted

into their drill hall, but the council dropped the plan. Shanghai, while boasting parallels with the great cities of Europe and America, could not have been less comparable on the point of open spaces. While European cities engendered public spaces such as Paris's Place de la Concorde and Rome's famous piazzas, Shanghai had none. Its land was too precious to waste on public enjoyment. 'Nowhere a fine avenue, spacious park, an imposing central square. Nowhere anything civic at all.'[70] The French Park offered more spacious surroundings, but was still woefully inadequate for the size and needs of the city. While New Yorkers could relax in 843 acres of Central Park and Londoners revelled in 630 acres of Hyde Park, Shanghailanders rubbed shoulders in the single acre Public Garden – its vapidity matched only by its title. Nonetheless, they made the most of what they had and built a bandstand in the centre of the park, which made 'an infernal racket'[71] every evening to entertain the city's social elite and convince them, at least for a few short hours, that they were somewhere else. The collective composition of foreshore and Public Garden reinforced the Occidental's absurdly blinkered feeling of ascendancy, as Ricalton states:

> As we pass along we are amazed at the evidences of up-to-date conditions – well-paved streets, magnificent modern buildings, street lamps, electric lights, public gardens with music stands. We can scarcely realize we are in the land of the Chinaman … The buildings are not Chinese; well-paved streets lined with

Enlarging the Public Garden by reclaiming land from the junction of the Whuangpu River and Souzhou Creek: before, in 1905 (**left**) and after, in 1906 (**below**).

Above The Public Garden

Below The first Garden Bridge, with drawbridge

strained one. For a long time after the British arrived, there was no bridge over Suzhou Creek at this point. The residents of Hongkou, mostly American at the time, relied on a ferry to take them across the creek. In October 1856 two men by the names of Wills and Cunningham constructed the first foreign bridge across Suzhou Creek, which became known as Wills' Bridge. Made entirely in wood, the 394 foot long and 26 foot wide structure had a 'draw' near the Hongkou side to allow larger boats to pass and was open to anyone who could pay the small toll, a 'thing hateful to the Shanghai public'. The bridge was replaced in 1871 by one of iron, which collapsed before it was completed due to the nature of Shanghai's infamously sodden soil, described in 1906 by Thomas Kingsmill as 'a water-logged, highly micaceous sand of extreme fineness and of alluvial deposit and generally under pressure with no more consistency than a quicksand'.[72] Others believed that the collapse of the bridge was caused by the instability of its pillars, which were standing on the boats and bodies of countless refugees that had sunk and drowned in the creek after a huge storm during the Taiping Rebellion.

Following the bridge's collapse, a wooden bridge designed by Farnham was built in 1873 and purchased by the Municipal Council as a free bridge. Despite being widened in 1890, it had outlived its usefulness by the early 20th century. The bridge's age and the advent of trams and motorcars in Shanghai necessitated a larger structure. Though the demolition of this historic structure was 'regretted by many', in 1905 invitations for tenders requested specifications for a steel bridge lasting 40 years or a wooden bridge lasting 30 years. Numerous proposals, including a wooden bridge made of Tasmanian timber and single, double and triple span

shade-trees, and the green lawns near the river, in the distance, are not Chinese; just beyond, at the end of the promenade next the water, you see a small round dome that is just within a paling that surrounds beautiful public gardens; they are not Chinese … on the riverfront, at least, little can be seen to tell you we are in China or even in the Orient.

Beside the Public Garden, straddling the former British and American Settlements, is the **Garden Bridge** (I4). The history of Shanghai's most important bridge, providing a vital link between the city centre and Hongkou, is a typically

bridges, were rejected in favour of a steel structure in two sections, each 171 feet long and 60 feet wide, 20 feet wider than the previous bridge. The bridge's utilitarian design, which minimised the horizontal thrust applied by arched structures, overcame the problems caused by the poor foundations and weak embankments, but its functional success was achieved at the cost of its appearance – perhaps, it was queried, 'an arched type would have been desirable'[73] (see pages 156 and 187). The bridge was designed by Howarth Erskine Ltd of Singapore, whose employees started construction on 4 August 1906. When it was formally opened on 20 January 1908, it was the 'most substantial structure in China',[74] providing 11 feet of clearance to boats and with a 37 feet wide carriageway with cantilevered walkways either side.

Another bridge, the Zhejiang Road Bridge (G4) across Suzhou Creek was opened the following month, west of the old Lao Zha Bridge, at the end of Fujian Road. The Zhejiang Road Bridge had a span of 196 feet, a width of 40 feet, and an 11 foot clearance. The approach roads needed to be raised to a gradient of 1 in 20, thereby creating the city's steepest and highest hill. Eight years later, in May 1916, an entirely new style of bridge was built across Suzhou Creek by the United States Steel Products Company of New York and Shanghai, which had 'a substantial rigid steel structure [and] light graceful lines',[75] providing an important link between Stone Bridge Road and the suburb of Chapei, where the British army had crossed Suzhou Creek on their way to invade Shanghai in 1842.

Hongkou

Improvements in transportation and infrastructure in Hongkou and Chapei inevitably hastened the development of more affluent institutions in these formerly inferior suburbs. One of the first major buildings to take advantage of this situation and built on one of the most 'attractive and desirable sites in the city' was the **Astor House** (I4) hotel, described in its first advertisement as the 'Waldorf Astoria of the Orient' and regarded by some as 'the pride of Shanghai'. This sumptuous hotel, designed by Atkinson & Dallas, was built in 1903 and extended according to designs by Davies & Thomas in a Renaissance style. The newly refurbished hotel was opened in January 1911 and became Shanghai's premiere hotel, surpassing the Bund's Palace Hotel.

Such was the desirability of the land along the river front in Hongkou that the panoramic views afforded by the Astor House were short-lived. Having outgrown its former residence on the Bund in a building owned by the Sassoon family, the **Russian Consulate General** (I4) was opened on the banks of Suzhou Creek, in front of the Astor House, on 14 January 1917. Since land in Shanghai was limited and therefore very expensive there were often few options for countries seeking prestigious sites for their consulates. For this reason, the site for the new Russian Consulate General designed by the architect Hans E Lieb was relatively small, yet it accommodated the consular offices and the residential quarters for the consul-general, two vice-consuls and minor officials.

Astor House

With 211 rooms and seven suites on five floors, the Astor House had sweeping south-facing views of the Bund and Whuangpu, enjoyed in particular by those in the two-storey dining hall, which occupied the full length of the first and second floors. At 154 feet long and 49 feet high, the 500-capacity dining hall was among the most luxurious places to eat in Shanghai. Skirted by galleries containing serviced private rooms, the cavernous interior was lit during the day by the barrel-vaulted ceiling of glass and at night by 6,000 candle power electric lights. The hotel spared no expense in providing every modern innovation to improve the comfort of its guests. All the rooms were electrically heated in winter and cooled in summer, access to the five floors was provided by two-speed lifts designed to prevent 'the unpleasantness of violent starting and stopping', and all the clocks in the building were synchronised by the master clock in the manager's office every 30 seconds. The manager's office was located at the east end of the building, with the secretary's office on a mezzanine above. The entrance was located in the centre of the main elevation, which led directly to a grand marble staircase with red and white marble panels up to a marble dado. Terrazzo floors, provided by Messrs Stolz & Kind, were used throughout the building. The ground floor also contained ladies' cloakrooms, a reading room, a sitting room and a private buffet with a quadrant-shaped teak bar and billiard room designed by Arts & Crafts Ltd of Shanghai. The building was laid out around a quadrangle containing a hairdresser and writing rooms. As with many buildings of this period, the kitchens, sculleries and storerooms were located in the attic and connected to the dining areas by six electric service lifts.

Top The Astor House Hotel
Above An artist's impression of the Astor House Hotel

Above The barrel-vaulted glass roof of the dining hall

The Russian Consulate's compact design was the brainchild of the architect, who solved this spatial problem by placing the kitchens, storerooms and servants' quarters in the basement, contrary to the usual practice of locating these in the attic, which in this case served as accommodation for consular staff. Consular offices, a courtroom and assembly hall, the latter two handsomely decorated in teak, occupied the ground floor. The first floor, paved in Japanese marble, contained reception and living rooms, two large drawing rooms, two large dining rooms, and a study. The second and third floors contained living quarters for the consul, vice-consul and other foreign staff. Expenditure in the First World War may have been the cause of the relatively humble nature of this building. Constructed in reinforced concrete by the Chinese contractor Chow Soey Kee, the exterior was finished in chiselled concrete blocks to give the appearance of real stone, and the interior fittings were simple.

Abutting the Russian Consulate was the **German Consulate** (14). Built in 1884, this too overlooked the Bund, but the premises were confiscated in 1917 along with other German assets. Next in line was the American Consulate. The United States of America was worried about being perceived

as a second-class power because of the lowly condition of its back street consulate behind the Bund, which was 'so utterly unfit for any kind of human occupancy'[76] and contained a gaol in a 'cruel and inhuman'[77] condition. The American Association of China believed American passivity to be the cause of America's relegated position in China and in the minds of the Chinese, and acknowledged Japan's expedient use of military force to achieve its objectives during the Sino-Japanese War. The following observation predated the mainstay of American foreign policy 50 years later: 'America, the greatest commercial nation in the world, debarred by her traditional policy from asserting her position by force of arms, has wilfully deprived herself of the natural advantages derivable from her wealth.'[78] Demanding a consulate 'worthy of the dignity of the United States [that] will demonstrate to the Oriental world the best ideals of American architecture',[79] the American community in Shanghai leaned sentimentally towards relocating to the former 'American Settlement', for which they had been seeking from Congress a new site and buildings. In August 1916, they received the necessary funds to purchase a 1 acre site on the junction of Suzhou Creek and the Whuangpu, with a 250 foot river frontage directly opposite the Public Garden. Unfortunately, since the funds did not extend to building the necessary **Consulate, Court and Post Office**, it was suggested that a temporary building be erected. The American community, who felt it a folly to waste money on a building that would have a very limited lifespan, rejected the idea outright. Robert Trimble, a US government architect, formulated a new design in 1929 in the Colonial style and partly modelled on Independence Hall 'in order that Americans may immediately feel at home'.[80] Some land had been reclaimed from Suzhou Creek so that the complex, comprising three buildings, would fit on the site, but the building was never realised and the consulate remained behind the Bund, while even in 1950 hopes of building a 'massive and dignified' consulate remained high.

At the end of Hongkou's consulate row stood the **Japanese Consulate** (14), which was built on the site of an old

wooden wharf between August 1909 and March 1911. The Japanese had recently obtained extraterritorial rights in China and by 1915 comprised the largest foreign population in Shanghai, creating in Hongkou a 'Little Tokyo'. From the turn of the century the rapid and staggering rise of this once fiercely insular nation had been altering the political and commercial dynamics of Shanghai. By 1916, when there were over 7,000 Japanese residents in Shanghai, the Municipal Council felt compelled to hire 30 Japanese constables from Japan to police Hongkou. The focal point of the Japanese community was its club, founded in 1906, and a clubhouse built in Hongkou in 1913 and opened in 1914. A Japanese temple, built in 1908, was also in the same area. To cater for this growing community, the Japanese architect Yajo Hirano made preliminary designs for a new consulate in

Above left Robert Trimble's unfulfilled design for a new American Consulate in 1929

Above The Russian Consulate (with Astor House Hotel behind)

Left The former German Consulate

1908 in a European Renaissance style 'according to English standards'. Hirano, like several other Japanese architects practising in Shanghai at the time, was educated in America. Hirano graduated from California University and established a firm in Hongkou in 1904, from where he designed many buildings and cotton mills. The adoption of Western designs by Japanese, as a result of their American training, preceded a similar phenomenon among Chinese architects by more than two decades.

In the first decades of the 20th century, Hongkou's cheap land prices helped to attract all manner of foreign and Chinese residents, who settled along Woosung Road, the extra-settlement road linking the city centre with Hongkou Park, and built large villas, as they had done in the western districts. Woosung Road was laid in 1904 and became 'typical of Shanghai life. Chinese, Japanese, foreign, semi-foreign buildings, are utterly mixed up. Chinese and Japanese shops, bars to catch "Jack ashore", bamboo huts and hovels, good foreign houses all rub up against one another for a good distance. No one can say it is a dull road.'[81] The diverse communities in the neighbourhood around this road built also a wide range of important cultural buildings. Chinese guilds and temples, Catholic, Protestant and Russian Orthodox churches (the Russian Orthodox Church was destroyed during the Japanese bombing of Chapei in 1932), Japanese temples, Jewish synagogues, and even a Sikh gurdwara served the needs of a multi-religious community. The gurdwara's construction was delayed by lengthy diplomacy required to permit the removal of graves in the area, but it finally opened on 30 June 1908. Designed by Robert Turner, it was built for the Sikh police and represented the centre of Sikh religious life in Shanghai. The Jewish synagogue of Shearith Israel, which opened on Seward Road in 1900, operated also as a religious school and served the growing Sephardi Jewish community, which included a number of very prominent figures in Shanghai, such as the families of Sassoon, Hardoon and Kadoorie. An older synagogue, Beth-El, on Beijing Road had been constructed in 1887. Another synagogue, Ohel Moishe, also on Seward Road, served Shanghai's other Jewish community, the Ashkenazi, from the start of the 20th century. On the west side of Hongkou on North Henan Road was the Shanghai Bankers' Guild, reputedly 'the most sumptuous Chinese building in the Settlement',[82] and not far from Hongkou Park (11). Hongkou Park, designed by Donald MacGregor, was one of Shanghai's primary parks, with extensive gardens, waterways, sports facilities and a swimming pool, which provided an invigorating recreational area for Shanghai's confined residents. Completed in 1909 and extended in 1917, Hongkou Park was second only to the larger Jessfield Park outside Shanghai's western boundary (A3–4). Jessfield Park was part of the farmland owned by the Scotsman Mr Hogg of Hogg Bros from the 1860s. In 1879 he sold 14 acres

The Japanese Consulate

The Japanese Consulate was a project as multinational as Shanghai itself: a European-style building designed by an American-trained Japanese architect with floors, doors, frames and sashes of Bangkok teak and Singapore hardwoods treated with French polish and Ningbo varnish. Oregon pine was used in the construction of the floors and roof and the roof garden was lined with French tiles. The main rooms were finished with English wallpaper and Lincrusta, and decorative fixtures such as mirrors, window glass and wired glass came from London. The overall plan comprised three independent units in one building: the main administrative building, the staff quarters and a connecting wing. In case of fire, steel rolling shutters could be used to isolate the three buildings. The administrative building faced east and contained a court, offices and anterooms on the ground floor and part of the first floor. The residence of the consul-general occupied the remainder of the first floor. The second floor was divided into two equal-sized apartments, one for the vice-consul and the other for the assistant consul-general. The attic space was used as a children's playground. The staff quarters, on the west of the block, were designed in a 'Colonial plan and style' and contained 12 apartments on four storeys with separate baths, kitchens and servants' quarters and an entrance on Whuangpu Road, as well as a graceful five-storey tower on the northwest corner. The connecting two-storey building contained three cells on the ground floor and three bedrooms on the top floor, with an external iron veranda. The foundations consisted of 4 feet of brick and concrete, with pile footings supporting the walls. All the walls were surfaced with red brick, cement mortar and decorative stone of native granite and limestone. Internally, all stairs, cornices, beams and columns were built in reinforced concrete. A central heater with ducts to each room provided heating and electric ceiling and desk fans provided ventilation, except in the cells and stables, which relied on natural ventilation. The buildings formed three sides of a courtyard, which contained gardens and a circular macadamised drive opening out on to the river front through two main gates with green stone gateposts set in a red brick wall. Drainage was emptied directly into the Whuangpu and partly into Hongkou's newly constructed public sewer.

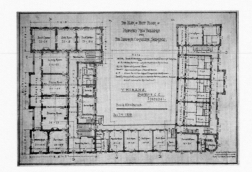

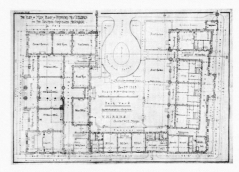

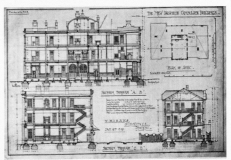

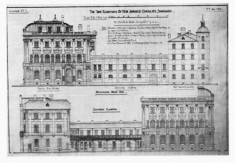

Above Hirano's drawings for the Japanese Consulate

Left The former Japanese Consulate designed by Yajo Hirano and completed in 1911

Right The Fitch Memorial Church in Hongkou (I2), designed in a Chinese style, unlike most churches in Shanghai

Far Right The church today, called Hong De Tang, on Duolun Road,

Right The former Ohel Moishe Synagogue, founded in 1907, moved to this site in 1927

Right The former Sikh Gurdwara

of land to the American bishop Mr SLJ Schereschewsky, who established St John's College. At the turn of the century, St John's and the Shanghai Municipal Council bought Hogg's remaining land, the Council turning it into Jessfield Park.

Industrial development

Hongkou, while showing signs of becoming an important commercial and residential suburb, was more renowned for its industrial character. Foreign industries were quick to establish themselves in Hongkou's cheap outskirts and the Japanese in particular expanded their interests, which quickly grew from small-scale businesses to substantial industrial facilities. Working conditions in Shanghai's factories were appalling. Workers were often children bought from families for $20, working 12 to 14 hour shifts for little or no pay but food and a place to sleep. Industrial accidents were common and uncompensated. Life was too cheap. 'In the accumulator factories, half the children have the blue line in their gums which is a symptom of lead poisoning. Few of them will survive longer than a year or eighteen months. In scissors factories you can see arms and legs developing chromium-holes. There are silk-winding factories so full of steam that the fingers of the mill-girls are white with fungus growths … There is a cotton mill where the dust in the air makes T.B. almost a certainty.'[83] Cotton had long been a leading industry in Shanghai, but modern cotton manufacturing processes were introduced in 1890 and were increasingly employed after the Sino-Japanese War. The British, keen to make Shanghai the 'Manchester of the Far East', vied for dominance of the Chinese market with the Japanese, who wished to satisfy a domestic demand with this cheap source of cotton from China. One of the largest cotton mills in Shanghai was the Ewo Cotton Mill, owned by Jardine & Matheson and extending over 14 acres of land in Hongkou. It started in 1897 and produced 180 tons of cotton per week and by the 1920s employed over 5,000 workers. By the late 1920s, the capital investment in the cotton industry in Shanghai was worth $250 million and employed 119,547 Chinese workers. Most of the modern cotton mills were two-storeyed concrete structures designed by architects working with Chinese building contractors who 'have become very efficient in putting up modern buildings'.[84] Japanese mills tended to be single storey and made of brick, which is better at reducing heat and damp. Their system of managing the mills was better than in the British mills as they employed Japanese foremen who spoke Chinese, unlike the British who rarely used the language in any of their business activities, relying instead on the comprador. The Japanese gradually came to dominate the cotton industry and by the late 1920s had over 4,400 out of their 25,000 population working directly in the industry.

With the massive investment in industry in the first two decades of the 20th century, many Chinese industrialists chose to establish factories in the sanctuary of Shanghai's foreign settlements. Despite having no natural resources itself, Shanghai became China's primary industrial city, congesting Hongkou's cheap outer districts, Pudong and, later, the banks of Suzhou Creek, all of which combined to form Shanghai's industrial heartland. So much industrial activity necessitated the construction of the Riverside Power Station on the banks of the Whuangpu in eastern Hongkou to augment the small Fearon Road Power Station, and this provided an electricity supply that was deemed one of the most efficient in the world. The French Concession had a separate electricity supply generated from what was said to

be the greatest diesel engine power plant in the world, located on Avenue Dubail. By the early 20th century, Asia's cheapest electricity supply and the city's superior infrastructure made Shanghai the manufacturing and industrial base of China. By the 1920s Shanghai had more than 250 modern factories, employing about 300,000 industrial workers, creating a skyline 'unlike other cities of China, which are noted for their pagodas and temples', but with 'hundreds of smoke-stacks and chimneys'.[85]

Improved transportation, the construction of China's railways and the upgrading of Shanghai's harbour added further to Shanghai's industrial skyline. Raw materials and products could now be brought to and from the city with greater efficiency to the one resource Shanghai never lacked – labour. Shanghai's status as a major world port had long been threatened by one of the world's most treacherous approaches and a sandbar at Woosung that forced modern large seagoing ships to offload their cargo into 'lighters' for the remaining 15 mile journey to Shanghai. China was very aware of this inconvenience and had used it to oppose passively the foreign community, but following the Boxer Rebellion was forced to consent to demands for the formation of the Whuangpu Conservancy Board, which was established in 1901. After abortive attempts to set up a Conservancy Board in the 1880s, the new body was charged with dredging the Whuangpu and addressing the problem of the 'Woosung Bar'. Improvements also were made to Shanghai's port facilities. Many proposals to make Shanghai one of the biggest ports in the world were devised. These included a scheme to cut a channel through Pudong to the sea, to cut a channel to Hangzhou Bay in the south and build a port on the coast, and to transform the whole of Pudong

Right A realty development plan near to Hongkou Park

into a vast port area, but local politics, financial constraints, lack of long-term planning and vested interests at Woosung conspired to thwart such grandiose plans. Shanghai's harbour therefore became its river fronts in the French Concession, in the former American Settlement and in Pudong – the city's neglected backyard.

Pudong's river front was occupied entirely by wharfs and warehouses separated by creeks, on which many of the native population, many of whom were Catholic converts, lived in houseboats. Pudong prospered from Shanghai's industrial development, accommodating by the 1920s factories, wharfs, oil refineries, godowns and many other industrial buildings. The Pootung Engineering Works and the Shanghai Dock & Engineering Company both occupied a large portion of the river front opposite Hongkou, but it was Hongkou that was Shanghai's major docklands, with three sections allocated to mooring up to 24 vessels along a 2 mile waterfront of wharfs and newly established shipbuilding companies. In 1918, a report by H von Heidenstam, the Chief Engineer of the Whuangpu Conservancy Board, concluded that Shanghai's port 'should be developed at whatever cost' to ensure that Shanghai reached its potential as a centre of world shipping based on the projected growth of pan-Pacific commerce. To achieve this, the report estimated $100m should be invested over 30 to 40 years to turn the Whuangpu into an enormous wet dock capable of taking ships of 40 foot depth by building locks at Woosung to prevent the Yangtze's vast deposits of silt clogging the river. Such a visionary scheme was lost on Shanghai's administration, which was content with dredging the Whuangpu as long as it assuaged demands for longer-term solutions. Thus Shanghai's port, like its road network, was hindered, through misguided administrative expediency.

On land, infrastructure developments faced similar resistance. The haphazard construction of China's railways caused Shanghai to be the linchpin between the country's northern and southern rail networks. Shanghai's North Station served the north of China, reaching Suzhou by July 1906 and Nanjing on 8 March 1908, while the South Station linked Hangzhou and the southern railway network in 1915. On 9 December 1916, these two networks were linked by a 10 mile stretch of track skirting the western boundary of the settlements, connecting Shanghai's two stations and, via Siberia, making Shanghai 'one of London's remote suburbs'.[86] The North Station (G3) was located in the district of Chapei, a Chinese-administered suburb stretching to the north of the city, comprising mainly makeshift hovels and home to the generally impoverished classes, such as factory workers, *jinrikisha* drivers and coolies. The suburb's impecuniousness belied its strategic importance, which would cause it to be the centre of much unwanted attention in the years ahead.

Social life

Although Hongkou Park and Jessfield Park were established in the early 20th century, Shanghai continued to suffer chronically from a lack of parks inside the settlements, especially the International Settlement, which was more congested than the relatively vacant and verdant French Concession. The only significant open space within the settlements where Shanghailanders could engage in any degree of sporting activity was the Recreation Ground. By the 1920s, this voluminous site accommodated horseracing, cricket, baseball, golf, swimming, tennis, football, polo and lawn bowls. Twice a year, the only event ever to halt the rampant hum of business was the Shanghai races, where the Chinese gambled to their hearts' content and Shanghai's social elite paraded in a rare display of common interest.

Despite the diversification of Shanghai's community, the segregationist attitude characterising most events, clubs and societies in Shanghai persisted well into the 20th century. Residents from various nations happily accommodated each other's presence, but the abundance of social clubs based on national interests proved less the city's enlightened character, and more the absence of it. Shanghai, to some, was a city in

Below Panorama of Hongkou showing its industrial development

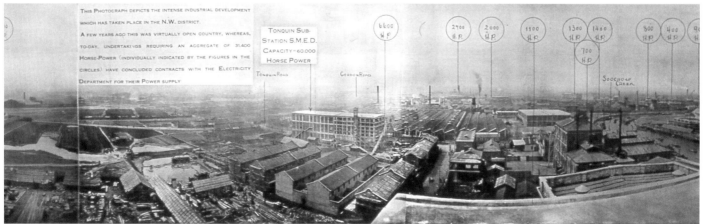

which cosmopolitanism was a myth, where 'each national group builds a wall round itself' and where 'group and national interests usually come before the community interest'.[87] People from every corner of the globe could mix with their own in all manner of clubs or societies such as the American Club, Jewish Club, Union Jack Club, Circolo Italiano, Japanese Club, Helvetia Société Suisse en Chine, Irish Association, Club Portuguez, Deutscher Gartenklub, Association of Lancastrians in Shanghai, St David's Society, Oxford and Cambridge Society, Swiss Rifle Club, Association of British Colonials in the Far East and Société Belge de Bienfaisance. There were also assorted cultural institutions such as the Photographic Society, Horticultural Society, Philharmonic Society and Royal Asiatic Society, the last of which established the International Settlement's only museum, an unsurprisingly pathetic affair in a city whose interminably rapacious desire for commerce always 'failed to realize the intellectual needs of her residents', it being said in 1925 that 'Shanghai, as a community, does practically nothing for science and still less for art'.[88]

Institutions that pandered to the needs of Shanghai's social elite were more numerous, their snobbish members, along with mosquitoes, being described by a griffin as one of Shanghai's 'two evils'. For some, an invitation to dinner with this set was the height of privilege and a mark of achievement, while for others it 'compared very unfavourably with a visit to the dentist'.[89] Nonetheless, privilege, that construct 'more effective than nationality in segregating a caste',[90] favoured Shanghai as much as Shanghai favoured the privileged, and no social institution catered for them better than the Country Club, the Columbia Country Club and, arguably 'the most popular institution in Shanghai', the Cercle Sportif Français, on what is now Nanchang Road. The building was designed by the French Municipal Council architects Wantz & Boisseron in a 'rustic style'[91] with verandas on the first floor providing excellent views over the numerous tennis courts and French Park beyond, where the

French troops had camped during the Boxer Rebellion. The club offered a wide range of sporting activities, while providing the highest standards in service and comfort. After tennis, fencing, boxing, or bowls, members could waltz in the huge dancehall, take a drink on the roof terrace, or dine to the strains of the resident orchestra.

The Chinese, though barred from such institutions, had their own clubs and societies, from which foreigners were banned. There were also a growing number of Chinese adaptations of Western clubs such as the International Recreation Club and the Young Men's Christian Association (YMCA). The International Recreation Club was founded by two Chinese millionaires, who objected to their exclusion from the Race Club in the heart of Shanghai, so established in 1911 a new race club near Hongkou Park (11). In 1929 the International Recreation Club was rebuilt in a Classical style

Above An advertisement from the late 1930s for coal – the main source of Shanghai's cheap electrical supply

Below The former Racecourse on Race Day

according to designs prepared by Palmer & Turner. The new design comprised several buildings, including a north wing which housed a gymnasium on the first floor above a bowling alley on the ground floor, and a main building which housed a large hall and bar, reading rooms, billiard, mah-jongg and card rooms, and office space. Ladies' rooms were on the first floor, with servants' quarters and kitchens on the top floor. The equally popular YMCA became one of the most successful social institutions to transcend Eastern and Western cultures. In 1920, it had as many as 3,400 members and 3,000 affiliated students. The organisation's first offices, designed by Albert Edmund Algar (1873–1926), were opened in 1907 on Sichuan Road. Algar was born in Quebec and studied in China before becoming an apprentice to Thomas Kingsmill, with whom he worked until 1896, when he gained employment for the Chinese government planning the city of Hangzhou. His firm was later involved in the design of many buildings in Shanghai including Grosvenor House and the modernisation of the old offices of the British American Tobacco company, which was one of Shanghai's first Modern-style buildings (H4). He became a Licentiate of the RIBA in the year before he died.

Social institutions and the buildings designed to house them presented a milestone in the building types starting to appear in China and in Shanghai from the beginning of the 20th century. New technologies heralded new types of buildings that required new materials, designs and techniques. Unique buildings such as telephone exchanges, cinemas, power stations, post offices, hospitals, railway stations, museums and even dog racing tracks were being

Right The former YWCA headquarters in Yuen Ming Yuan Road (H4). The interior was very elaborately decorated using traditional Chinese patterns and motifs which can still be faintly seen

built in China, and Shanghai was often the first city to receive such innovations. The Shanghai Telephone Exchange, for example, started in 1881 with 25 subscribers, but by 1920 there were over 9,000 telephones in Shanghai, albeit operating under a service that was 'a direct road to doddering insanity if taken seriously'.[92] Few technological innovations made such an impact on China in the early 20th century as the moving picture. China's first cinemas appeared in Hongkou in 1907 when construction started on two 'cinematograph halls', one on Yuenfong Road and the other owned by the Colon Cinematograph Company on Haining Road. The Victoria Cinema, seating 700 and situated at 24 Haining Road, and the Apollo Cinema, located at 52–7 North Sichuan Road (H3), were Shanghai's two foremost cinema film houses until 1920, despite the construction of the Olympic Cinema in 1914. Films, 'interspersed with songs and musical sketches',[93] could also be seen in an open-air cinema in the spacious grounds of the St George Hotel (C5), at the end of Bubbling Well Road. By the late 1920s, a rage for the cinemas had swept the city, with a huge increase in the number of permits requested from the Municipal Council for their construction and for that of theatres. By the 1930s, an industry had been created that made Shanghai famous all over the world.

Municipal matters

The paradox of Shanghai's lust for modernity and its opulent social institutions on the one hand and its antediluvian infrastructure on the other illustrates its administrative apathy. As Shanghai's buildings grew in stature and sophistication, Shanghai's Public Works Department struggled to keep pace. The Waterworks, established in 1893, had the dubious responsibility of decontaminating the Whuangpu's infamously turbid water, which, with its 20 million bacteria in every glassful, was judged 'probably the worst water it is possible to conceive',[94] bringing some to muse somewhat maliciously that the abundant Scottish community thrived in Shanghai 'because they drink nothing but whiskey'.[95] While, for some, there were alternatives to drinking water, there was no avoiding its consequences. Shanghai's sewage system – or lack of it – was a triumph of maladministration. The ears of the Municipal Council were deaf to public calls so desperate that they became inscribed in verse:

> It rains and it rains
> Till blocking our drains
> For sewers we've none in the EAST
> A 'symphony' of smell
> No language can tell
> But yet we return to the EAST
> To filth we are blind
> Benumbed is the mind
> But still we go back to the EAST.[96]

British American Tobacco Co Ltd

British American Tobacco Co Ltd (BAT) was one of the largest companies in Shanghai, with a cigarette factory employing thousands of staff. Their offices were originally constructed in 1907 at the corner of Museum and Suzhou Roads and served ostensibly as a godown. By the 1920s, the building proved inadequate for the growing administrative requirements of the company, who shared the premises with Mustard & Co. In 1924–5, the building was revamped with an extra floor being added and the interior and facade completely redecorated. The two principal elevations displayed a distinct departure from the predominantly Renaissance styles popular in Shanghai at the time. The aesthetic of the design was definitely modern, its red and cream plaster and coloured cement giving the building a distinctly Italianate character and providing a burst of colour against the grey granite facades of many of the buildings in the area. The modern theme was continued throughout the interior, which was devoid of decoration except for the use of black and white ceramic floor tiles and wall tiles up the dado rails in the public areas. Designed by John Wilson of Algar & Co, and built by Sing Jin Kee, this building is distinguished for being among the earliest modern-style facades in Shanghai.

The British American Tobacco Co building shortly after its upgrade in 1924–5 (*above*) and in 2005 (*below*)

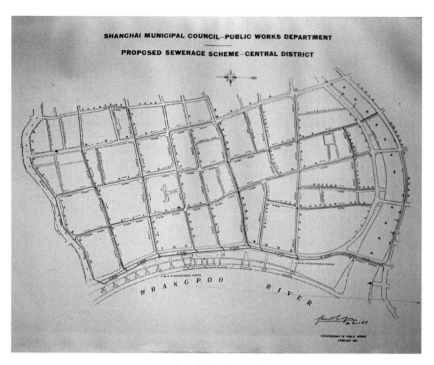

Above Map of proposed sewage system in Shanghai's Central District

Shanghai's first public sewer was laid in 1904 along Hongkou's Broadway, but the whole experience was fraught with problems, which deterred further improvements. Shanghai continued without a main sewage system until the 1920s, relying instead on the night soil collector who diligently worked the streets emptying the buckets placed outside each building, and sold his nightly harvest to appreciative peasant farmers who used it to grow their vegetables. This often poisonous crop was in turn sold to the city dwellers, whose restaurants and dining room tables served 'death-dealing cholera, typhoid and dysentery germs'.[97] This 'medieval, insanitary and disease-spreading practice' was rigidly protected by vested interests in the Municipal Council, who, besides displaying the customary reluctance to stretch the public purse strings, also reaped a handsome revenue from the sale of the city's waste. In 1908, 77,000 tons of ordure were sold to peasant farmers by the International Settlement, producing, in 1909, a 'handsome income' of Tls 47,000 for the public treasury, an annual contribution that had risen to $200,000 by 1920. In the same pages of the council's permanently optimistic annual reports that boasted construction of all manner of new public buildings including a health department, Town Hall and municipal hospital, the system of night soil collection was lauded as being, 'as regards the economy of nature, nearly perfect'.[98]

As Shanghai grew, so too did the Municipal Council's night soil revenue, while the 'oligarchy of landlords who are the real rulers of the Model Settlement' rubber-stamped the planning applications for larger buildings designed without

any regard for modern sanitary requirements. A deeply unsatisfactory status quo was maintained by the wealthy landlords represented on the Council, who were able to persuade the population that collecting night soil by hand was the best, most economical and sanitary method. The revenue from four years of public faeces effectively paid for the new hospital, while the prolongation of this practice 'so thoroughly drilled into a passive community' kept it more than busy. In the Health Officer's report for 1913, on the subject of night soil he stated: 'One recalls to memory the ghostly procession that yearly departs life in Shanghai, or goes home physically wrecked from these causes, it is extraordinary that more attention is not given to this important matter by the public generally.' This commercial city and the businessmen who ran it once again focused only on profit. 'No consideration for public health was involved.'[99]

Elsewhere, efforts to improve living conditions were being made. The creeks and dykes interlacing the settlement had forever been used to dump sewage and domestic refuse, diluted by the daily tides, but development had caused some to be blocked. With an increasing population and what the Shanghai Municipal Council described as the 'reckless and indiscriminate interference' with the original creeks, this practice became the cause of severe health risks, as well as curtailing the antics of the Shanghai Paper Hunt whose participants relied on the 'water jumps' to enliven their daft capering. In 1905, 12,950 tons of mud and refuse were removed from Defence Creek while similar problems with silt and refuse occurred in the waterways around the old Chinese city and the Yang Jin Bang. Since houses had been built along the banks of these waterways, it was deemed prudent to fill them in and convert them into streets. In 1914, Defence Creek was filled and became a widened Tibet Road, and in 1916 the Yang Jin Bang became King Edward VII Avenue – the two widest streets in Shanghai. The creeks criss-crossing the western districts faced a similar fate, the paths on their former banks becoming tracks, then being widened to roads when the creeks were eventually filled in – a haphazard process that explains the often meandering course of many of Shanghai's roads. As the pattern of the city's streets was laid down and the land around them built on, Shanghai was well positioned for its next chapter of development.

The emergence of an architectural dialectic

The first two decades of the 20th century had witnessed the culmination of much early progress. The International Settlement's vast Eastern and Northern Districts, which stretched for miles along the Whuangpu and into Hongkou, had nurtured Shanghai's industrial base. The Central District remained the focus of business activity, attracting the highest rents and thriving on the city's ever-expanding trade. The Western District and the recently extended French Concession continued to attract residents from increasingly diverse national and political backgrounds. Into this melting pot, ideas, products and people from all over the world were hurled together as Shanghai became an engine for change in China.

By 1920, Shanghai's physical form was defined. Most of the roads within the settlements had been laid, the boundaries of both settlements had reached their limits and the land use in each area of the city was defined. A similar juncture had been achieved in the architectural realm, which had emerged from an amateur trade, in which most plans for new buildings were prepared by 'inexperienced people'[100] causing the Public Works Department 'considerable difficulty', to become an organised and professional industry with a representative body, the Shanghai Society of Engineers and Architects (which changed its name a number of times until the 1940s) and numerous architectural firms. Atkinson & Dallas, Scott & Carter, Becker & Baedeker, Davies & Thomas, Moorhead & Halse, Palmer & Turner, and Yajo Hirano had all designed landmark buildings in Shanghai and become well established firms or professional practitioners.

The foundation of these first significant architectural firms coincided with important technological developments, including improved construction techniques and the shift from the use of brick and stone to reinforced concrete and steel frame structures. However, despite the rapid development in materials and techniques, the stylistic treatments and design philosophies remained rooted in European conservatism. Architectural practice in Shanghai, though markedly improved since the 19th century, was still finding its feet.

In the early 1900s, 95 per cent of the International Settlement's buildings were Chinese and therefore designed and built without an architect, despite a huge escalation in foreign-designed buildings, of which there were over 2,000 structures reflecting 'Western Renaissance' styles. Nonetheless, it was noted by Charles Mayne, Chief Engineer and Surveyor of the Municipal Council, in his annual report for 1904 that there was 'a distinct improvement in the quality of the materials used in the construction of native buildings [and] an improvement in the class of property being erected, small one-storey buildings being replaced by better class two-storey houses'.[101] With chaos surrounding Shanghai soon after the revolution of 1911, the real estate market was boosted once again by huge numbers of Chinese arriving in the settlements and demanding better and more modern standards of living. The Municipal Council's report for 1912 remarked of the 'appreciable boom in the building trade … [that it was] almost entirely confined to the construction of Chinese houses … The class of building now being erected shows that a serious attempt is being made to provide a better house than has been the case in the past, and there is a strong tendency towards providing a "Foreign air" to the structures.'[102] In one case in 1916, a property developer built 1,000 Shi Ku Men replete with modern conveniences and

sold them all before the first had been constructed (see pages 159–65).[103] However, with a concentration on quantity, building quality was declining. The high demand meant that there was a proliferation of untrained Chinese developers, who designed and built 'the cheapest class of building permissible under the building rules, caring little for the comfort and safety of the tenants'.[104] The rapid evolution of the lane house, for good or for ill, was underway, carrying with it Shanghai's real estate market.

A fusion of Eastern and Western design practices and styles had started to emerge with the construction of new building types, encouraging a degree of innovation in design and use of materials. The adoption of Western building types and styles by Chinese in this period, illustrated by a 'growing tendency to embody features of a foreign-style house in those of Chinese construction',[105] marked the most profound development from which all subsequent interpretations of Western design by Chinese architects and designers would evolve. This transformation also forced a revision of the Municipal Council's building regulations, which were different for Chinese and foreign structures. Similar trends, though only superficial, were witnessed in reverse too, with foreign missionaries and educational establishments starting to build new structures in Chinese styles to attract greater numbers into their fold.

The first two decades of the 20th century can be regarded as providing all the necessary ingredients for the sudden and dramatic changes that would take place in the 1920s. With the foundation laid, the following two decades would witness a city ripened for the picking. With so much political uncertainty, it was unclear as to who, from Shanghai's multinational menagerie, would reap the biggest harvest.

Below The Bund bridge over the Yang Jin Bang, dismantled when the Yang Jin Bang was filled in in 1916

RISE AND FALL, 1921–1941

Rise and Fall, 1921–1941

Shanghai was nothing but a swamp through which flowed innumerable creeks connecting the large fertile plains beyond and forming a breeding place for the mosquito and malaria. With true British characteristics this place was turned from a useless swamp until to-day, boasting magnificent roads, and every modern convenience, except sewerage, priding itself on its local government and the modernity seldom excelled either in Europe or America.

Far Eastern Review, 1919

Below The Bund in the late 1930s

Shanghai had always been a commercial city and excelled at trade. Both foreigners and Chinese, despite various differences and antagonisms, had reaped handsome rewards from their commercial cohabitation, but by the 1920s Shanghai's mercantile character was being superseded by political forces, and for the first time foreign dominance was being undermined.

Notwithstanding the sinister political backdrop occasioned by the activities of the warlords, Nationalists, Communists and foreign interests, the 1920s and 1930s proved Shanghai's defining age – a fantastical era of glamour, intrigue, adventure and overindulgence. While much of China was consumed with militarism, Shanghai once again provided a safe haven for seekers after peace and prosperity, and just as many willing to exploit their misfortunes. A continuous stream of Chinese refugees provided an unlimited demand for real estate, an infinite supply of labour and immeasurable capital, while international refugees also started joining the migration to Shanghai. The trickle began with the White Russians fleeing the Russian revolutions and subsequent discrimination in Soviet Russia. This turned into a flood when more arrived due to conflict in northern China, followed by thousands of European Jews fleeing Nazi persecution.

This infusion had a profound affect on Shanghai's residents culturally and numerically. Accommodating a rapidly expanding population caused rampant speculation in real estate, consuming the city with wealth and leaving it paralytic in its own excess. With unbridled riches, international allure and an incomparably shameless nightlife, it had everything a city could dream of. In the minds of a far removed international public, Shanghai had evolved from being an Asian backwater into a global phenomenon. However, by the 1930s, the politics it was inadvertently incubating began to devour the city. The two decades of the 1920s and 1930s saw the birth of China's Communist Party, the establishment of China's Nationalist government, the Great Depression, Japan's invasion of China, and the start of the Second World War. The dream turned into a nightmare, but the foreign settlements 'went on dancing',[1] as if sensing this was their final fling. Shanghai became a victim of its own success – a success that reached its zenith in the years immediately before its fall, when the Japanese brought down the curtain on Shanghai's final encore.

Few cities on earth exude such empathy for a past defined by such a short space of time. The intemperance of Shanghai in the 1920s and '30s remains the abiding memory for most foreigners fortunate to have experienced this unique period, while the buildings that define this epoch stand as ageing memorials that jog faint recollections or stir the imagination of subsequent generations, only hinting at what most people missed.

In the eye of the storm

The prosperity which Shanghai had enjoyed from the mid-1910s and during the Great War continued well into the 1920s. Peace in Europe brought renewed confidence to business globally and a protracted civil war in China channelled investment into neutral Shanghai, where the emerging progressive Chinese banks, dominated by the traditional banking communities from Ningbo and Shanxi, had amassed enough capital to support big businesses and a burgeoning property market. The better organised Chinese refugees had come a long way since the chaotic days of the Small Swords and Taipings and, together with the Chinese residents of the settlements, were becoming a powerful and increasingly cohesive force. However, the heaving bank vaults also contained the fortunes of the warlords and their cronies, thereby sustaining their destructive ways. As was noted in the 1920s, 'The foreign banks, like the concessions, contribute largely to the amenity of Chinese civil war and political strife. Once loot is turned into money and deposited with them by the looter it is sacred and beyond public recovery.'[2]

With their wealth secure in the settlements, the warlords could enjoy shopping for arms with relative impunity. In 1922, the Christmas sales arrived early for these iniquitous bargain hunters. A fleet of 15 Russian ships under the command of Admiral Iurii Stark arrived in Shanghai, carrying

Previous pages Photo from the late 1930s showing the buildings overlooking the racecourse (left to right) the Grand Theatre, Park Hotel, Foreign YMCA and China United Apartments

Left Cigarette advertising showing (behind) the racecourse, the Foreign YMCA and China United Apartments

Below Map of Shanghai, 1923, showing maximum area of the foreign settlement extensions, outlying countryside and creeks

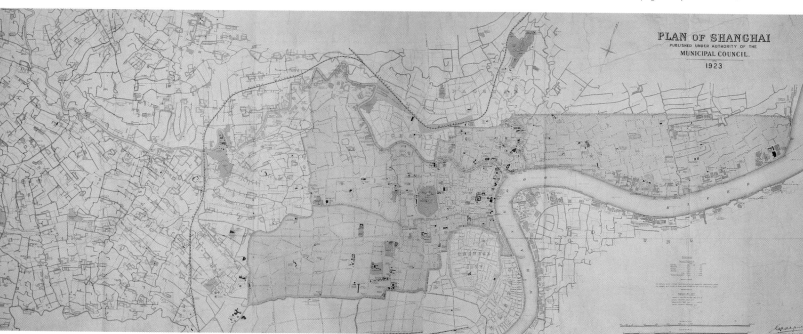

PLAN OF SHANGHAI
PUBLISHED UNDER AUTHORITY OF THE
MUNICIPAL COUNCIL.
1923

Right Cartoon by the renowned Austrian artist Frederick Schiff from the 1930s illustrating the inevitable result of too many servicemen in one place!

remnants of the White Russian army and large quantities of armaments rescued during their withdrawal from the port of Vladivostok. Intent on setting up a new home in the Philippine archipelago, the White Russian fleet fled their homeland as the Red Army swept across Russia. En route to the Philippines, supplies and moods became exhausted. Over 2,000 refugees, including soldiers, sailors, orphans, families and former officials, had been confined on board as they sailed past Korea and northern China. In Shanghai, they met with an anxious reception, particularly because of their cargo of munitions, the sale of which could replenish supplies. However, these stocks proved a mere appetiser for China's hungry warlords, who devoured weapons with the same rapacity with which they devastated China's embattled provinces. In September 1923, more Russian ships, this time under the command of Lieutenant General Fedor Glebov, delivered a veritable banquet of bombs, grenades, machine guns and 2 million rounds of ammunition. Shanghai's lucrative and debauched arms trade that fed all the contrafactions in and beyond the region was shaken 'to the very marrow.'[3]

Added to this potentially explosive mix was the growing political activism among an emergent urban working class, who with energetic students formed a willing audience for the doctrines served them by political agitators. In a manner dissimilar to previous disturbances the city had had to tolerate, Shanghai's growing stature was now drawing the foreign settlements towards the eye of the storm, as China's politically active ogled Asia's greatest prize.

In 1924, warlords from the neighbouring provinces of Zhejiang and Jiangsu started the fight. Some 120,000 soldiers made Shanghai's outer districts their battlefield in what was 'the beginning of a long chain of events that changed the face of China'.[4] One after another, China's provinces declared their allegiances and the conflagration engulfed most of the country. With so many armies on the march, engaged in battle or facing defeat, the flood of refugees and ensuing turmoil caused increasing unease in Shanghai. When the governor of Zhejiang was routed and fled to Japan, he left his army of tens of thousands to fend for themselves. On 9 September, the prospect of a large leaderless army encroaching on the city caused the Shanghai Volunteer Corps to be dragged out once again. A cordon was erected around the city's perimeter, safeguarding the foreign community and its business interests in a ring of barbed wire and sandbags.

To make matters worse, the Jiangsu army fell a month later and, also leaderless, joined their former foes in the swelling ranks of disillusioned, hungry and homeless soldiers camping on Shanghai's doorstep. Without a government and accommodating up to 80,000 armed restless soldiers, the Chinese areas of Shanghai were a tinder box awaiting a spark. In a desperate attempt to prevent a

conflagration, the Chinese merchants underwrote the cost of food and shelter, while the Chinese areas of Shanghai 'changed hands militarily five times' in a single month.[5] Finally, a notorious figure named Hsu Shu Tseng, or 'Little Hsu', threatened to ignite the blaze by uniting the soldiers and holding the foreign settlements to ransom in a planned hold-up of gargantuan proportions. With so much at stake, the Settlement police were elated when they managed to arrest Hsu, the only man ever to have been refused political asylum by the Municipal Council. To the enormous relief of the foreign community, the threat passed. A resumption of hostilities between the two provinces at the end of the year served to maintain the Volunteer Corps' vigilance, but, like the previous troubles, required only a massive disarming operation. While over 200,000 refugees flocked to the settlements, the greatest inconvenience for the foreign community during these turbulent times was the restrictions on venturing out beyond the settlement limits, curtailing their beloved paper hunts and shooting parties.

However, social and political life inside the settlements were also changing perceptibly. The lack of Chinese representation on the foreign councils, their exclusion from public parks, and the Mixed Court were the cause of growing unrest among the Chinese population, and it was inevitable that this problem would 'become the obsession of the masses'.[6] Their grievances crystallised on 30 May 1925 during a student demonstration against an incident at a Japanese-owned cotton mill, in which a Chinese worker was killed by a guard. The demonstration held on Nanjing Road on a busy Saturday afternoon was a politically motivated affair, illustrating graphically the scale of Chinese discontent and a growing political awareness among Shanghai's burgeoning working classes and students. The police arrested some of the protestors and detained them at Louza Police Station, near Nanjing Road. When the demonstrators besieged the station, the police panicked and fired on the crowd, killing four students and wounding 12 others.[7] To rub salt into the wounds of a deeply scarred Chinese community, a delegation from the Chinese Chamber of Commerce approached the Municipal Council with a sincere proposal to avert disaster. With arrogance and indignation, the Municipal Council ignored their proposals. The reaction the following day was instant and effective. The Chinese staged an anti-British and anti-Japanese boycott, which quickly evolved into a movement against British imperialism that lasted over a year, hitting the Settlement's rulers where it hurt most: in the Treasury. Britain and Japan were impotent in the face of this new form of passive resistance and responded in the only way they knew: with force. Once again, the Shanghai Volunteer Corps was called out in an attempt to restore law and order, but the damage was done and further action only made matters worse. China very successfully managed to divide the foreign powers in order to break their ranks. Britain, for the first time in its history in Shanghai, felt alone and isolated. This single event encapsulated Shanghai's condition in the minds of the Chinese: subservience to an unjust system of foreign domination symbolised by British imperialism, rising Japanese industrial interests in China, and China's growing nationalist and economic influence in dealing with these ills. For foreign-dominated Shanghai, the writing was on the wall, but few had the vision to read it.

Dr Sun Yat Sen, the founding father of the Republic of China, recognised the inevitability of this tide, but the question before him was how to exploit it. He had come to realise that the only viable way for his revolution to succeed was to unite China and defeat the warlords. From his provincial government headquarters in Canton he plotted the Northern Expedition, in which his Nationalist army of the Kuomintang would sweep through China, cleansing it of its ills and unifying its disparate provinces under the banner of communism. However, it took several years before this dream could be realised. Following Dr Sun's death in 1925, the command of the Nationalists had passed to the young General Chiang Kai Shek, who led the Northern Expedition from Canton in early 1927. City after city capitulated without resistance as news spread among the Chinese peasantry that the Nationalists were bringing new hope and lasting change. Never in the history of China had a single force made such rapid progress.

Shanghai once again became apprehensive. Over 40,000 foreign troops comprising Americans, British, French, Japanese and Italians, arrived for the defence of Shanghai from all over Asia, not because of the military success of the Nationalists, but because of its political doctrine. One of its stated intentions was to rid China of foreign imperialism and abolish special privileges inscribed in the treaties. Hankow, 600 miles up the Yangtse River and a former British concession, was overrun by the Nationalists on 3 January, as was another river port, Jiujiang, on 6 January, forcing Britain to surrender treaty rights at the two ports. Though vastly inferior in stature to Shanghai, these two cities symbolised to some the prospect facing Shanghai, as the foreigners were left to

Left Aerial view of the 1920s Bund and downtown Shanghai. Note the Custom House clock is being installed

gaze at the inevitable rise of Chinese nationalism, then masked in communism.

By March 1927, the Nationalist army had reached the outskirts of Shanghai, which 'had become a garrison town overnight',[8] with all the major powers representing the vested interests in Shanghai pouring troops into the city. The local governor and warlord, Marshall Sun Chuan Fang, promised to defend the city in the same breath with which he fled to Nanjing. On 21 March, the Nationalists claimed the Chinese areas of Shanghai, followed by Nanjing, where 'foreigners and their properties were assaulted, confiscated and plundered'.[9] General Chiang Kai Shek appeared in Shanghai for the first time on 26 March. The age of military feuding warlords, which represented a 'gigantic and agonising fester'[10] on the body of China, was coming to an end, only to be replaced by an equally destructive political feud between the Nationalists and Communists.

The seeds of this colossal dispute, whose consequences are still being felt acutely internationally, were sown in Shanghai. The communist activist Chou En Lai was a former student agitator and member of the Shanghai-based Socialist Youth Group, the forerunner of the Communist Party, which held its first conference in Shanghai on 23 July 1921. Chou had succeeded Li Li San, who had helped organise the student demonstration on Nanjing Road on 30 May 1925 and the subsequent general strike. He had primed Shanghai's workforce for the Marxist revolt he had long envisioned. To undermine Marshall Sun's authority, Chou had called a strike one month before the Nationalists arrived on the outskirts of Shanghai, but the strike failed, and to deter others from joining the cause, the strikers were decapitated and their heads suspended in bamboo cages attached to telephone poles. However, by the time the Nationalist army was threatening Marshall Sun's front, Chou had called another strike to undermine his rear. Over 100,000 workers answered the call, and Shanghai was paralysed by the collective action of over 300 labour unions, again supported by the students. The speed and success of this uprising surprised even Chou. The Chinese areas of Shanghai were under communist control, including government buildings and police stations. China's greatest prize was in the hands of the Communists, who were not going to relinquish it easily to the Nationalist army approaching from the south.

When the Nationalist army entered Shanghai from the south, the Chinese population greeted them with adulation. The Nationalists' 'blue sky and white sun' flag was waved feverishly from every window and street corner, and banners proclaimed impassioned slogans, all from the copybook of an imported Soviet propaganda machine. However, the Nationalist soldiers, led by three generals, Li Tsung Jen, Ho Ying Chin and Pai Chung Hsi, found the city already in the hands of an army comprised of Shanghai's industrial workers, mobilised by Chou.

When the Nationalists requested the Communists to lay down their arms, the Communists refused and the minor cracks that had threatened to separate the two sides became an unbridgeable chasm. A cosmopolitan band of soldiers, consisting of elements of the Nationalist army, mercenaries paid by Shanghai's wealthy merchants and gang members, set out to break the Communists and deliver Shanghai to Chiang Kai Shek. The events that followed may yet prove to be of longer lasting significance than almost any other incident in the 20th century. In the evening of 12 April 1927, the Communists' desperate resistance was broken when over 400 workers were slaughtered in the Labour Union Headquarters on Paoshan Road in Chapei. The journalist Percy Finch drew a fitting conclusion from the enormity of the massacre: 'Historically, the price Chiang paid for Shanghai was too high. From that tragic April night, he was headed for Formosa [Taiwan].'[11]

Shanghai had claimed another victim. Although the city offered so much to so many, it never gave everything to anyone. In the first three decades of the 20th century alone, the Qing Dynasty lost it to various warlords, who thought they owned it until the Communists fleetingly took it from them only to have it snatched by the Nationalists. The cycle did not stop here. Up to this point, the fighting had been only for the control of Shanghai's periphery. The settlements, the jewel in its crown, remained elusive.

The Nationalists mercilessly mopped up the remnants of Communist resistance in Shanghai killing over 10,000 in Shanghai's streets before advancing on Hankou, where the communist factions of the Nationalists held out in a last stand that attracted immense admiration from the world's Communists, who flooded to China to witness what they believed was the first step in the communist conquest of Asia. Before boarding ships for the 600 mile journey up the Yangtse, 'French, German, Japanese, American, British, Hindu, Turkish, and Javanese communists, flitted in and out' of Shanghai's hotels that were abuzz with international political intrigue.[12] On 10 July 1927, Chiang's army occupied Hankou, overthrowing the communist faction of the Nationalists, and severed China's ties with the Russians, who had sponsored his advance northwards.

The Nationalist government consolidated their gains throughout China, while the foreign community remained timid and unsure whether or not this was a government with which they could do business. The eviction from China of foreigners was high on the Nationalist agenda, and foreign missionaries were considered easy targets. Many hundreds were killed or harassed throughout the Nationalists' Northern Expedition, causing countless missions to close, striking a blow to the propagation of Christianity in China from which it never recovered. Numerous other incidents between foreigners and Nationalists in the months following their occupation of Greater Shanghai tested the new relationship,[13] and throughout 1927 business was at a standstill while

Shanghai's merchants tried to gauge the policies of China's new government.

It became obvious that the Nationalists needed Shanghai as much as Shanghai needed the stability that they could provide. On 8 October 1928, the Nationalist government was formally established in Nanjing. The new government stoked a growing anti-Japanese sentiment, which replaced anti-British sentiment, as the Chinese sensed Japan's interests extended beyond mere trade. The status quo in Shanghai reasserted itself as Chiang Kai Shek embarked in a volte-face of shameless proportions, siding with Shanghai's wealthy merchants, bankers and industrialists who funded his government and bankrolled its campaigns with early loans worth approximately $50 million. The marriage was an expedient one, suiting the Nationalists in their attempts to crush the Communists, while supporting Shanghai's business interests, including those of the gangs hiding out in the settlements, who enjoyed almost unlimited freedoms with which to operate their various rackets, including a revived opium trade. The foreign community was happy to turn a blind eye to these dubious arrangements as long as they too could share the spoils. With comparative peace in China, Shanghai enjoyed immeasurable prosperity, and the city revelled in it.

The foreign community in Shanghai proved willing to make some amendments to its 'anachronistic, unsuitable, and irritating' constitutions.[14] The Chinese had long been omitted from the Municipal Council and though they paid taxes and resided in the settlements, they had no official representation. This injustice was viewed by the foreign and Chinese communities in starkly different ways. The multinational utopia, a 'cosmopolitanism without peer … a veritable League of Nations'[15] pictured by the Council and its paymasters, was seen by Chinese only as a place in which 'the fire of discontent and hatred smoulders'.[16] What the foreigners failed to yield to – to their considerable eventual cost – was aptly summarised by Hsia: 'The greatest stumbling block to that spirit of unity in Shanghai is the constant friction between the Chinese and the foreign communities which divide themselves perpetually into two camps. The central problem really is, what is the status of Chinese in the Settlement?'[17] The former British Prime Minister, David Lloyd George, shared this view, asserting prophetically in a speech on 15 September 1927: 'Our interests and China's interests are identical. We both want peace and we both want trade. If we continue to insult and exacerbate each other we are likely before long to have neither.'

Reluctantly, the Municipal Council was waking up to its responsibilities. Although the Chinese contributed 55 per cent of municipal tax revenues, they were banned from the public parks and had no representation in the administration of the city. On 13 April 1927 a Council resolution was finally passed that stated 'Jessfield and Hongkew Parks, the Public

Gardens, the Bund Lawns and Foreshore, and Quinsan Square to be opened to Chinese from June 1, 1928, on the same terms as foreigners'. A small toll was designed to 'prevent their being overrun by persons of an undesirable class'. This tardy response to 'a very invidious social discrimination'[18] that had long irked the Chinese was matched by equally pressing constitutional matters, including the admission of three Chinese councillors onto the Shanghai Municipal Council in 1928 and two more in 1930. The British majority on the Council was lost for the first time as its new membership comprised five British, five Chinese, two Japanese and two Americans. On 1 January 1927, the Mixed Court was replaced by a Provincial Court, which had no foreign influence. A district court and a branch high court replaced this in 1929 and, like their predecessors, they dealt with Chinese and nationals of non-treaty powers. These included Germany and Russia, the latter voluntarily rescinding their extraterritoriality after the Bolshevik Revolution. In hindsight, these steps appeared to be too little too late. Nonetheless, the Chinese were being heard and, equally importantly, they were making positive steps towards establishing a system of government for the Chinese areas of Shanghai. The Greater Shanghai Municipal Government was established, headed by the first Mayor, Huang Fu, which set about devising a plan for a new Civic Centre to the north of Shanghai (see pages 182–185). From out of the political turmoil, there appeared to be some semblance of order emerging.

The property market

While the broader political issues facing China were unfolding in and around Shanghai throughout the 1920s,

Above Biplanes of the RAF on the Racecourse in 1927

supply of Chinese refugees. As had occurred at the time of the Small Swords, the Taipings, the 1911 revolution and numerous other minor disturbances, the strength of Shanghai's property market was due to the foreign settlements being 'an island of safety [where] the well-to-do Chinese take refuge and materially increase the demand for living-quarters'.[19]

This phenomenon of settlements as sanctuaries had started in the 1850s during the Small Swords' Rebellion, when foreigners constructed meagre buildings along the banks of the Yang Jin Bang on the boundary of the British Settlement and sold them to the Chinese refugees, as they did on a far greater scale the following decade during the Taiping Rebellion. Both occasions gave the city a taste of the enormous profit to be made from real estate, a business that began informally, but quickly became one of Shanghai's major industries, cluttering the city with rent-bringing buildings. Despite inevitable ebbs and flows in the property market, in the steady evolution of the settlements a trend could be observed for development westward, unofficially at first along extra-settlement roads, and then officially as the settlement boundaries were extended. The Municipal Council had long pressurised the Chinese authorities for further Settlement extensions, and in 1915 a draft agreement laid out plans to incorporate Chapei and western areas up to the railway line into the International

the development of the city was undergoing equally profound change. Unperturbed by the chaos outside the settlement boundaries, the business community inside the settlements enjoyed a prosperous decade and Shanghai continued to develop at a breakneck speed. Underpinning the prosperity of the 1920s and early 1930s was the unfailing property market, propped up, for the first time, by large numbers of foreigners moving into the settlements from the extra-settlement roads areas and the continuous

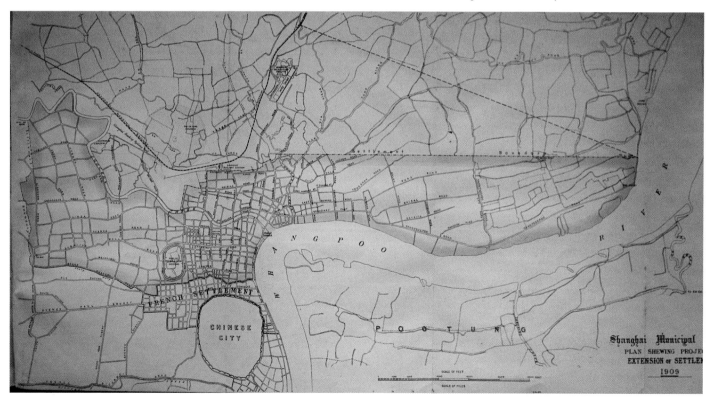

Settlement, but this agreement was never ratified. Shanghai's tight confines created a captive and artificially inflated property market characterised by 'two counter forces'. These were explained in a speech to the China Society in London in 1916: 'One impelled natives to acquire land within the Settlement (to secure the immunities and advantages which were to be obtained by living in territory controlled and policed by foreigners) the other drove foreigners to live outside their own Settlement (to get away from the bustle and stir of the busy port, and to enjoy country life outside of office hours)'.[20]

With the onset of the Jiangsu–Zhejiang War, many of the 7,000 foreigners living in extra-settlement areas at the time moved within the city's boundaries, where the city came 'to an abrupt end among acres of paddy fields and rice-patches'. The strict delineation of these two areas gave Shanghai the idiosyncratic character whereby within 'fifteen minutes one can leave behind the second largest bank building in the world and stand beside a mud-hut with scrubby little natives caressing mangy, mongrel dogs'.[21] At the more up-market end of this peculiar thoroughfare, the most conspicuous changes in the city were taking place, transforming the city's skyline into the 'Manhattan of the East'.

The Bund

Shanghai had long boasted about the Bund, using this granite curtain to symbolise the city's prominence rather than mask its squalor, which began immediately behind with 'a sordid and shabby mob of smaller buildings'.[22] In the 1920s, the reality finally started catching up with the superlatives. In that decade, 11 buildings were constructed and ageing structures such as the Palace Hotel were seen as outdated and in need of replacement. 'Never a thing of beauty', it was 'hoped that it [would] soon give way to something better'.[23] Among the first new Bund buildings of the 1920s was the massive and unassailable **Hongkong & Shanghai Banking Corporation** building on the corner of Fuzhou Road (H5). The response from the chief manager when asked by the chief architect, George Leopold Wilson (1880–1967), for a further $1 million to enhance the building, was unambiguous: 'spare no expense, but dominate the Bund'.[24] The 66,000 square foot structure had a 300 foot facade and 220 foot depth and served as 'a monument to the commerce and prosperity of the world'.[25] In the centre of the 'Neo-Grec' facade, the unmistakable dome soaring 180 feet above street level overshadowed the rest of the Bund, fulfilling completely the managing director's brief.

The HSBC building was the most expensive building ever contructed in Shanghai up to that time. It was designed by the Hong Kong-based Palmer & Turner, an enterprise that became the city's most prolific architectural firm, designing 9 of the 13 buildings constructed along the Bund from 1920. Established by William Salway in Hong Kong in 1868, Palmer

Metropole Hotel

A 14-storey steel framed structure, the Metropole Hotel was designed by Palmer and Turner and built in a record time of three months by Sin Jin Kee. It was tapered towards the top to comply with building bylaws, giving the structure its lofty appearance. The entrance is in the centre of the concave facade, which replicates the floor plan of the neighbouring Municipal offices to provide maximum space at this intersection. The building was rare in having a basement, which housed an Old English Grill and Bar, barbershop, lavatories and stores. The hotel reception and manager's office were on the ground floor, with a large banqueting hall on the first floor. The upper floors were all occupied by private rooms, each with a bathroom and suites with roof terraces on the uppermost floors where the building's profile starts to taper. The building was one of the first in Shanghai to use Aerocrete in the construction of internal walls, which was a much lighter material than concrete and therefore suited to Shanghai's poor foundation.

HSBC Building

This massive structure, designed by George Wilson of Palmer & Turner and built by Trollope & Colls, replaced HSBC's original Shanghai office, which had been designed by William Kidner in 1877. The two offices mark a transition in the city's physical, cultural and commercial character between the end of the 19th and early 20th centuries. Kidner's Classically styled three-storeyed structure stood in a compound with an open space around the building and Chinese staff and service quarters located at the rear. The new building provided the same services as its predecessor, but on a vast scale, occupying three times as much land and forgoing its spacious compound. The various amenities, Chinese bank and staff quarters all had to be incorporated in the main building, but concealed from view of the main public areas. Both buildings provided residences for the manager or high-ranking staff on the top floor.

The site of the new building occupied the ground on which three former buildings had stood: the former HSBC building, the Kelly & Walsh building, and the offices of Thomas Simmons & Co. The original plans were more decorative than the finished building, the facade of which is devoid of excessive ornamentation. The central portion of the structure comprised a triple-arched main entrance with the keystones carved to

Above The first offices of HSBC on the Bund, designed by William Kidner in 1877

Below Artist's impression of the new HSBC building, early 1920s

represent the faces of Agriculture, Industry and Shipping, though the original plan boasted six sculptures: Industry, Agriculture, Labour, Time, Justice and the Arts. Each archway had a bronze gate weighing 5 tons. Above this, a six-columned Ionic colonnade spanned three floors and supported the huge concrete dome covered with marble mosaic. The dome, which later housed the RAF Association Club, was deliberately placed at the front of the building, set back slightly from the facade, which was interrupted at this point. The combined effect was designed to amplify the sense of prominence from the street. Either side of this portion of the building were two 100 foot high symmetrical wings, at each end of which were two pilasters protruding slightly from the main facade. A heavy cornice skirted the building above the third floor, linking the building's three parts and setting apart the top floor.

Two bronze lions, designed by Henry Poole, lay beside the main entrance, the paws of which were said to bring good fortune if rubbed. Portents of luck also adorned the interior, access to which was gained by passing through a marble portico and bronze rotating doors into a main entrance hall. The bronze work throughout, as was the case elsewhere in Shanghai, was of a very high standard, it once being

Above HSBC under construction (1921–3)

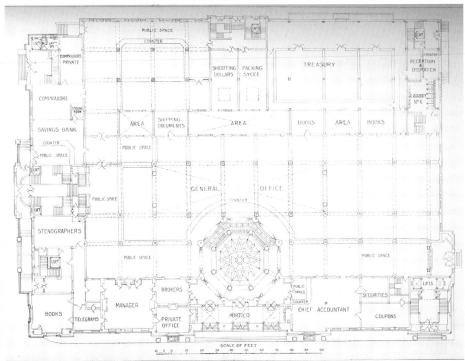

Left The former HSBC building
Below The original designs were more elaborate
than the eventual outcome

Above Ground floor plan

noted that 'nothing finer can be seen anywhere in the world'.[26] The octagonal plan of the hall satisfied both practical necessity and Chinese superstition, which associates the number eight with prosperity in business. 'Eight heraldic lions in gold, the Swastika (good fortune), Solomon's Seal (wisdom), Ceres, the Goddess of Plenty or Abundance; Helios, the God of the Sun; Artemis, the twin sister of Helios, the

Goddess of the Moon' also adorned the entrance hall, crowned with a 52 foot wide dome supported by eight Siena marble columns, their bases and capitals made of bronze. Venetian mosaic was used to decorate the dome and flooring throughout the building. Around the base of the dome, on each side of the octagonal form were painted panels representing the banking centres of the world: London,

depicted by Britannia; Paris, depicted by The Republic; Calcutta, depicted by Mysticism with the Star of India on her forehead; Bangkok, depicted by Fertility; Hong Kong, depicted by the Union Jack as a symbol of British colonial rule; Shanghai, depicted by Sagacity; Tokyo, depicted by Learning; and New York depicted by Bartholdi's Statute of Liberty. Between the panels were Chinese inscriptions from classical Chinese literature and the inscription running around the dome's base: 'Within the Four Seas all Men are Brothers'.

The building's interior layout radiated from the marble-panelled arcade around the entrance hall in 'the happiest simplicity'.[27] On the ground floor to the south of the entrance were the brokers' room, manager's office, private room, waiting room and other administrative rooms. The Chinese Bank and comprador's office were situated at the rear of the building, along with the treasury. The main banking hall dominated the central portion of the ground floor, occupying almost the entire length of the building and was amply lit by natural light through careful fenestration and the barrel-vaulted glass roof lit artificially from above. No expense was spared in the decoration of this hall: walls and columns were faced with grey Italian marble, including four monolithic

>

columns each weighing 7 tons, a 300 foot marble-faced counter supported bronze grilles, along the western wall an arcade was lined in Siena marble, and a large double staircase on the south wall was made of white and Sienna marble, underneath which was a marble entranceway into Fuzhou Road. All the marble, except for the Devonshire marble used to decorate the accountant's department, was shipped from Italy. The staircase provided access to a mezzanine floor leading to staff rooms, stationery rooms, telephone exchange, lavatories and changing rooms, and a tiffin room. The Chinese bank was a 'blaze' of Chinese decoration in a 'riot of pure decoration for the laughing joy of colour',[28] designed through the architect's bold scheme to use Chinese decoration in a Western building, which was the first time in Shanghai that such a scheme was attempted in a modern building. The upper four storeys housed offices and two apartments on the top floor with their own roof garden.

The building was the first in Shanghai to use cranes during its construction, greatly speeding up the construction process. With the building weighing approximately 50,000 tons, over 10 per cent of which were light-toned Hong Kong granite supported on 2,600 Oregon pine pillars up to 40 foot long to stop the whole building sinking into the alluvial depths, one of the greatest engineering problems to be overcome in designing the foundations was the great fluctuation in the weight of the treasury at the northwest corner of the building (stocks of silver could vary enormously at any given time and, if excessive, could cause the building to capsize). A reinforced raft was constructed to support the building, which was built 12 inches higher

than its desired height so that settling would bring it down to street level after some time. Temporary steps were built up to the main entrance and removed as the building settled. In the first year, the building sank between 4 and 6½ inches.

Above left Marble-panelled arcade inside the main entrance, beneath the dome
Above The ornate interior above the entrance hall showing the mosaics and painted ceiling inside the dome
Below left Interior of the ornately decorated Chinese Banking Hall
Below The sumptuous Main Banking Hall

& Turner set up their Shanghai office under the supervision of George Wilson, a partner and assistant architect of the firm from 1908 to 1914. Wilson was born in England in November 1880 and graduated from the Surveyors' Institute in 1905 before travelling to Hong Kong. He formed his own independent practice in 1914 with which he continued to work with Palmer & Turner. He became a Fellow of the RIBA in 1926 and retired in 1952. Through his work with Palmer & Turner, he had a hand in many of Shanghai's landmark buildings, the first of which was the Union Assurance Company of Canton (1916) on the Bund (see page 107). Most of Palmer & Turner's projects were rooted in Neoclassicism, since many of their jobs were eminent buildings for conservative clients, though their work does reveal a later proclivity towards Modernism. However, as with many of Shanghai's architects, Modernist pretensions were generally skin-deep, since the firm also designed mock-Tudor offices and the faux-Tudor Cathay Mansions at the same time as they were producing their best Modern work, such as Sassoon House (1929), the Royal Asiatic Society (1932) (right), Beth Aharon synagogue (1927), the Metropole Hotel (1934) (see page 135), Hamilton House (1934), Embankment Building (1933), Cavendish Court and Grosvenor House (1934). Their most prominent early work includes the Wing On department store (1918) and the International Recreation Club building (1929), but it is along the Bund where their work dominates. The Custom House (1925–8), Bank of Taiwan (1926), Chartered Bank (1923), Yokohama Specie Bank (1924), Yangtsze Insurance building (1920), and the Glen Line building (1922) were all built in the 1920s, while the Bank of China was completed in 1937. Their elevations for Sassoon House mark a departure from the design of previous buildings in Shanghai and, on the Bund at least, represent a shift from the decorative and conservative to simplistic modernity. The refined verticality of Sassoon House and its modern decorative motifs contrast with the explicit Renaissance designs and ornamentation that adorn most of Shanghai's larger structures built before the mid-1920s.

Custom House (H5) (1925–8). Ever since the first foreigners settled in Shanghai, the site of the Custom House has remained the same. The first Custom House in the foreign settlements was a 'cramped and unhealthy'[29] Chinese structure consisting of a central building with two perpendicular wings. Its successor, built in 1893, retained a similar floor plan, though the building was in a Tudor style with a central clock tower that rang out the Westminster chimes (see page 35). The new Custom House was built by Sing King Kee and designed by Edwin Forbes Bothwell of Palmer & Turner. Bothwell became an Associate of the RIBA in 1915 and a Fellow in 1922, and also worked for the Shanghai-based architectural firm Lester, Johnson & Morris. The new Custom House retained a clock tower, the bells now

ringing to 'The East is Red', but the building was massive, yet completed in a 'restrained classical manner' pertaining to the Doric style and apparently inspired by the Parthenon at Athens. The bold portico, with its four Doric columns, provided a base for the vertical arrangement of the building, designed to accentuate its height and draw attention to the huge clock tower, its apex standing nearly 300 foot above

Above, left Tudor-style office behind the Bund designed by Palmer & Turner in the 1930s

Above George Wilson

Left The former Royal Asiatic Society Building, 1932, showing oriental decorative motifs on a restrained modern facade. Note the faint outline of 'RAS', on the stone tablet at the top of the facade

street level. The huge building occupied an entire block and contained over 500 rooms; upon opening it was described as 'massive in design, massive in structural detail, and massive in size'.[30] An elongated central courtyard provided light to the building's interior spaces and divided it into three principal portions: the east, north and south, and west. The eastern elevation was the tallest with ten storeys, while the other elevations had either six or five storeys. Access to the upper floors was provided by 12 passenger lifts, six of which were located at the entrance from the Bund, which also provided access to the main stairway. The building's principal elevation was faced with granite, while the other facades were finished in brick. An exceptionally high standard of bronze work was used throughout the building for decorative purposes, such as window frames, lights, lift enclosures and the three massive ornamented doors at the main entrance.

General offices were located on the first floor, with the ground floor being occupied by waiting rooms, godowns, garages, workshops and servants' dormitories. The second to fourth floors were reserved for private offices and, to the rear of the building, staff quarters, kitchens, laboratories and separate lavatories for Chinese and foreign staff. On the second floor was the world's longest counter, 610 feet in length. The fifth floor was occupied by the Whuangpu Conservancy Board. The sixth floor contained five staff apartments, serviced by servants who lived on the seventh floor. The same arrangement was repeated on the eighth and ninth floors, though the eighth floor had just two very large apartments, each with four bedrooms and three bathrooms. The clock, 'Big Ching', crowning the building, was said to be 'one of the finest ever installed anywhere in the world'[31] and was made by JB Joyce & Co Ltd of London, its bells manufactured at the Taylor Bell Foundry in Loughborough, England.

The sheer size of the structure and the weight of the clock tower posed unique engineering problems in the design of the foundation. As for the other tall structures on the Bund, the foundation was a raft of reinforced concrete, here 16 inches thick, increasing to 24 inches under the clock tower. The arrangement of the raft's reinforced concrete beams allowed the building's steel superstructure to be fixed at the intersection of the beams, so providing maximum support. This solution was satisfactory only for the building, but not for the clock tower, whose 6,700 tons of steel and granite had to be dispersed by 225 additional concrete piles, each 50 feet long and 16 inches wide, which provided enough friction in the soft mud to prevent the clock tower collapsing. Although settling of the building was inevitable, calculations for the foundation had to be correct so that settling was even throughout the building. If the clock tower had settled faster and deeper than the rest of the structure, it would effectively have snapped the building in half.

Chartered Bank of India, Australia, and China (H5) (1923). The Chartered Bank started business in Shanghai in

1857 near the south end of Sichuan Road before moving to the Bund in 1892. The new five-storeyed Chartered Bank, completed in 1923, was designed by GL Wilson of Palmer & Turner and built by Trollope & Colls. Like Wilson's HSBC building, this structure was labelled 'Neo-Grec' and bears other similarities to this style, though diminutive in comparison (see page 142). The symmetrical structure, central Ionic colonnade above the main entrance, granite facade rusticated on the ground floor, and window pediments are all evocative of his work on the HSBC building. Inside the main entrance was a square vestibule with four columns of Brescia marble, walls panelled in a rich cream-coloured Pavonazzo marble and the floor in Roman marble mosaic. The building was constructed using a steel frame and reinforced concrete on a foundation consisting of a concrete raft and 25 foot Oregon pine piles.

Yokohama Specie Bank (H5) (1924). Originally based in Nanjing Road from May 1893, their offices moved to the Bund in 1894, where business was so good that the bank moved to larger Bund premises in 1900. These new offices, designed by Palmer & Turner and built by Trollope & Colls in

1924, were described as 'Neo-Grec', but their design was also said to display a 'freshness and vigor [sic] [and] a severe, chaste, and broad character'³² (see page 142). Although certainly uncomplicated compared with many of the other buildings on the Bund, the six-storey Yokohama Specie Bank was undeniably Classical in form, with a strict delineation of the building's components. The symmetrical facade was composed of three vertical sections, and the central recessed portion containing two massive Ionic columns spanning three floors stands above the three main entranceways. At the top of the building a cornice decorated in an Oriental style provided a unique departure from the Classical motifs adorning the building's predecessors. The bank was built using a steel-framed structure, with reinforced concrete roof and floors and Japanese granite facing.

Glen Line building (I4) (1922). Designed by Palmer & Turner and built by Trollope & Colls, the 90 foot high Glen Line Building occupied 300 feet of Beijing Road and the Bund, on the site of Siemessen's old hong (see page 143). The building and its foundation were constructed entirely in reinforced concrete with granite columns either side of the main entrance, which was located in the centre of the facade on the Bund. The offices were panelled in teak and oak and the floors surfaced in black and white marble terrazzo. The Glen Line offices occupied most of the ground floor, while the remaining office space was rented out. Access to the upper floors was via a stairway and two lifts in the centre of the building's north side, while coolies used a separate staircase that doubled as a fire escape. The top floor consisted of a residential suite for the General Manager of Glen Line. After the Second World War, the building was substantially redecorated by its new tenants, the United States Navy, but when they vacated it in the late 1940s, it became for a short while the American Consulate.

Sassoon House (H5) (see page 143). Construction of the Sassoon House, built by Sin Jin Kee and designed by George Wilson of Palmer & Turner, started in 1926 and presented some unique problems. Two houses, also belonging to Sassoon, that formerly occupied the site, had to be demolished and the site reconfigured to provide greater access to Nanjing Road, the course of which was very narrow because it was formerly a creek. As a result, the building had a peculiar ground plan, making Nanjing Road wider. Over 1,000 wooden piles were driven into the ground to support the foundation comprising a reinforced concrete raft 325 feet by 188 feet. Nine of the 12 storeys spanned the full width of the building, while the top three floors tapered up to the distinctive pyramid roof, which rose to a height of 240 feet. The building was originally designed to accommodate offices, but the owner decided half way through construction that its primary function would be as a hotel, so the plans were altered, with two floors being added. The fourth to eighth floors became the Cathay Hotel. The interiors of the

suites facing the Bund were designed to represent various different national and design styles including Jacobean, Georgian, Indian, Chinese, Japanese, modern French, and ultra-Modern. One suite was even named 'The Coward Suite' after Noël Coward, who had spent four days there writing *Private Lives*. The eighth floor contained the hotel reception and the renowned ballroom that became one of the most salubrious venues in Shanghai. The ninth floor was occupied by a Chinese restaurant and roof garden, and the tenth floor had an English-style banqueting hall with private dining rooms on the eleventh floor. On the ground floor a rotunda provided access to entrances on the Bund, Nanjing and Jinkee Roads via shopping arcades for upmarket outlets. Ten lifts ascended to the upper floors, at the top of which was a private apartment belonging to the owner, the eponymous Victor Sassoon.

The building's interior and exterior were designed with Modernist undertones, its tall narrow windows and slender surface detailing giving it a sense of verticality, in contrast to the often horizontal configurations elsewhere on the Bund. Modern and Oriental motifs were also adopted in the granite

Right and far right The former
Yokohama Specie Bank

Right and far right The former
Chartered Bank

Far left and left The former Glen Line Building

Far left and left The former Sassoon House (right), now the Peace Hotel (left)

Right The Jacobean Suite of the
Cathay Hotel in the former
Sassoon House

Far right The Indian Suite of
the Cathay Hotel in the former
Sassoon House

carvings and bronze work throughout the building, marking a distinct departure from the Classical motifs employed on previous buildings along the Bund.

Other buildings erected along the Bund from 1920 include the **North-China Daily News** (1924) and **Nisshin Navigation Company** (1921), both designed by the architectural firm Lester, Johnson & Morris; **Jardine & Matheson** (1922) designed by the architectural firm Stewardson & Spence; and the **Transport Bank** (1937–48) designed in 1937 by Hungarian architect CH Gonda. The firm Stewardson & Spence was established in 1919 by Robert Ernest Stewardson and Herbert Marshall Spence who had both worked in HM Office of Works. Stewardson qualified as an architect and became an Associate of the RIBA in 1904, working with London County Council before going to Shanghai. He became a Fellow of the RIBA in 1921. His professional partner, Spence (1883–1958) trained in Newcastle, England, and worked with several firms before joining HM Office of Works, for which he went to Shanghai to work in their China Branch from 1911 to 1919. He became an Associate of the RIBA in 1907 and a Fellow in 1929. Another architect, Bryan Watson, who died in 1927, worked with Stewardson & Spence from 1924 to 1926. In 1928, Stewardson & Spence disbanded, with Spence going on to join HGF Robinson, CFS Butt and JE March as Spence, Robinson & Partners from 1928 to 1958, relocating to Hong Kong in 1950. The partner Harold Graham Fector Robinson started his professional training with the Shanghai architectural firm Scott & Carter from 1905 to 1910, qualifying as a professional architect in 1911. He became an Associate of the RIBA the following year and a Fellow in 1929.

Another striking addition to the Bund was the **Peace Memorial** in memory of the fallen of the Great War and situated, prudently, on the boundary of the International Settlement and French Concession. A competition for the design of this was arranged, and three entries chosen. The winning design incorporated a huge granite plinth supporting a large bronze statue representing the angel of peace, at the foot of which were two orphaned children. The statue was unveiled on 16 February 1924.

The North-China Daily News building (H5) (opposite), known as 'the Old Lady on the Bund', was to be the tallest structure in Shanghai but by the time it was completed it had already forfeited this claim. Since the city's building regulations prohibited the construction of buildings taller than one and a half times the width of the street they fronted, the Bund's broad width allowed for a greater height of building and it was here that the city's tallest structures were first erected. The site occupied by this building was long and narrow, with a frontage of 61 feet against a depth of 170 feet. The narrow facade had entrances in each corner set in Cyclopean rusticated granite blocks. The building comprised two sections. The front portion had eight storeys topped by gilded cupolas at each corner, the combined height of which was over 140 feet, while the rear portion had seven storeys, separated from the front by a cavity wall to deaden the sound of the printing presses housed in the rear building. The entire structure was constructed in reinforced concrete and faced in artificial granite. The concrete frame allowed for open-plan floors that could be subdivided according to the needs of the occupants. The upper floors were reserved for offices, including the editorial offices on the fifth floor.

Jardine & Matheson (H5) was the first company to occupy a site in Shanghai, then No 1 the Bund, in 1844 for £500; its estimated land value in 1900 was £1 million. Their first offices, built in 1850 from designs 'sent up from the south' served them well, but although at the time 'many China residents will view with regret the demolition of this stately old building',[33] they were very outdated and inadequate for the needs of the business by 1920. Known to Chinese as 'Ewo', Jardine & Matheson was one of Shanghai's most illustrious trading firms and it was on this site that many of their projects were planned, including the first railway in China. Located on the south corner of Beijing Road, the new offices, designed by AW Graham-Brown of Stewardson & Spence, were 80 feet high, but their five-storey reinforced

Far left The former Transport Bank (1937–46)

Left The Nisshin Navigation Company

Left Former offices of the North-China Daily News

concrete structure was designed to carry an extra floor if necessary. The roof was even designed to be removed and put back on when an extra floor was required. Two floors have since been added on separate occasions, giving the building a height of just less than 120 feet. Designed in a 'free Renaissance' style, the building mirrored many of its neighbours along the Bund, in terms of its symmetry, granite facing and rusticated ground and first floors, Classical colonnade and heavy dentilled cornice (see page 146). The main entrance of the building was in the centre of the principal facade, while secondary entrances were provided at the corner of the building and down Beijing Road for compradors, coolies and lower-ranking staff. Inside, the staircase and walls were all finished in marble and bronze.

The Nisshin Navigation Company building (H5) was to house the offices of Japan's leading shipping company in China, Nisshin, which operated the routes between Japan and China, as well as along the Yangtze as far as Hankou and up the coast to Tianjing. The six-storey building has since had an extra floor added, though this addition is set back from the front of the building and so does not affect the appearance of the front elevation (above right). The overall composition is a rather muddled collection of elements that includes arched doorways beneath inset bay windows that rise to a heavy cornice, pediments and balustraded roof terrace.

The Transport Bank (H5) (above) was designed in 1937, but the Japanese invasion of China stalled construction until 1946 when Allied Architects were invited to amend the plans. The building was completed in 1948 and, with its distinctive symmetrical and stepped outline reflecting an aesthetic that would later be defined as Art Deco, is noticeably the last structure to have been built on the Bund in the former International Settlement. The bright white facade with its conspicuous vertical detailing presents a rather awkward composition against the massive black marble entrance and squat windows. This lack of refinement perhaps reflects the problematic design process to which the building was subject.

Inside the French Concession, the Bund retained its

Above left and right Former offices of Jardine, Matheson & Co Note the extra two floors that have been added.

mercantile character, with the frantic activity along its many wharfs discouraging the development of gardens and stately buildings. The French Consulate remained prominent at the head of Rue du Consulat until 1936, when construction was started on the very large **Messageries Maritimes** building

(1936–9) (H6), whose simplistic Modernist outline contrasted starkly with the Bund's whimsical 'Renaissance' piles further north (see opposite). The architect responsible for resisting the trend for traditionalism along the Bund was René Minutti, a late arrival to Shanghai's architectural fraternity,

Aurora University

Designed by Minutti & Co in a Modern style with strong vertical lines accentuated by the tall windows set in grey stone on a base of crimson tiles, this building opened on 12 September 1936. Built next to the auditorium of the university, it was designed to be the first component in a three-stage project that would create a massive symmetrical structure, of which this element would form the eastern wing. The central portion and the identical western portion were never built.

Aurora University was founded in February 1903

following the collaborative efforts of Chinese scholars and French Jesuit missionaries. It started in Xu Jia Hui with just 20 students taught in Latin, but in 1908 moved to its present location in Loukawei, which then 'seemed like a desert [with] hardly a house in the neighbourhood'.[34] By the 1930s, it was the second largest privately organised university in China. No theological or ecclesiastical studies were undertaken there; its role was merely to provide further education for boys of all races and creeds. In

1930 a new Museum of Natural History, designed by Léonard & Veysseyre, was built and named after Father Heude, who had collected specimens for over 60 years. The former Heude Museum was in Xu Jia Hui and built in 1883. The campus occupied land on both sides of the road, which is now a major highway. The heavily adapted former Église St Pierre, also designed by Léonard & Veysseyre, built between 1932 and 1935 and north of the campus, stands with its eastern end abutting the elevated freeway.

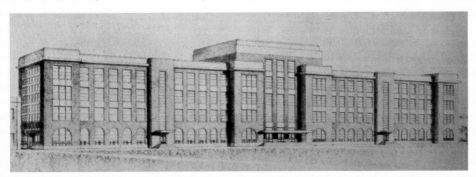

Above Concept drawing of the proposed building in Aurora University. Only one of the wings (left) was ever built.

Above The Aurora University

who did not carry the burden of traditionalism in architectural design. Born in Geneva in March 1887, Minutti came to Shanghai in 1920 after graduating from the Polytechnic School of Zurich and working in Europe, South America and Asia as a civil engineer. In Shanghai, he helped establish Ledreux, Minutti & Co, Civil Engineers and General Contractors, a firm that specialised in structural engineering, bridges, factories and industrial installations, including the Canidrome dog track and the French Waterworks. In 1930, he established Minutti & Co Civil Engineers and Architects, with whom he completed some of his best work, including the Picardi Apartments (B7) (1935) and a new building in Aurora University (F7) (1936).

Construction boom

Away from the Bund, development in Shanghai was equally dramatic, but the buildings were of a smaller scale before the 1930s. The erection of Chinese residences inside the International Settlement had peaked in 1915 when 6,134 were built, but a decreasing supply towards the 1920s and an increasing demand fuelled by Chinese refugees had forced rents up dramatically. By the early 1920s, this demand started to be satisfied by an upsurge in building activity, which set a

Above René Minutti

Left Concept drawing of the former offices of the Compagnie des Messageries Maritimes

Far left The former offices of the Compagnie des Messageries Maritimes

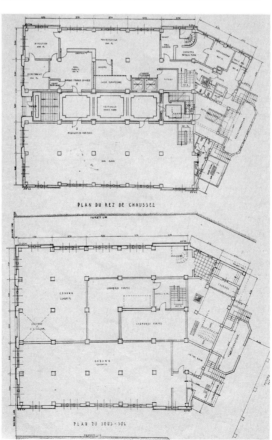

Left Floor plans from the original design of the Messageries Maritimes building

new record in 1925, when 7,734 Chinese Li Long were built.

However, the approach of the Nationalist army in 1927 threatened the stability of the foreign settlements, undermining confidence completely and halting construction almost overnight. The only major development involved the use of 300 tons of barbed wire in the erection of a 12 mile barricade and 126 barbed wire gates around the settlements. Building projects that had been planned were postponed and buildings in the process of construction were left half-finished. The number of Chinese houses built in the International Settlement in 1927 was just 2,640, and foreign residences just 48. With the Nationalist government firmly established by the end of 1927, the year marked a watershed in the evolution of Shanghai's built environment. This was due primarily to the relief felt among Shanghai's foreign community, who realised that their treaty rights would remain intact and their presence in Shanghai, at least for the near future, was assured.

This milestone not only put an end to the warring factions, but also brought confidence to the banking system, whose efficient operation depended on an effective central government. By the mid-1920s, Shanghai's foreign and Chinese banks had matured enough to issue mortgages, where formerly they had only granted loans to their foreign merchant clients. As the returns on these loans had proved increasingly profitable, more and more banks engaged in this activity and speculation increased. With the advent of the Great Depression at the end of the 1920s, international trade came to a standstill, and in China a currency crisis decimated the value of silver, on which the Chinese currency was based. With nowhere else to place their money, speculators ploughed it into land and property. Chinese and international money, seeking a safe haven where it could ride out the storm, stimulated speculation further. While the rest of the world was suffering severe economic hardship, Shanghai experienced a property boom of unimaginable proportions, which during 1930 the Shanghai Municipal Council claimed was 'without parallel in the history of the Settlement'.

Many businesses amassed fortunes overnight, but few benefited more from this rampant speculation than Shanghai's economic heavyweights and the well-established real estate companies such as Shanghai Land Investment Co Ltd, Asia Realty Co, and many new Chinese companies, such as Jin Xin Realty Co. Many of these firms established their own in-house architectural and engineering teams, as in the case of the Asia Realty Company, the Architectural and Building Department of which was founded by an Austrian architect, Joseph Hammerschmidt in July 1931. Hammerschmidt was trained at the Polytechnic University in Vienna and Adolf Loos's School of Architecture (bringing to his work stylistic influences expressed by aesthetic simplicity) and gained considerable experience in the Public Works Department of

Vienna before the First World War. Like several other foreign architects who arrived in Shanghai after the First World War, Hammerschmidt made his way to China via captivity in Siberia and worked his way to Shanghai via Tianjing.

Among the greatest property magnates was one of Shanghai's highest flyers, Ellice Victor Sassoon, whose trading roots stretched back to late 18th-century Baghdad. Victor made an indelible mark on Shanghai, sponsoring its biggest buildings and bankrolling its most lavish parties. The Sassoons were among the most influential Jewish families in India and Mesopotamia in the early 19th century, but it was Victor's grandfather, David Sassoon, who had established the family firm, David Sassoon & Sons, in Shanghai in 1844. After the death of the family patriarch, David's second son, Elias David, formed his own company, ED Sassoon, and the 'old' and 'new' Sassoons went on to make a fortune in opium and later in property that helped turn Shanghai into 'the centre of Jewish entrepreneurial activity in the East'.[35] Sir Jacob Sassoon and his two brothers, Meyer Elias and Sir Edward Elias, formed the next generation of the house of Sassoon. In 1877 ED Sassoon & Co started its real estate interests by purchasing the site on the Bund where the unassailable Sassoon House would later be built. By 1880, ED Sassoon & Co was the biggest property owner on Nanjing Road and was Shanghai's wealthiest property owner for over three decades. When Victor took over the business interest in 1924, following the death of his father Edward, he assumed the reins of one of the most affluent and powerful family businesses in Asia, with a property portfolio spread across multiple companies under the Sassoon umbrella.

Another Jewish property magnate was Silas Hardoon, 'one of the most distinguished foreigners in the Far East' and 'generally rated the richest individual in the Orient'.[36] He arrived in Shanghai in 1873 and worked for David Sassoon and then ED Sassoon & Co until 1911, looking after the company's property interests. His success was supreme and he amassed a personal fortune through real estate, owning more property than anyone else in the city for 18 years. Hardoon's private garden, Ai Li Yuan, on Bubbling Well Road was created in 1909 and was without doubt Shanghai's most extensive and luxurious garden (D5). It contained a network of streams and bridges linking lakes that were overlooked by 'innumerable and quaint' teahouses and summerhouses, a number of pagodas, a Chinese theatre and an aviary. The entire garden was richly decorated with 'every specimen of vegetation that could possibly be coaxed to grow in China ... orange trees, willows, firs, Japanese pines, luxuriant wisteria, beautiful mimosa, hydrangea, peach, cherry trees, magnolias, oleanders, palms, bananas, acacias, elms, maples, and bamboos of many variations'.[37] Hardoon died in June 1931 leaving all his property to his Eurasian wife, Luo Jialing, with whom he had adopted and raised many children. With no direct descendants, many distant relatives from around the

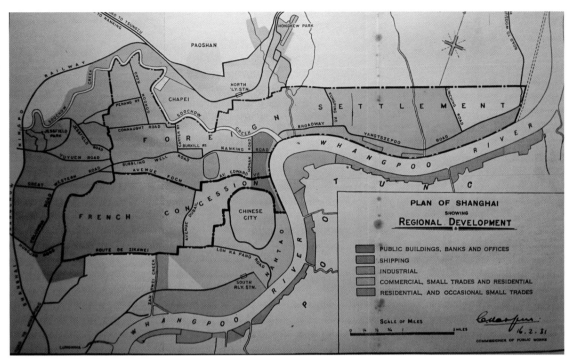

Left 1931 plan of Shanghai showing
regional development

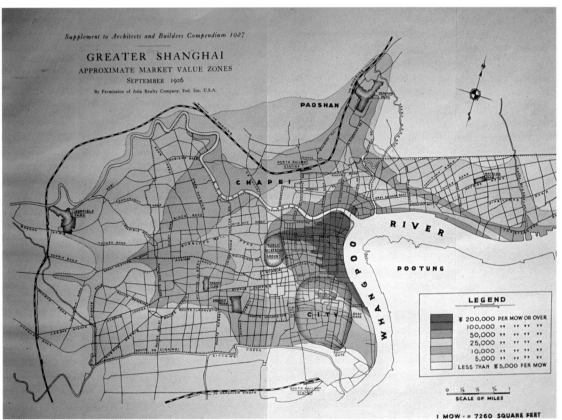

Left Map of land values in
Shanghai in 1926. Note the highest
prices are along the Bund and
Nanjing Road.

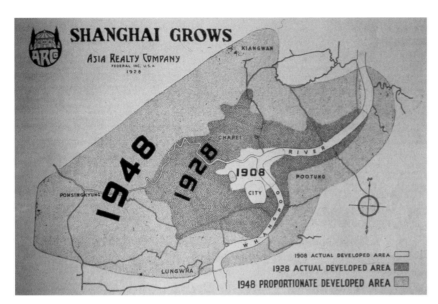

SHANGHAI GROWS

ASIA REALTY COMPANY
FEDERAL INC. U.S.A.
1928

1908 ACTUAL DEVELOPED AREA
1928 ACTUAL DEVELOPED AREA
1948 PROPORTIONATE DEVELOPED AREA

Above Optimistic projections of one of Shanghai's primary development companies made during the construction boom in the late 1920s

Above Silas Hardoon

Right One of many pavilions in Hardoon's famous garden

world visited Shanghai to claim a portion of Hardoon's vast fortune, which had already attracted a Tls 17 million tax bill from the British government. Hardoon's philanthropic character earned him some of the highest honours ever bestowed on a foreigner by the Chinese government. His garden parties, which regularly hosted up to 8,000 guests, were legendary. He also financed the construction of various institutions, including schools and the magnificent Beth Aharon synagogue (H4) in Museum Road, which opened in 1927 for the Shephardi community, outdoing the Ohel Rachel synagogue (D4), designed by Moorehead & Halse and built in 1921. The Ohel Rachel synagogue, on North Shanxi

Road, which included a Jewish school, was once the centre of Jewish life in Shanghai, along with the Jewish Club Ahduth, which was also constructed in 1921. This club served both the Shephardi and the Ashkenazi communities, despite being some considerable distance from the latter, who were based primarily in Hongkou.

In the midst of this boom between 1927 and 1930, the construction of foreign stores increased by over 1,000 per cent, foreign residences by 800 per cent, apartment buildings by 400 per cent, and Chinese houses by 250 per cent. Not only was the unmitigated progress numerical, but fundamental changes were also taking place in the design and construction of new buildings. The booming construction industry had attracted many new foreign architects to Shanghai, and the first wave of foreign-educated Chinese architects were returning, eager to implement new ideas, which was turned into reality by Shanghai's legions of building contractors who were practically all Chinese. Modern standards of living demanded that new buildings replete with contemporary conveniences replaced old and dilapidated structures. These new structures, employing new construction methods, materials and engineering techniques, allowed for thinner walls, taller structures, and a greater efficiency in the use of space, internally and externally. These advances were particularly suited to construction of the apartment building, an entirely Western concept that had only recently appeared in Shanghai. With high land values, a rising population and large numbers of foreign residents seeking modern, comfortable alternatives to the insecurity of living beyond the settlement boundaries, the apartment building flourished under Shanghai's unique circumstances (see page 155). However, one problem with this type of building was its exposure to the extreme heat of the afternoon sun in summer, hence the orientation of these tall buildings became a key consideration in their design. Of the hotels that occupied high-rise structures, two fifths had to close their rooms with western aspects in the summer as they became too hot. The first purpose-built high-rise apartment building in Shanghai, according to municipal records, was built in 1924, and although none were built in 1925, there were five built the following year. From then until 1934, 55 apartment buildings were constructed in Shanghai, some of which were then the biggest buildings in Asia including the Embankment Building, Hamilton House, Cavendish Court, Grosvenor House, Cathay Mansions, Medhurst Apartments, Carlton Apartments, Arco Apartments, Majestic Apartments, Broadway Mansions, Eddington Apartments and Astrid Apartments designed by W Livin.

Arco Apartments (E6) (see page 152). This nine-storey building planned in 1932 for the northeast corner of Shanxi and Changle Roads was owned and designed by Asia Realty Company. It contained 18 two-three-and-four bedroom apartments, each equipped with modern facilities including electric stoves and refrigerators. Shanghai's architectural uncertainty can be seen in the proposed interior design of each floor, some of which were said to be distinctly Spanish, while others were English or Italian in style.

Embankment Building (H4) (1933). When constructed, this building with its 194 apartments was the largest in Shanghai, containing 6 million cubic feet (see page 152). All apartments had a living room, one kitchen and bathroom, and built-in cupboards, but 62 apartments had two bedrooms and 132 had one bedroom. It was eight storeys high with shops and a swimming pool on the ground floor, offices on the first floor and apartments on the upper floors.

Hamilton House (H5) (1934). Opposite the Metropole Hotel (see page 135) and identical to it is Hamilton House, also designed by Palmer & Turner and built by Sin Jin Kee. Owned by ED Sassoon, the building was completed on 1 October 1932 and housed offices on the first three floors and luxury apartments ranging from one to four bedrooms on the upper floors, except on the sixth floor, which was an annex to the Metropole Hotel. Both buildings are of a steel frame construction faced in Suzhou granite up to the second floor and artificial stone thereafter.

Grosvenor House (E6) (1934). The building is set back quite a distance from the road so that residents will 'not be

Above The former villa of Victor Sassoon in Shanghai's far western suburbs

Beth Aharon

Built in 1927 by Fong Saey Kee and designed by George Wilson and EF Bothwell of Palmer & Turner, the Beth Aharon synagogue was a gift to the Jewish community from one of Shanghai's wealthiest residents, Silas Hardoon. The building was designed in a distinctively Modern style and had an elliptical plan. The site was 80 feet by 52 feet, with the building rising to a maximum height of 75 feet to the top of the steel-framed dome. The ground floor accommodated lecture halls, reading rooms and meeting rooms, while the main auditorium was on the first floor, reached by a flight of stairs. The synagogue was 36 feet high from floor to ceiling and had a gallery two thirds of the way around the outer wall.

During the Second World War, the synagogue provided a refuge for the famous Mirrer Yeshiva, 'the most complete yeshiva to escape Nazi Europe', making Shanghai 'one of the most active centres of Jewish studies in the world'.[38] The building was destroyed in the 1980s to make way for one of Shanghai's first high-rises built during the Communist period from 1949.

Right The Beth Aharon synagogue (demolished in the 1980s)

annoyed by the street noise or dust'.[39] The building preserved a residential character in harmony with the nearby Cathay Mansions, but projected a distinctly more modern appearance externally (opposite). The massive symmetrical structure comprises a towering central portion 21 storeys high, stepping down to expansive wings each of 12 storeys, all of which are decorated with vertical features including ornamented buttresses. The imposing character is created by both its height and its floor plan, which is arranged in a quadrant around the large private gardens to the south of the building. All flats have a southern exposure, while the flats on the upper floors, designed to be luxury apartments, had roof terraces. There were no corridors in the building, access being provided directly from the express lifts into the apartment. Palmer & Turner and Algar & Co were joint architects on the project.

Cathay Mansions (E6). This 14-storey residential hotel building overlooking the former French Club was designed by Palmer & Turner and built by Wing Kor Sung & Sons using tapestry brickwork and steel casements, and is typically idiosyncratic for Shanghai (see page 154). The Tudor-styled structure was built using a steel frame weighing 2,500 tons, placed on a concrete raft foundation with 288 piles. Despite these not inconsiderable precautions, the once 170 feet high building has sunk more than most in Shanghai, with its ground floor now at least 3 feet below ground level. The ground floor was reserved for shops facing the street, with a lobby serving four lifts inside the building. The first to tenth floors were occupied by private suites, with a dining room and other public rooms situated on the eleventh floor. Six food

Right The Embankment Building

lifts served food to the 279 private apartments throughout the building from the kitchens on the twelfth floor.

Broadway Mansions (14) (1932–4). This 22-storey building was owned by Shanghai Land Investment Company and designed in a distinctive Modern style by Bright Fraser under the supervision of Palmer & Turner (see page 154). Fraser was awarded a 'Victory Scholarship' in 1921 and the following year became an Associate of the RIBA. He became a Fellow in 1930 and worked for the Shanghai Land Investment Company. His Broadway Mansions once housed offices, shops and apartments, but today is a hotel. The floor plan is said to have replicated the Chinese character for the number eight, which symbolises prosperity and helped give the building its characteristic pyramidical outline. When it was built, it boasted of being the tallest building in Shanghai, but the Park Hotel and Grosvenor House are probably taller, though 60 years of subsidence may have changed these facts. After the Second World War, Broadway Mansions became the headquarters of the US Military Advisory Group and the Foreign Correspondents' Club of China before being renamed Shanghai Mansions. In the 1980s, the name reverted to Broadway Mansions.

A similar revolution was experienced in the construction of office buildings. Up until the 1920s, offices had been built on demand by the land renter, as has been seen along and behind the Bund since the 1840s. With a thriving property market during the 1920s, developers began constructing

Left Illustration of Grosvenor House

Left The imposing Grosvenor House

Left The former Eddington House apartments (D5)

Far left Apartments on the corner of Nanjing and Shimen Roads (E5)

Second left Willow Court (C6)

Third left Medhurst Apartments (E4)

Left Gascogne Apartments (D6)

offices specifically for the purpose of renting to companies. This was evidenced by a number of major office developments in the Central District which were fundamentally modern both in their building function and style compared to their conservative predecessors.

The Commercial Bank of China (H5) (1934) was built by the Metropolitan Land Company and designed by Davies, Brooke & Gran (right). Its concave facade completed the circus at the junction of Jiangxi and Fuzhou Roads, which was started by the construction of the Municipal Council offices.

The Liza Hardoon Building (H5) (1938) designed by Percy Tilley on Sichuan and Nanjing Roads was once described as 'the most up-to-date office building in the entire city'[40]. This structure is comprised of two parts, both designed in a Modern style with few decorative features and a sense of verticality expressed by the alignment and configuration of the windows and subtle surface detailing. The nine-storey portion of Nanjing Road fronts the taller 12-storey tower on Sichuan Road.

Above and right Concept drawings of the Commercial Bank of China

Left The rooftops of Shanghai's once ubiquitous Li Long, here showing Hongkou (Suzhou Creek can be seen in the bottom right of the photo and Hongkou Creek at the top right)

Below Li Long rooftops in Shanghai's old town

Bottom Decorated Shi Ku Men

Shi Ku Men Li Long

While this affluent epoch was apposite for the construction of larger structures, allowing for reasonable returns on capital investment, they were not the most lucrative building type in Shanghai. The most profitable and by far the most numerous were the Chinese lane houses. The Chinese generally were accustomed to living in single- or two-storeyed accommodation and no large apartment buildings were designed with the Chinese in mind. Instead, the Chinese occupied the vast swathes of high density tenement housing known as Li Long, which once covered the city like a vast blanket of patchwork rooftops. In boom times, the Li Long provided any investor with an instant fortune, and when the market was stagnant, a reasonable return on rent could still be guaranteed. The outlay on one two-storey Li Long house, 120 of which can be built on an acre of land, was approximately $300. The return on the investment in the building alone could be as little as two years, compared to ten years on an apartment building. This provided a population density of 600 people per acre, which was comparable to the most densely populated metropolitan area

Left and below Different styles of Shi Ku Men Li Long

Opposite The inner lane of a three-storey new-style Li Long compound showing the front entrance with metal gate (left) and back entrance (right) of each unit

in the world at the time, Eleventh Ward of New York City, which boasted skyscrapers in order to sustain 696 people per acre. So high was the population density in some areas of Shanghai that a new regulation was enforced in 1929 that forbade more than three families to live in one house, or five in a pair of houses. With an almost unlimited source of tenants, the Chinese Li Long proved a reliable investment, regardless of the market condition: 'The rule is, profit lay in the direction of cheap living.'[41]

Shi Ku Men is the name given to the individual unit characterised by a stone-framed wooden doorway, and Li Long is the collective term given to the overall layout of each unit along a network of lanes and alleyways. Architecturally, the Li Long represents one of the most prolific innovations unique to Shanghai and reflects an interesting marriage of Eastern and Western architectural design. In its simplest terms, the Shi Ku Men Li Long is an amalgamation of the English terrace house and a Chinese courtyard house. The evolution of this building type can be traced to the Small Swords' Rebellion when large numbers of wooden lane houses were built for Chinese refugees. In response to the increasing fire hazards posed by these structures, which had multiplied enormously during the Taiping Rebellion, the first tenements built using stone, brick and wood appeared from 1870, marking the advent of the Shi Ku Men Li Long. Arranged in terraces and usually two storeys high, the internal arrangement of the first Shi Ku Men was influenced

Right Plan of Gong Shun Li, a typical early Shi Ku Men, built in 1876 on Guangdong Road

Far right Plan of East Si Wen Li, a typical late Shi Ku Men Li Long, built between 1914 and 1921 on Xinxha Road. With over 300 units in the development, this was the largest Li Long compound in Shanghai at the time.

Above An entrance to a Li Long compound

Above, right A typical Horse Head wind-fire wall in the Yangtze Region

by the traditional dwellings from south of the Yangtze River, and allowed for very high densities of economical living.

The early Shi Ku Men's stone doorway provided access into each unit from a lane. Above the door there were often triangular, semi-circular or rectangular decorative motifs, but the walls always remained unadorned. The interior of early Shi Ku Men was arranged symmetrically along a central axis; inside the doorway was a small courtyard, sometimes as small as 1 metre square, three sides of which were surrounded by rooms. A reception room was always located in the centre of the building, connected to the courtyard and flanked by two rooms that formed the sides of the courtyard. Depending on the size of the Shi Ku Men, the ground floor would serve as a public area at the front and a kitchen at the back, where a rear entrance provided egress, often directly into a public alleyway. In the centre of the building, behind the reception room, a stairway gave access to the upper floor. Between the stairs and the kitchen was a rear rectangular courtyard in the same orientation as the front courtyard. Early Shi Ku Men were approximately 15 metres deep and 4 metres wide, separated by firewalls called Feng Huo Qiang (wind-fire wall), which protruded from the roofline and were decorated in the traditional Horse Head or Guang Yin Dou style.

The configuration of early Shi Ku Men changed gradually to accommodate a utility area at the back of the

building, resulting in the reduction in size of the rear courtyard, which became a narrow corridor leading from the rear entrance and orientated perpendicularly to the front courtyard. The primary consideration for the layout of the early Shi Ku Men was density, with little concern for light, ventilation and the close proximity of neighbouring buildings. By the 1910s, as standards improved, the density of the units was reduced by widening the lanes and designing better layouts for the overall compound. These compounds started to accommodate much larger numbers of units as demand rose. Whereas early Shi Ku Men had been built in small compounds comprising between 10 and 20 units, by the late 1910s as many as 500 units were being built in one development.

The exponential increase in demand for better accommodation among the Chinese population living in the foreign settlements led to improvements in the design of the Shi Ku Men in the early 20th century. This heralded the advent of the new Shi Ku Men Li Long, which had a similar configuration to its predecessor, but with an artificial stone frame replacing the stone doorframe leading from the lane; new materials were used in the construction of the building and modern facilities provided improved living standards. The new types of doorway were often decorated with Western motifs, such as Baroque mouldings in high relief.

The wooden frame and brick walls were replaced by reinforced concrete, faced in red or black brick, allowing for more floors, though the floor to ceiling height was reduced. The symmetrical alignment of the rooms inside the building along a central axis was replaced by an asymmetrical floor plan with the stairway on one side of the unit, an extra room halfway up the stairs known as a *ting zi jian*, and the loss of the rear courtyard. This isolated room became an important feature of Shanghainese life and is renowned for its use by writers who produced the 'Ting Zi Jian Literature' during the 1920s and 1930s. The diminutive room suited the humble needs of the lowly elements of Shanghai's literary community, who were able to live and write out of this single rented space and whose work reflected their modest surroundings against China's most glamorous backdrop. Architecturally this marked an important departure from the layout of traditional Chinese houses when the reception room was no longer positioned in the centre of the building. Improvements in living standards were achieved in a number of ways, including the incorporation of bathrooms, toilets, utility rooms and the introduction of electricity, water and gas. Also, lighting and ventilation were improved by increasing the width of the lanes to above 4 metres and reducing the height of the external walls of each unit. Concrete floors replaced wooden flooring throughout the

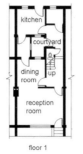

floor 1   floor 2   floor 3

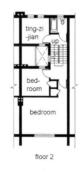

floor 1   floor 2   floor 3

Above, far left This terrace illustrates the poorer residences made of wood and brick that were superseded by Shi Ku Men Li Long

Above left, top and above Different styles of stone doorways leading to each unit of the Shi Ku Men Li Long.

Left, above Si Ming Cun, a new style Li Long, built in 1927–32 on Central Yanan Road (note the *ting zi jian*)

Left Jing Hua Xin Cun, a new-style Li Long, built in 1938 on Julu Road (note the *ting zi jian*)

Right Group of 16 apartments in a garden compound built in 1940 in the former French concession

ground floor, except in the reception room, which used wooden boards or ceramic tiles. Concrete was also used to surface the lanes in front of and behind each unit, improving drainage and sanitation.

After 1920, a new type of Li Long started to be built in which the front doorway and high wall of the old Shi Ku Men were replaced by a metal gate and fence, though the interior layout remained similar to its predecessors. The next significant development in the evolution of this building type was the introduction of the Garden Li Long in the 1930s. Although their interior layout retained the Shi Ku Men's key characteristics, the front gate and courtyard were replaced by a large garden area, giving the unit the appearance of a terraced town house. This more desirable version of the Li Long evolved into more lavish configurations, including semi-detached and detached units. These modern residences were only found in Shanghai, for throughout the rest of China, Chinese families, while also enjoying modern conveniences, preferred to live in one- or two-storeyed houses built in traditional styles often around a single or multiple courtyards.

For those without the resources to purchase the more luxurious versions of the Li Long, there was the Apartment Li Long, which proved popular throughout the 1930s and early 1940s. This type of Li Long was often on a small scale, with two to four storeys to a building and two apartments on each floor accessed by a central staircase. Until the 1940s, no other building proved more popular in Shanghai than the Li Long, which gave the city its characteristic low-rise, high-density residential appearance. However, it was commonly acknowledged that the lower class of residences with 'drearier interiors, narrower and dirtier courtyards' than other types of housing in China gave Shanghai 'living standards among the lowest in the world' for industrial workers. [42]

Tens of thousands of Li Long were built all over the city in various different forms and permutations, ranging from

sumptuous to meagre lodgings, often doubling as the setting for cottage industries producing small items for an unlimited local market. For those unable to afford even a Li Long, there were straw and bamboo huts that could be erected anywhere at any time. In 1929, Shanghai had an estimated 21,000 such makeshift hovels catering for the most desperate classes, highlighting the housing problem that Barz believed to be 'one of the greatest problems yet to be solved in Shanghai and so much more in other parts of the country ... In this large city of Shanghai apartment houses are needed with one, two or three roomed flats, perhaps with a kitchen and a sort of a bathroom. But at present they are still herded together in small areas and narrow alleys.'[43] Although the lifespan of a bamboo hut was minimal, nearly all Shanghai's Li Long survived until the 1980s, when they found themselves in the front-line of Shanghai's contemporary construction boom and started to be demolished to make way for modern high-rise developments.

Residential diversity

Although highly profitable for the investor, the Li Long represented what some perceived to be a 'useful though ugly' development strategy and the lowest rung in Shanghai's architectural hierarchy.[44] Success and affluence had to translate into bricks and mortar. For an era defined by unbridled wealth, landmark residences were becoming as popular among Shanghai's elite as White Russian prostitutes. Though equally dolled up, these extravagant villas often lacked the same class. Importing a menagerie of architectural styles, hacked up and reconfigured in often ghastly compositions, the fairytale aesthetic all too often created a Frankenstein's monster – the hideous result of a life's dream that destroyed its creator. Neoclassical porticos, ersatz Tudor facades, Spanish 'Colonial Revival', American Colonial and Baroque interiors were frequently jumbled together on this piece of China, as far removed in time and place as anywhere in the world at any time in history. Indeed, one resident spoke

of Huai Hai Road's 'architectural wonderland ... where such local architects as are of a humorous temperament erect brick and stone jokes in proof of the fact, and then drive their friends out that way and enjoy a good laugh'.[45] One of the most famous cases of reckless architectural fantasy occurred with the creator of Shanghai's Marble Hall, the home of the wealthy Kadoorie family (C5–D5). The 14-year-old Eleazer Silas Kadoorie (later Sir) arrived in Shanghai in 1881 and worked as an assistant to David Sassoon. His career in business enabled his renowned philanthropic activities in education and health throughout Asia. In 1920 he bought a plot of land on which a club had started to be built, but it burned down before it was completed. Construction of the Marble Hall started as Kadoorie and his family left for Europe for three years, leaving the project in the hands of an architect with ideas more impressive than his expertise. After numerous telegrams from the architect had exasperated Kadoorie, he finally wrote back saying 'do only what is absolutely necessary'.[46] On his return to Shanghai, Kadoorie found 'enraged contractors, the architect an alcoholic in hospital with DTs, and a ballroom 65 foot high, 80 foot long and 50 foot wide lit by 3,600 different-coloured electric light bulbs'.[47]

For many owners, conflict, the cost of construction, or the upkeep caught up with them in the end. 'These private palatial quarters were not money makers and until this day they have only served as adornments, involving the owners in a great deal of outlay which they could never recover.'[48] Although these 'old-style English homes, modern mansions, terraced and elaborate, quaintly gabled and of semi-Oriental architecture'[49] were lauded among Shanghailanders, the reality was often less glamorous: these 'magnificent and massive mansions undermine and swallow up, in their undertow, giant moneys, like dragons with an insatiable maw. If one only envisages the cost of maintenance and running of these modern triumphs, when left unused, it is heartbreaking.'[50]

Far left A Garden Li Long (E6)

Above The former Kadoorie residence, now a district Children's Palace

Right Moorish-style villa in Hongkou, once occupied by the Finance Minister of the Kuomintang, Song Zi Wen

Far right One of many Spanish-style villas in the former French Concession

Right Eclectic-style villa built for the Minister of Communications of the Kuomintang, Sheng Xuan Huai, in 1934

Far right American Colonial-style villa designed by a Chinese architect, Xi Fu Quan, and built in the former French Concession in 1936

Right French Renaissance-style villa built for a French lawyer in 1922

Far right Eclectic-style villa built in 1936 for a Jewish businessman, Eric Moller

When Shanghai prospered, as it did from 1927, its western suburbs brimmed with new residences, and the owners of formerly expansive residences subdivided their gardens and cashed in on the demand for land, or the residences were demolished to make way for the new. Insatiable land purchasing forced 1,000 per cent price rises between 1924 and 1934. From 1925 to 1930, 11,838 Chinese and 972 foreign buildings were demolished to make way for new developments – even the famously spectacular Majestic Hotel, the 'stately and exquisite work of art, an imperial aspiration' where Chiang Kai Shek married Soon Mei Ling in late 1927, was 'tragically torn down' in 1936 for being 'not in keeping with Mr Shanghai Lender's pocket'.[51] The Western District of the International Settlement, Shanghai's traditionally popular residential suburb, remained consistently more expensive than elsewhere, which explains the proliferation of a huge variety of accommodation in the cheaper but equally accessible and spacious French Concession, accommodating everything from high density Li Long, through capacious villas, to high-rise modern apartment buildings.

The work of one architectural firm, Léonard, Veysseyre & Kruze, dominated the skyline of the French Concession. The firm was formed by Paul Veysseyre and Alexandre Léonard. Veysseyre, who was born in Auvergne, France, in 1896,

studied architecture first under Maître G Chedanne in 1912, and then spent two years at the École Nationale des Beaux Arts in Paris. His journey to Shanghai, like that of many of his peers, began with enlistment in 1914. Following a brief spell in Poland after the First World War, he arrived in Shanghai in January 1921 and served in the Armoured Car Company of the Shanghai French Volunteer Corps. During this posting, he met Léonard and they formed Léonard & Veysseyre, which became Léonard, Veysseyre & Kruze in January 1934. Léonard, born in November 1890, was also educated at the École Nationale des Beaux Arts, but having started in 1908, he did not graduate until 1919 because of his service in the Great War. He arrived in Shanghai as professor at the French Concession's renowned Franco-Chinese Institute in 1921. Like many architects in Shanghai during the 1920s and 1930s, his work drew from traditional ideas and forms, evidenced in the Baroque Cercle Sportif Français (1924–6), 'the largest club in the Far East and one of the finest in the world',[52] before the firm embraced Modernism, becoming one of its principal and most successful exponents in Shanghai. Its forte, the apartment building, provided an exceptional medium for Modernist expression. Entirely new layouts, materials, construction techniques, decoration, compositions and functions could all be explored in what was Shanghai's first

Far Left British Tudor-style cottage

Left Modern villa in the former International Settlement built in 1939 for the Pei family

Above Paul Veysseyre

Above Alexandre Léonard

Above middle The former French Club, now part of the Garden Hotel (behind) (E6)

Above right Gascogne Apartments (D6)

Below The former French Club in its heyday

brush with contemporary design ideas. Their most noted works include the Gascogne Apartments (1935), Dauphine Apartments (1935), Bearn Apartments (1930), Edan Apartments and the Chung Wei Bank.

The diversity of the French Concession's buildings reflected the diversity of its residents, who represented every rung of Shanghai's social ladder and every race and creed. The largest foreign community comprised the Russians. Russians had lived in Shanghai from the mid-19th century, but it was not until the turn of the century that they became a prominent community, with many traders supplying materials to Russian interests in northern China. Most came from Manchuria and lived in Hongkou, where life was cheap, but following the Bolshevik Revolution their numbers increased dramatically and the community shifted to the French Concession. Thousands of former soldiers, professionals, aristocrats and officials were forced to settle and eke out new careers for themselves, most notoriously as the city's highest class of prostitute, though they were far more illustrious in their preferred trades, excelling in all manner of occupations, such as art, music, medicine, law,

publishing and business, enhancing significantly Shanghai's cultural character. At the end of the 1920s, seeking better living conditions away from the discrimination imposed on them by the Soviets while working on the railways in Harbin, and from the subsequent turmoil in that region at the end of the decade, many more Russians arrived in Shanghai. The community settled around Avenues Foch and Joffre, dubbed 'Little Moscow', where Orthodox domes sprouted, and shops displayed the names of such owners as Baranovsky and Grigorieff, and where Russian was 'heard more frequently than French and English'.[53] The Russian community built two Orthodox churches, both of which were designed by Yaron. One, St Nicholas's Church (E6), was built for former Russian servicemen as a memorial to Tsar Nicholas II and his family, while the much larger Russian Orthodox Cathedral (D6) (1931–2) on Xinle Road, seating 2,000, was built for and funded by the Russian community. This influx did much to transform Avenue Joffre into an important and prosperous commercial centre by the late 1920s, attracting regional branches of banks, shops and offices. This marked a shift in the demographics of the city caused by greater numbers of

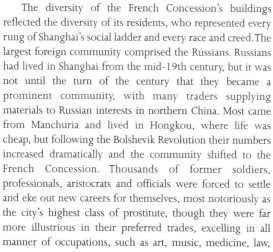

people migrating there as available land in the International Settlement became scarce. Even Bubbling Well Road's esteemed residential character was transformed by a westward shift of Nanjing Road's influence, causing the demise of the formerly large gardens and villas 'although architecturally they are no loss'.[54]

Consequently, the French Concession became 'dotted with palatial residences, luxurious private clubs, spacious parks and sporting grounds',[55] and 'the adobe of the wealthiest', but the serenity of its leafy avenues masked more ominous activities. Behind the fences of bamboo and iron and the thick hedges and brick walls, dissent stirred among the more sinister residents who vied for control of Shanghai, and of China. The French Concession became a breeding ground for Shanghai's gangsters who controlled anything from opium smuggling to labour unions, while China's opposition political parties, outlawed by the Nationalist government, enjoyed relative freedom and immunity in the neutral Concession. Of the many eminent residents who had enjoyed asylum in the French Concession, few would have such an impact on the course of China's development as Sun Yat Sen, Du Yue Sheng, Mao Tse Dong and Chou En Lai. As Ransome remarked: 'Foreign settlements and concessions have come to play a very important part in Chinese politics. A politician can at any moment assume a cap of invisibility by crossing a street. He is close at hand, surrounded by Chinese territory, can keep in close touch with events, and yet be inviolate. The unequal treaties have thus built up a system of political sanctuary from one end of China to the other.'[56]

Social Shanghai

Flush with money and a growing population, Shanghai began to assume the character of a truly international metropolis, far removed from its famously bland disposition of the 19th century throughout which it had suffered from a woeful lack of females. From the first days of foreign settlement, when only seven women were recorded in a foreign population of over 100, things improved little in subsequent decades and worsened during the 1860s epidemic, which appeared 'especially fatal to the female constitution'.[57] The consistently high numbers of male sailors and vagabonds in port and the institutional practice of employing young unmarried men from Europe and America to staff the big trading firms exacerbated the problem. For many years, these 'griffins', as they were called, were tempted out to Shanghai to make their fortune, but found only a wretched existence at the bottom of the foreign social ladder and few sources of entertainment to take their minds off home. (A 'griffin' was also the name given to the Mongolia ponies used for racing in Shanghai.) One young griffin wrote in 1910: 'Just sufficient vice is permitted to find an outlet that will act as a safety valve, and no more.'[58] In the days before Shanghai lost its innocence, the prejudiced words of one prominent missionary in 1872 prophetically

Left The Russian Orthodox Cathedral

underestimated the consequence of the male foreigners' self-imposed exclusion: 'our countrymen in China need the presence of a woman to humanize them, and to counteract the demoralizing influences which are inseparable from association with inferior races.'[59] By the 1920s, the preponderance of a female antidote to these demoralising influences consumed the city and intoxicated its male population to such an extent as to become synonymous with Shanghai, the 'Whore of the Orient'.

In a city with more prostitutes per capita of female population than anywhere else in the world, sex was easy to find, whether staying in a suite in the Cathay Hotel, where customers could bathe in a marble bathtub, full to the brim with spring water flowing through silver taps, or with a lowly homeless coolie on Fuzhou Road. The Cathay delivered premium ladies to the room with a dash of opium if so desired, while over 120,000 prostitutes of all classes catered for the general public. As Shanghai had always operated on a chit system, sex was even available on a tab. A man could go to an establishment such as the famous 'Gracie's' behind the British Consulate, hire the most

Left 1930s promotional advertisement for the Columbia Circle residential development by the Asia Realty Company

Paramount Ballroom

Paramount Ballroom (1934), distinctively Modern in design and replete with modern interior features, is conspicuous for its stepped tower rising above the main entrance, both of which were lit profusely by neon at night and served as a beacon to frivolous customers. These revelled in one of the most fashionable interiors in Shanghai, which boasted two dance floors, one made of glass and lit from below, and the other made of wood and sprung. This distinctive building was constructed in the grounds of what was once the St George's Hotel. St George's used to be one of Shanghai's most favoured hotels, as it was considered to be in the country, away from the bustle of the busy city. Set in 4 acres of land, the hotel served its own milk and butter from 18 Australian and Chinese cows.

Above right Paramount Ballroom with its stylish main dancehall (*right*) and gallery (*below*)

expensive whore in town, and cover his debt, at least temporarily, by a simple slip of paper 'which brings more joy than Aladdin's lamp — until the day of judgment when the shroff or bill collector is on hand'.[60] Failure to pay up could ruin a career. Blackmail was rife in a place where there were 'far too many who purchase expensive wickedness on Saturday night, go to church next day, put 20 cents in the plate, talk to the parson, and run down everything that is not as goody-goody as they pretend to be'.[61] The most adept temptresses and certainly the most expensive were the White Russians, many of whom, having trekked across Siberia selling all they owned just to survive, found themselves in no position to demand the nature of their employment in their new home, but thrived in their adopted trade, much to the chagrin of their Chinese counterparts.

The Lyceum Theatre

The Lyceum Theatre (E6) has an illustrious history in Shanghai, as the settlements' first foreign theatre, established in 1867 as a wooden structure built on Minghong Road. On 2 March 1871 it burnt down and a New Lyceum Theatre was built on the corner of Hongkong and Museum Roads, opening on 27 January 1874. It was the 'only theatre in the east' tall enough to allow the scenery to be lifted rather than rolled up and the only building in Shanghai 'really devoted to the entertainment of foreigners'.[62] Actresses were permitted on stage two years later, when anyone was allowed join the Amateur Dramatics Society, which was not the case in the French Concession, where only French performers were permitted until 1892. The theatre moved once again to a new building in the French Concession designed by Davies & Thomas and opened in 1931, where it was home to the Municipal Opera and Orchestra. Architecturally the building comprises an eclectic blend of detail, with few distinguished features, but with a prominent triple-arched window above the main entrance overlooking the junction on which the building stands.

More conspicuous and less sleazy than Shanghai's staple night trade was the plethora of new entertainment venues such as cinemas, theatres, dancehalls, nightclubs, singsong bars and sports clubs. These new establishments, serving a modern clientele, superseded the stuffy establishments that characterised Shanghai's past like the Shanghai Club and the Country Club. On the western edge of the International Settlement, the distinctive Paramount ballroom (C5), the largest and among the most elaborate dancehalls in Shanghai, was the first to allow mixed patronage on the dance floor where jazz and swing in a Chinese rhythm knocked out the latest tunes of Nelson Eddy and Jeannette MacDonald. A huge selection of elaborately titled cabarets reflected Shanghai's cultural diversity. Ladow's Casanova, Vienna Ballroom, Palais Café, St Anna Ballroom and Ciro's were interspersed among an equally diverse assortment of cinemas and theatres built for both Chinese and foreign audiences. With cavernous interiors and state-of-the-art facilities the Grand, the Capitol, the new Lyceum, the Metropole, the Carlton, the Embassy, the Isis, the Nanking, the Paris, the Peking, the Ritz, the Strand and the Cathay satisfied an inexhaustible audience among the Chinese. Equally well liked by the Chinese were the ever-popular races at both the International Recreation Ground and the Race Club. In 1936, the Race Club received a face-lift and had a new clubhouse and clock tower built.

The Cathay Theatre, a diminutive but distinctive Modernist structure built on Avenue Joffre in 1932, was designed by Gonda, who also designed the East Asia Bank (1927), the Shahmoon Building (1926–8), the Transport Bank (1937–48), and made his mark with one of Nanjing Road's major department stores, Sun Sun (1926), 'the store with the needle

Opposite, above Sun Sun department store (G5)

Opposite, below Gonda's Cathay Theatre (E6)

The Race Club

Designed by Spence, Robinson & Partners, the new Race Club (F5) was opened on 28 February 1934. Its sumptuous interiors included marble staircases, teak floors and huge tearooms. The old clock was replaced by the distinctive clocktower, known as 'Big Bertie'. After the Second World War the Race Club was closed as Chiang Kai Shek banned all forms of gambling. The building became a mortuary for a short while after the war, housing the bodies of American pilots shot down over China that awaited repatriation.

The Shahmoon Building

The Shahmoon Building (**H4**), constructed by Chang Yue Tai and designed by CH Gonda, was built for SE Shahmoon & Co at the corner of Museum and Suzhou Roads and housed the first major theatre in downtown Shanghai. The 102 foot structure contained a theatre which could seat 1,000 and could be adapted into a cinema, above which stood five floors of offices and apartments – the first time such a configuration was employed in Shanghai. The building's reinforced concrete design pre-empted the need for columns in the auditorium while supporting the floors above. Since the concrete frame held up the building, the walls were structurally superfluous, and so the windows could afford to be much larger. This was one of the first buildings in Shanghai to embrace the possibilities available to the architect for fundamental design changes as a result of developments in technology and materials. Shanghai's first purpose-built

film vault was constructed in the roof to provide safe storage for the rolls of film. The building's location was made prominent by the construction of the new bridge over Suzhou Creek. The graceful curve of the building provides an interesting profile, on top of the corner of which is a small ornamental tower. (Gonda used a similar arrangement in his design of the Bank of East Asia on the corner of Sichuan and Jiujiang Roads.) George Wilson, the senior architect at Palmer & Turner, claimed this building 'an example of ultra modern architecture', achieved 'not by superfluous ornaments taken from a bygone building period, but through simplicity in expression of modern technical achievements'.[63] Inside, the firm Arts & Crafts Ltd completed the plasterwork, while Mr Koppany completed the sculptural work, and Mr Podgorsky, the Russian artist responsible for the 'grotesque'[64] murals in the French Club, executed the decorative painting.

Right A jocular moral message by the cartoonist Schiff

tower'. New, modern department stores of the latest design rivalled the ageing giants and sold all the latest imports from Paris, London and New York, as international sophistication suffused Shanghai and its reputation for business and pleasure surpassed all other cities in Asia. Residents, businessmen and visitors gorged on the city's diverse nightlife, and basked in the retail heart of Nanjing Road. Not everyone approved of the quality of these developments. Foreign residents had long derided 'the miserable Chinese tinsel and tinder apologies for shops'[65] that lined Nanjing Road before the 1920s, until they started to disappear. Just like the opium dens on Fuzhou Road, Nanjing's modernisation was met with a certain nostalgic pining. 'With one or two exceptions, the new buildings on Nanjing Road … are appalling examples [that] show no vestiges of architecture and lack the picturesqueness of the old carved and gilded fronts.'[66] Among the most explicit departures from the two-storeyed shop fronts of old were the Sun department store, the Continental Emporium and the Wing On department store's hotel extension comprising a 21-storey Modernist tower designed by Elliott Hazzard and ESJ Phillips and linked to the original building by an overhead walkway. Hazzard designed several Modernist buildings in the 1930s, marking a departure from his earlier work, which included the Foreign YMCA overlooking the racecourse.

Foreign YMCA

Shanghai's building regulations restricted the height of buildings to no more than one and a half times the width of the street, which allowed certain areas of the city to grow taller than elsewhere. This growth occurred first on the Bund, but soon spread to the western area of the city around the Racecourse, where the Foreign YMCA building (**G5**) was built in 1928 by Whay Ching Kee to a design by Elliott Hazzard and Adamson. The building was constructed in two sections: the main nine-storey building fronting Bubbling Well Road, and a four-storey building at the rear housing a gymnasium and swimming pool. The main entrance was provided from Bubbling Well Road on the ground floor, leading to the main lobby on the first floor. A mezzanine level provided accommodation for offices, social areas and reading rooms, above which the third floor contained a dining room, library and kitchen. The upper floors comprised 253 guest rooms. The reinforced concrete structure was built on a raft supported by Oregon pines up to 80 feet in length and faced in brick, laid in a diamond chequered pattern.

Continental Emporium

This large building on the corner of Nanjing and Shandong Roads (H5) was financed by the Continental Bank in response to the demand for affordable modern office space in the Central District, where land prices had reached such astronomical levels that few new buildings were erected. Completed in April 1932 and designed by T Chuang, the massive six-storey structure has a 318 foot frontage along Nanjing Road and 222 foot along Shandong Road finished by an imposing tower at its northeast corner. Shops and showrooms occupied the ground, first and second floors, with offices occupying the upper floors, and there was a roof garden. Owing to the success of the building, an additional floor was added within a year of its opening.

Right Sketch of Hazzard and Phillips' design for the extension of the Wing On department store (G5)

Far right A former department store in Hongkou (H3)

The Central Post Office

The Central Post Office made an obvious landmark on the north side of Suzhou Creek on North Sichuan Road (**H4**). Architects, Stewardson & Spence, won an open competition to design the building, which opened on 1 December 1924, dispensing with Shanghai's previously inefficient postal system that had operated from seven different national post offices. Although the new post office was, as Barz suggested, 'modern in its structure [and] modern in its service', it was one of the most explicitly Classical structures in Shanghai, with its long Ionic colonnades skirting its principal facades and rising 50 feet from street level to the entablature. The cupola above the clock tower rose to 150 foot, at the base of which is a statue of Hermes holding his caduceus flanked by two 1920s-looking maidens designed and manufactured by the Shanghai-based Arts & Crafts Ltd.

Even the formerly mediocre suburb of Hongkou was acquiring a certain cachet, with modern department stores and hotels springing up on North Sichuan Road, which was coming to rival Nanjing Road for the Chinese, and with Broadway becoming a renowned centre for Chinese curios. It also hosted the new Central Post Office, which had replaced Shanghai's peculiar postal system that operated from seven different national outlets. The first Chinese Post Office, located in Beijing Road, started operations on 4 November 1907 adjacent to the British Post Office, which had been built in 1874 and began service in 1875. France, Russia, Germany, Japan and America all operated their own services from their respective consulates before the latter relocated to separate premises.

Hongkou even hosted Shanghai's first school of architecture, the Henry Lester Institute of Technical Education, which opened on 1 October 1934. The school had two components: the Lester School (D4) on Beijing Road, founded in November 1932, taught Medical Sciences, and the Henry Lester Institute of Technical Education (J4) on Seward (Changzhi) Road in Hongkou provided secondary and tertiary education in civil engineering, building and architecture. The two educational buildings present a departure from the formerly traditional structures designed by the firm. The Institute of Technical Education, with its central circular foyer and two wings with vertical buttressing giving the building a sense of lift in an Expressionist approach, is

Sun Department Store

This was the last of Nanjing Road's large modern department stores from the pre-war period (**G5**). Designed by Kwan Chu in 1932 and built in 1933, it was the first building to instal an escalator, of which *Far East Magazine* reported that 'thousand upon thousands crammed this ascending staircase, enjoying the unique ride for the first time in their lives'.[67]

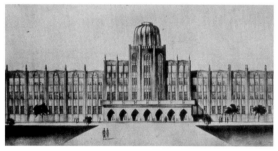

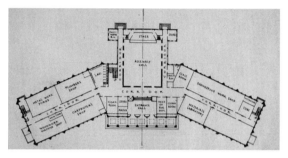

particularly idiosyncratic. Both were established through the benevolence of Henry Lester, a former resident of Shanghai and a civil engineer and architect involved in numerous projects as well as being one of Shanghai's first property investors. Lester died in May 1926, leaving Tls 1 million and several properties to the Shandong Road Hospital, for whom his architectural firm was appointed to draft the plans for a new six-storey building (see page 51).

The Japanese Incident

The most discernible change to affect Hongkou during the 1920s and 1930s, aside from the enormous escalation in industrial development, was the rising Japanese population. By 1930, Hongkou was dubbed 'Little Tokyo', as the Japanese population in Shanghai reached 18,478. From petty traders and waitresses in the late 19th century, the Japanese, largely ostracised and overlooked by the preoccupied European powers, had risen to ascendancy in Shanghai. Since 1915, they had become the city's largest foreign community and their trade with China had reached an all-time high during the anti-British boycott of 1925–6. However, their trade was stifled by the anti-Japanese movement, which had been formalised by the establishment of the Anti-Japanese Association in 1928 caused by the presence of Japanese troops in northern China and the inability of China and Japan to break the deadlock reached in negotiating their withdrawal. Despite improved relations in late 1929–30, the anti-Japanese

boycotts resumed with a far greater intensity in late 1931, when the Japanese overran Manchuria. Japanese interests in Shanghai were threatened severely and the population became anxious, even 'aggressive … desperate and bellicose'.[68] By early 1932, feelings boiled over in the Chinese district of Chapei, when a group of Japanese, including two Buddhist monks, was attacked by a large number of Chinese on 18 January, and two Japanese were killed. Some reports from testimonies given by Japanese officers in 1956 suggest that the fatal attack that started this chain of events was staged by the Japanese to provide the necessary spark that would ignite a firestorm. Whatever the stimulus, the Japanese retaliated immediately. Members of the Japanese Youth League burnt a Chinese towel factory believed to be a hotbed of anti-Japanese dissent. On 22 January, Japan sent 15 warships to Shanghai, including an aircraft carrier and two destroyers.

The longest period of uninterrupted peace that Shanghai had enjoyed for decades, and by far the most prosperous, came to an abrupt end on the evening of 28 January, when in Chapei, which had been drawn up as the defence line of the International Settlement, nearly 2,000 members of a Japanese naval landing party clashed with the 33,500-strong Chinese 19th Route Army.[69] Intent on teaching the Chinese a stern lesson, the Japanese planned to smash their resistance within two days. Dug in around the North Railway Station, the Chinese army was more than prepared for the defence of their territory. The Japanese began to realise the magnitude of their miscalculation: imperial prestige was being undermined by a force perceived by the Japanese military as a bunch of bandits. These 'bandits' were about to inflict 'the biggest military black-eye Japan had ever received'[70]. For five weeks the battle raged. On 13 February, the Japanese landed their army in Shanghai through the International Settlement, using the wharfs in Hongkou. At the same time, the Japanese Air Force heralded the start of an entirely new and brutal form of warfare that was to be repeated only three years later by Italy in Africa, setting 'a precedent for Mussolini's son to exalt sadistically over the thrills of chasing native spearmen across the plains of Ethiopia in his fighter-bomber and to write glowingly of the glorious sunburst of exploding bombs'.[71] Aerial bombardment in modern technological warfare was as incongruous in this wooden-built suburb of the Chinese peasant as chemical bombs were in the African highlands – and equally as devastating. Shanghai, in another first, had been the scene of a grim precedent that in its first outburst caused immense damage to property and killed thousands of innocent civilians as Chapei was razed under shellfire and incendiary bombs. Chiang Kai Shek refrained from putting the full weight of the Chinese army into the defence of Shanghai and eventually the Japanese broke through the Chinese lines. The terror that had befallen Shanghai's northern suburbs was cleverly glossed over as 'an incident' rather than a declaration of war, as Shanghai desperately tried to cling to the good old days.

Turbulent times

However, the 1932 'incident' marked the beginning of the end of Shanghai's heyday. The Japanese invasion of Manchuria at the close of 1931 undermined business confidence and when the hostilities spread to Shanghai practically all building work stopped. The destruction of Chapei had ruined

hundreds of businesses and struck a severe blow to Shanghai's industrial base, as well as destroying many properties belonging to companies in the building trade. In addition to the incident itself, the political situation in Shanghai and in China was of equal significance. The sense among foreigners that their days of privilege were numbered was affecting long-term confidence. As early as 1932, 'many large projects which had been about to be launched were abandoned or postponed indefinitely … during the first five months of 1932 the market was practically dead'.[72] Although land prices retained their over-inflated values, momentum was lost and Shanghai was sliding into the abyss.

The early–mid 1930s showed some signs of progress in the development of the city, but not on the same scale as the halcyon years before 1932. Continuing problems with the

Above A huge project proposed by the China Merchants Group would have dominated the Bund, but it was never built

Joint Savings Society Headquarters

On the corner of Sichuan and Hankou Roads, the Joint Savings Society building of Yienyieh Kincheng Continental China and South Sea Banks was designed by Laszlo Hudec and built by Kung Yih in 1927–8. The building is distinctive for its liberal use of different materials on the facade. The facade, to a height of 45 feet, was faced with Carrara marble and designed in a Classical manner employing Classical columns, window pediments and cornices. The next three floors were faced in a deep red brick, contrasting strongly with the white marble below and white stone on the top floor.

The main entrance, beneath the distinctive cupola, is contained in a massive double-arched doorway forming the rounded corner of the building, a design feature that satisfied the municipal requirement that all buildings in these narrow streets have rounded corners to maximise space at intersections. The tower above the main entrance was said to have 'emerged from memories of the rural renaissance in Upper Hungary'[78].

Right The former Joint Savings Society Headquarters on Sichuan Road

jurisdiction of the extra-settlement roads areas under the new government kept land prices rising, with the largest increases in the western districts. With so little available space and the high cost of land, the foreign residents of Shanghai became flat-dwellers as several landmark apartment buildings rose above the swathes of Li Long and villa rooftops.

Larger than all of these, however, and built in the midst of a deepening depression in Shanghai, was the Joint Savings Society Building, Asia's tallest building at the time. Completed in 1934, the soaring structure overlooking the Racecourse was funded by the Joint Savings Society of China and represents arguably the zenith of architectural achievement in Shanghai, and also in the career of its Shanghai-based architect, Laszlo Hudec. Hudec arrived in Shanghai in 1918, where he enjoyed the most prolific years of his career, marked by a transition from the traditional European styles adopted during his formative years to an espousal of Modernism from the early 1930s. His successful adoption and implementation of Modernist principles, epitomised in his design for the Joint Savings Society Building, set him apart from most of his peers in Shanghai.

Born in Banskabystrica, then in Hungary (now in Slovakia), in 1893, Hudec received a Beaux Arts training at the Royal Technical University of Budapest from 1911 to 1914 before being drafted into the Hungarian army during the Great War. His journey to Shanghai began when he was captured by the Russians and sent to Siberia. Along with so many White Russian refugees in the area at the time, Hudec doubtless heard about Shanghai and the opportunities it presented, and managed to escape and work his way down the railway being built in northern and eastern China around Harbin. Shortly after his arrival in Shanghai, all Germans and Austrians were deported, so, as

Joint Savings Society Building (Park Hotel)

The Joint Savings Society was arguably the most successful and influential Chinese financial institution in Shanghai. The rapid rise of modern Chinese banking institutions since the First World War provided the Chinese with a secure place to deposit their money, and therefore the Chinese banks had amassed huge capital by the late 1920s. The Joint Savings Society Building on Bubbling Well Road embodied the acme of China's financial institutions and represented the potential strength of Chinese business, surpassing in height all foreign structures in Shanghai. Designed by Hudec and built by Voh Kee Construction Company, the Joint Savings Society Building, housing the Park Hotel, opened in December 1934 and was 'the tallest building in the Far East and … one of the finest hotels in the world'[75]. The building consisted of two elements: a 21-storey tower at the front and a lower section to the rear. The structure comprised a 300 foot high-tensile steel frame supported on 400 wooden piles, each 150 feet long, and a 24 foot deep reinforced raft,

which has proven effective since the building's subsidence is negligible compared to many other smaller structures in Shanghai. The building's basement, a rare feature in Shanghai, is said to have contributed to the stability of the structure since it helps to distribute the pressure bearing down on the soil.

The banking hall was designed on the ground floor with the main entrance in the centre of the front elevation. Bank offices were on the first floor and vaults in the basement. A large dining hall panelled in oak occupied the second floor with views across the racecourse. The hotel occupied most of the upper floors, access to which was provided via an entrance on the southeast corner of the building to five express elevators, two for services and three for guests. From the third to the 13th floors were guest rooms. The 14th floor housed the grill room, which was panelled in Austrian walnut with silver inlay, with velvet draperies and gold ceiling. The 15th through 18th floors contained private apartments ranging in size from one to two bedrooms. The Board of Directors of the Joint Savings Society enjoyed exclusive use of the 19th floor. The 20th and 21st floors contained the water tanks, lift machinery and air-conditioning equipment. On top of the tower was an octagonal observation deck where guests could enjoy the views from Asia's tallest building.

The building's soaring tower was accentuated by the vertical detailing employed throughout the exterior of the structure. This was achieved in a number of ways, including tapering the tower's outline, using slender windows separated by continuous vertical bands of brick from the fourth floor to the top of the building, and employing heavy buttressing above the 13th floor, the contours of which are maintained down to the second floor, again by brick detailing. Above the third floor, the building is finished in tessellated brick and tiles with contrasting brown hues, the effect of which has

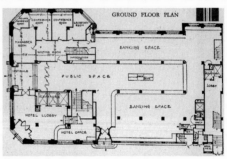

Top Hudec's sketch of the Joint Savings Society Building, with comparative illustrations of the heights of other tall buildings in Shanghai

Above Ground floor plan

Left The Joint Savings Society Building (Park Hotel)

subsequently become concealed by decades of pollution. The first three floors of the building faced in native black granite provide a base for the tower and are emphasised by their horizontal form, bound by parallel bands of granite that skirt the building. The tower, above the 14th floor, represents an interesting series of design solutions that allow the building to taper to the top floor while retaining the integrity of the details, such as the buttressing and other vertical forms. As each floor reduces in size, the loss of internal space is compensated by additional external space in the form of balconies for the private apartments.

a Hungarian, Hudec remained wary in his new British-dominated environment. Professionally, his associations with Germany and its allies proved a boon, as in China 'there [was] no foreigner as popular as the German',[73] who made an effort to integrate with the Chinese and with whom the Chinese shared an affinity. This was further underlined after the Great War when Germany renounced its extraterritorial rights, shedding any imperialistic connotations. This subtle condition later served Hudec well, as he won many contracts from Chinese clients.

Hudec's first work in Shanghai was undertaken with the American architect RA Curry and included projects such as the American Colonial-style new American Club (H5) on Fuzhou Road (1924), the French-owned International Savings Society building (B7) (1919) and the McGregor Hall of the McTyeire School (B4) on Edinburgh Road. In 1925 he established his own practice where he retained his traditional style, as seen in such projects as the Joint Savings Society Building (H5) on Sichuan Road (1928), and the new Moore Memorial Church (G5) (1926) , which replaced the old church erected in 1887 by KP Moore of Kansas City. The church shared the same compound as the McTyeire home, founded by a Southern Methodist bishop of the same name. By 1930, at the height of the construction boom in Shanghai and, importantly, following a trip to America, Hudec abandoned his traditional style in favour of more modern expressions, firstly toying with Expressionist and Gothic styles. Projects such as the China Baptist Publication Society building (H4) (1930), the Christian Literature Society building (H4) (1930), the German Evangelical Church (1931), the unexecuted Ambassador Apartments (1931) and the Chapei Funerary Chapel (1932) are good examples of

this transitional phase. Thereafter, Hudec appears to have embraced more overt Modernist styles. Among the first exponents of these was the newly rebuilt 2,100-seater Grand Theatre (F5) on Nanjing Road, which was conspicuous in its rejection of the traditional forms so evident in Shanghai. A comment in the China Architect's and Builder's Compendium for 1933 described the theatre as 'an experiment in modernistic design which may not please everyone, but is undoubtedly an interesting and striking building'.[74] Only months later, and adjacent to the Grand Theatre, rose arguably his best work. The Joint Savings Society Building (F5) , housing the Park Hotel, was an important milestone in the architectural development of the city. His most explicit Modernist work came later, when construction in Shanghai was in decline. The end of Shanghai's surging property market meant that few of these projects got further than the drawing board, including the Chao Tai Fire and Marine Insurance Building and the new NYK Building, though Shanghai was endowed with his designs for Herbutus Court (1935–7), the Aurora University Women's Institute building (Rue Bourgeat/ Changle Lu, inaugurated in April 1939), 'the finest school building in the city', and the villa of Dr Woo on Beijing Road (D4) (June 1938), 'one of the largest and richest residences in the whole of the Far East'.[76] It is a curious anomaly that the villa he designed for himself in a mock-Tudor style (1931) should be so incongruous in the face of his new design philosophy at the time. He also designed many villas for private clients, as well as industrial facilities and institutions, such as the Columbia Circle for the Asia Realty Company, Chapei Power Station, Union Brewery, Country Hospital, Paulum Hospital and the Margaret Williamson Hospital.

Far left Ambitious but unrealised proposal for the colossal Japanese NYK Office on the Bund

Left Proposal for the Chao Tai Fire and Marine Insurance Building

Far left Aurora University Women's Institute

Left Former villa of Dr Woo

Far left Hudec's villa

Left Former Union Brewery

Herbutus Court

The design of this apartment building had to address two key factors that are pertinent to Shanghai and that have necessitated particular design solutions to many of its buildings. The extreme heat of the summer and the provision of servants' quarters were both important considerations in the design of residential buildings in Shanghai, but these two factors were accentuated in the design of high-rise apartments. This site, in the western districts of the city, was once occupied by Chinese houses, which had to be cleared before construction began. Hudec's design for the nine-storey Herbutus Court contains two residents' apartments on each floor, with combined servants' quarters around airshafts on the north face of the building. Each apartment contained two bedrooms, dining room, living room, kitchen, bathroom and a large balcony. The building was oriented in a northwesterly direction to minimse the effects of the extreme heat of the afternoon sun in summer. The building, now a hotel, once contained a garden and playground at the rear, which has been converted into a car park. The front elevation has been obliterated by the construction of the elevated highway only metres from the windows of what were once the most expensive apartments on the upper floors of the building.

Far right Map of Shanghai showing the new Civic Centre to the north

The period following the construction of landmark structures such as the Joint Savings Society Building was described in the *China Architect's and Builder's Compendium* for 1935 as 'one of the worst experienced for some considerable time'. Property transactions per month in 1930–1 were double those which changed hands in the whole of 1935. With real estate undergoing 'the dullest period in many, many years', people began to realise that Shanghai was 'overbuilt' and apartment construction 'overdone'.[77] Land values decreased and many formerly affluent households were forced to downgrade into apartments or smaller houses. The depressed situation in the foreign settlements was in stark contrast to the Chinese areas of the city, where the value of building activity in 1934 totalled $23.73 million, only $4 million less than in the International Settlement and nearly twice the French Concession's $12.77 million. This was fuelled considerably by the reconstruction of Chapei and the government's plan in 1929 to develop an entirely new city, at the heart of which was a Civic Centre. Located in the Jiangwan District between Shanghai and Woosung and 4 miles from the Bund, the plan anticipated a shift of activity towards the mouth of the Yangtze, while attempting also to draw influence away from the foreign settlements.

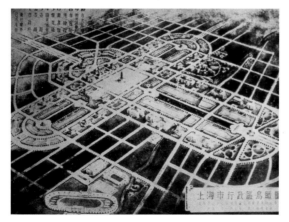

Right Proposal for the heart of the Civic Centre

Mayor's Building

Four storeys and 102 feet high, 310 feet long and 80 feet wide, the Mayor's Building was constructed in reinforced concrete and steel in a Chinese style and designed to 'include all the Oriental beauty in architecture'.[79] The ground floor housed the entrance hall, offices, dining room and kitchen, above which a library and conference rooms occupied the first floor. The mayor's office was located on the second floor, with staff offices, servants' quarters and store rooms in the attic.

The new Civic Centre and China's first architects

For the first time in history, Shanghai was being furnished with an urban plan in which streets, administrative buildings, public buildings and residential areas would all be carefully laid out according to the plans of the Chief Architect, Doon Da You. The first plans were published in 1931, after two years of consultation between architects and engineers in the Greater Shanghai Municipal Government's Planning Commission, headed by Dr Shen Yi, a former student trained in Germany, and by international advisors from San Francisco, Washington and Berlin. This entire development was a monumental, grandiose project, covering 16,700 acres of land, with far-reaching social, economic and political consequences. The buildings, constructed using modern materials and techniques, were all designed in a traditional Chinese style that was to be an example of 'Chinese Renaissance' architecture. The Civic Centre was planned in the shape of a cross covering 330 acres, at the centre of which was to stand a 200 foot pagoda and around which nine government offices were to be built. The roads intersecting at this cross were to be 60 metres wide in an east–west and north–south axis. On the

Far left Aviation Building in the former Civic Centre

Sketches of the former Shanghai Museum (**left**), the library (**bottom left**) and the gymnasium (**bottom right**) in the Civic Centre

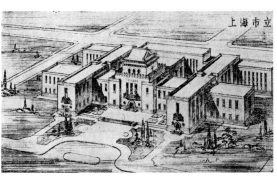

Ba Xian Qiao YMCA

This new nine-storey structure was designed in a classical Chinese style with upturned eaves and decorative Chinese features including carved stonework and elaborately painted interiors. It was built by Kaung Yue Kee and replaced the former building on Szechuan Road, which was opened in October 1907. The large distinctive brick structure overlooking the former racecourse had two banks, a swimming pool and changing rooms on the ground floor; and lobby, offices, library, billiard room, and a 500-seat auditorium on the first floor. The second floor contained offices, above which were five storeys of dormitories sleeping 230 people. The dining hall and social areas were on the eighth floor, with a penthouse above.

southern approach to the Civic Centre was a 2,500 foot long reflecting pool, whilst two smaller pools marked the east and west approaches.

The Mayor's Building was the first to be built, its foundation stone laid on 7 July 1930, the anniversary of the formation of the City Government of Shanghai, and was completed in 1934. The foundation stones for the library and museum were laid by the mayor in December 1934. Both buildings were two storeys high and constructed using reinforced concrete. Both featured imitations of the traditional Chinese gate tower in their centre portions, flanked by wings containing reading rooms and exhibition spaces respectively, as well as offices and lecture halls. A massive sports stadium, seating 70,000 spectators, formed

Above Doon Da You

Above right and right Former Nanking Theatre (**right**) and moved 200 yards to its new setting and renamed Shanghai Music Hall (**above right**)

Far right Sketch of the former Young Brothers Banking Corporation. showing the incorporation of Chinese motifs on modern buildings

Shanghai Mercantile Bank

This six-storey building was designed by Chao and Chen and built by Shun Chong in 1932–3 to be 'modern in every respect' and demonstrates the progress of China's leading architects towards producing modern designs (H5). It was said at the time of construction to possess 'the very spirit of modern German and Dutch architecture and yet in its restraint and in the study of its details the architects show the tastefulness of those with a true classical background'.[81] The building's exterior was finished in natural stone and the interior in bronze and marble.

the centrepiece of a Sports Centre comprising also a swimming pool and gymnasium all set in 50 acres of land with additional land reserved for lawn tennis courts and a baseball ground.

No expense was spared to embellish the site with 'gardens, monuments, pools, fountains, bridges and the like, the whole to form, with the future courthouses, museums, art galleries, auditorium and post office, a monumental and beautiful ensemble',[80] much of the budget deriving from the sale of private land in the new district. Residential, industrial and business districts were planned in specific zones around the Civic Centre, which were connected to one another by a network of roads radiating from the centre and an extension of the railway to link the port of Woosung, where harbour improvements were planned to ensure that this became the principal port of Shanghai. A bridge across the Whuangpu was even planned, an idea that had already been discussed in 1930 by Shanghai's business community, who proposed to fund the construction of a 600 metre steel bridge from the former walled city to Pudong.

Doon Da You, the man behind the plans for the Civic Centre, was a young and aspiring Chinese architect and among the first to return from America to practise in China. Doon was born in Hangzhou in February 1900, though he spent much of his youth in Japan and Europe before returning to China to study at Tsing Hua College. Following his graduation in 1921, he went to America, where he embarked on postgraduate studies at the University of Minnesota and Columbia University in New York. In 1928, Doon returned to China and, after a short period working with ESJ Phillips, started his own practice in Shanghai, before becoming Chief Architect of the City Planning Commission for the Civic Centre. Like many of his Chinese peers, Doon struggled to marry traditional Chinese architecture with modern construction techniques, materials and uses.

The same issue troubled Chao Shen, one of the first graduates of the American educational programme with Tsing Hua College. Attempts to combine Eastern tradition with Western technology can be seen most explicitly on the Bank of China building on the Bund (Lu Qian Shou and George Wilson) and on the roof of and throughout the Ba Xian Qiao Young Men's Christian Association (YMCA) building (G6) on Tibet Road, which Chao designed with an American-Chinese architect Poy Gum Lee. Chao was also noted for winning two prestigious prizes in 1930. The first was for the design of the Mausoleum of Dr Sun Yat Sen in Nanjing, and the other was for the plan for the Municipality of Greater Shanghai, which he designed with Hsi Ming, though Doon Da You completed the design and execution of this project. Chao was born in Jiangsu Province in September 1899 and graduated from Tsing Hua College in 1919. He obtained his postgraduate education from the University of Pennsylvania in 1923, then worked in America and travelled in Europe before returning to Shanghai in 1927 to begin architectural practice. He first teamed up with fellow Chinese architect Robert Fan, before establishing his own practice in 1930, which became known as Allied Architects. Allied Architects, including also fellow Pennsylvania graduates Chen Zhi and Tong Jun, was among the first and most influential Chinese architectural firms and embraced Modern design principles. Chao's most renowned projects include the Kiangnan Naval Hospital, on which he worked with the prominent American architect Henry Murphy, the Metropole Theatre (G4) on Tibet Road, the Shanghai Mercantile Bank (H5), the YMCA on Tibet Road and the Nanking Theatre (G6) (1928), the last two of which he designed with Robert Fan.

Robert Fan, described as 'one of the most distinguished architects in China',[82] was a young man who, having spent many years designing Western-style buildings with Chinese details, became renowned for his renunciation of both Western and Eastern traditionalism in architecture. Born

Above Robert Fan

Below Poy Gum Lee

Bank of China

On the site of the former German Club Concordia, the Bank of China (1937) **(H5)** was the last building on the Bund to be constructed before the Second World War and stands next to Sassoon House. The original 34-storey design towered over the Bund, but an urban myth suggested that Victor Sassoon objected to the building overshadowing his hotel and apartment, so, being one of the Settlement's most influential residents, he managed to have the height reduced to 18 storeys. However, it seems more likely that the financial crisis that began in the early 1930s played a greater role in diminishing the bank's size. The entire plot of land extends from the Bund to Yuen Ming Yuen Road, occupying much of the land once owned by Gibb, Livingston & Co. The building's original design was overtly Modernist, comprising a simple rectilinear form with no decorative features. However, the revised plan, by Palmer & Turner with the assistance of the Chinese architect Lu Qian Shou, though retaining its obviously Modernist appearance was decorated using Oriental motifs, including the patterned windows, carved stonework and rather awkward blue roof. Lu was one of the first Chinese architects to gain membership of the RIBA, becoming an Associate in 1930.

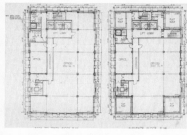

in Shanghai in October 1893, Fan graduated from Shanghai's St John's University in 1917 before attending the University of Pennsylvania until 1921 and gaining valuable experience with the American architects Day & Klauder and CF Durang. On his return to Shanghai, he started his own practice in 1927, where he tended towards traditional expressions in architecture. In the mid-1930s, he denounced traditionalism in design by calling on contemporary architects to design buildings from 'inside out', not 'outside in', believing that the scientific should precede the aesthetic – a tough moral stand in a city renowned for giving style precedence. The following year he travelled to Europe before returning to Shanghai and effecting his transformation to Modernism when he designed the Georgia and Yafa Apartments, the Astor Theatre (1939) and the Majestic Theatre (1941), far removed from his early eclectically Classical work on the Nanking Theatre with Chao.

The YMCA building also involved the American-Chinese architect Poy Gum Lee. Born in New York City in January 1900 to Cantonese parents, Lee was a graduate of Pratt Institute and gained further training at the Massachusetts Institute of Technology in 1921 and Columbia University in 1922. Lee's first major assignment was with the National Council of the YMCA, who sent him to China as assistant architect in the YMCA Building Bureau. Besides his work with Chao Shen and Robert Fan, he was also involved in the design of the Navy YMCA and Foreign YMCA buildings. In 1927 he established his own practice in Shanghai, designing the National Committee of the Young Women's Christian Association (YWCA) (see page 122), Nantao Christian Institute, the Institute for the Chinese Blind and the Cantonese Baptist Church.

Another American architect who flourished in the field of missionary architecture was Henry Murphy. Born in August 1877 in New Haven, Connecticut, Murphy was sent

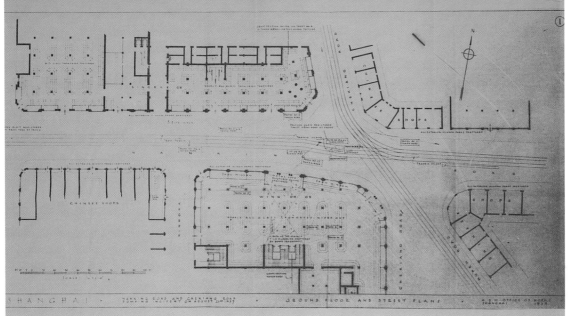

to Asia in 1914 by the Episcopal Board of Missions and the Yale Foreign Missionary Society in connection with a college in Tokyo and the 'Yale in China' programme in Changsha. He became an expert in educational and missionary buildings, designing the American School in Shanghai, where he worked as an associate architect in the Realty Investment Company of Shanghai and designed the Robert Dollar Building, St Mary's Hall and the National City Bank. He was famed for his determination to see 'the revival of the ancient architecture of China into a living style by adapting it to meet the needs of modern scientific planning and construction'.[83] This conviction stood him in good stead when missionaries began to adopt Chinese styles from the early 1910s, in a bid to stay abreast of their changing educational programmes after the Chinese revolution. His most prolific work was during his post as Architectural Advisor to the National government, during which he was involved with the city planning of the new capital, Nanjing.

The start of the Second World War

Though many architects enjoyed flourishing practices in Shanghai in the 1930s, the statistics from the mid-1930s onwards paint a grim picture of Shanghai's condition. However, the property market's pulse was kept beating by those who kept faith with the true spirit of the city, believing that the next boom was imminent. As long as it focused on trade, Shanghai had always managed to prosper, and to some there was no reason to think its predicament in the late 1930s was any different. After months of rising tension, this hope was shattered on 13 August 1937. China and Japan went to war, but this time there was no cosy title to veil the awful truth of the events unfolding in Shanghai's northern suburbs. Shanghai was in the frontline of the first major fighting of the Second World War. On 14 August 1937, remembered ominously in the annals of Shanghai as 'Bloody Saturday',[84] the city's past finally caught up with Shanghai's foreign community.

Anticipating a repeat of the horrors of 1932, hundreds of thousands of residents of Hongkou, Chapei and Shanghai's outlying areas flooded across Garden Bridge to seek sanctuary in the foreign settlements on the Saturday morning. With nowhere to go, most settled in streets, doorways and parks, transforming the Bund into a makeshift refugee camp. Within hours, the International Settlement was awash with desperate Chinese refugees, as it had been on various occasions since the 1850s. Only yards away, moored in the Whuangpu near the Japanese Consulate, was the aged cruiser *Idzumo*, the flagship of the Japanese fleet, busy shelling Chinese positions around Woosung. Chiang Kai Shek ordered his air force to attack the *Idzumo*, which they did with little effect. In the afternoon, the bombers returned, releasing two bombs too early. These smashed into the side of the Cathay Hotel, where thousands of people were seeking refuge. The consequence was horrific in every detail. Such barbarous scenes of unmitigated terror from the air had never before been witnessed. The exact numbers of killed and wounded were

beyond counting, but certainly exceeded 1,500. Bodies and human flesh lay strewn over Nanjing Road, the Bund and on the walls of Asia's most luxurious hotel in 'the worst single calamity outside Hiroshima'.[85]

The already desperate situation was compounded by a third bomb landing directly at the junction of Tibet Road and Edward VII Avenue, in front of the entertainment Mecca, The Great World. In a similarly horrific manner, over 1,000 people were killed and over 500 wounded. The neutral sanctity of the foreign settlements was blown to smithereens by the events of this fateful Saturday afternoon. A further incident occurred on 23 August, when a bomb fell midway along Nanjing Road in front of the Sincere and Wing On department stores, killing over 600 people. Foreign residents, no longer immune to the horrors beyond their hallowed boundaries, were evacuated to Hong Kong. For nearly a century, they had been able to amass considerable fortunes, hide behind foreign immunity and climb to the top of the highest building to witness events unfolding on the Chinese beyond the settlement boundaries, but the morning of 14 August 1937 forced them to look at the world in a new light. Shrapnel from anti-aircraft fire rained down on the settlements for weeks, and incendiary devices and faulty petrol tanks falling indiscriminately from aircraft operated by inexperienced pilots showed no regard for extraterritoriality. The Municipal Council imposed a curfew between 10 pm and 5 am, and Shanghai's famed nightlife was extinguished. The closeted cosiness of foreign life in Shanghai was raw and exposed, and no amount of gin in the Shanghai Club could convince anyone that life would ever be so comfortable again.

The Chinese fought a bitter battle for Shanghai offering the toughest resistance, but eventually they were forced to retreat, surrendering first the newly built and exposed Civic Centre, then the northern suburbs of Hongkou and Chapei where a bitter struggle for the North Railway Station again took place as it had done in 1932 (27

October), then Pudong (6 November), followed by the western districts (9 November), and lastly the former Chinese city (12 November). The marauding Japanese army ruthlessly laid waste all in their path, turning Chapei into an inferno that left a skyline that appeared 'as a jagged array of meaningless architectural forms'.[86] While 1932 had been appalling in its destructiveness, the force and brutality of the fighting in 1937 was 'vastly greater'.[87] The northern and eastern suburbs of the International Settlement, comprising more than half the area, lay in ruins. Street after street of former terraces were razed, transforming huge tracts of land into scorched earth and rubble. To rub salt into the wounds of a reeling community, the Japanese staged a 'Victory March' through the International Settlement on 3 December to boast a conquest that had destroyed 70 per cent of the city's industry, rendered over half a million people unemployed and caused $800 million worth of damage to Shanghai's factories. Desperate though the plight of Shanghai was, it paled in comparison to Japan's broader invasion of China, the ruthlessness of which caused the death of millions of civilians, often under the most barbarous conditions and most notoriously in the 'Rape of Nanjing', when hundreds of thousands of women and children were raped and murdered in a matter of days by Japanese troops. As the wave of war rolled westwards, Chiang Kai Shek withdrew his government from Nanjing to Chongqing, and Shanghai, clinging on to its extraterritorial status, that 'excrescence abhorrent to the Chinese',[88] was left to cater for millions of homeless refugees and former soldiers.

The introduction of new, horrifying and indiscriminate methods of warfare in Shanghai was countered by one of the greatest humanitarian achievements of the Second World War. In the 1932 hostilities, a Jesuit Priest, Father Jacquinot, had successfully negotiated a temporary ceasefire so that thousands of trapped Chinese refugees could escape the

Below left The smoke from Chapei rising over Shanghai

Below right Extent of destruction caused by incendiary bombs on the wooden structures of Hongkou and Chapei

battlefields in Chapei and Hongkou and pass into the International Settlement. Buoyed by the success of this remarkable achievement, in the war of 1937, Father Jacquinot managed to negotiate with the Japanese a sanctuary in the former Chinese city, which was to be respected by the Japanese as a safe haven for Chinese civilians. From 5 November, the northeastern corner of the former walled city became known as the Jacquinot Zone and proved against all odds that in wartime civilians can be excluded from the field of conflict.

The character of Shanghai following its greatest ever calamity changed significantly as it tried to adapt to its new situation. The Japanese controlled all the land around the settlements. Based in the Northern and Eastern Districts, they occupied over half the International Settlement, controlling the vital services such as electricity and the water supply and 90 per cent of its river front. They also employed armies of Chinese coolies to remove systematically all the scrap metal from these areas, and shipped it to Japan for the wider war effort. Foreigners were not allowed back into the areas north of Suzhou Creek until 27 December that year, though it remained banned to Chinese, making it very difficult for the factories to operate. Japanese sentries guarded all the bridges across Suzhou Creek, checking the papers of everyone crossing into the Japanese areas. Their presence on these border posts was notorious, as they delighted in humiliating those going about their business, especially the Chinese, many of whom were killed simply trying to go home after a day's work, just for the amusement of the Japanese troops.

The ruin of the Northern and Eastern Districts caused industry to migrate westwards. The Western District of the International Settlement and the extra-settlement roads areas, once home to the city's most luxurious villas, now started to accommodate heavy industry and small factories that belched noxious fumes. At the end of 1938, the areas of the Western, Central and Northern Districts of the International Settlement and the extra-settlement roads area that had escaped the actual fighting contained 3,880 factories employing over 150,000 workers, compared with the war-torn areas of the Northern and Eastern Districts, which had just 371 factories employing 74,119 workers.[89] Although statistics vary, there is no doubt that the migration of industry and workers into the settlements south of Suzhou Creek, bringing with them their dependants, caused considerable congestion and an explosion of illegal shanty-type structures, which the Municipal Council was unable to counter. The presence of over a quarter of a million additional residents reliant on the settlements for their living transformed formerly residential or partially industrialised districts.

While Chinese workers and refugees flooded into the international areas, the Japanese, with remarkable

foresight, saw an opportunity to reconstruct the former battlegrounds of Chapei and Hongkou. The only people on earth whose predicament was worse even than the Chinese peasantry at this time, and who were willing residents of Shanghai's most wretched district, were the European Jews escaping the horrors of Nazi Germany. Compared with the Nazis, even the Japanese, whose conduct in China stretched the bounds of human depravity, were a welcome reprieve. Jewish roots in Shanghai were very deep, going back to the first days of the settlement and the arrival of the Sassoons, but subsequent Jewish merchants had done much to strengthen the city's ties with the Jewish faith. The various synagogues in Hongkou and the International Settlement attest to this illustrious history, but among the most important associations, especially in the light of the Japanese invasion of Shanghai, had been the Jewish support of the Japanese war effort against Russia in 1904. A wealthy American Jewish banker from New York, Jacob Schiff, had bankrolled a large portion of the Japanese expenditure in the hope that a Russian defeat would help the plight of the 30,000 Jewish conscripts in the Russian army, who were treated as a sub-class in the military ranks. Japan never forgot Schiff's contribution, so when thousands of European Jews started to arrive on Shanghai's doorstep in the late 1930s, they were willingly received, at least for a while.

The Third Reich's increasingly aggressive direct action against the Jewish community in Germany and Austria made many Jews realise that their continued existence in their homeland was not viable. From 1938, many started packing their possessions and seeking whatever means they could to escape to less hostile countries. As the stream of Jews from Central Europe turned into a flood, many potential destinations closed their doors. Shanghai, the constitutional anomaly that demanded no visa to enter, was one of the last refuges that would accept them. Word of this

Right Aerial photograph showing Hongkou (top), central Shanghai and racecourse (middle) and the former walled city (bottom right)

lone haven quickly spread. Numbers of Jewish refugees arriving in Shanghai increased from 1,374 in 1938 to 12,089 in 1939.[90] Every available berth was taken on ships from Europe that made the often long voyage via the Cape of Good Hope, reaching Shanghai between one and three months later. On arrival in Shanghai, the thousands of refugees were processed in Victor Sassoon's Embankment Building before being settled in the burnt out areas of Hongkou. Recognising that these desperate people were often skilled professionals and industrious workers, the Japanese were ready to benefit from the efforts of the Jewish community to reconstruct the area. For those who were in no position to obtain their own accommodation, six refugee camps were established in the Northern and Eastern Districts of the Japanese-controlled International Settlement, housing over 2,500 people – approximately 20 per cent of the refugee population. Within months, European Jews had rebuilt large areas of Hongkou, turning it into 'little Vienna', with boutiques, bakeries, music halls, shops and cafes rising from the rubble, exhausting available living space. As the numbers of arrivals showed no signs of decreasing, the Japanese and foreign settlement authorities became anxious about Shanghai's open door policy. Hongkou's affordable rates also made it an attractive destination for Chinese refugees, more White Russians and thousands of returning Japanese. The Jewish tide began to be stemmed. With the onset of the Second World War and growing ambivalence towards the Jewish question, Shanghai, for the first time in its history, began to close its door to refugees.

The end of the 1930s was a desperate time in Shanghai and in the world in general. The grim foreboding of one local observer in the 1920s proved harrowingly prophetic: 'The wonderful future of Shanghai painted in glowing colours by local scribes is merely a castle in the air, a mirage conjured up by publicity optimists which fades away before the cold light of everyday facts.'[91] The appalling destruction caused by war, which had so often been a boon for foreign Shanghai, had finally caught up with the city. Short of invading the settlements, the Japanese were unable to harass the foreign community more than they did at the foreigners' weakest point – the extra-settlement roads areas beyond the Western District. This formerly cosy and idyllic area, suffused with opulent villas, was transformed into a haven for gangland activities and became known as Shanghai's 'Badlands'. Crime soared as the rule of law waned under the pressures of mere survival, and Shanghai's 'invisible government' underworld thrived on drugs and arms racketeering, kidnappings and extortion.

Now, the steady tempo of building activity was kept alive only by the needs of the desperate. As the glory days slipped from the grasp of an increasingly impoverished foreign community, nostalgic reminiscences evoked mythical bygone times. Whereas the annals of foreign Shanghai were filled with tales of glorious advances in construction and development, they now reflected only on the embattled and industrial monster that had been created:

> Shanghai today an industrial city stilled by the God of War, with sprawling factories rearing their ugly, plain walls over wide areas, was even known for its beauty in those far-gone days … There, thousands of plum trees were planted and a canal thread[ed] its way around them … Beflagged, colourful junks came down the Hutuh Canal, or Soochow Creek as it came to be known, and with pipe and lute and verse … For then there were no cotton or flour mills, and iron foundries

Below Suzhou Creek from the Embankment Building looking east towards the Central Post Office (far left), Hongkou skyline (centre) and Broadway Mansions (centre-right)

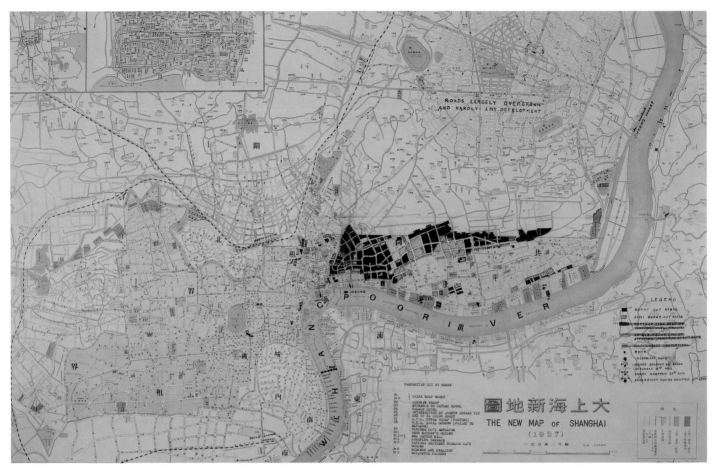

Above Map showing the extent of destruction caused by Japanese bombing in 1937

did not spout black smoke over a green countryside, turning fresh grass black with soot and poisoning trees and flowers with noxious gases.[92]

On 8 December (Shanghai time) 1941, Japan launched its attack on Pearl Harbor, ringing the final death knell on foreign Shanghai. That morning, columns of Japanese troops advanced on the International Settlement and formally took control. Resistance was futile. The British frigate HMS *Petrel* (sic) refused to surrender and was sunk in the Whuangpu before sunrise, symbolising aptly the descent of British power that had for so long ruled over this patch of Chinese territory and the naive desperation with which it tried to cling to its former role. The Municipal Council continued to function, albeit only symbolically, for a further year before being dismantled. The Rising Sun ruled over Shanghai, while the French Concession, representing the neutral Vichy government, retained a degree of autonomy, but only on paper. Shanghai's iniquitous plutocracy was replaced by inhuman military rule.

The end of an era

The period from the 1920s to 1941 represents Shanghai's maturity and decline, both in the broader socio-political sphere and in architecture. The city's unprecedented growth during the warlord period, tempered only briefly by the uncertainty of the Nationalist victory, up to the beginning of the Japanese hostilities was described by the architect George Wilson as 'nothing short of amazing' and marks the height of design activity in Shanghai. However, its relative eminence remains questionable. The Municipal Council and, to a lesser extent, the French Council 'at no time made an attempt to enforce harmony in any locality', resulting in the architectural 'conglomeration' on 'the Bund and buildings generally throughout Shanghai'.[93] In addition to this lack of regulation, the city's culturally diverse population resulted in an inevitable propensity for professionals to maintain their 'own ideas of architecture and city planning'.

There is no doubt that some remarkable buildings of a high standard were created in this period, but in a time when European and American design schools were undergoing revolutionary transformations in theory, philosophy and practice, architecture in Shanghai, like everything else, played second fiddle to commerce, as architects became 'slaves to "Copybook architecture"'. The client, with unprecedented financial influence, dictated form, employing the skills of the 'unfortunate' architect, more often than not, to turn fanciful dreams into reality.[94]

Those who tried to impose original styles often 'ignored everything produced in the past' and created only 'ugly and grotesque results'.[95] The result is Shanghai's 'architectural wonderland',[96] where Modernist piles shared the same drawing board as faux-Tudor villas and Neoclassical palaces to create streets containing encyclopaedic assortments of architectural references. This loose design philosophy permeated most private firms. The evolution of this architectural menagerie is easily traced through the 1920s and 1930s, a period that began rooted in conservatism defined by Neoclassical and quasi-European forms and ended with a proliferation of progressive styles articulated by Modernist references, both externally and internally. The trend towards traditionalism in Shanghai up to the 1920s can be attributed partly to the supremacy of Britain, which in the field of architecture was famously conformist and especially so in her overseas dominions, where symbols of power, wealth and order were rooted in conservatism. Even by 1930, one British architect doubted whether the 'extreme Modernism of Corbusier will find much favour with Shanghai residents'.[97] 'It was not until the decade ending 1925 that buildings were put up on principles in vogue in the United States'[98] – modern design made little impact on Shanghai's architectural landscape until the end of the 1920s, and even then much of it was 'anything but successful'.[99] It improved considerably into the 1930s, with the greater variety of foreign architects working in Shanghai and Chinese architects embracing the new style.

Ironically, the copious Classical styles were, to the Chinese, symbols of modernity. In the days of the new Republic, everything that was 'foreign' was by its very nature 'modern', and so when the first Chinese-designed modern buildings appeared, it was no surprise that they boasted Classical motifs. This was true of the work of both the untrained and the trained Chinese architects, the latter of whom were beginning to return from America during this period. They were pioneers in their field and returned to a building boom that offered exceptional opportunities for such young and relatively inexperienced architects. These architects were firmly established in Shanghai by the end of the 1930s, representing over 30 per cent of the city's architectural practices and rivalling Western firms, who were finding it increasingly difficult to work in the ever more hostile environment in which the foreigner's position was becoming untenable.

This trend in architecture, as with every other part of life in Shanghai, was merely an illustration of China's growing strength and organisation. Extraterritoriality, the iniquitous principle upon which the constitution of Shanghai was founded, was nothing more than a tumour slowly destroying its host. Ransome's summary of the Shanghailander's self-destructive character provides a pertinent conclusion:

> They seem to have lived in a hermetically sealed and isolated glass case since 1901. The people 'think imperially' in the manner of the Rand magnates at the time of the South African War. They think of 'anti-foreignism' as China's original sin, to be exorcised by periodical penances. They look round on their magnificent buildings and are surprised that China is not grateful to them for these gifts, forgetting that the money to build them came out of China. Controlling the bottle-neck through which the bulk of Chinese trade must pass, they prosper upon it coming and going and forget that it is the trade that is valuable to England and not the magnificent buildings which big profits and low taxes have allowed them to erect … Extremely conservative, like most business communities in foreign countries, they are prepared to have their country go to war for them rather than to adjust themselves to inevitably changing conditions.

The arrogant and 'conspicuous lack of endeavour on the part of the foreigner to broaden his contacts with the native'[100] had undermined the foreigner's position, and it was only a case of when and not if the 'unequal Treaties' would be rescinded and control of China's sovereign territory restored. Shanghai was a place to make money and, latterly, to have fun. Beyond that, very few foreigners saw any reason to expend any more energy on its future welfare. The fact that Japan emerged to claim Shanghai was, in the long and peculiar life of this city, just another chapter that would surely pass into the annals of history. Like all the city's rulers before it, Japan would surely not own Shanghai for long.

Below Modernist villa built in 1939 in the former French Concession, now a district Children's Palace

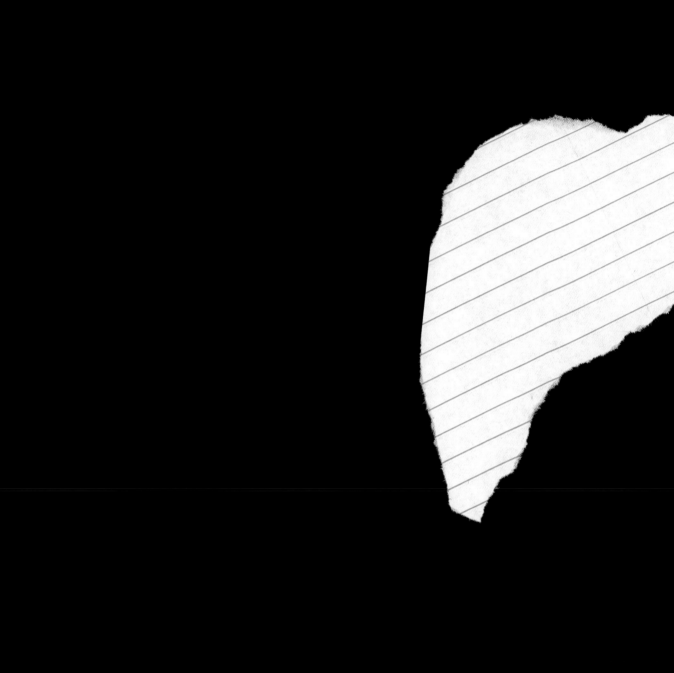

Anti-Design

Shanghai would have been a great city had there never been a foreigner in the place [and] would continue to be a great city even if the foreigners should vacate their modern buildings and go home.

China Weekly Review, 4 December 1926

Below Japanese map of Shanghai

For all the glamour, adventure and allure that Shanghai evoked during the 1920s and 1930s, the introductory pages of a 1941 guidebook exemplified the city's swift decline. Shanghai's bars, clubs, hum of business, and breathtaking structures were relegated to inconsequential titbits as visitors journeying up the Whuangpu could 'behold the shell-holed factory stacks and shell and fire torn structures on either bank'. Shanghai, it seemed, was reaching its lowest ebb.

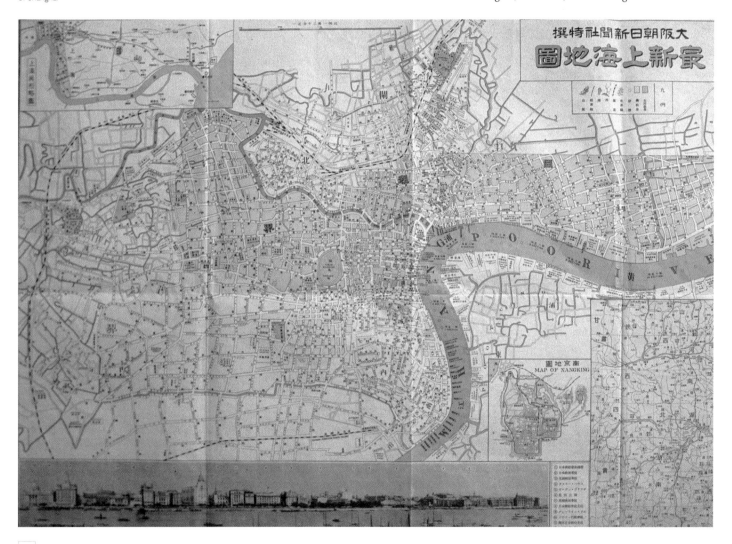

Despite bouts of optimism, time stood still for Shanghai from the early 1940s. The Second World War had barely ended before China's civil war condemned the Nationalist government to Taiwan, heralding a Communist government and the People's Republic of China. Shanghai's capitalist character and liberal spirit proved incongruous with the new mould, forcing its once formidable economic prowess to be reined in under a veil of political absolutism, from which it would emerge in tatters over half a century later.

Through neglect, inexperience and devastating political expedience, Shanghai regressed – buildings were not maintained and little new was constructed. While architecture and design are practices concerned with progress, their absence in Shanghai from 1949 was significant not only in the paucity of new structures but also in the failure of the political system that prevented their application. This reached its nadir in the long, dark years of the Cultural Revolution – a period of anti-design in an age of devolution, where society almost but not entirely consumed itself.

The Second World War

From the end of 1941, following their occupation of the International Settlement, the Japanese administration at first honoured the rights of foreigners. The Municipal Council continued its duties for a short while, maintaining the illusion of relative normality where 'Britons and Americans could mingle with enemies and friends alike'.[1] However, this state of limbo proved short-lived. The Allied members on the Council resigned in the opening days of 1942 against a backdrop of Allied capitulation throughout Asia. With business interests in Shanghai terminated or under Japanese control, the priority for most foreign residents in Shanghai was survival. Some were repatriated in the middle of 1942, but by the end of the year the first round-ups began for internment in the 'civilian assembly centres'. The first and worst of the centres was the military Haiphong Road Camp, reserved for 'political suspects, often former Municipal Police officers and ex-servicemen'.[2] Another seven camps catered for over 8,000 foreign civilians. Internees were given ten days to pack their belongings and register at Holy Trinity Cathedral, which became an assembly point before individuals were assigned their destination.

The conditions in the civilian camps were bad but bearable and as time passed the internees created liveable communities, though their captivity could not be compared with the weeks of confinement endured by Allied diplomats following Pearl Harbor. They awaited their fate at the expense of the Japanese government in the city's premiere hotels such as the Cathay and Metropole.

As the repatriations and internments continued, Shanghai's infamously stratified social structure was turned on its head. The citizens of Allied nations had been condemned to the bottom of the social ladder and bore armbands marking their status, while citizens of neutral countries acted as mediators and Axis powers enjoyed new-found privileges as favoured nations of Japan. Shanghai's clubs, businesses and institutions were commandeered by the Japanese and distributed among their various imperial offices. Hamilton House became an office for the Kempeitai, the much feared Japanese military police, headed from August 1942 by the dreaded Kinoshita. The Shanghai Club was appropriated by the Japanese Naval Landing Party. Jardine & Matheson's offices on the Bund became the Japanese Naval Intelligence Bureau. Even Hitler's propaganda ministry joined the free for all and found a home in the city's tallest building, the Park Hotel. While the inevitable confiscation of property meant that many of Shanghai's most famous landmarks assumed different roles under the new administration, the most terrifying changes occurred in lesser known establishments. Seemingly innocuous addresses, such as 76 Jessfield Road and Bridge House, a former hostel on the northern banks of Suzhou Creek, became institutions of torture and abuse so cruel that 'some victims implored the Japanese to kill them in order to end their suffering'.[3]

The Japanese authorities had also to contend with the internment of thousands of European Jews. Rendered officially stateless by German law in November 1941, the Shanghai Jews faced an uncertain fate. After much deliberation, it was decided in May 1943 that this group of approximately 20,000 'stateless refugees'[4] would be confined to an area of Hongkou known as a *shitei chiku*, an area that was 'neither a ghetto nor jail, but an area which is full of hope' (see map pages 8–9).[5] From August 1943, Jews needing to exit the *shitei chiku* had to obtain passes from the infamous and appalling Japanese official, Ghoya, self-proclaimed 'King of the Jews' and notorious psychopath. Life in Hongkou throughout the war proved primitive, but, like most other foreigners, the Jews, or '"Jude-men" – as the Chinese call them', managed to eke out a living in order to survive their ordeals, transforming one of Shanghai's poorest areas into 'a kind of tourist attraction'.[6]

For others, survival was far from assured. Life in Shanghai during the Second World War descended into a morass of anarchy and political struggle. Nationalists and Communists fought one another and both fought the Japanese. Private armies of Sikhs, White Russians and Chinese were hired to do what the Municipal Police had long since lost the will or capacity to do, while enjoying the opportunity for retribution against their former paymasters, under whom they had forever been racially segregated at work. No one was safe, not least complicit Chinese officials working for the Japanese or Chinese patriots blacklisted by the puppet regime in Nanjing. The formerly esteemed New Asia Hotel (H4) in Hongkou became home to Shanghai's 'Yellow Way Society'. This group of gangsters collaborated with the Japanese and 'used the

Previous pages Cultural Revolution poster depicting the Revolutionaries and Red Guards parading outside the Workers' Headquarters by the former racecourse

Right The New Asia Hotel

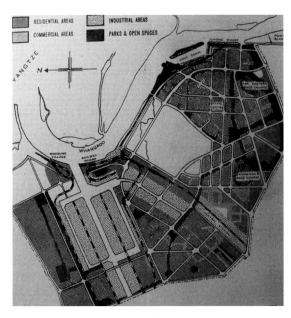

bathroom for the decapitation of Chinese who refused to play ball with conquerors and puppets'.[7] For those with a hint of freedom of movement, international espionage provided one way to strike a retaliatory blow at the Japanese administration, while others chose to collaborate with their captors.

The start of 1943 saw Shanghai become a free city for the first time in 100 years, at least on paper. America and Britain rescinded their extraterritorial rights to Chiang's government in Chongqing on 11 and 13 January 1943 respectively, and the French Vichy government followed suit on 30 July, by revoking France's rights under China's puppet regime. France formally abandoned extraterritoriality with the Chongqing government on 11 February 1946. However, Shanghai's real rulers, having assumed control over a veritable hornets' nest, were struggling to maintain their supremacy. As the tide of war started to turn against the Axis powers, insurgency increased. The Park Hotel's renowned restaurant on the 14th floor was the venue for a bombing on 4 May 1944, which killed several Japanese officers. A year later, Hongkou was once again the site of the worst incidence of bombing in Shanghai. On 17 July 1945, American planes attacking Japanese positions in Hongkou missed their targets. According to the memoirs of eyewitness Ernest Heppner, the bombs, landing in one of the most densely populated areas on earth, killed at least 30 Jewish refugees, 300 Japanese and an estimated 4,000 Chinese, and left over 700 refugees and thousands of Chinese homeless.

As the destruction caused by war weighed heavily on Shanghai's tired population, construction in Shanghai during the Second World War stalled. The Japanese drew up several grandiose plans for the city – more symbolic than practical. The most realistic plan was produced in 1939 by engineers of the Home Department of the Japanese government and the army and was based on the former Civic Centre scheme of the 1930s. The proposal, like its predecessor, intended to draw influence away from the foreign settlements and was put forward as a plan of China's 'Reformed Government', but in reality it was a Japanese plan employing Japanese companies and serving the Japanese population in Shanghai, which was expected to reach 300,000 by the end of the 1940s. One of the more drastic schemes involved the complete razing of the former International Settlement from the Bund to its former western boundary, to be replaced by a monumental central east–west axis of broad roads, state buildings and gardens overlooking a reorganised Pudong. The architect's plan was as ludicrous as Japan's vision of world domination, and equally fruitless.

Allied liberation

Japan had little time to implement any of its schemes for Shanghai. On 7 September 1945, following the atomic bombs on Nagasaki and Hiroshima, Shanghai was surrendered by Japan. Despite the united front presented by the Nationalists and Communists in their fight against Japan, the Nationalists quickly filled the power vacuum after the war, taking control of China's major cities, but losing out on much of the war bounty that was taken over by the Communists in northern China. Chiang Kai Shek and the Nationalist government had control of China's greatest prize, but not the means to retain it.

Returning foreigners faced a city in which they no longer enjoyed special privileges and in which their former homes were looted or in ruins. Many, broken in spirit and in health, decided then that their future lay not in Shanghai, but in the country stated on their passports – a place that some had never seen. Others chose suicide. A small minority of the various refugee communities stayed behind, but most made their way to America, Canada, Australia, the Philippines, or

Above and right Shanghai's progressive Modern era was interrupted by the Second World War with few notable Modernist buildings built in the 1940s. This villa on the outskirts of Shanghai, designed by Wang Min Xin in 1948, is one of the exceptions

first floor

ground floor

back to their former homes in Europe. After 1948, the Jews also had the choice of moving to Israel. There were also those who believed Shanghai would rise again and was approaching 'the biggest boom you can possibly imagine'.[8]

With the economy in tatters, industry at a standstill and hyperinflation producing China's first $100,000 banknote, such assertions seemed preposterous. However, just at this time when Shanghai faced bankruptcy, 50,000 American GIs arrived on the city's doorstep, with weeks of unspent pay and a determination to have a good time. As the American dollar restored life to the city, even the old trading houses and banks resumed a certain semblance of business. The Hongkong and Shanghai Bank found its 'lucky lions' in a godown and resumed business in its palatial residence on the Bund, while Jardine & Matheson created order from the chaos wrought to its wide-ranging business interests, and quenched Shanghai's thirst by resuscitating the Shanghai Brewery. The sense of revival, combined with huge grants in aid from the United Nations and the United States, created an atmosphere of 'riotous abundance'.[9] One American businessman boasted in *Fortune Magazine*: 'You watch. Shanghai will snap back faster than any city in the world. You won't know the place in a year,' echoing the famous words of the Nationalist government's finance minister, Soong Tze Wen: 'We must make Shanghai the show window of the New China.'

However, beyond the blustering and far from the American-funded shallow economic miracle, the reality for the Chinese was unemployment, starvation and hyperinflation in the face of appalling governmental corruption and fiscal negligence. In 1944, the US dollar had been worth 20 Chinese Yuan, but by 1948 it had topped a million. Thousands of homeless Chinese slept and died on Shanghai's streets, to be collected by trucks each morning and dumped like refuse in the city's outskirts. Such scenes played into the hands of the Communists and their army of over a million soldiers led by Mao Tse Dong.

Communist liberation

By April 1949, the whole of China north of the Yangtze was under Communist control and Shanghai was under curfew. Without an extraterritorial cloak for protection, foreigners in Shanghai with their considerable business interests once again feared for their livelihoods. By May, the Nationalist army started moving into defensive positions, occupying key vantage points provided by the tall apartment buildings and hotels such as Cavendish Court and the Cathay, while the nightclubs such as Paramount, Ciro's and the Majestic were commandeered for army barracks. Barbed wire and sandbags were put up all over the city, just as they had been when the Japanese had attacked Hongkou, and the former Public Garden hosted a battery of guns, as it had done in 1842 when the Chinese had tried to repulse the British. In the former extra-settlement roads areas to the west of the city, residents

Above The USS Helena at Shanghai on 20 September 1946. Note Sassoon House and the Bank of China in the background.

were again awaiting their fate while two huge armies faced each other across lines of picket fences and privet hedges. Generals Li Tsung Jen and Ho Ying Chin, two of the generals who had led the march on Shanghai in 1927, were now implicated in its downfall. While General Li attempted to negotiate a truce with the advancing Communists, General Ho was organising the city's defence. Unbeknown to anyone but Chiang, a few trusted aides and bank officials, a line of coolies one night at the end of April filed out of the Bank of China on the Bund, laden with the country's gold reserves to be taken to Taiwan. With fitting irony the looting of China's wealth was literally carried out on the backs of its poorest class on the former towpath that had come to symbolise foreign exploitation. Chiang, like the foreign businesses before him, fled China with much of its wealth in tow.

The ensuing Battle for Shanghai was similar to the Battle of Muddy Flat 95 years earlier, as one force capitulated at the first show of strength from the other, handing the reins of power in Shanghai to yet another ruler with little damage to property. A brief but spirited display of resistance occurred at the mouth of Suzhou Creek, overlooked by Garden Bridge, the former Public Garden and Broadway Mansions. As the Nationalists played for time and prolonged their retreat by two days, Shanghai characteristically continued business as normal a few streets behind the Bund, while machine guns, mortars and grenades raged on and around Garden Bridge.

By 27 May 1949, Shanghai was a communist city, its new rulers claiming to have liberated it 'from a semi-colonial and semi-feudal society'. In the eyes of the city's pro-communist newspapers like the *Shang Pao* (Commerce Daily), Shanghai had been transformed in three days from a city in which 'bandits let loose slaughter and plunder' to 'a paradise in which there is freedom, democracy, stability, and prosperity'.[10] Feverish flag-waving greeted the peasant army, whose unquestionable proficiency in the field of combat did little to prepare them for China's most modern metropolis, despite 'a great deal of effort into training PLA [People's

Liberation Army] troops assigned to capture cities'.[11] Towering skyscrapers, escalators, American films, foreign language schools, neon lights and rail-less trams confronted these rural peasants, and confirmed in them their nascent suspicions about this evil and decadent city. Nonetheless, these rural youngsters were noted for behaving impeccably in their alien abode, paying for everything and showing a sincere courtesy towards their urban neighbours.

On first impressions, some were misled by this charming display of rustic innocence, which was undermined only by the conversion of the racecourse into an execution ground for racketeers and Nationalist sympathisers. As the city acquainted itself with its new rulers, the Communist General, Chen Yi, was named Mayor of Shanghai. The Picardie and Gascoigne apartments in the former French Concession were rented out to the city council, who housed peasant soldiers in them so as to honour Mao's promise that they would sleep in skyscrapers. The lifts, flush toilets, electric stoves and, especially, the bidets provided no end of entertainment for the soldiers, whose tenancy changed every couple of weeks in a cunning move designed to exploit the free propaganda emanating from their excited gossip after their tour of duty in Shanghai. For foreign and Chinese residents who had experienced Shanghai in its heyday, the city was becoming tedious. Chiang's naval blockade stifled trade and Communist policies impinged on formerly liberal social activities. The British Consulate's Senior Architect, TSM Terrace, described the scene in Shanghai in 1949:

> I should say that the broad picture of Shanghai today is that conditions are not too pleasant, and the possibility of Shanghai ever returning to its normal way of life is very doubtful. Despondency prevails and the general feeling is that Shanghai is finished so far as the foreigner is concerned. The general atmosphere is indeed depressing and it looks as though Shanghai with its wonderful reputation for recovery has had its time.

Two decades earlier, when asked how China could solve its own problems, the illustrious American shipping magnate Robert Dollar replied, 'By a strong dictator who will set up a strong Government.' On 1 October 1949, Chairman Mao announced the founding of the People's Republic of China. Only months later, foreign governments one by one officially recognised China's new rulers. China was, according to Dollar's reasoning, finally in a position to solve its own problems. With Communist tradition rooted in peasant communes, village organisations and rural administration, it was questionable whether this fledgling government could cope with administering large, complex, industrialised urban centres, despite Mao's assertions that the time for communism to operate 'from the city to the village' had arrived. An immediate nationalisation programme reined in China's most commercial city, which had always relied on merchants, traders and industrialists for its prosperity. Construction had always been underpinned by the assumption that 'there [was] hardly a likelihood, should a new State step in, for it to confiscate the individual's right to property'[12] in Shanghai. With this worst-case scenario now becoming reality, construction halted.

At the time, Shanghai's housing stock comprised 52.7 per cent old lane houses (mostly within the former settlement boundaries), 19.8 per cent new lane houses, 13.7 per cent temporary huts (in the outlying suburbs), 9.5 per cent garden houses and 4.3 per cent apartments. With the help of Soviet advisors, the Communists forged ahead with land and property reform, slicing up China's urban real estate. At the onset of the Korean War in June 1950, followed by an edict demanding that all public buildings were to be handed in to the government by January 1952, the last remaining foreigners realised that this was the end. Britain, after over one hundred years of trade in China, pulled the plug on its $900 million stake in the country. The exodus from Shanghai pumped untold wealth into Hong Kong, which thrived on the sorry predicament facing Shanghai's former businesses, many of which went on to become very powerful enterprises in their new home. Those with most to lose were the last to leave. The 14 May 1954 marked the end of a century of Shanghai's famously turbulent property market. Over 15,000 foreign properties were appropriated by the Communist government, which used the same excuse again and again to legitimise its policy: properties were taken as collateral against outstanding debts. The nature and size of the debts were irrelevant. A century of ignominy caused by foreign exploitation was being avenged with swift and brutal retribution, delivering a fatal blow to Shanghai's commercial spirit.

One by one, Shanghai's former landmarks were taken. The Shanghai Club, after nearly a century of plying the city's elite with alcohol, was ordered to pay commodity tax on its liquor stocks, which it did, only to be fined 430 million

Yuan by the Tax Bureau, bankrupting the club. This 'melancholy story', as the British Ambassador described it in 1952, was repeated throughout Shanghai's former foreign settlements. Almost a hundred years to the day after the Battle of Muddy Flat, the Race Club, on the site of the battle itself, was taken against debts. HSBC fell the following year, against debt. Kadoorie's villa was appropriated and converted into a Children's Palace. The former empires of Sassoon and Hardoon were all taken against debt, the massive garden of the latter being converted into the unmistakable Sino-Russian Friendship Building (D5) – an absurdly decorative Soviet structure that fits well into Shanghai's architectural muddle.

Although there were many exceptions to the rule, depending usually on how much influence an individual or family could wield, nationalisation of housing was carried

Left and below The distinctive Sino-Russian Friendship Building (**left**) later renamed the Shanghai Exhibition Centre (**below**)

Right The Great World in 1960, adorned with decorations celebrating the 11th anniversary of the establishment of New China

out according to three vague categories. The first was 'enemy property'. These were confiscated outright. The second was former capitalist property, which was taken coercively from individuals such as the city's businessmen, entrepreneurs and non-Party members. The third and largest category contained the properties of most ordinary people, who had to revoke their property rights, albeit 'voluntarily', to prove their allegiance to the new Communist government.

Former mansions, villas, lane houses and workplaces were dutifully handed over, subdivided and assigned to government offices or formerly landless peasants, as Shanghai's population and area increased dramatically. 'A ring of new industrial suburbs' with rows of Soviet-styled concrete block apartments encircled the former settlements, reflecting a 'heavy dependence upon Soviet industrial planning and design'.[13] Although Master Plans were devised for a sprawling Shanghai, now covering 5,910 square kilometres, they became purely symbolic gestures of progress in a political climate that disfavoured improvement based on anything but political ideology. Shanghai's population grew by 44 per cent from approximately 5 million in 1949 to 7.2 million in 1957, while housing standards 'declined sharply ... reaching intolerable levels' for many.[14] At the same time, government offices and bureaucrats acquired the city's finest residences appropriated during nationalisation, and the military requisitioned almost 10 per cent of the city's property. With Mao's guerrilla mindset preoccupied with global conflict, Shanghai was transformed into a military base. As a result of despotic paranoia, combined with the Communists' concerns about overpopulation and ingrained distrust of large urban centres, much of Shanghai's industrial capacity was moved to other parts of the country away from the eastern seaboard, which Mao believed was vulnerable to attack.

While the Party boasted that 'the calamity-ridden port town was greeting a grand resurrection', others saw only descent into the political morass, as the Communists imposed their political ideology through vague doctrines that swayed with the political mood. Shanghai's towering edifices, so long the source of bravado, had come to serve as ideal billboards for political slogans and sites for committing suicide. The last had become so common that 'the police tried to stop the suicides by erecting nets which jutted out from first-floor windows over the pavement, but this only made them more determined. Instead of jumping from windows, they took running jumps from the roofs of tall buildings, so they would land in the street beyond the range of the netting.'[15] This bleak reality presented a grim foreboding for the years ahead, during which millions would take their own lives to escape their suffering.

Left The facade of one of Shanghai's offices in the former Central District with the faded slogan 'Long Life Great Leader Chairman Mao' painted on the central pilaster

Below The Modern staircase of one of Shanghai's former apartment buildings where many attempted suicide during the Cultural Revolution

Above The compound of the former British Consulate in 2005

Opposite, above and below The former Union Church before (above) and after (below) the Cultural Revolution

Below The former Shanghai Workers' Headquarters opposite the former racecourse

The Great Proletarian Cultural Revolution

Political campaign followed political campaign, as Shanghai and China were brought to the brink of civil war by the infighting within the Communist Party, concluding in the Great Proletarian Cultural Revolution (GPCR), launched in Shanghai in 1966. This year marked one of the lowest points of China's ostensible 5,000 years of civilisation. For ten terrible years, China's descent into chaos caused unfathomable misery, as countless millions were pitted against one another as pawns in a political crusade that, in the totality of its mercilessness, outdid all previous rebellions, wars and insurgencies within the Chinese empire. Shanghai's forte, for

so long its economic prowess, was now its political stature as Mao's power base, forming the vanguard against Beijing's power elite.

From August 1966, the notorious Red Guard, a mobilised body of lawless students devoted to Mao, ran amok on the streets in a frenzy designed to rid Shanghai of symbols of feudalism, capitalism and colonialism. Foreign language signage, statues and decorative features on walls were wiped from the face of Shanghai. Next in the firing line were the properties of 'landlords', 'rightists', 'capitalists', 'imperialists', 'anti-revolutionists', 'feudalists' and religious institutions. No one was innocent, as rampaging students smashed their way into homes, looted and destroyed possessions and seized properties for their own use or operational headquarters. In one example, the property of the former owner of Wing On department store was raided seven times. The British, the first foreigners into Shanghai, were among the very last to leave. The British Consulate was breached and forced to vacate the premises that had occupied the city's most hallowed piece of real estate. On leaving the consulate compound for the final time, Britain's last diplomatic staff in Shanghai, Mr Hewitt and Mr Whitney, were 'struck, kicked, had glue poured on them and clothes torn' in a 'clearly organised'[16] staged humiliation designed to wreak vengeance on the hapless foreigners unfortunate enough to be the last out of Shanghai. They arrived in Beijing on 24 May 1967 'battered but unbowed', having surrendered the consulate compound and its 'unlawful activities' against all manner of fines and taxes at which the Foreign Office philosophically concluded: '122 years without rent isn't bad going.'[17]

For the wretched Chinese unable to escape the social and political turmoil, Shanghai had become a battleground for the various political elements, each claiming to be more revolutionary than the other. By December 1966, the Revolutionists had occupied 360,000 square metres of housing and granted it to 19,500 families. On the last evening of 1966, the Red Guard carried out further raids on even more properties, as well as all those commandeered in the first raids in August. The following week, the Revolutionists, spearheaded by the Workers' Headquarters (G5), declared war on the government's municipal authority, and after the 'January Revolution' claimed control of Shanghai. The GPCR's impact throughout China had turned from being a war of words into a war of deeds. Beijing had lost control of Shanghai, as Mao and his cohorts, Jiang Ching (his wife), Zhang Chun Chiao, Yao Wen Yuan and Wang Hong Wen (later known as 'The Gang of Four'), oversaw the Party's downfall and the establishment of the Shanghai People's Commune on 5 February, which was renamed the Shanghai Revolutionary Committee on 23 February.

In the prevailing mayhem, nearly one and a half million square metres of homes, occupied by 40,501 families, and over one hundred religious sites were stolen in three appalling years.

Xiao Tao Yuan Mosque

The Xiao Tao Yuan Mosque, situated in the western part of the former walled city, had been one of Shanghai's most renowned mosques. The land for its complex was donated to the Muslim community by one of the Shanghai islamic mosque directors, Jin Zi Yun, in 1917. Construction of the present mosque began in 1925 and was completed in 1927. Like most religious sites in China, the mosque was severely damaged during the GPCR, though it escaped the worst atrocities since the Muslim communities from Pakistan and Iran, with whom China had amicable relations at the time, managed to avert much of the devastation that was inflicted on other similar sites.

Below The Xiao Tao Yuan Mosque

Schools and universities were closed for a decade, factories and workplaces were disrupted, and cathedrals, churches and temples were seized and desecrated. Among others, Xu Jia Hui, Holy Trinity Cathedral and Union Church lost their spires. Jing An, Jade Buddha and Lung Hua Temples were smashed and their statues and ancient scriptures destroyed, along with countless other temples and religious sites, including the Xiao Tao Yuan Mosque (H7) in the former walled city.

In the chaos, rural peasants descended on the city, occupying former garden and lane houses. Unable to pay the rent or adapt to the lifestyles intended for these properties, many continued their rural ways, cooking with charcoal fires on the ground, oblivious to the teak parquet flooring and decorative inlaid motifs designed to satisfy the whims of former owners with very different modes of living. While the government's nationalisation programme after 1949 had attempted to redistribute property to the masses in accordance with their version of the law, the Red Guard and Revolutionists ran riot in a ten-year rampage of pillaging and butchery that laid waste to China's cultural landscape and social fabric. In the name of political ideology, tens of millions were murdered or took their own lives.

Shanghai had faced many vicissitudes, but all previous experiences, however appalling or immoral, fostered at least a grain of progress – a seed from which new life could emerge. The GPCR contained no such hope. Instead, it demonstrated only that man's 'constant falling back into the uncivilised makes a mockery of any notion of a fundamental evolution of the species', surpassing perhaps even war as 'the most extreme case of ontological designing'.[18] While architecture and design represent human endeavour in pursuit of progress, the GPCR proved only to be its antithesis.

The death of Chairman Mao in 1976 coincided with the end of the GPCR and led to the almost immediate arrest of the infamous 'Gang of Four', under which soubriquet their names were collectively inscribed in the histories of China and the Communist Party as those responsible for the GPCR. China, it appeared, was turning a crucial corner. However, the complexities underlying the political squabbling within the Party were not as simple as to be the work of four individuals. Shanghai's radical administration was replaced with Party diehards, whose priority was not economic revival, but the purging of 'Gang of Four' sympathisers from Shanghai's bureaucracy. The economic lifeblood of Shanghai, laden with political burdens, was sapped from the city, while China began slowly to move forward.

Out of the mire

Following the Cultural Revolution, Shanghai was a city in which it appeared 'that not a single structure has been erected' since 1949.[19] In 1979, Shanghai was denied the opportunity to join a select few 'economic zones' in the south of China, handpicked by Beijing to lead China forward through its Open

Door policy. As southern China enjoyed special privileges, Shanghai, for the first time since the1840s, was losing its primacy among China's cities.

The Communist Party knew it could not ignore Shanghai and the tax revenue which the city fed to the treasury's coffers, but its officials were wary of its latent potential and the threat it could pose to the Party's power base. With Party allegiances playing a critical role in defining the fortunes of a region or city in China, it was unfortunate for Shanghai that in the early 1980s its leaders had no strong connections with Beijing's elite, and so cast the city into the political wilderness. When the mayor, Wang Dao Han, pressed Beijing to support a plan to develop Pudong into an economic development zone, the proposal was ignored. Instead, piecemeal steps were taken to improve living standards in spite of there having been practically no improvements for three decades. The sale of public property started in 1981 with the lowest-quality lane houses. A year later a new regulation was implemented that allowed tenants to improve their living conditions by adding structures to existing properties, as long it did not affect detrimentally the structure of the building or the appearance of the street and neighbourhood. Although many buildings had had floors added since 1949, approximately 70,295 square metres of extra living space were created by these makeshift structures. In the same year, a census showed that Shanghai's population had reached 5.86 million, housed in 28.6 million square metres of property. On average, every resident of Shanghai had a little less than 5 square metres of space, making the centre of Shanghai one of the most densely populated places on earth.

History, it seemed, had enveloped Shanghai and was bent on suffocating it. The city's ageing infrastructure and degraded housing stock were a burden that its rivals in the

Above, left and right The three–storey fire station (C5) built in the 1930s near the former Bubbling Well (old) and in 2005 with an extra four storeys. The building has sunk by over two feet.

Opposite An example of sub-divided living in a former villa, now housing many families

Left Extra floors and enclosed balconies are common methods of increasing living space.

Right Extra floors and enclosed balconies are common methods of increasing living space

south did not endure, while the politics that had infused the city from the 1920s had inflicted unmitigated destruction on the city's social and economic fabric. During the first three decades of Communism, it 'appears that not a single structure was erected in the former International Settlements and French Concession'.[20] Old properties suffered from multiple occupancy and a total lack of maintenance, causing a legal minefield in property ownership that could not be addressed without opening the floodgates to millions of claimants. Once the symbol of progress in China, its residents synonymous with modernity, dynamism and the fashionable, Shanghai emerged from the GPCR sorely abused and dispirited with a population stifled and downtrodden.

The tragedy that China and Shanghai endured through the GPCR might be viewed from a macro-historical perspective as yet another cycle of political turmoil caused by China's unruly rulers. Even in such relatively recent times as the 1870s, Walter Medhurst, a former British Consul to Shanghai observed prophetically:

> I firmly believe they ['the ruling and influential classes'] would hail the day when they could see (were such a thing possible) the last foreign factory razed to the ground, and the last ship dismissed the coast ... But it by no means follows that progress is to be despaired of in the future of China. Further shocks and awakenings through collisions with foreign powers must occur ... And whenever such collisions take place, they must inevitably be followed by the forcible introduction of new ideas, to the disruption of old-established

and cherished usages. We can only hope that when the shock does come, the aggressive influence may be wielded by a wise and humane power, and that it may be so directed as to accomplish what is needed for the country with the least possible amount of loss and calamity to its unhappy people.

The damage done by decades of foreign domination and arrogance cannot be underestimated in terms of its consequence on the Chinese psyche and their desire for retribution, summed up by Finch as 'modern history's most colossal failure of East–West relations' or, as Miller stated in 1937, 'The Dragon sleeps with one eye open and his tail slowly wagging in anticipated retaliation. The forces of retribution are slowly but surely gathering momentum.'

However, the backlash after 1949 was more to do with domestic politics than vengeance for a century of international subjugation and humiliation. Vociferous anti-foreign rhetoric was chiefly political expedience, emanating from a Communist Party beset with internal power struggles, which spilt out into the public domain through disastrous political campaigns that caused untold suffering to the masses. Being in the frontline, Shanghai bore the brunt of the political infighting and had the most to lose. This once economic colossus suffered bitterly during the first three decades of Communism, but the inevitable change of political tide was bringing with it hopes of resurgence. With China once again engaging in international trade, Shanghai's innate potential for trading would soon be unleashed.

The Giant Awakes

Through the exercise of will power and reason on the part of exceptional individuals, society's decline can be arrested and even reversed.

Plato, *Republic*

Men of experience and foresight have predicted that in another 50 years Shanghai may become the greatest city of the world. This is not the fantastic dream of an untravelled mind. The future holds something great for Shanghai, and that greatness will outstrip all its past achievements, marvellous as they have been.

Ching-Lin Hsia, *The Status of Shanghai*, 1929

Shanghai has grown accustomed to high praise and high expectations. The city's vaunted pre-eminence has been anticipated for over a century, yet Shanghai has never achieved genuine supremacy on the world stage. However, just as happened in the late 1920s, few cities have attracted such public fascination and media attention as Shanghai has over the past decade. The widespread interest generated by the current resurgence of China's most illustrious city is noteworthy on many levels: Shanghai's affinity historically with 'the outside world', its political and economic influence, and the sheer scale of recent regeneration have transfixed global audiences.

These factors, while transcending many themes, are central to urbanism and bound inextricably to historical experience. First, the linkage between Shanghai and the West, despite a severance of nearly half a century, has transformed into acquiescent nostalgia, forming the central pillar of the foreigners' awareness of Shanghai in the 21st century. Second, China's political and economic ascendancy, in which Shanghai plays a central role, are drawing attention both for the opportunities and for the threats they present internationally. Third, Shanghai's urban renaissance cannot fail to impress even the staunchest cynic for the audaciousness of its plans for the future, yet these plans

remain just ideas. In true Shanghai tradition, the relative grandiosity of its buildings casts little more than a design message. A structure's true worth is secondary to the image it conveys.

Just 50 years after the Nationalist government first proposed that Shanghai should become the 'show window' of China, the Communist government has deliberately turned one of the most capitalist metropolises on earth into China's unassailable showcase city.

The nod of approval

The permanent suppression of Shanghai, China's leading connection to the rest of the world, is an implausible ambition. The inevitable resurgence of China's most powerful city was only a matter of time, whether years, decades, or centuries. In a country controlled by a central government, Shanghai needed only the nod of approval that would release the shackles of political bondage that had done so much to undermine its former prowess. Beijing knew it had much to gain from a prosperous Shanghai, and could not afford to keep it constrained. In 1984, Shanghai received its chance to regain lost ground on its southern rivals when the government declared 14 cities open to foreign development. Shanghai was among this group. The following year Beijing appointed Jiang Ze Min as Secretary to the Party in Shanghai and two years later Zhu Rong Ji as Mayor. These two highly educated, influential figures gave Shanghai direct representation in the uppermost echelons of Beijing's political structure. These crucial appointments proved doubly significant when in the 1990s these men were promoted to the top of the Party – Zhu to Premier and Jiang to Chairman.

It was no coincidence that almost immediately Shanghai started to receive financial privileges comparable to its southern competitors. From 1988, it showed signs of closing the gap on the upstart cities that had stolen its primacy. Then in 1989 the student demonstrations in Beijing's Tian An Men Square took the government by surprise and unsettled the Party's higher echelons. As China reeled in the aftermath of governmental suppression, the students in Hong Kong, a stone's throw from China's key economic zones, protested vigorously and vocally. Shanghai, under the strict watch of Jiang and Zhu, remained conspicuously acquiescent.

Months later, during the Spring Festival of 1990, the

Party Chairman Deng Xiao Ping visited Shanghai and urged the municipal government to progress with the development of Pudong, Shanghai's neglected backyard across the Whuangpu from the Bund. Shanghai, it seemed, had earned its reward for compliance during Tian An Men's fallout. Two months later, on 18 April, China's premier, Li Peng, publicly announced the launch of the Pudong development project. After 40 years of neglect, Shanghai was on the rise once more.

Beijing chose Pudong over an area to the south of the former walled city to be the site of Shanghai's modern development area, though it took a couple of years before Shanghai was able to capitalise on its newfound allegiances. China's economy was in the doldrums until 1992, when further economic reforms and the continued collapse of Communism in Europe's Eastern bloc propelled China forward.

Shanghai continued to benefit and prosper under special privileges sanctioned by Beijing, including 18 'super-special' policies announced in September 1995, which catapulted the city into the forefront of urban development in China. Tax breaks, foreign investment incentives and access to huge government loans ensured the rapid transformation of Shanghai, but most especially of Pudong: Shanghai's backyard had become China's show window.

Pudong

'Town Planning' in its true sense would be difficult to apply in Shanghai.
Shanghai Municipal Council Annual Report for 1910

In 1991, in a deft move that exploited the media's thirst for the next big China story, the Shanghai Development Corporation (SDC) invited five international architectural firms to submit proposals for the development of a new business sector for the city. As the firms Dominique Perrault, Massimiliano Fuksas, Richard Rogers Partnership, Shanghai Joint Design Team, and Toyo Ito & Associates focused on Shanghai, it seemed the city had come of age. The SDC's design brief called for a masterplan for a massive area of approximately 2 square kilometres that was to house over a million residents and comprise 50 per cent office space. The plan, it was hoped, would draw the centre of Shanghai across the Whuangpu into a newly designed city, integral to but not dependent on the old Shanghai. With familiar grandiosity and ambition, Shanghai was again being furnished with another masterplan.

Pudong had been eyed for development since the early 20th century. Shanghai's poorest suburb had grown accustomed to the visionary carving up of its pronounced

Above Rows of high-density workers' accommodation

peninsula with imaginary lines backed by empty words of optimism. In the early 1920s, Pudong was to have been transformed into one enormous harbour facility as Shanghai strove to be the greatest port in the world. By the 1940s, the Japanese envisioned an ostentatious plan radiating from Pudong along monumental boulevards that advanced across a razed former British Settlement. After 1949, Pudong, near to the city's industry and shipping, seemed destined for a lacklustre future as it provided an ideal location for housing workers in regimented rows of concrete apartments that would march monotonously out across former peasants' fields.

At the close of the second millennium, after a century of false starts, Pudong's moment seemed finally to have arrived as it became the focus of 'one of the greatest urbanistic reflections of our times'.[1] Not only was this dilapidated corner of Shanghai garnering attention from the world's media and the world's greatest design minds, but Shanghai was also on the brink of receiving its first truly considered urban plan.

In 1993, the submissions from around the world were presented to the SDC. Against a fanfare of media-fuelled hype, Shanghai and the Communist Party basked in the positive story that was the future of China's gateway. The five designs submitted to the SDC were diverse in their approach to the problem.

The proposal from the British architectural firm Richard Rogers Partnership (RRP) concentrated on the idea of a

Right and below right Richard Rogers's plan for Pudong (bottom) and transport diagram (top)

Below The financial ghetto of Pudong, a fundamentally different urban scale to Shanghai

Diagram Illustrating the Overall Network of Transport Systems

'sustainable compact city'² that was sympathetic to the needs of a dynamic metropolis of which it was to be a central part. Forming the focal point of the future development of Shanghai, the concept concentrated on addressing the growing environmental crisis, of which China at that time had little awareness. The idea of housing 1 million people in over 5.3 million square metres, 50 per cent of which was reserved for office space, would have an inevitable and huge environmental impact locally, regionally and globally. Resource efficiency was paramount to RRP's proposal, which aimed to maximise the effective use of transportation and land through the careful arrangement of buildings and open spaces. With a central park forming the hub, the plan resembled a wheel with six avenues radiating outwards from the centre, intersecting three concentric rings for transportation: the first and smallest designed for cars and through traffic, the second for trams and buses, and the third for pedestrians and cyclists. Between the avenues, six nodes of mixed-use development were served by an underground public transport system. The city's commercial, cultural and social activities were concentrated in these areas, while residential, educational and health facilities were located along the river. The close proximity of residential, service and commercial areas was designed to maximise public transport, bicycle and pedestrian use, while the varied height of buildings and their even spacing between the six major avenues ensured maximum use of natural light and ventilation, so reducing energy consumption and pollution. The plan, calculated to 'reduce overall energy consumption by 70 per cent compared with that of conventionally designed commercial developments of a similar scale',³ was a major departure from established urban planning schemes that rely on islands of tower blocks intersected by major roads – for so long considered the symbol of progress by many.

Another plan, from the Italian firm Massimiliano Fuksas, adopted an evolutionary approach using a 'highly significant program aimed at dense development, to be realized in phases over a long period'. 'Viewed as no more than a point of departure', the proposal was intended to provide the foundation for future development in different phases, therefore designed to be flexible and adaptable to the city's inevitably changing needs. The concept also attempted to use traditional Chinese elements by drawing inspiration from 'the traditional Chinese house, with its framework based on the relationship between nature and construction.'⁴

A third proposal, by the French architectural firm Dominique Perrault, was founded on an approach that embraced continuity of the city's historical context while building something entirely new across the river. The overall concept, described as 'Towards a living urbanism', focused on 'the void' between the past and the future and the need to protect this 'in-between' to ensure the continuity of our cityscapes. It drew inspiration from the layout and texture of

Above and left The plan for Pudong from Dominique Perrault

the existing city, including its characteristic street pattern, the course of which was continued in the new areas of Pudong. This principle was intended to ensure that the network of roads and streets in the area could be 'naturally linked' to the existing city.⁵ The plan proposed the construction of two lines of high-rise development perpendicular to one another and joining opposite the Bund and contrasting with it, like the 'yin and yang'. A great park was designed to sit at the water's edge in front of the new development, while behind was a new town providing 2 million square metres of office space and other facilities.

Armed with five proposals for the masterplan of China's powerhouse, the subsequent development of Pudong continued apace using none and all of the suggested designs. The government had what it needed to move forward on its own in what it believed was a continuum of 'two decades' unremitting effort' that had 'presented before us a brand new modern metropolis full of energy and vitality' with rows of

Right The high-rise developments springing up from Pudong's older houses

tall new buildings 'orchestrating a superb march of today'.[6]

Shanghai had been a mercantile city until the 1920s and a political city thereafter, but the development of Pudong presented the first opportunity for the city to attend to its social needs, becoming more adaptable, complex, sensitive and liveable. However, the 'march of today' was orchestrated by politics and economics, the dual influences that had

forged, abused and helped characterise Shanghai. The city's chance to become a truly great metropolis was sacrificed by big business and politics. Money ensured that ill-considered short-term plans and vacuous designs won approval for Pudong, turning the show window of China into a grisly spectacle of brash and irrelevant structures whose sole yet empty claim was their height. The familiar prattle about

Right Pudong's world- famous skyline

Left The parcelled land of Pudong with the older quarters of Shanghai beyond the Whangpu River

soaring structures, so much a part of Shanghai from the late 19th century up to the 1930s, had reappeared on a scale unimaginable to the city's forefathers, who said: 'Shanghai engineers say that the soil will stand nothing higher than fifteen storeys. So Shanghai escapes the menace of what had been called the greatest mistake of modern architecture, the skyscraper. She faces in the future no such makeshifts was [sic] triple-deck streets with ramps, arcades, elevated railways, subways, leap-frog aerial bridges and the like'.[7]

Pudong and its politically motivated and economically fuelled expansion blew such hopes away. Richard Rogers's 'sustainable strategies' were buried under billions of tons of market-driven urban development laid out in extraneous grids sold to the highest bidder. Wide roads marooned islands of land on which pedestrians are stranded alone with towering structures, one such to a plot. Basic concepts of urban planning were swept aside as China rushed to reach the future by building a city of the past. Forewarned that 'unless the government of China shows real resolve and commits itself to planning for sustainable cities, it will soon be faced with massive congestion, pollution and social dissatisfaction on an even larger scale than is endemic to the cities it is using as role models',[8] Pudong represents one of the single greatest missed opportunities in China's recent urban renaissance. The failure to adopt a successful model that meets the future needs of one of the world's largest cities from a blank canvas boded ill for the regeneration of the former settlements with their well-established network of roads, houses and services.

The former settlements

From 'East and West'
For ages past they've been outclassed,
For speed and comfort too;
But times have changed and now, though strange,
They're building as we do.

Shamus A'Rabbitt, *Ballads of the East.*

While the plans for Pudong were being drafted and disregarded, the Municipality of Shanghai's policy towards the rest of the city resembled something of a gargantuan land auction. Also, troublingly, the land being sold was occupied by millions of people whose residence in Shanghai ranged from decades to days. The swathes of Li Long houses that had each supported all manner of occupants from multiple families with up to four generations to a room, to small industries and dormitories for immigrant labour were being bought up by developers keen to enter what was potentially Asia's most lucrative property market.

The demand for new housing and office space was conspicuously top–down, with the wealthy foreign investor, armed with unlimited foreign expense accounts, enticed to Shanghai by its commercial opportunities, and having nowhere to live and few places to work. Foreign businessmen and diplomats rented hotel rooms on long-term leases, while their future homes and offices sprouted from Shanghai's fertile soil, and the city's infrastructure underwent one of the largest urban transformations in history.

Shanghai's massive investment in infrastructure and

buildings through the 1990s was astonishing in its scope. New communications systems, the city's first subway and first highways, the world's two largest single-spanned bridges, a new airport, 1,300 kilometres of roads, improved water systems, more than 4,000 high-rise buildings and better housing, hotels and public facilities were earnestly planned and built. Shanghai's transformation was undertaken with an almost revolutionary fervour, changing permanently the face of the city in a matter of years. The formerly low-rise Li Long skyline, punctuated by the occasional 1930s high-rise, had given way to the developer's dream – a modern city with elevated highways, underground subways, high-rise apartment living and modern office buildings. However, the haste in attaining the developer's vision echoed the

China's potentially vast automotive market is today backed up by a deliberate government espousal of the motorcar both as a symbol of growing affluence among China's middle classes and as a means of offsetting huge unemployment in areas of China formerly dominated by inefficient state-owned industries. Almost a century ago, one writer in the *Far Eastern Review* foresaw this potential in the context of Shanghai:

> When one stops to think of the great number of cars running on the streets of Shanghai and remembers that these cars are practically all owned by foreigners one must be impressed with the great possibility for the sale of cars when the Chinese population of about 1,000,000 is seized with the ambition to own motor cars … from a Motor Car manufacturer's point of view, there is an unlimited amount of business to be done some day.

Although the construction of the highway necessitated the demolition of large numbers of buildings, the east–west section of the highway, named Yan An Lu, was constructed over the former Yang Jin Bang, which had divided the British Settlement and the French Concession. The culverting of this creek as late as 1916 meant that the former King Edward VII Avenue, the road built over the former creek, became Shanghai's widest road after the Bund. Hence, when the decision was made to construct an elevated highway nearly 80 years later, the breadth of the route made it an obvious choice. Furthermore, the idea of an elevated transport system was not new to Shanghai. The idea had been mooted in the

Above The northern half of People's Square in the 1950s, showing the former racecourse transformed into a public park with lakes and walkways

instantaneousness of a drug-induced high, leaving Shanghai with a hangover that might last decades.

The construction of an elevated highway that carved its way through much of downtown proved China's adoption of the motorcar as the primary means of transport in the future, a dubious policy if accepted by China's hundreds of millions of cyclists. The dream of Western manufacturers to tap into

Right The southern half of People's Square looking east showing the Municipality (F5/G5) (left) and the Shanghai Museum (right) (G5)

Above The rather bleak People's Square, showing the Municipality (right), the Shanghai Grand Theatre (left) and a diverse range of skyscrapers in the background

1910s, but it was not until 1921 that Sidney Powell, a renowned civil engineer, architect and surveyor, put together a proposal for two rings of elevated railway radiating from the Bund and connecting with the mainline railway network. The plan obviously failed to impress the ratepayers enough to secure its implementation, but nonetheless it does demonstrate an early desire for improved transportation in the downtown district, which had for so long been crippled by the ineffectiveness of the 1850s Committee for Roads and Jetties. The improvement of Shanghai's roads, cycle-ways and pavements remains a major challenge if car drivers, cyclists and pedestrians are to share equally in the upgrading of Shanghai's streetscape.

One of the largest intersections of elevated roads, rising to four decks of swirling concrete high above the neighbouring buildings, looks down on the former racecourse, now reincarnated as People's Square. This huge area of land, once the only sizeable open space in Shanghai, had hosted countless sporting events including horse races, cricket matches, baseball games, swimming galas and golf tournaments, as well as being the site of the Battle of Muddy Flat, a makeshift Royal Air Force base when Chiang Kai Shek was approaching Shanghai in 1927, and a communist execution ground after 1949. It enjoyed arguably its most valuable incarnation as Ren

Left With few public parks, Shanghainese are accustomed to being creative when seeking a secluded place to find peace and quiet!

Min Gong Yuan, or People's Park, from the early 1950s, when trees and lawns interspersed with artificial lakes and streams offered the public a pleasure area in the heart of the city on a scale and of a beauty that the foreigners in Shanghai had never achieved. However, following Shanghai's resurgence, People's Park was too valuable and its location too symbolic to be reserved for the sole purpose of amusing the public. In the centre of the park, overlooking People's Avenue, a pompous parade ground that severs the park into two isolated halves, the new offices of the Municipality of Shanghai were constructed. The design of this monolithic structure, clearly inspired by the traditional Chinese practice of providing a central location for the seat of authority, and like so many of Shanghai's landmark buildings constructed since the 19th century, concentrated more on making a statement than on addressing the needs of its occupants or its surroundings. The building represents a horizontal wall of white marble that disconnects the two portions of Shanghai's only downtown park, turning the remaining open spaces into diminutive parcels of irrelevant formality disguised as public spaces. Shanghai, long acquainted with the maladministration of its local government, had not only lost its one significant open space, but also had it taken by the very body charged with improving the city. Following People's Park, now called People's Square and a quasi-showroom illustrating the city's

newly found confidence, further monumental structures were quick to take root. The Shanghai Grand Theatre (F5), the $72 million museum (G5) and the Urban Planning Exhibition Hall (F5/G5) now nestle alongside the Municipality (F5/G5), forming the four pillars of Shanghai's primary public realm, whose very existence has been undermined by their construction.

Shanghai's history is replete with a consistent lack of regard for public spaces, despite repeated claims to the contrary from the administrations charged with their improvement. People's Square represents a catastrophic abuse of power or lack of experience on the part of urban planners, whose piecemeal attempts to rectify the paucity of public spaces by bulldozing entire blocks of housing will never return Shanghai's primary park to the people. Instead, power and money have dominated the decision-making process, and the influence and inexperience of the developer have proven too potent. Nowhere is this more evident, more controversial and more destructive than in the area of housing.

Shanghai's nationalised housing stock, once a windfall for the government, had stood almost completely neglected for half a century and so had become a tiresome burden. The sale of these properties for redevelopment provided a means of alleviating this pressure on the public purse. Plots of land were sold to developers in a deregulated land-use system that offered no incentive to safeguard the physical and social cohesion of the city, but instead rode roughshod over public concerns and individuals' rights: 'The more money they made by selling leases, the more money each district had to spend on infrastructure development.'[9] In four years from 1993, Shanghai sold leases for 1,334 land parcels covering 78.4 million square metres to developers. This coincided with, and was dependent on, large-scale relocations, which began in 1993. Former parcels of Li Long were pulled down to make way for high-rise developments.

In 1990, the population of Shanghai was approximately 13 million. Today, it is close to 20 million, yet the individual living space has nearly trebled from under 5 square metres per person to 13.8 square metres in 2003. With an enormous increase in the city's population, many of the high-density residential areas in or near the downtown, comprising 4.281 million square metres of 'shabby and dilapidated houses', were razed. In the name of urban regeneration, 900,000 households and countless communities were removed from the city's most desirable areas and relocated to the city's outskirts, creating massive urban sprawl. Nonetheless, an enormous housing programme provided 16.2 million square metres of accommodation in under two decades, equating to 53 per cent of the gross housing in Shanghai and 'exceeding the total housing construction area in the first 30 years of the New China'.[10]

While it was claimed that these new residential areas provided an environment in which 'man reaches unprecedented harmony with society and nature',[11] the destruction of large areas of high-density city centre housing was, for the first time, threatening the unique texture of Shanghai's urban fabric – a texture formed over many decades by the amalgam of disparate communities coming together to conduct business. Vast swathes of land were leased by government, bulldozed and redeveloped for an entirely new type of clientele. The buildings, erected in place of the intimacy provided by former alleyways, houses, shops and small businesses, have been largely exclusive, homogeneous, unilateral developments denying public access, participation and interaction. Plot by plot, the dense grain of Shanghai's streets and their seemingly irrepressible social character were being eroded by anonymous glass facades or gated complexes that created a barren wilderness at street level –

Left New residential towers being built north of Suzhou Creek

Right Shanghai's older houses are often overshadowed by newer high-rise apartments

Far right, above The character of one side of this street contrasts starkly with that of the other, illustrating the old character of the Shanghai street life (left) and the new high-rise character (right), divided by multi-lane roads that sever the city metaphorically and literally.

Far right, below Typical old-style Shanghainese frontages with high densities of living and activities

Below Dismantling the old and building the new

the most important and dynamic component of Shanghai.

The process continued almost unchecked until the late 1990s, when dissenting voices could no longer be ignored. In the depths of the Asian financial crisis, Shanghai, confronted with an unprecedented oversupply of office space fuelling dramatic rent reductions, faced genuine fears of a property crash. The slowing development offered a temporary reprieve as official policies shifted towards a greater awareness of public needs. Murmurings of architectural preservation, sustainable urban development and rights of property owners were concepts now acknowledged, though little understood, in the corridors of power, and not just used with brazen abandon in government exhibitions and in official reports. Designated 'excellent historical architectures in 12 historical and cultural regions',[12] 398 structures were assigned the title 'Heritage Architecture', a title intended to provide protection to these buildings from demolition and adverse modification. Although it contained intrinsic problems, this measure marked an important phase in the evolving debate that continues to reclaim a focus on the public realm from the dual influences of finance and politics. However, the power and influence of politics remain absolute, so whether or not a site is culturally or historically significant, if it conflicts with political interests, it will be removed. The only truly sacred sites are those that conform with or have historical links to the prevailing political process. The epitome of such a process is the site of the first congress of the Communist Party, which is now attached to a kitsch tourist redevelopment. These two sites alone epitomise the state of current architectural preservation and urban regeneration in Shanghai. Politics and economics rule, while the local population, who know nothing of or care little for the tawdry idiocies encouraged by self-proclaimed design gurus, are routinely excluded or forcibly removed from their homes and banished to the suburbs in order that tourists can be served bland versions of historical events that led to one of the most divisive periods of Chinese history or wealthy visitors can sip coffee in a faux-traditional environment and claim they have experienced the real Shanghai.

It is still too early to judge whether or not these attempts at architectural and urban rehabilitation of the thousands of buildings built in Shanghai since the 1980s will improve Shanghai's character and texture, and it is premature to analyse individual contemporary structures. History will be the judge of their success. Some of the more inappropriate structures built in the 1980s are already being pulled down and replaced by buildings that are more sensitive to their immediate surroundings. Mistakes that have been made are being acknowledged, and this encourages constant improvements in the quality of design practice and theory. The new generation of Chinese architects, like those who returned from America in the 1920s, are pioneers in a new and exciting period of development in their country. They have had much to learn in a very short space of time, but they

no longer lack experience. The knowledge and skills they have acquired are finally being translated into qualitative improvements in architecture and urban design.

Seeing through the charade

There is certainly nothing more wonderful in the East than the rapid growth of this place.

Sir Rutherford Alcock, Capital of the Tycoon, 1863, p 128

Despite the many conflicting forces, Shanghai has continued to grow, and still boom has not turned to bust. Shanghai, in its own irrepressible way, has managed to stoke the superlatives that satiate an ever-eager global audience that feeds on the city's aura. The world's first commercial magnetic levitation train whisks travellers to the airport at speeds in excess of 400 kilometre per hour, high-speed rail links to Beijing are expected to cut travel times in half, the city's airport is getting a second terminal, elevated railways have been added to the expanding subway network, plans for the world's largest port have been drafted that will house a million workers, and a number of satellite towns accommodating up to a million residents each are designed to satisfy the projected population increases in a city that has already grown by 400 per cent in two decades. Shanghai, as always, shows no sign of stopping. The plans for the future provide captivating viewing and present awesome problems, but one cannot fail to be impressed by the determination of the Chinese to succeed.

Nonetheless, the amazing statistics, the awe-inspiring architectural models and the sci-fi computer visuals that are employed at public exhibitions or official presentations to

Left The scale model of Shanghai in the Shanghai Urban Planning Exhibition Centre

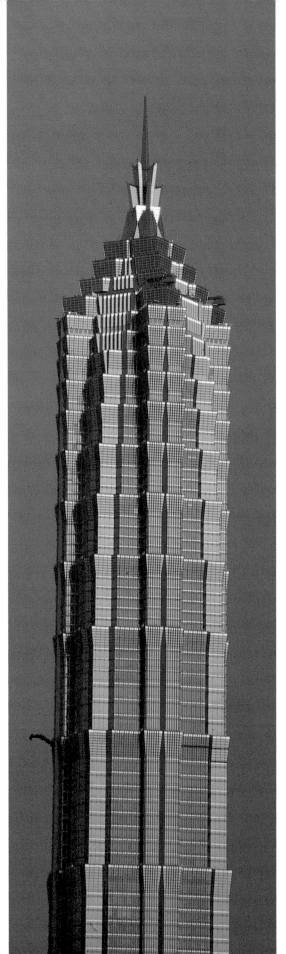

boast the city's future deal only with the tangible aspects of development and often neglect the intangible. As Yatsko puts it, Shanghai remains 'a city often stuck in control-oriented, authoritarian ways. Closer examination reveals Shanghai's fixation on building the hardware or physical infrastructure of an international economic hub, while undervaluing the importance of the necessary software, including … access to accurate information'. This neglect is certain to have a detrimental effect on public opinion, which is already aggrieved at the lack of representation, consultation and dialogue from those involved with the development process. Neglecting the city's social, cultural and legal needs might yet undermine all the effort that has gone into building the concrete and glass towers that so captivate foreign and domestic tourists.

When one stands on the Bund beneath Pudong's showcase towers, or wanders along Nanjing Road at night with its ubiquitous flashing neon, or sits in People's Square contemplating the vastness of the encircling urban landscape, there is certain to be a Chinese peasant or foreign equivalent gawping, open-jawed, at the awesome sights before them. Ironically, none of the sights is new. They are the same spectacles that captivated visitors to Shanghai nearly a century ago, only on a different scale. Shanghai's 1930s 'modern skyscrapers, the highest buildings in the world outside of the Americas, and its straw huts shoulder high' have been replaced by their modern-day equivalents.[13]

'Software' has always been the neglected partner to awe-inspiring 'hardware' that projects the sensational and the superficial. People will forever come to Shanghai and marvel at its science fiction landscape, unaware that it is all a show, a charade of fantastic proportions to convince others of the enchantment of a city that has never really existed. While other great cities evolve over centuries, taking time to mature as their fortunes ebb and flow, Shanghai, the 'vast brilliantly-hued cycloramic, panoramic mural of the best and the worst of the Oriental and Occidental',[14] revels in the idealism of its infancy. At the dawn of the third millennium, Shanghai has changed little in its approach. As Harold Acton commented in 1948, when he spoke of Shanghai's architecture contrasting with that of other cities:

> You may not like the architecture [of other cities] but you have to admit its integrity and a certain splendour. Each is a product of its own civilization; these monuments are habitable by the sort of man who made them: they have personality. But the buildings along the Shanghai Bund do not look man-made: they have little connexion with the people of China; they are poisonous toadstools sprung up from the mud, a long line of pompous toadstools raised by anonymous banks, trusts and commercial firms. Imposing from the river with their turrets and clock-towers, but essentially soulless: no court or government had designed them and given them life. There they stand trying to give materialism importance, but they fail.

Above and left These two photos show how much Shanghai has changed in 30 years. The old photograph was taken in the 1960s, showing the northeast corner of People's Square with the Park Hotel (until the 1980s, China's tallest building), the former Foreign YMCA, China Apartments and Moore Memorial Church, and the Sun Department Store protruding above the sea of low-rise Li Long houses. The new photograph, taken from the same angle, shows the extent of high-rise development since the 1980s. The Park Hotel is just visible to the right of the base of the large dark building (top middle-right). None of the other buildings is visible.

SHANGHAI'S FUTURE

Shanghai's Future

Architecture is the constructed expression of history that reflects the tensions and aspirations of a society.

Mario Botta, *San Francisco Modern*, Zahid Sardar, foreword

Previous pages The layers of Shanghai at the turn of the new millennium – old gives way to new, while a young child ponders his role in this extraordinary transformation

The history of Shanghai is saturated with the tensions and aspirations of myriad individuals and successive societies whose collective experience has created one of the largest cities in the world, its heritage embodied in a complex yet profoundly rich urban form and fascinating architectural character. If architecture and urban form are the constructed expressions of history, then equipped with a better understanding of these, the design process can more effectively sustain Shanghai's heritage into the future. To provide such an understanding has been the primary purpose of this book.

Right Shanghai's new developments are skirted with hoardings often boasting the ridiculous. Two Shanghainese sit in front of 'Rich Gate'.

Much has been said and written about the sensational development of China's cities since the 'Open Door' policy, yet relatively little is known internationally about the tangible and intangible heritage of these urban environments. This degree of unawareness has allowed urban growth to be lauded without scrutinising adequately the development process or its consequences. Many who have experienced what has happened in Shanghai since the 1990s are starting to question developers' practices and believe that these projects and their sheer quantity threaten to destroy the essence of this most remarkable Chinese city.

In the light of Shanghai's historical experience, the phenomenal commercial success which has fuelled its growth in the 21st century presents a curious paradox: can the very processes by which Shanghai was created and has prospered really be threatening its heritage? As this book has shown, it would be naive to think that Shanghai is averse to rapid development; on the contrary, Shanghai's character has always thrived on change. Furthermore, for centuries Shanghai's success has also been one of its main problems. Adversity and development are bedfellows in Shanghai. Progress has often followed terrible experience: from the ravages of the Japanese pirates, through the threat and assault of Britain's Royal Navy; from the violent uprising of the Small Swords, Taipings and China's warlords, to the corrupted Nationalists; from the unspeakable belligerence of the Japanese, to the repression of the Communists. Today, though the ruler's flag remains the same as that of 1949, Shanghai's administrators can lay no claim to Marxist Communism. After centuries of bitter experience, Shanghai the city (not the commodity squabbled over by competing rulers) is growing faster than ever before because it has been allowed to do what it does best: trade.

Historically, trade more than any other influence has shaped Shanghai's evolution and forged its character. It is central to almost every facet of Shanghai, from its origins through to its rapid expansion in the 21st century. Trade has brought renewed wealth and an unquestionable improvement in the general standard of living. Perhaps, then, this phase of development is not a threat, but merely the recurring cycle of history in which the city is remodelling itself in order to catch up with modern trends after half a century of degeneration. There is plenty of evidence to support this argument: signs of history repeating itself are everywhere, as

Shanghai's ascendancy is celebrated and dutifully promoted through the world's media. Although Shanghai continues to change rapidly, much remains the same.

Foremost in this cycle of historical recurrence is nostalgia, that irrational sentiment in architectural observation. Nostalgia has returned to occupy many a Western mind in Shanghai, as constructed vestiges of the past provide tantalising associations with a time and a place that, to many, are comfortingly un-Chinese. So captivating is the aura of Shanghai's past that the demand among foreigners for accommodation in old houses has driven up their value to rival the highest property prices in the world. Yet, once acquired, these residences have to be completely overhauled to make them habitable. In their attempts to own a slice of old Shanghai, 21st-century taipans are forced to erase the past while creating costly contemporary Western-style homes encased in nostalgic shells.

Shanghai's allure is also attracting modern-day adventurers. The 'griffin', that single young male who was for so long the workhorse of foreign firms in Asia and who was expelled from China's shores by the Communist Party, has returned with a vengeance. Thousands of young foreign men and women are now working in China's greatest city, tempted there by the prospect of high wages and a dash of the exotic. The luxury residences of foreign workers, financed by foreign expense accounts, are springing up in the distant suburbs, where peace and quiet and a Western lifestyle can be enjoyed without being spoilt or interrupted by the Chinese and their ancient habits which continue to cause offence to certain elements of the Western population in China. Exclusive gated compounds for expatriate communities present the modern equivalent of Shanghai's former Western District, western French Concession and extra-settlement roads areas, and serve foreign residents while, to paraphrase the former British Consul, Walter Medhurst, writing in 1872, 'they concentrate their efforts to forget that they are an exile from home'. Also housed in these sprawling suburbs are legions of resident nannies and domestics – the modern equivalent of the once ubiquitous amah. These local girls represent a fraction of the millions of Chinese drawn to live and work in Shanghai in their attempt to escape a worse plight outside. Modern-day refugees, they are fleeing not the warring factions that have so blighted China's past, but the contemporary peril of rural poverty. An estimated 3 million out of Shanghai's population of 20 million are part of this transient workforce.

China's enormous population has forever been both a blessing and a curse for Shanghai. The 3 million non-residents of Shanghai who have come to seek financial salvation in China's city of dreams represent a similar proportion of China's total population to those who sought refuge in the city during the Taiping Rebellion in the 1860s.

Left The courtyard house in the old city (foreground) is perhaps Shanghai's oldest building and the last remaining courtyard house in the city. The city's Municipality claims it does not have the resources to preserve this architectural remnant of Shanghai's past.

Right Shanghai's architectural menagerie continues today, as Chinese architects commonly draw inspiration from the references left behind by their Western counterparts of old.

Now, as then, there are countless Chinese in Shanghai living below the poverty line, whose sole objective is survival. Many of these are either local residents whose subsistence way of life does not conform to the current rush to get rich, or impoverished workers from China's other provinces seeking work. Today, Shanghai's economic stature has replaced extraterritorial sanctuary as the city's primary attraction for China's transient population.

But as Shanghai expands to accommodate ever larger numbers of resident, non-resident and foreign workers, the city absorbs ever more land, as valuable countryside is built on. The country around Shanghai is among the most fertile in China and it has helped to support the densest regional populations in the world's most populous country. Abundant rains and traditional farming have always combined to feed Shanghai's growing population, but as the city expands and the countryside contracts, the fine line between self-sufficiency and dependence will be breached. When Shanghai can no longer survive from the resources in its own vicinity, it will demand more and more from resources ever further afield. In a country of 1.6 billion people, this concentrated demand on resources could have catastrophic consequences.

In the early 2000s, in addition to the swathes of high-rise apartments that house residents displaced from the city centre or a domestic workforce, there are the new suburbs of foreign communities and wealthy Chinese, who enjoy the perceived luxury of living in new residential complexes shamelessly designed to evoke homes from abroad. 'Copybook architecture' has returned to Shanghai in the form of property developments deliberately designed as overt expressions of German, French, British, Italian and American architectural styles. The Classical column, Renaissance dome, ornate pediment, Baroque plasterwork, faux-Tudor tarred beams, American Colonial-style decking, and the decorative folly crowning a building are all re-emerging as foreign and Chinese architectural firms abandon experience and reason to deliver what the client demands. This trend echoes the behaviour of architects from the affluent 1930s, who were regarded then by colleagues such as George Wilson as guiltless – the 'unfortunate' 'slaves' to wealthy clients.

Pertinent to both foreign and Chinese architects before the Second World War, this question of aesthetic pliability which is endorsed by many foreign and Chinese architects practising in Shanghai is re-emerging as a point of debate. The first Chinese architects working in Shanghai from the 1920s bore the responsibility of developing their own style while addressing the needs of an emergent nation, and the results of this have been documented in Chapter 5. The Chinese architects of today have a similar duty and are grappling with comparable issues. Foreign architects face a similar dilemma. Although now they are often designing for Chinese clients, their counterparts in the early 20th century

were conscious of this 'very complex question'. The English viewpoint was posited in 1929: 'When an Englishman settles down in a foreign country … he is often at a loss to know in what style to build a house. How far is it desirable that building [sic] designed by Englishmen abroad should bear the characteristics of our English civilisation?'[1]

The answer remains as elusive today as it always was. Foreign architectural firms are flocking to China in order to share in the spoils of the country's rapid development. Like their predecessors from the early 20th century, many such firms, operating far from the scrutiny of the international architectural fraternity and in an environment with less stringent regulations than those imposed in Europe or America, are failing to deliver the quality of work that would be demanded of them outside of China, and many are willing to transgress stylistically and qualitatively in order to complete the job. The increasingly pressing concerns for the environment, culture or local population are ignored, while the project is pursued in isolation. This is evidenced from the dearth of knowledge of these issues displayed at the planning stage of many projects. The principle that guides most developers in Shanghai has not changed for over a century: big is best.

The city's administration supports this view of size for size's sake, believing it to be the symbol of modernity. However, among Chinese architects 'modern' has always been synonymous with 'foreign', as it was foreigners who brought new ideas to China, irrespective of whether or not these ideas were manifested in symbols of ancient Greece and Rome. If China's architects can transcend this outmoded perception of modern, perhaps they will be able to reconcile their own traditional designs with the needs of the future and arrive at an entirely new architectural paradigm. In the meantime, foreign architectural firms benefit from almost free rein while enjoying the fruits of Shanghai's success, a success which growing numbers believe is in danger of creating, in the case of Pudong, a 'private financial ghetto',[2] and in older parts of the city massive fracturing of established communities and urban spaces.

To counter this international architectural free-for-all, the responsibility for delivering quality projects which respect the local conditions lies with the new generation of Chinese architects, just as it did in the late 1920s. Their immediate predecessors never had the opportunity to practise in a liberalised economic environment. China's young architects, therefore, have an enormous responsibility to marry the needs of the past with the demands of the future. Up to now there has been little success, as the demands of the client in an under-regulated construction industry prove too powerful, but there are signs that this is changing. A growing sensitivity towards urban continuity, sustainable development, architectural preservation, adaptive reuse of old buildings and community participation is emerging.

On a broader scale, the failure to implement an overall plan for the city from the 1840s onwards has led to incoherent and inconsistent development strategies that have left Shanghai fractured and muddled. Shanghai's historical lack of central planning is evident in the 21st century, with the city's division into local districts creating discordant patterns of development as different regional administrations work in isolation from and in competition with neighbouring districts. Superimposed upon this problematic framework is the monopolistic character of government-related departments associated with urban development. From academia through professional practice, to central government, the process is answerable, ultimately, to politics, which does not always concur with the needs of a growing city. This disjointed policy demonstrates a continuum of maladministration, whose consequences were predicted by the Municipal Council in their annual report of 1908, then framed in relation to Shanghai's outlying districts. It was feared then that they would 'be rapidly built over without any proper control' making 'the development of the settlement on systematic lines … impossible'. While a few individuals and developers gain from the sale of land and increase in property prices under such conditions, those who stand to lose most are the general public. Since the 1990s, many have been forcibly removed from their homes so that developers can make fortunes from new residential and office developments that garner handsome returns for officials whose job it is to rubber-stamp planning applications. The increasingly violent protests emanating from the communities, who feel isolated from and disillusioned by the political process, conflict with the sanguine rhetoric of the city's Urban Planning Bureau, who remind the paying public that one such redevelopment project 'is the blueprint the designers are planning, the prospect that the people are delightfully talking about, and the dream that children are dreaming as well'. As Shanghai undergoes massive change, pulling down the old to make way for the new, we are reminded comfortingly of our own thoughts: 'while dwelling upon the wonders that time has bestowed on Shanghai, we are at the same time looking forward to her glorious future'.[3]

This type of language and lack of accountability cause some in the architectural and design community to suggest that the political process is central to the problem. They believe that until China comes to terms with its past, it will find it difficult to respect the structures or the 'constructed expressions' that have become its heritage. This is problematical as China remains hindered by contradictions that emanate from outdated political ideologies. The Urban Planning Exhibition continues to celebrate the city's 'excellent historical architectures [sic]' that are said to 'represent the Shanghai characteristic cultural background combining oriental and western culture into a perfect match', while dismissing this cultural background as 'semi-colonial and semi-feudal' – the premise behind the destruction of many old structures that has already taken place. Coming to terms

Below As the physical structures of the past are replaced by new ones, so are the ideologies bringing about this change. The slogan 'Long Life Chairman Mao' is just visible on this former shopfront in the process of being demolished.

Left Countless residents have been evicted from their homes to make way for new developments. This mother and her child stubbornly resist the inevitable tide.

with the colonial or semi-colonial experience in many countries has often resulted in the eradication of colonial structures, precipitating the wanton destruction of property and of the public realm. In China, the only manifestation of this phenomenon occurred during the Cultural Revolution, but although this response seems to have passed, there remains a contradiction as to how former foreign buildings should be treated. Nowhere is this contradiction more explicit than on the Bund, the quintessence of foreign exploitation, where 'semi-colonial' structures are lauded above all other sites in Shanghai. The Bund, along with the Pudong skyline, has become the city's showpiece.

As these issues evolve and are deliberated, the reality persists that Shanghai's hunger for trade since the 1980s has resulted in a period of growth which has witnessed the largest urban development programme in history. Shanghai's recent experience has proved so phenomenal that many now fear boom will turn to bust. As the city's property prices outstrip those of Manhattan, Laurie's admonition of 1866 that 'Shanghai remains a mighty warning to the sanguine and a deathblow to undue speculation' should perhaps be heeded. This statement once again suggests that history is only repeating itself, that Shanghai will continue to experience highs and lows, and all the while will thrive on adversity and prosper on trade. But can such a process continue forever?

This leads us to return to the paradox. Can the city's exceptional commercial character as evidenced in this period of development undermine its unique heritage? If it can, this suggests that the material result of this rampant growth is not merely repeating the past, but creating a profoundly different urban environment through a process that is qualitatively and quantitatively different. Although Shanghai has negotiated many periods of rapid expansion, each of these phases has been a response to the needs of the population, however desperate or financially driven they have been. Despite the prevalence of appalling iniquity in the municipal administration since the 1840s, the consequence of previous development endorsed and relied on the Chinese living in the city centre, a course that has given Shanghai its distinctive character. Shanghai has never been a foreign city, nor has it not been the 'real China' as many have suggested and continue to suggest. 'Can a city of several millions of Chinese not be Chinese?'[+]

However, Shanghai's condition at the beginning of the 21st century illustrates a significant qualitative difference from what has occurred during previous periods of growth. Large portions of the population are being removed from the city centre. Whereas former phases of development have been broadly inclusive and complementary, the dismantling of traditional lifestyles in Shanghai is now causing a homogenisation of the city centre and a uniformity of the suburbs driven by forces that are exclusive and divisive. These

forces can be broadly observed by two new phenomena: one concerns process, the other design. First, the process of removing high-density low-rise housing from the city centre because of the value of the land it occupies and forcing local residents to relocate to the distant suburbs is new. Second, the design of modern high-rise apartment living is fundamentally at odds with the way of life which predominates in Shanghai and for which the city has become renowned. However high the buildings, life in Shanghai has always occurred at street level. Shanghai's population is famed for thriving in the shadow of the skyscraper, but contemporary architecture and urban planning have failed to safeguard the integrity of this facet of the public realm. They have designed instead exclusive structures which serve a wealthy minority and are often disconnected from their surroundings, and have created insipid parks containing manicured vegetation where blocks of housing once stood, ousting the former residents and displacing them to the city's outskirts. These two facets of contemporary development, rather than assimilating with existing structures and ways of life, have become so absolute that the sustenance of the city's rich texture, based on a diversity of characteristics encompassing street patterns, intimate public spaces, accommodation, transportation, recreation, the workplace and spiritual wellbeing, is being threatened fundamentally.

In addition to the totality of current development, the environmental impact of conurbations is a matter of serious concern when one considers a city the size of Shanghai. The demands on an increasingly depleted and diminished ecosystem threaten to destabilise the quality of life inside the city and beyond its boundaries, where demand for resources is eroding the systems that support the city. One environmental issue that is already proving critical to Shanghai is the overuse of groundwater, the excessive pumping of which is causing Shanghai to sink at a rate of 2.5 centimetres (1 inch) a year. When this is combined with Shanghai's natural flaw of having no solid foundation on which to erect tall buildings, the potential consequences are terrifying.

And so to re-engage with the original paradox. The first position, based on historical experience, suggests that Shanghai will always overcome adversity, even thrive on it, and that the 21st-century explosion in property development is just another phase that will augment the remarkably fascinating texture of the city. In contrast, the second position suggests that such development is fundamentally dissimilar to previous experiences and, despite historical lessons, does jeopardise the city's unique character.

Although it may still be too early to draw any firm conclusions, it is essential that we acknowledge the existence of these two opposing views of development and understand their potential consequence. In designing for Shanghai's future, developers, architects and planners should be aware of the city's rich heritage and aim to enhance it, and not succumb to the lure of short-term financial gain. A city born from a lust for wealth can hardly claim to need protection from it, but the rule of money does seem to have proved overwhelming.

It remains to be seen whether money will in fact consume the city and transform its extraordinary heritage into a bland, homogeneous and soulless urban form, or whether it will embellish, refine and enrich the city and its character as it has done in the past. The early attempts at large-scale redevelopment, such as in Pudong, certain areas of the former foreign settlements and the former walled city, have proved almost comprehensively negative, relying on enormous land clearance and population dispersal and replacing established patterns of life and environment with poorly designed and planned buildings and inadequate infrastructure. Nonetheless, Shanghai has always shown a resilience to man's recurring ineptitude, and thrives on hard times.

It is comforting therefore to conclude by considering Shanghai's most endearing quality: the city possesses an incorporeal characteristic that has ensured its survival through countless vicissitudes. Despite its inimitable tangible heritage manifest in its menagerie of buildings and rich urban environment, its intangible heritage is most beguiling and defies domination. As Percy Finch and history suggest: 'Shanghai has had many conquerors, but Shanghai conquers the conquerors.'

Shanghai will continue to consolidate its role at the centre of China's remarkable transformation, but it will always retain its autonomous character. Whether Shanghai will suffer or gain from China's recent experience only time will tell, but as a microcosm of global politics in the past, it is perhaps fitting to ask the same question of the world – will the world suffer or gain from China's recent experience? Perhaps we can learn this lesson from the annals of China's gateway:

> Fortunately for the human race there is a natural law which prevents any people attaining a world-mastery until such nation has achieved a very high state of mental development … China is not yet qualified, but when she is – as indeed she will be some day – she should rule the world. Inasmuch, however, as development of intellect is universal, we have cause to hope that by the time China is in a position to rule, that natural flower of intellect, universal peace, will be a feasibility, if not the obvious necessity it is rapidly proving itself to be.[5]

NOTES AND REFERENCES

Introduction

1. Percy Finch, *Shanghai and Beyond*, Charles Scribner's Sons (New York), 1953, p 14.

CHAPTER ONE The Origins of Shanghai

1. Hosea Ballou Morse, *The International Relations of the Chinese Empire,Vol 1–3*, Longmans, Green (London, New York), 1910–18, Vol 1, p 347.
2. II Kounin and Alex Yaron, *The Diamond Jubilee of the International Settlement of Shanghai*, Post Mercury Co (Shanghai), 1940, Foreword.
3. H Lang, *Shanghai Considered Socially*, Shanghai American Presbyterian Mission Press (Shanghai), 1875, p 35.
4. Hang-Jia-Hu is named after the cities of Hangzhou, Jiaxin and Huzhou whose wealth was derived from the trade of silk and tea.
5. Lang, *Shanghai Considered Socially*, p 6, says that the settlement 'Shanghai Chin' (meaning the market of Shanghai) receives a mention in archives dated 1015, but the source is not stated.
6. *General Description of Shanghai and its Environs*, Mission Press (Shanghai), 1850.
7. Some records put this date at 1292, 1279 and even 1366.
8. Quoted by Chang Che Seang, *General Description of Shanghai and its Environs*, p 43.
9. Ibid, p 44.
10. Some sources give a date of 1543.
11. Carlos Augusto Montalto de Jesus, *Historic Shanghai*, Shanghai Mercury (Shanghai), 1909, p xvii.
12. There remains some ambiguity as to when the city wall was actually built. Montalto de Jesus, *Historic Shanghai*, p xviii and Kounin and Yaron, *Diamond Jubilee*, give

1544; *General Description of Shanghai and its Environs*, gives 1552; John Wharton Maclellan, *The Story of Shanghai from the Opening of the Port to Foreign Trade* (North-China Herald, Shanghai, 1889), gives 1555 and Lang, *Shanghai Considered Socially*, states 1570. It seems likely that the wall was built in haste following the attacks in 1553 and would have been improved thereafter.
13. *Shanghai Xian Zhi*, Qin Dynasty, Jia Qin reign,Vol 19, miscellaneous.
14. Robert Fortune, *A Journey to the Tea Districts of China*, John Murray (London), 1852, p 12.
15. George Lanning and Samuel Couling, *The History of Shanghai*, Kelly &Walsh (Shanghai), 1921, p 271.
16. *General Description of Shanghai and its Environs*, p 73.
17. Linda Cooke Johnson, *Shanghai: from Market Town to Treaty Port, 1074–1858*, Stanford University Press (Stanford, CA), 1995, p 71.

CHAPTER TWO Establishing and Legalising the Foreign Settlements

1. James Vivian Davidson Houston,*Yellow Creek: the Story of Shanghai*, Putnam (London), 1962, p 18.
2. John Wharton Maclellan, *The Story of Shanghai from the Opening of the Port to Foreign Trade*, North-China Herald (Shanghai), 1889, p 5. H Lang, in *Shanghai Considered Socially* (Shanghai American Presbyterian Mission Press, Shanghai, 1875), states 21 June.
3. Carlos Augusto Montalto de Jesus, *Historic Shanghai*, Shanghai Mercury (Shanghai), 1909, p 2.
4. Ibid, p 3.

5. Arnold Wright, *Twentieth Century Impressions of Hong Kong, Shanghai and Other Treaty Ports of China*, Lloyds Greater Britain Publishing Company (London), 1908, p 62.
6. Maclellan, *The Story of Shanghai*, p 7.
7. Lang, *Shanghai Considered Socially*, p 14.
8. Montalto de Jesus, *Historic Shanghai*, p 10.
9. Ibid, p 14.
10. George Lanning and Samuel Couling, *The History of Shanghai*, Kelly & Walsh (Shanghai), 1921, p 266.
11. Ibid.
12. Montalto de Jesus, *Historic Shanghai*, gives 1,000 men; FL Hawks Pott, *A Short History of Shanghai* (Kelly & Walsh, Shanghai, 1928), gives 2,000.
13. Lanning and Couling, *History of Shanghai*, p 271.
14. Montalto de Jesus, *Historic Shanghai*, p 21.
15. With the exception of Russian treaties concerning the northern border areas.
16. Hosea Ballou Morse, *The International Relations of the Chinese Empire,Vols 1–3*, Longmans, Green (London, New York), 1910–18, Vol 1, p 299.
17. Lanning and Couling, *The History of Shanghai*, state 8th; William Richard Carles, *Some Pages in the History of Shanghai* (East & West, London, 1916), gives the 5th; and Montalto de Jesus, *Historic Shanghai*, gives the 9th.
18. Charles M Dyce, *Personal Reminiscences of Thirty Years' Residence in the Model Settlement, Shanghai, 1870–1900*, Chapman & Hall (London), 1906, p 95.
19. Lang, *Shanghai Considered Socially*, p 26.
20. Morse, *International Relations of the Chinese Empire,Vol 1*, p 348.
21. Lanning and Couling, *The History of Shanghai*, p 283.

22. Ibid, p 283.

23 Charles B Maybon and Jean Fredet, *Histoire de la Concession Française de Changhai*, Plon (Paris), 1929, p 25.

24. Maclellan, *The Story of Shanghai*, p 26.

25. *North-China Herald*, 1868.

26. Maclellan, *The Story of Shanghai*, p 100.

27. Lang, *Shanghai Considered Socially*, p 25.

28. Maclellan, *The Story of Shanghai*, p 96.

29. II Kuonin, *Eighty-Five Years of the Shanghai Volunteer Corps*, Cosmopolitan Press (Shanghai), 1938, p 13.

30. Montalto de Jesus, *Historic Shanghai*, p 94.

31. George Lanning, *The History of Shanghai*, Kelly & Walsh (Shanghai), 1920, p 69.

32. Mr Bruce to Mr Medhurst, 8 Sept 1862. In Morse, *The International Relations of the Chinese Empire, Vol 2*, p 125.

33. Lanning, *The History of Shanghai*, p 163.

34. Montalto de Jesus, *Historic Shanghai*, p 217.

35. The number of councillors and national representation varied throughout this period, though in summary: originally consisting of seven members (five British and two American), it was increased in 1869 to nine members (seven British and two Americans). One German member replaced an American before the First World War, then, after 1914, the British seats decreased and a Japanese councillor was admitted. Until 1928, the nine members consisted of five British, two Americans and two Japanese. In 1928, three seats for Chinese were added, followed by two more in 1930, bringing the total membership to 14.

36. Montalto de Jesus, *Historic Shanghai*, p 222.

37. *Shanghai: 1843–1893: the Model Settlement: Its Birth, its Youth, its Jubilee*, Shanghai Mercury (Shanghai), 1893, p 1.

38. Quote by Dr Koo in Lanning and Couling, *The History of Shanghai*, p 453.

39. Robert Barnet, *Economic Shanghai: Hostage to Politics*, Institute of Pacific Relations (New York), 1941, p 6.

40. *All About Shanghai and its Environs*, University Press (Shanghai), 1934–5, p 23.

41. Barnet, *Economic Shanghai*, p 7.

42. *Report of the Right Honourable Richard Feetham C.M.G.*, North-China Daily News & Herald, 1931, p 113.

43. Lanning, *The History of Shanghai*, p 77.

CHAPTER THREE Constructing Shanghai, 1843–1899

1. Peter George Laurie, *The Model Settlement* (Shanghai), 1866, p 1.

2. James Ricalton, *China through the Stereoscope: a Journey through the Dragon Empire at the time of the Boxer Uprising*, Underwood & Underwood (New York and London), 1901, p 77.

3. Carl Crow, *Foreign Devils in the Flowery Kingdom*, Harper & Bros (no publisher or date), p 178.

4. Laurie, *The Model Settlement*, p 2.

5. Ibid.

6. Ibid.

7. Ricalton, p 77.

8. Laurie, *The Model Settlement*, p 1.

9. *Far Eastern Review*, Vol 27, No 8 (August 1931), p 469.

10. Crow, *Foreign Devils in the Flowery Kingdom*, p 179.

11. Rutherford Alcock, *The Capital of the Tycoon*, Longman, Roberts & Green (London), 1863, pp 37–8.

12. *Shanghai – 1843–1893, The Model Settlement: its birth, its youth, its jubilee*, Shanghai Mercury Office, 1893, p 2.

13. Rodney Gilbert, *The Unequal Treaties*, John Murray (London), 1929, p 166.

14. James Vivian Davidson Houston, *Yellow Creek: the Story of Shanghai*, Putnam (London), 1962, p 32.

15. J Thompson, *Ten Years' Travels, Adventures and Residence Abroad*, Marston, Low & Searle (London), 1875, p 400.

16. Carlos Augusto Montalto de Jesus, *Historic Shanghai*, Shanghai Mercury (Shanghai), 1909, pp 27–8.

17. Ibid, p 27.

18. John Wharton Maclellan, *The Story of Shanghai from the Opening of the Port to Foreign Trade*, North-China Herald (Shanghai), 1889, p 16.

19. George Lanning and Samuel Couling, *The History of Shanghai*, Kelly & Walsh (Shanghai), 1921, p 279.

20. H Lang, *Shanghai Considered Socially*, Shanghai American Presbyterian Mission Press (Shanghai), 1875, p 23.

21. Ibid, p 21.

22. Montalto de Jesus, *Historic Shanghai*, p 32.

23. R Barz, *Sketches of Present-day Shanghai*, Centurion Printing Co (Shanghai), 1935, p 5.

24. Charles Ewart Darwent, *Shanghai: a Handbook for Travellers and Residents to the Chief Objects of Interests in and around the Foreign Settlements and Native City*, Kelly & Walsh (Shanghai), 2nd edn, 1920, p 1.

25. Maclellan, *The Story of Shanghai*, p 93.

26. *Shanghai – 1843–1893, The Model Settlement*, p 7.

27. FL Hawks Pott, *A Short History of Shanghai*, Kelly & Walsh (Shanghai), 1928, p 22.

28. Thomas Kingsmill, 'Early Architecture in Shanghai', in *Social Shanghai*, Vol 12 (July–Dec 1911), North-China Daily News & Herald (Shanghai), 1911, pp 76–7.

29. Charles M Dyce, *Personal Reminiscences of Thirty Years' Residence in the Model Settlement, Shanghai, 1870–1900*, Chapman & Hall (London), 1906, p 34.

30. Arnold Wright, *Twentieth Century Impressions of Hong Kong, Shanghai and Other Treaty Ports of China*, Lloyds Greater Britain Publishing Company (London), 1908, p 85.

31. Maclellan, *The Story of Shanghai*, p 30.

32. William Richard Carles, *Some Pages in the History of Shanghai, 1842–1856: a paper read before the China Society*, East & West (London), 1916, p 16.

33. II Kounin and Alex Yaron, *The Diamond Jubilee of the International Settlement of Shanghai*, Post Mercury Co (Shanghai), 1940, p 90.

34. James Vivian Davidson Houston, *Yellow Creek: the Story of Shanghai*, Putnam (London), 1962, p 35.

35. Maclellan, *The Story of Shanghai*, p 28.

36. Ibid.

37. Wright, *Twentieth Century Impressions of Hong Kong, Shanghai and Other Treaty Ports of China*, p 379.

38. Lang, *Shanghai Considered Socially*, p 21.

39. Laurence Oliphant, *Narrative of the Earl of Elgin's Mission to China and Japan in the Years 1857, '58, '59* (Edinburgh and London),

1859 in Maclellan, *The Story of Shanghai*, p 47.

40. Maclellan, *The Story of Shanghai*, p 94.

41. Lang, *Shanghai Considered Socially*, p 24.

42. ES Elliston, *Ninety-five Years, a Shanghai Hospital 1844–1938* (no publisher) 1941, p 12.

43. Kingsmill, 'Early Architecture in Shanghai', p 80.

44. Wright, *Twentieth Century Impressions of Hongkong, Shanghai, and Other Treaty Ports of China*, p 378.

45. Lang, *Shanghai Considered Socially*, pp 39–40.

46. Darwent, *Shanghai: a Handbook for Travellers and Residents*, p 17.

47. Lanning and Couling, *The History of Shanghai*, p 276.

48. Ibid.

49. Lang, *Shanghai Considered Socially*, p 21.

50. Kingsmill, 'Early Architecture in Shanghai', pp 80–1.

51. FO 676/558, Public Record Office, London.

52. *Shanghai – 1843–1893, The Model Settlement*, p 7.

53. Maclellan, *The Story of Shanghai*, p 20.

54. Darwent, *Shanghai: a Handbook for Travellers and Residents*, p 92.

55. Maclellan, *The Story of Shanghai*, states Nicholas Massa, though some 20th-century sources quote Jean Ferrand.

56. Ibid, p.19.

57. *North-China Herald*, 19 March 1853.

58. Darwent, *Shanghai: a Handbook for Travellers and Residents*, p 74.

59. Quote from the *North-China Herald* in Maclellan, *The Story of Shanghai*, p 29.

60. Wright, *Twentieth Century Impressions of Hong Kong, Shanghai and Other Treaty Ports of China*.

61. *North-China Herald*, 1868.

62. Ibid.

63. Eugene Boardman, *Christian Influence upon the Ideology of the Taiping Rebellion 1851–1864*, University of Wisconsin Press (Madison), 1952, p 9.

64. Montalto de Jesus, *Historic Shanghai*, p 120.

65. Ibid, p 206.

66. Maclellan, *The Story of Shanghai*, p 81.

67. Laurie, *The Model Settlement*, p 4.

68. Maclellan, *The Story of Shanghai*, p 59.

69. Alcock, *The Capital of the Tycoon*, pp 37–8.

70. George Lanning, *The History of Shanghai*, Kelly & Walsh (Shanghai), 1920, p 163.

71. Laurie, *The Model Settlement*, p 4.

72. Maclellan, *The Story of Shanghai*, p 60.

73. Laurie, *The Model Settlement*, p 2.

74. Kounin and Yaron, *The Diamond Jubilee of the International Settlement of Shanghai*, p 109.

75. On 30 June 1870, of 1,666 foreigners living in the International Settlement, 894 were British; cf Charles M Dyce, *Personal Reminiscences of Thirty Years' Residence in the Model Settlement Shanghai, 1870–1900*, Chapman & Hall (London), 1906, pp 31 and 42.

76. Ibid, p 46.

77. The other nationalities represented in the International Settlement in 1870 were, in descending numerical order: 104 Portuguese, 104 Portuguese Eurasians from Macao, 46 Spanish, 16 French (not including the French Concession), 9 Danish, 8 Swedish, 7 Austrian, 7 Swiss, 7 Japanese, 5 Italian, 5 Dutch, 3 Greek, 3 Norwegian, 1 Belgian, 1 Brazilian and 155 Indians, Malays and other Asians.

78. Laurie, *The Model Settlement*, p 2.

79. Paolo Rossi, *The Communist Conquest of Shanghai*, Twin Circle Publishing and Crestwood Books (Arlington, VA), 1970, p 87.

80. J Thompson, *Ten Years' Travels, Adventures and Residence Abroad*, Marston, Low & Searle (London), 1875, p 407.

81. Lang, *Shanghai Considered Socially*, p 40.

82. *The East of Asia Magazine*, North-China Herald (Shanghai), 1904, Vol 3, p 29.

83. *St Francis Xavier's College Diamond Jubilee Souvenir Album 1874–1934* (no author, publisher or pages)

84. JD Clark, *Sketches in and around Shanghai, etc.*, Shanghai Mercury and Celestial Empire Offices (Shanghai), 1894, p 120.

85. Ibid, p 118.

86. Wright, *Twentieth Century Impressions of Hong Kong, Shanghai and Other Treaty Ports of China*.

87. *Shanghai Mercury*, 18 August 1884.

88. JD Clark, *Sketches in and around Shanghai, etc.*, Shanghai Mercury and Celestial Empire Offices (Shanghai), 1894, p 120.

89. HB Morse, *The International Relations of the Chinese Empire*, Vol 3, Longmans, Green (London, New York), 1910–18, p 76.

90. Lang, *Shanghai Considered Socially*, p 33.

91. Laurie, *The Model Settlement*, p 1.

92. Lang, *Shanghai Considered Socially*, p 37–8.

93. Lanning, *The History of Shanghai*, p 164. Dr Johnson in 1874 speaking of Peking Road near the gaol.

94. Darwent, *Shanghai: a Handbook for Travellers and Residents*, p 11.

95. Laurie, *The Model Settlement*, p 4.

96. 'Bank building in Shanghai, China', *The Architect*, 6 October 1877, p 185.

97. Kounin and Yaron, *The Diamond Jubilee of the International Settlement of Shanghai*, p 144.

98. Ibid.

99. Lanning and Couling, *The History of Shanghai*.

CHAPTER FOUR Becoming a City, 1900–1920

1. *Far Eastern Review*, Vol 13, No 4 (Sept 1916), p 144.

2. James Vivian Davidson Houston, *Yellow Creek: the Story of Shanghai*, Putnam (London), 1962, p 112.

3. Ernest Otto Hauser, *Shanghai: City for Sale*, Harcourt, Brace (New York), 1940, p 110.

4. The total number of permits is distinct from the number of permits for houses, the figures for which appear in each annual report of the Shanghai Municipal Council and reflect the ebb and flow of the building industry (see table, p 251).

5. Arnold Wright, *Twentieth Century Impressions of Hong Kong, Shanghai and Other Treaty Ports of China*, Lloyds Greater Britain Publishing Company (London), 1908, p 62.

6. *Shanghai Municipal Council Annual Report*, Kelly & Walsh (Shanghai), 1911, p 113.

7. Wright, *Twentieth Century Impressions of Hong Kong, Shanghai and Other Treaty Ports of China*, p 382.

8. Charles Ewart Darwent, *Shanghai: a Handbook for Travellers and Residents to the Chief Objects of Interests in and around the Foreign Settlements and Native City*, Kelly & Walsh (Shanghai), 2nd edn, 1920, pp 70–1.

9. *Gow's Guide to Shanghai*, North-China Daily News & Herald (Shanghai), 1924, p 40.

10. Arthur Ransome, *The Chinese Puzzle*, George

Allen & Unwin (London), 1927, p 147.

11. *Far Eastern Review*, Vol 13, No 4 (Sept 1916), p 144.

12. *Far Eastern Review*, Vol 9, No 9 (Feb 1910) p 424.

13. JD Clark, *Sketches in and around Shanghai, etc.*, Shanghai Mercury (Shanghai), 1894, p 64.

14. R Barz, *Shanghai – sketches of present-day Shanghai*, Centurion Printing Company (Shanghai), 1935, p 37.

15. *Far Eastern Review*, Vol 24, No 12 (Dec 1927), p 550.

16. II Kuonin and Alex Yaron, *The Diamond Jubilee of the International Settlement of Shanghai* (Shanghai), 1938, p 136.

17. *Far Eastern Review*, Vol 9, No 3 (Aug 1912) p 140.

18. Tasman Ile, *Shanghai Night*, Shanghai, p 159.

19. *Wanderings in China Vol II*, William Blackwood (Edinburgh), 1886.

20. Darwent, *Shanghai: a Handbook for Travellers and Residents*, p 33.

21. *Far Eastern Review*, Vol 13, No 5 (October 1916), p 183.

22. John Otway Percy Bland, *Houseboat Days in China*. Edward Arnold (London), 1909, p 45.

23. *Gow's Guide to Shanghai*, North-China Daily News & Herald (Shanghai), 1924, p 21.

24. Wright, *Twentieth Century Impressions of Hong Kong, Shanghai and Other Treaty Ports of China*.

25. Noel Barber, *The Fall of Shanghai*, Macmillan (London), 1979, p 25.

26. Darwent, *Shanghai: a Handbook for Travellers and Residents*, p 21.

27. *Far Eastern Review*, Vol 23, No 10 (Oct 1927), p 446.

28. *Far Eastern Review*, Vol 1, No 5 (Nov 1904), p 35.

29. *Gow's Guide to Shanghai*, p 36.

30. Clark, *Sketches in and around Shanghai*, p 55.

31. Darwent, *Shanghai: a Handbook for Travellers and Residents*, p 22.

32. Clark, *Sketches in and around Shanghai, etc.*, p 59.

33. *Far Eastern Review*, Vol 13, No 4 (Sept 1916), p 144.

34. *Shanghai by Night and Day*, Shanghai Mercury Ltd, 1902, p 35.

35. *Far Eastern Review*, Vol 13, No 4 (Sept 1916), p 146.

36. Ibid.

37. Darwent, *Shanghai: a Handbook for Travellers and Residents*, p 15.

38. *Far Eastern Review*, Vol 14, No 5 (Oct 1918), p 425.

39. *Far Eastern Review*, Vol 12, No 7 (Dec 1916), p 255.

40. Darwent, *Shanghai: a Handbook for Travellers and Residents*, p 29.

41. *Far Eastern Review*, Vol 10, No 11 (April 1914), p 36.

42. *Shanghai by Night and Day*, p 54.

43. *Far Eastern Review*, Vol 1, No 6 (Nov 1904), p 35.

44. Reginald Luff, 'Buildings in Shanghai', in *Social Shanghai*, Vol 6, July–Dec 1908, North-China Daily News & Herald (Shanghai), 1908, p 26.

45. Kuonin, *The Diamond Jubilee of the International Settlement of Shanghai*, p 163.

46. Wright, *Twentieth Century Impressions of Hong Kong, Shanghai and Other Treaty Ports of China*, p 376.

47. *Far Eastern Review*, Vol 8, No 12 (May 1912), p 448.

48. *Far Eastern Review*, Vol 13, No 5 (Oct 1916), p 183.

49. *Far Eastern Review*, Vol 13, No 4 (Sept 1916), p 150.

50. Peter George Laurie, *The Model Settlement* (Shanghai), 1866.

51. John Wharton Maclellan, *The Story of Shanghai from the Opening of the Port to Foreign Trade*, North-China Herald (Shanghai), 1889

52. *Far Eastern Review*, Vol 7, No 11 (Feb 1911), p 326.

53. Ibid.

54. Wright, *Twentieth Century Impressions of Hong Kong, Shanghai and Other Treaty Ports of China*.

55. *Far Eastern Review*, Vol 1, No 6 (Dec 1904), p 22.

56. Ibid.

57. Jay Denby, *Letters of a Shanghai Griffin to his Father and Other Exaggerations*, China Printing Company (Shanghai), 1910, p 138.

58. *Far Eastern Review*, Vol 1, No 6 (Nov 1904), p 35.

59. Mitchell in Darwent, *Shanghai: a Handbook for Travellers and Residents*, p 8.

60. Wright, *Twentieth Century Impressions of Hong Kong, Shanghai*, p 604.

61. GL Wilson, 'Architecture, Interior Decoration and Building in Shanghai Twenty Years Ago and Today', *China Journal of Science & Arts*, Vol 12, No 5 (May 1930), p 249.

62. Wright, *Twentieth Century Impressions of Hong Kong, Shanghai and Other Treaty Ports of China*, p 371.

63. Quoted in a pamphlet by Sidney J Powell in Darwent, *Shanghai: a Handbook for Travellers and Residents*.

64. Lang, *Shanghai Considered Socially*, p 33.

65. Darwent, *Shanghai: a Handbook for Travellers and Residents*.

66. *Far Eastern Review*, Vol 3, No 2 (July 1906), p 66.

67. James Ricalton, *China through the Stereoscope: a Journey through the Dragon Empire at the time of the Boxer Uprising*, Underwood & Underwood (New York and London), 1901, p 77.

68. Wright, *Twentieth Century Impressions of Hong Kong, Shanghai and Other Treaty Ports of China*, p 371.

69. Harold Acton, *Memoirs of an Aesthete*, Methney (London), 1948, p 292.

70. WH Auden and Christopher Isherwood, *Journey to a War*, Faber and Faber (London), 1939 (revised edn, 1973), p 227.

71. Denby, *Letters of a Shanghai Griffin*, p 113.

72. *Far Eastern Review*, Vol 3, No 2 (July 1906), p 66.

73. *Far Eastern Review*, Vol 5, No 11 (April 1909), p 393.

74. *Far Eastern Review*, Vol 4, No 6 (Nov 1907), p 186.

75. *Far Eastern Review*, Vol 12, No 12 (May 1916), p 485.

76. *Far Eastern Review*, Vol 13, No 5 (Oct 1916), p 185.

77. *Far Eastern Review*, Vol 4, No 9 (Feb 1908), p 271.

78. Ibid.

79. *Far Eastern Review*, Vol 13, No 5 (Oct 1916), p 184.

80. *China Weekly Review*, 9 February 1929, p 448.

81. Darwent, *Shanghai: a Handbook for Travellers and Residents*, pp 55–6.

82. Wright, *Twentieth Century Impressions of Hong Kong, Shanghai and Other Treaty Ports of China*, p 379.
83. Auden and Isherwood, *Journey to a War*, p 236.
84. *Far Eastern Review*, Vol 24, No 5 (May 1928), p 225.
85. Hsia Ching-Lin, *The Status of Shanghai – a Historical Review of the International Settlement*, Kelly & Walsh (Shanghai), 1929, p 118.
86. Bland, *Houseboat Days in China*, p 5.
87. Hsia, *The Status of Shanghai*, p 138.
88. Arthur de C Sowerby, *China Journal of Science and Arts*, Vol 3, No 5 (May 1925), p 247.
89. Denby, *Letters of a Shanghai Griffin*, p 145.
90. Ransome. *The Chinese Puzzle*, p 148.
91. Darwent, *Shanghai: a Handbook for Travellers and Residents*, p 79.
92. Denby, *Letters of a Shanghai Griffin*, p 2.
93. Wright, *Twentieth Century Impressions of Hong Kong, Shanghai and Other Treaty Ports of China*.
94. *Far Eastern Review*, Vol 19, No 3 (March 1923), p 178.
95. Denby, *Letters of a Shanghai Griffin*, p 3.
96. From 'The Lure of the East' by Shamus A'Rabbitt in *China Coast Ballads*, AR Hager (Shanghai), 1938, p 116.
97. *Far Eastern Review*, Vol 11, No 5 (Oct 1914), p 144.
98. *Shanghai Municipal Council Annual Report*, 1911, pp 12 and 13.
99. *Far Eastern Review*, Vol 11, No 5 (Oct 1914), p 145.
100. *Far Eastern Review*, Vol 2, No 1 (June 1905), p 4.
101. *Municipal Council Report for 1904*, Kelly & Walsh (Shanghai), 1905, p 238.
102. *Municipal Council Report for 1912*, Kelly & Walsh (Shanghai), 1913, p 17b.
103. *Far Eastern Review*, Vol 13, No 4 (Sept 1916), p 144.
104. *Municipal Council Report for 1914*, Kelly & Walsh (Shanghai), 1915, p 3b.
105. *Municipal Council Report for 1914*, Kelly & Walsh (Shanghai), 1915, p 238.

CHAPTER FIVE Rise and Fall, 1921–1941

1. Tasman Ile, *Shanghai Nights* (no publisher or date), p 1.
2. Arthur Ransome, *The Chinese Puzzle*, George Allen & Unwin (London), 1927, p 123.
3. Percy Finch, *Shanghai and Beyond*, Charles Scribner's (New York), 1953, p 77.
4. Ibid, p 21.
5. Ibid, p 25.
6. Anatol Kotenev, *Shanghai: Its Municipality and the Chinese*, North-China Daily News & Herald (Shanghai), 1927, p 173.
7. It is acknowledged that the figures for the killed and wounded do vary, though this was not the first time the police had shot demonstrators outside this building. Several Chinese were killed in a similar event on 18 December 1905 when the station was 'severely damaged by fire' by Chinese aggrieved at an alleged unfair decision in the Mixed Court (Municipal Report for 1906). A proposal to erect a 'semi-military' wall around the exposed sides of the building was later dropped. Louza Police Station was designed by Mr Dallas and completed in November 1889.
8. Tasman Ile, *Shanghai Nights*, p 1
9. Harumi Goto-Shibata, *Japan and Britain in Shanghai 1925–31*, Macmillan (London), 1995, p 49.
10. Finch, *Shanghai and Beyond*, p 140.
11. Ibid, p 158.
12. Ibid, p 165.
13. One such incident occurred on 16 August when a British Royal Air Force (RAF) reconnaissance aircraft was forced to land outside the settlement boundary. The RAF collected the fuselage and returned it safely to their makeshift airbase on the Racecourse in the centre of the Settlement. When they returned to collect the wings, they found them guarded by Chinese troops who refused to hand them over. With British authority in Shanghai and the RAF losing face, General Duncan, commander in charge of the Shanghai Defence Force, threatened to pull up the railway tracks of the Shanghai–Ningbo railway line unless the wings were returned. The line was strategically vital to the Nationalists, so when the deadline passed and the tracks were pulled up, it came as little surprise when the Defence Force Headquarters in the Kalee Hotel in front of Trinity Cathedral received a message of assurance that the wings would be returned safely. The tracks were duly re-laid and the situation was defused.
14. Hsia Ching-Lin, *The Status of Shanghai – a Historical Review of the International Settlement*, Kelly & Walsh (Shanghai), 1929, Foreword.
15. Tasman Ile, *Shanghai Night*, p 11–12.
16. Hsia, *Status of Shanghai*, Foreword.
17. Ibid, p 139.
18. *Report of the Right Honourable Richard Feetham C.M.G.*, North-China Daily News & Herald (Shanghai), 1931, p 143.
19. *Far Eastern Review*, Vol 13, No 4 (Sept 1916), p 145.
20. William Richard Carles, *Some Pages in the History of Shanghai 1842–1856*, East & West (London), 1916, p 1.
21. Tasman Ile, *Shanghai Nights*, p 11.
22. WH Auden and Christopher Isherwood, *Journey to a War*, Faber and Faber (London), 1939 (revised edn, 1973), p 227.
23. GL Wilson, 'Architecture, Interior Decoration and Building in Shanghai Twenty Years Ago and Today', *China Journal of Science & Arts*, Vol 12, No 5 (May 1930), p 248.
24. F King, *The History of the Hongkong and Shanghai Banking Corporation, Volume III: The Hongkong Bank between the Wars and the Bank Interned* (Cambridge), 1988, p 132.
25. *Far Eastern Review*, Vol 20, No 7 (July 1923), p 453.
26. Ibid, p 455.
27. Ibid, p 453.
28. 'The Hongkong and Shanghai Bank', *Architects' Journal* (13 May 1925), p 730.
29. Thomas Kingsmill, 'Early Architecture in Shanghai', in *Social Shanghai*, Vol 12 (July–Dec 1911), North-China Daily News & Herald (Shanghai), 1911, p 75.
30. *Far Eastern Review*, Vol 24, No 2 (Feb 1928), p 72.
31. *Far Eastern Review*, Vol 24, No 2 (Feb 1928), p 72.

32. *Far Eastern Review*, Vol 20, No 4 (April 1923), p 245.
33. *Far Eastern Review*, Vol 16, No 1 (Jan 1920), p 55.
34. *Far Eastern Review*, Vol 32, No 9 (Sept 1936), p 394.
35. M Ristaino, *The Port of Last Resort*, Stanford University Press (Stanford, CA), 2001.
36. *Men of Shanghai and North China*, University Press (Shanghai), 2nd edn, 1935.
37. *Social Shanghai*, Vol 14 (July–Dec 1912), North-China Daily News & Herald, 1912, p 117.
38. Ristaino, *The Port of Last Resort*, pp 143–4.
39. *Far Eastern Review*, Vol 28, No 11 (Nov 1932), p 515.
40. Bruno Kroker, 'The Building Industry in Shanghai', *China Journal of Science & Arts*, Vol 30, No 5 (May 1939), p 315.
41. Arthur Sopher and Theodore Sopher, *The Profitable Path of Shanghai Realty*, Shanghai Times (Shanghai), 1939, p 90.
42. Olga Lung, *Chinese Family and Society*, Yale University Press (New Haven and London), 1946, p 90.
43. R Barz, *Shanghai – Sketches of Present-day Shanghai*, Centurion Printing Company (Shanghai), 1935, p 151.
44. Sopher and Sopher, *The Profitable Path of Shanghai Realty*, p 90.
45. Jay Denby, *Letters of a Shanghai Griffin to his Father and Other Exaggerations*, China Printing Company (Shanghai), 1910, p 13.
46. Harriet Sergeant, *Shanghai*, John Murray (London), 1991, p 124.
47. Ibid.
48. Sopher and Sopher, *The Profitable Path of Shanghai Realty*, p 318.
49. Tasman Ile, *Shanghai Night*, p 159.
50. Sopher and Sopher, *The Profitable Path of Shanghai Realty*, p 90.
51. Ibid, p 155.
52. *Men of Shanghai and North China*, pp 328–31.
53. Barz, *Shanghai – sketches of present-day Shanghai*, p 33.
54. Wilson, 'Architecture, Interior Decoration and Building in Shanghai', p 249.
55. Tasman Ile, *Shanghai Nights*, p.11
56. Ransome, *The Chinese Puzzle*, p 121.
57. Lang, *Shanghai Considered Socially*, p.55–6.

58. Denby, *Letters of a Shanghai Griffin*, p 58.
59. Walter Henry Medhurst, *The Foreigner in Far Cathay*, Edward Stanford (London), 1872, p 25.
60. Shamus A'Rabbitt, *China Coast Ballads*, AR Hager (Shanghai), 1938.
61. Denby, *Letters of a Shanghai Griffin*, p 138.
62. Charles Ewart Darwent, *Shanghai: a Handbook for Travellers and Residents*, Kelly & Walsh (Shanghai), 1st edn, 1916, p 152.
63. *Far Eastern Review*, Vol 23, No 6 (June 1927), p 261.
64. Wilson, *Architecture, Interior Decoration and Building in Shanghai*, p 257.
65. *Shanghai Times*, October 1904; in *Far Eastern Review*, Vol 1, No 6 (Nov 1904), p 35.
66. Wilson, *Architecture, Interior Decoration and Building in Shanghai*, p 248.
67. *Far East Magazine*, Vol 3, No 1 (1936).
68. Goto-Shibata, *Japan and Britain in Shanghai 1925-31*, p 136.
69. Ibid. Goto-Shibata quotes 33,500, while Finch, *Shanghai and Beyond*, quotes 16,000. Whatever the actual figure, it was numerically far superior to the Japanese force.
70. Finch, *Shanghai and Beyond*, p 244.
71. Ibid, p 245.
72. TW Brooke and RW Davis, *The China Architect's and Builder's Compendium*, North-China Daily News & Herald (Shanghai), 1932, p 107.
73. Tasman Ile, *Shanghai Nights*, p 17.
74. Brooke and Davis, *The China Architect's and Builder's Compendium*, p 108.
75. *Far Eastern Review*, Vol 31, No 10 (Oct 1935), p 396.
76. Kroker, *The Building Industry in Shanghai*, p 315.
77. Brooke and Davis, *The China Architect's and Builder's Compendium*, p 127.
78. Lenore Hietkamp, *The Park Hotel, Shanghai (1931–34) and its Architect, Laszlo Hudec (1893–1958)*, University of Guelph, 1989, p 26.
79. *Far Eastern Review*, Vol 27, No 6 (June 1931), p 350.
80. Ibid.
81. *Far Eastern Review*, Vol 28, No 11 (Nov 1932), p 519.
82. *Men of Shanghai and North China*, p 163.

83. *China Weekly Review*, Vol 47, No 4 (22 Dec 1928), p 159.
84. Journalist and eyewitness Percy Finch calls it 'Bloody Saturday' (*Shanghai and Beyond*, p 252), though other later sources call it 'Black Saturday'.
85. Ibid.
86. *North-China Daily News*, 5 November 1937.
87. FC Jones, *Shanghai and Tientsin*, Oxford University Press (London), 1940, p 62.
88. *Far Eastern Review*, Vol 28, No 4 (April 1932), p 156.
89. Jones, *Shanghai and Tientsin*, pp 103–4.
90. Ristaino, *The Port of Last Resort*, p 103.
91. *Far Eastern Review*, Vol 20, No 10 (Oct 1924), p 474.
92. II Kuonin, *The Diamond Jubilee of the International Settlement of Shanghai* (Shanghai), 1938, p 32.
93. *Far Eastern Review*, Vol 23, No 6 (June 1927), pp 254–5
94. Wilson, *Architecture, Interior Decoration and Building in Shanghai*, p 250.
95. Ibid.
96. Denby, *Letters of a Shanghai Griffin*, p 13.
97. Wilson, *Architecture, Interior Decoration and Building in Shanghai*, p 251.
98. Sopher and Sopher, *The Profitable Path of Shanghai Realty*, p 23.
99. Wilson, *Architecture, Interior Decoration and Building in Shanghai*, p 250.
100. Kuonin, *The Diamond Jubilee of the International Settlement of Shanghai*, p 228.

CHAPTER SIX Anti-Design

1. Peter Clague, 'Bridge House', *South China Morning Post*, 1983, p 27.
2. Bernard Wasserstein, *Secret War in Shanghai*, Profile Books (London), 1999, p 138.
3. Clague, 'Bridge House', p.47
4. This term applied to the European Jews who had arrived in Shanghai after 1937 and not to the many former Russian refugees who arrived in Shanghai long before 1937 but were also stateless.
5. *Shanghai Jewish Chronicle*, 9 May 1943, in

Marcia Reynders Ristaino, *Port of Last Resort*, Stanford University Press, 2001, p 199, which is an excellent resource for providing a detailed account of refugee life in Shanghai during the Second World War.

6. Paula Eskelund and F Schiff, *Squeezing Through! – Shanghai Sketches, 1941–1945*, Hwa Kuo Printing Co (Shanghai), 1946, no page numbers.

7. OSS X-2 Branch, 'Shanghai: Counter-Espionage Summary', 12 August 1945, FOIA/CIA in Wasserstein, *Secret War in Shanghai*, p 25.

8. Cornelius Starr, owner of the Shanghai *Evening Post and Mercury*, quoted in *Fortune Magazine*, February 1946, p 142.

9. Noel Barber, *The Fall of Shanghai*, Macmillan (London), 1979, p 36.

10. Richard Gaulton, 'Political Mobilization in Shanghai, 1949–1951', in Christopher Howe (ed), *Revolution and Development in an Asian Metropolis*, Cambridge University Press (Cambridge), 1981, pp 41–2.

11. Ibid, p 40.

12. Arthur Sopher and Theodore Sopher, *The Profitable Path of Shanghai Realty*, Shanghai Times (Shanghai), 1939, p 213.

13. Ka-iu Fung, 'The Spatial Development of Shanghai', in Howe (ed), *Revolution and Development*, p 274.

14. Christopher Howe, 'Industrialization Under Conditions of Long-Run Population Stability: Shanghai's Achievement and Prospect', in Howe (ed), *Revolution and Development*, p 171.

15. Barber, *The Fall of Shanghai*, p 223.

16. File Number: FO 676/558, National Archive, London.

17. Letter dated 16 September 1967 in FO 676/558, National Archive, London.

18. Tony Fry, *A New Design Philosophy – an Introduction to Defuturing*, University of New South Wales Press (Sydney), 1999.

19. Howe (ed), *Revolution and Development*, p xv.

20. Ibid.

CHAPTER SEVEN The Giant Awakes

1. Dominique Perrault, 'Liu Jia Zui Business District, Shanghai 1992', presentation document.
    .   Richard Rogers Partnership, 'Lu Jia Zui, Shanghai, China, 1992–1994', presentation document.

2. Ibid.

3. Massimiliano Fuksas, 'Urban development of the International Trade Center of the Lu Jia Zui-Pudong zone, Shanghai' (1992), presentation document.

4. Perrault, *Liu Jia Zui Business District, Shanghai 1992*.

5. Shanghai Urban Planning Exhibition, 2005.

6. *Far Eastern Review*, Vol 23, No 10 (Oct 1927), p 448.

7. Richard Rogers, *Cities for a Small Planet*, Faber and Faber (London), 1997, pt 2, p 53.

8. *China Daily*, 22 January 1988.

9. Shanghai Urban Planning Exhibition, 2005

10. Ibid.

11. Ibid.

12. *All About Shanghai and Environs*, University Press (Shanghai), 1934–35, p 43.

13. Ibid.

CHAPTER EIGHT Shanghai's Future

1. 'New House in Shanghai', *Architect and Building News*, 28 June 1929, p 883.

2. Richard Rogers, *Cities for a Small Planet*, Faber and Faber (London), 1997, pt 2, p 45.

3. Shanghai Urban Planning Exhibition, 2005.

4. Marie-Claire Bergère, 'The Other China: Shanghai from 1919 to 1949', in Christopher Howe (ed), *Revolution and Development in an Asian Metropolis*, Cambridge University Press (Cambridge), 1981, p 34

5. Jay Denby, *Letters of a Shanghai Griffin to his Father and Other Exaggerations*, China Printing Company (Shanghai), 1923, p 121.

BIBLIOGRAPHY

Alcock, Rutherford, *Capital of the Tycoons: A Narrative of a Three Years' Residence in Japan*, Longman (London), 1863

A'Rabbitt, Shamus, *China Coast Ballads*, AR Hager (Shanghai), 1938

Auden, WH and Isherwood, Christopher, *Journey to a War*, Faber and Faber (London), 1939 (revised edn, 1973)

Baker, Barbara, *Shanghai: Electric and Lurid City: an Anthology*, Oxford University Press (Hong Kong and Oxford), 1998

Ball, Samuel, *Observations on the Expediency of Opening a Second Port in China*, PP Thoms (Macao), 1817

Barber, Noel, *The Fall of Shanghai*, Coward, McCann & Geoghegan (New York), 1979

Barnet, Robert, *Economic Shanghai: Hostage to Politics*, Institute of Pacific Relations (New York), 1941

Barz, R, *Sketches of Present-day Shanghai*, Centurion Printing Co (Shanghai), 1935

Bickers, Robert A, *Empire Made Me: an Englishman adrift in Shanghai*, Allen Lane (London), 2003

Bland, John Otway Percy, *Houseboat Days in China*, Edward Arnold (London), 1909

Brooke, TW and Davis, RW, *The China Architect's and Builder's Compendium*, North-China Daily News & Herald (Shanghai), 1932

Buissonnet, Eugéne, *De Pékiná Shanghai: Souvenirs de voyages* (Paris), 1871

Carles, William Richard, *Some Pages in the History of Shanghai, 1842–1856: a Paper Read before the China Society*, East & West (London), 1916

Carrie, WJ, *Report of the Shanghai Refugees Committee*, Shanghai Refugees Committee (Shanghai), 1938

Champly, Henry, *The Road to Shanghai: White Slave Traffic in Asia*, John Long (London), 1934

Cheng, Nien, *Life and Death in Shanghai*, Grove Press (New York), 1986

Christian Cooperation in China, National Christian Council of China (Shanghai), 1937

Clancy, PJ, *The Secret of Shanghai*, Mellifont Press (London), 1938

Clark, JD, *Sketches in and around Shanghai*, Shanghai Mercury and Celestial Empire Offices (Shanghai), 1894

Clemow, Valentine, *Shanghai Lullaby*, Hurst & Blackett (London), 1937

Clifford, Nicholas R, *Spoilt Children of Empire: Westerners in Shanghai and the Chinese Revolution of the 1920s*, Middlebury College Press (Hanover), 1991

Clifford, Patrick, *West from Shanghai: a Story of Shanghai and the Japanese War*, Mellifont Press (London), 1937

Clune, Frank, *Sky High to Shanghai: an Account of My Oriental Travels in the Spring of 1938*, Angus & Robertson (Sydney and London), 1939

Cumming, Gordon, *Wanderings in China*, William Blackwood (Edinburgh and London), 1886

Darwent, Charles Ewart, *Shanghai: a Handbook for Travellers and Residents*, Kelly & Walsh (Shanghai), 1912

Darwent, Charles Ewart, *Shanghai: a Handbook for Travellers and Residents*, Kelly & Walsh (Shanghai), 2nd edn, 1920

Davis, Charles Noel, *A History of the Shanghai Paper Hunt Club, 1863–1930*, Kelly & Walsh (Shanghai), 1930

Denby, Jay, *Letters of a Shanghai Griffin to his Father and Other Exaggerations*, China Printing Company (Shanghai), 1st edn, 1910

Dong, Stella, *Shanghai: The Rise and Fall of the Decadent City 1842–1949*, William Morrow (New York), 2000

Dyce, Charles M, *Personal Reminiscences of Thirty Years' Residence in the Model Settlement, Shanghai, 1870–1900*, Chapman & Hall (London), 1906

Elliston, ES, *Ninety-five Years, a Shanghai Hospital 1844–1938* (npub), 1941

Eskelund, Paula and Schiff, F, *Squeezing Through! – Shanghai Sketches, 1941–1945*, Hwa Kuo Printing Co (Shanghai), 1946

Fairbank, John King, *Trade and Diplomacy on the China Coast: the Opening of the Treaty Ports, 1842–1854*, Harvard University Press (Cambridge, Mass), 1953

Feetham, Richard, *Report of the Hon. Richard Feetham to the Shanghai Municipal Council*, Shanghai, North-China Daily News and Herald (Shanghai), 1931

Fortune, Robert, *A Journey to the Tea Districts of China*, John Murray (London), 1852

Fortune, Robert, *A Residence among the Chinese*, John Murray (London), 1857

Fortune, Robert, *Three Years' Wanderings in the Northern Provinces of China*, John Murray (London), 1847.

Foster, Arnold, *Municipal Ethics: an Examination of the Opium-license Policy of the Shanghai Municipality*, Kelly & Walsh (Shanghai), 1914

Foster, Arnold, *The International Commission for the Investigation of the Opium Trade and the Opium Habit in the Far East to be held in Shanghai, February 1909*, Hodder & Stoughton (London), 1909

Fry, Tony, *A New Design Philosophy – an Introduction to Defuturing*, University of New South Wales Press (Sydney), 1999

Gamewell, Mary Ninde, *The Gateway to China*, FH Revell (New York), 1916

General Description of Shanghai and its Environs, Mission Press (Shanghae), 1850

Gilbert, Rodney, *The Unequal Treaties: China and the Foreigner*, John Murray (London), 1929

Gordon, Charles George, *Gordon's Campaign in China: by Himself*, Chapman & Hall (London), 1900

Goto-Shibata, Harumi, *Japan and Britain in Shanghai 1925–31*, Macmillan (London), 1995

Green, Owen Mortimer, *Shanghai of To-day: the Model Settlement*, AS Watson (Shanghai), 1927

Green, Owen Mortimer, *The Foreigner in China*, Hutchinson (London), 1943

Harfield, Alan, *British and Indian Armies on the China Coast 1785–1985*, A & J Partnership (London), 1990

Hauser, Ernst Otto, *Shanghai: City for Sale*, Harcourt, Brace (New York), 1940

Henderson, James, *Shanghai Hygiene*, Presbyterian

Mission Press (Shanghai), 1863

Heppner, Ernest G and Gunther, Ernest, *Shanghai Refuge: a Memoir of the World War II Jewish Ghetto*, University of Nebraska Press (Lincoln, NB), 1993

Hietkamp, Lenore, *The Park Hotel, Shanghai (1931–34) and its Architect, Laszlo Hudec (1893–1958)*, University of Guelph (Ontario), 1989

Hill, Henry Berry, *Chinnery and China Coast Paintings*, F Lewis (Leigh-on-Sea), 1970

Hill, Henry Berry, *George Chinnery, 1774–1852: Artist of the China Coast*, F Lewis (Leigh-on-sea), 1963

Hinder, Eleanor M, *Life & Labour in Shanghai* (npub, np), 1944

Houston, James Vivian Davidson, *Yellow Creek: the Story of Shanghai*, Putnam (London), 1962

Howe, Christopher (ed), *Revolution and Development in an Asian Metropolis*, Cambridge University Press (Cambridge), 1981

Hsia, Ching-Lin, *The Status of Shanghai: a Historical Review of the International Settlement, its Future Development and Possibilities through Sino-Foreign Co-operation*, Kelly & Walsh (Shanghai), 1929

Hsu, Shu-his, *Japan and Shanghai*, Kelly & Walsh (Shanghai), 1938

Ile, Tasman, *Shanghai Nights* (npub, np, nd)

Johnson, Linda Cooke, *Shanghai: from Market Town to Treaty Port, 1074–1858*, Stanford University Press (Stanford, CA), 1995

Johnston, Tess, *A Last Look Revisited*, Old China Hand Press (Hong Kong), 2004

Johnstone, William Crane, *The Shanghai Problem*, Stanford University Press and Oxford University Press (London), 1937

Jones, FC, *Shanghai and Tientsin: with Special Reference to Foreign Interests*, Royal Institute of International Affairs (London), 1940

Kahler, William R, *Rambles round Shanghai*, Shanghai Mercury (Shanghai), 2nd edn, 1905

Knight, Sophia, *Window on Shanghai: Letters from China, 1965–67*, Andre? Deutsch (London), 1967

Kotenev, Anatoly M, *Shanghai: its Mixed Court and Council*, North-China Daily News & Herald (Shanghai), 1925

Kotenev, Anatoly M, *Shanghai: its Municipality and the Chinese*, North-China Daily News & Herald (Shanghai), 1927

Kounin, II and Yaron, Alex, *The Diamond Jubilee of the International Settlement of Shanghai*, Post Mercury Co (United States), 1940

Kranzler, David, *Japanese, Nazis and Jews: the Jewish Refugee Community of Shanghai, 1938–1945*, KTAV Publishing House (Hoboken, NJ), 1976

Lang, H, *Shanghai Considered Socially*, npub (Shanghai), 1875

Lanning, George, *The History of Shanghai*, Kelly & Walsh (Shanghai), 1920

Lanning, George and Couling, Samuel, *The History of Shanghai*, Kelly & Walsh (Shanghai), 1921

Laurie, Peter George, *The Model Settlement*, npub (Shanghai), 1866

Lee, Leo Ou-fan, *Shanghai Modern: the Flowering of a New Urban Culture in China, 1930–1945*, Harvard University Press (Cambridge, Mass and London), 1999

Lei, KN, *Information and Opinion Concerning the Japanese Invasion of Manchuria and Shanghai from Sources Other than Chinese*, Shanghai Bar Association (Shanghai), 1932

Li, Ling Hin, *Privatization of Urban Land in Shanghai*, Hong Kong University Press (Hong Kong), 1996

Lo, Wen Kan, *China's Case: on the Demonstration in the International Settlement at Shanghai, 30th May 1925*, Union of Chinese Associations in Great Britain (London), 1925

Lung, Olga, *Chinese Family and Society*, Yale University Press (New Haven and London), 1946

MacCormick, Elsie, *The Unexpurgated Diary of a Shanghai Baby*, Chinese American Publishing Co (Shanghai), 2nd edn, 1927

MacFarlane, W, *Sketches in the Foreign Settlements and Native City of Shanghai*, Shanghai Mercury (Shanghai), 1881

Maclellan, John Wharton, *The Story of Shanghai from the Opening of the Port to Foreign Trade*, North-China Herald (Shanghai), 1889

Maybon, Charles and Fredet, Jean, *Histoire de la Concession française de Changhai* (Paris), 1929

Medhurst, Walter Henry, *The Foreigner in Far Cathay*, Edward Stanford (London), 1872

Men of Shanghai and North China, University Press (Shanghai), 1933, 1935

Michie, Alexander, *The Englishman in China During the Victorian Era*, William Blackwood (Edinburgh and London), 1900

Miller, GE, *Shanghai: the Paradise of Adventurers*, Orsay Publishing House (New York), 1937

Montalto de Jesus, Carlos Augusto, *Historic Shanghai*, Shanghai Mercury (Shanghai), 1909

Moule, Arthur Evans, *Personal Recollections of the T'ai-P'ing Rebellion, 1861–63*, Shanghai Mercury (Shanghai), 1898

Murphey, Rhoads, *Shanghai, Key to Modern China*, Harvard University Press (Cambridge, Mass), 1953

Oliphant, Laurence, *Narrative of the Earl of Elgin's Mission to China and Japan in the years 1857, '58, '59* (Edinburgh and London), 1859

Pal, John, *Shanghai Saga*, Jarrolds (London) 1963

Pan Lynn, *In Search of Old Shanghai*, Joint Pub. Co. (Hong Kong), 1982

Pease, Howard, *Shanghai Passage*, Doubleday, Doran (Garden City, NY), 1929

Peters, Ernest William, *Shanghai Policemen*, Rich & Cowan (London), 1937

Plain Speaking on Japan, Commercial Press (Shanghai), 1933

Pott, Francis Lister Hawks, *A Short History of Shanghai*, Kelly & Walsh (Shanghai), 1928

Private Diary of Robert Dollar on his Recent Visits to China, WS Van Cott (npl), 1912

Ransome, Arthur, *The Chinese Puzzle*, G Allen & Unwin (London), 1927

Reconstruction in China – a Record of Progress and Achievements in Facts and Figures, China United Press (Shanghai), 1935

Ricalton, James, *China through the Stereoscope: a Journey through the Dragon Empire at the time of the Boxer Uprising*, Underwood & Underwood (New York and London), 1901

Ristaino, Marcia Reynders, *Port of Last Resort: Diaspora Communities of Shanghai*, Stanford University Press (Stanford, CA), 2001

Rivers, William A, *Eurasia: a Tale of Shanghai Life*, Kelly & Walsh (Shanghai), 1907

Rudinger, St Piero, *The Second Revolution in China, 1913: My Adventures of the Fighting around Shanghai, the Arsenal, Woosung Forts* (Shanghai), 1914

Schiff, Friedrich, *Maskee: a Shanghai Sketchbook*, Yellow Hall (Shanghai), 1940

Scott, John William Robertson, *The People of China: Their Country, History, Life, Ideas, and Relations with the*

Foreigner, Methuen (London), 1900

Sergeant, Harriet, *Shanghai*, John Murray (London), 1991

Shanghai: 1843–1893: the Model Settlement: Its Birth, its Youth, its Jubilee, Shanghai Mercury (Shanghai), 1893

Sheldon Wilkinson, Edward, *Shanghai Country Walks*, North-China Daily News & Herald (Shanghai), 1932

Sopher, Arthur and Sopher, Theodore, *The Profitable Path of Shanghai Realty*, Shanghai Times (Shanghai), 1939

Speakman, Harold, *Beyond Shanghai*, Abingdon Press (New York and Cincinnati), 1922

Taire, Lucian, *Shanghai Episode: the End of Western Commerce in Shanghai*, Rainbow Press (Hong Kong), 2nd edn, 1958

Tata, Sam, *Shanghai 1949: the End of an Era*, Batsford (London), 1989

The Battle of Muddy Flat 1854: an Historical Sketch of that Famous Occurrence, North-China Herald (Shanghai), 1904

The Boxer Rising: a History of the Boxer Trouble in China, Shanghai Mercury (Shanghai), 1900

The Foreigner in China, North-China Daily News & Herald (Shanghai), 1927

The History of Freemasonry in Northern China, 1913–1937, Kelly & Walsh (Shanghai), 1938

The Jubilee of Shanghai, 1843–1893 (Shanghai), 1893

Thornhill, WB, *Shanghai*, Stanley Gibbons (London), 1895

Wasserstein, Bernard, *Secret War in Shanghai*, Profile Books (London), 1998

Wheeler, LN, *The foreigner in China*, Griggs (Chicago), 1881

Willis, Helen, *Through Encouragement of the Scriptures: Recollections of Ten Years in Communist Shanghai*, Christian Book Room (Hong Kong), 1961

Wood, Shirley, *A Street in China*, Michael Joseph (London), 1958

Wright, Arnold, *Twentieth-century Impressions of Hongkong, Shanghai, and Other Treaty Ports of China: their History People, Commerce, Industries and Resources*, Lloyd's Greater Britain Publishing Co (London), 1908

Yang, Simon and T'ao, LK, *A Study of the Standard of Living of Working Families in Shanghai*, Social Research Publications (Peiping), 1931

Yates, MT, *The T'ai-Ping Rebellion: a Lecture Delivered at* the Temperance Hall, Celestial Office (Shanghai), 1853.

Yatsko, Pamela, *New Shanghai: the Rocky Rebirth of China's Legendary City*, John Wiley (New York), 2001

Yeung, Yue-man and Sung, Yun-Wing, *Shanghai: Transformation and Modernization under China's Open Policy*, Chinese University Press (Hong Kong), 1996

Pamphlets, periodicals and newspapers

Addresses presented by the English and American Communities of Shanghai to the Hon. J. Ross Browne: Material Progress in China (Shanghai), 1869

China Architect's and Builder's Compendium (Shanghai), 1924–35

China Quarterly (Shanghai), 1936–38

China Weekly Review (Shanghai), 1928, 1929

Chinese Recorder, Mission Press (Shanghai), 1919–24

Decennial Reports on the Trade, Navigation, Industries of the Ports open to Foreign Commerce in China and Corea, and on the Condition and Development of the Treaty Port Provinces, 1882–1891 and 1902–11, Departments of State and Public Institutions, Inspectorate General of Customs (Shanghai), 1893–1913

Desk Hong List, North-China Desk Hong List (Shanghai), 1875, 1876, 1878, 1884, 1903, 1922, 1931, 1933–39

Far Eastern Review, 1904–39

Harbour Regulations for the Port of Shanghai, Departments of State and Public Institutions, Inspectorate General of Customs (Shanghai), 1913

Hell over Shanghai: Eye-witnesses' Reports, Modern Books (London), 1932

Ladies' Directory: Red Book for Shanghai, North-China Herald (Shanghai), 1876

Land Regulations and Bye-Laws for the Foreign Settlement of Shanghai, Shanghai Municipal Council (Shanghai), 1936

Lester School and Henry Lester Institute (Shanghai), 1938?

Letters, Notices from the Imperial Commissioner Ho, and Other Chinese Authorities, upon the General Extension of the Foreign Customs Establishment, North China Herald (Shanghai), 1860

Miscellany or Companion to the Shanghai Almanac for 1857 (Shanghai), 1856

Municipal Council Report, Shanghai Municipal Council (Shanghai), 1882–1939

Municipal Gazette, Shanghai Municipal Council (Shanghai), 1911–41

Persiflage: Being a Shanghai Almanack for 1889, Kelly & Walsh (Shanghai), 1888

Port of Shanghai, Whangpoo Conservancy Board (Shanghai), 1936

Problems of the Pacific: Proceedings of the Second Conference of the Institute, 4th Conference in Hangchow & Shanghai, 1931, University of Chicago Press (Chicago), 1928

Proceedings of the Society and Report of the Council: Shanghai Society of Engineers and Architects (Shanghai)

Proclamation of Sir H. Pottinger and the Text of the Order and Other Documents Relative to Merchant Vessels under British Colours Trading with any Other Port of China, except the Five Declared Open by Treaty (Hong Kong), 1843

Puck: the Shanghai Charivari (Shanghai), 1871

Report of the Hon. Richard Feetham to the Shanghai Municipal Council, Shanghai Municipal Council (Shanghai), 1931, 1932

Report: Whangpoo Conservancy Board Shanghai, Shanghai

Scenic Shanghai, AS Watson (Shanghai), 192–

Shanghai Almanac for the Year 1862 (Shanghai), 1862

Shanghai Weekly Review, (Shanghai)

Shen Bao, (Shanghai)

Social Shanghai, North-China Daily News & Herald (Shanghai), 1907–12

Statistics of Shanghai, Shanghai Civic Association (Shanghai), 1933

Statistics of Trade at the Treaty Ports for the Period 1863–1872, Departments of State and Public Institutions, Inspectorate General of Customs (Shanghai), 1873

Symposium on Japan's Undeclared War in Shanghai, Chinese Chamber of Commerce (Shanghai), 1932

The Shanghai Incident, Press Union (Shanghai), 1932

The Silk Reeling Industry in Shanghai: a Preliminary Report on Shanghai Industrialization, the Fifth Biennial Conference of the Institute of Pacific Relations (Shanghai), 1933

The Sino-Japanese War in Shanghai, North-China Daily News & Herald (Shanghai), 1932

PHOTO CREDITS

Every effort has been made to credit every photograph and illustration in this book. The publisher will ensure that any omissions will be amended in subsequent editions. Unless stated otherwise, illustrations are from private collections.

All contemporary photographs are by Edward Denison, all rights reserved.

General Description of Shanghai (Mission Press), 1850: pp.18, 19, 20

British Library: Front Cover, pp.21, 27

The Builder: pp.147 (right), 174 (left), 184 (bottom right), 186 (right),

The China Architect's and Builder's Compendium, (Shanghai), 1924-1935: pp.88 (bottom), 158 (bottom left and right), 159 (top), 160, 176 (bottom),

Chinese Architect: pp.155 (top right), 170 (left, middle and bottom)

Dian Shi Zhai Hua Bao: pp.22, 50, 90 (right),

The Far Eastern Review, 1904-1939: pp.84, 92 (right and bottom), 99 (bottom and top right), 100 (top and bottom right), 102 (bottom right), 103 (top), 111, 113, 114 (bottom), 141 (right), 142 (right), 150 (top), 182 (bottom left), 199 (top),

R. Feetham, *Feetham Report*, (North China News and Herald, 1931: pp.86, 149,

Rev.F.Graves, *St John's 1879-1919*, (Oriental Press), 1919: p.

O.Green, *Shanghai of Today*, (Kelly and Walsh), 1927: pp.53 (top right), 54, 151,

Martyn Gregory Gallery, London: pp.36-7, 40-1, 46, 48(top and middle),49, 52, 55 (bottom), 61 (top), 68, 80,

HSBC, Group Archives: pp.48 (bottom), 136, 138,

Hudec Collection Courtesy of Lenore Hietkamp and the University of Victoria Special Collections: pp.179 (right), 180-1 (except

contemporary photographs),

I.Kounin and A.Yaron, *The Diamond Jubilee of the International Settlement of Shanghai*, (Post Mercury Co.), 1940: p.121

G.Lanning, and S.Couling, *The History of Shanghai*, (Kelly and Walsh), 1921:pp.43, 46, 55 (top left), 77 (bottom), 78-9, 88, 89, 91, 94, 106 (bottom), 143 (top right), 146 (top right), 168, 175,

C.Maybon and J.Fredet, *Histoire De La Concession Francaise De Changhai*, (Paris), 1929: pp.60, 61, 74-75 (bottom),

Men of Shanghai and North China, (The University Press, Shanghai), 1933&1935: pp.139 (right), 148, 150 (right), 168 (left), 184 (left), 185 (bottom),

C. Montaldo de Jesus, *Historic Shanghai*, (Shanghai Mercury), 1909: p.33

The National Archives, UK: pp.44, 45, 55 (top right), 81, 125, 187 (top), 188 (right), 192,

Norma in *Shanghai Life – Shanghai Cartoonist Club* (Tai Ping Publishing Co), 1942: p.15

B.Perlin in *Fortune Magazine*, 1946: pp.199

Dominique Perrault: p.217

RIBA Library: pp.117, 137 (left and bottom),

Reconstruction in China – a record of progress and achievements in facts and figures, (China United Pres, Shanghai), 1935: p.182 (bottom right), 183 (bottom),

Richard Rogers Partnership: p.216,

San Pa Jou: pp.134,

Social Shanghai (North China Daily News and Herlad), 1907-12: pp.53 (bottom), 69, 76 (right), 83, 96, 101 (top), 122, 150 (bottom left), 207 (top left),

F.Schiff, *Maskee: A Shanghai Sketchbook*, 1940: pp.130, 172,

Shanghai Municipal Council Annual Report, 1882-1939: pp.72 (right), 82, 98 (bottom), 110, 125, 119 (bottom), 120, 209 (top left),

St Francis Xavier's College Diamond Jubilee Souvenir Album 1874-1934: p72 (left),

STATISTICS

sources: Feetham Report, 1931 and Shanghai Municipal Council Annual Reports

NUMBERS AND NATIONALITY OF FOREIGNERS, BY YEAR

Settlement and external roads area	1865	1870	1876	1880	1885	1890	1895	1900	1905	1910	1915	1920	1925	1930
British	1372	894	892	1,057	1,453	1,574	1,936	2,691	3,713	4,465	4,822	5,341	5,879	6,221
Japanese	–	7	45	168	595	386	250	736	2,157	3,361	7,169	10,215	13,804	18,478
Russian	4	3	4	3	5	7	28	47	354	317	361	1,266	2,766	3,478
American	378	255	181	230	274	323	328	562	991	940	1,307	2,264	1,942	1,608
Portuguese	115	104	168	285	457	564	731	978	1,331	1,495	1,323	1,301	1,391	1,332
German	175	138	129	159	216	244	314	525	785	811	1155	280	776	833
French	28	16	22	41	66	114	138	176	393	330	244	316	282	198
Polish	–	–	–	–	–	–	–	–	–	–	–	82	198	187
Italian	15	5	3	9	31	22	83	60	148	124	114	171	196	197
Spanish	100	46	103	76	232	229	154	111	146	140	181	186	185	148
Danish	13	9	35	32	51	69	86	76	121	113	145	175	176	186
Greek	7	3	2	4	9	5	7	6	32	26	41	73	138	121
Swiss	22	7	10	13	17	22	16	37	80	69	79	89	131	125
Czechoslovak	–	–	–	–	–	–	–	–	–	–	–	65	123	100
Norwegian	4	3	4	10	9	23	35	45	93	86	82	96	99	104
Dutch	27	5	5	5	21	26	15	40	58	52	55	73	92	82
Korean	–	–	–	–	1	–	–	–	–	–	20	46	89	151
Latvian	–	–	–	–	–	–	–	–	–	–	–	43	88	106
Roumanian	–	–	–	–	–	–	–	–	12	15	16	47	69	54
Swedish	27	8	11	12	27	28	46	63	80	72	73	78	63	87
Austrian	4	7	7	31	44	38	39	83	158	102	123	8	41	88
Hungarian	–	–	–	–	–	–	–	–	–	–	–	8	27	37
Esthonian	–	–	–	–	–	–	–	–	–	–	–	47	35	27
Belgian	–	1	3	1	7	6	21	22	48	31	18	30	34	27
Turkish	–	–	–	3	4	18	32	41	26	83	108	9	33	13
Brazilian	–	–	–	–	4	2	–	3	8	7	5	8	27	13
Persian	–	–	–	–	1	1	4	2	6	49	39	7	20	48
Armenian	–	–	–	–	–	–	–	–	–	–	5	6	13	34
Lithuanian	–	–	–	–	–	–	–	–	–	–	–	–	12	28
Syrian	–	–	–	–	–	–	–	–	–	–	–	–	12	2
Serbian	–	–	–	–	–	–	–	–	–	–	–	–	11	12
Finnish	–	–	–	–	–	–	–	–	–	–	–	–	10	4
Arabian	4	–	–	–	–	–	–	–	–	14	–	2	7	1
Argetinian	–	–	–	–	–	–	–	–	–	–	–	–	4	3
Peruvian	1	–	–	–	–	–	–	–	–	–	–	–	4	3
Chilean	–	–	2	1	2	–	–	–	–	–	–	–	2	–
Jugoslav	–	–	–	–	–	–	–	–	–	–	–	–	2	9
Egyptian	–	–	–	–	–	–	–	–	–	11	8	2	1	12
Bulgarian	–	–	–	–	–	–	–	–	–	–	2	1	–	8
Filipino	–	–	–	–	–	–	–	–	–	–	–	–	–	387
Montenegrin	–	–	–	–	–	–	–	–	–	–	2	–	–	–
Venezuelan	–	–	–	–	–	–	–	–	7	–	–	–	–	–
Iraquan	–	–	–	–	–	–	–	–	–	–	–	–	–	56
Indian	–	–	–	4	58	89	119	296	568	804	1,009	954	1,154	1,842
Malay	–	–	–	–	–	28	32	157	171	–	–	–	–	2
Mexican	1	–	–	–	–	–	–	–	–	–	–	–	–	4
Sundries	–	155	47	53	89	3	270	17	11	9	13	18	11	6
Total	2,297	1,666	1,673	2,197	3,673	3,821	4,684	6,774	11,497	13,536	18,519	23,307	29,947	36,471

POPULATION BY YEAR

Year	Foreign Settlement	External Roads	Grand Total
1844	–	–	50
1849	–	–	175
1855	–	–	243
1860	–	–	569
1865	2,235		2,297
1870	1,517	52	1,666
1876	1,581	44	1,673
1880	1,974	164	2,197
1885	3,286	330	3,673
1890	3,360	389	3,821
1895	4,174	441	4,684
1900	6,557	80	6,774
1905	10,639	505	11,497
1910	12,051	1,260	13,536
1915	15,709	2,532	18,519
1920	19,746	3,661	23,307
1925	22,850	7,097	29,947
1930	26,965	9,506	36,471

DETAIL BUILDING STATISTICS 1915-1930

	1915	1916	1917	1918	1919	1920	1921	1922	1923	1924	1925	1926	1927	1928	1929	1930
Chinese houses	6,134	5,903	3,342	2,313	2,336	2,470	4,064	4,267	5,634	5,293	7,734	5,160	2,640	3,508	5,282	6,818
Foreign buildings	41	89	58	75	101	109	66	84	208	73	141	108	43	–	–	–
Foreign stores	–	–	–	–	–	–	–	–	–	–	–	–	–	77	310	298
Hotel buildings	–	–	–	–	–	–	–	–	–	–	–	–	–	7	1	3
Office buildings	–	–	–	–	–	–	–	–	–	–	–	–	–	24	33	35
School buildings	–	–	–	–	–	–	–	–	–	–	–	–	–	3	1	6
Theatres	–	–	–	–	–	–	–	–	–	–	–	–	–	7	6	6
Apartment buildings	–	–	–	–	–	–	–	–	–	–	–	–	–	4	8	5
Foreign residences	–	–	–	–	–	–	235	128	162	128	127	97	48	55	380	327
Factories	–	–	–	–	28	51	41	25	14	20	13	22	19	45	53	27
Godowns	27	41	36	55	52	84	55	28	38	27	19	21	14	53	52	64
Miscellaneous	690	734	490	525	614	828	883	955	1,216	1,152	932	839	856	928	1,460	1,247
Totals	6,892	6,767	3,926	2,968	3,131	3,542	5,344	5,487	7,272	6,693	8,966	6,247	3,620	4,711	7,586	8,836
Estimated Value in Taels (million)	5	6	5	4	6	11	21	16	13	12	15	21	9	20	25	46

BUILDING PERMITS FOR HOUSES ISSUED BY THE SHANGHAI MUNICIPAL COUNCIL

Year	Total
1890	1,436
1891	1,773
1892	1,733
1893	2,096
1894	2,353
1895	3,400
1896	3,297
1897	3,401
1898	3,263
1899	2,026
1900	1,368
1901	2,703
1902	3,767
1903	4,330
1904	4,931
1905	5,370
1906	5,411
1907	4,888
1908	3,081
1909	2,080
1910	2,367
1911	1,253
1912	3,513
1913	4,435
1914	8,824
1915	6,892
1916	6,767
1917	3,926
1918	2,968
1919	3,131
1920	3,542
1921	5,344
1922	5,549
1923	7,361
1924	6,820
1925	8,966
1926	6,247
1927	3,620
1928	4,711
1929	7,586
1930	8,836
1931	8,699
1932	3,439
1933	5,130
1934	4,571
1935	2,252
1936	1,513
1937	1,126
1938	3,291

FOREIGN NATIONALS RESIDING IN SHANGHAI, 1930

Nationality	Foreign Settlement	External Roads	French Concession	Total
America	1,145	463	1,541	3,149
Arabia	1	–	–	1
Argentina	3	–	1	4
Armenia	29	5	33	67
Austria	64	24	44	132
Belgium	25	2	61	88
Brazil	9	4	14	27
Britain	4,606	1,615	2,228	8,449
Bulgaria	8	–	2	10
Cuba	–	–	2	2
Czechoslovakia	88	12	39	139
Denmark	143	43	164	350
Holland	42	40	108	190
Egypt	12	–	–	12
Esthonia	23	4	40	67
Philippines	356	31	–	387
Finland	4	–	23	27
France	159	39	1,208	1,406
Georgia	–	–	4	4
Germany	524	309	597	1,430
Greece	109	12	64	185
Hungaria	27	10	22	59
India	1,758	84	–	1,842
Italy	168	29	123	320
Iraq	56	–	–	56
Japan	12,788	5,690	318	18,769
Jugoslavia	9	–	5	14
Korea	139	12	–	151
Latvia	88	18	–	106
Latvia	–	–	48	48
Lithuania	27	1	32	60
Luxembourg	–	–	2	2
Malaya	–	2	–	2
Mexico	4	–	3	7
Norway	84	20	69	173
Persia	16	32	9	57
Peru	2	1	–	3
Poland	159	28	156	343
Portugal	847	485	267	1,599
Roumania	46	8	32	86
Russia	3,113	374	3,879	7,366
Serbia	11	1	33	45
Spain	116	32	73	221
St Dominica	–	–	4	4
Sweden	44	43	31	118
Switzerland	93	32	81	206
Syria	2	–	25	27
Tonkin	–	–	941	941
Turkey	12	1	19	32
Sundries	6	–	–	6
Total	26,965	9,506	12,335	48,806

INDEX